More Acclaim for David Hackett Fischer's *Washington's Crossing*

Named one of the Best Books of 2004 by
The Los Angeles Times, The Boston Globe, The Chicago Tribune, The Washington Post

An English Speaking Union Ambassador Book Award
for American Studies

A New Jersey Council of the Humanities Book Award for 2005

Winner of the New Jersey State Historical Commission's
Richard P. McCormick Prize

Winner of The Society of the Cincinnati Book Prize

"In a fascinating narrative of the moves and countermoves of American, British, and Hessian forces, Fischer persuades us that the war itself was the source of political and social developments that continue to this day. His mastery of the historian's craft enables him to embody his argument in telling us what happened and who it happened to, taking care not to clog the story with lengthy didactic interruptions. He thus resuscitates Washington's reputation as a field general and at the same time demonstrates his role in establishing an American way of warfare and in fixing the place of the military in the republic that the Revolution created." —Edmund S. Morgan, *The New York Review of Books*

"In Fischer's narrative, the reader . . . cannot help but be caught up by the spirit of these events. *Washington's Crossing* is history at its best, fascinating in its details, magisterial in its sweep. . . . superb features . . . add depth and insight to Fischer's narrative."
—*The Boston Globe*

"Fischer's thoughtful account describes how Washington, in a frantic, desperate month, turned his collection of troops into a professional force, not by emulating the Europeans but by coming up with a model that was distinctly American." —*The New Yorker*

"A tale told with gusto, punctuated by finely rendered accounts of battles and tactics. If it remains part of the historian's obligation to make scholarly writing accessible beyond the academy, David Hackett Fischer deserves to be recognized for a job well done. Not least because it helps us understand anew a great American icon."
—Fred Anderson, *The Los Angeles Times Book Review*

"A vivid, fast-paced narrative that is further characterized by impressive research and new interpretations. . . . Washington's crossing that stormy night has never been told with more clarity or stirring detail." —Donald Higginbotham, *The Chicago Tribune*

"Fischer's vision of the crossing is every bit the masterpiece Leutze's is. . . . The most dramatic moments come as the history Fischer presents outshines the myths you've been told. The Hessians for example, were not drunk on Christmas ale that night. And they were highly skilled, significantly more experienced than their American adversaries. Even Fischer, after 42 years of teaching American history, was surprised to learn how close the Americans came to losing. But perhaps most valuable is Fischer's portrait of Washington. Instead of presenting the Napoleonic hero of the painting, he shows a proud youth who evolved into a humble democratic leader. (The moment when Washington weeps as he watches the Americans surrender in New York is especially poignant.)" —*Newsweek*

"*Washington's Crossing* is history in the heroic mode. Fischer . . . offers ample evidence of the tenacity and bravery of Continental troops and militia, the determined efforts of New Jerseyites to drive the enemy from the state, and the sheer brutality of eighteenth-century warfare. The result is a complicated, compelling, sometimes breathtaking, narrative of events and their impact, which is interspersed with leisurely paced biographical sketches and other digressions." —Jean B. Lee, *Virginia Magazine of History and Biography*

"Fischer knows how to make an argument . . . readers will find it simply delightful; many scholars of the American Revolution will find it indispensable."
—David Waldstreicher, *American Historical Review*

PIVOTAL MOMENTS
IN AMERICAN HISTORY

Series Editors

David Hackett Fischer
James M. McPherson

James T. Patterson
Brown v. Board of Education:
A Civil Rights Milestone and Its Troubled Legacy

Maury Klein
Rainbow's End:
The Crash of 1929

James M. McPherson
Crossroads of Freedom:
Antietam

Glenn C. Altschuler
All Shook Up:
How Rock 'n' Roll Changed America

WASHINGTON'S CROSSING

DAVID HACKETT FISCHER

OXFORD

UNIVERSITY PRESS

OXFORD
UNIVERSITY PRESS

Oxford University Press, Inc., publishes works that
further Oxford University's objective of excellence
in research, scholarship, and education.

Oxford   New York
Auckland   Cape Town   Dar es Salaam   Hong Kong   Karachi
Kuala Lumpur   Madrid   Melbourne   Mexico City   Nairobi
New Delhi   Shanghai   Taipei   Toronto

With offices in
Argentina   Austria   Brazil   Chile   Czech Republic   France   Greece
Guatemala   Hungary   Italy   Japan   Poland   Portugal   Singapore
South Korea   Switzerland   Thailand   Turkey   Ukraine   Vietnam

First published by Oxford University Press, Inc., 2004
198 Madison Avenue, New York, New York 10016
www.oup.com

First issued as an Oxford University Press paperback, 2006
ISBN-13: 978-0-19-518159-3

Oxford is a registered trademark of Oxford University Press

The Library of Congress has cataloged the cloth edition as follows:
Fischer, David Hackett, 1935–
Washington's crossing / David Hackett Fischer.
p. cm. — (Pivotal moments in American history)
Includes bibliographical references and index.
ISBN-13: 978-0-19-517034-4

1. Delaware River Valley (N.Y.–Del. and N.J.)—History—
Revolution, 1775 — 1783
2. Washington, George, 1732–1799—Headquarters—
Pennsylvania—Valley Forge.
I. Title. II. Series.
E263.P4 F575 2004   973.3'32—dc22   2003019858

7 9 8

Printed in the United States of America
on acid-free paper

For Anne, with love

CONTENTS

[Handwritten annotations:]
types of fighters
the major defeat
regroup/ reorganization → rise in morality & motivation
the journey → events before the Battles
Battle of trenton
Battle at princeton
Conclusion → thesis
goal 4/4
goal 4/5

MAPS

EDITOR'S NOTE

This volume is part of a series called Pivotal Moments in American History. Each book in this series examines a large historical event or process that changed the course of American development. These events were not the products of ineluctable forces outside the boundaries of human choice; they were the results of decisions and actions by people who had opportunities to choose and act otherwise. This element of contingency introduces a dynamic tension into the story of the past. Books in the Pivotal Moments series are written in a narrative format to capture that dynamic tension of contingency and choice.

The design of the series also reflects the current state of historical writing, which shows growing attention to the experiences of ordinary people and increasing sensitivity to issues of race, ethnicity, class, and gender in the context of large structures and processes. We seek to combine this new scholarship with old ideas of history as a narrative art and traditional standards of sound scholarship, mature judgment, and good writing.

No single day in history was more decisive for the creation of the United States than Christmas 1776. On that night a ragged army of 2,400 colonials crossed the ice-choked Delaware River from Pennsylvania to New Jersey in the teeth of a nor'easter that lashed their boats and bodies with sleet and snow. After marching all night, they attacked and defeated a garrison of 1,500 Hessian soldiers at Trenton. A week later the Americans withstood a fierce British counterattack in Trenton and then stole away overnight to march fifteen miles by back roads to Princeton, where they defeated British reinforcements rushing to Trenton.

These victories saved the American Revolution from collapse. Without them there would have been no United States, at least as we know it. Of all the pivotal events in American history, none was more important than what happened on those nine days from December 25, 1776, through January 3, 1777. During the previous five months the American rebels had lost every battle. They had been driven from Long Island to Westchester and across the Hudson and Delaware Rivers to Pennsylvania. George Washington's army had lost 90 percent of its strength. Many of the remaining troops intended to go home when their enlistments expired at the end of the year. Citizens in New Jersey and elsewhere were taking the oath of allegiance to the king. The bold declaration of July 4, 1776, seemed all but dead. Washington's crossing of the Delaware was an apparent act of desperation. But it paid off in a huge way. The battles of Trenton and Princeton heralded the triumph of independence six years later.

The story is full of twists and turns, of contingent moments when events seemed likely to move in one direction but then swung in another, when leaders made key choices between two or more alternatives. The storm on December 25–26 delayed the crossing so long that Washington almost called off the whole operation. But the same storm masked the Americans' approach to Trenton and curtailed the normal alert patrolling of the Hessians (Fischer disposes of the old canard that the Hessians were sleeping off a Christmas drunk). A hard freeze on the night of January 2–3 made passable the road taken by the Americans from Trenton to Princeton that had been knee-deep in mud the previous day. Many other contingencies large and small await the reader of this dramatic story.

Washington's Crossing is a vivid narrative of a military campaign that shaped the future not only of America but also of the world. The Hessians emerge here in sharper, clearer focus than in any previous study. David Fischer has written much more than a military narrative, however. He sets the story in the social and political context of a major transformation in the history of the Western world. The American Revolution pitted an amateur army fighting for a new order of liberty and independence against two professional armies (British and Hessian) defending an old order of hierarchy and discipline. Until Washington crossed the Delaware, the triumph of the old order seemed inevitable. Thereafter, things would never be the same again.

James M. McPherson

Washington's Crossing

Washington Crossing the Delaware, painting by Emmanuel Leutze (1851). Metropolitan Museum of Art, Gift of John S. Kennedy, 1897.

INTRODUCTION

❧ The Painting

> That was the residence of the principal citizen, all the way from the suburbs of New Orleans to the edge of St. Louis. . . . Over the middle of the mantel, engraving— Washington Crossing the Delaware; on the wall by the door, copy of it done in thunder-and-lightning crewel by the young ladies—work of art which would have made Washington hesitate about crossing, if he could have foreseen what advantage to be taken of it.
>
> —Mark Twain, 1883[1]

WASHINGTON'S CROSSING!" the stranger said with a bright smile of recognition. Then a dark frown passed across his face. "Was it like the painting?" he said. "Did it really happen that way?"

The image that he had in mind is one of the folk-memories that most Americans share. It represents an event that happened on Christmas night in 1776, when a winter storm was lashing the Delaware Valley with sleet and snow. In our mind's eye, we see a great river choked with ice, and a long line of little boats filled with horses, guns, and soldiers. In the foreground is the heroic figure of George Washington.

The painting is familiar to us in a general way, but when we look again its details take us by surprise. Washington's small boat is crowded with thirteen men. Their dress tells us that they are soldiers from many parts of America, and each of them has a story that is revealed by a few strokes of the artist's brush. One man wears the short tarpaulin jacket of a New England seaman; we look again and discover that he is of African descent. Another is a recent Scottish immigrant, still wearing his Balmoral bonnet. A third is an androgynous

1

figure in a loose red shirt, maybe a woman in man's clothing, pulling at an oar.

At the bow and stern of the boat are hard-faced western riflemen in hunting shirts and deerskin leggings. Huddled between the
thwarts are farmers from Pennsylvania and New Jersey, in blanket
coats and broad-brimmed hats. One carries a countryman's double-
barreled shotgun. The other looks very ill, and his head is swathed
in a bandage. A soldier beside them is in full uniform, a rarity in
this army; he wears the blue coat and red facings of Haslet's Delaware Regiment. Another figure wears a boat cloak and an oiled hat
that a prosperous Baltimore merchant might have used on a West
Indian voyage; his sleeve reveals the facings of Smallwood's silk-
stocking Maryland Regiment. Hidden behind them is a mysterious
thirteenth man. Only his weapon is visible; one wonders who he
might have been.[2]

The dominant figures in the painting are two gentlemen of
Virginia who stand tall above the rest. One of them is Lieutenant
James Monroe, holding a big American flag upright against the
storm. The other is Washington in his Continental uniform of buff
and blue. He holds a brass telescope and wears a heavy saber, symbolic of a statesman's vision and a soldier's strength. The artist in-
vites us to see each of these soldiers as an individual, but he also
reminds us that they are all in the same boat, working desperately
together against the wind and current. He has given them a common sense of mission, and in the stormy sky above he has painted a
bright prophetic star, shining through a veil of cloud.

Most Americans recognize this image, and many remember its name.
It is *Washington Crossing the Delaware*, painted by Emanuel Leutze in
1850. Today it hangs in New York's Metropolitan Museum of Art.
Visitors who are used to seeing it in reproduction are startled by its
size, twelve feet high and twenty feet wide.

The painting itself has a history. The artist was a German American immigrant of strong liberal democratic principles, who returned
to his native land and strongly supported the Revolutions of 1848.
In the midst of that struggle Emanuel Leutze conceived the idea of
a painting that would encourage Europe with the example of the
American Revolution. His inspiration was a poem by Ferdinand
Freiligarth called "Ça Ira," which created the image of a vessel filled
with determined men:

"You ask astonished: "What's her name?"
To this question there's but one solution,
And in Austria and Prussia it's the same:
The ship is called: "Revolution!""[3]

In 1848 and 1849, Leutze began to work on the great canvas. An early study survives, complete only for vivid figures of Washington and Monroe and a single soldier. It is painted in strong primary colors, bright with hope and triumph. After he started, the European revolutions failed, but the artist kept working on his project in a different mood. The colors turned somber, and the painting came to center more on struggle than triumph. Leutze recruited American tourists and art students in Europe to serve as models and assistants. Together they finished the painting in 1850.[4]

Just after it was completed, a fire broke out in the artist's studio, and the canvas was damaged in a curious way. The effect of smoke and flame was to mask the central figures of Washington and Monroe in a white haze, while the other men in the boat remained sharp and clear. The ruined painting became the property of an insurance company, which put it on public display. Even in its damaged state it won a gold medal in Berlin and was much celebrated in Europe. It became part of the permanent collection of the Bremen Art Museum. There it stayed until September 5, 1942, when it was destroyed in a bombing raid by the British Royal Air Force, in what some have seen as a final act of retribution for the American Revolution.[5]

Emanuel Leutze painted another full-sized copy, and sent it to America in 1851, where it caused a sensation. In New York more than fifty thousand people came to see it, among them the future novelist Henry James, who was then a child of eight. Many years later he remembered that no impression in his youth "was half so momentous as that of the epoch-making masterpiece of Mr. Leutze, which showed us Washington crossing the Delaware, in a wondrous flare of projected gaslight and with the effect of a revelation." Henry James recalled that he "gaped responsive at every item, lost in the marvel of wintry light, of the sharpness of the ice-blocks, the sickness of the sick soldier." Most of all he was inspired by the upright image of Washington, by "the profiled national hero's purpose, as might be said, of standing *up*, as much as possible, even indeed of doing it almost on one leg, in such difficulties."[6]

The great painting went to the city of Washington and was exhibited in the Rotunda of the National Capitol. Northerners admired it as a symbol of freedom and union; southerners liked it as an image of liberty and independence. When the Civil War began, it was used to raise money for the Union Cause and the antislavery movement. The presence of an African American in the boat was not an accident; the artist was a strong abolitionist.

In 1897, private collector John S. Kennedy bought the painting for the extravagant sum of $16,000, and gave it to the Metropolitan Museum of Art. There it remained until 1950, when romantic history paintings passed out of fashion among sophisticated New Yorkers. It was sent away to the Dallas Art Museum in Texas, and then to Washington Crossing State Park in Pennsylvania, where it stayed until 1970.

Among the American people the painting never passed out of fashion. Many cherish it as an image of patriotism, and they have reproduced it in icons of wood, metal, ceramics, textiles. It appeared on postage stamps, dinner plates, place mats, key rings, coffee mugs, and tee shirts. By the mid-twentieth century the painting was so familiar that artists quoted its image without explanation, not always in a reverent way. Cartoonists invented angry satires of Nixon Crossing the Delaware, Ronald Reagan Crossing the Caribbean, Feminists Crossing the Rubicon, and Multiculturalists Rocking the Boat.[7]

American iconoclasts made the painting a favorite target. They studied it with a skeptical eye and asked, "Is this the way that American history happened? Is it the way that history ever happens? Are people capable of acting in such a heroic manner?" Some answered all of those questions in the negative. Postmodernists deconstructed the painting in a different spirit, and insisted that it was a figment of the artist's imagination rather than a representation of objective historical reality, in which they deeply disbelieved. Debunkers attacked the painting in its details with high enthusiasm. Leutze's work, they argued, was riddled with historical error. The flag was inaccurate (the Stars and Stripes were not adopted until 1777). The boat was not correct (a ship's longboat, rather than the rivercraft that the army used). The river was wrong (more like the Rhine than the Delaware). The light was mistaken (the crossing took place at night). The ice was not right (jagged blue bergs rather than rounded white river floes). Washington was too old, and James Monroe was not young enough. The debunkers' favorite complaint was about the same detail that had inspired young Henry James: George Washington was not only standing in the boat, but standing on one leg, which they regarded as utterly ridiculous.[8]

The debunkers were right about some of the details in the painting, but they were wrong about others, and they rarely asked about the accuracy of its major themes. To do so is to discover that the larger ideas in Emanuel Leutze's art are true to the history that inspired it. The artist was right in creating an atmosphere of high drama around the event, and a feeling of desperation among the soldiers in the boats. To search the writings of the men and women who were there (hundreds of firsthand accounts survive) is to find that they believed the American cause was very near collapse on Christmas night in 1776. In five months of heavy fighting after the Declaration of Independence, George Washington's army had suffered many disastrous defeats and gained no major victories. It had lost 90 percent of its strength. The small remnant who crossed the Delaware River were near the end of their resources, and they believed that another defeat could destroy the Cause, as they called it. The artist captured very accurately their sense of urgency, in what was truly a pivotal moment for American history.

Further, the painting is true to the scale of that event, which was small by the measure of other great happenings in American history. At Trenton on December 26, 1776, 2,400 Americans fought 1,500 Hessians in a battle that lasted about two hours. By contrast, at Antietam in the American Civil War, 115,000 men fought a great and terrible battle that continued for a day. The Battle of the Bulge, in the Second World War, involved more than a million men in fighting that went on for more than a month. By those comparisons, Washington's Crossing was indeed a very small event, and the artist was true to its dimensions.[9]

But the painting also reminds us that size is not a measure of significance. The little battles of the American Revolution were conflicts between large historical processes, and the artist knew well what was at stake. He understood better than many Americans that their Revolution was truly a world event. We shall see that Washington's Crossing and the events that followed had a surprising impact, not only in America but in Britain and Germany and throughout the world.

Emanuel Leutze also understood that something more was at issue in this event. The small battles near the Delaware were a collision between two discoveries about the human condition that were made in the early modern era. One of them was the discovery that people could organize a society on the basis of liberty and freedom, and could actually make it work. The ideas themselves were not new in the world, but for the first time, entire social and political systems were constructed primarily on that foundation.

Another new discovery was about the capacity of human beings for order and discipline. For many millennia, people had been made to serve others, but this was something more than that. It was an invention of new methods by which people could be trained to engage their will and creativity in the service of another: by drill and ritual, reward and punishment, persuasion and belief. Further, they could be trained to do so not as slaves or servants or robots, but in an active and willing way.

These two discoveries began as altruisms, and developed rapidly in the age of the Enlightenment, not only in Europe and America but in Ch'ing China and Mughal India and around the world. Together they define a central tension in our modern condition, more so than new technology or growing wealth. As ideas they were not opposites, but they were often opposed, and they collided in the American Revolution. In 1776, a new American army of free men fought two modern European armies of order and discipline. When the conflict began in earnest, during the late summer and fall of 1776, the forces of order won most of the major battles, but an army of free men won the winter campaign that followed. They did so not by imitating a European army of order, a profound error in historical interpretations of the War of Independence, but by developing the strengths of an open system in a more disciplined way.

Emanuel Leutze's painting shows only one side of this great struggle, but the artist clearly understood what it was about. He represented something of its nature in his image of George Washington and the men who soldiered with him. The more we learn about Washington, the greater his contribution becomes, in developing a new idea of leadership during the American Revolution. Emanuel Leutze brings it out in a tension between Washington and the other men in the boat. We see them in their diversity and their stubborn autonomy. These men lived the rights they were defending, often to the fury of their commander-in-chief. The painting gives us some sense of the complex relations that they had with one another, and also with their leader. To study them with their general is to understand what George Washington meant when he wrote, "A people unused to restraint must be led; they will not be drove."[10] All of these things were beginning to happen on Christmas night in 1776, when George Washington crossed the Delaware. Thereby hangs a tale.

THE REBELS

～ Washington's Dilemma: An Army of Liberty

> Men accustomed to unbounded freedom, and no
> controul, cannot brook the Restraint which is in-
> dispensably necessary to the good Order and Gov-
> ernment of an Army.
>
> —George Washington, 1776[1]

IT WAS MARCH 17, 1776, the mud season in New England. A
Continental officer of high rank was guiding his horse through
the potholed streets of Cambridge, Massachusetts. Those who
knew horses noticed that he rode with the easy grace of a natural
rider, and a complete mastery of himself. He sat "quiet," as an equestrian would say, with his muscular legs extended on long leathers
and toes pointed down in the stirrups, in the old-fashioned way.
The animal and the man moved so fluently together that one observer was put in mind of a centaur. Another wrote that he was in-
comparably "the best horseman of his age, and the most graceful
figure that could be seen on horseback."[2]

He was a big man, immaculate in dress, and of such charis-
matic presence that he filled the street even when he rode alone. A
crowd gathered to watch him go by, as if he were a one-man parade.
Children bowed and bobbed to him. Soldiers called him "Your Excellency," a title rare in America. Gentlemen doffed their hats and
spoke his name with deep respect: General Washington.

As he came closer, his features grew more distinct. In 1776, we
would not have recognized him from the Stuart painting that we know

7

too well. At the age of forty-two, he looked young, lean, and very fit—more so than we remember him. He had the sunburned, storm-beaten face of a man who lived much of his life in the open. His hair was a light hazel-brown, thinning around the temples. Beneath a high forehead, a broad Roman nose bore a few small scars of smallpox. People remembered his soft blue-gray eyes, set very wide apart and deep in their sockets. The lines around his eyes gave an unexpected hint of laughter. A Cambridge lady remarked on his "appearance of good humor." A Hessian observed that a "slight smile in his expression when he spoke inspired affection and respect." Many were impressed by his air of composure and surprised by his modesty.[3]

He had been living in Cambridge for eight months and was a familiar sight in the town, but much about him seemed alien to New England. Riding at his side on most occasions in the war was his closest companion, a tall African slave in an exotic turban and long riding coat, also a superb horseman. Often his aides were with him,

George Washington with his slave companion, William Lee, painting by John Trumbull (1780). Metropolitan Museum of Art, bequest of Charles Allen Munn.

mostly young officers from southern Maryland and northern Virginia who shared the easy manners and bearing of Chesapeake gentlemen.[4]

It was Sunday afternoon, March 17, 1776, and George Washington had been to church, as was his custom. At his headquarters the countersign was "Saint Patrick" in honor of the day, but nobody was bothering with countersigns, for that morning the shaky discipline of the Revolutionary army had collapsed in scenes of jubilation. American troops had at last succeeded in driving the British army from Boston, after a long siege of eleven months.[5] The turning point had come a few days earlier when the Americans occupied Dorchester Heights overlooking the town. The British garrison organized a desperate assault to drive them away. As both sides braced for a bloody fight, a sudden storm struck Boston with such violence that the attack was called off on account of the weather. The Americans seized the advantage and greatly strengthened their position. On the night of March 16 they moved their heavy guns forward to Nook's Hill, very close to Boston.[6]

The next morning, March 17, British commanders in Boston awoke to the disagreeable sight of American batteries looming above them and decided that the town was untenable. While Yankee gunners held their fire, the British troops evacuated the town "with the greatest precipitation." Altogether about nine thousand Regulars boarded transports in the harbor, along with 1,200 women and children of the army, 1,100 heartsick Tories, and thirty captive Whigs. The ships paused for a few anxious days in Nantasket Roads, while Americans worried that it might be a ruse. Then the ships stood out to sea, and the largest British army in America disappeared beyond the horizon.[7]

When the British troops sailed away, many Americans thought that the war was over, and the hero of the hour was General Washington. Honors and congratulations poured in. Harvard College awarded him an honorary degree, "in recognition of his civic and military virtue." In Dunstable, Massachusetts, the sixth daughter of Captain Bancroft was baptized Martha Dandridge, "the maiden name of his Excellency General Washington's Lady." The infant wore a gown of Continental buff and blue, with "a sprig of evergreen on its head, emblematic of his Excellency's glory and provincial affection."[8]

As spring approached in 1776, Americans had many things to celebrate. Their Revolution had survived its first year with more success than anyone expected. The fighting had started at Lexington Green in a way that united most Americans in a common cause.

Untrained militia, fighting bravely on their own turf, had dealt heavy blows to British Regulars and Loyalists on many American fields: at Concord and Lexington on April 19, 1775, Ticonderoga in May, Bunker Hill in June, Virginia's Great Bridge in December, and Norfolk in January of 1776. North Carolinians had won another battle at Moore's Creek Bridge in February, and the new Continental army had gained a major victory at Boston in March. Another stunning success would follow at South Carolina in June, when a British invasion fleet was shattered by a small palmetto fort in Charleston harbor.

In fourteen months of fighting the Americans won many victories and suffered only one major defeat, an epic disaster in Canada. By the spring of 1776, royal officials had been removed from power in every capital, and all but a few remnants of "ministerial troops" had left the thirteen colonies. Every province governed itself under congresses, conventions, committees of safety, and ancient charters. A Continental Congress in Philadelphia had assumed the functions of sovereignty. It recruited armies, issued money, made treaties with the Indians, and controlled the frontiers. European states were secretly supplying the colonies, and American privateers ranged the oceans. Commerce and industry were flourishing, despite a British attempt to shut them down.

In the spring of 1776, the goal of the American Congress was not yet independence but restoration of rights within the empire. They still called themselves the United Colonies and flew the Grand Union Flag, which combined thirteen American stripes with the British Union Jack. Many hoped that Parliament would come to its senses and allow self-government within the empire. More than a few thought that the evacuation of the British army from Boston would end a war that nobody wanted. The members of the Massachusetts General Court were thinking that way on March 28, 1776, when they thanked George Washington for his military services and wished that he might "in retirement, enjoy that Peace and Satisfaction of mind, which always attends the Good and Great." The implication was that his military work was done.[9]

Tories persisted in every state, but they were not thought to be a serious threat. Americans laughed about a Tory in Kinderhook, New York, who invaded a quilting frolic of young women and "began his aspersions on Congress." He kept at it until they "stripped him naked to the waist, and instead of tar, covered him with molasses and for feathers took the downy tops of flags, which grow in the meadow and coated him well, and then let him go." For the young women of Kinderhook, the Revolution itself had become a frolic.[10]

In that happy moment, one might expect that George Wash-ington would have shared the general mood. Outwardly he did so, but in private letters his thoughts were deeply troubled. To his brother he confided on March 31, 1776, "No man perhaps since the first Institution of Armys ever commanded one under more difficult Cir-cumstances than I have done. To enumerate the particulars would fill a volume—many of my difficulties and distresses were of so pe-culiar a cast that in order to conceal them from the enemy, I was obliged to conceal them from my friends, indeed from my own Army."[11]

Washington understood that every American success deepened the resolve of British leaders to break the colonial rebellion, as they had broken other rebellions in Scotland, Ireland, and England. He was sure that the Regulars would soon return, and he was very clear about their next move. As early as March 13, 1776, four days before the British left Boston, Washington advised Congress that the enemy would strike next at New York and warned that if they succeeded in "making a Lodgement," it would not be easy to evict them.[12]

The next day, while most of his troops were still engaged around Boston, George Washington began to shift his regiments to Man-hattan. He informed Congress that when the last British troops left Boston he would "immediately repair to New York with the remain-der of the army." To save his men the exhaustion of marching on the "mirey roads" of New England, he ordered his staff to plan trans-port by sea.[13]

The defense of New York was a daunting prospect. Since Janu-ary, Washington and his officers had discussed the supreme diffi-culty of protecting an island city against a maritime enemy who commanded the waters around it. They knew the power of the Royal Navy and respected the professional skill of the British army. But Washington was more concerned about his own army than that of the enemy. The problem was not a shortage of men or munitions. Half a million free Americans were of military age. Most were ready to fight for their rights, and many were doing so. The great major-ity owned their own weapons, and Europeans were happy to supply whatever they lacked.

Washington's dilemma was mainly about something else. He did not know how he could lead an amateur American army against highly skilled Regular troops. After a year in command, Washing-ton wrote "licentiousness & every kind of disorder triumphantly reign."[14] The problem was compounded in his mind by the diversity of his army. He wrote, "the little discipline I have been labouring to

establish in the army, is in a manner done away by having such a
mixture of troops." They came from many parts of America. They
joined in the common cause but understood it in very different ways.
This great "mixture of troops" who were used to no control presented
George Washington with a double dilemma. One part of his problem
was about how to lead an army of free men. Another was about how to
lead men in the common cause when they thought and acted differently from one another, and from their commander-in-chief.[15]

Part of George Washington's difficulty rose from his own origins
and upbringing, in a very special American place called the Northern Neck of Virginia. It was a huge tract of five million acres between the Potomac and the Rappahannock rivers, so large that it
spanned three degrees of longitude from the Chesapeake Bay to
the mountains of western Virginia.[16] In 1649, the Northern Neck
was created by England's Charles II as a reward to some of his most
faithful royalist supporters. One of them, Thomas Lord Culpepper,
bought out the rest and passed the land by inheritance to the Fairfax
family, an interesting and eccentric clan who combined Cavalier
manners with Roundhead principles in the English Civil War. After
much litigation, a British court ruled in 1745 that the entire Northern Neck belonged to one man, Thomas Fairfax, sixth Baron Fairfax
(1693–1781). He liked it so well that he moved there from England
and built a rural retreat called Greenway Court in the Shenandoah
country at the western end of his domain.[17]

The family interests were managed by Lord Fairfax's cousin
Colonel William Fairfax, who built a great house at Belvoir next to
Mount Vernon. The gentry of the Northern Neck became agents of
the Fairfaxes and great landholders in their own right. These families of Carters, Lees, Marshalls, Custises, Washingtons, and Fairfaxes
intermarried, as George Washington's older stepbrother Lawrence
married Colonel Fairfax's daughter Anne Fairfax Washington. They
looked after one another, and when young George Washington lost
his father, Lord Fairfax and Colonel Fairfax took a fostering interest
in the young man. They became his mentors, and their houses were
his schools. They were quick to recognize his promise and watched
over his development, not always with an approving eye.[18]

From these men George Washington learned the creed he followed all his life. It valued self-government, discipline, virtue, reason, and restraint. Historians have called it a stoic philosophy, but it
was far removed from the ancient Stoicism of the slave Epictetus,
who sought a renunciation of the world, or the emperor Marcus

Aurelius, who wished to be in the world but not of it. The philosophy that Washington learned among the ruling families of the Northern Neck was a modern idea. It was a philosophy of moral striving through virtuous action and right conduct, by powerful men who believed that their duty was to lead others in a changing world. Most of all, it was a way of combining power with responsibility, and liberty with discipline.

Much of this creed was about honor: not "primal honor," not the honor of the duel, not a hair-trigger revenge against insult, or a pride of aggressive masculinity. This was honor as an emblem of virtue. These gentlemen of the Northern Neck lived for honor in that sense. The only fear that George Washington ever acknowledged in his life was a fear that his actions would "reflect eternal dishonour upon me."[19]

A major part of this code of honor was an idea of courage. The men around young George Washington assumed that a gentleman would act with physical courage in the face of danger, pain, suffering, and death. They gave equal weight to moral courage in adversity, prosperity, trial, and temptation. For them, a vital part of leadership was the ability to persist in what one believed to be the right way. This form of courage was an idea of moral stamina, which Washington held all his life. Stamina in turn was about strength and endurance as both a moral and a physical idea.

These men of the Northern Neck believed that people were not born to these qualities but learned them by discipline and exercise. Washington himself was a sickly youth, and he suffered much from illness. He was taught to strengthen himself by equestrian exercise and spent much of his life outdoors on the back of a horse. Whenever he had the time, he went hunting three times a week. Even in his last years, he walked several miles every night to keep fit. By exercise Washington acquired extraordinary stamina and strength. The painter Charles Willson Peale remembered a moment at Mount Vernon in 1772 when he and other men were pitching a heavy iron bar, a popular sport in the Chesapeake. Washington appeared and, "without taking off his coat, held out his hand for the missile, and hurled it into the air." Peale remembered that "it lost the power of gravitation, and whizzed through the air, striking the ground far, very far beyond our utmost efforts." Washington said, "When you beat my pitch, young gentlemen, I'll try again."[20]

Even as commander-in-chief, Washington joined his men in games of strength and skill, always developing his stamina in a disciplined way. In times of great stress he could keep going when others failed. His brother officer John Armstrong wrote that he "maintains full possession of himself, is indefatigable by day and night."[21]

This modern creed of the Fairfaxes and Washingtons was linked to an idea of liberty. Washington thought of liberty in the Stoic way, as independence from what he called "involuntary passion." He was a man of strong passions, which he struggled to keep in check. For him the worst slavery was to be in bondage to unbridled passion and not in "full possession of himself."

George Washington also thought of liberty as a condition of autonomy from external dominion, but not as we do today. He believed that only a gentleman of independent means could be truly free. This way of thinking was widely shared by the gentry of the Northern Neck, and it made liberty into a system of stratification. Gentlemen of honor and independence such as the Fairfaxes and Washingtons had great liberty; small freeholders had not so much of it. Tenants had little liberty, servants less, and slaves none at all. This was a hierarchical world where liberty and slavery coexisted— to us a contradiction because we do not share the assumption of inequality on which it rested.

Washington grew up among many inequalities, and he accepted most of them. He was very conscious of social rank. Washington was a very sociable man among his peers, at his ease with others of his class, and often in their company. From 1768 to 1775 he entertained two thousand people at Mount Vernon, mostly "people of rank," as he called them.[22] He deliberately kept others at a distance and advised his manager at Mount Vernon always to deal that way with inferiors. "To treat them civilly is no more than what all men are entitled to," Washington wrote, "but my advice to you is, to keep them at a proper distance; for they will grow upon familiarity, in proportion as you sink in authority."[23] Washington had been taught to treat people of every rank with civility and "condescension," a word that has changed its meaning in the modern era. In Washington's world, to condescend was to treat inferiors with decency and respect while maintaining a system of inequality.

His world was also a hierarchy of wealth, and Washington acquired a large share of it. When his brother died, he became the master of Mount Vernon at the age of twenty-two, leasing it from his sister-in-law, then owning it outright. At thirty-six he married Martha Parke Custis, a very beautiful and gracious woman, and one of the richest widows in Virginia. By skillful management and good luck his property increased rapidly before the Revolution. Public service diminished his wealth, and he was forced to sell large tracts of land to pay the expenses of his presidency. Even with that burden he built one of the largest family fortunes in America, with a net worth of more than a million dollars. In 1799, his estate with that of his wife included many thousands of acres and 331 slaves.[24]

Part of his world was a hierarchy of race. In his early years Washington owned many slaves and actively bought and sold them. Before the Revolution he shared the attitudes of his time and place and fully accepted slavery, but after 1775 his thoughts changed rapidly. He began to speak of slavery as a great evil, and by 1777 he wrote of his determination to "get clear" of it. After much thought and careful preparation, he emancipated all his slaves in his will.[25]

Even as Washington was a farmer and slaveowner, he also decided to follow a profession of arms. In his youth he bought books on military subjects. His military career started at high rank in 1752, when by virtue of his social standing he was commissioned a major in the Virginia militia at the age of twenty. In 1753, he volunteered to lead a party deep into the Ohio country through mountainous terrain in wintry weather to deliver an ultimatum from the governor of Virginia to a French commander who was thought to be trespassing on Virginia land. Washington and a frontier guide were nearly murdered by an Indian, whom they overpowered. The guide wanted to kill the Indian, but Washington refused. After many adventures he got home again and submitted a report that made him a world figure, "the talk of two hemispheres."[26]

The French and Indian Wars were a hard school for a young soldier. Washington experienced a humiliating defeat at Fort Necessity, then a disaster with General Braddock, where the young Virginian had two horses shot from under him and four bullets through his coats and survived without a scratch. Through it all his reputation kept growing. In 1755, he was promoted to colonel and appointed commander-in-chief of Virginia forces. At the age of twenty-three, young Colonel Washington was something of a martinet, with a deep concern for order and discipline. To the governor of Virginia, he complained of "insolent soldiers" and "indolent officers." He raged against the undisciplined militia, demanded more rigorous military laws, and tried to organize a new First Virginia Regiment on the model of British Regulars. Washington wrote to his captains in 1757, "Discipline is the soul of an army. It makes small numbers formidable; procures success to the weak, and esteem to all."[27] His American troops did not respond with enthusiasm. In one draft of 400 recruits, 114 deserted. Washington clapped his men in irons, locked them in a "dark room," and made heavy use of the lash. When that failed, he hanged some of them on a special gibbet that he raised forty feet high. It was a monument to his concern for discipline, and also to his frustration.[28]

Washington led his men in hard campaigning along the western frontier. In ten months his Virginia regiment fought twenty battles against the Indians and lost a third of its strength, but the civil population suffered less on the Virginia frontier than in other colonies. Washington was often in extreme peril, riding fearlessly with a few men through deep woods controlled by hostile Indians. Again he emerged unscathed.[29]

When the Revolution began, some of Washington's closest connections were Loyalists. He had large investments in the empire, with assets in Bank of England securities. But when he heard the news of the bloodshed on Lexington Green, he joined the Revolution and sent a letter of explanation to George William Fairfax. "Unhappy it is though to reflect," he wrote, "that a Brother's Sword has been sheathed in a Brother's Breast, and that the once happy and peaceful plains of America are either to be drenched with blood, or Inhabited by Slaves. Sad alternative! But can a virtuous man hesitate in his choice?"[30]

These were his alternatives in 1775: liberty or slavery, virtue or corruption, honor or disgrace, courage or cowardice. In his own way this gentleman of the Northern Neck was as radical as any Revolutionist in the country. He was ready to "shake off all connections with a state so unjust and unnatural," nearly four months before the Continental Congress was prepared to do so.[31]

When the Congress searched for a commander-in-chief of the army on June 15, 1775, Washington was not everyone's first choice. High-toned Whigs such as Elbridge Gerry and Joseph Warren preferred Charles Lee, the former British officer whose radical rhetoric was more to their taste. Other New Englanders thought that the commander should be one of their own, and half a dozen Yankees were eager for the job. But Samuel Adams counted the votes and told his friends that "southern" delegates would support a Continental army only if a Virginian were to lead it. Washington was the available man: the only Virginian with experience of command and young enough to take the field. He was the only member of Congress who wore a uniform, and it suited him. One congressman wrote of his "easy soldier-like air." His "modesty" and "independent fortune" were mentioned in his favor, a reassuring combination to these gentleman Whigs. Perhaps the decisive element was his air of Stoic calm; he was a man Whigs could trust with power. The Adams cousins proposed and seconded the nomination. Congress made it unanimous. Everyone was happy except George Washington, who turned to Patrick Henry and said, "Remember, Mr. Henry what I now tell you: from the day I enter upon the command of the American armies, I date my fall, and the ruin of my reputation."[32]

Washington surrounded himself with a staff who shared his values. Most were bright and able young gentlemen of his own rank and region. Of twenty-two aides-de-camp and military secretaries who served him from July 1775 to July 1777, twelve were Virginians and Marylanders. They were chosen for character, manners, efficiency, and courage under fire, where they had a major function. Washington called them his "military family." They formed bonds of intimacy and affection with one another and their chief.[33] His military secretary was Robert Hanson Harrison, a hunting companion before the war and a member of the Fairfax County militia. He was recruited through other members of the Washington family and

George Washington, Layayette, and Tench Tilghman by Charles Willson Peale (1784). Maryland Commission on Artistic Property, Maryland State House.

became "the indispensable headquarters secretary" from 1775 to 1781.[34] His closest aide was Tench Tilghman, a bright young Maryland gentleman of a family close to the Washingtons. He had made his fortune as a Philadelphia merchant and served without salary. Washington was very fond of him and wrote later, "In August [1776] he joined my family and has been in every action in which the main Army was concerned. He has been a zealous servant and slave to the public and faithful assistant to me for near five years."[35]

Often with the general was his wife, Martha, who traveled back and forth in high style between Mount Vernon and the army's headquarters, with slave coachmen and postilions in the brilliant scarlet and white livery of the Washington family. In winter she sometimes traveled in an elegant sleigh. She was a canny manager of land and slaves and became her husband's best friend and most intimate advisor. In the army's headquarters she pitched in with the paperwork, and he came to rely on her support.

Another close companion was Washington's slave William Lee. Washington bought him in 1767 and made him his manservant, but he was more than that. Washington called him "my fellow." He was a comrade, a friend, and a brilliant rider in a class with Washington himself. Before the war they hunted together across the Northern Neck. William Lee was said to be as fearless as Washington himself,

Martha Washington, by James Peale (1796), watercolor miniature on ivory, 1-9/16 x 1-1/4 inches. Mount Vernon Ladies Association.

and the two men "would rush, at full speed, through brake or tangled wood, in a style at which modern huntsmen would stand aghast." William Lee rode with Washington through the war, and early paintings showed the two men together in battle. Washington later emancipated him "as a testimony for his attachment to me and for his faithful service during the revolutionary war."

Throughout the war, Washington's "military family" surrounded him with the culture in which he was raised. Male and female, slave and free, they reinforced his values and beliefs, which were very different from those of others in the American army.[36]

Those differences began to emerge when Washington took command in Massachusetts. As he rode into New England he wrote of the landscape as if it were a foreign country. In camp he was appalled by New England soldiers. "The officers generally speaking are the most indifferent kind of people I ever saw," he confided to Lund Washington. "They are an exceeding dirty and nasty people." He often complained of the "levelling spirit" of New England, where "the principles of democracy so universally prevail."[37]

New England was more fluid in its society than the Northern Neck of Virginia. In 1776, officers often rose from the ranks and sometimes returned to them. An example was William Bostwick, who enlisted in the Seventh Connecticut Regiment as a company clerk and was commissioned as first lieutenant in October 1776, then went home when his enlistment expired, enlisted in the Connecticut militia, and served as a captain in "all alarms to the close of the war."[38]

Another example was Joseph White, who joined the army as a private at the age of eighteen. He acquired an officer's coat and wangled an appointment as "assistant adjutant" in a regiment of artillery, a rank and office of his own invention. One day he was sent to pick up orders from General Washington, who was surprised by White's youth and asked, "Pray sir, what officer are you?" White answered that he was assistant adjutant of the regiment of artillery. "Indeed," said the general, "you are very young to do that duty." White replied, "I told him I was young, but was growing older every day." He remembered that Washington "turned his face to his wife, and both smiled."[39]

Men such as Joseph White and William Bostwick became the core of the New England army. To Washington, the "levelling spirit" of New England appeared as indiscipline and disorder. New Englanders in turn did not like his hierarchical attitudes, and Washington began to feel that he could not do his job without rendering himself "very obnoxious to a gre[at] part of these People."

This difference was a problem in the army, for as late as June 1776 two-thirds of Continental regiments under Washington's command were New Englanders. Yankee farmers and mechanics turned out in large numbers. In the town of Concord in Massachusetts, nearly all able-bodied men of military age served willingly in the years from 1775 to 1777, and more than 75 percent saw combat at

New England Troops (1775), frontispiece for H. H. Brackenridge, *The Battle of Bunkers-Hill*, Philadelphia (1776), one of very few original contemporary American images of American soldiers early in the Revolution. The kneeling figure in the foreground wears small clothes and a gentleman's riding coat with dragoon sleeves. The soldiers behind him are wearing hunting shirts and leggings. Their broad-brimmed hats are cocked in ways that represent the individuality of these men. Library of Congress.

Bunker Hill and subsequent battles. It was much the same in most New England towns, which strongly supported the war at heavy cost.[40]

Most of these New England soldiers came from yeoman families with land and property. They were expected to equip themselves with the help of their families. When Joseph Plumb Martin of Milford, Connecticut, joined the state levies for six months, his grandfather said, "Well you are going a soldiering then, are you? . . . I suppose you must be fitted out for the expedition." Private Martin was equipped by his grandparents with "arms and accouterments, clothing, and cake, and cheese in plenty, not forgetting to put my pocket Bible into my knapsack."[41]

In 1776, these Yankee regiments may have been the most literate army in the world. Nearly all New England privates could read and write. Even young recruits such as Martin, who was just sixteen, were caught up in the great public questions that were debated in kitchens, taverns, and town meetings. "During the winter of 1775–76, by hearing the conversation and disputes of the good old farmer politicians of the times, I collected pretty correct ideas of the contest between this country and the mother country, (as it was then called)," he wrote. "I thought I was as warm a patriot as the best of them."[42] These New England men were raised to a unique idea of liberty as independence, freedom as the right of belonging to a community, and rights as entailing a sense of mutual obligation.

George Washington and the New England men slowly found a way to work together. Washington learned to listen, to reason, and to work through councils of war in which a majority of officers were Yankees. New Englanders learned that an army was not a town meeting, that somebody had to give orders, and that orders had to be obeyed. The result was an untidy and unstable compromise, which allowed an army of cantankerous Yankees to operate under a gentleman of Virginia.

George Washington had a special problem with a Yankee regiment that was by all accounts one of the best in the army. The Fourteenth Massachusetts Continentals were raised in Marblehead and recruited from fishing towns on the north shore of Massachusetts, especially Beverly, Salem, Lynn, and Marblehead.[43] Their colonel was John Glover, prosperous owner of sloops and schooners in the Atlantic trade and member of the tight "codfish aristocracy" who dominated the north shore of New England. He was not a radical by nature, but he and his townsmen felt the sting of tyranny in writs of assistance, corrupt customs officers, and illegal impressments of Marblehead crews by the Royal Navy. These repeated acts turned a conservative ship captain into a revolutionary.

Many of his men were seamen and fishermen. One was described as wearing "a blue coat, with leather buttons, and tarred trousers." They were very well armed, and many had bayonets. John Glover ran his regiment like a taut ship with the same system of command that prevailed at sea. A Pennsylvania officer observed that "there was an appearance of discipline in this corps; the officers seemed to have mixed with the world, and to understand what belonged to their stations."[44]

The regiment also reflected the ethnic composition of New England maritime towns. Indians and Africans sailed in Yankee ships and settled in the seaport villages. They also enlisted in Glover's regiment. He knew these men as shipmates and welcomed them to his command. Others in the army did not approve. An officer from the middle states, Alexander Graydon, wrote of Glover's men, "In this regiment there were a number of negroes, which to persons unaccustomed to such associations, had a disagreeable, degrading effect."[45]

At first George Washington was not happy about the enlistment of African Americans, but after much discussion he worked out a sequence of compromises. The first was to allow African Americans to continue in the ranks but to prohibit new enlistments. The second was to tolerate new enlistments but not to approve them. By the end of the war, African Americans were actively recruited, and some rose to the rank of colonel in New England. Washington's attitudes were different from those of Colonel Glover, but here again he worked out a dynamic compromise that developed through time. It also kept the peace within the army, allowed men of different views to fight the war together, and encompassed another idea of freedom in the American Revolution. In that process the Continental army, beginning with the Marblehead regiment, became the first integrated national institution in the United States.[46]

George Washington had another problem with regiments of riflemen who came from the backcountry of western Pennsylvania, Maryland, and Virginia. Of all the units in the American army, none were more fascinating to their opponents. In the summer of 1776, British troops captured a rifleman and took him aboard the flagship of Admiral William Howe. British officers gathered to study the man, his clothing, and especially his weapon. They took a keen professional interest in the American long rifles that fired a small but lethal half-ounce ball with astonishing accuracy over great distances. Admiral Howe's secretary Ambrose Serle noted that his weapon was "a handsome construction, and entirely manufactured in America."[47]

Many tales were told about the accuracy of these weapons in the hands of backcountry marksmen. American riflemen loved to give demonstrations, aiming at a small mark the size of a man's eye or the tip of his nose, and hitting it repeatedly from a distance of 250 yards. British and Hessian officers lived in fear of American riflemen. Lieutenant Johann Heinrich von Bardeleben noted that "most of our officers must cut the rank insignia from their uniforms, supposedly because the rebel riflemen had their greatest interest in officers."[48]

One of the most formidable units was a regiment of Pennsylvania riflemen, famous for their black hunting shirts. Their leader was Colonel Edward Hand (1744–1802), an Irish immigrant, trained in medicine at Trinity College Dublin. He came to America in 1767

A Backcountry Infantryman, ca. 1776, an "accurate representation by a German officer in British service." This backsettler carries a musket and bayonet. Anne S. K. Brown Military Collection, Brown University Library.

as surgeon's mate in the Eighteenth Royal Irish Regiment and settled as a physician in Lancaster, Pennsylvania. He strongly supported the Revolution and was elected colonel of the regiment.[49]

Backcountry regiments from western Virginia were called "shirt men," from their homespun backcountry hunting shirts made of sturdy tow cloth that had been "steeped in a tan vat until it became the color of a dry leaf." In woods or high grass they were nearly invisible. Congress recommended on November 4, 1775, that their hunting shirts and leggings be adopted for the entire army.[50]

One backcountry company came from Culpeper County, in western Virginia on the east slope of the Blue Ridge Mountains. They called themselves the Culpeper Minutemen and mustered three hundred men with bucktails in their hats and tomahawks or scalping knives in their belts. One of its members wrote that they wore "strong brown linen hunting-shirts, dyed with leaves and the words 'Liberty or Death,' worked in large white letters on the breast." They armed themselves with "fowling pieces and squirrel guns" and marched to Williamsburg, where tidewater Virginians were not thrilled to see them. One Culpeper man remembered, "the people hearing that we came from the backwoods, and seeing our savage-looking equipments, seemed as much afraid of us as if we had been Indians."[51]

Part of their "savage-looking equipments" may have been their flag. A sketch of it by a historian in the mid-nineteenth century shows the dark image of a timber rattlesnake, coiled and ready to strike, and the words "Don't Tread on Me." The same symbol was adopted at the same time by the backcountry militia of Westmoreland County in Pennsylvania and by other western units.[52] Here was another idea of liberty, different from the collective consciousness of New England towns, and the liberty-as-hierarchy among the Fairfax men, and liberty for African Americans among the Marblehead mariners. The backsettlers spoke of liberty in the first person singular: "Don't Tread on *Me*."

When the backcountry regiments joined the Continental army outside Boston, they made much trouble for George Washington. He wrote that "some of them especially from Pennsylvania, know no more of a Rifle than my horse." They were difficult men to lead. The social attitudes of a Fairfax gentleman did not sit well with them, and they were utterly defiant of discipline and order. Washington grew so angry with them that he ordered some to be tried for mutiny and threatened them with capital punishment. The backcountrymen responded by coming close to a full-blown insurrection.[53]

They also started more serious trouble with New Englanders. It happened in Cambridge when a regiment of Virginia riflemen in "white linen frocks, ruffled and fringed," met Glover's Marblehead regiment in "round jackets and fisher's trousers." There were mutual shouts of derision, and then something worse. Many of the Virginians were slaveowners, and some of the Marblehead men were former African slaves. Insults gave way to blows, and blows to a "fierce struggle" with "biting and gouging." One spectator wrote that "in less than five minutes more than a thousand combatants were on the field." Americans from one region began to fight Americans from another part of the country, on a larger scale than the battles at Lexington and Concord.

Washington acted quickly. A soldier from Massachusetts named Israel Trask watched him go about it. As the fighting spread through the camp, Washington appeared with his "colored servant, both on horseback." Together the general and William Lee rode straight into the middle of the riot. Trask watched Washington with awe as "with the spring of a deer he leaped from his saddle, threw the reins of his bridle into the hands of his servant, and rushed into the thickest of the melees, with an iron grip seized two tall, brawny, athletic, savage-looking riflemen by the throat, keeping them at arm's length, alternately shaking and talking to them."

Talking was probably not the right word. The rioters stopped fighting, turned in amazement to watch Washington in action, then fled at "the top of their speed in all directions." The trouble ended without courts, irons, or whips that were more terrible than death to a proud backsettler. In a few moments George Washington and William Lee had restored order in the army. Trask remarked that "hostile feelings between two of its best regiments" were "extinguished by one man."[54]

Washington had some of his deepest and most persistent differences with yet another unit, called the Philadelphia Associators. They were a volunteer militia that had begun as another of Benjamin Franklin's many inventions in 1747, when Britain was at war with France and Spain. Quaker Pennsylvania had no militia and was unable to defend itself from privateers that cruised the coast. The Quakers in the legislature were faithful to their testimony of peace and refused to act. In Philadelphia, Benjamin Franklin proposed to defend the town with a voluntary association, which men could freely join or not as they pleased. They were to supply their own weapons, elect their own officers, and choose a military council for short terms.

Costs would be borne by voluntary subscription. Discipline would be done without corporal punishment, but only by "little fines . . . to be apply'd to the purchasing of drums, colours, etc.," or "to refresh their weary spirits after exercise." Incredibly, it worked. Franklin recruited ten companies of one hundred men in Philadelphia, then a hundred companies in the counties. He raised a subscription for artillery, established a lottery to pay for fortifications, sold muskets and bayonets in his shop, and even designed the colors.[55]

The Associators, as they were called, functioned in time of war and faded away. In 1775, Pennsylvania still had no militia and most Quakers remained true to their testimony of peace. In an hour of need, Philadelphians turned out in huge mass meetings and agreed to revive Franklin's organization as the "Associators of the City and

Pennsylvania Associators in plain brown and gray uniforms intended to "level all distinctions." Anne S. K. Brown Military Collection, Brown University Library.

Liberties of Philadelphia." In the city itself, they raised five battalions of infantry and two batteries of artillery. Many other battalions were organized in the rural counties of Pennsylvania.

The Philadelphia Associators were a cross-section of the city's diverse population. Alexander Graydon remembered that his company included men from five nations and many religions. Even a few "Free Quakers" enlisted.[56] Many members were mechanics, artisans, shopkeepers, and laborers who were radical Whigs and democrats. They agreed to elect their officers by secret ballot and adopted an egalitarian dress. In May 1775, a "considerable number of the Associators" called for a uniform that would "level all distinctions" and cost no more than ten shillings.[57]

These men applied a revolutionary idea of direct democracy to military units. On September 15, 1775, they organized a Committee of Privates in every battalion: five or seven men elected for six-month terms, to meet with representatives from every company, perhaps a hundred men in all. The Committees of Privates convened in the city's schoolhouses and met regularly through 1776. Most of the committeemen were of middling social rank: schoolmasters, shopkeepers, artisans, one college professor. They discussed the organization of their units, supported families of men on active service, and debated political questions such as the Constitution of Pennsylvania. They had a major impact on the design of the Pennsylvania government, which in 1776 was the most radical in the world, with a unicameral legislature and more democracy than any other instrument of government.[58]

At the same time, it is interesting that the Associators chose their highest leaders from the city's wealthiest and most powerful men. Their senior officer was Colonel John Cadwalader of the Third Battalion, who became their brigadier. Some thought he was the richest merchant in Philadelphia. His portrait shows a man of extraordinary dignity and refinement, far from the egalitarian spirit of the Committees of Privates. Washington offered him a commission as general in the Continental army, but Cadwalader turned it down and remained an officer in the Associators. Company commanders were also men of high prominence. One of them was the artist Charles Willson Peale, who helped to equip and uniform some of his men and to provide for their families out of his own pocket. There were tensions here, and much strife later in the Revolution, but in 1776 Philadelphians of different classes worked together in a common cause that belonged neither to the rich nor the poor. Here was yet another way of thinking about liberty and freedom, in a

manner that was true to the founding principles of Pennsylvania
and to an idea of liberty that was inscribed on the Great Quaker Bell
of Liberty in 1751. It bore a verse from Leviticus: "Proclaim Liberty
throughout the land, unto all the inhabitants thereof." This was an
idea of liberty as reciprocal rights that belonged to all the people, a
thought very different from the exclusive rights of New England
towns, or the hierarchical rights of Virginia, or the individual autonomy of the backsettlers.[59] George Washington was dubious about
the Associators. Their version of liberty was more radical in thought
and act than any other unit's in the army. But these men were devoted to the American cause and willing to fight in its defense. Later
they would prove themselves to be excellent troops, and they would
play a major part in campaigns that followed.

Yet another problem for Washington appeared in the silk-stocking
regiments that joined the army. One of them came from Maryland. It
was called Smallwood's regiment after Colonel William Smallwood, a
wealthy planter's son and a strong Whig, who recruited the regiment
from the sons of planters, lawyers, and merchants in Baltimore and
Annapolis. First to form was a company called the Baltimore Independent Cadets. The names on its muster roll were English, Irish,
Scottish, French, German, and Dutch, but most were men of wealth.
Their leader, Captain Mordecai Gist, wrote that the company was
"composed of gentlemen of honour, family and fortune, and tho' of
different countries animated by a zeal and reverence for the rights of
humanity."[60] Every member signed a contract, swearing to resist "the
oppressive unconstitutional acts of Parliament to deprive us of liberty." They agreed to elect their officers, to be bound by "sacred ties
of Honour and love and justice due to ourselves and our country,"
and to submit to martial discipline, but "not to extend to corporal
punishment." Here was another idea of liberty as a voluntary agreement, much like the commercial contracts these men made routinely
in Baltimore and Annapolis. The Baltimore Cadets equipped themselves lavishly, with "a scarlet uniform coat with buff facings, trimmed
with gold or yellow metal buttons, half boots, a good gun, cartouche
pouch, a brace of pistols, a cutlass, four pounds of powder and sixteen pounds of lead." They promised to be ready to march to "the
assistance of our sister colonies on 48 hours notice."[61]

     The entire regiment marched to Philadelphia on July 17, 1776,
and John Hancock described them "upwards of a thousand strong . . .
an exceeding fine body of men."[62] They made a strong impression in
the camp. A Pennsylvania militiaman described them as "city bred

Marylanders" who were "distinguished by the most fashionably cut coat, the most macaroni cocked hat, and the hottest blood in the union." Other Americans remarked on their dress uniforms of scarlet and buff, which were thought to be "not fully according with the independence we had assumed."[63]

These gentleman Whigs of Maryland were deadly serious about their soldiering. When they joined George Washington's army, they put aside their scarlet coats, and every man "from the colonel to the private all were attired in *hunting shirts*." But even privates in the Batimore Cadets expected to be treated as gentlemen, with privileges of their rank such as immunity from corporal punishment and the right to resign from the army if the terms of their contract were not honored. George Washington learned that he could work with these men, but only with extreme care. They became one of the great fighting regiments in the army.[64]

On July 6, 1776, the Continental Congress sent George Washington one of the first copies of the Declaration of Independence and ordered him to "have it proclaimed at the Head of the Army in the way you shall think it most proper."[65] Washington was quick to obey. On July 9, he ordered that "the several brigades are to be drawn up this evening in their respective parades, at six o'clock, when the declaration of Congress, shewing the grounds and reasons of this measure is to be read with an audible voice."[66] Washington's aide Colonel Samuel Blachley Webb wrote in his diary, "The Declaration was read at the head of each brigade, and was received with three Huzzas by the Troops—every one seemed highly pleased that we were separated from a King who was endeavoring to enslave his once loyal subjects. God grant us success in this our new Character."[67]

That evening a jubilant mob of troops and townsmen removed the royal arms from New York's public buildings. They pulled down a handsome equestrian statue of George III on New York's Bowling Green, cut off its head, and carried the body through the town, "among many Spectators, Fifes and Drums all the way, beating the Rogues march." George Washington was appalled. He issued an order approving "zeal in the public cause" but reprimanded the entire army for "want of order."[68]

Washington ordered that "in future these things shall be avoided by the Soldiery, and left to be executed by proper authority." The Soldiery were unrepentant. When they discovered that the statue was made of lead, they broke it into pieces and sent it to the women of Litchfield, Connecticut, to be melted into musket balls. A small fragment of the horse's tail survives in the collections of the New-York Historical Society.[69] There was little malice in these republican rituals. Captain Alexander Graydon observed, "had even George [III] himself been among us, he would have been in no great danger of personal injury, at least from the army. We were, indeed, beginning to grow angry with him; and were not displeased with Paine for calling him a royal brute, but we had not yet acquired the true taste for cutting throats."[70]

In 1776, Americans were less interested in pulling down a monarchy than in raising up a new republic. Washington's leadership was becoming a major part of that process within the army. Men who came from different parts of the continent were beginning to understand each other. And Washington was learning how to lead them. He learned that the discipline of a European regular army became the enemy of order in an open society. To impose the heavy flogging and capital punishments that were routine in European armies would destroy an army in America. The men would not stand for that abuse. When the backcountry riflemen were convicted for mutiny, Washington did not impose the death penalty that was customary in the British service. He fined the guilty riflemen twenty shillings each and appealed to honor, reason, pride, and conscience. They in turn declared themselves "heartily sorry" and promised to reform, at least a little. Slowly this army of free men was learning to work together. They were also coming to respect this extraordinary man who was their leader, if not quite their commander-in-chief. They had come a long way toward forming an army, but was it enough? George Washington knew that they were about to meet some of the most formidable troops in the world, and the outcome was very much in doubt.[71]

THE REGULARS

❧ The Kings Own: An Army of Order and Discipline

> The more confident a man is of his own capacity,
> with so much the greater resolution he will act. . . .
> Hence then it is that discipline becomes necessary
> . . . as well to encourage them to a due discharge
> of their duty, as to prevent their being intimidated.
>
> —Captain Bennet Cuthbertson, Fifth Foot,
> *A New System of Military Discipline*, 1768[1]

PRIVATE DANIEL McCURTIN of the Maryland Line was there when the Regulars arrived. It was June 29, 1776, a quiet summer Saturday in New York. He had just received his discharge from the army and was sitting in a house overlooking the lower harbor, getting ready to go home. About nine o'clock in the morning he looked out and admired the view across an empty sheet of water. A few minutes later he looked again. To his amazement, the bay had filled with ships. "I could not believe my eyes," Private McCurtin wrote. "Keeping my eyes fixed at the very spot, judge you of my surprise when in about ten minutes, the whole bay was full of shipping as ever it could be. I declare that I thought all London was afloat."[2]

In the van were big British ships of the line, cleared for action with red gunports open, batteries run out, and huge white battle ensigns streaming in the breeze. Behind them came transports crowded with troops. They advanced at a majestic pace, as if nothing in the world could stop them. Inside Sandy Hook they dropped

*A View of the Narrows between Long Island and Staten Island, with Our Fleet at Anchor
and Lord Howe Coming In.* The ship in the distance is Admiral Howe's HMS
Eagle, which arrived on July 12, 1776. The drawing is attributed to Captain
Lieutenant Archibald Robertson, Royal Engineers. It may be the work of
another British officer, Captain Thomas Davies, Royal Artillery. Spencer
Collection, The New York Public Library, Astor, Lenox and Tilden Foundations.

anchor so close together that they reminded Private McCurtin of
"something resembling a wood of pine trees trimmed."

For two days the ships continued to arrive, more than a hundred
full-rigged vessels and a swarm of smaller craft, all gathering inside
the Hook. Then, on July 1, 1776, bright signal flags blossomed from
British halyards, and gray canvas billowed beneath black yardarms.
The great armada sailed slowly up the bay, anchored near the low
coast of Long Island, and made preparations for landing.[3] American troops rushed from New York City to Brooklyn. When the defenders were in place the British ships moved again, this time very
quickly across the harbor to Staten Island. Three nimble British
frigates slipped inshore, and a flotilla of small boats splashed into
the water. Thousands of British Regulars swarmed ashore with
scarcely a shot fired. It was a brilliant maneuver. The Royal Navy
and British army had carried out a complex amphibious operation
with harmony and high professional skill. The Americans were made
to feel like helpless amateurs in the complex art of modern war.[4]

The landing on Staten Island was only the beginning. In the
next six weeks, five hundred transports and victualing ships arrived

in New York's lower harbor. They brought twenty-three thousand British Regulars, plus ten thousand German troops, many civilian workers, and several thousand women of the army. Another thirteen thousand troops were sent to Canada. By late August two-thirds of the British army were in the colonies. Supporting these troops were seventy British warships in American waters, half the fighting strength of the Royal Navy. In 1776, it was the largest projection of seaborne power ever attempted by a European state.[5]

Still more remarkable was the quality of this great force. A military observer thought that the British army on Staten Island was "for its numbers one of the finest ever seen." Every man was a long-serving volunteer. This was a modern professional army, with much experience of war. Its fifteen generals were on the average forty-eight years old in 1776, with thirty years of military service. By comparison, the twenty-one American generals who opposed them in New York were forty-three years old, with two years of military service. In British infantry regiments, even privates had an average of nine years' service in 1776. Most American troops had only a few months of active duty.[6]

Except for the late unpleasantness in the colonies, the recent service of the British army was an experience of victory without equal in the world. Its senior officers and sergeants were seasoned veterans of a great world conflict called the Seven Years' War in Europe and the French and Indian War in America. From 1755 to 1764, the British army fought on five continents and defeated every power that stood against it. Regimental honors told the story: Minden and Emsdorf in Europe, Plassey and Pondicherry in India, Louisbourg and Quebec in North America, Guadeloupe and Martinique in the West Indies, Moro and Havana in Cuba, Minorca in the Mediterranean, Manila in the Philippines, Senegal in Africa. In 1776, the British army was full of pride and confidence. An American who knew it well thought it was "the most arrogant army in the world," and it had much to be arrogant about.[7]

As a social institution, the British army in 1776 was a bundle of paradoxes. Regimental badges and colors proclaimed that it served the king, but it was entirely the creature of Parliament. The army cherished its traditions but operated under a law called the Mutiny Act that expired every twelve months. The British people took pride in its achievements but deeply feared the power of a standing army and kept it on a short leash.

The officers of the army made another paradox. Many were highly skilled professional soldiers who studied war as a science and followed it as a career, but they cultivated the casual air of a country gentleman, and in most regiments they acquired their commissions by purchase. The cost was high: in a line regiment 500 pounds sterling for a lieutenant, 1,500 for a captain, 2,600 for a major, and 3,500 for a lieutenant colonel. Cavalry and guards were even more expensive. Later generations condemned this "purchase system" as organized incompetence and institutionalized corruption, but its purpose was to ensure that British officers had a stake in their society and were not dangerous to its institutions. The purchase system kept the army firmly in the hands of Britain's governing elite, mainly its small aristocracy, who controlled much of the wealth and power in the nation. Of 102 regimental colonels in 1769, more than half came from an aristocracy of two hundred families in a nation of seven million people.[8]

Yet another paradox appeared in the structure of the British army, which was both bureaucratized and decentralized. It was one of the first global bureaucracies, with specialized departments for barracks, boatmen, commissaries, engineers, hospitals, ordnance, and quartermasters. Around the world, officers toiled long hours at field desks, filling out the statistical reports that still survive in redbound elephant folios at the Public Record Office near Kew Gardens. But the army was also deliberately decentralized. Even in the late twentieth century a British brigadier described it as "a collection of semi-nomadic tribes" and explained the reason why. "There's no such thing as *the* British Army," he wrote. ". . . That's why there could never be a coup in this country."[9]

The army's tribes were its many regiments and special battalions. More than forty of these tribal units came ashore on Staten Island. Every one of them was encouraged to believe that it was absolutely the best in the army at what it did. That feeling was especially strong among the first units that landed on the beaches of lower New York.

In the first wave at Staten Island were battalions of British grenadiers, the storm troops of the army. They were tall, heavy-set men and were made to appear even taller by grenadier caps that were designed to add an extra foot to their height. Every British infantry regiment had a company of grenadiers, specially selected for size and strength. On active service, British generals combined these companies into composite battalions and used them to lead assaults on fortifications, to break an enemy line, or to make landings on hostile beaches. Casualties were heavy in grenadier companies, but numbers were kept up by a steady flow of replacements. Altogether the four

A British Grenadier and *British Light Infantry*, pencil sketches by De Loutherbourg. (1778). Anne S. K. Brown Military Collection, Brown University Library.

battalions of grenadiers who came to Staten Island were one of the largest concentrations of these units in the history of the army.[10]

Landing with the grenadiers at Staten Island was the light infantry, another proud elite, called the "Light Bobs" in the army. This was a new invention by British officers who had served in the French and Indian War. General Thomas Gage formed an entire regiment of light infantry in America, dressed it in drab uniforms, and trained it to fight in open order. After the war General William Howe persuaded the king to authorize separate light infantry companies in every regiment.[11] They also were chosen men, selected not for size but for intelligence, energy, and marksmanship. They were trained in "leaping, running, climbing precipices, swimming, skirmishing through woods, loading and firing in different attitudes, and marching with remarkable rapidity." In 1774, General Howe organized a camp at Salisbury where light infantry companies learned to work together in composite battalions of special forces.[12]

Every light infantry company wore the badges and facings of its parent regiment, with distinctive short jackets, light equipment, and a small helmet or cap in place of the usual broad-brimmed cocked hat. As emblems of their special role, some companies added jaunty green feathers, which gave the Light Bobs another nickname. The Green Feathers of 1776 were the ancestors of Green Jackets in the nineteenth century and Green Berets in the twentieth, all highly mobile light troops.[13] British commanders made frequent use of these men, and by 1776 they were already hardened by heavy service in America. The first wave included the same units who had marched to Lexington and Concord and led the assault on Bunker Hill. In New England they had taken heavy losses from an enemy they despised, and they were in no mood for gentle measures. The four battalions of light infantry at New York were the largest deployment of these light troops to that date.[14]

While General Gage and General Howe were developing light infantry in this modern army, other British officers invented new units of light horse. The central figure was Colonel John Burgoyne. In 1757, he raised a new regiment called the Sixteenth Light Dragoons. They were meant to be highly mobile and heavily armed. Every trooper carried two pistols, a short-barreled carbine, and a long cavalry sword.[15]

Burgoyne was a top-down reformer who despised equality, insisted that his officers must be of high social standing, and opposed promotion from the ranks. He demanded that his officers think of themselves as professional soldiers, required them to write English with "swiftness and accuracy," ordered them to learn French, and compelled them to make time for "reading every day." He expected them to become highly skilled in tactics, weapons, and horsemanship down to "each strap and buckle." They were required not to abuse their horses or "swear at their men." His troopers welcomed Burgoyne's reforms and called him "Gentleman Johnny," partly for his extravagant personal tastes, but mostly for the courtesy that he showed to inferiors in a hierarchical world.[16]

In 1762, Burgoyne's light horse saw heavy service in Portugal and won a reputation for slashing attacks on larger Spanish forces. They came home in triumph, and George III ordered six regiments of light dragoons to be formed on their example. They proved use-

Officers of Heavy Cavalry and Light Dragoons (ca. 1780). The
Trustees of the National Museum of Scotland.

ful in keeping restless civil populations in order, a major task of the
British army in a world without professional police.[17]

Another proud elite who came to Staten Island was the Royal
Regiment of Artillery, in dark blue uniforms that contrasted with
the red of the British infantry. Three battalions of Royal Artillery
landed on Staten Island, with a strength of seventy-two guns. Even
their enemies acknowledged them as the best and most modern
field artillery in the world. Officers were appointed not by purchase
but merit and trained as "gentlemen cadets" at the Woolwich Military Academy, which the army called "the Shop." They studied al-
gebra, trigonometry, quadratic equations, chemistry, engineering,
and logistics and became an intellectual elite in the army.[18]

Woolwich-trained officers were highly innovative and drew upon
the flow of invention in Britain's early Industrial Revolution. In the
early 1770s, William Congreve and James Pattison developed a new
generation of mobile brass field guns with light but sturdy carriages
and interchangeable parts. Some of these new weapons, called "grasshoppers," could be moved on pack horses or carried by eight men.

They were designed for mobility on American terrain.[19] Congreve also ran the Royal Powder Factory and developed munitions in great variety: hollow shells with bursting charges, incendiary "carcasses" for use against buildings, canister and grapeshot against infantry, illuminating rounds and smoke shells. From the experience of the American war, Lieutenant Henry Shrapnel would invent in 1784 an exploding shell that still bears his name.[20]

Other British gunners developed new ways of using artillery in battle. Among them was William Phillips, who would be prominent in the American War of Independence. He was commissioned lieutenant-fireworker in 1747 and made his reputation at Minden, moving his guns with speed and concentration that turned the battle. When the French infantry fell back, the British artillery pursued them, driving their big battery horses into a trot, and turned a retreat into a rout.[21] Phillips took a leading role in the American war. The development of mobile artillery on a large scale was a shock to the Americans, and had a major impact on the campaigns that followed.

Most British troops who landed on Staten Island were infantry of the line, in twenty-six "marching regiments." Some of these units had existed for more than a century, others for only a few years. All cherished their traditions, and most were recognized as having a distinct regimental character. The Fifth Foot were called "the Shiners," from the money that their patrons, the opulent dukes of Northumberland, lavished on their turnout. The Tenth Foot were known as "the Springers," from their "readiness for action." These characteristics were imposed on all men in a regiment. In the Shiners, all men must shine. Among the Springers, every man must spring. Other British regiments gained nicknames from American events. The Twenty-ninth Foot became "the Ever Sworded" after an unarmed party was massacred in America in 1746; for two hundred years the regiment carried swords in the mess. The Fifty-fourth Foot were called "the Flamers," for the American houses they put to the torch.[22]

Each British regiment reinforced its character by doing its own recruiting. In 1776, this was an army of volunteers, but some of its methods gave new meaning to volunteering. More than a few felons were given a free choice between prison and the army, or occasionally (and illegally) between a rope and a red coat. Many enlisted in the face of poverty and even starvation. In the Thirty-third Foot, recruiters attracted men by raising oatcakes on their swords. The regiment was known as "the Havercake Lads."[23]

Most soldiers were in the army because they wanted to be there. Recruits were drawn by the promise of adventure and the attractions of a martial life. Regiments were able to select men with discrimination, and officers' manuals offered much advice on that subject. "Country lads" of sixteen to nineteen were favored as "more tractable." Young men of pleasure, "bred up amidst the corruption and vices of a metropolis," were "not to be desired." Army recruiters believed that "seamen and colliers never make good soldiers," and they refused to take men who had been discharged for misbehavior, or even those who had served in another regiment. Contrary to persistent myth, British soldiers were not an army of outcasts, criminals, and psychopaths. Most were farmers, weavers, and laborers with clean records.[24]

Before the American Revolution, British soldiers enlisted for life. In 1776, most were veterans of long service. The regiment became their home, and they were fiercely proud of it. Later in the war, recruiting became more difficult, and the army took on a different character. It reduced the term of service to three years, and some regiments increased the bounty from the obligatory king's shilling to a golden guinea or more. By 1778, the supply of recruits ran so low that Parliament passed an Army Press Act, carefully exempting all parliamentary voters from the draft. The law was intended mainly to stimulate voluntary enlistment. Always it was thought that British soldiers should enlist as an act of choice.[25]

When British regiments came to America in 1776, recruiting parties remained at home and sent a flow of new soldiers across the Atlantic throughout the war. To read the muster rolls in the Public Record Office is to be amazed at the complex global system that kept British regiments throughout the world strong enough to function, if rarely at full strength.

While the army assembled on Staten Island, training went on at an urgent pace. It was a process vital to this modern army. Every British regiment did its own training, each in its own way, but most British units shared a similar approach that set them apart from European armies. Colonel John Burgoyne observed that the Prussian method was to train men "like spaniels by the stick," and the French method "substituted honour instead of severity." He thought "a just medium between the two extremes to be the surest means to bring English soldiers to perfection."[26]

British officers studied the process of training with great care and analyzed it in many manuals and treatises. Captain Bennet Cuthbertson of the Fifth Foot wrote one of the most widely read works, *A System for the Compleat Interior Management and Œconomy of a Battalion of Infantry*. First published in 1768, it was reprinted in 1776 and purchased in bulk by regimental agents. Another important work was the anonymous *A New System of Military Discipline, Founded upon Principle by a General Officer*, attributed to Richard Lambert, the Sixth Earl of Cavan, also reprinted in 1776.[27]

The ideas in these British military books were very far from the values of the American Revolution, but in their own way they were also part of the Enlightenment. Most were written in a spirit of improvement and humanitarian reform. Instead of centering on liberty, they were mainly a search for order and regularity through discipline. They thought of disciplined soldiers not as "robots" or "human machines" or "automatons," as writers such as Michel Foucault mistakenly believed, but as men who actively engaged their minds and wills in the performance of their duty. This was particularly the case in the British army.[28]

British treatises on military discipline began by reflecting on the purposes of military training. They agreed that its end was "to enforce obedience, and to preserve good order." The object was to create a spirit of "subordination," on the assumption that "no authority can exist where there is not a proper submission." In the British army this was not to be done primarily by the stick or the lash but in more constructive ways. The goal was to train a soldier to think of himself as part of a tightly integrated unit. It was also to teach him to act willingly and even creatively in support of others. To those ends, the soldier's will was not broken but bent or guided in the direction of his duty. One of the most commonly used praise-words in British (and later American) armed forces was and still is "presence of mind." Men were encouraged to have presence of mind and to use it on a battlefield in a disciplined way.[29]

It is interesting to see how this was achieved. Basic training in the British army took a new recruit through a sequence of instructors. All of them taught specific skills and a general attitude. First came the corporal, who trained new-caught men to stand and walk with "a military bearing." The object was to make the recruit the "master of his person," which meant learning to "carry himself" with "self-possession," which was an idea of internal discipline. He was trained to do these things with pride and strength and confidence, as a member of his regiment. Unlike some other methods of training, it did not begin by trying to break a man down but from the start worked to build him up, and to make him stronger.[30]

The Twenty-fifth Foot at Minorca, 1771, by an unknown artist. At the far right is
Lord George Lennox, colonel of the regiment, talking with the sergeant major.
The drummer, fifer, infantry and grenadiers (to the left) are marching with the
Prussian step. National Army Museum, London.

After learning to stand and walk like a soldier, a recruit was
taught to march: first alone, then in a file with others. In 1776, most
British soldiers learned the "Prussian step," with stiff knees and
straight legs. Each foot was extended horizontally to fall flat on the
ground, toes out, arms straight at one's side, chest out, stomach in,
head up, spine stiffened, chin straight, and face frozen—while a
corporal was shouting in one's ear. The Prussian step seemed at
first an unnatural gait, but it was comfortable when learned, and
most men could do it with order and regularity. British recruits were
taught to do this "soldier's step" with short paces and long paces, in
"slow step" and "quick step." They practiced until they could do it
without thinking. Slow learners were called "the awkward men" and
made to practice in extra hours until they got it right.[31]

After mastering this movement, a recruit was trained to march
in step, to the beat of the drum. Marching in time was a recent re-
invention, inspired by the ancient memory of Roman legions and

by the modern example of the Prussian army under Frederick William I. For more than a century British troops had been doing some movements in step. Pikemen had long done so. As early as 1662, British infantry were trained to advance on the battlefield by starting on their left foot and counting paces. During the mid-eighteenth century, marching in time spread very rapidly through European armies. In 1763, a manual observed that "marching in cadence" was "now practised by some of the British troops," though not by all of them. Old soldiers did not like it, and some complained that it was "too much like dancing," but it was found to be useful on the battlefield and important for the mastery of discipline. By 1776, marching in step and cadence had become general throughout the British army.[32]

Every marching movement was elaborately studied and taught until men could move together in close order under any conditions, especially on a field of battle. Here again the object was to engage a soldier's will in this process of discipline and control and to make the "motions of the will" as regular as those of a disciplined body. It was observed that many recruits found pleasure in mastering these movements, responding instantly to commands, and choosing to become one with others in the regiment.

Recruits also learned to respond willingly to the beat of a drum, which in the eighteenth century was made without muffles so that it could be heard over the noise of battle. In 1768, Thomas Simes's *The Military Medley* listed many drum signals that every British soldier had to learn. Some established daily routines such as reveille and taptoo (ten o'clock in summer and nine o'clock on winter nights). Other drum-calls assembled an entire command, or summoned sergeants or officers. Many signals were for maneuvers on the battlefield. One stroke with a flam (made by striking the drumhead with both drumsticks almost but not quite simultaneously) meant turn or face right. Two strokes and a flam meant turn left. Three strokes were the signal for turn right about; four meant left about. Altogether British regiments used 170 drum signals, and soldiers were drilled to move instantly on hearing them. It was discovered that in moments of stress men were more responsive to drum signals than to voice commands. "Military musick" also had another function: It welded men into units. Drummers and fifers had a broad repertoire of marching tunes, regimental songs, and popular ditties that men sang together to the beat of the drum, creating a strong sense of regimental identity and a spirit of belonging.[33]

After a corporal taught the recruits to march in time, a sergeant took over and instructed them "in the use and management of arms." They were trained to follow a set of rules called the Manual Exercise, "ordered by His Majesty" in 1764 for the "handling of firelocks." There were thirty-five different commands, and each command was analyzed into many separate motions. The simple command "Ground your firelocks!" required a sequence of fourteen motions, which had to be done with perfect precision so that men could perform them together in close formation.[34]

After recruits mastered the manual exercise, they learned volley firing, first by "snapping" unloaded weapons, then by using "squibs," or blank cartridges, and finally by firing powder and ball. Where supplies of ammunition allowed, men were taught to load and fire very rapidly, which was the key to the success of British infantry. Then they learned to fire in formation, first in a single line, then in two ranks, and finally in the three ranks that were often used by British infantry in 1776 and not easy to master. Soldiers had to learn to fire and reload very quickly while standing very close to one another. Their

A Perspective View of an Encampment for a British Regiment, ca. 1777. In the right foreground recruits are being trained in the Manual Exercise and Close Order Drill. Note the many women and children in the camp. Some are cooking (right foreground), returning laundry (far left), and officers' ladies are visiting (in the center). A senior officer's marquee appears in the background. The camp displays the high standard of cleanliness and order which existed in the British army. Anne S. K. Brown Military Collection, Brown University Library.

movements had to be controlled and synchronized with great care, for an entire formation could be disrupted by one clumsy soldier. They also learned to "lock" their formation, so that "the front rank knelt down, the second rank shifted slightly to the right, and the third moved a half-pace" to the right. The object was to concentrate the largest volume of fire on the smallest possible front.[35]

Some regiments and commanders trained their men in aimed fire, though there was no command for "Take aim" in the Manual Exercise and no effective sights on standard-issue muskets. A special effort was made to control the elevation of the weapon, which was the key to effective volley firing. In 1779, a test was made of volley firing by a battalion of Norfolk militia. At a distance of seventy yards, only 20 percent of the shots struck a target that was eighty feet wide and two feet high. The problem was to train men to level their weapons and not to fire high, which even trained troops tended to do under stress. At Boston in 1775, General Thomas Gage had his men firing at marks in the Charles River.[36]

The last part of basic training was in the hands of the regimental adjutant, who taught the men to form a line, a column, and a square. Incessant drilling continued through a soldier's entire term of service, in "manual exercise, platoon exercise, evolutions, firing and manouevres." This was followed by frequent inspections, culminating in an annual inspection of the entire regiment, with a written critique by a higher authority.[37]

Another part of a recruit's basic training was to maintain his uniform and equipment, a complex and difficult task. Much attention was given to meticulous regulation of the smallest details of dress. The rules were unimaginably elaborate. "It is impossible to be too exact and particular," one manual advised. Close attention to neatness and uniformity was thought important "for the support of discipline." The theory was that "small lapses should be corrected and punished quickly to prevent larger ones" and to accustom men to working with others in a willing way.[38]

Soldiers were also taught to keep a high standard of cleanliness, a vital factor for the health and safety of the army. The British army was very well trained that way, with a high standard of camp sanitation, which was literally a matter of life and death. An historian writes that "by comparison with some eighteenth-century armies and with contemporary civilian populations, the British Army in the War for American Independence seems to have enjoyed exceptionally good health." This was so on Staten Island, even in a long, hot American summer that made field sanitation very difficult.[39]

Training and drill were reinforced by discipline, which varied broadly from one unit to another. In some regiments much use was made of flogging, and discipline was brutal beyond imagining. The Forty-eighth, Fifty-fifth, and Fifty-seventh Regiments of Foot were all called "steelbacks" from the heavy floggings that they endured. Others were called "bloody backs." But most regiments were moving toward different methods of discipline and used flogging with moderation. In the Thirty-third Foot it was said of Lord Cornwallis, the colonel of the regiment, that "he never used the lash to break a man's spirit, but he never hesitated to use it to instill discipline."[40]

Yet another approach prevailed in the Fifth Foot, where Lord Percy and the officers made little use of flogging and preferred rewards to punishments. As early as 1769, the Fifth Foot introduced regimental medals of merit. A soldier who stayed out of trouble for seven years received a medal with the inscription "seven years military merit" in a circle of laurel leaves, to be displayed by a ribbon from his lapel. For fourteen years of meritorious service, a soldier received a silver medal. In the Fifth Foot, much use was also made of shame. Cuthbertson recommended that a "slovenly soldier" should be dealt with by "disgracing him before his brother soldiers and exposing him in a publick manner to their derision."[41]

In the British army as a whole, discipline was regulated by a code of military law called the Articles of War. Commanders worried mainly about two offenses: desertion and mutiny. When desertion increased, higher authorities made examples by punishments of extreme brutality. Men who deserted repeatedly were sometimes sentenced to a thousand lashes, administered in many floggings, which destroyed the flesh on a man's back and broke his will. Other deserters were sentenced to death by firing squad, with comrades as executioners and the regiment looking on. The most dreaded punishment was to be sentenced to "perpetual banishment in the corps of infantry stationed on the coast of Africa," a death sentence by another name.[42]

Even more severely punished than desertion was mutiny, which included any act of "sedition," any hint of violence against a superior, or any knowledge of such a thing. The penalty for mutiny was death. The two articles on desertion and mutiny were required to be read to every recruit on enlistment, in solemn ceremonies where each soldier was instructed in his duties and also in his rights. But the Articles of War also had another purpose. They established the rights of British soldiers, who could not be arrested or imprisoned for more than eight days without due process of law. Officers were required to act as gentlemen and treat their men decently. Any soldier who thought himself abused by his commanding officer could demand a court-martial, but woe unto him if his complaint was found to be without merit.

Another purpose of the Articles of War was to protect civilians from depredations by the army. Soldiers were forbidden to abuse women, to commit crimes against the civil population, or to steal or spoil property, "unless by order" to "annoy Rebels or other Enemies in arms against us."[43] These rules were enforced on Staten Island. Young American women were at high risk near British camps, and one officer made a joke of it. Francis Lord Rawdon, a captain in Percy's Fifth Foot, wrote home from Staten Island in an infamous letter, "The fair nymphs of this isle are in wonderful tribulation, as the fresh meat our men have got here has made them as riotous as satyrs. A girl cannot step into the bushes to pluck a rose without running the most imminent risk of being ravished, and they are so little accustomed to these vigorous methods that they don't bear them with the proper resignation, and of consequence we have the most entertaining courts-martial every day."[44]

Lord Rawdon's remarks are often quoted in histories of the Revolutionary War as evidence of what the Americans were fighting against. They also tell us that courts martial met every day on Staten Island, in a sustained effort to enforce the rule of law, and to establish some measure of due process for soldiers and civilians. In the British army, military justice was thought to be vitally important to discipline.

～ An Army Within the Army: The Highland Regiments

An enduring strength of the British army, and another application of its modern idea of discipline, was its ability to enlist its most formidable enemies as entire regiments or corps, with their own customs and traditions intact but with a high standard of order. The first of many groups were the warrior clans of the Scottish Highlands, who as recently as 1745 had been mortal foes of the English army. After the battle of Culloden, Scots were forbidden to wear the kilt or carry weapons. Only a few years later they were enlisting in the British army. Highlanders who had long been faithful to the house of Stuart began to serve throughout the empire as loyal soldiers of a Hanoverian king.[45]

Two regiments of Scottish Highlanders joined the British army on Staten Island. One was the Forty-second Foot, or Royal Highland Regiment, better known since 1861 as the Black Watch. It was raised to keep order in the Highlands and renowned through the empire for winning more battle honors than any other regiment in the British army. The other was the Seventy-first or Fraser's Highlanders, raised in 1757 and revived in 1775 by the family of Lord Lovat, who had been executed as a rebel in the Forty-five.

Each Scottish regiment was as big as a British brigade. In 1776, the Forty-second and Seventy-first each recruited three battalions for American service, 3,248 men in all. When English regiments were having trouble attracting men for American service, recruiters went through the Highlands, and men flocked to the colors. Part of it was the poverty of Scotland and the size of the bounty—a golden guinea and a crown, later raised to three guineas—but most young Scots had been bred to a warrior tradition, and they leaped at the chance to join a Highland regiment. At the start of the American Revolution, the *Scots Magazine* reported that sixty-five thousand men came forward to enlist.[46]

An Officer and Soldier of the Forty-second Foot, The Royal Highland Regiment, watercolors by Edward Davies (ca. 1780). Two large battalions of this regiment, later known as the Black Watch, saw active duty in the American War. We are grateful to Lieutenant Colonel S. J. Lindsay of the Black Watch and Allan Carswell at Edinburgh Castle for helping with these two paintings. National War Museum of Scotland.

They were recruited by groups from the glens, often with the help of clan leaders. Many served with their own kin. In the Second Battalion of the Seventy-third Foot, twenty of about thirty-five officers were named Mackenzie. In the Forty-second Foot, which recruited from the glens and lochs of the central Highlands, especially from Perthshire, a large part of the regiment was named Campbell, Stewart, or Stirling.[47] Many new recruits spoke only Gaelic. In the eighteenth century, Highland regiments ran their own schools "under the management of an old soldier," to teach the men to read and write English so that they could communicate with the rest of the army.[48]

The men were often desperately poor, but they were very proud and often of high standing in their clans. In the early years of the Forty-second Foot, English officers observed with amazement that privates arrived on the parade ground with gillies, or servants, carrying their weapons. In Highland regiments many of these men rose from the ranks to be officers. Colonel David Stewart of Garth remembered that in his seventeen years with the Forty-second Foot, twenty-eight sergeants became commissioned officers, an extraordinary number in comparison with English regiments in which the number of officers commissioned from the ranks approached zero.[49]

Arms were the profession of these men, and many served for life. The record for long service belonged to Private Donald Macleod, who enlisted in the Royal Scots, and joined the Independent Companies (later the Forty Second Foot) ca. 1730. He served for 75 years and was living in London at the age of 103. His children were said to range in age from eighty-three to nine.[50]

Some of these men joined for the uniform, which was a thing to behold: a short red jacket of a military cut, the regimental kilt, a plaid (Gaelic for blanket) draped from the back of the left shoulder, bright red and white caddis stockings, a sporran of badger skin or leather, and a bonnet either of black bearskin or the feathers of an eagle, vulture, or black cock. Scottish infantry were armed to the teeth. In the Forty-second Foot, the Crown supplied each soldier with a musket and bayonet. The colonel of the regiment added a brace of pistols and a Highland broadsword at his own expense. For close work the men equipped themselves with belted dirks and hidden black knives. Sergeants carried Lochaber axes eight feet long, which in strong hands could cleave a man from crown to groin. American troops were not properly intimidated by this weapon, and it was replaced by carbines or fusees in the New World.

In 1775, it was observed that Highland recruits knew the use of all their weapons except the musket, and they were drilled by candlelight before they sailed to America. The very able commander of the Forty-second Foot, Lieutenant Colonel Thomas Stirling, had long experience in America. He prepared his men for service in the New World by personally teaching them how to fight in open formation. In America the Highland battalions were used as light infantry with great success.

Highland regiments had a distinct method of discipline that centered mainly on honor and reputation among kin. One soldier in the Forty-second Foot wrote that a Highlander regarded "any disgrace which he might bring on his clan or district as the most cruel misfortune." One officer, yet another Colin Campbell, announced that if any man left the field to carry a wounded comrade, "his name shall be stuck up in the parish church," which was more dreaded than whips or chains. Flogging was rarely used in the Forty-second Foot. It was recorded that "no instance of corporal punishment occurred" for many years. In five years only one man deserted from the regiment. When he was brought back, his comrades refused to mess with him.[51]

A Highlander's fierce pride and loyalty to his regiment appeared in an incident that happened during the American Revolution. A large body of recruits for Fraser's Highlanders and the Royal Highland Regiment were ordered to the Eightieth and Eighty-second Foot, which were regiments of lowland Scots who spoke English and did not wear the kilt. The Highlanders refused, insisting that they had enlisted only to serve with their own kin. A large force was sent to arrest them, and the recruits drew up by regiments on the shore in Leith and prepared to defend themselves. A battle followed. Of the Regulars who tried to arrest them, nine were killed and thirty-one wounded by a force of raw recruits.

The Highlanders were at last overpowered and eventually court-martialed in Edinburgh Castle. Several men spoke in their own defense. Archibald MacIver of the Forty-second Foot said that he and his friends came from Inverness and Argyll, spoke only Gaelic, were "ignorant of the English tongue," and always used the kilt and had "never worn breeches," which were inconvenient for all healthy men to wear and "impossible for a native highlander." The military court was unmoved by this appeal and sentenced them to death, but King George III intervened and granted the men "free pardon" to join their regiments in America. His Majesty may not have understood about an American and his taxes, but he knew not to come between a Highlander and his kilt.

These Scottish soldiers were also Regulars, with a strong sense of discipline, but in a different way from English regiments. They were bound together less by rituals of drill and order and more by kinship, reputation, and a fierce sense of loyalty that flowed through family, clan, and chiefs and upward to the king himself. A constant principle was personal loyalty. In 1775, many thousands of High-landers swore allegiance to George III and turned out to fight for him with a feeling of personal obligation and some considerable disgust for the American rebels. When a group of American soldiers was captured by the Forty-second Foot in 1776, a kindly Scottish sergeant scolded them, "Young men, ye should never fight against your king."[52]

Scottish and English Regulars shared important values in com-mon with American rebels, but in other ways their principles were far apart. The writings of soldiers and officers show that these men, even the Whigs among them, believed deeply in the British monar-chy. On enlistment they swore a personal oath "to be true to our Sovereign Lord King George, and to serve him honestly and faith-fully." The army celebrated many special days with rituals of loyalty and obeisance. It observed the official birthdays of the queen on January 18 and the king on June 4, the restoration of the monarchy on May 29, the coronation of George III on September 22, and his accession to the throne on October 25. Individual regiments also had their own days that celebrated a connection with the Crown. These rituals represented ideals of loyalty, fidelity, honor, duty, dis-cipline, and service that were as sacred to British Regulars as the cause of liberty was to the American rebels. For men on both sides who actually did the fighting, the war was not primarily a conflict of power or interest. It was a clash of principles in which they deeply believed.

THE HESSIANS

❧ The Landgraf's Dream: An Army of Honor and Profit

> Honor and Gold await us!
> If Heaven will lead us back home. . . .
> But if we die as brave soldiers there,
> Earth will cover us as well as here.
>
> —Hessian marching song, 1776[1]

ON AUGUST 15, 1776, yet another European army came to New York. Two large convoys arrived with eight thousand Hessian troops on board. Many more would follow. Altogether about twenty thousand Hessians served in the American War of Independence, plus ten thousand soldiers from other German states, and other men who were recruited individually for service in British regiments. Their saga is an important part of our story, and a fascinating subject in its own right.[2]

Even before the Revolution began, British ministers in London had tried to hire them for service in the colonies. It is startling to discover from French and German sources that as early as the winter of 1774–75, British envoys held secret negotiations at the Hessian palace of Hofgeismar for the employment of large numbers of German troops to control the American colonies, many months before the first shots were fired at Lexington and Concord. The talks failed because Hessian price was high and the parties could not agree on terms.[3]

When the American fighting began in 1775, the British government tried to hire twenty thousand Russian troops, thinking that they would be cheaper than Germans. A British officer in America added that Russians were "the most eligible" in another way, as "not understanding the language, they are less likely to be seduced by the artifice and intrigue of these holy hypocrites." But Empress Catherine the Great wanted no part of it and wisely refused. British ministers approached the Netherlands and asked to rent their Scottish Brigade, with no success. Prussia's Frederick the Great also refused to rent his army and wrote to Voltaire that selling one's subjects to the English was like selling "cattle to have their throats cut." Lacking other sources, members of Parliament suggested that perhaps an army of Moors might be hired from the fez of Morocco.[4]

In desperation the British government returned to the small states of Germany, who were the largest suppliers of troops in the world, if also the most expensive. The "soldier trade," or *Soldatenhandel* as Germans called it, was a big business in middle Europe, where small states maintained large armies and had long rented them to other rulers when not in use at home. Nobody was more successful in that commerce than Friedrich Wilhelm II, Landgraf of Hesse-Cassel. In 1760, he became the absolute ruler of his small state in west-central Germany. It was an impoverished country of about 2,750 square miles and 275,000 people. More than 90 percent of the population were farming families who made a precarious living on poor soil. Much of the land was forest, and the climate was thought to be exceptionally dark and wet.

Hesse-Cassel was not on the main arteries of trade in middle Europe. Its towns were stagnant and declining in the mid-eighteenth century, and the region had been much fought over in major European wars. As late as 1750, visitors noted that Hesse-Cassel had not yet recovered from the horrors of the Thirty Years War, which ended in 1648, more than a century earlier. Another terrible war began in 1757, and once again Hesse was a battleground. The city of Cassel changed hands eight times in the fighting, and Marburg fifteen times. The countryside was ravaged by French, British, and German armies, and the death rate trebled in ten years.[5]

The ruler of this small state had very large ambitions. Friedrich Wilhelm II was an interesting and complex man. He had been raised to the warrior ethic of German nobility, and his childhood governor August Moritz von Donop trained him to be a soldier. Friedrich Wilhelm loved the discipline of martial life and spent much of his early adulthood fighting in incessant European wars. Prussia was his country's ally, and Frederick the Great became his hero.

GERMAN TROOPS IN THE AMERICAN WAR, 1776–83

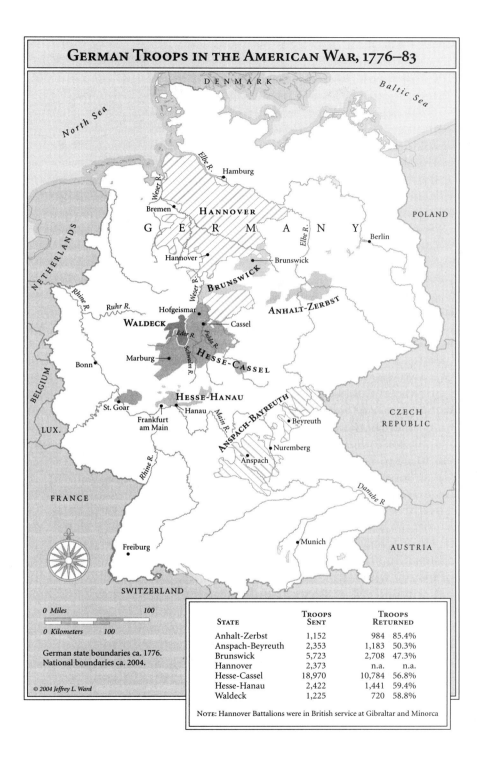

STATE	TROOPS SENT	TROOPS RETURNED	
Anhalt-Zerbst	1,152	984	85.4%
Anspach-Beyreuth	2,353	1,183	50.3%
Brunswick	5,723	2,708	47.3%
Hannover	2,373	n.a.	n.a.
Hesse-Cassel	18,970	10,784	56.8%
Hesse-Hanau	2,422	1,441	59.4%
Waldeck	1,225	720	58.8%

NOTE: Hannover Battalions were in British service at Gibraltar and Minorca

0 Miles 100

0 Kilometers 100

German state boundaries ca. 1776.
National boundaries ca. 2004.

© 2004 Jeffrey L. Ward

*Friedrich Wilhelm II,
Landgraf of Hesse-Cassel*, a
painting by Johann
Heinrich Tischbein the
Elder. Staatliche Museum,
Kassel.

Like his Prussian model, Friedrich Wilhelm was a man of the
Enlightenment. He corresponded with Voltaire and studied in
Geneva with Jean-Jacques Burlamaqui, who taught him to believe
in a world ruled by natural law and reason. Another major force in
his life was religion. Hesse-Cassel had long been a Calvinist state,
but in 1749 Friedrich Wilhelm shocked his people by converting to
Catholicism. He made pilgrimages to Rome and devoted himself to
his new faith, even while his subjects remained staunch Protestants.
The three great influences in his life were the Prussian army, the
Roman Catholic Church, and the European Enlightenment. All centered on what he called the "love of order," an ideal that he served
all his life. Friedrich Wilhelm put his thoughts on paper in a series
of essays, which he called his *Pensées*. They laid out a creed for an
enlightened ruler. Most of all they celebrated reason and order, fidelity and loyalty, discipline and regularity.[6]

As Landgraf of Hesse-Cassel and head of the Hessian army,
Friedrich Wilhelm II put these ideas to work. He became the model
of an enlightened prince, and a social reformer in his orderly way.
Though absolute power was firmly in his hands, he consulted with
the Hessian *Landtag,* or Assembly, and worked to establish the rule
of law in his realm. Like many enlightened despots he read Cesare
Bonasana Beccaria with great attention and restricted the use of

torture in his realm. For his subjects he created a system of social welfare, organized a "collegial bureaucracy" to administer the country, built roads and canals, dredged the Fulda River, sponsored trade fairs, reconstructed towns, encouraged agricultural reform, founded schools, and encouraged universities and gave them *Lernfreiheit* and *Lehrfreiheit*, freedom to learn and freedom to teach. He also reduced taxes and was popular with his people.[7]

At the same time, Friedrich Wilhelm II expanded the Hessian army. It was important for security in a dangerous neighborhood. More than that, Friedrich Wilhelm thought of the army as a school of discipline. Many visitors remarked on his "passion for the military" and his devotion to the Prussian system. Every day he drilled his troops himself, even Sundays and holidays. On wet days he drilled them in the dining hall of his palace. Friedrich Wilhelm's *Pensées* celebrated the martial virtues. He encouraged the aristocracy to send their sons into the army, and most did so, as did the sons of the upper middle class. One leading scholar, Charles Ingrao, discovered that "more than two-thirds of all Hessian nobles receiving government pay were in the army."[8]

The Hessian army expanded very rapidly. In the early 1770s, it had twelve thousand regulars in the field army and twelve thousand militia on active duty in its garrisons. The ratio of active-service soldiers to civilians in Hesse-Cassel was 1:15. By comparison the ratio was 1:30 in Prussia and 1:300 in England. In proportion to population, the Hessian army was the largest in Europe, perhaps the largest in the world. It was also one of the best. The officers were professional soldiers who took a personal oath of loyalty to the Landgraf, made a career of military service, and kept a strict code of honor. Many were sons of serving officers and began their careers as cadets, as early as the age of eleven. They were highly educated in their profession. By the early 1770s, Hessian officers were attending the Collegium Carolinum in Cassel, where they studied languages, engineering, and mathematics. They were expert at military cartography, tactics, and logistics, more so than British or American officers. Advancement was by merit, and promotions were made in the field for outstanding service. Most officers were men of long experience. In the Regiment Alt von Lossberg, majors and captains averaged twenty-eight years of service in 1776; even the lieutenants had been in the army for ten to fifteen years.[9]

The highest-ranking officers tended to come from the Hessian aristocracy. One officer who would play a major role in the American war was Colonel Carl Emilius von Donop, thirty-six years old in

Carl Emilius Ulrich von Donop, a portrait by the younger Tischbein. This Hessian aristocrat was the personal adjutant to the Landgraf, and was given command of the Jäger Corps in America. This painting shows him as a hunter pointing to his prey. At his side is a dog marked with his initials, C. E. U. Westfälisches Landesmuseum für Kunst und Kulturge-schichte, Münster.

1776, the son of one of Hesse-Cassel's great noble families. Donop was tall, blond, handsome, ambitious, arrogant, and self-assured. He was well connected in the courts of Europe. One of his friends and correspondents during the American war was the Prince of Prussia and he was personal adjutant to the Landgraf of Hesse-Cassel when the American Revolution began. Donop asked leave to serve in America, and the Landgraf gave him the coveted command of the Jäger Corps. The young officer had expansive dreams of power and glory. He wrote to the prince of Prussia that after the colonial rebellion was subdued he hoped to remain in America, fight a new war "against all the powers in this part of the new world" and seize the wealth of Mexico and Peru.[10]

Colonel von Donop had a highly developed sense of social hi-erarchy. To his superiors he was very deferential and addressed them in a courtly French. To inferiors and to Hessian officers of lower social standing, he wrote in a harsh and curt language of command.

Behind a surface of civility, he was brutal and very cruel. He ordered his men to take no American prisoners and threatened to have them severely beaten if they did so. Colonel von Donop was thought to be an able officer, but he was not much loved by those who soldiered under him.[11]

Most Hessian officers came from the middle class. One of them was Colonel Johann Gottlieb Rall. In 1776, he was fifty years old, a veteran of thirty-six years' service in the Hessian army. The son of a military officer, he joined his father's regiment as a cadet, or *Freikorporal*, in 1740. His manners were rough and unpolished, and he spoke an earthy barracks-room German. Rall was a fighter. He saw much active service with the Hessian army and became a soldier of fortune in eastern Europe and Turkey. He won distinction as a combat soldier and was given command of a regiment before the American war.[12]

Colonel Rall was very much liked by his men. He stood up for them and showed them sympathy and kindness. A junior officer wrote that "considered as a private individual, he merited the highest respect. He was generous, magnanimous, hospitable, and polite to everyone; never grovelling before his superiors but indulgent with his subordinates. To his servants he was more friend than master. He was an exceptional friend of music and a pleasant companion."

His men especially remembered Colonel Rall's passion for music, in which the Hessian troops excelled. They organized vocal and instrumental groups in America. "In Europe we should not have got much honor by our music," one wrote, "but here we passed for masters." Colonel Rall delighted in directing his regimental band and its six oboes. An officer wrote that he sometimes neglected the details of barrack-room soldiering, "but oh, the hautboists. That was his affair!"[13]

Not so happy were Rall's relations with superiors who lacked his experience of combat. He let them know what he thought of them; they resented his attitude and despised his manners. Colonel von Donop and other aristocratic officers treated him with hostility, but Jäger Captain Johann Ewald commented that when it came to fighting they were not fit to carry Rall's sword.[14]

Colonel Rall's regiment were called *Landgrenadiere* and derived from the old Hessian *Landmiliz*, or militia. They were not thought to be an elite regiment. Most were young farm workers, very short in stature. Grenadier Johann Reuber, aged seventeen, was five feet one inch tall. His schooling was limited, but he kept a diary in a Hessian country dialect that revealed his feelings. Grenadier Reuber

Hessian Brass Fusilier's Cap from the American War. Armed Forces History Collection, Smithsonian Institution.

was fiercely proud of his commander and his regiment. Colonel Rall's leadership made it one of the best combat units in the Hessian army. In the spring of 1776, Colonel William Faucitt got to know Rall in Germany and described him as "one of the best officers of his rank in the Landgrave's army."[15]

Other Hessian officers were of more humble origins and rose from the ranks. One who did so and became prominent in America was Lieutenant Andreas Wiederholdt. He served in the Knyphausen regiment, reputed to be one of the most efficient in the army, with a strong cadre of senior sergeants. Wiederholdt enlisted as a private, rose to the rank of sergeant major in 1760, won distinction in battle during the Seven Years' War, and was made an officer. He was no youngster, as some American historians have inferred from his rank. In 1776, Lieutenant Wiederholdt was forty-four years old and a veteran of twenty-five years' service. During the American war he kept a journal that showed him to be hypercritical of his commanders, but he was very attentive to his men and his duty. In the field he was given much responsibility, and later he was promoted to captain, but there was a limit to how high he could climb in the Hessian army. After the war he left the Hessian service and became a general in the Portuguese army.[16]

These three officers, Donop, Rall, and Wiederholdt, represented three paths to command in the Hessian army. Different as they may have been in origins, education, and social rank, they all believed deeply in hierarchy, order, and discipline. In America they shared a deep contempt for the *Rebeller*, as they called their opponents. They despised the American language of liberty and freedom as the cant of cowards, traitors, and poltroons. They were skilled professional officers, proud to serve in the Hessian army. Though they hoped to make their fortunes in America, they were not mercenaries in the usual sense. These were men of courage and honor who believed in service to their prince, and they lived and died by a warrior's creed.

Hessian privates who came to America shared these attitudes. They were recruited in a complex process that was designed mainly to serve the needs of the state. All male children in Hesse-Cassel registered for military service at the age of seven. At sixteen they appeared for examination by recruiting officers. Between the ages of sixteen and thirty they were required to register every year at Easter. Decisions on their military service were made by servants of the state. Hessians who were thought to be more valuable in their civil occupations were declared "indispensable personnel" (*unabkömmliche Mannschaft*) and forbidden to join the army. Among them were skilled artisans, farmers with more than fifty acres, and anyone who made a major contribution to the Hessian economy.[17]

Hessian Jäger Corps (ca. 1776), hand-colored engraving by Müller in uniforms of green and red. Anne S. K. Brown Military Collection, Brown University Library.

Most other young males were strongly urged to enlist, especially younger sons of poor peasant families, who made up the rank and file of Hessian infantry regiments. Jägers, the Hessian equivalent of light infantry, tended to be sons of gamekeepers and foresters. Artillerists were sons of industrial workers in the cities. Recruits received many inducements for enlistment. The pay of a private soldier was higher than that of a servant or unskilled farm worker. The monthly wage was large enough to buy a cow or two pigs. Military families were exempted from some of the most onerous taxes and allowed various small liberties. Many recruits appear to have joined willingly, for they also shared a warrior ethic that was very strong in Hesse-Cassell. A Swiss scholar observed in 1781 that nearly all peasants had served in the army, and "everywhere they talk of war."

Other young Hessians were judged to be "expendable people" (*entbehrliche Leute*) and were forced into the army. They included "masterless servants," school dropouts, bankrupt tradesmen, the idle, the unemployed, and wandering youth, who were seized by recruiting parties on the roads. One victim was a student named J. G. Seume, who had left the University of Leipzig after a falling-out with university administrators and was making his way to Paris with a knapsack on his back and a few classics in his pockets. As he crossed Hesse-Cassell he was caught by a press gang and found himself in the army. Seume protested and brought out his matriculation papers, but a soldier ripped them up and told him that he was on his way to America. He was put under restraint with a bankrupt merchant from Vienna, a magistrate from Meiningen, a lacemaker from Hannover, and even a monk from Würzberg, all kidnapped on the road. None of them wanted to be there, and discipline was brutal. Some of his friends planned to desert and were betrayed. Two men thought to be ringleaders were summarily hanged. The rest were severely beaten by an entire company. "It was simple butchery," Seume wrote.

Like most recruits, Seume realized that resistance was futile. "I surrendered to my fate," he wrote, "and tried to make the best of a bad situation." He began to internalize the strict discipline of the Hessian army and took pride in being part of it. "I improved daily," he wrote, "and soon I got the reputation of being the man who knew perfectly all the manual and how to execute quickly and easily all the evolutions and military formations on the drill ground." The Landgraf's system of order and dominion worked on him. This restless university dropout and "masterless man" became a good soldier. He was promoted to sergeant and soon was helping to discipline other conscripted recruits.[18]

The Hessian system of discipline was different from the British army's. It made more use of corporal punishment with cudgels and clubs. A common penalty was thirty strokes with a stick. For more serious offenses the dreaded sentence was "the gauntlet," in which a soldier was severely pummeled by his peers. For serious infractions a soldier could be made to run the gauntlet twelve or twenty times. British officers who often used the lash rejected the cudgel as unfit even for animals, but it was widely used in the Hessian army.[19]

More use was made of capital punishment than in other armies. Hessian soldiers were hanged for leaving their post. They also knew that their families at home would be punished for their misconduct. Field discipline was relentless, more so than in the British or American armies. A case in point was an incident that involved three armies in America. On October 27, 1776, a Hessian soldier "straggled from camp" was captured by the Americans. He was brought to General Washington, who told him that "Hessians would get great encouragement" if they changed sides. The American commander-in-chief gave him a guinea and dismissed him to go back to his corps. The Hessian made his way back to British lines and was taken to General Howe. The German soldier explained what had happened, and Howe "likewise gave him a guinea" for coming back. Then he returned to his own commanders and explained once more what had happened. The Hessian general listened, then "ordered him to be flogged," for straggling from camp in the first place. One wonders who kept the golden guineas.[20]

By savage discipline and endless drill the Hessian army developed the dark art of training men to a condition of instinctive and unquestioning obedience.[21] It worked. At the battle of White Plains the Knyphausen regiment was ordered to advance against heavy musketry through a field of high grass. The grass caught fire, but the Hessian infantry kept advancing through the burning field, carrying their cartridge boxes over their heads so that their ammunition would not explode. They were stopped by heavy American volleys and driven back, but they came forward again and carried the day with heavy losses. Hessian soldiers were legendary for their discipline, courage, and obedience—as long as their officers and sergeants were there to lead them, sometimes by inspiring a greater fear.[22]

But it was not mainly fear that drove them. Hessian soldiers came to believe deeply in the values of order and obedience, which were taught to them in a very hard school. Their journals show that they also shared a sense of service and honor that Germans called *Dienst*.

Regiment von Knyphausen (ca. 1776), hand-colored engraving by Müller. This unit, reputed to be one of the best in the Hessian army, fought at Trenton. Anne S. K. Brown Military Collection, Brown University Library.

They also felt a sense of personal obligation to their Landgraf Friedrich Wilhelm II. Each man swore a personal oath to serve him. His livery was their uniform, and his name was engraved on their weapons and equipment. Their regimental and company colors carried mottos such as *Pro Principe et Patria*, "For Prince and Fatherland."

In America, Hessian diarists were amazed by the abundance of the New World and the affluence of even ordinary homes. By comparison with the poverty of Hesse, the New World seemed a land of plenty. From the Landgraf himself to the lowest private, they dreamed that they could grow rich from the American war, and sang about it in their marching songs.

> Frischauf, ihr Brüder, ins Gewehr,
> 's geht nach Amerika.
> Versammelt ist schon unser Heer
> Vivat Viktoria!
> Das rote Gold, das rote Gold
> Das kommt da nur so hergerollt,
> Da gibt's auch, da gibt's auch, da gibt's auch bessern Gold![23]

> Be quick, brothers, to arms!
> Let us go to America.
> Assembled is our army.
> Long live victory!
> That red gold, that red gold
> That comes rolling out from there
> There we'll all get it, get it, there we'll all get more gold.

Another barrack-room ballad repeated the same idea in soldiers' slang.

> Geht mit nach Amerika,
> Da wird sein genug allda.
> Es wird sein Silber, Gold und Geld,
> Was man suchet in der Welt
> Alles, was man suchet da
> Ist jetzt in Amerika.
>
> Go with us to America.
> There will be enough for all.
> There will be silver, gold, and money,
> Everything that man seeks in the world
> All that a man seeks there
> Is in America.[24]

That attitude was shared in Hesse-Cassel from the top to the bottom of the society, and with good reason. The treaty that Friedrich Wilhelm made with Britain was, in the words of one minister, "the deal of the century." He received a total of 21 million talers, for a net profit of 12.6 million talers. The Landgraf invested much of the money in British and Dutch stocks and in loans to other kingdoms, which brought a large annual income. Some of these returns were passed on to the people of Hesse-Cassel in the form of reduced taxes and increased public spending. The soldier trade and subsidy treaties had long been a leading source of income for Hesse-Cassel, and for many of its subjects. Far from being the tyrannical act of a despotic ruler, it was strongly supported by the Hessian *Landtag*, which urged Friedrich Wilhelm to negotiate more treaties and to rent the army more often.

Officers and privates also expected to make money out of the American war, and many did so. Captain Johann Ewald wrote that his pay as a company commander in the Jäger Corps was "more than one Guinea daily, without counting booty money, and everyone was well paid in proportion." He observed from long service that many officers made their fortunes in America. Even the private

Regiment von Alt Lossberg (ca. 1776), hand-colored engraving by Müller. This distinguished Fusilier regiment saw heavy service in the New York campaign and was present at Trenton. Anne S. K. Brown Military Collection, Brown University Library.

soldiers in his Jäger company received one pound sterling a month. Ewald wrote, "Never in this world was an army as well paid as this one during the civil war in America. One could call them rich."[25]

Hessian troops also had another source of income from "booty" that came to them as prize money and was officially sanctioned. Every man received his share, from generals to privates. Another source of gain was "forage." If a Hessian soldier consumed British rations, six shillings a month were deducted from his pay; if he supplied himself by foraging on the countryside, his pay was not docked. Every man had a vested double-interest in forage.

Then there was "plunder." It was officially forbidden, but officers often looked the other way and sometimes joined in. Hessians were punished for plundering, but typically because some other act was committed at the same time, such as arson. As we shall see, there is abundant evidence from Hessian sources that they plundered on a very large scale. Altogether Hessian soldiers in America sent more than a million talers home to their families. The state also paid more than nine million talers to families of soldiers.[26]

There was a tension in the Hessian army. It was a highly disciplined professional force, with strong values of obedience and service. At the same time, it was an army of entrepreneurs who assumed risk for the sake of profit. This was so from the Landgraf who was its commander-in-chief to the lowest private in the ranks. These attitudes shaped the conduct of Hessian soldiers in America and made a difference in the course of events. They also created other tensions between the British and Hessians, with serious consequences for their commanders and for the outcome of the war.

THE PLAN OF THE CAMPAIGN

~ The Howe Brothers in America

> Some persons condemn me for having endeavoured to con-
> ciliate His Majesty's rebellious subjects, by taking every
> means to prevent the destruction of the country.... I acted
> in that particular for the benefit of the King's service.
>
> —Sir William Howe, 1779[1]

FIRMLY IN COMMAND of British and Hessian forces at New
York were two brothers, Admiral Lord Richard Howe and
General William Howe. Both were officers of high ability and
long experience in the ways of war. They were also complex characters, deeply "interesting" in the eighteenth-century sense of engaging sympathy. How they came to their position and what they did
with it is a strange story.[2]

The Howe brothers were of an upwardly mobile aristocratic family, one of the most powerful in England on the eve of the American
Revolution. They were also of royal blood, in a convoluted way. The
Howe family rose from the Protestant gentry of Nottinghamshire,
where their ancestors accumulated large estates, held many offices,
sat in Parliament, and became eminent in the county. In the seventeenth century their grandfather Scrope Howe became a leader in
Parliament and strongly supported the Whig Revolution of 1688 at
a critical moment. In gratitude the new King William III raised him
to the peerage as the first Viscount Howe. His son, the second Viscount Howe, was also an important Whig in Parliament. He briefly
became governor of Barbados and was the father of the Howe brothers who commanded at New York.[3]

As prominent as these men had been, the Howe family owed its prominence in 1776 mainly to its women. The maternal grandmother of the Howe brothers was a very handsome German aristocrat who became the royal mistress of George I. Their mother, Sophia Kielmansegge, was believed to be the illegitimate daughter of the king. She was a strong and attractive woman, and the royal family accepted her as a blood relation. She became the friend and traveling companion of the mistress of George II. Later, as the dowager Countess Howe, she lived in the household of George III and received a large annual pension from the Crown. As the daughter of one king, the friend of another, and family advisor to a third, Countess Howe was said to be one of the strongest people around the king.

Under the watchful eye of this formidable lady, her sons grew up at court. They became friends and companions of the future King George III. He thought of them as cousins, which they were by blood if not by blessing. The Howe brothers were educated by private tutors and schooled at Eton, but neither was a great scholar. It was decided at an early date that they would follow military careers.[4]

Richard Howe was sent to the navy. He was enrolled by his family at the age of thirteen and went to sea as a midshipman the following year. His first cruise took him around Cape Horn and through the South Seas with Lord Anson, who became his patron. The Royal Navy, like every other British institution, showed deference to the high aristocracy and especially to blood relations of the Crown, but it also required its officers to be very good at their jobs. At sea young Richard was Mister Midshipman Howe, like any other "Snotty," as they were called in the navy.

He had to make his way by merit, and did so very rapidly. As a junior officer, Richard Howe won a reputation as a superb seaman, a fighter of high courage in wars against the French and Spanish, and one of the most able young officers of his generation. British newspapers were full of his exploits. As commander of a small sloop he helped drive off a larger French force in the Irish Sea. As a young post captain he fought a big French ship in the fog of the St. Lawrence River and defeated her. He became a legend for battering a French fortress on the Isle of Aix, rescuing a British army in a gale on the lee shore of Saint Cas, assaulting the massive defenses of Cherbourg, and sailing boldly into the dangerous shoals of Quiberon Bay to silence one French ship of the line and sink another.

Richard Howe became a hero to the nation and to his own men, who admired him as a fighting captain and respected his quiet integrity. The navy affectionately called him "Black Dick" for his dark complexion and his saturnine moods. On the morning of the first of June, 1794, one seaman was heard to tell another, "I think we shall have a fight today. Black Dick has been smiling."[5]

He became the youngest admiral in the navy and a leader of the service. Behind a forbidding exterior, Admiral Howe was a man of humanity who looked after his crews. He was no egalitarian, but in an age of hierarchy he treated his seamen as human beings and was known for "goodness" and "condescension" in that special eighteenth-century sense. In a world of inequality, Lord Howe showed a genuine attitude of decency and concern for his inferiors. He did not talk much about it. Lord Howe was famous for his extreme economy of speech. He never used a sentence where a single word would do. Horace Walpole remarked that he was as silent as a stone. But in his quiet way, Richard Howe worked for the welfare of British seamen, sought to raise their pay, and improved the conditions of their lives.[6]

He was also a naval reformer in other ways. As treasurer of the Admiralty he was a highly skilled administrator and set a new standard for honesty, accuracy, and ethics in public office. He promoted technical innovations in seamanship and designed new boats, sails, rigging, and weapons. In 1776, Lord Howe introduced to his American squadron a new system for maneuvering fleets by flag hoists that allowed an admiral to "converse" with his captains. An historian of the Royal Navy writes that this single change introduced a "new era" of command and control at sea.[7]

In 1758, he inherited the family title as the fourth Viscount Howe, which brought many responsibilities for his large family and its estates. But he continued his career in the Royal Navy, and he so loved the sea that he built a library in his country house as an exact replica of his cabin in HMS *Queen Charlotte*, his favorite flagship. When Lord Howe took command at New York in 1776, he was fifty years old and a veteran of thirty-six years' service. His opportunities came by privilege, but his achievements were won by merit. His brother officers and seamen under his command regarded him with respect and genuine affection. There was an authenticity about him, and not a hint of scandal. He was one of the best naval commanders of his age, a faithful friend, and a formidable opponent.[8]

While Richard Howe made his way in the navy, his younger brother, William Howe, was rising in the army. The family bought him a commission in 1746. He became a lieutenant when he was eighteen, a captain at twenty-one, and lieutenant colonel at the age of twenty-eight. As with his brother, privilege opened doors, but

Richard Lord Viscount Howe of the Kingdom of Ireland

Admiral Richard Lord Howe, the Fourth Viscount Howe, a 1778 mezzotint by James Watson, after a painting by Thomas Gainsborough. Boston Public Library, Print Department.

merit took him through them. During the Seven Years' War, William Howe distinguished himself for courage and leadership in actions along the coast of France. He joined the attack on Quebec, and General James Wolfe chose him to lead the vanguard of a small British army up the narrow goat's path to the Plains of Abraham, opening the way for the glorious victory that followed. Other laurels were won at Louisbourg, Havana, and Belle Isle, and he had a growing reputation as a brilliant and highly skilled tactician. When the war ended, William Howe came home a national figure and the model of a martial hero, six feet tall, dark, strong, and as silent as his brother. According to legend he returned to England in American buckskins and Indian moccasins, and his family nicknamed him "the savage."[9]

William Howe continued his career in time of peace and was regarded as one of the ablest field-grade officers in the army, but something happened to him during the French and Indian Wars.

There was also another brother in the family, the eldest son, George Augustus Howe, the third viscount. He was killed in a skirmish near Ticonderoga in 1758. By all accounts he was a man of rare and special spirit, much loved by those who knew him. Even the penurious people of Massachusetts taxed themselves for a handsome memorial in Westminster Abbey. His death was a heavy blow to the Howe family. Both of his brothers were deeply shaken, and each responded differently to loss and grief. Richard Howe became more austere and aescetic. William Howe went another way. At night he was often seen at faro tables in London surrounded by gamblers, courtesans, and others of that sleazy upper-class underworld that Thomas Jefferson called "the tinsel aristocracy." In the daytime he continued his career in the army. He became a leader in the reform of the service, and gave much attention to refinements of discipline and drill and to the development of light infantry.[10]

The Howe brothers sat in Parliament for many years, as did many high military officers. Richard Howe represented the navy town of Dartmouth from 1757 to 1782, and William Howe sat for Nottingham from 1758 to 1780. The politics of the Howe brothers, and their opinions on American affairs, were surprising to their relatives at court. Like others of the high aristocracy in the eighteenth century, they were staunch English Whigs who cherished their own liberty and believed deeply in the Revolutionary settlement of 1688, with its idea of a King-in-Parliament. They believed deeply in the human rights that were affirmed by the Glorious Revolution and also in the supremacy of Parliament, which put them squarely on both sides of the American question. In the 1760s they voted as moderate Whigs and did not support strong measures against America. Both believed deeply in the British Empire as an engine of progress and an instrument of law. At the same time, they sympathized with American demands for the rights of Englishmen within the empire.[11]

Through it all, the general and the admiral remained very close to King George III, but far from his opinions on the colonies. On one occasion, Richard Howe was traveling with the king and got into a flaming argument about America with him while they were dining in a tavern. Tempers rose so high that Richard Howe sharply rebuked the king's "persevering and invincible obstinacy" toward the colonies. George III replied in good humor that "it was imprudent to curse one's king before waiters in a public inn."[12]

William Howe shared the feelings of his brother. In 1774, he told the electors of Nottingham that the ministry had pushed its

American policy too far, that the entire British army could not conquer America, and that he would refuse a command there.

Events took a different turn. The king himself intervened and asked the Howes to go to America and resolve the dispute. On those terms the Howe brothers reluctantly agreed to serve, to the surprise of William Howe's constituents. He told them, "My going thither was not of my seeking. I was ordered, and could not refuse. . . . Every man's private feelings ought to give way to the service of the public."[13]

The Howe brothers went to America to restore the empire, by peaceful means if possible and war if necessary. William Howe was first on the scene in Boston in 1775, one of many generals who served under the command of General Thomas Gage. A council of generals decided that a strong demonstration of force would over-awe the colonists and return them to their allegiance. Something like that method had worked in many insurrections throughout

General the Honourable William Howe, pointing hopefully toward the American interior. This engraving, by an unidentified artist, is undated, but was done shortly after General Howe was made Knight of the Bath for his victories in the New York campaign (ca. 1777). Massachusetts Historical Society.

England, Wales, and Scotland during the eighteenth century. William Howe's part in that decision is not clear, but he volunteered to command the attack.

The result was the battle of Bunker Hill. William Howe led the assault himself. The result was a victory that turned into a disaster. The American peasants, as they were contemptuously called, fought with a determination that experienced British officers had never seen in them before and defeated two attacks. On the third assault, the British infantry marched up the hill through high grass so thick with blood that their gaiters were stained red. General Howe himself went with them, followed by a servant carrying a wine decanter on a silver tray. They won the hill, but nine hundred Regulars fell dead or severely wounded.

General Howe escaped without a scratch, but Bunker Hill had a profound effect on him. His opponent, the American General Henry Lee, observed in a very wise book on the American Revolution that "the sad and impressive experience of this murderous day sunk deep into the mind of Sir William Howe; and it seems to have had its influence upon all his subsequent operations with decisive control."[14]

After the battle, General Howe was celebrated for his courage and promoted to commander-in-chief of the British army in America. But he was increasingly reluctant to fight another general engagement against a highly unpredictable enemy, unless he could do so on his own terms without risking heavy losses. Always as taciturn as his brother, he became more silent about his purposes and acts. After Bunker Hill, he lost himself more than ever in mindless dissipation, indulging heavily in food and drink. He gave way to his passion for gambling every night, testing his luck over and over again in games of chance. There was something deeply melancholy about the frantic gaiety night after night at Sir William Howe's gaming table, while officers and men he cared deeply about were dying on his orders. Perhaps he was obsessed with the strange outcome of that greater game of chance in war itself, where so many worthy comrades risked everything and lost, while he survived.

William Howe also sought solace in the company of Elizabeth Lloyd Loring, a "flashing blonde," the young wife of New England Tory Joshua Loring. She was widely reported to be Howe's mistress in America, and her complaisant husband received a lucrative job as commissary of American prisoners, whom he cruelly abused in a horrific way. Satirists in Britain and America had a field day:

> Awake, arouse, Sir Billy,
> There's forage in the plain,
> Ah, leave your little Filly,
> And open the campaign.
> Heed not a woman's prattle
> Which tickles in the ear,
> But give the word for battle,
> And grasp the warlike spear.[15]

Others laughed, but here was another sad sign that this British commander-in-chief was not in command of himself.

William Howe's private affairs did not diminish his standing with his men or his attention to duty in working hours. Even his enemies conceded that "as an executive soldier . . . he is all fire and activity, as brave and cool as Julius Caesar."[16] He made a special effort to treat his subordinates with kindness and sympathy, an important clue to his character and conduct. Later in the campaign, a very green Hessian captain made a tactical mistake and was "sharply reprimanded" by his German superiors. General Howe went out of his way to speak kindly to the young officer, "to express his satisfaction" and to encourage him with words of support that were deeply appreciated. His men thought him "a good general," and in August 1776 he was described as "the Idol of the Army."[17]

In America, the Howe brothers were struggling with a very difficult problem. Their assignment was to end the rebellion and restore the American colonies to their allegiance. When they agreed to serve, they insisted on appointments not only as military commanders but also as peace commissioners, with powers to negotiate with American leaders and authority to grant pardon and amnesty. The king reluctantly agreed, but a powerful minister, George Germain, intervened against them. Germain took a very hard line against the Americans and did all in his considerable power to prevent compromise or conciliation. The Howe brothers were not allowed to grant substantive concessions and could not guarantee any of the rights for which the Americans were contending.

In London during the winter of 1774–75, Admiral Richard Howe had searched for a solution in conversations with Benjamin Franklin. They were brought together by the Howes' sister Caroline, an intelligent and attractive woman who met with Doctor Franklin ostensibly for games of chess but mainly for a political purpose. The British admiral and the American doctor got on well, and for many weeks they tried to find a way to settle the imperial dispute.

George Sackville Germain, First Viscount Sackville, an undated miniature by Nathaniel Hone. In the British government Germain took a very hard line against America. National Portrait Gallery, London.

But Franklin observed that any solution acceptable in America would require Parliament to stop taxing the colonies without their consent and allow Americans to manage their own affairs. This, Admiral Howe pointed out, was unacceptable in London. The negotiations ended in friendship and political failure.[18]

While Admiral Howe was talking with Franklin, General Howe had another solution in mind. He wrote to his constituents in Nottingham early in 1775 that many Americans "do not agree to a taxation from hence," but "do not wish to sever themselves from the supremacy of this country." He added hopefully, "This last set of men, I should hope, by their being relieved from the grievance, will most readily return to all due obedience of the laws."[19] He appears to have thought that a system of American self-taxation might be devised in a way that was consistent with parliamentary supremacy. Once again the king and his ministers did not agree, and the Howe brothers were not authorized to make any such agreement.

When the Howes came to New York, they attempted many negotiations with leaders in Congress and the Continental army. But given their instructions from London, they were fully aware that peace and reconciliation could be achieved only by the application of force. To that end, many plans were put before them. Some believed that the best way to defeat the rebellion was by blockade. The Americans were vulnerable to such a strategy. They traded actively throughout the Atlantic world. On the eve of the Revolution a larger part of per capita income in the colonies came from foreign trade than in any other era of American history. The Americans also needed foreign trade to make war. They could manufacture ships and firearms and cannon, but in the spring of 1775 they could not make their own gunpowder or even supply their own flints. Both had to be imported.[20]

For these reasons, several high officers in the Royal Navy thought that a blockade was the most promising solution. Lord Howe did not agree. He observed in 1776 that a full blockade of America was beyond the power of even the world's largest navy, which was burdened with many other tasks. Britain in 1776 was a world power without allies. France and Spain were spoiling for revenge from the last war and had more ships of the line than Britain possessed. A large part of the Royal Navy had to be kept close to home against the danger of European war and even invasion. The navy also supported British troops in America, escorted convoys, and protected commerce against American privateers. The Atlantic coastline of North America was more than three thousand miles long, and in 1775 a partial British blockade failed miserably. West Indian planters, European traders, and even merchants in Britain itself conspired to keep American commerce flowing. Between privateering and trade, American ports were busier and more prosperous than ever.

Other British leaders favored a different strategy, which Germans call *Shrecklichkeit*. This was the deliberate use of extreme violence and terror to break the American will to resist. In 1775, Major John Pitcairn, Admiral Samuel Graves, and General John Burgoyne recommended that British forces should sack and burn New England towns until the colonists gave up. This policy was supported by other British leaders such as George Germain who had experience of war in central Europe, where *Shrecklichkeit* was widely used. It also found support among officers who had served in Ireland and Scotland, where hard measures against civilian populations were routine.

Several officers actually applied this policy at the start of the Revolution. Admiral Graves ordered his men to burn the town of Falmouth in Maine, and General Burgoyne deliberately burned Charlestown during the attack on Bunker Hill. The only result was an explosion of American anger. The Howes rejected this approach. As good English Whigs they believed that the systematic destruction of civilian life and property was unlawful and inhumane. They also thought that it was unwise and ineffective. The Howe brothers forbade men under their command to act in such a way. General Howe ordered the execution of soldiers who attacked civilians and burned private property. Admiral Howe severely punished some of his men who sacked Naushon Island near Martha's Vineyard. *Schreck-lichkeit* was not their way of war. They would have no Irish scenes in North America.

A third strategy, strongly recommended by William Howe's second in command, General Henry Clinton, was to make war relentlessly against the rebel army, to seek it out and destroy it completely. Before the battle of Bunker Hill he urged other British generals to land troops behind the Americans at the base of the Charlestown peninsula, cut off the American army, and capture it. Afterward, Clinton advised Howe to pursue the retreating American army with the same object. Clinton repeated that argument many times in New York, suggesting operations that might destroy the American army. This was always Clinton's advice, and the Howes always rejected it. After Bunker Hill, General Howe appears to have felt that the Americans in arms were an elusive adversary: Their armies could melt away into the civil population, and even if one army were captured or destroyed, two more would rise in its place. In a general engagement against these dangerous enemies, even a victory could come at a ruinous price.

In the spring of 1776, William Howe sent a letter to London that is a key to his thinking. "The scene here at present wears a lowering aspect," he wrote, "there not being the least prospect of conciliating this continent unless its armies are roughly dealt with; and I confess my apprehensions that such an event will not readily be brought about, the rebels get on apace, and knowing their advantages, in having the whole country, as it were, at their disposal, they will not readily be brought into a situation where the King's troops can meet

General Sir Henry Clinton, an undated stipple engraving by A. H. Ritchie. This officer was a strong critic of the Howes' strategy in America. William L. Clements Library, University of Michigan.

them upon equal terms. Their armies retiring a few miles back from the navigable rivers, ours cannot follow them from the difficulties I expect to meet with in procuring land carriage." And so he rejected General Clinton's strategy.[21]

Yet another approach might be called the spreading-ink-stain strategy. It was to seize small strategic areas in the colonies and to expand them until the rebellion came to an end. Some British leaders wished to occupy the colonial seaports of New York, Philadelphia, Charleston, Savannah, Newport, and Boston, as bases for control of the countryside. The conquest of the maritime towns lay within the reach of British arms, but the second task was supremely difficult. The American colonies, as Daniel Boorstin has written, were a culture without a capital. More than 95 percent of the population lived outside the major cities. The spreading-ink-stain strategy was also very slow and it required more troops for occupation duty than Britain could supply.

A variation on this strategy seemed more promising. Many officers proposed to seize and hold major corridors and river lines, especially the line of the Hudson River. British leaders believed that New England was the seat of the rebellion. If the Hudson could be held, that incendiary region could be separated from the rest of the colonies, and the rebellion could be defeated in detail. This method of divide and conquer looked very promising to the Howe brothers. It made the best use of limited resources and allowed them to concentrate their strength against a divided enemy.

Yet another plan was to support Loyalist Americans against the rebels. A leading advocate of this idea was General James Robertson. He wrote, "I never had an idea of subduing the Americans. I meant to assist the good Americans to subdue the bad."[22] The Howes shared this way of thinking. William Howe wrote to his constituents, "You are deceived if you suppose there are not many loyal and peaceable subjects in that country. I may safely assert that the insurgents are very few, in comparison of the whole people." They saw a major opportunity here.[23]

From these various possibilities, the Howe brothers put together a strategy of their own. It appeared in letters that General William Howe sent to George Germain in London early in 1776. He proposed that the British army be greatly reinforced in America. With the navy, it should seize and hold the city of New York and make it a major base of operations. A smaller force should be sent to Canada with orders to move south, and the two forces should take control of the Hudson Valley.

General Howe believed that the key was speed and skillful maneuver. He wrote, "the army at the opening of the campaign, being in force, would probably by rapid movements bring the rebels to an action upon equal terms, before they could cover themselves by works of any significance." The object was to catch them off balance and win a series of actions without the heavy losses of a pounding match. He wrote hopefully of "a decisive action, than which nothing is more to be desired or sought for by us, as the most effectual means to terminate this expensive war."[24]

After New York and the Hudson were taken, Howe proposed that a small garrison might hold the city while British forces moved in two directions to seize Rhode Island and New Jersey. By that method, three American colonies would be brought under British control. American moderates would be offered amnesty if they swore allegiance to the Crown, and Loyalists would be granted protection. In that way, the colonies could be recovered one by one. Howe was thinking of the war as a contest for American opinion, not as a hammering match. The Howes also hoped that their superiors in London would agree to reasonable concessions on taxation as the colonies were recovered. Indeed, the ministers did authorize a policy of voluntary American contributions in lieu of imperial taxation, but they ordered the Howes not to speak of this possibility until the Americans had agreed to end the rebellion.

Altogether it was an intelligent plan and well within the material resources at hand. With help from Germany, the British government was able to send General Howe more troops than he requested. Admiral Howe was given nearly half the Royal Navy. It was also a humane plan, which proposed to treat the civil population with decency and restraint and to avoid *Schrecklichkeit* at all costs. It sought to make an overwhelming show of force, but to use it without brutality, and to offer free pardon for all who returned to allegiance.

While the Howes were planning their campaign, George Washington and his generals searched for a counterstrategy. This also was a very hard question. They knew what was coming their way but not how to stop it. Americans in Congress and the army offered a great array of possibilities, as broad as the choices before British leaders.

In some ways the American task was the easier of the two. To win the war Britain had to conquer the colonies; the Americans needed only to survive. The Americans also had another opportunity. If they could draw the major European powers into the conflict, they were very likely to win. Britain had made many enemies in the last great European war. Most rulers in Europe thought that Albion should be cut down a notch or two. But the Europeans were not sure about the Americans. Some worried that the American rebellion would fail. Others feared that it might succeed and spread to their own countries. But in many European capitals, hatred of British power was stronger than fear of American ideas. Most observers agreed that if the Americans could have some success against Britain, others would come to their aid.

One American strategy was to make economic and maritime war on Britain, mainly through the use of privateers. This began to be done by private enterprise more than by public means, and it proved to be highly successful. American privateers took to the seas in growing numbers. They captured twice as many British ships as were in the Howes' New York armada and inflicted millions of pounds in losses on British merchants. But this strategy had a weakness: Commercial losses did not fall heavily on the king or the aristocracy or the country gentlemen who controlled Parliament. It had comparatively little impact on decision makers in London.

General Horatio Gates proposed another American strategy: a Fabian defense, after Fabius Cunctator, the Roman general who fought a delaying campaign against the Carthaginians. Gates believed that the Americans should avoid a big battle, retreat into the interior, even to the Appalachian Mountains, and wear down the European armies by slow attrition. This idea had the merit of clarity, but it failed the test of politics and public opinion.

A third strategy was favored by Continental General Charles Lee. He also believed that Americans should avoid a major battle against British Regulars and suggested that smaller forces should resist by fighting an irregular war, which could take a steady toll of British and German strength and do fatal injury to a regular army. Lee's idea was not a partisan war or a guerrilla war, but a war of small, highly mobile forces under independent command of officers such as Lee himself.

A fourth strategy was favored for a time by George Washington. He called it "a war of posts." This was a defensive idea, in which the enemy would be invited to attack strong positions. The object was to avoid a general action on open ground where everything could be lost in an afternoon. It promised the same results as Bunker Hill but required an obliging enemy.

Yet another approach would be called the offensive-defensive in another American war. It was to keep a strong Continental army and navy in being and attack wherever an opportunity presented itself, while offering no opening to an enemy. Canada and the northern frontier offered one opportunity. The West Indies were another. Centers of Tory strength were a third. This approach combined the tactical and operational offensive with a strategic defensive. George Washington thought well of it.

A fifth strategy was a perimeter defense. It was to defend all of the American colonies and every main town. This made no military sense at all, but in a representative republic it became a political favorite. Whenever any part of America became vulnerable to British attack, citizens protested, journalists raged against decision makers, aliens and dissenters joined in, the open institutions of the country operated as amplifiers, and ambitious politicians made it an issue. The political pressures for a perimeter defense were sometimes irresistible, even as it was a military absurdity.

Which strategy did American leaders choose? In the end, all of them. Every plan would be tried at one time or another. For a start, George Washington and the leaders of the Continental Congress all agreed that New York was likely to be attacked and must be defended. John Adams called it the "nexus of the Northern and Southern Colonies" and observed that it was the "key to the whole Continent, as it is a Passage to Canada, to the Great Lakes, and to all the Indian Nations." The loss of New York would be a heavy defeat for the Cause— for its support at home and for its standing abroad. But was New York defensible? The answer would not be long in coming.[25]

THE FALL OF NEW YORK

~ A Cataract of Disaster

> O doleful! doleful! doleful!—Blood! Carnage! Fire!
>
> —American Chaplain Philip Fithian, August 27, 1776
>
> They will never again stand before us in the field. Everything seems to be over with them and I flatter myself now that this campaign will put a total end to the war.
>
> —British General Hugh Percy, September, 1776[1]

AT THE BEGINNING of 1776, Congress and the commander-in-chief had assigned the defense of New York to General Charles Lee, the most experienced senior officer in the Continental army. He was overwhelmed by the job and did not believe that it could be done. To George Washington he confided, "the consequences of the Enemy's possessing themselves of New York have appear'd to me so terrible that I have scarcely been able to sleep."[2]

Like most towns in the British colonies, New York was open and largely unfortified. Its prosperity grew from the free flow of commerce, and its location provided easy access by water from every side: the Hudson River from the north and west, Long Island Sound from the east, the Atlantic Ocean from the south. For many years the seaport towns of British America had not needed fortifications, because they were secure behind the wooden walls of the Royal Navy. Now their old protector had become the enemy, and every approach to New York was an avenue for a seaborne invader. Charles Lee put the problem succinctly: "What to do with the city, I own puzzles me," Charles Lee wrote; "it is so encircl'd with deep navigable water, that whoever commands the sea must command the town."[3]

Lee studied the problem at length, as did a committee of the Continental Congress, and New York's Committee of Safety. All concluded that "to fortify the Town against shipping" was impossible.

Instead, they resolved to "fortify lodgments" at vital points to guard the approaches to the city. The result was an ambitious plan of fortifications on lower Manhattan, Brooklyn Heights, and Paulus Hook (now Jersey City), all to control access from the south. Lee also planned to block approaches from the east by fortifying both banks of the East River at Hell Gate. He also proposed to control the Hudson River by building strong forts on very high ground at the north end of Manhattan and on the Jersey Palisades across the river.[4]

Most American leaders agreed with this idea of a point-defense, but the more they thought about it, the more vital points they discovered. Worse, in this free and open American world, other military commanders began to act independently on their own initiative. One of them was a cantankerous Connecticut Yankee, General Israel Putnam. He appeared in New York on April 7, 1776, and sent a letter to Congress asking permission to fortify Governor's Island in New York's upper harbor. Putnam thought that his idea was such a good one that he did not wait for a reply. At "candlelighting," on the evening of April 8, 1776, he put a thousand troops into boats and sent them to Governor's Island on his own initiative.[5]

On April 13, 1776, George Washington arrived in Manhattan and took command. He wrote that "The plan of defence formed by General Lee is, from what little I know of the place, a very judicious one."[6] As troops arrived, he put them to work building fortifications, at first on Lee's design. Large forts began to rise at the northern tip of Manhattan and Fort Lee on the Jersey Palisades. Massive entrenchments were constructed on the high ground of Brooklyn Heights against attack by land and by sea.

Major-General Israel Putnam, an engraving by Miss A. Hall (1818) after a drawing by John Trumbull. Putnam was a free spirit in the American army, as autonomous as his New England troops. Author's collection.

Washington consulted widely with others. As he did so, Lee's plan began to change. Local leaders urged fortification of New York City itself, which Lee had rejected. Washington yielded to strong urgings and gave the orders. American troops tried to make the city itself into a fortress. Batteries and barricades rose along the East River and the Hudson.

By midsummer, Lee's original plan was scarcely recognizable. As reinforcements arrived, Washington organized them in ten brigades and distributed seven of them in a tight perimeter defense of lower Manhattan: two along the Hudson, two more along the East River, one inside the town, and two more in reserve. Two brigades were put to work on Fort Washington and King's Bridge. Two brigades went to Long Island, and two regiments to Governor's Island.[7]

The British commanders on Staten Island were quick to observe the dispersion of Washington's army and actively encouraged it. They sent small British forces to harass the American defenders in many places. Small parties raided New Jersey. Others ranged the coast of Long Island. On the afternoon of July 12, Admiral Richard Howe seized the opportunity of a south wind and flowing tide and ordered two frigates, HMS *Phoenix* and HMS *Rose*, to force a passage up the Hudson River. As the frigates got under way with three tenders, the American army flew to arms and opened fire with every gun that would bear. The British ships were hit many times but suffered few casualties and no major damage. As the frigates came abreast of Governor's Island and Paulus Hook, they returned fire in crashing broadsides. Some gunners on Paulus Hook abandoned their positions and ran for cover. Others worked their guns so frantically that they neglected their swabs, and one gun blew up, with a heavy loss of American life.[8]

The ships continued north past lower Manhattan, and Alexander Hamilton's guns opened fire from the Battery. The frigates replied, and British round shot went flying through New York and the village of Greenwich. The *New York Gazette* reported that three cannonballs entered "Captain Clarke's House at Greenwich" and one "lodged at the head of Miss Clarke's Bed in her Chamber." A panic spread through the town, especially among "Women, Children and the Infirm." Washington wrote, "when the Men of War passed up the River the Shrieks and Cries of these poor creatures running every way was truly distressing and I fear will have an unhappy effect on the Ears and Minds of our young and inexperienced Soldiery."[9]

The action continued for two hours, until the ships sailed beyond American fortifications and anchored defiantly in the Tappan

Zee. There they threatened to stop traffic on the river and to start a Loyalist rising in the Hudson Valley. The Americans tried to destroy them with fire-ships, but they sailed south again past the American defenses with impunity. One British seaman climbed a masthead and remained there through the action, openly displaying his contempt for the rebels. The Royal Navy had demonstrated its complete control of the waters around New York. The Americans were shocked by the weakness of their defense at one of its strongest points.

The event was also a reminder that British forces possessed the initiative and could attack where they pleased. Some American officers urged an immediate attack on Staten Island. Several wanted to destroy the water supply on the island by polluting it with "stove black," but that idea was unanimously rejected. Nobody could think of a way to seize the initiative. Lacking an alternative, American defenders began to dig and fortify more frantically than ever.

Washington was desperately short-handed, and yet he had more troops in and around the city than he could supply. Other units, mostly militia from New England and Pennsylvania, were marching

The Phoenix and Rose Engaged by the Enemy's Fire Ships, an engraving by Sir James Wallace. The American failure to keep these ships out of the Hudson River demonstrated the British control of waters around New York. The Mariners Museum, Newport News, Virginia.

to his support, but in July he instructed them to remain at a distance. The Philadelphia Associators, to their dismay, received orders to stay in New Jersey. These men were able, highly motivated, and ready to fight, but Washington held them in what was called Flying Camp, where they had nothing to do and began to think about going home. Robert Morris wrote later, "our Associators had been much disgusted with their service in the Flying Camp, and their spirit had gone to sleep." The New England militia were held north of the city at White Plains. They also demanded leave to go home and were allowed to do so by New York authorities. So were the Jersey militia, who were sent to Perth Amboy and, after sitting there in idleness, asked to go home and attend to the harvest.[10]

The American troops were growing restless. Discipline, never their strong point, rapidly diminished. These thousands of armed Americans loved to fire their weapons and often did so, maddening the commander-in-chief. His general orders complained that "constant firing in camp, notwithstanding repeated orders to the contrary, is very scandalous, and seldom a day passes but some persons are shot by their friends."[11]

Washington's temper was growing short. He began to have run-ins with entire regiments in his army, especially the militia. One unit that got under his skin was an ancient and very honorable New England regiment called the Connecticut Light Horse, commanded by Lieutenant Colonel Thomas Seymour. Its troopers joined the army as volunteers, and were described as "truly irregulars." One was taken prisoner by the British and asked to explain his duties. He answered that they were "to flank a little and carry tidings," much to the hilarity of his captors. Some described these Connecticut cavaliers as "old fashioned men, probably farmers and heads of families . . . beyond the meridian of life." They wore fragments of uniforms from colonial wars and carried long-barreled fowling pieces rather than carbines and sabers. But some of them were fit and able, and they were five hundred strong, a useful addition to the American army.[12]

The Connecticut Light Horsemen were the only large body of cavalry that Washington had. He needed them more than he knew for scouting and intelligence, especially on Long Island. But these mounted Connecticut countrymen did not fit Washington's idea of a soldier or his plan for the defense of New York. When they arrived full of "zeal" and "attachment to the cause," Washington told them that their horses were in the way and he could not pay their upkeep. They were men of "reputation and property" and offered to pay for themselves and their horses. Washington replied that "they could not be of use as horsemen" and asked them to serve as infantry, a mortal insult to a cavalryman. They were ordered to get rid of their horses and to start "fatigue duty" and "garrison duty," digging fortifications with the rest of the army.[13]

The Connecticut cavalry agreed to "do duty as foot till the arrival of the new levies," but when more infantry arrived, Washington insisted that they continue to serve dismounted. This time the Connecticut cavalry refused, and on July 16, 1776, the field officers gave him a letter explaining that "by the law of Connecticut they were expressly exempted from staying in garrison or doing duty on foot." They demanded to be dismissed from the army. Washington was infuriated. He wrote back, "if your men think themselves exempt from the common duties of a soldier . . . they can no longer be of use here where horse cannot be brought into action." He added, "I do not care how soon they are dismiss'd."[14]

The result was the departure of a large part of Washington's cavalry, "fine men and as well spirited as any on the ground." Washington explained to John Hancock, "their assistance is much needed, and might be of essential service in case of an attack, yet I judged it advisable . . . to discharge them." The commander-in-chief was fearful that their refusal to do "fatigue duty" would spread through the army. Some of the Connecticut cavalry quietly remained with the army, and many served honorably later in the war, but most were lost to this campaign.[15]

As the summer wore on, ill health began to plague the army. It had plenty of salt meat and hard bread but desperately lacked fresh food and green vegetables. The farmers around New York had a plentiful harvest in 1776 and began to bring their crops to the city. Undisciplined soldiers were so desperate that they seized the food on sight. Washington issued strict orders against this practice but could not enforce them, and the farmers stopped coming. In the midst of plenty, the army began to suffer from malnutrition, even from scurvy in the summertime.

Other diseases spread through the Continental camps. New York, like other seaport towns in the eighteenth century, supported many prostitutes. A survey by the town government shortly after the Revolution found that 20 percent of women of childbearing age in New York City were prostitutes. Some of Washington's troops were quartered on Holy Ground, the center of the flesh trade in the city. Washington issued stern warnings against "lewd women," but his troops in New York suffered an epidemic of venereal disease.

Other illnesses were even more destructive. As the weather grew warmer, thousands of troops began to fall ill of gastrointestinal diseases. Monthly strength reports told a dismal story. In the spring of 1776, the army had been very healthy. During the month of June, only 9.7 percent of the troops were reported sick, a low number for any army in the eighteenth century. As the summer came on, and the troops were concentrated in close-built camps around New York, the sick list surged to 17 percent in July, 25 percent in August, and 32 percent in September. These numbers included only "ineffectives" who were too sick to serve. Many men were ill but remained on duty.[16]

Most armies and navies suffered that way in the eighteenth century. In the close-packed mess decks of British warships in American and West Indian waters during the Revolution, the sick lists were almost as large as in Washington's army. But the disciplined and highly professional British Regulars and Hessian troops on Staten Island were described as very healthy (with some exceptions). Hessian Lieutenant Johann von Bardeleben of the Donop regiment wrote in his diary, "Our camp site was excellent. The smell of cedar, sassafras, and other local woods made it very pleasant." The camps on Staten Island were carefully laid out on good ground, their water supply was protected, and sanitation was strictly enforced. Their diet lacked fresh food but included antiscorbutics such as pickled sauerkraut.[17]

The American camps were by all accounts much worse than those of the British and Hessians. American officers understood the importance of field sanitation but were unable to enforce it. The results were horrific. Nathanael Greene described "the stench that rose from the American camps" and wrote that the troops were "easing themselves in the ditches of the fortifications, a practice that is disgraceful to the last Degree."[18]

American troops lacked experience and camp discipline, and they paid a terrible price. They polluted their camps and fouled their water supply. The result was a polydemic of dysentery, "putrid fevers," typhoid fever, malaria, and enteric diseases. The diary of Philip Fithian, a Presbyterian chaplain with the New Jersey militia, was a heart-rending story of illness in the army. In New York on July 19, 1776, he wrote: "The vile water here sickens us all. I am very sick; troubled with a continued lax & fearful of a confirmed flux. I kept my bed most of this day." By July 22, he was feeling better but wrote that many in camp were ill of "dysentery" and "other putred disorders." On July 26, he visited three regimental hospitals and found "every apartment" crowded with men "in the utmost distress."[19]

The same diseases spread among American troops at Fort Washington and King's Bridge, where General Heath observed that "in almost every farm, stable, shed, and even under fences and bushes were the sick to be seen."[20] On Long Island, General Nathanael Greene reported to Washington, "the troops in general are exceeding Sickly, great numbers taken down every day."

Greene worked tirelessly among his men, taught them to dig "necessary vaults," and urged them to practice elementary camp sanitation, but in late August Greene himself fell dangerously ill and was unable to lead his men. The command system of the American army on Long Island was crippled by his loss. Joseph Reed wrote, "on General Greene's being sick, Sullivan took the command, who was wholly unacquainted with the ground or country." Sullivan began to make changes that were not approved at headquarters, and Washington appointed yet another commander, Israel Putnam, which compounded the confusion.[21]

As if all that were not enough, the American intelligence system failed miserably in New York. Washington's army at Boston had used many sources: pickets, patrols, raids, interrogation of prisoners and deserters, civilian informants, and others. None of these methods worked well in New York. Some reliable information came from the Pennsylvania Riflemen of Colonel Edward Hand, who were posted along the southwestern coast of Long Island to watch the flow of shipping into the lower harbor. But with the exception of a few British deserters and escaped American prisoners, Washington had little information about enemy dispositions. He ordered General Hugh Mercer, commanding at Perth Amboy, to send spies to Staten Island, but without success. Mercer reported that he could "procure no certain Intelligence of their situation—No person has yet come over to us, nor is it easy to find one of our Friends duely qualified or ready to undertake the business of a Spy on the Island."[22]

As late as August 12, Washington wrote to Hancock that the army had no intelligence about the enemy's movements, "nor have we any further intelligence of their designs." He expected the Howe brothers to attack any day and kept his weary troops on high alert. The result was the exhaustion of his army. Philip Fithian rejoined his regiment on Long Island, which suffered much from false alarms and nervous commanders. On August 15, they were awakened at three o'clock in the morning by reports of an attack. "Our hard-fated men," Fithian wrote, "stood there more than two hours under Arms, some without Blankets or even a coat it raining hard all the

Time." The attack never came, and the next morning Fithian was sick again.[23]

Washington was baffled. On August 19, he wrote, "there is something exceedingly misterious in the conduct of the enemy." Some scraps of information reached his headquarters. On August 21, Governor William Livingston of New Jersey wrote "in utmost haste" that a spy had at last got across to Staten Island. He reported that the whole force of the enemy was thirty-five thousand, and all but fifteen thousand had left their camps and were "embarqued" for an uncertain destination—probably Long Island or the Hudson River, or both. The spy believed that the remaining fifteen thousand would invade New Jersey.[24]

Later on the same day, Colonel Hand's riflemen at the Narrows reported much activity in the British fleet. Admiral Richard Howe's flagship received "a large company on board," and late in the afternoon the transports began to stir. Other sources reported variously that the enemy would first attack the Hudson, or the East River, or New Jersey, or New York City itself, which Washington thought most likely. Accurate indicators of British movements were lost in a cloud of rumor and false reports.[25]

The British commanders had been taking their time. The Howe brothers wanted to give conciliation a chance, but mainly they were waiting for the Hessians to arrive. Finally, on August 15, 1776, two convoys reached New York on the same day, and the German troops came ashore. Their officers reported that the men needed a week to recover their land legs after the long Atlantic crossing. General Howe gave them six days and prepared to attack.

The disorganized American troops were now widely scattered around New York, on three islands and six riverbanks. The Howe brothers resolved to strike quickly and to concentrate all their strength against a small part of Washington's dispersed army. On the night of August 21, six days after the Hessians had come ashore, the Howe brothers set their army in motion. The first to move were the British light infantry, grenadiers, Highland battalions, and Hessian Jägers, all under the command of General Cornwallis. Under cover of darkness, these elite units boarded transports, sailed across New York's lower bay, and anchored on the coast of Long Island. It was a short step, but the step of a giant. The Royal Navy supplied a massive covering force. It also furnished much specialized amphibious equipment, including a flotilla of broad, flat-bottomed landing barges, each carrying twenty seamen and fifty soldiers. Some of these eighteenth-century landing craft had ramps, for guns and horses

British Landing Barge, contemporary model. These amphibious craft were developed by the Royal Navy and used in many operations during the New York campaign. National Maritime Museum, London.

and wagons. Supporting the troops were specialized bomb vessels, small warships with very large mortars that fired huge explosive shells.[26]

At six o'clock the next morning, August 22, the British warships opened fire on the beaches and the fields of southwestern Long Island while the soldiers climbed down into their special landing barges and assembled behind the hulls of the transports. As a thin screen of American pickets retreated from the water's edge, British troops came ashore in overwhelming force. Light infantry raced across flat and open fields, and light dragoons ranged far inland, driving small parties of American pickets before them. When the beaches were secure, and carefully masked from American observation, the main body of the British army came ashore—fifteen thousand men on the first day. Three days later the Hessian troops followed. Here was another display of overwhelming power and professional skill. No other armed forces in the world could have done what the British army and Royal Navy did together that day. It was also done with efficiency, and the Howe brothers were very careful with the lives of their highly trained Regulars.[27]

At American headquarters on August 22, Washington learned quickly of the British landing, but his information was faulty. He believed that the Howes had committed only eight or nine thousand troops out of their total strength of thirty-five thousand, and he suspected that it was "a feint upon Long Island to draw out forces into that quarter."[28]

Washington believed that the major attack would probably come on Manhattan, but he was not certain. Lacking other intelligence, he searched for clues in the conduct of the British troops on Long Island. On August 22, they moved within three miles of American lines. Then they stopped and did not advance for two days. That pattern suggested to the American leaders that Long Island was not their major attack and that the operation was designed to draw American troops away from Manhattan.

Washington was racked by doubt and indecision. He decided to send six battalions from New York to Long Island, and four more the next day, but he also sent boats to bring them back instantly if the British moved toward New York City. He kept the bulk of his troops on Manhattan and held most American troops out of action, expecting the major British attack to fall elsewhere.

Once again American intelligence failed. Washington still believed that the British commanders were holding back 26,000 men, with as many as 12,000 already embarked on transports, ready to strike at another point. He was doubly mistaken. Howe's army was also suffering from illness, and had a little less than 25,000 effective troops, not 35,000 as Washington believed. The British commanders committed nearly all of their army to Long Island, not 9,000 as the Americans mistakenly thought, but 22,000 out of 24,464 effectives, More than 90 percent of Howe's force was ashore on Long Island, not 25 percent as Washington reckoned. It was a fatal miscalculation by American leaders.[29]

Other errors followed in the American camp. Hedging his bets, Washington sent ten regiments as reinforcements for Long Island and included two of his most disciplined units, Haslet's Delaware Continentals and Smallwood's Maryland regiment. But he ordered the commanders of these regiments to remain in New York. Lieutenant Colonel Herman Zedwitz, a Prussian officer, had been caught attempting to sell American intelligence to British officers for two thousand pounds. Washington was so outraged by Zedwitz's betrayal that he ordered thirteen senior officers, including Haslet and Smallwood, to leave their commands and sit as a court-martial on August 25 and 26. Then came the British attack. The officers of the Delaware and Maryland regiments desperately wanted to be with their men, but Washington wanted to be done with Colonel Zedwitz and

William Smallwood, a portrait
by Charles Willson Peale
(1781–82), the colonel of the
Maryland regiment, one of
the best disciplined units in
the American army.
Smallwood was appalled by
the disorder that he observed
in the Continental Army on
Long Island. Independence
National Historical Park,
Philadelphia.

would not let them go. The officers protested. Smallwood wrote later,
"I waited on General Washington, and urged the necessity of attending our troops, yet he refused to discharge us, alleging there
was a necessity for the trials coming on." The court martial sat so
late on the twenty-sixth that it was impossible for the officers to get
over that day. They finally joined their units on the twenty-seventh
and were appalled to find their regiments in great danger.[30]

The American command was in extreme disorder. General Nathanael
Greene had planned a defense on the high ground of Brooklyn
Heights, but he was still very ill and unable to lead it. His replacement, General John Sullivan, was unclear about the plan, uncertain
of the terrain, and uninformed about the location of his own army.
Washington visited Long Island on August 23 and walked the ground
with Sullivan. The two of them decided together to make a major
change in the American position. They agreed to move a large part
of the army, about three thousand men, forward from their entrenchments around Brooklyn Heights and post them on a ridge called
the Heights of Guana, several miles to the south facing the British
and Hessian forces.

This was good ground for defense: high, steep, and thickly
wooded. It was a very strong position against a frontal attack and

could be crossed only at four passes where country roads ran between scattered villages. But the ridge was very long, nearly ten miles altogether, and it could not be held in strength by three thousand troops. Washington and Sullivan decided to post their men on high ground near the passes, in the hope that the British troops might be enticed to attack as they had done at Bunker Hill. The American troops were not expected to hold their posts, but to sell them at a price that the British and Hessians could not afford to pay.

After these decisions were made, Washington decided to change generals yet again. He replaced Sullivan with Israel Putnam, who knew Long Island well but had little knowledge of the American positions. In five days, the American troops at Long Island went through three commanders. At the same time, more confusion arose from an attempt by Washington's headquarters to reshuffle its regiments into brigades. So tangled was command and control that units were uncertain about their commanders and not sure of the positions they were to defend. Many units began to move on their own. Sullivan reported that "American troops were wandering about western Long island, sometimes miles beyond their position." Information-gathering in Washington's headquarters was so weak that he did not know the movements of his own army. No senior officer knew how many American troops were actually on Long Island or exactly where they were posted. Estimates by historians have ranged from sixteen to thirty-one regiments, 9,450 to 11,000 men.[31]

Washington returned to Manhattan and on August 25 sent a letter to Putnam, urging him to get a grip on the army, to "form a proper line of defense on good ground," to keep the men "in or near their respective camps," and yet again to impose "order and discipline." Washington added, "the distinction between a well regulated army, and a mob, is the good order and discipline of the first, & the licentious & disorderly behavior of the latter." The army that Washington had seen on his visit to Long Island looked more like a mob.[32]

Putnam tried to do as he was told. He posted about a third of his army on the Heights of Guana, several miles in front of the fortifications on Brooklyn Heights. The right of the line was commanded by Stirling. The left was led by Sullivan, and its flank was in dense woodland. On August 26, Washington visited Long Island again, studied Putnam's dispositions, and approved them.

At last Washington began to realize that Long Island was Howe's major effort, but American intelligence failed yet again. Washington and his commanders did not know where the enemy was and did not patrol actively. The American army had very little cavalry

William Alexander, Lord Stirling, a portrait by Bass Otis after an early engraving. This American leader claimed a peerage that was recognized by Scottish courts but denied by the British House of Lords. On Long Island, he led an American brigade with great courage, and served in the New York and New Jersey campaigns. Independence National Historical Park.

after the loss of the Connecticut Light Horse and was unable to screen the front and flanks of its own position.[33]

British light cavalry and light infantry were quick to dominate the ground between the armies and began to probe American positions. On August 24, Hessian troops led by Colonel von Donop skirmished with small parties of American troops. An American rifleman caught the Hessian commander in his sights and took aim at close range, but his rifle misfired. Donop coolly raised his weapon and "shot the rifleman through the head." The Jägers took losses, but the American riflemen got the worst of it and were driven in. Once again American patrols were unable to get intelligence of enemy movements.[34]

The British commanders were better informed about the Americans and the ground, thanks in large part to Long Island Loyalists who came forward to help them. They observed the American positions on the Heights of Guana and discovered that the northern flank of the American army was not secure. From that knowledge a plan emerged. Its author was probably General Henry Clinton. As always, his purpose was to cut off the American army, block its retreat, and destroy it.

Clinton proposed to divide the British forces in three parts. To the south (the British left), General James Grant would lead troops forward toward the American line in a noisy demonstration. In the center, the Hessians under General Leopold von Heister would do the same. To the north, Clinton would lead nearly half the British army in a broad sweeping movement around the American flank and attack them from the rear. At the same time, the Royal Navy would take a position off Brooklyn Heights and batter the American fortifications from the water.

The British commander agreed. On the night of August 26–27, Howe, Clinton, and Cornwallis marched with about ten thousand men, mostly British infantry, on the long flanking movement to the north. Their guides were three Loyalists who led them through a tangle of field lanes and country roads to the Jamaica Road, which ran across the heights well north of the American positions. The only Americans they met were five militia officers who surrendered without a shot.

In the morning Grant led his demonstration to the south, and Heister did the same in the center. On the north Clinton led the major attack behind the American flank. The British troops had to cut a path through the woods with saws and axes. Even so the Americans did not discover them. The British burst out of the woods on the flank, and the American left collapsed. Sullivan was captured; his troops broke and ran. Colonel William Smallwood saw sixty British light infantrymen put to flight two Connecticut brigades. Washington and Putnam hurried forward to stop the rout. Smallwood watched in amazement as the American troops, "from the Brigadier-General down to the private sentinel, were caned and whipped by the Generals Washington, Putnam and Mifflin, but even this indignity had no weight, they could not be brought to stand one shot."[35]

On the right, Stirling saw Sullivan's line fall apart and ordered a retreat. To cover the withdrawal he led forward two of the best American regiments: Smallwood's Marylanders and Haslet's Delaware Continentals. They made a desperate stand in a ploughed field and stopped the British advance long enough for other units to get away. Washington watched them and cried, "Good God! What brave fellows I must this day lose." Both regiments suffered severely. Colonel Smallwood wrote afterward, "I could wish the transactions of this day blotted from the annals of America. Nothing appeared, but fright, disgrace, and confusion."[36]

There were pockets of strong resistance. A British observer wrote that some Americans, "more bold though not more brave, fired as they ran or as they could find cover, from walls and hedges." Altogether General Howe estimated that he lost 370 men killed and wounded, and his casualty counts were always on the low side.[37] But

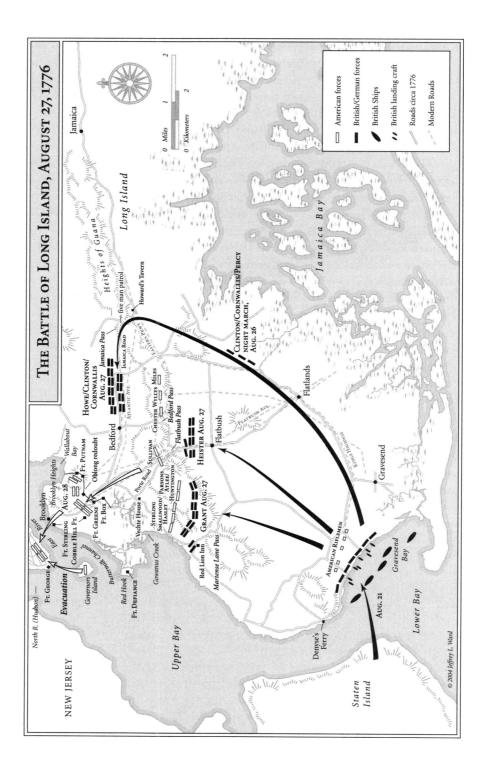

THE BATTLE OF LONG ISLAND, AUGUST 27, 1776

American forces
British/German forces
British Ships
British landing craft
Roads circa 1776
Modern Roads

0 Miles 1 2
0 Kilometers 2

Jamaica

Long Island

Heights of Guana

Howard's Tavern

five man patrol

Jamaica Pass

Jamaica Road

EASTERN ROAD

Howe/Clinton/
Cornwallis
Aug. 27

ATLANTIC AVE.

Chester Wyllys MILES

Bedford Pass

Bedford

Flatbush Pass

Heister Aug. 27

Flatbush

CLINTON/CORNWALLIS/PERCY
NIGHT MARCH,
AUG. 26

Flatlands

FLATBUSH AVE.

Gravesend

KINGS HIGHWAY

Sullivan

Porte Road

Parsons
Atlee
Huntington

Grant Aug. 27

Wallabout
Bay

Ft. Putnam

Oblong redoubt

Ft. Box

Ft. Greene

Brooklyn Heights

Brooklyn

Aug. 28

Fort Stirling

Cobble Hill Ft.

Vechte House

Stirling
Smallwood/ Haslet

Red Lion Inn

Martense Lane Pass

American Riflemen

Gravesend
Bay

Aug. 21

Denyse's
Ferry

Lower Bay

Staten
Island

East River

Ft. George

Evacuation

Governor
Island

Red Hook

Ft. Defiance

Gowanus Creek

Buttermilk Channel

Upper Bay

North R. (Hudson)

NEW JERSEY

© 2004 Jeffrey L. Ward

Jamaica Bay

all along the line, the American units could not stand against the Regulars. Chaplain Philip Fithian watched in horror as a disaster unfolded around him. He scribbled in his diary: "O doleful! doleful! doleful!—Blood! Carnage! Fire! . . . Many, many we fear are Lost. . . . Such a dreadful Din my ears never before heard!—And the distressed wounded came crying into our Lines."[38]

An eyewitness on the other side was Ambrose Serle. He wrote that "the rebels abandoned every Spot as fast, I should say faster, than the King's Troops advanced upon them." The English, Hessians, and Scottish troops followed and "cut them down in a terrible manner." In some cases the Regulars refused to allow the Americans to surrender. An English officer wrote, "The Hessians and our brave Highlanders gave no quarters, and it was a fine sight to see with what alacrity they despatched the rebels with their Bayonets, after we had surrounded them so that they could not resist. . . . We took care to tell the Hessians that the Rebels had resolved to give no quarters to them in particular, which made them fight desperately and put to death all who fell into their hands."[39] A Hessian colonel confirmed that "the English did not give much quarter, and constantly urged our people to do the like." He went on: "The riflemen were mostly spitted to the trees with bayonets. These people deserve pity rather than fear."[40]

The American rebels got little pity that day. British and German Regulars were quick to discover that green American troops had a special fear of the bayonet, the terror weapon of the eighteenth century. British bayonets were a fearful sight, with their long blades gleaming in the light, and many American troops had no bayonets of their own. After the battle, Howe issued a general order on the subject: "Soldiers are reminded of their evident superiority on the 27th of August by charging the rebels with their bayonets even in the woods where they had thought themselves invincible. The General therefore recommends to the troops an entire dependence upon their bayonets"[41]

As the chase went on, more Americans were allowed to surrender, sometimes entire units. The Hessian Rall regiment surrounded a formation of about fifty men with colors flying. Colonel Johann Rall shouted orders to form and prepare to fire, and Americans "saw what was in store and dropped their weapons." A Hessian grenadier seized an American liberty flag, just as General von Mirbach came up and claimed it for his trophy. Colonel Rall intervened. "Nothing doing, General," Rall said. "My grenadiers captured the flag and they shall keep it, and no one will take it from them." It was the sort of thing that endeared Rall to his men.[42]

The British command put the prisoners to work. "As long as we had no horses," a Hessian remembered, "the prisoners were harnessed in front of the cannon." He recalled that "among the prisoners were many called colonels, lieutenant colonels, majors, and other officers, who, however, are nothing but mechanics, tailors, shoemakers, wig-makers, barbers, etc. Some of them were soundly beaten by our people, who would by no means let such persons pass for officers."[43]

The Connecticut regiment of Lieutenant Jabez Fitch was caught between two "severe fires" and surrounded by Hessian troops. The regiment came apart, and many were captured. Fitch was confined in a barn with "a great number of prisoners of different regiments." He found himself next to Captain Joseph Jewett, who had a mortal bayonet wound in his abdomen and suffered terribly for two days, often repeating that "it was hard work to die." On his last night, he worried for his family and asked his friends to "write the circum-stances of his Death to his Wife." The next morning Captain Jewett passed away, as dawn rose on another cruel day in New York.[44]

Altogether, the Americans counted their losses at about 300 killed and 1,097 captured, with no reliable estimates of the wounded. General Howe thought he had inflicted 3,400 casualties. Half that number would be closer to the mark. The plan of British General Henry Clinton had succeeded brilliantly in a tactical way but did not achieve its strategic goal of destroying the rebel army. Most of the Americans on the Heights of Guana got away. Ambrose Serle wrote of Howe's army, "In one thing only they failed—could not run as fast as their Foe."[45]

The American army had been routed. Its commanders had made many grievous errors, and even its best infantry could not win a pitched battle against a seasoned regular army. In an ordeal by combat on Long Island, the forces of order made short work of an army of liberty. But some British and Hessian officers were quick to see that something else had happened. The Americans had been driven from the field, but most of them survived to fight another day. Those who talked with American prisoners also reported that even though they had suffered a heavy defeat, they did not feel defeated. In the eyes of the Regulars, the rebels had lost all honor, but many retained their pride and determination even as prisoners, to the irritation of their captors. They believed deeply in their cause and were confident that they would win in the end. It was madden-ing to professional soldiers. These American "peasants" were so ignorant of war that they didn't know they were beaten. It was clear, even to the winners, that the battle of Long Island was only the beginning.[46]

After the battle of Long Island, the Howe brothers were confident that they had trapped a large part of the American army, perhaps ten thousand men, on Brooklyn Heights, with the Royal Navy in their rear.

The position of the Americans was strong. They had been working on their fortifications for months. They held the high ground with clear fields of fire, with double palisades, trenches and half trenches, redoubts and star forts at intervals along the line, and small fortresses at critical points. The Americans had abundant provisions, plenty of ammunition, and many guns.[47]

Some British officers wanted to storm the American lines, but William Howe refused to repeat the error of Bunker Hill. He was not about to risk his highly trained Regulars in a frontal assault on a fortified position. Instead he ordered his military engineers to make "regular approaches" in siege lines and field redoubts, "which the nature of the ground favored extremely." The British sappers moved methodically forward and soon discovered weak points in the American line.[48]

While siege operations advanced, the Howes tried yet another peace initiative. They released General Sullivan from captivity, on condition that he carry a message to Congress calling for negotiations. American leaders in the Congress and army had none of it and were not pleased with Sullivan even for delivering a message. The peace feelers were rejected out of hand, in part because of the behavior of British and Hessian troops at Long Island. Stories were quick to spread of captives who were denied quarter and were shot or bayoneted in cold blood. Other tales began to circulate of prisoners who were severely maltreated. American attitudes were hardening. There was no thought of ending the war.

On Brooklyn Heights, General Howe advanced his siege lines methodically toward the American lines. Admiral Howe prepared to send his warships into the East River. Washington's army would soon be surrounded, and its destruction appeared to be only a matter of time. Then something happened that seemed of small importance to General Howe. There was a change in the American weather.

The first sign was a shift in the wind. The prevailing westerlies below New York backed around to the northeast, and the wind began to rise. Then came dark clouds, and a cold rain began to fall on August 28. On both sides it made life a muddy misery for private soldiers in sodden coats and flooded trenches. The next day was worse. The rain grew into a great storm, a classic American nor'easter with "such heavy rainfall as can hardly be remembered." That morning Washington rode to the forward positions on Brooklyn Heights. He studied the British entrenchments through the driving rain, and the soldiers hard at work as the storm beat down on them. The siege lines advanced inexorably, protected by folds in the ground that the Americans had not been able to cover.[49]

In the afternoon of August 29, Washington called a council of war at the Philip Livingston house. With him were seven generals from the Brooklyn position: Putnam, Spencer, Mifflin, McDougall, Parsons, J. M. Scott, and Wadsworth. As the rain wept upon the windowpanes, Washington posed a question: Should the army evacuate Long Island? He ran through many reasons for abandoning the position and withdrawing across the East River to Manhattan.

The council raised doubts and questions. Some argued that it could not be done. One officer observed that it was a desperate venture. The crossing was "a full mile wide," the current was strong and swift, boats were in short supply, the British army could attack at any moment, and the Royal Navy could catch the army on the water. Others thought that it should not be done. The fortifications were very strong. General Putnam observed, based on his experience, that the army would fight well behind entrenchments: "Give an American army a wall to fight behind and they will fight forever." Then Washington weighed in. After all the confusion and cross-purposes and blunders on Long Island, he was suddenly clear and firm. He had already begun to collect the boats, and the decision was made. Washington ordered that an evacuation was to begin immediately, in strictest secrecy. Nobody was to be told. His own men were kept deliberately in the dark. The army was told to pack up and prepare to change positions along the line. At ten o'clock that night in heavy rain the American units began to withdraw from their lines to the water's edge. Colonel Benjamin Tallmadge wrote, "It was one of the most anxious, busy nights that I ever recollect, and being the third in which hardly any of us had closed our eyes to sleep, we were all greatly fatigued."[50]

Anyone who has made a night march will recognize the scene. The weary men stumbled forward in mud and rain. Many were so tired that they scarcely seemed to care what happened to them. The American position was a sea of mud, and the guns sank to their hubs. Small cannon were dragged away by great effort. The larger ones were left behind.

The army had two regiments from the north shore of New England: the Marblehead mariners in John Glover's Fourteenth Massachusetts, and fishermen from Salem and Lynn in Israel Hutchinson's Twenty-seventh Massachusetts. They were ordered to man the boats and keep them moving against the wind and current in the darkness.[51]

The nor'easter masked Washington's movements and kept British ships out of the East River but also delayed the American crossing. At first light many of the best American troops were still holding their positions as a rear guard. Colonel Tallmadge's regiment was among them. They knew that when British patrols discovered what had happened they were doomed to captivity or death or both, given the barbaric treatment of prisoners.

Then, incredibly, there was another change in the weather. Tallmadge remembered that "a very dense fog began to rise, and it seemed to settle in a peculiar manner over both encampments." It was so thick that Tallmadge could "scarcely discern a man at six yards' distance." New Englanders received this event as a "providential occurrence." Virginians regarded it as a stroke of fortune.

The sun rose but the fog persisted, and in a strange yellow light the American army made its escape. Tallmadge even went back and rescued a favorite horse and was away again, some distance in the river, when the first British troops appeared on the brow of Brooklyn Heights. Another evacuation rescued the American garrison on Governor's Island. One boat was sunk by British artillery fire, but nearly all the troops survived. Tallmadge thought that "General Washington has never received the credit which was due to him for this wise and most fortunate measure."[52]

The loss of Long Island caused much soul-searching in the American camp. On September 6, George Washington reported the result to Congress and called a "council of the general officers" to "take a full and comprehensive view of our situation."[53] In Washington's thinking, the problem was to match a strategy to his soldiers. He concluded that it would be folly "to lead our young troops into open ground against their superiors, both in number and discipline." Further, he reported that "I have not found that readiness to defend even strong posts at all hazards." Washington observed that American troops were not willing to die for honor or duty. "The honor of making a brave defense does not seem to be a sufficient stimulus, when the success is very doubtful, and the falling into the enemy's hands probable."

From all this Washington concluded that "on our side the war should be defensive"; "we should on all occasions avoid a general action or put anything to the risque unless compelled by necessity." He resolved to keep his army in being, but it would be a "retreating army," defending what it could, yielding when it must, keeping the field and watching for an opportunity when "a brilliant stroke could be made with any probability of success."[54]

Washington decided not to abandon New York City but to move "all the stores and ammunition," and to remove the American sick by Albany sloops to Orangetown, New York.[55] Three days later, seven of Washington's generals asked for another council to reconsider those decisions. They voted to evacuate the city immediately. By the fourteenth of September their army was working frantically to save what it could, but they had too many stores, not enough wagons, and very little time. That day, Washington's scouts brought reports of "uncommon and formidable movements" in the British and Hessian camps. Manhattan was their next target, but where would they strike?[56]

Early on the morning of September 15, 1776, Admiral Richard Howe sent a squadron of the Royal Navy up the Hudson River and made a noisy demonstration "to draw the enemy's attention to that side." Washington and his aides thought it was a diversion. More subtle signs pointed to an attack at the northern end of the island on the East River, near the small country village of Harlem. Washington rode there and prepared to fight.[57]

Once again he was deceived by another of the Howes' ingenious strategems. While the Americans gathered near Harlem on northern Manhattan, other British ships sailed into the East River on the night of September 14–15 and anchored near Kip's Bay, at the present line of Thirty-third Street. Standing guard on that shore, in what was thought to be a quiet sector, were green Connecticut levies. Private Martin remembered, "we had a chain of sentinels quite up the river, four or five miles in length." Every half hour, he heard the American sentries repeat their watchwords: "All is well." He also heard a British voice in the river call out a reply: "We will alter your tune before tomorrow night."[58]

The next morning, Martin awoke to find five warships anchored in the river, with springs on their cables, gunports open, and main batteries run out. He remembered that "it was on a Sabbath morning, the day in which the British were always employed about their deviltry if possible."[59]

As the sun rose, a flotilla of flat-bottomed landing craft emerged from Newtown Creek across the river, near the old boundary be-

Kipp's Bay and the East River, near the present line of 33rd Street, a sketch by Archibald Robertson (1778). The artist was a witness to the British landing in this cove, September 15, 1776. Spencer Collection, The New York Public Library, Astor, Lenox and Tilden foundations.

tween Queens and Brooklyn. In one of them was an officer of the Welch Fusiliers, Frederick Mackenzie, who observed that "the officers of the Navy in each Boat, knew what corps, and the number of men he was to take on board, the whole was conducted without confusion." This was their third amphibious landing on a hostile shore in as many months. They were getting very good at it.[60]

On the Manhattan shore, Private Martin watched what was coming his way in complete fascination. "When they came to the edge of the tide," he wrote, "they formed their boats in line." Then the big frigates opened fire. Martin remembered that "all of a sudden there came such a peal of thunder from the British shipping that I thought my head would go with the sound. I made a frog's leap for the ditch and lay as still as I possibly could, and began to consider which part of my carcass would go first."[61]

Heavy broadsides from the five British warships crashed into the American lines. The American troops panicked and ran. Major Nicholas Fish wrote that as the British approached the shore, the Connecticut state levies departed: "These dastardly sons of cowardice deserted their Lines and fled in the greatest disorder." Fish watched the panic spread, and it "infected those upon the Right . . . as well Officers (& those of distinction) as Men, in so much that it magnified the Number of Enemy to thrice the reality & generated substances from their own shadows." Colonel William Weedon watched in disgust. "Two brigades of northern troops . . . ," wrote this Virginian, "run off without firing a gun."[62]

Washington and his aides came galloping down from Harlem and arrived as the Connecticut militia were running for their lives, their officers among them. Washington was enraged. He "three times dashed his hat on the ground," and shouted, "Good God, have I got such troops as those!" Weedon wrote that "the general was so exasperated that he struck several officers in their flight. . . . It was with difficulty his friends could get him to quit the field, so great was his emotions."[63]

Wave after wave of British troops came ashore. The light infantry charged the American breastworks to the north. The grenadiers stormed the high hill of Iclenburg (later Murray Hill). One determined American militiaman stood his ground and shot Major Vaughan in the thigh, "the only British casualty that day," said Mackenzie.[64] Then came the Hessians, first a thin screen of green-coated Jägers, followed by the dense blue ranks of the grenadiers. They advanced half a mile south toward the Watts farm (near what is now Twenty-third Street), met stubborn resistance in an orchard, and lost two killed and ten wounded. A little beyond, another party of Americans came forward "with an intention of surrendering." A British officer observed that the Hessians killed "about sixty of them, and took a few prisoners." Fish wrote, "It is remarkable that all our killed were shot thro' the Head, which induces the belief that they were first taken prisoners & then massacred."[65]

Then the British commanders made a strange decision. They stopped the advance at Murray Hill (just west of the present Lexington Avenue), instead of continuing west to cut the major road on which American troops were streaming out of southern Manhattan. Most of the Americans got away. According to the military surgeon James Thacher, who was in the retreating army, they owed their escape to Mary Lindley Murray, Quaker mistress of Murray Hill and a staunch Whig. Thacher wrote that Mrs. Murray invited the British commanders into her handsome house and "treated them with cake and wine, and they were induced to tarry two hours or more." General Henry Clinton explained that the real reason was an order by General Howe to halt until a "second embarkation" by British and Hessian troops could come ashore. It is possible that both accounts are correct.[66]

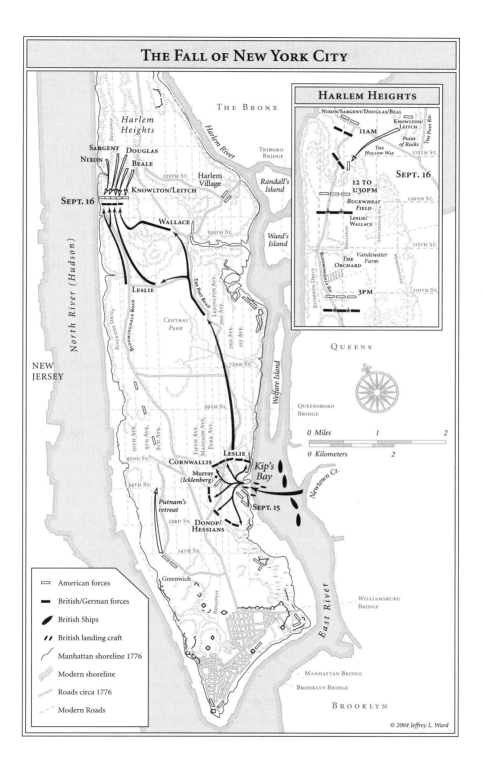

THE FALL OF NEW YORK CITY

HARLEM HEIGHTS

NIXON/SARGENT/DOUGLAS/BEAL

KNOWLTON/LEITCH

11AM

Point of Rocks

THE HOLLOW WAY

125TH ST.

THE POST RD.

SEPT. 16

12 TO 1:30PM

120TH ST.

BUCKWHEAT FIELD

LESLIE/WALLACE

115TH ST.

Vandewater Farm

THE ORCHARD

MORNINGSIDE

BROADWAY

AMSTERDAM AVE.

RIVERSIDE DRIVE

BLOOMINGDALE RD.

3PM

110TH ST.

THE BRONX

Harlem Heights

SARGENT

DOUGLAS

NIXON

BEALE

KNOWLTON/LEITCH

125TH ST.

Harlem Village

Harlem River

TRIBORO BRIDGE

Randall's Island

SEPT. 16

WALLACE

110TH ST.

Ward's Island

LESLIE

CENTRAL PARK

THE POST ROAD

LEXINGTON AVE.

3RD AVE.

2ND AVE.

1ST AVE.

BLOOMINGDALE ROAD

RIVERSIDE DRIVE

North River (Hudson)

NEW JERSEY

72ND ST.

Welfare Island

QUEENS

QUEENSBORO BRIDGE

59TH ST.

10TH AVE.

9TH AVE.

8TH AVE.

FIFTH AVE.

MADISON AVE.

PARK AVE.

0 Miles   1   2

0 Kilometers   2

42ND ST.

CORNWALLIS

LESLIE

Kip's Bay

SEPT. 15

Murray (Icklenberg)

34TH ST.

Newtown Cr.

Putnam's retreat

23RD ST.

DONOP/ HESSIANS

14TH ST.

Greenwich

WILLIAMSBURG BRIDGE

East River

BROADWAY

American forces

British/German forces

British Ships

British landing craft

Manhattan shoreline 1776

Modern shoreline

Roads circa 1776

Modern Roads

MANHATTAN BRIDGE

BROOKLYN BRIDGE

BROOKLYN

© 2004 Jeffrey L. Ward

The day was another disaster for the American army, but again most of the troops escaped and very few were captured. Even so, Nathanael Greene wrote, "we made a miserable, disorderly retreat," and "we lost a prodigious deal of baggage and stores." Everyone found somebody else to blame. Privates blamed their regimental officers. Joseph Martin remembered, "The men were confused, being without officers to command them. I do not recollect of seeing a commissioned officer from the time I left the lines on the banks of the East River in the morning until . . . evening. How could men fight without officers?" The regimental officers blamed the senior commanders. Benjamin Trumbull, a Connecticut officer, wrote, "The fault was principally in the general officers in not disposing of things so as to give the men a rational prospect of defence and a safe retreat." The senior officers blamed the privates. George Washington called them "disgraceful and dastardly." All were right. The fiasco at Kip's Bay was failure on every level of the American army.[67]

As the American troops retreated to the north, three of their officers wanted to destroy New York City. Nathanael Greene advised the commander-in-chief, "I would burn the city and the suburbs. . . . If the enemy gets possession of the city we never can recover the possession without superior naval force to theirs." Charles Lee was of the same mind. Washington agreed and wrote later, "Had I been left to the dictates of my own judgment, New York should have been laid in Ashes before I quitted it." But the commander-in-chief had already put the question to the Continental Congress in a secret communication. "I applied to Congress," Washington wrote, "but was absolutely forbid—that they will have cause to repent the order, I have not a moment's doubt."[68]

After they retreated from the city, a fire broke out at one o'clock in the morning on September 21, 1776. Fanned by a strong south wind, it raced through the close-built neighborhoods and grew into "an immense column of fire and smoke." The city was a scene of the apocalypse. The wooden steeple of Trinity Church became a "pyramid of fire." When its shingles burned, an onlooker remembered, "the frame appeared with every separate piece of timber burning until the principal timbers were burnt through, when the whole fell with a great noise." The inhabitants fled for their lives. One observer wrote, "The sick, the aged, women and children, half naked were seen going they knew not where. . . . The shrieks and cries of the women and children . . . made this one of the most tremendous and affecting scenes I ever beheld." The fire destroyed nearly all of the city west of Broadway, and more than six hundred houses of the thousand in the town.[69]

The British leaders were sure that "it was done by design," and they were probably right. They reported that the fire started simultaneously in many places during the middle of the night. Colonel Carl von Donop wrote that "thirteen of the actual incendiaries were captured in the act and imprisoned in order to learn about the whole conspiracy. Two were thrown into the fire by the mob, and sailors hanged one by his heels after his right hand (in which he had held a torch when caught setting fire to a house) had been cut off by a highlander." One horror led to another. This American war, like every other, was turning hard and ugly. The charred ruins of New York would be a symbol of that cruelty for many years to come.[70]

North of the city, Washington rallied his men on the high ground of Harlem Heights, near the present site of Columbia University. In front, on wooded ground, two brigades were posted as an advance guard. The next day, the British and Hessians moved north, driving the Americans before them. Washington sent Adjutant Joseph Reed to learn what was happening. Reed returned to report that the American infantry "behaved well, stood and returned fire till, overpowered by numbers, they were obliged to retreat. The enemy advanced very fast."[71]

Reed remembered that "by the time I got to him the enemy appeared in open view and in a most insulting manner sounded their bugle horns as is usual after a fox chase. I never felt such a sensation before; it seemed to crown our disgrace." This insult was keenly felt by the American commanders. Washington, outraged, forgot his defensive strategy and ordered his men to attack.[72]

Reed himself took the lead. Smallwood's Maryland regiment, the Connecticut Rangers, and the Virginia infantry took cover in a ravine, overgrown with bushes. On its western edge was a post-and-rail fence. The British light infantry came on, full of confidence. When they reached the fence, the Americans rose up and fired. The British infantry stopped, then fell back under heavy fire. The Americans came forward firing, and the British retreated with heavy losses. It was a small victory, but timely. An American officer wrote, "Our troops were in a most desponding Condition before, but now are in good spirits."[73]

After the fight at Harlem Heights, Tench Tilghman wrote, "The two armies are as quiet as if they were a thousand miles apart." But they were very close. Once again American intelligence failed. George Washington asked some of his officers to go spying behind enemy lines, and the result was an American tragedy. Captain Nathan Hale, an earnest young Yale graduate, volunteered to disguise himself as a Dutch schoolmaster and went into the enemy's camp with great courage, but little skill at espionage. He incautiously revealed himself to Colonel Robert Rogers, who had been playing both sides, and Hale was betrayed to British leaders. Incriminating papers were found in his possession, and New England Tories (probably including his own cousin) confirmed his identity. General Howe ordered a summary execution without trial on September 24, 1776. Before his death Nathan Hale repeated part of a passage from Addison's *Cato*, the great model for American Whigs:

> How beautiful is death, when earn'd by virtue!
> Who would not be that youth? What pity is it
> That we can die but once to serve our country.

British officers were moved by Nathan Hale's "gentle dignity," even as they left his body dangling at a rope's end. Americans were inspired by his selfless "sacrifice to his country's liberty," but he was yet another victim of amateur incompetence in the New York campaign.[74]

Washington was on the edge of despair. On September 30, his strength reports showed only 14,759 men fit for duty. Half his army had disappeared, and the enemy was "within a stone's throw." He confided to his cousin Lund Washington, "I was never in such an unhappy, divided state since I was born." He felt that he could not lead these troops to victory, and yet he was told that "if I leave the service all will be lost." Washington was baffled, exhausted, and angry, not least with himself. He wrote that he was "wearied to death all day with a variety of perplexing circumstances."

On one point he was very clear. "If the men will stand by me (which by the by I despair of)," he wrote to Lund, "I am resolved not to be forced from this ground while I have life, and a few days will determine the point." He expected the British army to attack again on Harlem Heights and kept his army posted on the high ground of upper Manhattan, hoping that he could entice the British and Hessians into a headlong assault.[75]

The Howe brothers had other ideas. They took a few days to shift their base to what remained of New York and put their scattered forces in order. The navy replenished its ships, and the army replaced its losses with an astonishing flow of recruits and "draughts" from regiments throughout the empire. Then the Howes planned to deal with the Americans who were sitting on the hills north of town. As always, they looked for a way to do it without the brutal butchery of a frontal attack on a prepared position. Once again the Royal Navy and British army would work together in a combined operation. Once more they would use their control of the waters around New York to trap the American army by a double envelopment.

On October 8, the Royal Navy moved up the Hudson River and stopped Americans from using it. Three days later, General Howe embarked his army on amphibious craft and small sloops in Kip's Bay and Turtle Bay and led them up the East River by boat. One boat capsized in the rough water of Hell Gate, but the rest got through. They came ashore at Throg's Neck on the mainland, north of Manhattan and about five miles from King's Bridge, the major crossing from Manhattan. If they could reach the bridge quickly, Washington's army would be trapped.

This time the British commanders made a mistake. The landing site at Throg's Neck was chosen as a compromise between the army who wanted a site farther northeast at New Rochelle where the roads were better, and the navy, who preferred Westchester Creek where the anchorage was more protected. They compromised on Throg's Neck without knowing the ground. When the troops landed on October 12, they found that Throg's Neck was a marshy island at high tide. The Americans had destroyed the bridge and causeway, and had fortified the only good ford. A small force of Edward Hand's Pennsylvania Riflemen were there again, with orders to bring down the British horses.

The morale of the American riflemen was remarkably high, given what they had recently been through. Hand wrote his wife a description of the British landing: "I suppose they think that movement will induce our Army to move further back, but I think they will find themselves much disappointed. Our late retreats were dictated by prudence not by a dread of their arms." At Throg's Neck thirty riflemen stopped the British army in their tracks, then held them while another 1,500 American infantry hurried to their support. The British army was stymied.[76]

The Howes decided to withdraw the troops and try a better landing. A heavy autumn storm disrupted their plan, and it was a week before they could get their men off. Washington moved quickly. He rode out along the coast, explored other landing sites, and posted some of his regiments to defend them. On October 18, he also decided to withdraw his army from Manhattan to the mainland. They started marching with all their equipment and supplies north to a strong position at White Plains.

On the same day, the Howe brothers retrieved their stranded troops and landed them again at Pell's Point, three miles north of Throg's Neck. Here they found John Glover's brigade of Massachusetts Continentals, posted a few days before by Washington. Glover had four small regiments: his own Marblehead mariners and county regiments commanded by Joseph Read, William Shepard, and Loammi Baldwin. All were much reduced by illness and battle, but the men who remained were hardened veterans, and their officers were among the best in the army. Baldwin was a Massachusetts country squire, polymath, civil engineer,and horticulturalist (developer of the Baldwin apple). He had an excellent eye for terrain. On the day of Lexington and Concord, Baldwin put his men on good ground along the Battle Road, caught the entire British column in enfilade, and stopped it at a critical moment.[77]

At Pell's Point, Baldwin and Glover watched the British force approach, and counted "200 sail" in four divisions. Glover's first thought was to send a letter to General Charles Lee asking for advice; "I would have given a thousand worlds to have had General Lee or some other experienced officer present," he recalled. But the British were ashore before an answer came. Glover and Baldwin improvised a defense. Their position was strong. The only way off the beach was by a narrow road through small fields lined with stone walls. The American commanders placed their regiments in echelon one behind the other, protected by the stone walls and very rough ground. The men were ordered to lie down until the British troops came within range, then to rise and fire volleys as fast as they could, and fall back behind the other regiments, using the walls for cover. In the first exchange the British troops received a withering fire, saw the Americans retreating, and went running after them with their bayonets, only to have another American line rise up in their faces. The British and Hessians suffered about two hundred killed and many wounded, more than they had lost on Long Island. The stubborn resistance allowed Washington to withdraw his troops north to the hills of White Plains. It also demonstrated the surprising stamina of the American troops. Even if they could not defeat the Regulars at their own game, they were learning that they could win in other ways.[78]

Howe came after Washington and found the Americans in a strong defensive position on very high ground behind the Bronx River. A key to the position was a "rocky height" 180 feet high. Howe deployed his army and made a spectacular display of about thirteen thousand men, arrayed across a broad field on a bright autumn day. Then he ordered his Hessian troops forward. In the van were three regiments that had been doing much of the fighting: Rall's land grenadier regiment, Knyphausen's Regulars, and the Regiment von Lossberg. They launched a heavy attack and suffered severe losses before Colonel Rall found an approach on a side of the hill that the Americans had neglected to defend. He led his grenadiers forward with great courage and took the hill at heavy cost. An unofficial reckoning by a British officer estimated 349 killed and wounded in his own army, probably many more. The Americans reported losing heavily as well. One Hessian volley alone from the Knyphausen regiment was observed to bring down ninety-two men.

Many British and Hessian accounts testified that the American troops were learning from their defeats. Lieutenant Bardeleben wrote that "the rebels had excellent positions at White Plains. They had made their defenses better than usual, and maintained their posts with extraordinary tenacity." The defeated Americans retreated in good order. The victorious British and Hessians gained the field but returned to Manhattan with a feeling that something had gone wrong.[79]

Howe took his army back to Manhattan to deal with the last remaining troops there, the garrison at Fort Washington, at the narrow northern tip of the island. Once again, the American commanders could not agree on what to do. Washington wanted to abandon the fort and pointed out that it was unable to stop British ships from passing up and down the Hudson River. Nathanael Greene wanted to keep it. He argued that the fort could not easily be captured, that the garrison could be ferried over the Hudson if need be, and that they tied down many British troops. Washington gave way to Greene, against his better judgment. It was a major error. The fort was impressive at first sight. It stood on a precipice 280 feet above the water's edge, with rivers on three sides and massive fortifications on the landward side.[80]

But in fact it was highly vulnerable. A British officer observed that the fortifications were "too extensive for the number of troops, as was generally the case with the Americans, who were indefatigable in constructing redoubts." The outer works were more than a mile in extent, far beyond the strength of its garrison, mostly Pennsylvania state levies and militia, with some Maryland and Virginia riflemen and Connecticut men.[81]

The fort had strong batteries, well stocked with guns and ammunition, and a two-month supply of dry provisions. But it had no

The Fall of Fort Washington

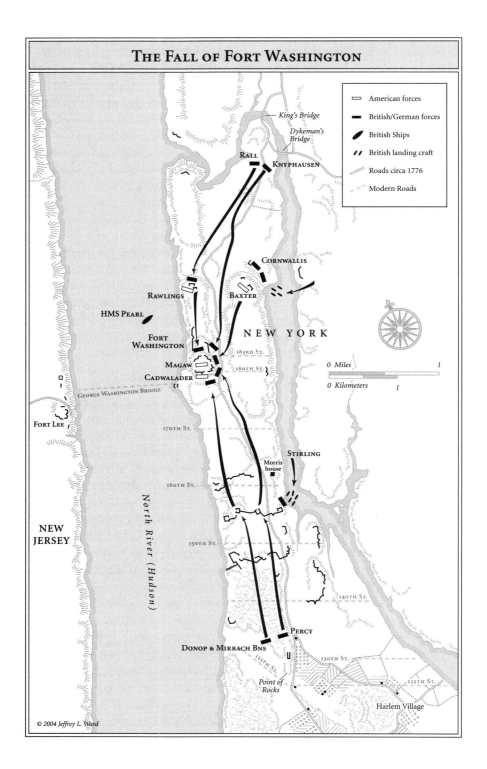

American forces

British/German forces

British Ships

British landing craft

Roads circa 1776

Modern Roads

King's Bridge

Dykeman's Bridge

RALL

KNYPHAUSEN

CORNWALLIS

RAWLINGS BAXTER

HMS PEARL

NEW YORK

FORT WASHINGTON

183RD ST.

MAGAW

180TH ST.

CADWALADER

GEORGE WASHINGTON BRIDGE

170TH ST.

FORT LEE

STIRLING

Morris house

160TH ST.

NEW JERSEY

North River (Hudson)

150TH ST.

140TH ST.

PERCY

DONOP & MIRBACH BNS

125TH ST.

130TH ST.

Point of Rocks

125TH ST.

Harlem Village

0 Miles   1

0 Kilometers   1

© 2004 Jeffrey L. Ward

well; water had to be brought up from the rivers below. The senior officers, Colonel Robert Magaw and Lieutenant Colonel Lambert Cadwalader, were good men, but they were betrayed by an American traitor. On the night of November 2, 1776, adjutant William Demont sneaked out of the fort and delivered its plans to the British commanders, along with much helpful information about the intentions of the Americans and the strengths and weaknesses of their defenses. To Frederick Mackenzie, the British officer who interrogated him, Demont reported "great dissensions in the Rebel army, everybody finding fault with the mode of proceeding, and the inferior officers, even ensigns insisting that, in such a cause, every man has a right to assist in council and to give his opinion."[82]

General Howe concentrated a large part of his army against the fort, thirteen thousand men altogether, four times the strength of the garrison. On November 15, he sent an officer under a white flag with a demand for the surrender of the fort and a warning that the garrison would be put to death if they resisted. The Americans remained defiant. Nathanael Greene rushed reinforcements across the river from Fort Lee.

At daybreak Howe's army launched their assault. British troops attacked in boats across the Harlem River, and four thousand Hessians stormed the fort on its landward side. The fighting was heavy where the Hessians met a large force of riflemen, and the German troops suffered many casualties. Inexorably the defenders were driven from the outer works into the central part of the fort, which became untenable, and the American commander surrendered. Some defenders were denied quarter. Mackenzie wrote, "The Hessians . . . were extremely irritated at having lost a good many men in the attack" and killed some of the riflemen after surrender, until officers intervened to stop the slaughter.[83] More than 2,800 American troops were lost, mostly to cruel captivity in the prison hulks of New York harbor. General Nathanael Greene was crushed by his error in recommending that the fort be held. He wrote, "I feel mad, vexed, sick and sorry. . . . This is a most terrible event: its consequences are justly to be dreaded."[84]

George Washington was shattered by the event. He was a witness to the final scenes, looking on helplessly from the Jersey Palisades across the Hudson River. Through his telescope he could see some of his troops fighting bravely, only to be driven back and defeated. The worst of it was to watch them surrender and see some of them put to the sword. This time there was no expression of anger by the American commander-in-chief. His feelings ran deeper than

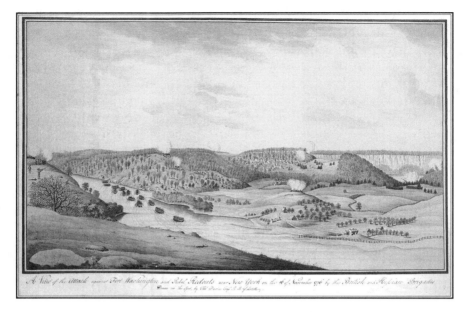

A View of the Attack against Ft. Washington, and Rebel Redoubts, near New York on the 16th of November, 1776, a drawing by Captain Thomas Davies, Royal Artillery. It shows the landing by British and German troops on the Harlem River. In the background on the right are the Hudson River, the Jersey Palisades, and HMS *Pearl.* I. N. Phelps Stokes Collection, The New York Public Library, Astor, Lenox and Tilden Foundations.

that. He blamed no one else for what had happened, took all the responsibility on his own shoulders, and judged himself more severely than anyone else could judge him.

As the full weight of the disaster fell upon him, he turned away from his lieutenants and began to weep "with the tenderness of a child." His aides did not know how to help, or even if they should. Some were beginning to doubt that he could lead them. Joseph Reed wrote afterward, "he hesitated more than I ever knew him on any other occasion, and more than I thought the public service admitted."[85] Charles Lee wrote in sadness, "Oh! General—an indecisive mind is one of the greatest misfortunes that can befall an army."[86] It was the lowest point of Washington's long career. In the agony of that moment he felt that he had lost everything: lost the war, lost the Cause, lost his own way. But then this extraordinary man reached deep into his last reserves of inner strength. Not much was left, but enough to shake off a terrible despair. He looked away from Fort Washington and rallied his aides around him. Together, they would try again.

THE RETREAT

❧ Cornwallis and the Conquest of New Jersey

> Let them go, my dear Ewald, and stay here. We do not
> want to lose any men. One Jäger is worth more than
> ten rebels.
>
> —General Charles Cornwallis, November 19, 1776[1]

> Now I perceived what was afoot. We wanted to spare
> the king's subjects and hoped to terminate the war
> amicably.
>
> —Jäger Captain Johann Ewald, November 19, 1776[2]

ON THE OTHER SIDE, the British commanders were preparing to strike again. The campaign for New York was coming to an end, and they were pleased with the result. But
now it was November, and the weather was turning damp and cold.
The question was, what next? The Howe brothers had the initiative,
and the choice was theirs.

Once again they received much advice from others. General
Henry Clinton, their able, ambitious, and immensely irritating subordinate, was quick to offer his opinion that they should strike a heavy
blow at the heart of the rebellion. Clinton made several proposals.
One was to seek out and destroy the fragments of Washington's broken army. Another was to move decisively against Philadelphia and
arrest the Continental Congress. His preference was to do both at
once, with Henry Clinton leading the campaign.[3]

Some historians believe that Clinton's strategy might have broken the rebellion. Others suspect that it might have broken Henry

Clinton. In any event, the Howe brothers had other ideas. One question in their minds was about how to continue their campaign for the pacification of the colonies. Another was a matter of logistics. They had to maintain the strength of a large army and navy a long way from home. The Howes had been trusted with more than half of the armed forces of the British Empire. After three months of active service, Admiral Howe's ships were worn, and General Howe's regiments were growing weary. Their handsome uniforms were torn and ragged. Some of the British infantry had worn out their shoes. The quartermasters were doing their best, but the line of communications was three thousand miles long. Supplies were running thin, and a hard American winter was approaching. General William Howe urgently needed housing, food, and forage for his army. New York City, with half its buildings burned, could serve only a small part of it, and the surrounding countryside had been picked clean by marching armies.

Admiral Richard Howe needed something else, a safe haven for his squadron. New York harbor was not ideal. In the bitter-cold winters of the late eighteenth century, the waters around Manhattan often froze solid. Henry Clinton wrote, with his usual air of disapproval, "The admiral wanted a winter station for his large ships and every other consideration must give way."[4]

The brothers put their heads together, and by early November they made a plan. With more than a month of autumn remaining, they decided to mount two quick campaigns before the winter closed in. Admiral Howe would move by sea and occupy Rhode Island as they had long planned: not the entire province but the island itself and the town of Newport. Its climate was mild, and its fine harbor was closer to the Gulf Stream and more nearly ice free than New York's. The prosperous farms on the island and the great plantations of the Narragansett country could supply much of the army through the winter. With Rhode Island occupied, another colony would be restored to the Crown, and a base constructed for the recovery of New England. And what a good place Rhode Island would be for General Henry Clinton! He would be given command, to his everlasting fury.

At the same time, the British commanders decided to send a second expedition in the opposite direction. General William Howe's army would occupy the eastern counties of New Jersey with great speed, and many troops would remain there through the winter. This was rich farmland, unspoiled by war. The army could find its food and forage in the Jersey countryside and shelter in its small towns. The remnants of Washington's ruined army were thought to be north of New York City and unable to resist. The object of the campaign would be to drive the Continental troops out of eastern New Jersey without a major engagement and to occupy it quickly before the Americans could lay waste to the countryside. Then a third colony would be recovered for the empire.[5]

It was a good plan in many ways. It provided for the army and the navy, protected the main base in New York, extended control over two more colonies, and offered support for Loyalists in areas where they were thought to be strong. At the same time, the Howes also maintained the initiative, kept up the momentum, and provided a strong flexible base for operations in 1777, if another campaign were to be necessary at all, which the triumphant British leaders were beginning to doubt. Some expected that the rebellion would not survive the winter. With that hope in mind, the Howes set their plans in motion with speed and resolve.

In the American camp, George Washington was in control again and studying his choices. He gave much attention to intelligence, with more success than before. As the British army occupied more territory, General Washington gained many sources of information. As early as November 7, he heard that General Howe was planning "an expedition to the Jerseys." On November 8, he wrote Nathanael Greene at Fort Lee that "various sources of intelligence" revealed British plans for a "penetration into Jersey." Greene was ordered to move his stores immediately from Fort Lee and to ask the inhabitants to "drive off their stock, and remove the Hay, Grain, etc." If they refused, he was to destroy it.[6] On November 9, Washington learned from the interrogation of British deserters that flat-bottomed landing craft were being brought through the Harlem River for a crossing of the Hudson, and that the British troops were ordered to have five days' provisions "ready dressed."[7]

That same day, Washington began to move his army across the Hudson River at Peekskill in preparation for the British attack. Three days later, he shifted his headquarters to Hackensack in northern New Jersey, at Judge Peter Zabriskie's great house with its three-foot stone walls on the town green. In his mind, this movement was not a retreat but a shift of front. Washington went into New Jersey to protect the state from attack.[8]

To lead the British conquest of New Jersey, Howe selected one of his finest officers, Charles Cornwallis, in his first independent command.

Jemina, Countess Cornwallis, mezzotint by Robert Laurie, after a portrait by Joshua Reynolds (1771). National Portrait Gallery, London.

Americans remember Cornwallis as a defeated general who lost an army at Yorktown and made possible the independence of the United States. Britons think of him as a victorious general who won another empire in the battle of Seringapatam, where he broke the power of Tipu Sultan, conquered a large part of India, and ruled it wisely as the first viceroy. The Irish know him in yet another way, as the viceroy of Ireland from 1798 to 1801, who ended the rebellion of 1798, defeated a French invasion, and resigned on principle when King George III refused to grant Roman Catholic emancipation. Europeans knew him as a peacemaker, who negotiated the peace of Amiens in 1802 and ended the bloody wars of the French Revolution. Altogether Charles Cornwallis was a man of many talents and one of the most appealing figures of his generation.[9]

He was of the high aristocracy, the son of the first Earl Cornwallis. He attended Eton, then went into the army and made a profession of soldiering in a very serious way. As a young officer Cornwallis hired his own Prussian military tutor, attended an Italian military academy at Turin, and bought a commission in the Grenadier Guards at the age of seventeen in 1758. He moved quickly to other marching regiments in search of opportunities for command, as a captain in

*Charles Cornwallis, Second
Earl Cornwallis*, portrait by
Thomas Gainsborough
(1783). National Portrait
Gallery, London.

the Eighty-fifth Foot, lieutenant colonel of the Twelfth Foot, and
colonel of the Thirty-third Foot, all by 1766. His active service was
mainly in Europe, where he won honors for gallantry in battle at
Minden and on many German fields.

In Britain, Cornwallis was well connected at court. He became
aide-de-camp to George III in 1765, lord of the bedchamber, and
constable of the Tower in 1770. He was also active in local affairs
near the family's great estate and became a member of Parliament,
sitting in the House of Commons for the family seat in the borough
of Eye, and later the House of Lords. In politics he was a staunch
Whig and strongly opposed hard measures against America.
Cornwallis wrote that Americans were "free Englishmen, such as
we, who are simply standing up for their rights." In 1766, he joined
a minority of men who voted against the Declaratory Act that asserted Parliament's power to tax the colonies and legislate for them
"in all cases whatsoever."

In 1768, Cornwallis did a strange thing by the standards of his
class. He married for love. Jemima Jones was the daughter of Colonel James Jones of the Third Regiment of Foot Guards, and a remarkable person in her own right. Her portraits show a beauty unlike
any other in the world. She was independent, intelligent, spirited,

witty, charming, and very outspoken on public questions. To her brother-in-law, Jemima wrote, "Don't laugh at my being political. I assure you I do not think a female *ought* to talk politics, but when it comes to husband, friends, &c., one must feel, and it will out." Cornwallis was deeply in love with her, and she with him. His biographers write that "the years they had together were extraordinarily happy ones." She gave birth to a son and a daughter, but her health was very fragile, and Cornwallis worried desperately about her.[10]

In 1775, when the American war began, Cornwallis followed his profession and returned to the army. He favored American rights but opposed the American rebellion. To Jemima's distress he volunteered for duty in America, seeking service at Cape Fear or in Canada, where he hoped to have an independent command. According to legend, Jemima pulled many strings to have his orders canceled, even asking her uncle the Archbishop of Canterbury to intervene, but in vain.[11]

In America, Cornwallis was very popular with his men. Henry Clinton described him as a "favorite not only with his own but with this army." He did not stand upon ceremony and once wrote that "no man despises the pompous etiquette of command more than I do." In the field he kept close to his men, and one of them remembered that "he lived and marched and suffered with the army." Always he led them by example. He made less use of flogging than other officers and intervened to reduce extreme sentences. His devotion to his men appeared in India, where he received 42,000 pounds sterling for his great victory over Tipu Sultan and gave the entire sum to his soldiers. His biographer writes, "As a man he displayed, far more than Clinton and others, qualities of honesty, justice, endurance, tolerance, humanity, and eagerness to better the life of those under him."[12] He was popular with junior officers, whom he often invited to share his table. Captain John Peebles of the Royal Highland Regiment remembered dining with him in an atmosphere of "ease and politeness" and of quiet moderation in all things. After one such occasion, Peebles wrote in his diary, "din'd with Lord Cornwallis. Good things with temperance & politeness is true Epicurism."[13]

At the same time, Cornwallis won the esteem of his superiors. At the beginning of the New York campaign, William Howe chose him for command of the elite battalions of light infantry, grenadiers, Highlanders, and his own Thirty-third Foot, who led most major assaults. Cornwallis was among the first men ashore on Long Island, and in the battle that followed he led the charge at Gowanus

Road, where his men exposed themselves to enemy fire with "almost reckless abandon."[14] He landed at Kip's Bay, and was on the right of the line at White Plains. At Fort Washington it was said that his "astute disposition of troops sealed the rebel escape route." Now he was given another job with the same men. His orders were to clear the rebel army from New Jersey without a major engagement, and to do it quickly before the weather changed.

The invasion of New Jersey began with a night river crossing, another extraordinary feat of soldiering. On the evening of November 18, the Royal Navy delivered a flotilla of landing barges and doubled-ended bateaux, "passing the enemy's posts undiscovered" on the Hudson River. The boats were hidden in the protected waters of Spuyten Duyvil, north of Manhattan.[15]

The next day General Howe's headquarters issued marching orders to twelve battalions of assault troops. They were always the same, on the cutting edge of the army: two battalions each of light infantry, guards, and British grenadiers, plus three battalions of Hessian grenadiers, two battalions of the Forty-second Highlanders, two companies of Hessian Jägers, and Cornwallis's own Thirty-third Foot. With them were the ubiquitous Royal Engineers and Royal Artillery, with eight field guns. Cornwallis also took along a hundred American Loyalists of Robert Rogers's corps. His force totaled about five thousand men.[16]

Their orders came late in the day to strike tents, load wagons, and be ready to march at nine o'clock on the evening of November 19, 1776. Every effort was made to preserve secrecy. Nothing was revealed about the destination. Cornwallis waited for complete darkness. Then he led the light infantry, the British grenadiers, the Thirty-third Foot and Forty-second Highlanders to the waters of Spuyten Duyvil, where they boarded the boats.[17]

At about eleven o'clock they started across the Hudson River. When they were on the water, a cold November rain began to fall. One light infantry officer remembered being soaked to the skin by a "thick heavy rain." On the great river a dense fog arose. The troops in their barges and bateaux glided through it as silently as ghosts.

Their guides were three New Jersey Tories. One is thought to have been John Aldington, a brewer in a settlement called the English Neighborhood, now the city of Leonia. The other guides were William Bayard, who ran the Hoboken ferry, and John Ackerson, a farmer in Closter. They knew the river well, and the dispositions of the American troops.

The Landing of the British Troops in the Jerseys, a drawing by Captain Thomas Davies (1776). This scene shows the second division of Cornwallis's force landing with artillery on the morning of November 20, 1776. Emmet Collection, The New York Public Library, Astor, Lenox and Tilden Foundations.

As the British force approached the Jersey shore, an officer in the lead company peered anxiously through the mist. Lieutenant Henry Stirke of the Tenth Light Infantry was amazed to discover that they had landed at the foot of huge vertical cliffs, rising high above the water and extending along the river as far as he could see. These were the New Jersey Palisades, a formidable obstacle. The Tory guides pointed through the mist to a long diagonal fracture that was barely visible in the rock. Lieutenant Stirke was ordered to lead his company forward and "push up the hill, with as much expedition as possible," then "to take post; and maintain it, till sustained." His men began to climb in the darkness, through rain and mist. They found themselves on a steep and slippery trail about four feet wide, with a grade of fifty degrees in some places. The ground must have been treacherous in the night, with rain cascading down the rock.[18]

The light infantry reached the top, ready for a fight, and found that the Palisades were entirely unguarded at that point. A Hessian who followed them thought that a few men armed with stones could have stopped the entire corps. The American General Nathanael

Greene had posted guards on other parts of the Palisades, but they had missed this place.[19]

Cornwallis's force followed Stirke's company in single file up the narrow trail. It took them much of the night, as the boats shuttled back and forth across the river. At daybreak another wave of Hessians and guards crossed from a long wharf at the Philipse Farm on Philipseberg Manor, a huge estate that spanned the east bank of the Hudson from Spuyten Duyvil to the Croton River. The second wave had an easier passage on the water in daylight but a harder task at the Palisades, where they were ordered to bring up the artillery: eight field guns, four three-pounders, two six-pounders, and two howitzers, which with their carriages weighed two thousand pounds. Gunners, sappers, soldiers, and seamen worked together, hauling the guns and limbers and ammunition boxes up the face of the steep cliff by brute force. The trail was impassable for artillery horses.

Royal Artillery, Hoisting the Guns over a Sheer Cliff, watercolor by William Congreve. The Royal Artillery Historical Trust.

At the top of the Palisades the men hauled the guns forward with drag ropes. [20]

Once again, with a good plan and skillful execution, British and Hessian forces achieved tactical surprise, even though the American leaders knew that an attack was coming. Even after they landed, nobody discovered them at the Palisades, though two thousand American troops were still at Fort Lee only a few miles south of the crossing point. Long after daybreak, when the second division began to cross, they were still not detected for many hours.

The British infantry quickly established a perimeter and began to send out patrols. At last they were observed, not by the American army but by a slave girl named Polly Wyckoff, who was working in the kitchen of Matthew Bogert's farm and saw the British approaching across the fields. She ran into the parlor and cried, "Bogert's fields are full of red coats."[21]

It was ten o'clock in the morning when an American officer galloped up to the Zabriskie house in Hackensack with the news that the British were over the river. George Washington was instantly in motion, and his first thought was to get his troops away from Fort Lee. After the disaster at Fort Washington, he could not lose another garrison that way. Urgent orders went to the fort, ordering the troops to leave instantly and march west across the Hackensack River.

Washington must have been unhappy with Nathanael Greene, who had been ordered to guard the Palisades and failed. Ten days earlier Greene had been urged to evacuate the fort and had moved slowly, complaining that he could not find enough wagons. He had been instructed to get the men away, but that morning they were still in their tents, with most of their equipment, and many heavy guns.

When the news of the British landing reached the fort, American discipline collapsed. Some of the men stopped to eat a leisurely breakfast, as if it were their last meal. Others broke into the rum supply. Many scattered into the woods. Washington and Greene galloped to the scene, got most of the men together in a column, and started them marching westward toward New-Bridge over the Hackensack River.

On the Palisades, Cornwallis formed his men in two columns and led them south at a quick march toward Fort Lee. Captain Johann Ewald's company of Hessian Jägers was sent out to cover the advancing army's right flank. Captain Ewald looked ahead and saw "a great glitter of bayonets and a cloud of dust in the distance." It was the garrison of Fort Lee marching toward New-Bridge. Ewald sent his Jägers running after them. They began to skirmish with American stragglers and sent a message back to Cornwallis for more light infantry. "Instead of the Jägers," Ewald wrote, "I received an order from Lord Cornwallis to return at once. I had to obey and informed him what I had discovered. Cornwallis replied, 'Let them go, my dear Ewald, and stay here. We do not want to lose any men. One jäger is worth more than ten rebels.'"[22]

Ewald was amazed. He returned to his troops and pushed them forward again, "in hopes of catching some baggage." They succeeded in capturing a coach and four, filled with fugitives who were retreating in grand style. Then Ewald was summoned again by Cornwallis and told to stay close to the column. At last he began to understand his British commander. "Now I perceived what was afoot," he wrote. "We wanted to spare the King's subjects and hoped to terminate the war amicably, in which assumption I was strengthened the next day by several English officers."[23]

Cornwallis allowed the American troops to march away and took his troops to Fort Lee. It was not a massive fortification like Fort Washington. Thomas Paine described it as a "field fort." The main part of it was an armed camp, with separate batteries on the cliffs overlooking the Hudson. The British troops found the fort in a shambles. The road to the west was littered with the debris of a fleeing army. Inside the fort, Cornwallis and his men found a few drunken stragglers and vast quantities of supplies. Greene had succeeded in getting most of the ammunition away, and all of the field guns. Left behind were nine hundred tents, all of the American army's entrenching tools, much heavy artillery, and an immense store of provisions. The British and Hessian infantry were surprised by the quantity of material in the fort. Cornwallis ordered his men to leave the booty for other troops that followed. He was mindful of his orders to keep the pressure on the retreating American army, without forcing it to battle.[24]

As night fell on November 20, the American troops crossed the Hackensack River and entered the village of Hackensack. An inhabitant remembered, "the night was dark, cold, and rainy, but I had a fair view of them from the light of the windows as they passed on our side of the street. They marched two abreast, looked ragged, some without a shoe to their feet, and most of them wrapped in their blankets." Many of these men had joined the army in July and August. They were still wearing summer clothing, which had been reduced to rags by hard campaigning. A British officer who found some of them along the road observed contemptuously, "No nation ever saw such a set of tatterdemalions."[25]

Washington posted guards at the crossing points over the Hackensack river, and stayed the night in Peter Zabriskie's house. With him were about four thousand Continentals and militia, who camped in the village. It was a miserable night for them. The men had lost their tents and tools at Fort Lee and huddled miserably together wherever they could find a bit of shelter.[26]

The British army was not far behind. The next morning the light infantry and Jägers came up to New-Bridge, about two miles north of the village. The American rear guard occupied houses on both sides of the river and put up a sharp fight at the bridge. Captain Ewald remembered that the Americans "defended themselves very well." Cornwallis's vanguard discovered to their surprise that Washington's ragged men did not behave like a beaten army. At New-Bridge they fought doggedly. Ewald wrote, "in spite of this the post was forced, and the greater part were killed, wounded, or captured." In other skirmishes along the road, small parties of American infantry resisted stubbornly against heavy odds. The Hessian Jägers and British light infantry were learning to treat these tatterdemalions with respect. At British headquarters, attitudes of "featherbed soldiers" toward American troops were very different from those of British and Hessian infantry on the sharp edge.[27]

Cornwallis continued his pursuit in a carefully measured way. He paused at New-Bridge while more troops came up. Howe sent him two more infantry brigades and elements of a third, plus the very useful troopers of the Sixteenth Light Dragoons. These reinforcements doubled the size of Cornwallis's command to nearly ten thousand men. That night they bivouacked along the east bank of the Hackensack River. An inhabitant of the town remembered that "we could see their fires about one hundred yards apart, gleaming brilliantly in the gloom of the night, extending some distance below the town and more than a mile toward the New Bridge."[28]

On November 22, Cornwallis's men pushed across the Hackensack River at New-Bridge and marched south to the town of Hackensack. That night the Hessians camped on the village green. Loyalists welcomed them as liberators and were shocked to be plundered by hungry German and British soldiers who did not share the war aims of the Howe brothers and could not distinguish a Tory from a Whig.[29]

Washington and his army had left Hackensack the day before. While the American rear guard was fighting at New-Bridge, the rest of the army headed west to the hamlet of Acquackanonk Landing on the Passaic River. The Americans crossed the river on a rickety

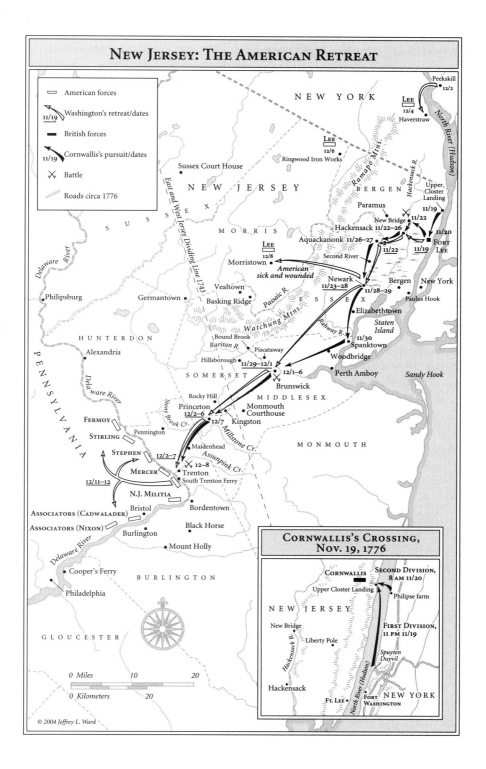

New Jersey: The American Retreat

Legend:

- American forces
- **11/19** Washington's retreat/dates
- British forces
- **11/19** Cornwallis's pursuit/dates
- ✕ Battle
- Roads circa 1776

NEW YORK

Peekskill • 12/2

LEE 12/4

Haverstraw

LEE 12/6

Ringwood Iron Works •

Sussex Court House •

NEW JERSEY

BERGEN

Upper Closter Landing

SUSSEX

East and West Jersey Dividing Line 1743

Ramapo Mtns.

Hackensack R.

North River (Hudson)

Paramus •

New Bridge **11/19** **11/22**

MORRIS

Hackensack 11/22–26 **11/20**

LEE 12/8

Aquackanonk 11/26–27

FORT LEE **11/19**

Morristown •

American sick and wounded

Second River

11/22

11/19

Delaware River

Philipsburg •

Vealtown •

Newark 11/23–28

Bergen • New York

11/28–29

Paulus Hook

Germantown •

Basking Ridge •

Passaic R.

ESSEX

Elizabethtown •

Staten Island

HUNTERDON

Alexandria •

Watchung Mtns.

Bound Brook

Raritan R.

Rahway R.

11/30 Spanktown

Woodbridge •

Hillsborough •

Piscataway •

11/29–12/1

Perth Amboy •

Sandy Hook

PENNSYLVANIA

Delaware River

SOMERSET

✕ **12/1–6**

Brunswick

MIDDLESEX

Stony Brook Cr.

Rocky Hill •

Princeton **12/2–6**

Monmouth Courthouse

FERMOY •

Pennington •

12/7 Kingston

MONMOUTH

STIRLING •

Millstone Cr.

STEPHEN • **12/2–7**

Maidenhead •

Assunpink Cr.

MERCER •

✕ **12–8**

Trenton •

12/11–12

South Trenton Ferry

N.J. Militia

ASSOCIATORS (CADWALADER) •

Bristol •

Bordentown •

ASSOCIATORS (NIXON) •

Burlington •

Black Horse •

Mount Holly •

BURLINGTON

Delaware River

Cooper's Ferry •

Philadelphia •

GLOUCESTER

0 Miles 10 20

0 Kilometers 20

© 2004 Jeffrey L. Ward

Cornwallis's Crossing, Nov. 19, 1776

CORNWALLIS

SECOND DIVISION, 8 AM 11/20

Upper Closter Landing

Philipse farm

NEW JERSEY

New Bridge •

Liberty Pole •

FIRST DIVISION, 11 PM 11/19

Hackensack R.

Spuyten Duyvil

Hackensack •

FT. LEE

FORT WASHINGTON

NEW YORK

North River (Hudson)

wooden bridge, then destroyed it, and camped on the other side in another cold November rain. British cavalry followed at a distance and came up to the river, but once again Cornwallis did not attack. He rested his army in Hackensack for two days and sent out foraging parties, who were astounded by the wealth of the New Jersey countryside and the prosperity of its farms. The foragers collected abundant supplies; in the Hackensack meadows they captured many thousands of cattle that had been driven from Pennsylvania and southern New Jersey for Washington's army.

Cornwallis's object was to keep Washington's small American army moving across New Jersey, not to bring it to battle. At headquarters in New York, Henry Clinton interrupted his preparations for Rhode Island, and urged yet again a different plan. As often before, he argued that the strategic purpose of the war should be to destroy the American army and capture the leaders of the rebellion. This time Clinton proposed to Howe that, instead of going to Rhode Island, he should be sent to Perth Amboy in New Jersey with orders to cut off Washington's retreat, or else he should be landed in the Delaware River so that he could strike at Philadelphia and the Continental Congress.[30]

The Howe brothers listened courteously and rejected his advice. They wanted Rhode Island quickly, and Clinton's orders stood. In New York harbor during the week of November 24, a fleet of fifty-one transports with an escort of twelve warships began to gather in the lower bay. Smaller craft started sailing eastward through Hell Gate to Long Island Sound.[31]

While British forces assembled for the Rhode Island expedition, Washington's army continued its retreat through New Jersey. On the west side of the Passaic River they turned southward and marched down the Passaic Valley toward Newark. This town had been settled by New England Puritans who had named it the New Ark of the Covenant. In 1776, their descendants were staunch Whigs who strongly supported independence. The American army found them busily moving their families and goods out of the town. Livestock were being driven away, and the roads were crowded with carts and wagons piled high with household goods and furniture. A Hessian officer wrote that "the greater part of the inhabitants have carried away their beds."[32]

In Newark, George Washington had a choice to make. One road led northwest to Morristown and the Watchung Mountains in the northwest, where he would be safe from attack but unable to protect the people of New Jersey. The other road ran southwest to Brunswick, Princeton, and Trenton, through the densely settled central corridor of the state. Washington instantly made his decision. The sick would go northwest to Morristown. The rest of the army would march south to Brunswick, where he hoped to join with other regiments and militia from the middle states. Washington got his weary men moving toward Brunswick on two roads, one by Woodbridge and the other by Springfield and Quibbletown. William Beatty remembered that the march was made in a very dark night, "which together with the Intolerable bad roads made this tour of duty very hard."[33]

The American troops reached Brunswick at noon on November 29, 1776. There they remained until December 1. The army was melting away. When it left Newark, Lieutenant James Monroe stood by the side of the road and counted the men as they passed by. He was shocked to discover that the army was reduced to three thousand men. At Brunswick it grew smaller, as many units came to the end of their service and went home. William Beatty's outfit was among them. He remembered, "Two or three days after our arrival at Brunswick, being the first of December, and the Expiration of the flying Camp troop's time, Our Brigade march'd to Philadelphia leaving our Brave Genl with a very weak army." Washington asked them to stay, but he reported that "all the men of the Jersey flying camp . . . have refused to continue."[34]

Another problem was General Charles Lee, who was at Peekskill and at last about to cross the Hudson River after many urgings. Lee's forces were also diminishing rapidly, from seven thousand a few weeks before to four thousand by the beginning of December. Lee was not responding to Washington's instructions, and he demanded an independent command. "I should be glad to receive your instructions," he wrote to his commander-in-chief, "but I cou'd wish you wou'd bind me as little as possible." The second ranking general in the American army was going into business for himself.[35]

Even with his depleted forces, Washington thought about making a stand behind the Raritan River and deployed his men along the bank. Some of his strongest units were artillery, and one of the best of these was an Independent Company of New York State Artillery. Its commanding officer was Captain Alexander Hamilton, a young West Indian undergraduate at King's College. He had organized the company, recruited its men, raised the money for full uniforms of Continental buff and blue with buckskin breeches, and imposed discipline with an iron hand and some use of the lash, all at the age

Captain Alexander Hamilton, the
commanding officer of the New York
Battery of Artillery. William S. Stryker
(1898), *The Battles of Trenton and
Princeton*, 16.

of twenty. While he led his company and fought in the battles around
New York, Hamilton used his paybook to take notes on reading in
Plutarch's *Lives* and Malachi Postelthwayt's *Universal Dictionary of
Trade and Commerce*, preparing himself to be a leader of the free re-
public for which they were fighting.[36]

By the fall of 1776, Hamilton had sixty-eight officers and men.
Recalling the long retreat across New Jersey, an officer in another
unit wrote: "I well remember the day when Hamilton's company
marched into Princeton. It was a model of discipline; at their head
was a boy and I wondered at his youth; but what was my surprise,
when struck with his diminutive figure, he was pointed out to me as
that Hamilton of whom we had already heard so much."[37]

In Brunswick, on December 1, 1776, Washington called on Hamilton's artillery to cover the crossings. Early that afternoon, British
light dragoons came in sight on the opposite bank at the Brunswick
ferry. Washington was writing yet another letter to Congress when he
heard the alarm, and added a quick note, "1/2 after 1. O'Clock P.M.
The Enemy are fast advancing, some of 'em are now in sight."[38] American troops tried to destroy a bridge over the Raritan River but were
only able to damage it before the British light infantry and Hessian
Jägers drove them away. American riflemen occupied houses along
the river and began to take a toll of the Jägers. Cornwallis wanted the
bridge, and the British brought up their artillery, which began firing
in an attempt to push the Americans back from the river.

Alexander Hamilton brought up his guns and unlimbered on what is now the campus of Rutgers University, and an artillery duel began across the Raritan. Lieutenant Enoch Anderson wrote, "in the afternoon . . . a severe cannonading took place on both sides, and several were killed and wounded on our side." Hamilton's counterbattery fire kept the British at a distance while the American troops withdrew.[39]

Enoch Anderson of Haslet's Delaware regiment remembered that the artillery continued until "near Sundown" when "orders were given for a retreat." The Delaware men had brought off their equipment in good order, including a hundred beautiful tents, but now they had no wagons. Anderson remembered that "Colonel Haslet came to me, and told me to take as many men as I thought proper, and go back and burn all the tents. 'We have no wagons,' said he 'to carry them off, and it is better to burn them than they should fall into the hands of the enemy.' Then I went and burned them—about one hundred tents. When we saw them reduced to ashes, it was night and the army far ahead. We made a double quick-step and came up with the army about eight o'clock. We encamped in the woods, with no victuals, no tents, no blankets. The night was cold and we all suffered much, especially those who had no shoes."[40]

While the Americans camped in the open at Kingston, thirteen miles to the south, Cornwallis held most of his army on the north bank of the Raritan until the next morning, when his men repaired the damaged bridge and marched into Brunswick. The British troops were hungry and had not been able to bake their flour into bread. Their horses were exhausted, and Cornwallis wrote, "I could not have pursued the enemy from Brunswick with any prospect of material advantage, or without greatly distressing the troops under my command."[41] Some of the Hessians were barefoot. In the Raritan River they captured two coastal sloops with "a large quantity of shoes and long trousers on board, which came at just the right time, because our men could no longer proceed in their boots."[42] General Howe ordered Lord Cornwallis "not to advance beyond Brunswick" until he arrived. The British army remained there until December 6, when Howe took command and decided to take West Jersey too.[43]

While the British and Hessians rested in Brunswick, Washington continued south to Princeton. Enoch Anderson remembered that "here we had comfortable lodgings in the College. The whole army was now about twenty-five hundred men, and as their enlistments expired, they went off by the hundreds."[44] In Princeton, Washington expected to find Charles Lee and his troops, or at least a message indicating when the two parts of the Continental army would be united. But there was nothing, and not a word for five days. Lee was distancing himself from his commander-in-chief, perhaps because he wanted to avoid the taint of an expected defeat, or probably because he wanted to run his own show.[45]

Washington would deal with Lee later. At the moment he was more concerned about getting his men south across the Delaware, twelve miles away. On December 2, he sent part of his army to the river at Trenton and left 1,400 men in Princeton to delay the enemy as best they could, for five days if possible. Washington himself marched with Haslet's Delaware men in the rear guard of the main body. Anderson recalled that "we continued on our retreat;—our Regiment in the rear, and I, with thirty men, in the rear of the Regiment, and General Washington in my rear with pioneers,—tearing up bridges and cutting down trees, to impede the march of the enemy. I was to go no faster than General Washington and his pioneers."[46]

Washington was worried that the enemy might trap his army against the Delaware River and destroy it. That idea was distant from the mind of General Howe, who seemed happy to see rebels disappear beyond the river, and all the better if it happened without a battle. On December 7, the British and Hessian troops finally started marching from Brunswick in three columns. The pursuit resumed its stately pace like a slow dance across New Jersey. The two armies moved in a military minuet, with Generals Howe and Cornwallis setting the beat. That same day, Washington's rear guard left Princeton at three o'clock in afternoon. At precisely four o'clock Cornwallis's infantry arrived. Howe's Hessian aide Captain Friedrich von Münchausen wrote, "Princeton is a nice little town, and has a fine college. . . . A remarkably excellent library has till now been spared by the war." But not for long. Sergeant Thomas Sullivan of the British Sixty-fourth Foot wrote, "Our army when we lay there spoiled and plundered a good library that was in it."[47]

While the British remained at Brunswick and Princeton, the bulk of the American troops arrived at the water's edge in Trenton around noon on December 2, 1776. Washington had sent orders ahead for boats, and many were waiting when they arrived. For the next five days the men labored mightily at getting their guns and supplies and wagons across the river. The crossing continued, day and night, by the light of large fires.

The Pennsylvania militia came to help. The Philadelphia Associators moved up the river in boats, using their tents for sails. One company was equipped and commanded by the American artist Charles Willson Peale. Watching from the Pennsylvania shore, he was shocked by what he saw of Washington's army struggling to cross the Delaware. Peale wrote that it was "the most hellish scene I ever beheld. All the shores were lighted up with large fires, boats continually passing and repassing, full of men, horses, artillery and camp equipage. . . . The Hollowing of hundreds of men in their difficulties of getting Horses and artillery out of the boats, made it rather the appearance of Hell than any earthly scene."[48]

As the Continentals marched past Peale, "a man staggered out of line and came toward me. He had lost all his clothes. He was in an old dirty blanket jacket, his beard long and his face full of sores . . . which so disfigured him that he was not known by me on first sight. Only when he spoke did I recognize my brother James." It was Ensign James Peale, who had joined Smallwood's Maryland regiment when it was more than a thousand strong and had fought in the battles around New York. Now he was one of a hundred survivors who crossed the Delaware.[49]

As the American army reached the west bank of the Delaware, Washington began to organize a defensive line on the Pennsylvania side of the river. He distributed his regiments along twenty-five miles

George Washington, by James Peale, after Charles Willson Peale (ca. 1787–90). The two figures on the left are the artists James Peale and Charles Willson Peale. Both served in the Trenton and Princeton campaign, James in Smallwood's Maryland regiment, and Charles in the Philadelphia Associators. The painting represents their deep respect for the American Commander in Chief. The left side of the painting, in dark shadow, represents the "black times" of the New Jersey campaign in which they fought. The right side of the painting is a bright scene of the victory of Yorktown. Independence National Historical Park.

of the west bank, guarding all of the major crossing points. Others on his staff warned him that to defend everything was to defend nothing. In the words of historian Douglas Southall Freeman, it was a "commitment that made him weak everywhere."[50]

But Washington had other strengths. As early as December 1, while still in Brunswick, he sent a secret order to Colonel Richard Humpton: "You are to proceed to the two ferry's near Trentown and to see all the boats there put in the best Order, with a sufficiency of Oars and poles, and at the same time to Collect all the Additional boats you [can] from both above and below and have them brought to those ferry's and Secured for the purpose of Carrying over the Troops and Baggage." Humpton was told to "particularly attend to the Durham Boats which are very proper for the purpose."[51]

At the same time, the Pennsylvania Council of Safety ordered Captain Thomas Houston of the Pennsylvania Navy to proceed up the Delaware in the galley *Warren* and remove all ships and boats to the Pennsylvania side of the river.[52] The New Jersey militia went to work on the same task above the Trenton falls. Captains Jacob Gearhart, Daniel Bray, and Thomas Jones and the men of the Second Regiment of the Hunterdon County militia searched the Delaware and Lehigh rivers for "boats of every kind" and hid them in creeks and behind wooded islands on the Pennsylvania bank.[53] Together these men collected all the boats along forty miles of the river. They did their work so thoroughly that when the Tory Joseph Galloway went searching for vessels on the Jersey shore, he found only one scow, two boats on a millpond, and four bateaux.[54]

Downstream, the Delaware River was dominated by a new fighting force called the Pennsylvania Navy. It operated a flotilla of thirteen low, sinister black-painted river craft variously called galleys or gondolas, with names such as *Burke, Camden, Chatham, Congress, Experiment, Franklin, Ranger,* and *Washington,* and a Pennsylvania naval flag sewn by Betsy Ross. These vessels were driven by two banks of oars and two lateen sails that could point close to the wind. On board were fighting crews of about thirty men, and the rowers were said to include Tory captives. They were small double-ended, flat-bottomed river craft, only about forty-seven to fifty feet long, but powerfully armed with a very large gun forward. Altogether, they carried one thirty-two-pounder, four twenty-four-pounders and eight eighteen-pounders, which outranged any other weapon in the Delaware Valley. When Washington brought his army to the river, Pennsylvania Commodore Thomas Seymour sent nine gallies to help carry men and stores, while four patrolled the river.[55]

Small as they were, these vessels of the Pennsylvania Navy controlled the river up to the falls at Trenton. The waters around New York City had been dominated by the Royal Navy, which gave the British commanders the initiative and the power to strike when and where they pleased. Along the Delaware, the Americans had the same advantages.

On December 8, the British entered Trenton. As General Howe and his aides rode into the town, Captain Münchausen wrote that "some inhabitants came running toward us, urging us to march through town in a hurry so we could capture many of the enemy who were just embarking."[56]

Howe and Cornwallis and three aides rode down to the river. As they came into the open, the American artillery on the opposite bank "opened a terrific fire." Münchausen counted thirty-seven guns in action. The Jägers and light infantry ran for cover, but General Howe made a point of remaining under the heaviest fire with "the greatest coolness and calm for at least an hour." Münchausen wrote that "wherever we turned the cannon balls hit the ground, and I can hardly understand, even now, why all five of us were not killed. A cannon ball landed so close to Captain Münchausen that the dirt splattered his body and face." Another ball took off the hind leg of the captain's horse, and the German officer wrote, "I had the honor to receive a small contusion on my knee."[57]

This ritual of European honor on the bank of the Delaware revealed something of what these aristocratic European officers were fighting for. While Howe and Cornwallis and Münchausen were making a display of gallantry, thirteen men were killed and maimed around them. On the other side of the river, the American artillery fire was a display of defiance by the Continental army, which was far from feeling defeated.

The British commanders made a show of searching for boats. Troops were sent up and down the river and found very few. One of General Howe's engineers asked Joseph Galloway to discover if materials were available in Trenton for making boats or pontoons or rafts. Galloway found "48,000 feet of boards, a quantity of wire, and there was timber enough about Trenton for that purpose." But General Howe had no interest in crossing the river. His forces were fully extended, even overextended. He had already decided to end the campaign and prepared to send his army into winter quarters.

Many British and Hessian officers were appalled by that choice. British General Vaughan offered to take a rowboat and continue the pursuit. Hessian Captain Ewald wrote, "It became clearly evident that the march took place so slowly for no other reason than to permit Washington to cross the Delaware safely and peacefully." Charles Stedman remarked in his account of the war, "General Howe appeared to have calculated with the greatest accuracy the exact time necessary for the enemy to make his escape."[58]

As the British and Hessian troops reached the Delaware River at Trenton, the capital city of Philadelphia was less than a day's march away. Its inhabitants gave way to a full-blown panic. Rumors swept the city. Many heard that the marching army of Howe and Cornwallis was "at least 12,000 strong, determined for Philadelphia."[59] Margaret Morris wrote that "a person from Philada told us the people there were in great commotion, that the English fleet was in the River & hourly expected to sail up to the city; that the inhabitants were removing to the Country."[60]

Others believed that the enemy was within. It was said that "several persons of considerable repute had been discovered to have formed a design of setting fire to the City & were summoned before the Congress and strictly enjoined to drop the horrid purpose." A woman who heard that report wrote, "My heart almost died within me, & I cried surely the Lord will not punish the innocent with the guilty, and I wished there might be found some interceding Lots and Abrahams amongst our People."[61]

On December 8, martial law was declared in the city, and General Israel Putnam was given summary powers to maintain order. On December 9, the shops were ordered to close, and the militia was ordered to patrol the streets. Many Philadelphians sought safety in flight. A lady remembered that when news arrived that the British were in Princeton, and then on the Delaware, many people fled for their lives. "Where shall we go; how shall we get out of town? was the universal cry. Few families had the means to leave town. Coaches were few and mostly owned by Loyalists who were happy to stay. Happy was he who could press a market-wagon, or a milk-cart to bear off his little ones." One woman who signed herself "H. T." left by "a small river boat called a wood flat," where her choice was to stay below in "a smoky cabin" or huddle in a blanket on a snow-covered deck. In the countryside refugees from the city were "thankful if they could find a hut or barn, in any region of security."[62]

Among some Philadelphians (not all or even most), political opinions shifted as often as the wind on the Delaware. Tories became more outspoken, and Whigs turned very quiet. A few changed their

The British Landing on Rhode Island, December, 1776, watercolor by John Cleveley Sr. (1777). National Maritime Museum, Greenwich.

allegiances altogether. The moderate Whig John Dickinson retreated to the country and advised his family not to accept Continental money. The Allen family, one of the richest and most powerful in Pennsylvania, changed sides and left Philadelphia to join the British. Washington wrote of these men, "the late treachery and defection of those who stood foremost in the opposition, whilst fortune smiled upon us, make me fearful that many more will follow their example."[63]

The mood in Philadelphia appeared to be spreading through the country. As far away as Leesburg, Virginia, Nicholas Cresswell observed that in early December many Whigs "had given up the cause for lost. . . . Their recruiting parties could not get a man (except they bought him from his master)."[64]

Then there was more bad news for the American cause. On December 7, the same day when Cornwallis and Howe drove Washington's troops out of New Jersey, a British fleet arrived in New England waters. A large British and Hessian force led by General Henry Clinton conquered Rhode Island and the city of Newport, without a battle. Now a third colony fell under imperial control. For the American Whigs, the six months since the British troops arrived on Staten Island had been a cataract of disaster. Many on both sides thought that the rebellion was broken and that the American war was over.

THE CRISIS

❧ Thomas Paine and the Black Times of 1776

> Panics in some cases have their uses; they
> produce as much good as hurt. Their du-
> ration is always short; the mind soon grows
> through them, and acquires a firmer habit
> than before.
>
> —Thomas Paine, *The American Crisis*

O N OCTOBER 28, 1776, when the American garrison of Fort
Washington was fighting desperately in New York, a middle-
aged man with ink-stained hands watched intently from the
New Jersey Palisades across the Hudson River. After the fort surrendered, he pulled out a sheet of paper and wrote an account with a
wooden pen on a drumhead. Then he sent it by express to Philadelphia, for publication in the *Pennsylvania Journal*.[1]

Thomas Paine joined the army as a volunteer in July and became an aide-de-camp and personal friend to General Nathanael
Greene. At the same time, he worked as a war correspondent, one of
the first in American history. His dispatches on the battles around
New York celebrated the struggles of the Continental army against
heavy odds.[2] Paine was a familiar figure in the army, welcomed by
generals and privates alike. He stayed with them through "the whole
of the black times of that trying campaign," as he called it. They liked
the way he soldiered with them and shared their misery on the long
retreat from New York to Pennsylvania. They specially valued what he
wrote about them. Captain Alexander Graydon remembered that he
"gave us a handsome puff in one of the Philadelphia papers."[3]

Thomas Paine, engraving by
William Sharp (1793), after
a painting by George
Romney. National Portrait
Gallery, London.

Most of all they respected his genius for explaining to the world
what they were doing and why they were there. His nickname in the
army was "Common Sense," after the pamphlet that "made him
conspicuous," as one soldier put it.[4] This was a literate army, and
the American privates read Thomas Paine. British soldiers read him
too. After the battle of Long Island, a Regular broke into the abandoned American entrenchments and found "some poor pork, a few
greasy proclamations, and some of that scoundrel Common Sense
man's letters, which we can read at our leisure."[5]

Thomas Paine and the men of the Continental army shared a
deep devotion to the American cause, but they thought about it in
different ways. From the greenest private to the commander-in-chief,
most men in the army were American Whigs, fighting for their own
rights. Paine was an English radical, fighting for everybody's rights.
Graydon remarked upon the difference. He observed Paine's friendship with George Washington and his "good reception at headquarters and acquaintance with the Commander-in-chief, whom he seems
to have considered from that time, as embarked with him on the
general cause of reforming, republicanizing, and democritizing the
world, than which nothing was more foreign to the views of the General, or those of the others who took a lead."[6]

As the army made its long retreat across New Jersey, Thomas Paine marched with it, thinking always about "the general cause." He did not doubt its final triumph, and believed that the "republicanizing and democritizing of the world" was inevitable, but he worried that Americans might draw the wrong lesson from the defeats around New York. After the war, Paine explained his thinking to his friend Samuel Adams. "The black times of *Seventy-six*," he believed, "were no other than the natural consequence of the military blunders of the campaign." But he feared that Americans might have seen them in another way, "as proceeding from a natural inability to support its cause against the enemy, and might have sunk under the despondency of that misconceived idea."[7]

Thomas Paine reflected on that problem as he retreated across New Jersey. He watched and worried as Continental regiments came to the end of their enlistments and decided to go home. The army was shrinking before his eyes, and the people of New Jersey were not turning out to support it. Paine concluded that something had to be done. "It was necessary," he decided, that "the country should be strongly animated."

On November 22, when the army was crossing the Passaic River, Paine came to a decision. He resolved to write another pamphlet, like *Common Sense* but with a different message. By his own account, he started to work on it when the army reached Newark and "continued writing it at every place we stopt," scribbling by firelight in makeshift camps along the road while exhausted soldiers slept around him.[8]

A rough draft was more or less complete by the time he crossed the Delaware River. He carried it to Philadelphia, but when he reached the city, he was shocked to find the houses shuttered, the streets deserted, "the public presses stopped, and nothing in circulation but fears and falsehoods." The air of panic in the town increased Thomas Paine's sense of urgency. He remembered, "I sat down, and in what I may call a passion of patriotism, wrote the first number" of his new pamphlet in a final draft.[9]

He called it *The American Crisis*. The first sentence had the cadence of a drumbeat. Even after two hundred years, its opening phrases still have the power to lift a reader out of his seat. "These are the times that try men's souls," Paine began. "The summer soldier and the sunshine patriot will, in this crisis shrink from the service of his country; but he that stands it NOW deserves the love and thanks of man and woman."

The American Crisis was a call to arms by an English radical who hated war with the passion of his Quaker forebears. Before the Revo-

The American Crisis, Number 1. This essay, drafted by Thomas Paine as he retreated with the American army across New Jersey, was first published in the *Pennsylvania Journal* on December 19, 1776. It had a major impact on the revival of the American cause in the week before the Battle of Trenton. Historical Society of Pennsylvania.

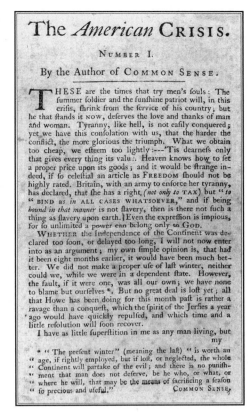

The *American* CRISIS.

NUMBER I.

By the Author of COMMON SENSE.

THESE are the times that try men's souls: The summer soldier and the sunshine patriot will, in this crisis, shrink from the service of his country; but he that stands it NOW, deserves the love and thanks of man and woman. Tyranny, like hell, is not easily conquered; yet we have this consolation with us, that the harder the conflict, the more glorious the triumph. What we obtain too cheap, we esteem too lightly:—'Tis dearness only that gives every thing its value. Heaven knows how to set a proper price upon its goods; and it would be strange indeed, if so celestial an article as FREEDOM should not be highly rated. Britain, with an army to enforce her tyranny, has declared, that she has a right, *(not only to* TAX*)* but "*to* "BIND *us in* ALL CASES WHATSOEVER," and if being *bound in that manner* is not slavery, then is there not such a thing as slavery upon earth. Even the expression is impious, for so unlimited a power can belong only to GOD.

WHETHER the Independence of the Continent was declared too soon, or delayed too long, I will not now enter into as an argument; my own simple opinion is, that had it been eight months earlier, it would have been much better. We did not make a proper use of last winter, neither could we, while we were in a dependent state. However, the fault, if it were one, was all our own; we have none to blame but ourselves *. But no great deal is lost yet; all that Howe has been doing for this month past is rather a ravage than a conquest, which the spirit of the Jersies a year ago would have quickly repulsed, and which time and a little resolution will soon recover.

I have as little superstition in me as any man living, but my

* "The present winter" (meaning the last) "is worth an "age, if rightly employed, but if lost, or neglected, the whole "Continent will partake of the evil; and there is no punish-"ment that man does not deserve, be he who, or what, or "where he will, that may be the means of sacrificing a season "so precious and useful." COMMON SENSE.

lution, Thomas Paine wrote to Edmund Burke, "I have seen enough of war and the miseries it inflicts to wish it might never more have an existence in the world, and that some other mode than destruction might take place to adjust and compose the differences that occasionally arise in the neighborhood of nations."[10]

But in the black times of 1776, Thomas Paine had come to believe that some evils in the world were even worse than war, and one of them was the tyranny that British ministers were attempting to fasten on their former colonies. *The American Crisis* was an attempt to awaken the people of the United States to that idea, and to its urgency.

Such was the panic and chaos in Philadelphia that it took Thomas Paine ten days to get his essay into print. Finally the first number of *The American Crisis* appeared in the *Pennsylvania Journal* on December 19, 1776. Four days later it was published as a pamphlet. Paine insisted that it be sold for two pennies, just enough to pay the printer's expenses. The author asked nothing for himself and encouraged printers everywhere to copy it freely. It traveled through the country as fast as galloping horses could carry it.[11]

Within a day of its first publication it was circulating in the camps of the Continental army along the Delaware River. Even Paine's bitter political rival James Cheetham testified to its impact. Cheetham wrote that *The Crisis* was "read in the camp, to every corporal's guard, and in the army, and out of it had more than the intended effect." The troops used its first sentence as a watchword and later as a battle cry. In his own state, Cheetham wrote, "the convention of New York, reduced by dispersion, occasioned by alarm, to nine members, was rallied and reanimated. Militiamen who already tired of the war, and straggling from the army, returned. Hope succeeded to despair, cheerfulness to gloom, and firmness to irresolution."[12]

Like *Common Sense*, the first number of *The American Crisis* owed its power to Thomas Paine's unique gift for expressing a popular feeling that was already stirring in other hearts. "'Tis surprising to see how rapidly a panic will sometimes run through a country," Paine wrote ". . . Yet panics in some cases have their uses; they produce as much good as hurt. Their duration is always short; the mind soon grows through them, and acquires a firmer habit than before."[13] That is exactly what happened in the United States during the dark weeks of December in 1776. In the black times, people began to think anew. Thomas Paine's pamphlet caught that spirit, and helped it grow.

The American Crisis was more than an exhortation. It was a program for action. Paine laid out the broad agenda for Congress and the states, for the army and the militia, for merchants and farmers, for Americans who were still free and others who were under the heel of a foreign conqueror. Most important, he concentrated the mind of a nation on the single most urgent task, which was to rebuild its army, and do it quickly.

The "December Crisis," as Paine called it, was critical in more senses than one. Everyone agreed that it was a perilous moment when things had gone deeply wrong for the American War of Independence. It was also a pivotal moment when great issues of the Revolution were hanging in the balance. Most of all it was a moment of decision, when hard choices had to be made. Thanks in part to Thomas Paine, it became a time when many Americans resolved to act, in ways that made a difference in the world.

There is an old American folk tale about George Washington and the Crossing of the Delaware. It tells us that the new American republics nearly failed in the winter of 1776, that George Washington crossed the Delaware on Christmas night, and that his victory at

Trenton revived the Revolution. All of this story is true, but it is not the whole truth. There was more to it. The great revival did not follow the battles of Trenton and Princeton, important as they were. It preceded them, and made those events possible (though not inevitable). Further, the revival did not rise solely from the leadership of George Washington himself, great as he was as a general and a man. He would have been the first to agree that it emerged from the efforts of many soldiers and civilians, merchants and farmers, leaders in the army and members of the Congress. Most of all it rose from the acts and choices of ordinary people in the valley of the Delaware, as Thomas Paine's *American Crisis* began to circulate among them.

This great revival grew from defeat, not from victory. The awakening was a response to a disaster. Doctor Benjamin Rush, who had a major role in the event, believed that this was the way a free republic would always work, and the American republic in particular. He thought it was a national habit of the American people (maybe all free people) not to deal with a difficult problem until it was nearly impossible. "Our republics cannot exist long in prosperity," Rush wrote "We require adversity and appear to possess most of the republican spirit when most depressed."[14]

An important part of this revival happened in the Congress. Then as now its members were very much maligned. They did nothing good for their reputation on December 12, 1776. When British troops appeared on the banks of the Delaware, Congress adjourned to the Patapsco. A week later they were meeting in Baltimore, then a rough and disorderly boom town. The congressmen were not happy to be there. Oliver Wolcott of Connecticut wrote his wife that Baltimore was "infinitely the most dirty place I was ever in." Benjamin Harrison of Virginia called it "the Damndest Hole in the World." But Samuel Adams, who signed himself "Puritan" in the public prints, took a perverse pleasure in its discomforts and thought that they improved the virtue of Congress. He wrote on January 9, 1777, "We have done more important business in three weeks than we had done, and I believe should have done, at Philadelphia, in six months."[15]

The disasters of the New York campaign persuaded the members of Congress to make a change in the direction of the war. For months they had thought that their duty was to manage the details of it themselves, and their intervention had driven the generals wild with frustration. On December 12, they agreed to change their ways and passed a resolution that "until Congress shall otherwise order,

General Washington be possessed of full power to order and direct all things relative to the department, and the operations of war."[16]

This self-denying ordinance marked a major change in the conduct of the war, but the generals wanted something more specific. On December 21, General Nathanael Greene sent a letter to President John Hancock. He wrote, "I am far from thinking the American Cause desperate, yet I conceive it to be in a critical situation." He recited a long list of problems: "the enemy in the Heart of our Country, the currency inflating, enlistments expiring, the disaffected daily increasing, and public sentiment at a stand." The immediate problem was to build "a new army."

General Greene urged Congress to grant George Washington "full Power to take such measures as he may find necessary to promote the Establishment of the New Army." He argued that "Time will not admit nor Circumstance allow of a Reference to Congress. The Fate of War is so uncertain, dependant on so many Contingencies. A Day, nay an Hour is so important in the Crisis of publick Affairs that it would be folly to wait for Relief from the deliberative Councils of Legislative Bodies."

He did not ask the members of Congress to surrender their authority over the army but proposed that they should authorize the commander-in-chief to act as necessary while "reserving to yourselves the Right of Confirming or repealing the Measures." Greene concluded, "I can assure you that the general will not exceed his Powers, altho' he may sacrifice the Cause. There never was a man that might be more safely trusted."[17]

Congress agreed. On December 27, 1776, it voted that the commander-in-chief should be given the powers that Greene asked for, for a period of six months.[18] Oliver Wolcott wrote of this measure, "the whole of the military department is put into his hand for six months. . . . The Preservation of the Civil Liberties of the People, at the present Time, depends upon the full exertion of the Military Power."[19]

Some in the country complained that Congress had made Washington "dictator," a word used at the time. It was not so. John Adams, who was very careful about such things, wrote that "Congress never thought of making him dictator or of giving him a sovereignty." It decided instead to do something new. It granted "large powers" to Washington but of limited scope (the department of war), for a limited term (six months), and with limited authority (always accountable to Congress). These men were radical Whigs. Their purpose was to protect a free republic. Their grant of new powers to George

Washington affirmed the rule of law, recognized the principle of civil supremacy over the military, and established the authority of Congress as representative of the states and the sovereign people. At the same time, it also established another principle: the conduct of military operations by military officers, subject to the general oversight of Congress but without Congressional interference in operations.[20]

This was an American compromise of some complexity. Other countries have gone a different way in the modern world. In many nations military officers took over the government by force of arms, and sometimes the army became the state. In Fascist and Communist regimes, civilian gauleiters and commissars controlled the military. The United States went a third way: civil control and military direction of its wars. Together Congress and the army created a new system that combined energy in government with republican institutions on a continental scale.

The officers of the army clearly understood the terms of this arrangement and carefully respected them. Washington set the example. He was quick to use the powers that were granted to him, but always with great care, explaining at length to Congress what he was doing and why he was doing it. On December 20, 1776, for example, he wrote to John Hancock that he had been waiting "with much impatience" for Congress to establish a Corps of Artillery. He said that the time had come when action could not be delayed, and so "under the Resolution of Congress bearing the date of the 12th inst." he was going ahead.[21] Washington added: "It may be said that this is an application for Powers that are too dangerous to be intrusted. I can only add that desperate diseases require desperate remedies. . . . The Enemy are daily gathering strength from the disaffected. This strength, like a Snowball rolling, will increase unless some means can be devised to check effectually the progress of the Enemy's arms."[22]

All this was an improvised solution to an urgent problem, but it established a precedent of enduring importance. In the black times of December 1776, leaders in the army and Congress found a way to combine energy and decision with the principles of a republican polity. Congress quickly applied the precedent to other problems in economic affairs. On December 21, it delegated authority to three respected Philadelphia merchants, Robert Morris, George Clymer, and George Walton. They were appointed "a Committee of Congress with Powers to execute such Continental business as may be proper and necessary to be done at Philadelphia."[23]

Here again Congress affirmed its own authority but delegated some of its powers to an executive body, composed of men who were highly qualified by knowledge, experience, and character. It was a step toward a system of separate legislative and executive powers— only a halting first step, but it started a long journey. Eleven years later, many of these same men in the army and the Congress joined together again to become the architects of a federal constitution.

While Congress and the generals developed new ways of managing military and economic affairs in this time of crisis, another major change happened within the army. At the beginning of December its command had fallen into disarray. Part of the problem rose from heavy pressure by governors and congressmen for a perimeter defense against every attack. A Continental Congress that could barely supply one army found itself maintaining twelve of them in 1776, each under its own commander. Most of these forces were larger than the main army under George Washington, the nominal "commander-in chief." In the returns for December 1, General Washington reported that the army under his "immediate command" had fallen to 3,765 men present and fit for duty. On the same day, General William Heath had 4,089 effectives in the highlands of New York. The northern army of General Horatio Gates included about 8,900 effectives in November; in December only a remnant of about 2,000 men remained at Fort Ticonderoga under Anthony Wayne. The largest Continental force in early December was Charles Lee's command in northwestern New Jersey, with 7,540 effectives. In Philadelphia, Israel Putnam commanded a sizeable force. Other Continental troops under General Adam Stephen were on the march from Virginia, where they had been dealing with Tories and Lord Dunmore's attempt to start a counter-revolution among the slaves. Continental troops were also at Savannah, Charleston, tidewater Virginia, the western frontier, coastal Connecticut, northern Rhode Island, and Massachusetts Bay. On December 1, 1776, the United States had more men under arms than General Howe, but they were scattered in small forces. The American army, like the American nation, was a loose and unstable confederation.

The problem was compounded by the attitudes of several high-ranking officers who were not happy about the generalship of George Washington. Two in particular were very open in their discontent. They had lived on the Virginia frontier in Berkeley County and had known Washington for many years. One of them was General Horatio Gates. He was a British emigrant, the son of a housekeeper to the duke of Leeds, who bought him a commission in the British army; he rose to the rank of major in the Sixtieth Royal Americans, then settled in western Virginia and strongly supported the Revolution. He was a decent man and a friend of Washington's, but in December Gates had grave doubts about the commander-in-chief.[24]

His aide, Major James Wilkinson, remembered that in December Gates was deeply worried about Washington's leadership, and wished to fight the war in a different way, by retreating deep into the interior of the country. Gates took his complaints directly to Congress, where some members were sympathetic to him. It was a direct challenge to Washington's conduct of the war by the third-ranking general in the Continental army.[25]

The second-ranking general challenged Washington's authority in a different way. General Charles Lee was a strange and turbulent character, bizarre beyond even a novelist's imagination. Born in Cheshire, the son of a British army officer, he was raised in an unhappy home and sent to school in Switzerland, where he broke out of the British mold. He never formed the manners of a gentleman or adopted the attitudes of his brother officers. He remained a loner, and rarely trusted others. Historian John Shy writes that "his sex life seems to have been of the transient kind." His closest friends were the dogs that always surrounded him.[26]

Major General Charles Lee, an engraving by A. H. Ritchie after a caricature by Rush Brooke. Print Collection, The New York Public Library, Astor, Lenox and Tilden Foundations.

At fourteen, a commission was bought for him in his father's regiment. He came to America at the age of twenty, as a lieutenant in the Forty-fourth Foot. He had his baptism of fire on Braddock's expedition, where he first met Washington, who detested him. In 1756, Lee was serving as a captain on the New York frontier. He settled among the Indians, lived with a Seneca woman, and was adopted by the Mohawks, who called him "Boiling Water." During the French and Indian War he rejoined his regiment in the disastrous attack on Ticonderoga, suffered a severe wound, and was sent home to recover. In 1761–62 he went to Portugal as major and lieutenant colonel of the new 103rd Regiment. While on detached duty with Burgoyne's new light cavalry, he had a brilliant success that made his military reputation. After the war, Lee went on half pay and served as a soldier of fortune in Poland, Russia, the Balkans, and Turkey. In 1771, he was back in England, where he fell out of favor in the army, quarreled even with his king, and moved to the Virginia frontier, where he became a radical Whig and joined the American army.

Washington called him "the first officer in Military knowledge and experience we have in the whole army" and noted that "he is zealously attached to the Cause, honest and well meaning" but also "rather fickle and violent I fear in his temper." Charles Lee was passionate for the principles of the Revolution but thought ill of its leaders and wrote that Congress was a "herd of stumbling cattle." In Charleston he compelled South Carolinians to work beside their slaves. During the New York campaign he became increasingly critical of Washington, and even openly contemptuous. On December 13, 1776, Lee wrote to Gates, "*entre nous*, a certain great man is most damnably deficient. . . . unless something which I do not expect turns up we are lost. Our counsels have been weak to the last degree."[27]

In December, Washington asked Lee to march with his troops from northwestern New Jersey and join him on the Delaware. Lee did not refuse outright but evaded and delayed. In curt notes he complained that his men were "ill-shod," that he had not explored the roads, that he did not know where the Delaware might be crossed, that he wanted to discuss various "schemes," and that the militia wished him to stay in Morristown.[28] Washington responded, "I have so frequently mentioned our situation, and the necessity of your aid, that it is painful to me to add a word upon the Subject. Let me once more request and entreat you to march immediately." The two top commanders of the Continental army were on the verge of an open break.[29]

Then fate intervened, in the form of a British dragoon. Lee at last started marching and got as far as Basking Ridge, New Jersey, where he stayed the night of December 12–13 at White's Tavern with his aides and about a dozen guards, several miles from the main body of his army. At about ten o'clock the next morning, Lee was busy with his correspondence and was just about to leave when British dragoons galloped up to the tavern "at full speed."

The British cavalry, led by Colonel William Harcourt, had been ordered to discover "General Lee's motions and situation." They rode about thirty miles and met several Loyalists, who told them that Lee was only four or five miles distant. The advanced guard of dragoons under twenty-two-year-old Banastre Tarleton was ordered forward at a trot, and they captured two American sentries and a light horseman. Tarleton wrote proudly to his mother that threat of "instant death" and "fear of the sabre extorted great intelligence" about Lee and his guard at White's Tavern. Tarleton surrounded the building and ordered his men to fire "thro' every Window and Door, and cut up as many of the guard as they could." Inside, several women offered to hide the general in a bed, which he "rejected with evident disgust." They heard Tarleton shout, "If the general does not surrender in five minutes, I will set fire to the house." Tarleton offered to let everyone else go if Lee would give himself up and threatened again with an oath that "the house should be burnt and every person, without exception would be put to the sword." Lee emerged, and Colonel Harcourt put him on a horse. A cavalry bugle sounded recall, and off they galloped "with all possible expedition." They returned to their base with their captive, having covered sixty miles on horseback in one day.[30]

Lee was taken to Brunswick, where his captors treated him with cold contempt as a traitor who had betrayed his king and comrades. He was kept under close confinement, with sentries "continuously in the room with him."[31] Lee sent word to Howe that he was ready to talk and offered unsolicited advice on how the Americans might be defeated. British leaders were appalled. Captain Münchausen wrote that Lee "repeatedly asked to see general Howe, but Howe will not see him nor speak to him." One infuriated British officer wrote of Lee, "He is as perfect in treachery as if he had been an American born. . . . They swallow their oaths of allegiance to the King and Congress alternately, with as much ease as your lordship does Poached eggs. . . . I think nothing but a total extirpation of the inhabitants of this country will ever make it a desirable object of any Prince or State."[32]

Americans knew nothing of this and received the news of Lee's capture as a major blow to the Cause. Washington responded in another way. He expressed contempt for Lee's folly, and no great sense of loss. "Unhappy man!" Washington wrote. "Taken by his own imprudence! Going three or four miles from his own camp to lodge and within twenty of the enemy."[33]

On the other side, British officers who were not acquainted with Lee exulted in his capture. Münchausen wrote, "Victoria! We have taken General Lee, the only rebel general whom we had cause to fear. . . . as to his ability and knowledge of the art of warfare, he is undoubtedly the first general."[34] But one English leader who knew Lee better wanted to give him back. Joseph Yorke, British minister to The Hague, wrote that he was "convinced from what I have seen and know of him, that he was the worst present which could be made to any army."[35]

The British capture of Charles Lee was a gift to the American cause. It delivered Washington from a very difficult problem of leadership. A week after Lee was taken, Washington at last succeeded in drawing together the fragments of his army. On December 20, the brigades that had been commanded by Lee and Gates began to arrive in the camps along the Delaware River. General John Sullivan brought in two brigades of two thousand men, mostly from Massachusetts, Connecticut, and New York, after a hard march through the hills of northwestern New Jersey. Two days later, another brigade of six hundred New Hampshire men came in after a longer and harder march from the northern frontier, where they had been serving under Gates. The reinforcements were pathetically small, but in a few days the size of Washington's army doubled.[36]

At the same time, the militia were turning out. In Northampton County, Pennsylvania, Presbyterian clergyman John Rosbrugh urged men from the pulpit to take up arms. He was sixty-three years old, but when the call went out, he left his young wife and five children and went off to the army as chaplain of the Third Battalion of the Northampton County militia. On December 27, while waiting to cross the Delaware, he seemed to have a premonition that he would not see his family again and put his thoughts in a letter.

"We are going over to New Jersey," he wrote. "You would think it strange to see your husband, an old man, riding with a French fusée slung at his back. This may be the last letter you shall receive from your husband. I have counted myself yours, and have been enlarged by our mutual love of God. . . . Pray for us. From your loving husband, John Rosbrugh."[37]

As the militia and the old one-year regiments assembled, a major long-term effort was under way to recruit new units with long terms of enlistment. On December 18, 1776, Washington confided to Augustine Washington, "If every nerve is not strained to recruit a new Army with all possible expedition, I think the game is pretty near up."[38]

It was to be a new army in several ways at once, a genuinely continental army, the first truly national institution after Congress itself, with officers commissioned by the United States. It would also be an army of volunteers, recruited for the length of the war or three years, with generous bounties and land warrants as an incentive. It was to be a large army. Congress in September 1776 authorized Washington to raise eighty-eight infantry battalions, a force nearly as large as the British army.[39]

So important was the new army thought to be that in December Washington sent some of his best officers and sergeants back to the states on recruiting duty at a moment when he desperately needed every man he could get on the Delaware. The recruiters succeeded even beyond the mandate of Congress. In Maryland, for example, the leading officers of Smallwood's regiment went back to Baltimore and Annapolis. Among them were Colonel Smallwood himself, still recovering from wounds, and Captain Samuel Smith, one of the ablest officers in the army. Their old regiment divided to become two new regiments, and then divided again to form five more in the state of Maryland, each with a cadre of battle-tested officers and sergeants. This effort was well under way in December 1776. Altogether it was not quite what Washington and Congress had hoped. They had asked for eight new continental regiments from Maryland, but by 1777 they got seven, all with veteran officers and noncoms, and the ranks began to fill slowly. In western Maryland some of these men mustered in heavy snowstorms during the month of December 1776 and began their own march to the Delaware River in bitter weather.[40]

Continental recruiters in other states did even better than Congress had asked. By 1777 they raised not 88 regiments as they were asked but 119. Some existed only on paper, and many would not be ready to serve until the spring of 1777, but recruitment began to revive in the black times of December 1776, before Washington's Crossing. Everywhere it was a response to an urgent need.

While the new army was recruiting, the old army came together in Pennsylvania. With his officers, Washington decided to reorganize it, mainly because he had to do so. In Robert Wright's words, he "shifted from the regiment to the brigade as the basic combat element," because "attrition had eroded the effective strength of most of his regiments to dangerously low levels."[41] This change had several consequences. It concentrated command and control of the army in the hands of a small number of Washington's most able senior officers, whom he trusted to carry out his wishes. Wright observes that "improved control paid particular dividends as brigades executed complex maneuvers at night and adjusted to rapidly changing battlefield conditions."[42]

Within the brigades, another consequence was to increase the ratio of officers and sergeants to privates. Wright notes that "only two of the brigades contained substantially more than the official strength of a regiment. On the other hand, the ratio of officers and sergeants to rank and file was higher than usual, with more staying power in combat." In December 1776, the American army had a large proportion of officers and sergeants to its total strength, and it maintained that pattern in the field.[43]

The British regiments were changing in the opposite direction. They tended to lose officers after a long period of active service in America. This was partly due to the unsporting American habit of aiming first at gorgets and gold lace, but mainly it was the routine wastage of illness and exhaustion and the difficulty of replacing troops in the New World. The Hessians also had a problem that way. They began with the Prussian model of big regiments with only four companies. To meet British requirements, they reorganized their regiments with a larger number of men and a smaller proportion of officers. The Hessians soon had a severe shortage of officers in America, where sickness and battle took a heavy toll, and the replacement chain stretched nearly 3,500 miles. As a consequence the Hessian and British armies had progressively fewer officers in proportion to men in marching regiments.[44]

The American system proved superior in another way. In the British and Hessian armies, infantry regiments were organized differently for administration and for fighting. British infantry in 1776 were grouped administratively in regiments of ten companies with strong identities and traditions. On active service, the grenadier and light infantry companies were removed from their parent regiments and formed in separate battalions. The marching regiments retained only their eight "battalion," or line, companies and were weakened by the loss of some of their best men. Hessian regiments in America mustered in four or five companies but fought in eight platoons, an awkward arrangement. By comparison, the American system was simple and flexible. The same units were used for marching, fighting, and administration.

Another change in American units appeared in the rapid promotion of officers of middle rank. Benjamin Rush wrote on December 21, 1776, that promotions in the army should go to men who combined a "genius" for command with an ability to hold "the confidence of their troops."[45] This actually happened, as new men rose rapidly in the army. Some were a long way from the image of a Continental officer and gentleman in smallclothes, silk stockings, and broadcloth coats.

One of these men was Charles Scott, the newly minted colonel of the Fifth Virginia Regiment, who joined the army just as it was retreating across New Jersey. Scott was a rough diamond from the Virginia frontier with little schooling and less polish. He had earned a reputation in the field during the old French War as "an excellent woodsman" and an able soldier. His regiment of Virginia infantry called him "Charley." They had a reputation for being "the most profane and disorderly" in the army, but they were hard and tough and fought tenaciously. Their colonel led from the front and was tougher and more profane than his men. He represented a new breed of combat leader in the American army.[46]

While the infantry was reorganized, another reform was made in the American artillery. The central figure was Henry Knox, who had become one of Washington's most trusted lieutenants. A Boston bookseller, he had taught himself the science of gunnery from treatises in his own shop. He was intelligent and highly inventive and became a valued advisor on questions of management and strategy in the army. A big, heavy set man with a booming voice, he was also a tested leader in battle. Washington wrote of him that "his genius supplied the deficit of means." Knox studied ways to minimize losses in one's own forces while raising the cost to the enemy.

Henry Knox integrated infantry and artillery and used his field guns as assault weapons. He assigned an additional company of artillery to each brigade of infantry. One historian observes that "the artillery company added materially to the firepower of each brigade, particularly in adverse weather. At Trenton, and at Princeton a week later, Washington's brigade commanders used both of these factors to advantage."[47] Muskets were difficult to fire in wet weather, and impossible in stormy conditions. Artillery could be protected with tampions and touchhole covers and fired using shielded slow matches.

Winthrop Sargent, a pencil sketch
by John Trumbull. This graduate
of Harvard (1771) was a Captain-
Lieutenant with the Massachusetts
Artillery during the New York and
New Jersey campaigns. He also
took an active and leading part in
the western movement, and in the
Federalist Party. National Portrait
Gallery, Smithsonian Institution.

Young captains of artillery companies began to emerge. Among
them was Winthrop Sargent (1753–1820), a New England Yankee,
Gloucester born, raised in wealth, and schooled at Harvard who had
served as captain of his father's ships. He was bright and high-
spirited, full of energy and ambition, a driver and a leader. At
Harvard he shared his books with his sister, Judith Sargent Murray,
who became one of America's first feminists. In 1776, Winthrop
Sargent was twenty-three years old, a captain-lieutenant of a company of Massachusetts artillery in the Continental line, and the
nephew of brigadier Paul Dudley Sargent.

Another promising young artillary officer was Captain Alexander Hamilton. On the retreat at the Raritan River, an old soldier
"noticed a youth, a mere stripling, small, slender, almost delicate in
frame, marching . . . with a cocked hat pulled down over his eyes,
apparently lost in thought, with his hand resting on a cannon, and
every now and then patting it as it were a favorite horse or a pet
plaything."[48] The efficiency of his company brought him to the notice of senior commanders.

In December, other improvements were made in the army's logistics. Without them, the Continental army could not have crossed

Judith Sargent Stevens Murray, a portrait by John Singleton Copley (ca. 1770–72). She was the sister of Winthrop Sargent, who strongly supported her education. During the Revolution she wrote and later published several of the earliest feminist writings in the United States (1779–84). Many families associated with the Continental Army have been identified as "conservative" for their later support of the Federalist party, but they were more radical on the rights of women and African Americans than their anti-Federalist and Jeffersonian opponents. Terra Foundation for the Arts, Daniel J. Terra Art Acquisition Endowment Fund, Chicago.

the Delaware and might have disintegrated. It is interesting to see how this was done. In some respects, the American army was well equipped, even in the black times. It had more than enough fire-arms, ammunition, and gunpowder. A separate supply service looked after munitions with high success. The army could draw on large "magazines" and never ran short of powder, flints, or ammunition in the winter of 1776–77.

In other ways it was miserably supplied. The worst shortages were of clothing, blankets, stockings, and shoes. Washington observed of his army that "many of 'em [were] entirely naked and more so thinly clad as to be unfit for service." American leaders had no idea of the requirements for a long campaign in cold weather and little conception of how rapidly a marching army could destroy its shoes and clothing. When Washington's army reached Philadelphia after their long retreat, many were in rags. In Quaker Burlington, one "peaceable man" watched American troops march by and observed that "if the War is continued thro the Winter, the British troops will be scared at the sight of our Men, for as they had never fought with Naked Men."[49]

The household economy of early America was incapable of sup-plying the army. In the fall of 1776 Congress took upon itself the task of supplying Continental troops with clothing and shoes. It agreed to supply every private each year two linen hunting shirts, two pairs of overalls, a leather or woolen waistcoat with sleeves, one pair of breeches, a hat or leather cap, two shirts, two pairs of hose, and two pairs of shoes.[50]

Much of what the army needed was imported from abroad, through the Dutch and French West Indian islands of St. Eustatius and Martinique. The new Continental navy took on the task of running supplies through a British blockade that was gradually growing more effective. The navy used small ships, heavily sparred and very fast. Their primary mission in these desperate months of the war was to bring in materials that the army most urgently needed.

The Continental sloop USS *Independence* sailed from Martinique with supplies for the army. She was intercepted by a British frigate and chased into Chincoteague, then made sail for the Delaware Capes, got through a British blockading squadron, and reached Philadelphia on the afternoon of December 20, with "near 1000 muskets and 856 blankets." The army had a surplus of weapons but desperately needed the blankets. Robert Morris found wagons and teamsters in Philadelphia, and the blankets arrived in the Continental camp on Christmas Eve, a welcome present for the army, and just in time.[51]

On December 23, the continental brigantine USS *Andrea Doria* also reached Philadelphia with more supplies for the army. She had left the Dutch port of St. Eustatius at the beginning of December and met a British sloop of war, HMS *Racehorse*. The British ship received three shots through her mainmast, lost her sails, and struck her colors after a long and bloody fight. *Andrea Doria* lost two men killed and several wounded. After repairs were made at sea, "the extreme vigilance of her captain brought her safe past the enemies ships." Her cargo was exactly what the army needed: 463 blankets, 208 dozen pairs of woolen stockings, and 106 dozen pairs of worsted stockings, which Robert Morris hurried to the army, along with large quantities of muskets, pistols, powder, and lead.[52]

For every ship that got through, others were lost or taken by the Royal Navy. The hazards of these missions and the determination of the new navy and its Continental marines are apparent in the story of the first USS *Lexington*, a small frigate of fourteen guns under the command of Captain William Hallock. In the West Indies, she took aboard a large and valuable cargo, sailed from Cape Francois, and headed home for Philadelphia. Near the Delaware Capes, she was captured by HMS *Pearl*, a British frigate more than twice her size. Most of the American officers were taken off as prisoners. In rising wind and heavy seas, the British frigate was only able to put aboard a prize crew of seven or fifteen men and lost her boat. *Lexington*'s crew, led by Captain Boyce of the Continental marines, rose against their captors, took over the ship, and brought her into Baltimore on January 2.

Lexington carried a cargo that demonstrated not only the broad dependence of the American states on European trade but also the rapid rise of industry in 1776: 386 blankets; 2,200 ells of fabric, 200,000 needles, and 636,000 pins to support household manufactures, as well as 366 reams of paper; 12-3/4 tons of sulphur and a barrel of saltpeter for the manufacture of gunpowder and cartridges; 7-1/2 tons of lead for the making of ammunition; 5,000 flints, 500 stands of arms, and 500 bayonets. President John Hancock of the Continental Congress wrote from Baltimore, "I shall order her to be immediately unloaded, and dispatch her cargo as fast as possible."[53]

The states also helped to supply the army. A case in point was Virginia, much the biggest state in 1776—nearly as big as the next two states, Pennsylvania and Massachusetts, combined. In the crisis of December, Virginia rallied to the common cause. On December 6, when the condition of the Continental army became known, the Virginia legislature passed an emergency resolution asking the governor to collect blankets throughout the Commonwealth.[54]

Governor Patrick Henry applied his eloquence to that task. On December 19, he sent letters to the heads of militia in every county of Virginia. One copy went to the county lieutenant of Albemarle, who was Patrick Henry's old rival Thomas Jefferson. The two men put their differences to the side and worked together in the common cause. Henry wrote to Jefferson, "In Pursuance of a Resolution of the Legislature, I am to appoint a fit Person in every County to collect from the Inhabitants of this Commonwealth all the BLANKETS and RUGS they are willing to spare for the Use of the Soldiery. I have to beg of you, Sir, to accept of that Appointment for Your county, and to draw upon me for the Amount of the Purchase. When it is considered that those who are defending their Country are in the extremest Want of Blankets, and that our Army cannot take the Field without a supply of that article, I have Hopes that our worthy Countrymen will spare from their Beds a part of that Covering which the exposed Situation of the Soldier teaches him to expect from the Humanity of those for whom he is to fight." Jefferson did as he was asked, and more blankets were on their way to the Continental army.[55]

New England states acted differently in the same cause, by taking the lead in creating new organizations and institutions. An example was Connecticut and the Trumbull family. One historian has written that "what Lee implied in Virginia, or Adams in Massachusetts, or Livingston in New York and New Jersey, Trumbull signified in Connecticut."[56]

Four Trumbulls, often confused, played leading roles in the American cause. The father of the family was Jonathan Trumbull, a Harvard graduate (1727), a deeply pious Congregationalist (he nearly became a minister), a hardheaded and highly prosperous merchant, and governor from 1776 to 1784. He gave strong support to George Washington, whose biographer writes, "Governor Trumbull was the State Executive from whom the commander-in-chief always had the best hope of succor in every emergency, whether the desperate need was of men or of meat."[57]

Three of Governor Jonathan Trumbull's sons held high office during the Revolution, supporting the cause in a variety of ways. The most renowned was the youngest son, John Trumbull, who went into the army and became Washington's aide for a time, then deputy adjutant general. A gifted artist, he left the army in February 1776 and for the rest of his life served the Revolution and the Republic with his palette and paintbrush. John Trumbull's heroic canvases of Bunker Hill, the signing of the Declaration of Independence, and the battles of Trenton and Princeton created an iconography of the American Revolution.

His brothers served in other ways. Jonathan Trumbull Jr. became paymaster of the army, a thankless task that he performed with honesty and efficiency. Joseph Trumbull, the eldest son, was commissary general of the Continental army from July 19, 1775, to the spring of 1777, with the rank and pay of colonel. Like his father, he was a Harvard graduate, a highly successful merchant, and an honest man. He was remarkably successful in constructing a Continental supply system from the states. The army thought highly of him. Washington wrote, "Few armies if any have been better and more plentifully supplied then the troops under Mr. Trumbull's care." Joseph Trumbull's quiet labors behind the scenes allowed Washington to keep an army in being. He made his greatest contribution during the black times of 1776.[58]

As numbers increased, the spirits of the army began to rise. A case in point was Lieutenant Colonel Samuel Blachley Webb, a Connecticut Yankee who had been wounded at Bunker Hill and twice at White

Plains, promoted to lieutenant colonel in the Continental army, and made aide-de-camp to George Washington, all by the age of twenty-three. On December 16, 1776, he took a moment from his work at headquarters to answer a letter from Joseph Trumbull. "You ask me our Situation," Webb wrote. "It has been the Devil, but is to appearance better. About 2,000 of us have been obliged to run damn'd hard before about 10,000 of the enemy. Never was finer lads at a retreat than we are. . . . No fun for us that I can see; however, I cannot but think we shall drub the dogs."[59]

Even after the army had lost four major battles and had been driven a hundred miles from New York to Pennsylvania, these men exuded an extraordinary optimism, even an optimistic fatalism. In late December, another officer from Connecticut wrote home, "Now is the time for us to be in earnest. . . . As for what few troops we have, you would be amazed to see what fine spirits they are in, and the continental troops really well disciplined, and you may depend will fight bravely, and doubt not before one week you will hear of an attack somewhere, when I trust we shall do honour to ourselves."[60] But everything hinged on events in New Jersey.

THE OCCUPATION

~ Americans under Foreign Rule

> The Virtue of the Americans is put to a tryal. . . . But
> I think it impossible that the Americans can behave
> so Poltroonish.
>
> —Nathanael Greene, December 4, 1776[1]

I N 1776, the intentions of the Howe brothers for New Jersey
were very clear and entirely honorable. Their instructions from
London were to "make peace if possible, and . . . war
if peace was out of the question." Their Whiggish purpose was to
restore the empire by a program of pacification, and New Jersey
was to be the first big test.[2]

Whether by peace or by war, their policy was to "enable the
Loyalists to recapture control of American affairs." The Howes had
been told that the rebellion was the work of a few "hot-headed de-
signing men." General James Robertson, who had served twenty
years in the colonies and was thought to be an expert, declared that
two-thirds of the Americans were loyal to the Crown. Pennsylvania
Tory Joseph Galloway estimated that the true proportion of Loyalists was closer to four-fifths.[3]

The first priority of the British leaders was to impose peace
and restore order throughout New Jersey. By the last week in November, General Howe believed that most of the fighting was over
in the state. He had broken the Continental army into pieces. One
fragment was retreating across the Delaware River. Another had fled
beyond the Watchung Mountains in northwestern New Jersey. A third
had been driven up the Hudson Valley, and a fourth had returned

to southern New England. British leaders thought that the rebels were not likely to return, except in small raiding parties.

General Howe decided that he could safely spread his forces across the Jersey countryside, so that they could maintain order and protect the loyal population. To that end he distributed his army in many small garrisons across the state. Each garrison in turn was ordered to maintain small outposts and to send active patrols of cavalry and infantry through the country. Altogether the troops occupied a belt of territory across the narrow waist of New Jersey, where a large part of its population lived.

The troops moved rapidly to their assigned places and met little resistance. The British commander-in-chief issued strict orders that reminded his army why they were there. Their task was to restore order and to help the great majority of loyal Americans to return to their rightful king. He ordered the army not to plunder, ravage, or abuse the population.

The next part of the pacification program in New Jersey began with a dramatic gesture. On November 30, 1776, the Howe brothers issued a proclamation that offered amnesty to all who returned to the Crown. Everyone was invited to take an oath of allegiance. Those who did so within sixty days and promised to remain "in a peaceful obedience to his Majesty" would receive "full and free pardon" for whatever they had done. They were also offered a certificate that guaranteed their lives and property.[4]

Many British leaders were not happy about the Howes' proclamation, which took them by surprise. In London, hard-minded and conservative men condemned it as "lenient" and even "liberal." George Germain thought it was weak and ineffectual. He believed that only hard measures would restore the empire. In New York high officers in the army and navy did not like the policy, and American Loyalists were outraged. Joseph Galloway raged against the Howes for allowing the radical Whigs who had persecuted his Loyalist friends to escape with impunity. But the Howe brothers stood firm, and it was done.

American Revolutionaries may have helped it along in an ironic way by responding with a policy of their own. To all who swore an oath of allegiance to the king, the Whigs promised free pardon if they would swear to abjure it. Altogether, it was a great encouragement to swearing in New Jersey.[5]

In the fall of 1776, many people of New Jersey accepted the terms that the Howe brothers offered them. Within a few weeks, British authorities reported that more than three thousand people had come forward to make an oath of allegiance to George III and take their "protection papers." They did so at a time when much of the countryside was still controlled by American rebels.

That estimate was probably an undercount, for any officer of His Majesty's Forces was empowered to issue certificates, and records were slow to reach headquarters. Even so, three thousand oaths of allegiance represented about 12 percent of households in New Jersey, and a larger proportion of its political population. As more people came forward to swear their oaths and receive their protection papers, the program appeared to be working. The Howe brothers were delighted. It seemed an excellent beginning.[6]

But beneath the surface, many people in New Jersey responded to the Howes' policy in other ways. A Continental soldier, Stephen Olney, noticed a difference by social rank. He wrote that "great numbers flocked to confess their sins to the representative of Majesty, and obtain pardon. It was observed, that these consisted of the very rich and very poor, while the middling class held their constancy."[7]

Other patterns followed ethnic and religious lines. The hard core of the Revolutionary movement in New Jersey consisted of English-speaking Calvinists. The Swedish Lutheran minister Nicholas Collin wrote, "By God there will never be any peace till the Whigs and Presbyterians are cut off."[8] New England Congregationalists in Essex County were strong supporters of the Revolution. So were the Presbyterians of Princeton, and the Scots-Irish in northwestern Morris and Sussex counties.

The Presbyterian leader was John Witherspoon, an eminent divine who emigrated from Scotland with his wife and five children in 1768 to become president of the College of New Jersey, later to be Princeton University. He was a dour character who once remarked that "he would almost as soon whip a boy for wit as for lying." Witherspoon was not a liberal man, but in 1776 he was strong for the liberty of America. As the Revolution developed, he became "a zealous whig" who served in the Continental Congress, the only member who wore clerical bands in 1776. He spoke with "uncommon eloquence" for independence, signed the Declaration, and published sermons on liberty that reached a large public in Britain and America.[9]

When the British army approached Princeton, John Witherspoon chose the response of flight and resistance. On November 29, 1776, he closed the college, sent the students home, bundled his books into a wagon, helped his wife into the "old family chair," and rode beside her on a sorrel mare to Pequea in Pennsylvania, where they moved in with their daughter and her husband, Samuel Stanhope Smith, a future president of Princeton. British leaders tried to capture Witherspoon, hoping to arrest the signers of the Declaration of Independence, and later thought they had killed him in Trenton. But he escaped and kept working for the Revolution. He remained a central figure in Congress, a member of the Board of War and the Secret Committee of Correspondence, and a relentless critic of British practices in the Revolution.[10]

Other Presbyterians and Congregationalists followed his example, moving west away from the British army so that they could continue to serve the Revolution. So large was the exodus from Princeton that Benjamin Rush described it as a "deserted village." It was said that only the Quakers remained. It was much the same in the Congregationalist town of Newark.

The British army occupied Princeton in great strength. They fortified the campus of the college and turned Nassau Hall into a barracks and a storehouse. The stone cellar below that seminary of enlightment became a dungeon. British troops rounded up recalcitrant Whigs and locked up "about 30 of our country people" who were accused of "being Rebels or aiding and assisting them." Their farmhouses were occupied and looted.[11]

In the face of this repression, some of New Jersey's affluent families made their private peace with Britain, and a few Whig leaders turned their coats. Among them was Richard Stockton, a lawyer, judge, landowner, and heir to one of the great estates in New Jersey. On the outskirts of Princeton he built a handsome country house called Morven, which became his pride and obsession. It was he who brought the College of New Jersey to Princeton, near his home.

Stockton joined the Revolutionary movement, became one of its leaders in New Jersey, and went to the Continental Congress as a moderate Whig. His son-in-law Benjamin Rush remembered him as a man who was "sincerely devoted to the liberties of his country" but who "loved law and order" and "once offended his constituents by opposing the seizure of private property in an illegal manner."

In 1776, Stockton signed the Declaration of Independence, became very active in committee work, and was given a commission as colonel in the Continental army. Then the British army arrived, and Stockton was a marked man as a signer of the Declaration. As the British troops approached his beloved Morven, Stockton lost his nerve and fled, not only from the British but also from the Revolution. His son-in-law observed that "he was timid where bold measures were

Richard Stockton (1730–81) and *Annis Boudinot Stockton* (1736–1801), master and mistress of Morven on the outskirts of Princeton. Stockton was the only signer of the Declaration of Independence who abandoned the American cause and swore allegiance to George III. Princeton University Art Museum.

required." Other Whigs retreated west to Pennsylvania, where they could continue to resist. Stockton went east and sought sanctuary at Federal Hall, another great Jersey country house, owned by his friend John Cowenhoven. It was a big mistake. Federal Hall was in Monmouth County, where many Loyalists lived. In the middle of the night a band of Loyalists broke into the home, seized Stockton, and carried him to British authorities. He was treated harshly, put in irons, and locked in a "common jail." Ill and badly frightened for his family and his home, he decided after a short stay in prison to accept the Howes' offer of amnesty. This signer of the Declaration of Independence now signed a declaration of allegiance to the king and gave "his word of honor that he would not meddle in the least in American affairs."[12]

Richard Stockton was released from prison and went home to Morven, which had been plundered in his absence. He also resigned from the Continental Congress and retired to private life. He was the only signer of the Declaration to turn his coat and came to be "much spoken against." A year later, in December 1777, Stockton completed his infamy when Whig leaders demanded that he take another oath of allegiance to Congress or leave Morven forever. Stockton agreed to an oath of adjuration and kept on at Morven, a

Morven, a nineteenth-century photograph. Historical Society of Princeton.

sad and pathetic figure, broken in spirit by the Revolution. He lingered a few years in declining health until his death in 1781. Morven survived, to become for a time the official residence of New Jersey's governors, and today the house is more handsome than ever.

Another response to the occupation appeared in the Dutch-speaking communities of Bergen County. As the advancing British armies entered the village of Hackensack, they were surprised to be welcomed by the inhabitants. The Hessian Lieutenant Andreas Wiederholdt described the town as "a place of about 160 houses and many well affected people, mostly Dutch." The same thing happened at New-Bridge, two miles north of Hackensack, where British Lieutenant Henry Stirke wrote that the "inhabitants came in to take the oath of allegiance."[13]

Many neighbors of other ethnic groups also made their peace with the strongest army. Lawyer John Ross (uncle-in-law of Betsy) was remembered to have said, "Let who will be king, I well know that I shall be the subject."[14] This was the old European tradition of passive obedience, much preached by medieval clergy, who argued that one must endure a tyrant or conqueror as a judgment by God on a sinful people. But in passive obedience, the operative word was "passive." It implied that a king was to be obeyed only as long as he was strong enough to command obedience.

While some chose the way of passive obedience, others tried the path of active neutrality. One of many people who made this choice was Nicholas Collin, the young Swedish Lutheran minister

Nicholas Collin, a Swedish immigrant
Lutheran minister in Raccoon, New
Jersey. He tried to remain neutral
during the American Revolution.
Authors' Collection.

in Raccoon, New Jersey. The occupation was a time of "much anxiety" and "constant alarm" for him. He wrote in his diary, "as the fire
came closer, many drew away, and there was much dissension among
the people. Many concealed themselves in the woods, or within their
houses, other people were forced to carry arms, others offered opposition and refused to go. The people were afraid to visit the church,
because the authorities took the opportunity to get both horses and
men."[15]

Many Swedish immigrants in New Jersey responded differently.
A congregation that had deeper roots in America, and called itself
the English Swedish Church, strongly supported the Revolution.
But after six years in America, Nicholas Collin still thought of himself as Swedish. "Being a Swedish subject," he wrote, "I could not
give my oath of allegiance to any but my own government."[16]

More than a few people in New Jersey tried to cultivate good relations and strong alliances with both sides. Among them was the Van
Horne family, who became highly skilled at this dangerous game.
Philip Van Horne was a New York merchant who left the city at the
start of the Revolution and moved to a country estate called Convi-
ial Hill or Phill's Hill near Bound Brook in Somerset County, New
Jersey, between the armies. He had a large fortune, a habit of hospitality, and five very attractive daughters. Philip's brother, John Van

Horne, died at the beginning of the Revolution, leaving a widow and three daughters more, who divided their time between New Brunswick, New York, and Convivial Hill in New Jersey. The two households visited back and forth and were often confused. Altogether there were eight young "Misses Van Horne," as they were collectively called, "all handsome and well bred." They attracted swarms of officers from every army.[17]

Philip Van Horne was a good friend of New Jersey's Whig governor William Livingston. He also maintained good relations with British and Loyalist officers and received them in his home when they were in the neighborhood. When the American army arrived, they were welcome too, and many American officers stayed in his house. Captain Alexander Graydon found that Mr. Van Horne "alternately entertained the officers of both armies, being visited by one and sometimes by the other. . . . His house, used as a hotel, seemed constantly full."[18]

It was, if nothing else, a considerable feat of scheduling. In the words of Leonard Lundin, the Van Hornes "performed prodigies in the difficult art of being all things to all people." Philip Van Horne carefully cultivated friendships with high officers in every camp. He kept up his friendships with leading New Jersey Whigs and cultivated connections with Loyalists and British leaders. He also made a point of doing favors for both sides. When Graydon was captured at Fort Washington, Philip Van Horne helped the soldier's mother to win his release.[19]

His beautiful daughters cultivated connections with younger officers on both sides. As the war went on around them, they danced and flirted happily with men in many uniforms. They encouraged visiting Americans to believe that they were "avowed whigs." British and Hessians took them to be secret Loyalists. Many knew what they were doing, but their combination of genteel Whiggery and sociable Toryism added to their attraction. They were known for "civility to the British officers, hospitality to Hessians, and sympathy for Americans."[20]

When the Misses Van Horne were in the country, they were courted by Continental officers. When they went to Flat Bush in New York, they were entertained by the British garrison and invited to balls for royal anniversaries. Sometimes the Van Horne sisters were with their uncle in New Brunswick, where Hessian gentlemen came to call. Colonel von Donop was a frequent visitor. Jäger Captain Johann Ewald fell madly in love with Jeanette Van Horne. He sent her gifts of "sausages made in the German manner," dead game birds that his men had shot, and passionate love letters in fractured

French. She saved the letters, and they still survive in the Library of Congress.[21] While that romance continued, a senior British artillery officer, General William Phillips, was much taken by Catherine Van Horne, so much so that he included her in his will and left her "a respectable bequest" when he died of a Chesapeake fever in the spring of 1781. A third sister, Mary Van Horne, was courted by an American officer, Colonel Stephen Moylan, and they were married in 1778.[22]

General Washington did not approve of the ambidextrous Van Hornes, and Philip Van Horne in particular. On January 12, 1777, he wrote sternly to Colonel Reed, "I wish you had brought Vanhorne off with you, for from his noted character there is no dependence to be placed upon his Parole." A few weeks later Washington thought that Van Horne should be ordered into British lines: "Would it not be best to Order P. Vanhorne to Brunswick—these people in my opinion can do us less injury there than anywhere else." But not even George Washington could restrain the Van Hornes. They remained at liberty and flourished happily in an eighteenth-century world where distinctions of rank and wealth sometimes proved more powerful than politics or war.[23]

The Quakers were another story. Their testimony of peace always infuriated men who lived by a warrior ethic. It happened again in the conquest of New Jersey, where they followed a long hard road. Many Quakers (not all of them) tried to keep out of the fight, and took the path of peace in a country at war. They deeply angered the American

Margaret Morris, a Quaker in Burlington, New Jersey, who tried to relieve the suffering of people on both sides in the American Revolution. Special Collections, Haverford College Library.

Whigs, who thought that the Society of Friends wanted to enjoy the blessings of liberty without bearing its costs. On the other side, the Quakers were also immensely irritating to the British and Hessians. Some Quakers were willing to affirm (never swear) their allegiance to the king, but they stubbornly refused to defer to their conquerors.

When British and Hessian troops came into homes, many people were careful to treat them with deference, but not the Quakers. On one occasion, when four Hessians entered a house, the Quaker who lived there refused to take off his hat as a gesture of respect. One Hessian "a stout fellow," attacked the Quaker, "laid hold of his hat on his head, and pulled it off." The Quaker, a "small man and between fifty and sixty years" but very strong, lost his Christian forbearance and "laid hold of their champion, and struck up his heels and threw him on the ground and clapt his foot on his Sword and Prevented his drawing it, and took his hat again." The three other Hessians drew their swords, and the Quaker was "obliged to Yield up a very good hat though he had a Protection several days before." The soldiers let him live but made him surrender many of his possessions. They also turned a peaceable subject who had taken the king's protection into an enemy, which happened more and more in New Jersey.[24]

African Americans in New Jersey, mostly slaves before 1776, responded in a more militant way. They fought on both sides, always in the hope of emancipation. Some found a promise of liberation in the Revolution itself. In New Jersey, slaves could win their freedom by serving in the militia as substitutes for their master, but more promises were made than kept. In Somerset County, a slave named Samuel made such an agreement in 1776 with his master Casper Berber and served through the Revolution. When the war was over, his dishonest master broke the agreement and sold him to another master. Samuel bought his freedom a second time, by twenty years' hard labor.[25]

Perhaps aware of experiences like Samuel's, many slaves rebelled against their rebel masters and found freedom with the British forces. Some joined units called Black Pioneers. Others organized their own partisan companies of former slaves and servants. One man who did so was a slave named Titus, owned by a Quaker named John Corlis, on the Navesink River near Shrewsbury. In 1775, the local Friends' Meeting urged Corlis to emancipate his slave without success, and Titus ran away. Three years later he reappeared as Colonel Tye, leader of a partisan band of fifty former slaves and servants, operating from a base called Refugeetown on Sandy Hook, with other havens in the cedar swamps of Monmouth County. Colonel Tye's men were allies of the British forces, but they were independent fighters for their own freedom. In 1780, while leading an attack on a brutal Whig leader and slaveholder, Tye was wounded and died of tetanus, but his band and other black partisans fought to the end of the war, and even beyond it. These actions by servants and slaves turned New Jersey's growing strife into a three-cornered conflict.[26]

Yet another response to conquest appeared among some New Jersey merchants and manufacturers, who thought of the British occupation as a new opportunity for business. Among them were some of the monied men of Trenton, who followed a course as torturous as the waters of Assunpink Creek, on which they built their mills. Some managed to stay in business during the war and traded with both sides as opportunities appeared. The "rich merchant of the village," in William Stryker's description, was Abraham Hunt. He was suspected of Tory opinions by the Whigs, and of Whig connections by Tories, but his closest neighbors knew him as a "a noncommittal man."[27] Mainly he was a businessman who lived for money and profit. In the summer of 1776, he was actively buying and selling muskets and scabbards as a commissioner of Hunterdon County. During the Hessian occupation of Trenton he dealt with the Hessians. On Christmas night Colonel Johann Rall was invited for a late supper in Abraham Hunt's house at the intersection of King and Second streets. After the battles of Trenton, Hunt was back in business supplying American militia and Continental troops.[28]

Abraham Hunt appears to have sworn oaths of allegiance both to the king and Congress. His property was not taken by either side. He received a protection paper signed by General Howe, and supplied the army of General Washington. Stryker wrote that "patriots, it is said, feared he was not altogether true to the cause, for they knew that their country's enemies ofttimes partook of his bounty, but it is never asserted that he took any active part against his country."[29]

It was the same again for Stacy Potts, who was described as "a wealthy gentleman who owned a large tannery nearby, and a steel works on Petty's Run near the river." This highly successful Trenton businessman also had good relations with both sides. Colonel Rall made his headquarters in Stacy Potts's big white frame house at the center of Trenton, and on Christmas afternoon the two men were playing a convivial game of checkers.[30]

For Abraham Hunt and Stacy Potts and others in Trenton, the Revolution was good for business. They made the most of their op-

Abraham Hunt, a businessman in Trenton who prospered by trading with both sides during the war. William S. Stryker (1898), *The Battles of Trenton and Princeton*, 121.

portunities, and both sides were happy to deal with them. Other businessmen were steadfast in their devotion to the Revolution or to the king, but more than a few followed their fortunes.

New Jersey's Loyalists made yet another story. When British forces appeared, they were quick to declare themselves for the king, sometimes too quick for their own good. Thomas Paine wrote that "many a disguised Tory has lately shown his head, that shall penitentially solemnize with curses the day on which Howe arrived on the Delaware."[31] In Monmouth County, Tories took up arms in numbers large enough to bring reactions from both British and American commanders. William Howe welcomed their support as a revolution against the rebellion and extended his chain of garrisons to protect them. Washington perceived it as a rebellion against the Revolution, which he called "an insurrection of the Tories in Monmouth County." On November 24, 1776, Washington sent an entire regiment under Colonel David Forman, himself of Monmouth, to suppress them. Forman's orders were "to march with your regiment" and "apprehend all such persons as from good Information appear to be concerned in any Plot or Design against the liberty or safety of the United States."

Washington's orders were open to interpretation. Forman was instructed "to attack any Body of men whom you may find actually assembled or in Arms" but to "be cautious against proceeding against any but such as you have the fullest ground of Suspicion." He was also ordered "not [to] suffer your Men to give the least molestation to the property of any in the Course of your March," but "if you find any Stock of Cattle or provision that you may judge in danger of falling into the hands of the Enemy, you are first to desire the Inhabitants to remove them, and upon their Refusal you are to have it done yourself."

Colonel Forman carried out his orders in a different spirit. He organized the Association of Retaliation, a vigilante group in Monmouth County, and became very active in the confiscation of Loyalist estates. He was remembered even by his brother Whigs for his "energy and merciless severity." The Tories called him "Black David." In Monmouth County, the American Revolution became a bitter civil war.[32]

Lord Richard Howe and Sir William Howe were highly intelligent men. They took satisfaction in the number of people who swore allegiance to the Crown, but they were well aware that the "furious whigs" had moved into the interior and the British army could not reach them. They knew that Tories who came into the open were always vulnerable to an attack by Whigs, and the army could not protect them. They soon learned that the few Whig leaders who took an oath of allegiance to the Crown were useless to them, and that complaisant New Jersey families such as the hospitable Van Hornes were not what they appeared. One night the Hessian Baroness von Riedesel was staying in the house of Philip Van Horne and his family, and they led her to believe that they were Loyalists. Later, she overheard the Van Hornes singing "God Save Great Washington! God Damn the King!"[33]

Admiral Howe was keenly aware that support for the Crown was very thin in America. As early as December 11, 1776, he told his private secretary, Ambrose Serle, that "almost all the People of Parts & Spirit were in the Rebellion." Serle was shocked. He believed deeply in the British cause and commented in his diary, "If this be true, it is another cogent argument, that, as we must regain Possession of this country by the Sword, by the Sword only we can expect to keep it."[34]

The pacification policy was running into other troubles, which rose indirectly from a problem of supply. Through the New York campaign, much of the provisions for the British and German troops were brought three thousand miles by sea. By the end of November, requirements had increased and supplies were running low. A British letter from New York on November 30 reported that "our army moulders away amazingly; many die by the sword, many by sickness, brought on by the bad provisions we have had from *Ireland*."[35]

In early December, General Howe ordered his garrisons in New Jersey to supply themselves with food and fuel by foraging in the countryside. He insisted that it be done with restraint, but the army had to be fed. Orders went from his headquarters in the elaborate top-down detail that was typical of Howe's command. Colonel Carl von Donop, who commanded the garrisons in Trenton, Burlington, and Bordentown, was told exactly what to do. First he was to take a census: "Order the farmers to give the exact Lists of their cattle, grain and forage, out of which you will please to form magazines for subsisting the Troops." Then he was to collect what he needed and pay with a paper receipt: "Any quantity of Salt provision or flour, exceeding what may be thought necessary for the use of a private family is to be considered as a Rebel Store, be seized for the Crown and issued to the troops as a saving for the Public."

The British command ordered their troops to "supply themselves with firewood. . . . Axes, wedges, and cross cut saw shal be sent from Brunswick." To keep the men happy in their work, a quantity of rum "shall be sent immediately for the troops under your command," but if it "can be found in the neighborhood, then it was to be taken too."[36]

The British commander for New Jersey, Major General James Grant, was charged with the execution of these orders. Much of his correspondence with officers in the field was an effort to establish territorial boundaries for foraging. His staff also prepared instructions on how the foraging must be done. The army was to offer payment for everything it took. A document from Grant's staff set prices, to be paid in gold and silver, for hay, grain, flour, and meat, with a bonus if the farmers delivered them to the troops. It added, "from the generous prices fix'd, it is to be hoped that the Inhabitants will cheerfully furnish the supplies, in order to prevent the disagreeable alternative of having them seized by Foraging parties."[37]

The system went quickly into operation, but not as the Howes intended. Most farmers were not paid in coin but given promissory notes, or sometimes nothing at all. Not many farmers volunteered to deliver their property to the army on those terms, and so the "disagreeable alternative" of compulsory foraging went into effect. Small parties of soldiers roamed the countryside with lists of supplies they were to collect. The lists grew ever longer as commanders added other urgent needs such as beds, bedding, blankets, stockings, and shoes.

Many inhabitants fled when the British army approached, taking everything they could carry, even their furniture. Colonel von Donop reported that "the houses here are built very poorly and as the greater part of the inhabitants have carried away their beds it will be necessary for the men to lie on straw beds upon the ground, otherwise they will perish with the cold."[38]

When the soldiers entered empty houses, foraging became plundering. There was always a thin line between the two. In New Jersey forage quickly disappeared. The most compelling evidence of plundering by British troops came from British officers. In 1779, the House of Commons launched an inquiry into the conduct of the Howe brothers. Major General James Robertson, who was in New York on Long Island, and briefly in New Jersey, was asked:

Q. Did the troops plunder the inhabitants as they passed through that country?
A. There was a great deal of plundering.
Q. What effect had this on the minds of the people?
A. Naturally it would lose you friends and gain you enemies.[39]

Howe grew very angry about plundering, which deeply threatened his policy of pacification. He tried to stop it by repeated orders. When they failed, he ordered "the Provost to go his rounds attended by an executioner, with orders to hang up, on the spot, the first man he shall detect in the fact, without waiting for further proof by trial. The commanding officers are to take particular care that the soldiers are acquainted with this order." Even this order had no effect, and the executions began. General Robertson testified in Parliament, "I saw some men hanged, by Sir William Howe's orders, for plundering."[40]

Hessian officers also tried to stop plundering by their men. Their commanding general, Leopold Philipp von Heister, intervened personally in some of the more egregious cases. He was amazed when a party of Jägers "pillaged an occupied house, and set fire to two others not a pistol's shot distance from Hessian headquarters." The general ordered them to be placed under arrest.[41]

American generals had the same problems. In every army, commanding generals issued strict orders against plundering. Howe, Heister, and Washington did so repeatedly. British, Hessian, and American soldiers all saw their opportunities and took them. But if every army plundered in New Jersey, they did not do so in the same way. The differences were important to the events that followed.

The diary of Sergeant John Smith of Lippitt's Rhode Island regiment is a running record of American plundering by himself and his friends. While on a march through New England on September 28, 1776, he wrote, "about midnight I was awaked by something pulling me & a voyce Crying turn out dam you. Look here see and Behold. I looked and saw five fat Geese. . . . I eat a hearty meal asking no Questions with the rest of my Brother Soldiers who Seamd Hearty in the Cause of Liberty of teaking what came in the way first to their hand Being Resolv'd to Live By their industry. By the Rhoad in the moerning we Eat the fragments & rested in our hut or Rather Den of Th——fs."

The next day, he "went out on a Patrole again & took up a Sheep & two Large fat turkeys not being able to Give the Countersign & Brought to our Castle where they was tryd by fire and Executed by the whole Division of the free booters then whilst the feast was Getting ready two of our Party went out and found a Boat & Crosed over the River to the other side and found a Boat afloat loaded with Oisters out of which they took about two Bushels." One soldier in his regiment "stole a Hive of Bees and carried it off with him."[42]

There was much of this American plundering in New Jersey. One man who lived near Princeton wrote, "It is a Provocation and grief to us to be Plundered by the Regulars our Professed enemies. Then how much more must it be so to the Sufferers that are Plundered by their Pretended Friends."[43] In general the plundering by friends ran to petty theft and careless destruction.

Hessian plundering was different. These troops from central Europe were past masters of the art. Their plundering was on a different scale.[44] When Hessians left a town, they were followed by convoys of wagons. At Trenton, the American army discovered that the Hessians had accumulated "twenty-one waggon loads of plunder."[45] Rall's brigade paled by comparison with Donop's men in Bordenton and Burlington. In two weeks, they filled "several hundred wagons and carriages with plundered goods." This came from the testimony of the Hessian officer who was sent by Donop to save the plunder when the Americans threatened to attack. Captain Ewald wrote that he was ordered to "escort the baggage to Crosswicks and "to protect it from any mishap." He found that it consisted of "several hundred wagons, carriages, and carioles—all loaded with plundered goods—and I very much wished that the enemy would take it away from me. I formed the rear guard and let the Jägers wander along both sides of the column to prod the drivers on with blows, to keep order, and to make them go faster."[46]

Americans reported that the Hessian women who accompanied the army were the most formidable plunderers of all. An example was given by Lieutenant Charles Peale in the American army. He was staying at Crosswicks, New Jersey, with the family of a Mr. Cooke, who told him that "the Hessians had taken every shirt he had, except the one on his back; which has been their general practice wherever they have been. They have taken hogs, sheep, horses and cows, everywhere; even children have been stripped of their clothes—in which business the Hessian women are the most active—in short the abuse of the inhabitants is beyond description."[47]

Similar testimony came from Martha Reed, whose house at Trenton was plundered by Hessians. She was a small child, and her father was away with the American army. She remembered that "one cold winter night, mother, and we two children were gathered in the family room; a great fire blazed in the chimney place. . . . Suddenly there was a noise outside, and the sound of many feet, the room door opened, and in stalked several strange men, and a couple of women, who looked like giants, and giantesses to us they were so tall. These were the dreaded Hessians, surely come. They jabbered away in harsh, gutteral tones, coming to the fire, spreading out their hands to the blaze.

"We children jumped up screaming, and clung to our mother. She was a brave little woman, and standing up, pointed to the door, telling them to go out. They understood the gesture, if not the words, and shook their heads doggedly. As they crouched about the fire, one of the women caught sight of the large silver buckles which mother wore in her shoes, as was the fashion of the time, and made signs for her to take off the shoe. Seeing her hesitate, the woman snatched at the buckle, and pulling off the shoe, rapped my mother in the face with the heel." An officer intervened and "rebuked the buckle snatcher." Martha Reed's mother misled the plunderers to believe that her husband was in the British army. "When they learned this, they treated us with rough kindness," but they kept plundering, searching the closets and cupboards. They killed a hog and cut it up on the mahogany dining room table. The plundering went on until the house was "ransacked and pillaged from garret to cellar."[48]

Plundering was never totally promiscuous. Even at its most extreme, it tended to operate according to customary rules, which were commonly observed by most armies. The customs were enforced by officers, who tended to intervene not to stop all plundering but to regulate it.

The first rule of customary plundering was that unoccupied houses could be stripped. Hessian Captain Ewald often described this principle in operation. He wrote of one town in New Jersey that "the village was deserted by the inhabitants, save for a few, and was therefore plundered clean." He noted in Newark, with its Whig population of New Englanders, that "the region is well cultivated, with very attractive plantations, but all their occupants have fled and all the houses had been or were being plundered and destroyed."[49]

A second rule was that resistance or even "impudence" was grounds for aggravated plundering. This was particularly the case if the resister was male. Plundering parties demanded to be treated with respect, even as they robbed families of their most cherished possessions. There are many accounts of people "falling on their knees" before a plundering party, in a ritual display of submission.[50]

A third rule of plundering was, in Ewald's words, that "personal effects and possessions taken from a military person were regarded as lawful booty; but these things if taken from a civilian were illegal and loot." This also applied when military stores were discovered, as in the neighborhood of Fort Lee, where "during the night all the plantations in the vicinity were plundered, and whatever the soldiers found in the houses was declared booty."[51]

The fourth rule of plundering was that families in their homes should not be plundered of all their food and possessions but left enough to survive. In New York, the British plunderers made a point of taking most of the cattle they could find, but left one or two milk cows for each family, so that they would not starve.

As the plundering increased, even these unwritten rules began to be broken. One problem was the drunken plunderer. Then none of the rules applied. Plundering became pillage and a carnival of destruction. There were also angry, demented, and even sociopathic plunderers. John Mott was horrified to see one Hessian "flaying a live cow for meat," a sight so outrageous that even a Quaker got a weapon and fired at the German soldier "with intent to kill."[52] The work of drunken and demented plunderers was beyond description. Lord Howe's secretary, Ambrose Serle, walked through the American countryside near Red Hook and wrote, "It is impossible to express the devastations, which the Hessians have made upon the Homes and Country Seats of some of the rebels. All their Furniture, Glasses, Windows, and the very Hangings of the Rooms are demolished or defaced. This, with the Filth deposited in them, makes the houses so offensive that it is a Penance to go into them."[53]

Plundering ran out of control in other ways. Lieutenant Johann von Krafft, a Hessian officer, wrote, "The English soldiers, especially those of Lord Rawdon's corps perpetuate daily the grossest highway-robberies and even kill." Krafft testified that Rawdon's men attacked their own allies. "One night," he wrote, "some English soldiers attacked a Hessian Grenadier Sergeant with their bayonets, wounded him in many places, robbed him of everything, and left him lying on the spot, where he soon after died. Innumerable like incidents occur, even in the day-time."[54]

As plundering became pillage, so pillage became rape. A Princeton resident, Robert Lawrence, testified from his own knowledge to an incident that happened in Penn's Neck, two miles from the college. Two British dragoons "Pretended to a Young Woman that they was Searching for Rebels, and had been Informed that some of them were Secreted in the Barn and desired her to go with them and Show them the most Secret Places there, and She (Knowing that no body was there) to convince them Went to the Barn with them to show them that no body was there. And when they had got her there, one of them Laid hold on her Strangled her to Prevent her crying out while the other Villain Ravisht her, and when he had done he Strangled her Again while the other Brute Repeated the horrid crime Upon her again. She is a Farmer's Daughter but her name with her father's must be kept secret to avoid the Reproach above Mentioned."[55]

These were not isolated cases. George Washington received reports of many rapes by British soldiers in the town of Pennington, New Jersey. A judicial inquiry confirmed that they had happened on a large scale. Mary Campbell, wife of Daniel Campbell, appeared before Justice Jared Saxton of the Hunterdon County Court and swore that she was raped many times by soldiers when she was "five months and upwards Advanc'd in her Pregnancy." Rebekkah Christopher testified under oath that she was raped several times by British soldiers and got away, only to find her ten-year-old daughter in a barn being raped by five or six others.[56]

Some incidents involved many victims. Six women and young girls testified before a magistrate that they were raped repeatedly for several days by gangs of British soldiers in the house of Edward Palmer. One of the victims was Palmer's daughter Mary Phillips. Another was his thirteen-year-old granddaughter Abigail, who said that she was held prisoner and raped for "three Days successively," along with two other girls, Elisabeth and Sarah Caine, by "a great number of soldiers belonging to the British army." When she screamed, the soldiers threatened to put out her eyes with their bayonets if she did not remain quiet. Others testified that a group of sixteen young women in Pennington tried to escape by hiding in the woods but were found and raped by British soldiers.[57]

The Continental Congress and the governors of New Jersey and New York launched formal investigations. More evidence was gathered by county justices and clergymen such as Alexander McWhorter in Newark and John Witherspoon at Princeton. They documented an epidemic of rape in New Jersey by British soldiers: "Three women were most horribly ravished by them, one of them an old woman nearly seventy years of age, whom they abused in a manner beyond description, another of them was a woman considerably advanced in her pregnancy, and the third was a young girl." Others described gang rapes not only by private soldiers but by officers: "British officers, four or five, sometimes more, sometimes less in a gang, went about the town by night entering into houses and openly inquiring for women."[58]

Americans were shocked by the number of cases, by their scale, and by the involvement of British officers. The Pennsylvania Council of Safety reported another such an incident near Woodbridge, New Jersey: A "gentleman in that part of the country was alarmed by the cries and shrieks of a most lovely daughter; he found an officer, a British officer in the act of ravishing her, he instantly put him to death; two other officers rushed in with their fusees, and fired two balls into the father," who was severely wounded.[59]

General Howe insisted that these reports were nothing but American propaganda, and that "one case only was reported to him and that in this instance the victim refused to prosecute."[60] Junior officers in his army knew better. Captain John Peebles, commander of a grenadier company of the Royal Highland Regiment, wrote sadly in his diary on Christmas Eve 1776, "In orders a man condemned to suffer death for a Rape, but pardon'd at the intercession of the injured party; the second instance, tho' there have been other shocking abuses of that nature that have not come to public notice. The story of the poor old man and his daughter in Long Island was very bad indeed, hard is the fate of many who suffer indiscriminately in a civil war."[61]

As acts of violence by occupying troops increased, the people of New Jersey took up their weapons and began to fight back. Small bands of armed men ambushed mounted British couriers on the road. They killed a British officer and his servant, attacked foraging parties in the countryside, and shot at Hessian sentries. Captain Friedrich von Münchausen wrote on December 14, 1776, "It is now very unsafe for us to travel in Jersey. The rascal peasants meet our men alone or in small unarmed groups. They have their rifles hidden in the bushes, or ditches, and the like. When they believe they are sure of success and they see one or several men belonging to our army, they shoot them in the head, then quickly hide their rifles and pretend they know nothing."[62]

Captain Münchausen and General Howe himself had such an encounter on a New Jersey road, and the British commander-in-chief nearly became another victim. "While my general was returning here today," Münchausen wrote, "I played the role of a dragoon. I took 20 light dragoons and deployed them all around the general, about a quarter of an hour's march from him, to search out any harm that might befall him I came upon five peasants with rifles who were lying behind a ditch. At that moment I had but one dragoon with me. They fired without hitting us, and then ran away. But we caught up with them. Two other dragoons, hearing the shots, rushed to our assistance. Two of the rebels were wounded, which must not be interpreted as cruelty, for a person is naturally hostile to anyone who has just endangered his life. Had I not intervened, all five of them would have been murdered."[63]

Now it was the turn of British officers to be outraged. By eighteenth-century European rules of war, civilians in arms could be put to death. The French called them *francs-tireurs*. Germans considered them *banditen*; English troops referred to them as banditti. These "laws of war" were ruthlessly enforced in European conflicts by summary execution. Even today, civilians not in uniform are forbidden to defend themselves against regular soldiers under the terms of the Hague Convention. Americans in 1776 rejected these rules. From the day of Lexington and Concord, men without uniforms believed that they had a natural right to take up arms in defense of their laws and liberties.

On the basis of the "law of war," in New Jersey General Howe announced a new policy: Anyone not in uniform who attacked his troops would be judged an "assassin" and put to death on the spot. Captain Münchausen noted, "It is now ordered that inhabitants who ventured, in mobs or individually, to fire at our passing men, would be hanged at the next tree without trial." The only result was that more infuriated American civilians took up arms, and more British and Hessian regulars died miserably on country lanes in New Jersey, far from home.[64]

As disorder spread through New Jersey, robbers and bandits infested the countryside. Some were stragglers from both armies. In early December, a gang of "three villains" was active on the roads in New Jersey. They appear to have been deserters from the American army. One was identified as an Irishman named John Watson who had deserted from the Pennsylvania Rifle Regiment. Near Princeton they broke into the house of a country merchant, and "after abusing the family in a barbarous manner," they carried away a large stock of goods in their knapsacks and bags. A reward was posted for their arrest.[65]

In occupied New Jersey, General Howe had proclaimed a peace, but there was no peace. The pacifiers found themselves at war with an infuriated population. On Christmas Eve, Howe instructed his men in New Jersey not to travel alone on the roads, but to restrict their movements to large convoys, a few days each week. As law and order collapsed, the people of New Jersey were also at war with one another. During the dark days of December 1776, the Revolution was a civil war, which became an anarchy of cruelty and violence. This was life without liberty or law in occupied New Jersey.[66]

THE OPPORTUNITY

～ The Rising of New Jersey

> The chain, I own, is rather too extensive, but . . .
> trusting to the general submission of the country
> to the Southward of this chain, and to the strength
> of the corps placed in the advance posts, I con-
> clude the troops will be in perfect security.
>
> —Sir William Howe, December 20, 1776[1]

HILE THESE EVENTS were happening in occupied New Jersey, another drama unfolded among the conquerors. The story was more tangled with underplot than an old Spanish tragedy. It involved three marching armies, two quarreling Hessian colonels, one incompetent British commander, and a beautiful widow in the village of Mount Holly. The Americans had their own tale to tell. Ordinary people in New Jersey came together to do something about their lost liberty. They were unable to break the grip of the conqueror in their state, but they created an opportunity for the Continental army. This part of the drama has never been written, but George Washington and his lieutenants understood what was happening, and they were quick to make the most of it.

The story began in Trenton on the morning of December 14, 1776, where General Howe, now Sir William for his victory on Long Island, was having breakfast with the officers who were to command his winter garrisons along the Delaware. The gathering included immaculate aides in bright scarlet and gold lace, and weary field commanders in uniforms faded and stained by hard service. A central figure was Howe's crusty engineering officer, Captain John

Montresor, with maps and plans in hand. Also present were Hessian Colonel Johann Rall in blue-black regimentals, and Colonel Carl von Donop in his uniform of Jäger green. Probably sitting in were two British regimental commanders: Lieutenant Colonel William Harcourt in the light cavalry uniform of his Sixteenth Light Dragoons, and Lieutenant Colonel Thomas Stirling of the Forty-second Highland Regiment, resplendent in a blue-green kilt, red jacket, black feathered bonnet, fur sporran, and Highland sword.

The affair must have been lively and sociable. A spirit of victory was in the air. But the conversation must have been difficult, if the correspondence of these commanders is a guide. In letters to one another, they communicated in three languages. Many British officers could only speak English. When they met people with different languages, some of them shouted English, on the Anglo-Saxon theory that aliens would understand what was said to them, if only it were said loud enough. Sir William Howe issued his general orders in English and French. Colonel Rall spoke neither English nor French but only a rough soldier's German, and he talked with his men in a Hessian dialect. Colonel von Donop wrote in French to English officers, and German to Hessian brothers, but also had no English. Colonel Stirling wrote in English to his superiors and spoke Gaelic with some of his Highlanders.[2]

One British officer had trouble understanding what was said to him in any language. Major General James Grant was a highly intelligent man, but he suffered from a selective form of social deafness: He could not hear what was said to him by people he despised as his inferiors. Grant had been born to high privilege in Scotland. He became a leader of his clan and laird of Ballindalloch Castle, one of the greatest Scottish country houses. He was very bright and in his youth had been a brilliant law student at the university at Edinburgh, but the subject did not attract him, and he went into the army as an ensign in the Royal Scots. Judgments about him were deeply divided. His superiors thought well of him, and he was exquisitely sensitive to their wishes. General Howe and members of the royal family all held him in high regard. But men who served under him, even Scottish officers of the same social standing, hated and despised him. Colonel Charles Stuart, son of the earl of Bute, wrote simply, "I detest the man." Major James Wemyss described him as "without abilities, or the least knowledge of his profession, he possessed a kind of cunning, invariably directed to the promotion of his own interest. . . . He was a Gamester, a Glutton and an Epicure. In short it may be truly said, that he lived only for himself."[3]

Major General James Grant, a caricature by Max Rosenthal after a drawing by John Kay. This officer was highly skilled in the art of pleasing his superiors, but was despised by men who served under him. He had a particular contempt for his American enemies and German allies. In December 1776 he was put in command of British and Hessian forces in New Jersey. Historical Society of Pennsylvania.

Grant was so absorbed in his own gratification that he traveled with his own chef, and required him to sleep in the same room so that he could receive Grant's desires for his next meal. He took little interest in others and was specially contemptuous toward American rebels and Hessian Regulars. His record of command during the American War of Independence was marked by repeated failures, and even disasters, but he was protected by people above him and was placed in many offices of responsibility. General Grant became commander of British and German forces in occupied New Jersey and was charged with carrying out the plans of the commander-in-chief.[4]

General Howe himself had already made the major decisions. The day before the breakfast in Trenton, the English commander-in-chief had decided to place German and Scottish battalions in forward positions along the Delaware River and to use his English regiments to occupy most of the Jersey countryside. Why he did so is not evident in the records; perhaps it was a question of language.[5]

Whatever the reason, it was typical of Howe and other high commanders in the British army that he and his staff began by making the major decisions in meticulous detail. Only then did they consult with others. On December 13, he drafted the general orders, and his aides prepared the final copies in a perfect copperplate hand. The next day, December 14, Howe discussed them at breakfast with the officers who were to carry them out.[6]

Howe had scouted the ground himself, riding up and down the Delaware under a hail of fire from American batteries across the river. He decided to hold the river line in strength, with three brigades forward on the river itself. Sir William chose the sites himself. He placed three brigades in towns about six miles apart, close enough to be mutually supporting, but sufficiently far apart to have their own fields for foraging.

The central post was at Bordentown on the extreme easternmost bend of the Delaware. There he posted Colonel von Donop, with three battalions of Hessian grenadiers and a detachment of Jägers, supported by six Hessian field guns (three-pounders). Six miles south at Burlington he stationed Colonel Stirling's Forty-second Highland Regiment and a Hessian battalion, with their own battalion guns, and they were promised two big eighteen-pounders to keep the Pennsylvania Navy at a distance. Seven miles north was Trenton, the most exposed position. Here General Howe placed a fighting officer, Colonel Johann Rall, with three Hessian regiments that had done well at White Plains and Fort Washington.

Twelve miles behind these forward positions, Howe sent a strong garrison to Princeton: a full brigade of British infantry, plus two battalions of light infantry and a regiment of light dragoons, all under Alexander Leslie. Farther north beyond Princeton were other occupying forces, mostly British troops and some Hessians and Waldeck troops, divided among fourteen garrisons in New Jersey. Each was ordered to maintain "such other posts as shall appear necessary to secure the communications of your cantonment." In overall command was General James Grant, with his main British base at Brunswick, thirty-five road miles from the Delaware River.

Howe knew he was running a risk by scattering his troops so widely across New Jersey, but he thought that the American army had been defeated and presented no major offensive threat. Grant believed so, too, and assured his officers on the Delaware River that they had nothing to fear. He wrote on December 17, "I can hardly believe that Washington would venture at this season of the year to pass the Delaware at Vessel's ferry as the repassing it may on account of the Ice become difficult."[7]

Grant was mainly interested in completing the pacification of New Jersey, and he sent his troops marching widely across the countryside. On December 17, 1776, he ordered Colonel Charles Mawhood to march "by Hillsborough towards Flemingtown" in Hunterdon County. General Leslie was told to make a circuit to Springfield in Essex County, then south through Bound Brook in Somerset County to Princeton. General Matthew was sent to Pluckemin, where he took prisoners in a skirmish and lost his guide, wounded in the foot.[8]

		Burlington	42.ᵈ Reg.ᵗ 2. Battalions. Hessian Grenadiers, 1. Batt.ⁿ Detachment of Jagers
	Colonel Donnop	Communication from Burlington to Bordens Town	Hessian Grenadiers, 1. Batt.ⁿ
		Bordens Town	Hessian Grenadiers 2. Batt.ⁿˢ Detachment of Jagers
	Colonel Raille	Trenton	Rall's Brigade 20. Dragoons 50. Jagers
	Brig.ʳ Gen.ˡ Leslie	Prince Town	2.ᵈ Brigade Light Infantry 2.Batt.ⁿˢ 3. Troops, 16. Dragoons
		Hillsborough, &c.ᵃ	3. Batt.ⁿˢ 4.ᵗʰ Brigade
		Brunswick	British Grenad.ʳˢ 2. Batt.ⁿˢ 3. Troops, 16. Dragoons
Major General Grant Commanding in New Jersey	B.ʳ G.ˡ Matthew	Landing	Guards.
		Spanktown	46.ᵗʰ Reg.ᵗ 1. Troop. 17. Dragoons.
		Amboy	33.ᵗʰ Reg.ᵗ
		Elizabeth Town	Waldeck Reg.ᵗ 1.Troop, 17. Dragoons
		Newark	2.Batt.ⁿˢ 71. Reg.ᵗ
		Aquakenunk	1. Batt.ⁿ 71. Reg.ᵗ
		Hackensack	26.ᵗʰ Reg.ᵗ
		New Bridge	7.ᵗʰ Reg.ᵗ
		Bergen	57.ᵗʰ Reg.ᵗ
		Paulus's Hook	50. Men from the 57. Reg.ᵗ

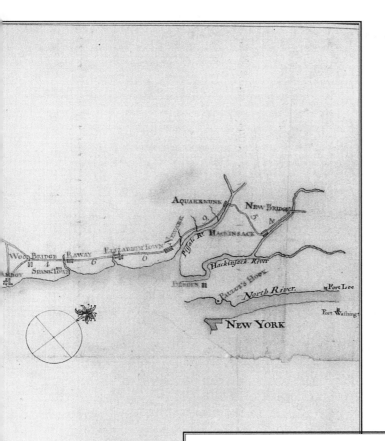

British and Hessian Garrisons in New Jersey, a manuscript map drawn ca. December 12–13, 1776, by Captain John Montresor, an Engineer on General Howe's staff. It shows Howe's decision to distribute his troops in seventeen posts from the Hudson to the Delaware. It also shows his keen attention to the distance between the garrisons. This copy survives in the papers of General Henry Clinton, who wrote the note in upper corner, "Capt. Montresor after the misfortune of Trenttown this Gentleman has forgot the Assonpink Creek, which is however here put in." Clinton himself added the creek and marked the crossing upstream. This map survives in the Clinton Papers, William L. Clements Library, University of Michigan.

All of these assignments expanded the reach of the occupation but diminished the strength of its detachments. The British commanders were coming up against a hard American reality, in the sheer size of the country that they were trying to control. William Howe's "extended chain" of garrisons reached from the Delaware River to the Hudson. His garrisons were hard pressed to control a corridor of about three hundred square miles. That area was less than 5 percent of New Jersey and a tiny fraction of the continent, and yet it stretched the resources of the British army to the limit.

Difficulties began to multiply from the start. At first they came not from the Americans but from strains among British and German commanders along the Delaware River, who felt that they did not have strength enough to do their jobs. They commanded the forward outposts of an embattled empire and felt exposed to attack from the rebels across the river. Bands of New Jersey militia were also roaming the countryside, and the Pennsylvania Navy controlled the river itself below Trenton Falls.

On December 11, Colonel Carl von Donop met another problem when he led his three Hessian battalions to Bordentown. The town was not big enough to hold his men. He occupied it with only one battalion and billeted the rest along the country roads. Colonel Stirling's Forty-second Highland Regiment and the Hessian Block Battalion had trouble of another kind at Burlington, which was under the guns of the Pennsylvania Navy's galleys, six of them anchored in the middle of the river. Stirling withdrew his men to the crossroads hamlet of Black Horse, about six miles south of Burlington, and they occupied barns and scattered farmhouses. None of these positions were easily defensible, and small patrols of Jägers were sent out. Captain Ewald led one of them to the south on December 13 and ran into a party of American militia who were rounding up cattle. Ewald took several prisoners, who told him that a thousand militia were just to the south.[9]

Other difficulties appeared when Colonel Rall led his brigade to Trenton, seven miles above Bordentown at the northwestern end of the outpost line. Rall's Hessian troops were not happy to be there. Lieutenant Wiederholdt wrote sarcastically, "On December 14, we marched to fabulous Trenton, a place I'll remember as long as I live." Another officer added, "This town consists of about one hundred houses, of which many are mean and little, and it is easy to conceive how ill it must accommodate three regiments. The inhabitants, like those at Princeton, have almost all fled, so that we occupy bare walls."[10]

The Hessian troops were exhausted. Lieutenant Colonel Francis Sheffer, commanding the Regiment von Lossberg, wrote, "We arrived in Trenton with our regiments torn apart and much fatigued. Major Ludwig von Hanstein asked Rall if these were the good winter quarters they had been promised." Rall said no. They would soon be in Philadelphia "across the ice of the river Delaware." The men looked forward to moving on. Grenadier Johannes Reuber wrote in his journal, "It was quiet here and we did the usual duties, as watches, etc. It started to freeze and we liked it. We thought to cross the river and take Philadelphia."[11]

Like most American communities, Trenton had no walls or fortifications. Its site was chosen for economic advantage, not military security. The town occupied an open site at the head of navigation on the Delaware River. It was an important center of commerce, with a flourishing river trade above and below Trenton Falls. Roads and ferries came into the town from six directions. Small industries flourished there, with several mills on Assunpink Creek.

There was much debate among Hessian officers about how Trenton should be defended. Several officers urged Rall to fortify the town. Two Hessian engineers, Captain George Pauli and Captain Wilhelm Martin, came to the village and recommended a redoubt at the upper end of the town and fortifications along the river. They drew up the plans, but Colonel Rall did not agree. Later Major von Dechow strongly urged the same thing, and Rall made him a rude reply. "Scheiszer bey Scheisz," he said in his soldier's speech. "Shit upon shit! Let them come. . . . We will go at them with the bayonet."[12]

Colonel von Donop, who had overall command of the brigades along the river, later claimed that he urged Colonel Rall to fortify the town, but he did not go there after the breakfast with General Howe. The two Hessian colonels did not get on. Within the small circle of the Hessian army, they were as different as two officers could be. Each of them despised the other. These two Hessian commanders appear not to have talked or met together, though they were only about six miles apart, and much hinged on their cooperation. Their letters to one another were correct but curt and very cold. Each addressed the other as "my brother," but there was no hint of brotherly love.[13]

A case in point was a small question of who would guard a bridge over Crosswicks Creek between their commands. It was a desolate spot in deep woods, four miles south of Trenton and two miles north of Bordentown. All agreed that the bridge should be protected. It was very close to Colonel von Donop, who had more troops than he could house at Bordentown, and far from Rall, who was desperately shorthanded. But Donop refused to commit his own troops and ordered Rall to send a detachment of a hundred men to the bridge and keep them there. Their mission was to keep open communications between the two Hessian brigades. If attacked by superior force, they were to retreat to Bordentown. Rall did as he was instructed; Donop did nothing.

A major factor in these plans was Hessian contempt for Americans. Lieutenant Jakob Piel of the Lossberg regiment wrote of Colonel Rall, "It never struck him that the rebels might attack us, and therefore he had made no preparations against an attack. I must concede that on the whole we had a poor opinion of the rebels, who previously had never successfully opposed us."[14]

On the morning of December 14, when Howe was dining with his officers in Trenton, George Washington was directly across the river, staying in the house of Thomas Barclay near Trenton Falls, so that he could keep an eye on the enemy. That day, after Howe left for Princeton and New York, Washington moved his headquarters ten miles up the river "to be near the main Body of my small army." He was also closer to the upper ferries across the river.[15]

He was deeply worried about the possibility of a British advance across the Delaware and knew better than anyone how little he had to stop it. At the same time, he was thinking of a "counterstroke" and confided his thoughts to a few trusted officers. Washington wrote to Horatio Gates on December 14 that Howe "beyond all question means if possible to possess himself of Philadelphia." He urged Gates to march from northern New Jersey and join him with his regiments as soon as possible. "If we can draw our Forces together I trust under the smiles of providence, we may yet effect an important stroke, or at least prevent General Howe from executing his Plan." Washington wrote much the same thing to General William Heath, urging him to move from New York into New Jersey. "If we can collect out force speedily, I hope we may effect something of importance, or at least give our Affairs such a turn as to make 'em assume a more promising aspect."[16]

But how could it be done? Where was the opportunity? It was the old story again. Every possibility that rose was blasted by events. Washington had hoped that he could turn Charles Lee's ambition to a constructive purpose, and urged him to raid Brunswick. No sooner had he proposed that idea than Lee was raided himself and made a prisoner.[17]

Washington's New Jersey aide Joseph Reed offered some constructive advice. "The River is not, nor I believe cannot be sufficiently guarded," Reed wrote. "We must depend upon intelligence of their Motions—to which no Expense must be spared." Reed himself had already sent patrols of "gentlemen of the Light Horse" into New Jersey without learning much of use.[18] Washington agreed and asked his officers for help. He ordered them to raise redoubts at every crossing point on the river and to work with local militia to stop crossings from Pennsylvania by people who might take intelligence to the enemy. They were also asked to create listening posts along the river and to send agents of their own into New Jersey.

Upstream, the Continental troops of Fermoy, Stephen, Mercer, and Stirling guarded "every suspicious part of the river" from Howell's and McConkey's to Coryell's Ferry. Downriver, the Philadelphia militia went to Dunk's Ferry. Cadwalader's Pennsylvania militia guarded the Bristol crossings. In the middle, Ewing was responsible for the ferry crossings at Trenton. Dickinson was sent to Yardley's Ferry; his orders were "Find out the fording place there and have a redoubt thrown up immediately. You and General Ewing must divide the Ground between Trenton falls and your post and establish the Proper Guards and Patrols to watch the enemy's motions, you will spare no pains or Expense to obtain Intelligence—all promises made or monies Advanced shall be fully complied with and discharged." Washington ordered them to send "every piece of intelligence worthy of notice" by express, and every brigadier was told to keep his men together "night and day," with three days' rations, ready to march at the "shortest notice."[19]

These officers were quick to obey. None was more active than Philemon Dickinson, the brother of John Dickinson, born to a family of great wealth with large holdings in four states. Just above Trenton on the Delaware River, he owned a handsome gentleman's farm called the Hermitage, which was famous for its gardens and greenhouses. Now it was occupied and plundered by Hessian Jägers. When his brother John Dickinson turned against independence, Philemon Dickinson strongly supported it. He became a general of New Jersey militia and devoted his resources to the Continental cause. From his headquarters in Pennsylvania he acted quickly on Washington's instructions and sent men across the river, into the countryside around Trenton itself. Dickinson wrote to Washington, "A Negro fellow whose master lives in Trenton, whom I have just seen, informs me they are building boats at Henry's Mills, a mile from Town,

Philemon Dickinson, a gentleman farmer who
lived near Trenton and became a General
in the New Jersey militia and helped to
organize the rising of the Hunterdon
men. From an old image published
in William S. Stryker (1898), *Battles
of Trenton and Princeton*, 83.

and that he was told by the Soldiers that there were many boats
coming from Brunswick. What degree of credibility is to be given to
this information I will not determine."

He added, "I have endeavoured to prevail with some intelligent person to go down into Trenton, but hitherto without success;
if 'tis agreeable to your Excellency, I will offer fifteen or twenty dollars to a good hand, who will undertake it, if such a one can be
found. People here are extremely fearful of the Inhabitants at Trenton betraying them."[20]

Dickinson found that many people in New Jersey were growing
very angry against the British and German invaders who were attacking their houses and plundering their property. In Hunterdon County,
one such man was Captain John Mott, who lived near Dickinson's
home outside Trenton. According to family tradition, Mott was a
Quaker who had married out of meeting, losing his "birth right in
the Society of Friends," and joined the militia. One of his daughters
recalled that on a bitter cold Sunday in December 1776 the family
was keeping warm by the fire when a party of six Germans approached
the house. Mott barricaded the door and sent the children to hide in
the cellar. The Hessians smashed the door with axes. Mott was a tall
man and very strong. He met the intruders as they entered and fought
them with a fireplace poker and tongs. In a terrific struggle he killed
three Hessians, and the others fled for their lives. One of the children
in the cellar "never forgot the tumult overhead" and told the story to
her own children, who recorded it. The family also recalled that this
lapsed Quaker "never spoke of the three Hessians whom he was forced
to kill, without tears, saying always that it seemed like murder."[21]

Others shared Mott's experience. The result was a spontaneous rising of the Hunterdon men. Mott himself recruited men who were ready to take up arms against the British and Hessians. Other leaders did the same. Colonel David Chambers of the Hunterdon militia led a band in Amwell Township east of Coryell's Ferry. These men did not go into the town of Trenton or attack its outposts, but when Hessian Jägers or British dragoons or small foraging parties left the town and went up the Delaware Valley along the River Road, or northwest toward Flemington and Lambertville, or north toward Princeton, the Jerseymen attacked. Colonel Rall began to lose men every day, and the strength of the militia increased. On December 16, Colonel Chambers sent prisoners across the river to George Washington: two Regulars, and one "Malitious Active Tory" who had "assembled and spirited the negroes against us." On December 17, a patrol of British dragoons went upriver toward Pennington and McConkey's Ferry. They were intercepted by the Hunterdon men, and one dragoon was "deadly wounded." On December 18, another dragoon was killed on the road to Maidenhead by a party that was reported to be more than a hundred strong. On December 19, three grenadiers in the Lossberg regiment were captured while out foraging. On December 20, Rall sent a patrol of Jägers and dragoons four miles upriver to Howell's Ferry, where they met 150 Hunterdon men commanded by Captain John Anderson; the Americans came off second best and lost three or four men.[22]

The Jerseymen forced Rall to send dispatches to Princeton with an escort of a hundred men, which some British commanders thought absurd. But the growing scale of attacks by the Hunterdon militia supported his judgment. Rall was rapidly losing control of the countryside, even to the outskirts of Trenton. He could not patrol up the river even to Howell's Ferry, four miles upstream, without losing men. McConkey's Ferry ten miles distant was beyond his reach. The Hessian commander could identify the American leaders by name, and he could defeat the Hunterdon militia in a stand-up fight, but he could not stop them from striking again and again, and vanishing into country that they knew so well. In all of this the Jersey men went far beyond instructions from Washington. This Hunterdon Rising was an autonomous event, by angry men against a hated oppressor.

While Philemon Dickinson and the Hunterdon men were taking control of the countryside upriver from Trenton, another American officer began to attack from a different direction. He was James Ewing, a

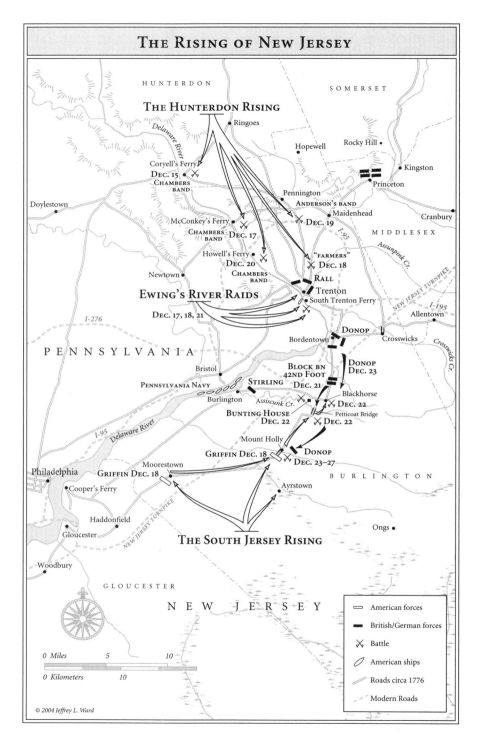

THE RISING OF NEW JERSEY

HUNTERDON

SOMERSET

THE HUNTERDON RISING

Ringoes

Hopewell   Rocky Hill •

Delaware River

Coryell's Ferry •
DEC. 15
CHAMBERS
BAND

Kingston •

Princeton

Doylestown •

Pennington

Maidenhead

Cranbury •

McConkey's Ferry •
CHAMBERS **DEC. 17**
BAND

ANDERSON'S BAND

DEC. 19

MIDDLESEX

Howell's Ferry •
DEC. 20
CHAMBERS
BAND

"FARMERS"
DEC. 18

Assunpink Cr.

Newtown •

RALL
Trenton
South Trenton Ferry

EWING'S RIVER RAIDS

DEC. 17, 18, 21

NEW JERSEY TURNPIKE

I-195

Allentown

I-276

DONOP

PENNSYLVANIA

Bordentown

Crosswicks

Crosswicks Cr.

Bristol •

BLOCK BN
42ND FOOT
DEC. 21

DONOP
DEC. 23

STIRLING
DEC. 21

PENNSYLVANIA NAVY

Burlington

Assiscunk Cr.

Blackhorse

DEC. 22
Petticoat Bridge

BUNTING HOUSE
DEC. 22

DEC. 22

I-95   *Delaware River*

Mount Holly

GRIFFIN DEC. 18

DONOP
DEC. 23–27

Philadelphia

Moorestown •

GRIFFIN DEC. 18

Ayrstown •

BURLINGTON

• Cooper's Ferry

Haddonfield •

NEW JERSEY TURNPIKE

Ongs •

Gloucester •

THE SOUTH JERSEY RISING

• Woodbury

GLOUCESTER

NEW JERSEY

	American forces
	British/German forces
	Battle
	American ships
	Roads circa 1776
	Modern Roads

0 Miles   5   10

0 Kilometers   10

© 2004 Jeffrey L. Ward

hard-driving Scotch-Irish border chieftain, who had been born and
raised in Lancaster County, Pennsylvania, when it was the western
frontier. He became a brigadier general of Pennsylvania militia, and
in December he commanded a brigade of five regiments, mostly
from Cumberland, York, and Lancaster counties. They had been in
the field since the summer and had lost 80 percent of their strength,
but Ewing still had a hard core of six hundred men, devoted to the
Cause. Washington posted them at Trenton Ferry directly across the
river from the town. Ewing's orders were to guard the river and collect intelligence. The commander-in-chief wrote, "spare no pains, nor
cost to gain information of the Enemys movements, and designs—
whatever sums you pay to obtain this end I will chearfully refund.
Every piece of information worthy of communication transmit to
me without loss of time."[23]

Like the Hunterdon men, Ewing and his Pennsylvanians went
beyond Washington's orders. They were well armed and had artillery, as many as thirty guns on the west bank of the Delaware. They
also had boats and felt that they owned the river. Their brigadier
had a fighting spirit, and just before dawn on December 17, 1776,
they launched a raid across the river. With supporting fire from a
heavy "cannonade," thirty men crossed the river in small boats,
stormed ashore, attacked a Jäger outpost at the Trenton ferry landing, and were back across the river before Colonel Rall knew what
had happened.[24]

Rall reinforced his men at the ferry. The next morning, December 18, Ewing's raiders hit them again with twice the force. The
Hessians were badly shaken. Adjutant Piel of the Lossberg regiment
wrote, "because they had boats and we had none, they could cross at
any point and harass us."[25] The morning after that, Rall woke the
entire garrison before dawn and sent a full company and two cannon to the ferry landing. The Americans did not come that day, and
the Hessians returned to their quarters. Every morning after that
Rall ordered his exhausted men to turn out before sunrise and haul
the cannon to the ferry landing, then pulled them back after sunrise. The Hessian guards at the ferry were ordered not to gather in
large numbers in daylight. Whenever they did so, the American artillery fired at them from the other side of the river. Rall was beginning to lose control of the town itself.[26]

On the night of December 21, Ewing's raiders attacked in a
different way. They rowed silently across the river, sneaked ashore
with blackened faces, set fire to several houses at the ferry landing,
and vanished into the dark. In the Hessian garrison, the strain was

beginning to show. Grenadier Reuber called the raiders with darkened faces "black Negroes and yellow dogs." He added, "We had to watch out. . . . They crossed the Delaware to our side, set some houses on fire, and then retreated. Again everything was quiet . . . but we had to watch out."[27]

The Hessian garrison suffered few casualties in these repeated raids from the river, but they lost sleep and confidence and their morale was badly shaken. Rumors of impending attacks multiplied. On December 20 or 21, Reuber remembered that "the inhabitants of the town circulated a rumor that the rebels wanted to surprise us. We did not have any idea of such a thing, and thought the rebels were unable to do so."[28] But their colonel took no chances. Reuber wrote, "Early in the morning Commander Rall selected a strong force from his brigade, also a cannon, and we must march in two divisions, along the Delaware, to see about the Americans attempting to cross the Delaware for an aggression. There was no sign of it, and we marched to near Frankfort, which was situated on the other side of the Delaware. There we could see Americans. Rall stopped us and we joined with the other divisions and returned to Trenton. All was quiet again."[29] Rall strengthened his six outposts around the town. Some of his officers urged him to build redoubts on the heights above Trenton and on high ground south of the town. Donop's engineers offered the same advice, but Rall rejected it. He explained to Donop, "I have not made any redoubts or any kind of fortifications because I have the enemy in all directions." For security the guns were kept in the center of town. Reuber wrote that every soldier was ordered to sleep "fully dressed like he was on watch. The officers and sergeants must enforce this order."[30]

Rall called for help. He sent many messages asking for assistance from Donop below Bordentown, General Leslie in Princeton, and Major General Grant at Brunswick. Rall reported that his Trenton garrison was exhausted, the town was indefensible, and attacks were increasing. Only one senior officer took Rall's worries very seriously: In Princeton, Alexander Leslie, an excellent officer, moved quickly. As early as December 18 he wrote to Rall, "I've ordered the first Light Infantry to be at Trenton tomorrow at 10 o'clock and I take the 2d Light Infantry and 300 Men of the 2d brigade to Maidenhead to be in the way if needed."[31] Leslie also sent troops on December 21. Reuber recalled, "Saturday afternoon before Christmas came three English regiments from Princeton to Trenton for reinforcement and when they came to town and Major Rall settled them, they were ordered to turn around and march back to Princeton."[32]

Brigadier-General Alexander Leslie, commander of the British brigade that occupied Princeton. He was a very able officer, much respected for his character, and was the only British or Hessian leader who responded to Colonel Rall's warnings and sent help to Trenton. From a caricature in William S. Stryker (1898), *Battles of Trenton and Princeton*, 71.

General Grant's reaction was very different. He had complete scorn for the Americans and wrote so contemptuously to Donop, "Tell the colonel [Rall] he is safe. I will undertake to keep the peace in Jersey with a corporal's guard." When he received three letters from Rall in one day, warning of attack and seeking help, Grant responded with open contempt for the Hessian commander and insisted that Rall exaggerated the danger. "I am sorry to hear your brigade has been fatigued or alarmed," Grant wrote to Rall. "You may be assured that the rebel army in Pennsylvania which has been joined by Lee's Corps, Gates's and Arnold's, does not exceed eight thousand men, who have neither shoes nor stockings, are in fact almost naked, starving for cold, without Blankets, and very ill-supplied with provisions. On this side of the Delaware they have not three hundred men. These are scattered about in small parties under the command of Subaltern Officers, none of them above the rank of captain, and their principal object is to pick up some of our light Dragoons."[33]

Rall asked specifically that the British troops establish garrisons closer to Trenton at Maidenhead to keep the road open. Grant refused again. "As General Howe does not approve of Maidenhead for a Post," he wrote, "I cannot send troops there, but I have desired General Leslie to send patroles frequently from Princetown to meet the Patroles from Trenton. . . . Ammunition shall be sent for the

Artillery & powder and Balls to make cartridges, which your men can do themselves at their leisure."[34]

Even as his garrisons along the Delaware were increasingly hard pressed, Grant continued to divide his forces and scatter them more widely over the countryside. He was oblivious to warnings and calls for support that were coming from many officers and sent blithe messages to both Rall and Donop insisting that all was well, while they were struggling to keep growing forces of angry Americans at bay. Grant was more concerned about his own superiors than he was about the enemy. On December 23, Grant wrote to Donop, "We are all in a great favour at home. His majesty has ordered Spruce Beer to be issued to the Troops without any stoppage." As long as his superiors were happy, General Grant was content.[35]

While trouble was building in Trenton, Colonel von Donop was also coming under heavy pressure from the south. Here another group of Jerseymen turned against their conquerors. This rising started with Samuel Griffin (1746–1810), a Virginia colonel without a command, who had been wounded in the heel in the retreat from New York. After the confusion of that campaign he found himself in southern New Jersey with a small force of Virginia artillery and a few Continental infantry from Pennsylvania. As reports of Hessian and British conduct spread, the militia rallied to him. By mid-December Griffin had about five hundred men from Cumberland, Salem, and Gloucester counties, and their numbers kept growing. Griffin led them to Moorestown, just south of the Hessians at Bordentown and the Highlanders at Blackhorse.

Donop learned of them and sent a Tory agent named Barzella Haines to have a look. Haines found the American troops at Mount Holly on December 21 and reported that "they were not above eight hundred, near one half boys, and all of them Militia a very few from Pennsylvania excepted,—That he knew a great many of them who came from Gloucester, Egg Harbour, Penns Neck and Cohansey. They were commanded by Colonel Griffin."[36]

Colonel Thomas Stirling, commander of the Forty-second Highlanders, also heard about them from a "a gentleman of credit," who reckoned "1000 of the rebels were certainly at Mount Holly" and "2,000 more were in the rear to support them." Stirling's men were widely scattered in small foraging parties. He began to concentrate his forces and reported his news to Donop.[37]

Donop asked Stirling for his advice. The Scottish colonel replied, "The rebels without doubt mean to beat up our Quarters and

Colonel Thomas Stirling, an undated miniature. This officer led two battalions of the Forty-second Foot (Royal Highland Regiment) in the New Jersey campaign. Marchioness of Tullibardine, *A Military History of Perthshire, 1660–1902* (Perth, 1908), 387.

drive us from hence from their approaching so near us. I am therefore of opinion, if it is necessary to keep this Country for the Winter, that we should not wait to be attacked. . . . You sir, with the troops at Bordentown, should come here and attack. I am confident we are a match for them."[38]

Donop followed the Scottish colonel's suggestion and decided to attack, resolving to "get rid of these troublesome guests." His Jägers found the Jersey militia at Petticoat Bridge on the approaches to Mount Holly, and a series of sharp skirmishes followed, with casualties on both sides. On the morning of December 23, Donop's main body came up and another engagement ensued. American militia, now outnumbered, retreated. The Hessians complained that the Americans "run so fast, they had not the Opportunity of killing any of them." But the Americans did not run far. They formed on a hill in the distance and remained there.[39]

Colonel von Donop decided to stay the night of December 23 at Mount Holly. Captain Ewald wrote that "because of its position, this town is a very excellent trading place and inhabited by many wealthy people. Since the majority had fled and the dwellings had been abandoned, almost the whole town was plundered; and because large stocks of wine were found there, the entire garrison was drunk by evening."[40]

Before the Hessians arrived, Margaret Morris wrote, "all the women removed from the Town except one widow of our acquaintance." Colonel von Donop moved into her house. Jäger Captain Ewald, who was there, took up the story. "The colonel, who was exceedingly devoted to the fair sex, had found in his quarters the exceedingly beautiful young widow of a doctor. He wanted to set up his rest quarters in Mount Holly, which to the misfortune of Colonel Rall, he was permitted to do."[41]

The colonel spent the night of December 23 in the widow's house. He decided to stay on Christmas Eve, and then on Christmas as well. He was supposed to be at Bordentown, within six miles of Trenton, close enough for mutual support in a major attack. Instead he remained for three days at Mount Holly, eighteen miles from Trenton. He kept his troops with him, more than a full day's march from Colonel Rall's garrison, out of touch and unable to render any assistance.[42]

Captain Ewald thought it may have decided the outcome of the campaign. He wrote, "This great misfortune, which surely caused the utter loss of the thirteen splendid provinces of the Crown of England, was due partly to the extension of the cordon, partly to the fault of Colonel Donop, who was led by the nose to Mount Holly by Colonel Griffin, and detained there by love. . . . Thus the fate of entire Kingdoms often depends upon a few blockheads and irresolute men."[43]

One wonders who the "exceedingly beautiful young widow" of Mount Holly was and what her purposes may have been. Was she sympathetic to the American cause? Could she have been an American agent? Continental officers, including Washington himself, were recruiting a great many agents in New Jersey, and some of them were women. Attempts to identify her have met with no success. Captain Ewald described her as the widow of a doctor, but none of the known physicians in the town fits the description.[44]

In December 1776, there was a young and very beautiful young widow, a "Free Quaker" strongly sympathetic to the American cause, who lived in Philadelphia, had family connections in Gloucester County, New Jersey, was married there, and often went back and forth. She was acquainted with Margaret Morris, and also with George Washington. Her name was Betsy Ross. One historian, Joseph Tustin, has raised the possibility she may have been the mysterious widow of Mount Holly. Her husband, John Ross, who had died in 1776, came from Gloucester County and may have been related to Doctor Alexander Ross, who was a physician practicing at Mount Holly in 1776. But Mr. Tustin is very careful to point out that no firm evidence has been found to support this hypothesis, or to settle the question. Whoever this lady may have been, the Hessian Captain Ewald believed that she had a major impact on the course of events.[45]

Each of these movements in New Jersey had different drivers. The rising of the Hunterdon men in the north and west, the river raids of

Ewing's Pennsylvania militia, the march and countermarch of Griffin's militia to the south, and the dalliance of Colonel von Donop with the beautiful young widow of Mount Holly all were spontaneous events. Historian Samuel Smith wrote, "The militia attacks from the north and south by generals Dickinson and Ewing were not planned and scheduled; rather it was left to each commander to determine the appropriate time to launch a harassing movement." More than that, the leaders were led by their men. Here again the campaign was a movement with a broad base and many autonomous actors.[46]

Washington was not the director of these events, but he and his staff were quick to recognize an opportunity. The rising of the Jersey militia in four counties, and the Pennsylvania raiders on the river, unhinged Sir William Howe's careful plans. The attacks kept the garrisons of Colonel von Donop and Colonel Stirling, and especially of Colonel Rall, in a continuous state of alarm. Rall's brigade was on alert for days and nights on end. The men were ill and exhausted, and deprived of sleep. The officers were quarreling with one another. Rall was in a state of fury, not against the rebels but against his English allies. Donop, who was supposed to be supporting Rall, allowed himself to be drawn away to the south for three crucial days. General Grant, their superior, was out of touch, ignorant of conditions along the Delaware, and the victim of his own arrogance. He was utterly unresponsive to their calls for help.

Washington and his staff had been looking for a chance to make a "counterstroke," and they were attentive to the flow of news as it arrived in their headquarters. Another New Jersey officer played a critical role in that process. He was Colonel Joseph Reed, Washington's adjutant. He and Washington had a difficult relationship, but one of high importance. Reed was in Bristol, Pennsylvania, on the Delaware River. His many contacts across the river kept him well informed about events in New Jersey. Reed was specially knowledgeable about the activities of Griffin's militia, the raids by Ewing's Pennsylvanians, and the effect of Dickinson's Hunterdon rising. More than that, he was highly intelligent in his analysis of the information that was brought to him. On December 22, 1776, he sent a message by express to Washington with an accurate summary of Griffin's activities. Reed reported that "Colonel Griffin had advanced up the Jerseys with 600 men as far as Mount Holly" and that "the spirits of the Militia are very high—they are all supporting him." Reed proposed a choice of actions. "We can either give him a strong reinforcement—or make a separate attack—the latter bids fairest for producing the greatest and best effects."

Colonel Joseph Reed, portrait by Charles Willson Peale from life (ca. 1783). Reed has had a bad historical press. George Bancroft falsely accused him of treason after confusing him with a Tory of the same name, and other scholars have judged him severely for his criticism of Washington's leadership in the New York campaign. Reed served as Adjutant of the Continental Army. He continued to work very closely with Washington and had a seminal role in planning the Trenton and Princeton campaigns. Independence National Historical Park.

The most important part of his letter was an exhortation to act quickly and decisively. He wrote to Washington, "We are all of the opinion my dear general that something must be attempted to revive our expiring credit, give our Cause some degree of reputation & prevent total depreciation of the Continental money which is coming on very fast." He insisted that "even a Failure cannot be more fatal than to remain in our present situation. In short some enterprize must be undertaken in our present Circumstances or we must give up the cause."

Reed had his own recommendation. "The scattered divided state of the enemy affords us a fair opportunity of trying what our men will do when called to an offensive attack." This had not been done before. "Will it not be possible my dear General for your troops or such part of them as can act with advantage to make a diversion or something more at or about Trenton—the greater the alarm the more likely Success will attend the attacks."

There was more. Reed wrote bluntly, "Our affairs are hasting fast to ruin if we do not retrieve them by some happy event. Delay is now equal to a total defeat. Be not deceived general with small flattering appearances; we must not suffer ourselves to be lulled into security and inaction." He ended, "Pardon the Freedom I have used, the Love of my country, a Wife and four Children in the Enemys Hands, the Respect and Attachment I have to you—the Ruin and Poverty that must attend me & thousands of others will plead my Excuse for so much Freedom."[47]

That letter reached Washington by courier on December 22, 1776; Washington called a council of war. The general announced that the army had grown stronger; all of the reinforcements from New England had now arrived. The meeting debated Reed's plan for crossing the Delaware and attacking one of the enemy's posts in New Jersey. The council agreed very quickly, and a long discussion followed on how it might be done. Much of the conversation was about the weather, the river, and boats. Colonel John Glover, who had long experience of maritime affairs, was consulted about the feasibility of the crossing. Glover told Washington "not to be troubled about that, as his boys could manage it." The next day secret orders went out to senior officers in the army. The operation was on.[48]

The next day, December 24, Joseph Reed was sent to New Jersey to check on the condition of Griffin's militia and the whereabouts of Colonel von Donop. Jäger Captain Johann Ewald remembered that on Christmas Eve, "a trumpeter arrived in Mount Holly from General Washington, who presented a proposal to Colonel Donop concerning the exchange of some of his officers who had been captured at Mt. Holly." Ewald was suspicious. He wrote in his diary, "The next few days would show that this was a ruse to find out whether the colonel was still in Mount Holly or was already marching back to Bordentown, which every reasonable man desired, since Trenton as well as Mount Holly were without any further support."[49]

Late on Christmas Eve, Washington convened his council of war again, this time in the Merrick house. Attending were Major Generals Greene and Sullivan; Brigadier Generals Stirling, Fermoy, Mercer, Stephen, and St. Clair; and Colonels Paul D. Sargent, John Stark, John Glover, and Henry Knox. The plans for the operation were worked out in detail.[50]

Unknown to George Washington, a British spy was at work in his headquarters. He or she reported the American meeting to the British high command within a day. Other British agents were also operating in the American camp. Their information stirred even General Grant to action. He sent a galloper to Colonel Rall, with an urgent message that reached Trenton on Christmas evening. General Grant wrote, "Washington has been informed that our troops have marched into winter quarters and has been told that we are weak at Trenton and Princeton and Lord Stirling expressed a wish to make an attack on these two places. I don't believe he will attempt it, but be assured that my information is undoubtedly true, so I need not advise you to be on your guard against an unexpected attack at Trenton. I think I have got into a good line of intelligence which will be of use to us all."[51]

Other warnings of an American attack arrived at Trenton. On Christmas Eve, two deserters came across the river and reported to Hessian officers that the American army was preparing to march. On that day or the next, a Loyalist physician who lived in the "doctor's house" on the river in South Trenton told Colonel Rall that "the rebels were going to cross the Delaware." On Christmas day, a countryman named Wahl came to see Johann Rall and said "Colonel, take care, they are going to attack you." Rall replied, "Let them come."[52]

Colonel Rall was confident that his garrison could deal with the rebels in an open fight, as they had done many times before. But he had to keep his men on constant alert. Every day and night, an entire regiment remained under arms, ready to muster at a moment's notice. The Regiment von Lossberg had that duty on December 23; Regiment von Knyphausen on December 24, and the Rall regiment on Christmas day and night. The outposts around Trenton were manned every night and heavily reinforced on Christmas day. The entire garrison was called out by special alarms on December 22, December 23, and again on December 25. Every morning, two hours before daylight, a reinforced patrol with two guns was sent out down to the river. On Christmas Eve, Captain Ernst von Altenbockum took a large patrol of 123 men up the Delaware River to Pennington and came under fire from militia in New Jersey and artillery in Pennsylvania.[53]

The pressure on the Hessian troops was relentless. With the constant alarms and many small attacks on patrols and outposts, the garrison was worn to exhaustion. An example was the company of Captain von Altenbockum, an outstanding young officer in the Regiment von Lossberg. His men had been "under arms three successive nights, and then off duty for one night." All three regiments were ordered to sleep in full equipment and had been ordered not to remove their cartridge belts. An officer wrote, "We have not slept one night in peace since we came to this place. The troops have lain on their arms every night and they can endure it no longer." But once again, Grant sent no aid.[54]

The men were about used up, and the officers even more so. The three regiments in Rall's garrison had lost 177 men in combat at White Plains and Fort Washington. Many officers had been wounded: Lieutenant Colonel Francis Scheffer, commander of the Lossberg regiment, Lieutenant Colonel Bretthauer of Rall's regiment, and Major von Dechow of Knyphausen's still were suffering from unhealed wounds. Others were ill in New York and Trenton.[55]

On the day before Christmas, Rall wrote to Donop that the "brigade was extremely fatigued because of the miserable weather and continuous service." The Trenton commander reported that only two officers in his own regiment were fit for duty and that the other regiments were also in bad shape, the Lossberg regiment especially. He warned that his command was "in no condition to defend the post without relief and reinforcements."[56]

Even on Christmas day there was no respite, no celebration, and no heavy drinking by the Hessians in Trenton, as has often been alleged. Rall visited his sentinels and outposts late in the afternoon, returned to his headquarters, and was playing a game of checkers with the American owner of the house, Stacy Potts, early on Christmas evening.

As darkness fell, a sudden spatter of musketry was heard in the distance on the northwest edge of town. Rall ran outside, mounted his horse, and galloped to the sound of the guns. Forty or fifty Americans had attacked an outpost, wounded six men, and vanished into the woods. The outposts were strengthened yet again. One soldier recalled that "100 men were placed all around the town. . . . Rall with two companies and a cannon marched forward through woodland and looked around but could not detect a thing. After Rall returned with his two companies we had to start over again."[57]

The Hessians were not sunk in sloth and idleness on Christmas. All but the sick were on duty that day. The outposts were reinforced, and the Rall regiment was sent out a patrol. Lieutenant Wiederholdt, commanding an outpost northwest of town, posted seven sentries. He wrote, "I sent out patrol after patrol and warned them to be on their guard." The patrols returned without incident, and "the night passed quietly." Later that night Rall was playing cards with the merchant Hunt. Major von Dechow proposed to send away the baggage. "Fiddlesticks!" Rall replied. "These clodhoppers will not attack us, and should they do so, we will simply fall on them and rout them."[58]

In the night, a winter storm hit Trenton. The garrison breathed a sigh of relief. After three days of constant alarms and little sleep, the Hessian duty officers all eased off a little. Major Dechow "issued orders canceling the next morning's predawn patrol because of the heavy storm." On the north side of town, Lieutenant Wiederholdt allowed his men to take shelter in the picket house. At last, in the midst of a howling northeaster, the Hessian garrison relaxed for the first time in eight days. Nobody thought that the enemy could attack in such weather.[59]

THE RIVER

∿ Henry Knox and the Delaware Crossings

> The force of the current, the sharpness of the frost, the darkness of the night, the ice which made during the operation, and a high wind, rendered the passage of the river extremely difficult, but for the stentorian lungs and extraordinary exertions of Colonel Knox.
>
> —Major James Wilkinson, 1816[1]

EARLY ON CHRISTMAS MORNING, the American camps along the Delaware River began to stir. Clouds of white smoke rose from kitchen fires where the women of the army were hard at work, with orders to prepare "three days rations ready cooked." Company officers and sergeants were instructed to see that every man had "arms, accoutrements and ammunition in the best order." Fresh flints were issued for each musket, with plenty of black powder and ball. A few lucky soldiers got the new blankets that had just arrived from Robert Morris and were much wanted on that winter day.[2]

The ground was white with frozen snow. For much of the morning the sun warmed the air a little, but temperatures stayed below freezing. In the shade one felt a damp cutting cold that chilled a man to his bones. At midday, the westerly wind shifted to the northeast, and this army of farmers and fishermen could read the signs of a change in the weather. During the afternoon they could feel it in the wind that was rising in the trees, and they could see it in the high thin clouds that raced across the sky.[3]

At the army's headquarters, there were clouds of another sort. On Christmas morning aide-de-camp Tench Tilghman copied a letter from George Washington to Robert Morris in Philadelphia. Its tone was different from most of the general's correspondence, and expressive of his state of mind. The letter began with thanks for the blankets, but mainly Washington was writing to inform his friend of troubling new intelligence. A message had been intercepted from a "person in the Secrets of the Enemy." It seemed to indicate that British commanders were planning "to cross the Delaware as soon as the Ice is sufficiently strong." Washington warned, "I mention this that you may take the necessary Steps for the Security of such public and private property as ought not to fall into their hands, should they make themselves Masters of Philadelphia."

The mood of the letter was dark but grimly determined. Washington continued as if he were musing to himself, "It is in vain to ruminate upon, or even reflect upon the Authors or Causes of our present Misfortunes. We should rather exert ourselves to look forward with Hopes, that some lucky chance may yet turn up in our Favour." At the end of the page, he dropped his accustomed mask of confidence and added sadly, "I hope the next Christmas will prove happier than the present to you and to Dear Sir Your sincere Friend and humble servant."[4]

About four o'clock in the afternoon an American drum began to beat; then another and another. Up and down the Delaware River, regiments turned out for evening parade. They had done it often before, but this muster was different. John Greenwood remembered that every man in his regiment was ordered to carry a musket, even officers and musicians such as himself. Greenwood was a fifer. He recalled, "I then had a gun, as indeed every officer had." All were given as much ammunition as they could carry. "Every man had sixty rounds of cartridges served out to him," Greenwood wrote. "I put . . . some in my pockets and some in my little cartridge box."[5]

Greenwood wrote that "none but the first officers knew where we were going or what we were going about, for it was a secret expedition." His regiment knew even less than the others, for they had arrived two days ago from the northern frontier. In October, they had been fighting near Montreal. By November they were living in misery at Ticonderoga. Of five hundred men who entered Canada, only one hundred remained. Most had come down with the "flux or camp distemper," and many had died "like rotten sheep." When the regiment marched south to Pennsylvania, Greenwood himself fell ill with the "fever and ague" of malaria. "What I suffered on the march cannot be described," he wrote. "They who were with us know best about these things, others cannot believe the tenth part, so I shall say nothing further."[6]

Now these men were on the road again in Pennsylvania and "knew not the disposition of the army we were then in, nor anything about the country." They did not know where they were going, and some were too miserable to care. Greenwood wrote of his shattered regiment, "I never heard soldiers say anything, nor ever saw them trouble themselves as to where they were or where they were led. It was enough for them to know that wherever the officers commanded they must go, be it through fire and water."[7]

Some of these men were on their last legs, but when they heard the order to march on Christmas day, Greenwood remembered that their spirits rose a little. He observed that "owing to the impossibility of being in a worse condition than their present one, the men always liked to be kept moving in the expectation of bettering themselves." Even after everything that had happened to them, they continued to be optimistic fatalists who believed that any change was for the best.[8]

Late in the afternoon, they began to move out of their camps in an operation that had been planned in meticulous detail. The infantry were ordered to march in compact columns "eight men abreast," so they would stay together on the road. General Washington ordered "a profound silence to be enjoined, and no man to quit his Ranks on pain of Death." Officers who had to carry out those orders softened them a little. Mercer repeated them as "no man is to quit his Ranks on pain of instant punishment."[9]

The officers were under orders to remain "fixed in their divisions" and to "have a white paper in their hats to be distinguished by," a custom that endured in the United States Army from the banks of the Delaware to the coast of Normandy, where officers and noncoms had white stripes painted on the backs of their helmets. It was a sign for the men to follow their leaders, and a signal to the officers that they were to lead from the front.[10]

Washington and his staff had planned the operation in great detail. He meant to cross the Delaware River on Christmas night and attack Trenton a little before dawn, with all the strength in his command. Field commanders were ordered to lead their men across the river in four separate movements, all at the same time.[11]

Washington himself and his veteran Continental regiments (about 2,400 men) were to cross at McConkey's and Johnson's ferries, about ten miles upstream from Trenton, and would attack the town from the north and west. A smaller force, James Ewing's brigade of eight hundred militia from rural Pennsylvania, were to cross the river at Trenton Ferry, just south of Trenton Falls very near the town. Their mission was to seize and hold the bridge across Assunpink Creek and block the only exit from the town to the southeast.

A third force down the river had another assignment. Colonel John Cadwalader's 1,200 Philadelphia Associators and about six hundred New England Continentals under Colonel Daniel Hitchcock were ordered to embark near Bristol in Pennsylvania and to land at Burlington in New Jersey, about twelve miles below Trenton. Their mission was to draw the attention of Colonel von Donop's brigade of Hessian grenadiers and Colonel Stirling's Highlanders and keep them occupied. Washington wrote to Cadwalader, "If you can do nothing real, at least create as great a diversion as possible."[12]

There was also some hope that Israel Putnam could lead another crossing from Philadelphia and join the South Jersey militia south of Mount Holly. About three hundred men had already gone over the river, but Putnam's crossing was always very doubtful, and remained on the margin of the operation.

No sooner had these forces mustered on Christmas afternoon than Washington's schedule began to come apart. The old army saying that "no battle plan survives contact with the enemy" is only half correct. Most plans do not survive contact with one's friends. Washington's plan miscarried that way during the first hour of the operation. He had wanted the army to march from their separate camps toward three crossing points on the Delaware River and assemble away from the water's edge, out of sight from New Jersey. It was urgently important to his plan that the troops should reach their assembly areas before sunset (about 4:41 P.M. that day), so that they could move to the river at nightfall and cross as soon as the sky was dark enough to hide their movements.[13]

Time was vital to the success of the operation. Washington reckoned that his Continental troops at the upstream crossing had to march about ten miles in New Jersey from McConkey's Ferry to Trenton. To achieve surprise, he wanted to attack the town before dawn, at five o'clock in the morning. The plan would work only if the army began to cross the Delaware just after dark and assembled in New Jersey ready to march no later than midnight, a very tight schedule. To that end, he ordered the army to parade in Pennsylvania "precisely at four in the afternoon."[14]

The schedule failed even before the march began. John Greenwood recalled that his regiment did not leave camp until after four o'clock, about half an hour before sunset. They were in Newtown, Pennsylvania, five miles from McConkey's Ferry. Many were ill, and more than a few were without shoes. Major James Wilkinson followed their trail from Newtown to the river and remembered that the "route was easily traced, as there was a little snow on the ground, which was tinged here and there with blood from the feet of the men who wore broken shoes." The men were burdened with packs, blankets, weapons, three days' provisions, and sixty rounds of ammunition. They also had artillery with them and did not reach the assembly area until well after dark, about six o'clock or later. Even so, Greenwood's regiment were among "the first who crossed."[15]

The same delays happened up and down the river. Chaplain David Avery's regiment got to the northern assembly area two hours after dark. Ewing's and Cadwalader's troops downstream were late as well. The men put down their equipment and rested their weary feet, while officers grew frantic with worry. Even before they reached the west bank of the river, they were more than two hours late. Washington was deeply concerned. Two hours' delay meant an attack in daylight, which made tactical surprise very doubtful and put the entire mission at risk.[16]

As if that were not trouble enough, a travel-stained officer rode up to George Washington just as he was leaving his quarters for the river and handed him a dispatch. The courier was Major James Wilkinson, who had ridden all day on treacherous roads from Philadelphia. Wilkinson remembered the moment when he reached the commander-in-chief. "I found him alone with his whip in his hand, prepared to mount his horse," he recalled. The major delivered a sealed letter, and the general was not happy to receive it. "What a time is this to hand me letters!" he said. Wilkinson apologized and explained that he was acting on orders from General Gates.

"General Gates!" Washington said. "Where is he?"

"I left him this morning in Philadelphia," Wilkinson replied.

"What was he doing there?"

"I understood him that he was on his way to Congress."

"On his way to Congress," the general said, as he opened the letter. The messenger departed hastily. "I made my bow," Wilkinson remembered, and he went quickly toward the river to join the crossing as a volunteer. The young major knew what was in the dispatch, and he preferred the wrath of the enemy to the fury of his commander-in-chief.

The letter he brought from Horatio Gates has not survived, but Wilkinson remembered that Gates had "appeared much depressed

General Horatio Gates, a portrait from life by Charles Willson Peale (1782). Independence National Historical Park, Philadelphia.

in mind, and frequently expressed an opinion that while General Washington was watching the enemy above Trenton, they would privately construct batteaux, pass the Delaware in his rear and take possession of Philadelphia." Wilkinson also heard Gates say that "General Washington ought to retire to the South of the Susquehanna, and there form an army; he said it was his intention to propose the measure to Congress at Baltimore." He asked Wilkinson to come with him, but the major wisely refused and made his way to George Washington.[17]

In the past several days, Horatio Gates had grown distant from Washington, even to the edge of insubordination. Just before Christmas, Washington had asked him to take a command in the Trenton operation. Gates begged off, pleading illness, and asked permission to go to Philadelphia on account of his health. Washington agreed but urged him to stop at Bristol on his way and help sort out some "uneasiness of command" between Hitchcock's Continentals and Cadwalader's militia there. Gates refused again, openly defying his commander-in-chief. He claimed he was too ill to stop at Bristol, but he was well enough to ride another hundred miles to Baltimore and seek out the president of Congress. Horatio Gates was going over the head of his commander-in-chief, seeking to persuade Congress to overrule Washington's plan of operations, and perhaps hoping to replace him. All this came to a head just at the moment when the army was crossing the Delaware. Washington was thunderstruck, and Wilkinson witnessed a flash of his formidable temper. But the general did not permit himself the luxury of rage against a wayward subordinate. With his iron self-discipline, Washington returned to the task at hand, which was to get his army across the Delaware.[18]

While the Continentals marched to McConkey's Ferry, the weather was changing very rapidly. John Greenwood recalled that when his regiment left their camp in Newtown a little after four o'clock, the sun was low on the horizon but still "shining brightly." As they marched along snowy roads in the gathering darkness, the sky clouded over. A little after sunset, Greenwood wrote, "it began to drizzle or grow wet." By the time they reached the river, the drizzle had become a driving rain. About eleven o'clock, a howling nor'easter hit them with terrific force. Greenwood remembered that "it rained, hailed, snowed and froze." He forgot to mention sleet. The wind rose so high "it blew a perfect hurricane," in his words. All this happened as the army gathered at the river.[19]

While Washington's Continentals were waiting to make the northern crossing at McConkey's and Johnson's ferries, other American forces were trying to get over the river downstream. General James Ewing's troops were set in motion late on Christmas day. Ewing's eight hundred Pennsylvania militia were on the road toward Trenton ferry, where they were to make the central crossing. They too were delayed and ran into the same storm. On the river they met another obstacle: a massive ice jam exactly at their crossing point. The Delaware River was tidal below the falls at Trenton. The floating ice that came downstream was caught by the incoming tide and driven upstream against the falls. Great cakes of ice were trapped between the rocks and the tide and compressed into a jumbled mass of frozen chaos. An expert on the river, New Jersey state geologist Kemble Widmer, writes from long experience that "it takes only four hours to pile ice five feet deep for nearly half a mile down the river [from Trenton falls], and across its entire width except for three or four narrow channels of rushing water twenty or thirty feet wide. There is no conceivable way for anyone to cross such an ice jam."[20] On Christmas night in 1776, Ewing's men could not move through the ice below Trenton Falls in their boats or walk over it on foot. They were unable to get across the river. Nobody could have done it that night, until the river cleared with a change in the weather or a shift in the tides.[21]

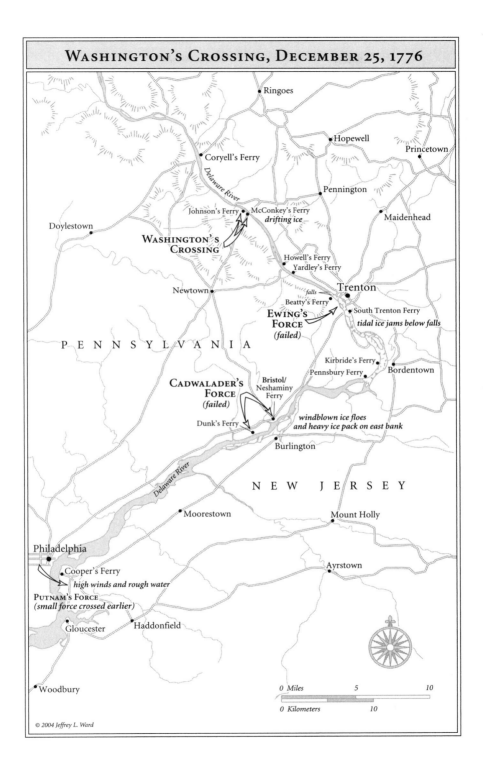

WASHINGTON'S CROSSING, DECEMBER 25, 1776

Ringoes

Hopewell

Princetown

Coryell's Ferry

Delaware River

Pennington

Johnson's Ferry • McConkey's Ferry
drifting ice

Maidenhead

WASHINGTON'S CROSSING

Doylestown

Howell's Ferry
Yardley's Ferry

Newtown

falls
Beatty's Ferry

Trenton

South Trenton Ferry

EWING'S FORCE *(failed)*

tidal ice jams below falls

P E N N S Y L V A N I A

Kirbride's Ferry
Pennsbury Ferry

Bordentown

CADWALADER'S FORCE *(failed)*

Bristol/
Neshaminy
Ferry

Dunk's Ferry

*windblown ice floes
and heavy ice pack on east bank*

Burlington

N E W   J E R S E Y

Moorestown

Mount Holly

Philadelphia

Cooper's Ferry

Ayrstown

high winds and rough water

PUTNAM'S FORCE
(small force crossed earlier)

Gloucester   Haddonfield

Delaware River

Woodbury

| 0 Miles | 5 | 10 |

| 0 Kilometers | 10 |

© 2004 Jeffrey L. Ward

Farther downstream, Cadwalader's Pennsylvania Associators and Hitchcock's New England Continentals met another problem. At their crossing point by Neshaminy Ferry, the great river was nearly a quarter mile wide, and the water was turbulent. The northeast wind kicked up a nasty chop directly in their faces. The river was swollen with rain, snow, and ice, and the currents were swift and strong. Captain Thomas Rodney and his company of Delaware light infantry had a rough time. He recalled, "The River was also very full of floating ice, and the wind was blowing very hard, and the night was very dark and cold, and we had great difficulty in crossing." Conditions were so bad that Colonel Cadwalader called off the crossing at Neshaminy Ferry and ordered his men to march six miles downstream to Dunk's Ferry.[22]

At eleven o'clock they began to move across the river with more success, but as the boats approached the Jersey shore they ran into yet another obstacle. The river made a ninety-degree turn to the west below Bordentown, then turned south and west again. The current and the tides drove the drift ice hard against the east bank of the river and created another jam. It was not as dense as that below the Trenton Falls, but the ice was so thick along the Jersey side of the river that boats could not reach land. Thomas Rodney remembered that "when we reached the Jersey shore we were obliged to land on the ice, 150 yards from the shore." His light infantry struggled across the ice on foot. Rodney reckoned that "about 600 of the light troops got over, but the boats with the artillery were carried away in the ice and could not be got over."[23]

The men made many attempts to break through the ice. Some succeeded in the First and Third battalions of the Philadelphia Associators. But as Charles Willson Peale's infantry in the Second Battalion tried to follow, they were defeated by the ice and the rising storm. Peale wrote, "When the 1st and 3rd were nearly landed on the other side the wind began to blow, and the ice gathering so thick at a considerable distance from the shore there was no possibility of landing, and they were ordered back."[24]

The men who had got ashore in New Jersey watched as things fell apart. Rodney remembered, "After waiting about three hours we were informed that Generals Cadwalader and Hitchcock had given up the expedition, and that the troops that were over were ordered back. This greatly irritated the troops that had crossed the River, and they proposed making the attack without both the Generals and the Artillery but it was urged, that if General Washington should be unsuccessful and we also, the cause would be lost, but if our force remained intact it would still keep up the spirit of America; therefore this course was abandoned."

The rank and file of the Associators made their own decision to return, but as the storm increased they found it as difficult to go back as it was to move forward. "We had to wait about three hours more to cover the retreat," Rodney wrote, "by which time the wind blew very hard and there was much rain and sleet, and there was so much floating ice in the River that we had the greatest difficulty to get over again, and some of our men did not get over that night. As soon as I reached the Pennsylvania shore I received orders to march to our quarters, where I arrived a little before daylight very cold and wet."[25]

On the Pennsylvania shore, Joseph Reed observed that the troops returned "with great reluctance. . . . By this time the ice began to drive with such force and in such quantities as threatened many boats with absolute destruction. To add to the difficulty, about daybreak there came the most violent storm of rain, hail, and snow intermixed in which the troops marched back to Bristol except a part of the Light Infantry which remained till next day."[26]

By midnight, the entire operation was on the verge of disaster. Of Washington's three forces, two were defeated by ice on the river. Only the northern force remained at McConkey's Ferry. But there, at the water's edge, one important part of the plan went right. "The boats were in readiness," Major Wilkinson remembered. A large flotilla of small river craft was waiting when the men arrived. The Jersey militia of Hunterdon County had done their work well. Parties led by

Durham Boats were widely used to carry bulk cargo on the Delaware River. In Washington's crossing they were used to move infantry across the river. Washington Crossing Historic Park, Washington Crossing, Pennsylvania.

Continental General William Maxwell and Captains Daniel Bray, Jacob Gearhart, and Thomas Jones had collected many boats from the upper Delaware and Lehigh rivers. Bray's men alone had rounded up twenty-five vessels of various shapes and sizes.[27]

Specially prized were the big Durham boats, sturdy freight boats built to carry heavy cargoes for the Durham Iron Works, after which they were named. They were used along the upper Delaware River for iron, grain, wood, and whiskey. William Stryker remembered them from his youth, big double-ended boats painted black with bright yellow trim. From a distance he thought that they looked "like large canoes." Some were thirty or forty feet long, and others as large as sixty feet. They were sharp-built fore and aft, flat bottomed and high sided, with a broad beam of eight feet and a shallow draft of only twenty-four or thirty inches. A crew of four or five steered them downstream with oars and long eighteen-foot sweeps, and pushed them upstream with long "setting poles." Some boats carried one or two collapsible masts and sails, which were useless in the storm that night. In all conditions the Durham boats were very stable on the river, and their shallow draft was well suited to the army's amphibious needs. After dark they were brought out of their hiding places behind Malta Island and were steered south through the ice to the landings at McConkey's Ferry and Johnson's Ferry, side by side on the river.[28]

Other boats were also pressed into service, probably any vessel that could float. One New England soldier who grew up near the water remembered crossing in a "flat bottomed scow," which does not sound like a Durham boat. It might have been one of the ferry boats, which were in some ways more useful to the army than the Durham boats. The big Delaware ferries were built to carry horses, wagons, and even the fabulous "Flying Machine," a coach that before the Revolution was traveling between Philadelphia and New York in a single day at the amazing speed of eight or even nine miles an hour, with a change of horses in Princeton. The ferries were best for the army's horses, artillery, and ammunition wagons. The Durham boats with their high sides and sharp ends were excellent for infantry.

Most of the men crossed the Delaware standing up. Big river ferries and freight boats had few seats or none at all. On a wet winter night, anyone who sat in the bottom of a Durham boat or ferry would have been sitting in ice water. There are accounts of other Delaware crossings in 1776 in which the men were ordered to jump up and down in several inches of watery slush to clear the ice from the boats and to keep from freezing. The legions of American debunkers who have made a mockery of George Washington for "standing up in the boat" might try sitting down in such conditions.

To manage the boats, the army recruited three groups of watermen. Most prominent were the men of Colonel John Glover's Marblehead regiment, salty seamen and fishermen from the North Shore of New England. They were highly visible in their short blue seamen's jackets, woolen caps, tarred trousers, and worsted stockings, now ragged and worn from heavy service. These were the same men who helped to rescue the American army from Long Island and fought in the campaigns around New York. Once again they were doing double duty as boatmen and infantry.[29]

Other mariners came to the army from the Philadelphia waterfront: seamen, longshoremen, block-makers, riggers, and ships' carpenters. Among them were eighty-two young men and boys, recruited by Captain Joseph Moulder for his battery of artillery. A third group were ferrymen and boatmen from New Jersey and Pennsylvania, who knew the river and could navigate it in the dark.[30]

The crossing was a challenge to all their skill that night. The river near Trenton was described in late December 1776 as "extremely rapid here and in general about two ells [90 inches] deep." At McConkey's Ferry, the width of the stream was about eight hundred feet, and the water was high and swift. Ice had formed on the river and had broken apart into floating cakes and floes. The current had

Colonel John Glover, an engraving by H. B. Hall, after a pencil drawing by John Trumbull. Glover's Marblehead men helped to ferry the American army across the Delaware, as also did New Jersey ferrymen, and Philadelphia seamen and longshoremen. Picture Collection, The New York Public Library, Astor, Lenox and Tilden Foundations.

jammed large pieces along the banks in thick jagged rows. The main stream was full of flat cakes of flow-ice, which came down the Delaware at surprising speed, spinning and turning in the whirls and eddies of the river. The temperature was falling; and more ice was forming in the river and even on the boats. Much use was probably made of setting poles that night.

Another problem was the darkness of the night. A bright moon had risen after sunset but was obscured by the storm. Visibility grew so poor that boatmen could barely see the opposite shore. Wilkinson recalled that "the force of the current, the sharpness of the frost, the darkness of the night, the ice which made during the operation, and a high wind, rendered the passage of the river extremely difficult." Washington thought that the "greatest fatigue" was "in breaking a passage through the ice" along the shore." Henry Knox believed that the worst of it was "floating ice in the river," which "made the labor almost incredible."[31]

Washington had given command of the crossing to Knox. He was a big, heavy man, taller than Washington and weighing in at nearly three hundred pounds. Many men remembered his "deep bass voice," which they could hear above the roar of the nor'easter. Several commanders of the army believed that the crossing would have failed "but for the stentorian lungs of Colonel Knox."[32]

Colonel Henry Knox was put in command of the Delaware crossing on Christmas night. From a lost painting, reproduced in Douglas Southall Freeman, *George Washington*, iv, 131f.

His hardest task was to deal with the frightened horses and eighteen pieces of artillery. The Durham boats would have been useless for that purpose. Only a few big ferries could carry them, which caused further delays in the crossing. In the end it was done "with almost infinite difficulty," in Knox's words. He wrote to his wife that "perseverance accomplished what at first seemed impossible."[33]

Another challenge was to get the infantry safely across the river. The great majority of the army, like other populations in eighteenth-century America and Europe, were unable to swim a stroke. Soldiers joked that they did not fear to drown, for they were born to hang. Even seamen did not learn to swim, much to the disgust of Benjamin Franklin, who was a great swimmer himself and tried in vain to teach his American generation to take to the water. There was a strange fatalism about those attitudes in the eighteenth century.

In the course of the crossing, some of the men tumbled into the icy water. One of them was Delaware's Colonel John Haslet. He was fished out in the nick of time, suffering much from exposure. This unconquerable man marched ten miles on severely swollen legs and fought a battle without complaint. In the end, not a man was lost to the river, but the guardian angels of the army were working overtime. Every artillery piece also arrived in good order on the Jersey shore, much to the relief of Henry Knox.

Not so happy was the commander-in-chief. According to tradition, Washington crossed the river with Glover's Marblehead mariners, in a boat commanded by Captain William Blackler, with Private John Russell at an oar.[34] On the Jersey shore Washington wrapped himself in his cloak, sat down on a wooden box that had once been a beehive, and brooded over the ruin of his plan. The operation was now three hours behind schedule. Later he wrote that the delay "made me despair of surprising the Town, as I well knew we could not reach it before the day was fairly broke." Sitting on his beehive, he watched his men struggling against the storm and ice and wondered if he should call it off. But desperate as the mission had become, he decided that it might be more difficult to abandon it. Washington wrote, "As I was certain there was no making a Retreat without being discovered, and harassed on repassing the River, I determined to push on at all Events."[35]

While Washington watched gloomily, the rest of the army got ashore. The men were shaking with cold and wet to the skin but in remarkably good spirits. Greenwood remembered that "we had to wait for the rest, and so began to pull down the fences and make fires to warm ourselves, for the storm was increasing rapidly." He added many years later, "I perfectly recollect, after putting the rails on to burn, the wind and the fire would cut them in two in a moment, and when I turned my face toward the fire my back would be freezing. . . . By turning round and round I kept myself from perishing before the large bonfire."[36] In those miserable circumstances, John Greenwood was struck by a feeling of elation that the men shared. He wrote, "The noise of the soldiers coming over and clearing away the ice, the rattling of the cannon wheels on the frozen ground, and the cheerfulness of my fellow-comrades encouraged me beyond expression, and, big coward as I acknowledge myself to be, I felt great pleasure, more than I now do in writing about it."[37]

The assembly of the army on the Jersey shore went slowly but without a major hitch. Washington's first concern was to protect the secrecy of the operation. He ordered Adam Stephen's Virginia brigade to move quickly inland and "form a chain of sentries round the landing place at a sufficient distance from the river to permit troops to form." They were told "not to suffer any person to go in or come out—but to detain all persons who attempts either."[38] Washington selected a secret password and wrote it himself on small slips for all the units in the army. Benjamin Rush visited him the night before the crossing and wrote, "While I was talking to him, I observed him to play with his pen and ink upon several small pieces of paper. One of them by accident fell upon the floor near my feet. I was struck with the inscription upon it. It was 'Victory or Death.'"[39]

THE MARCH

~ The Ordeal at Jacob's Creek

> Press on, Press on, boys!
> —George Washington, December 26, 1776 [1]

BEHIND A SCREEN of sentries on the Jersey shore, the Continental army began to form in line of march. Every commander received written orders before the crossing and knew his place in the long column. Leading the army were two small detachments of infantry, each of about forty men. Their instructions were to operate independently ahead of the main columns, to set roadblocks three miles outside Trenton, and to "make prisoners of all going in or coming out of town."

One of these advance parties was to move on the inland roads that led into Trenton from the north. It was led by Captain William Washington of the Third Virginia Regiment, a distant cousin of the commander-in-chief. When the war began he was a student of divinity. He was a big man of "great personal strength," with a jolly round face and the easy manners of a Chesapeake gentleman. His portrait has a different air from others of the same period: he was one of the few Revolutionary leaders who was painted with the hint of a smile on his face.

Captain Washington had been severely wounded in the battle of Long Island. His injuries were not healed, but he returned to his unit as a company commander in Adam Stephen's brigade. With him was Lieutenant James Monroe, who only a year ago had been a sophomore at the College of William and Mary. He served with distinction

William Washington, a portrait by
Charles Willson Peale (1781–82).
A cousin of the general, Captain
Washington commanded the
American vanguard in Greene's
division on the march to
Trenton. Independence National
Historical Park.

in the battles of Harlem Heights and White Plains and was a combat veteran at the age of eighteen.[2]

The other advance party went forward on a different route, with orders to block the lower River Road that ran beside the Delaware River to Trenton. The leader was Captain John Flahaven of the First New Jersey Continentals. Flahaven had already won a reputation as a "gallant and ambitious officer" who led his men aggressively from the front. With him were forty Jerseymen who were described as green "recruits," but they knew the terrain and were fighting on their own turf.[3]

Behind the independent companies came the infantry regiments of Adam Stephen's Virginia brigade. George Washington often put his Virginians on the sharp edge. Their instructions were to attack Hessian guards and sentries on the outskirts of Trenton, seize strong points and alarm posts, and storm any house where resistance was offered.[4]

After Stephen's brigade came the main body of the army in two divisions. They were ordered to march together in one column from the ferry landings, then to divide and enter Trenton by different roads. The right wing of the army was John Sullivan's First Division, mostly New England men in the brigades of Glover, Sargent, and St. Clair. They were to advance along the River Road and enter Trenton from the southwest.[5] The left wing was Nathanael Greene's Second Division. It included the brigades of Stephen, Mercer, and

Stirling. Their orders were to move inland and approach the town from the northwest, away from the river. One of their brigades was to advance to the Princeton road that entered Trenton from the northeast. They were to block that road and encircle the town.[6]

A vital element was artillery, which American leaders planned to deploy on a lavish scale. The standard practice in European armies during the eighteenth century was to use two or three "battalion guns" for every thousand infantry. The Americans advanced on Trenton with seven or eight guns for every thousand muskets, a very large proportion.[7] Altogether, Henry Knox brought eighteen guns across the river, and with his usual audacity, he intended to add even more guns by taking them from the enemy. On his orders the leading American units included a "detachment of the artillery without cannon." These men went into battle armed with drag ropes, handspikes, and hammers. Their orders were to seize the Hessian cannon at the start of the battle and turn them against the enemy. If that plan failed, their job was to disable the Hessian guns by driving iron handspikes into the touch holes and breaking them flush with the gun tube. This method of "spiking," if carefully done, prevented guns from being fired until a skilled metalworker could drill out the touch holes, a laborious operation.[8]

The American leaders intended to use their guns as shock weapons against the enemy and as supporting arms for their own infantry. The battles around Boston and New York had taught them that artillery was highly effective in both roles. It could break a formation of

Lieutenant James Monroe, a miniature by Louis Sene, Paris (1796). The future fifth President of the United States, Monroe was Captain William Washington's second in command. James Monroe Museum and Memorial Library, Fredericksburg, Virginia.

highly trained British and German Regulars, and it could also steady an amateur army of citizen soldiers and give them a fighting chance against disciplined troops.

With those purposes in mind, American commanders distributed their guns for maximum effect. The general orders for the campaign were highly specific. In the order of march, artillery was placed at the head of each infantry brigade. The leading brigades in each division were given four guns; supporting brigades, three guns; and reserve brigades, two.[9]

The field guns used in the Trenton campaign were drawn by artillery horses with civilian teamsters. Some guns had limbers, which were usually an extra set of wheels to which the heavy trails of the guns were secured. Other batteries hitched the trails directly to the horses that pulled them. The guns were meant to move quickly on the battlefield. For maximum effect, gunners were trained to seize every opportunity to fire along a rank or down a column. This was called *enfilade* firing. When it was done skillfully, a single iron cannon ball three inches in diameter could do terrible execution. There was a case on record of one shot hitting forty-two men.

Many armies in the eighteenth century had been trying to make their field artillery more mobile. The American army put this new

Artillery Piece with Side Boxes, sketched by Charles Willson Peale (1776). American Philosophical Society.

technology to work and improved it. Henry Knox encouraged the development of new gun carriages that were lighter and maneuverable, but this gain was made at a price. American gun carriages were fragile, and much plagued by broken axles and shattered wheels.

The abundance of American artillery was an infantryman's delight but a quartermaster's horror. Henry Knox commanded seven independent batteries from five American states. The guns included three-pounders, four-pounders, five-and-a-half pounders, and six-pounders. Ammunition was a persistent problem. Some of it was packed in side boxes on the guns themselves. More was carried in ammunition wagons, which in the American army tended to be small farm carts.[10] By comparison with heavy cannon in forts and ships, Henry Knox's field guns were very light, but for the men who had to manhandle them in boats and move them on icy and rutted roads, they were heavy and clumsy. A six-pounder weighed as much as 1,750 pounds for the barrel and carriage alone, and more than a ton with side boxes of ammunition and trail boxes for equipment. In the field the guns were a great strength, but on the march they were a major impediment for a mobile army. On Christmas night in 1776, the artillery caused many delays that put the operation behind schedule. Some accounts of the Delaware crossing reported that the infantry was across the river by two o'clock in the morning, but Washington wrote that "it was three o'clock before the Artillery could all be got over."[11]

In the end it was nearly four o'clock in the morning when the American army began to march. The mission was now four hours behind schedule. The road surfaces were so bad that the men walked in long files on the shoulders. The entire column, with horses, guns, and wagons, stretched more than a mile. At its head were mounted men in "plain farmer's habit," local residents who had offered their services as guides. Reports of the crossing spread quickly across the countryside, and many New Jersey men joined the army as volunteers. Among them were David Laning, John Guild, and John Muirhead, who lived nearby and knew the terrain.[12]

The guides led the army away from the river, on a road that climbed upward through a dark wood, similar to a sweep of woodland that stands there today. They were heading northeast straight into the teeth of the storm, which was still increasing. The weather was remembered as more violent on the march than it had been during the crossing. Some of the men had managed to dry themselves a little by fires near the river. Now they were soaked again from head to foot by heavy rain, thick squalls of snow, and the sharp sting of sleet that blew directly in their faces. But they were happy to be moving. "Finally our march began," Elisha Bostwick wrote. He remembered moving silently through a "constant fall of snow" in the forest, and "the torches of our field pieces Stuck in the Exhalters Sparkled and blazed in the Storm all night."[13]

The column advanced slowly on a track that meandered through the dark woods. John Greenwood remembered that "we began an apparently circuitous march, not advancing faster than a child ten years old could walk, and stopping frequently, though for what purpose I know not." To walk their route today is to discover the reason why. The track was (and is) rough and winding, as it climbs upward from the river to an elevation of about two hundred feet. Parts of the route were steep and icy. The track was bad enough for infantry in the dark. It was worse for artillery and horses that had not been roughshod for the winter.[14]

The army marched about a mile and half on that road and came to a crossroads at the Bear Tavern. Here the guides turned right ninety degrees into the Bear Tavern Road, which ran across a high flat tract of tableland, directly toward Trenton. Now they were moving southeast, and the storm was no longer blowing in their faces. The marching became easier for the men and it was better for the guns too. For a mile beyond Bear Tavern the surface of the road was remembered as "sleety" and "slippery," but the terrain was straight and level. The army began to make better time.[15]

Bear Tavern in a nineteenth-century photograph. William S. Stryker (1898), *Battles of Trenton and Princeton*, 142.

Then they came to a big stream called Jacob's Creek. Its tumbling waters had cut a deep ravine directly across their path. The road fell away in a steep decline, down the side of the ravine, toward a rocky creek bed a hundred feet below. The water was high and swift that night as it flowed toward the Delaware River. In a storm of snow and sleet and hail, the steep descent was difficult for marching men, and impossible for limbered guns and harnessed horses.[16]

Lieutenant Elisha Bostwick remembered that the column halted, and "our horses were then unharness'd & the artillery prepared." That arduous process, which he summarized in a few words, consumed precious time. The artillery's long drag ropes had to be brought out, and trees used as mooring posts for a mechanical advantage, so that the guns could be lowered slowly to the bottom of the ravine. On the other side of the creek, the guns had to be hauled up again by teams of men who were struggling to keep their own balance. Slowly the column inched its way down the slope to Jacob's Creek and up the other side, only to meet another deep ravine. It was a flooded tributary of Jacob's Creek, smaller but very steep.

George Washington rode up and down the column urging his men forward. Suddenly the general's horse slipped and started to fall on a steep and icy slope. "While passing a Slanting Slippery bank," Lieutenant Bostwick remembered, "his excellency's horse['s] hind feet both slip'd from under him." The animal began to go down. Elisha Bostwick watched in fascination as Washington locked his fingers in the animal's mane and hauled up its heavy head by brute force. He shifted its balance backward just enough to allow the horse to regain its hind footing on the treacherous road. Bostwick wrote that the general "seiz'd his horses Mane and the Horse recovered." It was an extraordinary feat of strength, skill, and timing; and another reason why his soldiers stood in awe of this man.[17]

At last the army passed the deep ravines of Jacob's Creek and came to a high open stretch of road that rose gradually to an elevation of 250 feet. Here the men faced another test. Throughout the march, the nor'easter raged with renewed fury, and the great swirling bands of the cyclonic storm struck them again and again. Greenwood wrote that "during the whole night it alternately hailed, rained, snowed and blew tremendously." From time to time the gale diminished, only to revive in another "violent storm of Rain, Hail and Snow intermixed."[18]

On the open road beyond Jacob's Creek the column was more exposed to the bitter wind, and the distances seemed to stretch interminably. The men were consumed by exposure and exhaustion.

Many were ill, and some could not keep up. The column began to straggle. At least two soldiers fell out and froze to death by the side of the road. Fifer John Greenwood was nearly a third. He wrote, "I recollect very well that at one time, when we halted on the road, I sat down on the stump of a tree and was so benumbed with cold that I wanted to go to sleep. Had I been passed unnoticed I should have frozen to death without knowing it, but as good luck attended me, Sergeant Madden came and, rousing me up, made me walk about. We then began to march again, just in the old slow way."[19]

The army crossed over the high plateau, and the road began to drop away, on a long smooth slope that stretched toward Trenton for the better part of a mile. In a happier time it might have made a perfect downhill run for the eighteenth-century sport of coasting, but on this stormy night it was another trial for the artillery. The drag ropes must have come out again, and the men hauled back on them to keep the guns from running away down the long icy hill, and crushing the horses in their traces. The only brakes on the gun carriages were the straining muscles of weary men who struggled to restrain them.[20]

At the bottom of the hill the head of the column came to a hamlet called Birmingham (now West Trenton). It was a little crossroads settlement at the intersection of a road that led to Howell's Ferry. Washington looked ahead and was distressed to see the first faint light of dawn in the eastern sky. The time was near six o'clock, and they were only halfway to Trenton. The men were very tired and cold and wet. Bostwick gratefully remembered that "a halt was made at which time his Excellency & Aids came near to front on the Side of the path where the soldiers Stood."

Washington talked with his men. Bostwick recalled, "I heard his Excellency as he was coming on, Speaking to and Encouraging the soldiers. The words he spoke as he pass'd by where I stood & in my hearing were these: 'Soldiers keep by your Officers. For Gods Sake, keep by your officers.' Spoke in a deep & solemn voice." The General paused near the house of Benjamin Moore, and the family brought him food and drink, which he accepted with thanks. There was no time for a dismount. He ate quickly on horseback, as senior officers gathered round him for an improvised Council of War.[21]

As they had planned, Washington ordered the army to divide at Birmingham crossroads. His generals knew their assignments. Nathanael Greene had the hardest task. He was to lead his division left at Birmingham crossroads to the Upper Ferry Road. It ran uphill away from the river to the Scotch Road and the Pennington

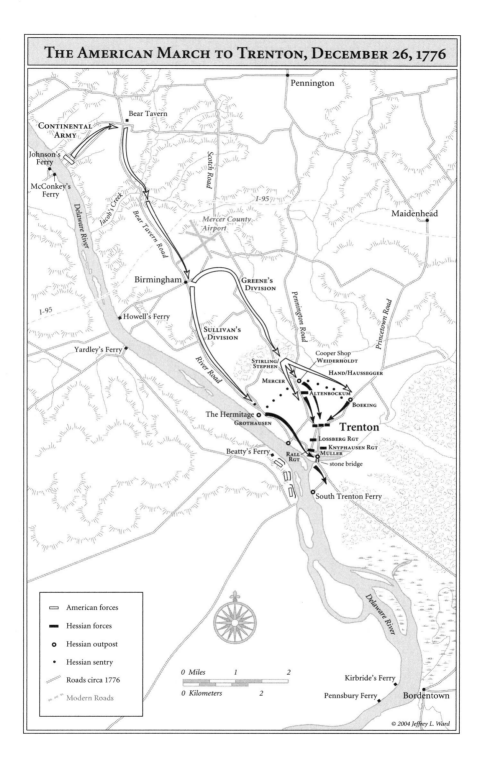

The American March to Trenton, December 26, 1776

Pennington

Bear Tavern

Continental Army

Johnson's Ferry

McConkey's Ferry

Delaware River

Scotch Road

I-95

Maidenhead

Jacob's Creek

Bear Tavern Road

Mercer County Airport

I-95

Birmingham

Greene's Division

Howell's Ferry

Yardley's Ferry

Sullivan's Division

Pennington Road

Princetown Road

River Road

Cooper Shop
Weiderholdt

Stirling/Stephen

Hand/Haussegger

Mercer

Altenbockum

Boeking

The Hermitage
Grothausen

Trenton

Beatty's Ferry

Lossberg Rgt

Rall Rgt

Knyphausen Rgt
Muller

stone bridge

South Trenton Ferry

American forces

Hessian forces

Hessian outpost

Hessian sentry

Roads circa 1776

Modern Roads

0 Miles   1   2

0 Kilometers   2

Delaware River

Kirbride's Ferry

Pennsbury Ferry

Bordentown

© 2004 Jeffrey L. Ward

Road, which would bring Greene's division into Trenton on its northern side. The other division of the army under Sullivan had orders to continue on the River Road and "enter the town by Water Street." Greene's roundabout uphill route was the longer and slower of the two. He was ordered to start first and move quickly. Washington rode with him, to help spur the men forward. As Sullivan had the shorter distance and a downhill road, he was told to "halt for a few minutes at the cross road which leads to Howell's Ferry," so that both divisions would reach Trenton at the same time.

Time was the critical factor. Captain William Hull of the Seventh Connecticut Regiment remembered that "the General gave orders that every officer's watch should be set by his, and the moment of the attack fixed." They tugged out their large pocket watches and matched them to the timepiece of the general, in one of the first recorded instances of synchronized watches in a military campaign.[22]

They hoped that the Pennsylvania and New Jersey militia would be crossing the Delaware River south of Trenton and approaching the town from the south and east. But of these other columns they heard nothing. Just in case, the lead brigade of Sullivan's division was ordered to move quickly across the town near the river and seize the roads from the east. On reaching the town, both divisions had the same instructions, which were to drive forward and attack with great speed and force. Washington wrote, "I ordered each of them, immediately upon forcing the out Guards, to push directly into the Town, that they might charge the Enemy before they had time to form."[23]

During the halt at Birmingham, the men of Glover's Marblehead regiment checked their weapons and discovered that even the "best secured arms" were "wet and not in firing condition." Others reported that "snow and sleet melted into the cartridge boxes," and the powder was wet as well. The news passed up the chain of command to the general officers, who had gathered on horseback during the halt.

"What is to be done?" John Sullivan asked.

"You have nothing for it but to push on and charge," Arthur St. Clair replied.

"Advance and charge," said George Washington.[24]

Within a few minutes, Greene's division marched off to the left, with Washington in the van, and Sullivan prepared his men to move forward. Ahead of the army, the American advance parties were already in place. They had been busy that night putting up roadblocks around Trenton, "cutting off all communication" between the town and the countryside to the west and north. Captain Flahaven and his Jersey recruits attended to the River Road and the Scotch Road. Captain William Washington and Lieutenant James Monroe led their Virginians to the Pennington Road and the highway between Trenton and Princeton. Monroe remembered that "Captain Washington executed his orders faithfully. He soon took possession of the point to which he was ordered, and holding it through the night, intercepted and made prisoners of many who were passing in directions to and from Trenton."[25]

Monroe's account of "the many who were passing" suggests a surprising flow of traffic on country roads in the small hours of a stormy night. It had been the same in Massachusetts on the night of Paul Revere's Ride. Both marching troops and midnight messengers found many people abroad on errands that could not wait on time or the weather. Farmers and woodcutters were delivering food and firewood to town. Young men were out courting. Midwives were delivering babies. Ministers were comforting their flocks, and in that distant era physicians were making house calls. All were rounded up by the Virginia infantry, as neither side could distinguish friend from foe in this American civil war.[26]

Lieutenant Monroe met a Jerseyman who came out to see why his dogs were barking. Monroe remembered that the man thought "we were from the British army, and ordered us off. . . . He was violent and determined in his manner, and very profane." Monroe told him to go back to his home or be taken prisoner. When the man realized that he was talking to American troops, his manner suddenly changed. He brought them food and offered to join them. "I'm a doctor," he explained, "and I may be of help to some poor fellow." The offer was accepted, and Doctor John Riker joined Monroe's infantry as a surgeon-volunteer.[27]

At about 7:30 A.M., a little after sunrise, the main columns of the army came up with their advanced parties, about two or three miles from Trenton. On the Scotch Road, Washington rode along the line of march, urging the men to pick up the pace: "Press on, Press on, boys!" he shouted to them.[28]

Then came a cry from the head of the column. A group of fifty armed men was spotted, approaching from the direction of Trenton. Washington hurried forward and discovered to his amazement that they were men from his own army. They were a party of Virginians from Adam Stephen's Fourth Regiment, led by Captain George

Wallis. They were not in any advanced party, and Washington asked why they were there. Wallis had a strange tale to tell.

A few days earlier, Hessian Jägers had killed one of Adam Stephen's men in a boat on the river. On Christmas Eve, before the army was informed of the Trenton mission, Adam Stephen acted on his own initiative and sent a raiding party across the Delaware River to "take revenge." Captain Wallis got the job. At twilight on Christmas day, while most of Washington's army was mustering in Pennsylvania, Wallis and his company went over the river into New Jersey, on a private mission unknown to their commander-in-chief. When darkness began to fall on Christmas night, they attacked a Hessian outpost at Trenton. The American raiders thought they killed four German soldiers and wounded eleven. The Hessians recorded none killed and four or six or eight men wounded. The alarm was sounded in Trenton, and the entire Hessian garrison, led by Colonel Rall, turned out very quickly to hunt down the attackers. A party of mounted men gave chase, but the Americans got away in the darkness, and the Hessians returned to their garrison. The raiders remained on the outskirts of the town and the next morning met the oncoming American army.

George Washington listened to the story of Captain Wallis with growing dismay. He was convinced that all his attempts to achieve surprise and secrecy had been wrecked by one of his own officers. He summoned Adam Stephen from the column and asked if it was so. Stephen confirmed the truth of it. The general grew very angry. "You, Sir!" he raged. "You, Sir, may have ruined all my plans by having put them on their guard." Others remembered that they had never seen Washington in such a fury. The more he thought about what Stephen had done, the more infuriated he became. Once again, the indiscipline of the American army and even of its high officers threatened his entire operation.

Washington may have wondered if it had been done deliberately. In western Virginia, Adam Stephen had been a thorn in Washington's flesh for years. Stephen was a brutal, ruthless, and highly successful entrepreneur on the Virginia frontier, where he had many dealings with Washington. He had been Washington's second-in-command during the French and Indian War, gained a reputation for drinking, whoring, and insubordination, and was severely reprimanded. He entered politics, ran against Washington for the House of Burgesses, and lost. Stephen thought of Washington as his rival, despised him as a "weak man," and always came off second best in war and politics and land speculation.

In December, Adam Stephen was ordered to take his brigade north from Virginia and join the Continental army on the Delaware, under Washington's command. Neither man was happy with that arrangement, but it was forced upon them by circumstances that they could not control. Then, on the day before Washington was about to mount the Trenton operation, Adam Stephen decided to start his own private war against the Hessians and sent his own small expedition across the Delaware to seek vengeance for the death of a soldier.

Stephen appears to have been absorbed in the old border and backcountry custom of *lex talionis,* the rule of retaliation. He was also true to the border tradition of acting quickly without consulting higher authority. In the realm of *lex talionis* there was a higher law of retribution, which took precedence over other obligations. For Stephen this was an act of blood revenge against the Hessians. But one wonders if he might have been taking another revenge against his commander-in-chief, who had inflicted many humiliations on him through the years.

These thoughts may have deepened Washington's fury. Witnesses remembered that it was a mighty thing to behold. But in a moment, Washington mastered his anger. He calmed himself by turning away from Adam Stephen and talking to the bewildered men in Captain Wallis's company. He spoke kindly to them and personally invited these proud Virginia soldiers to join his column. He would settle with Adam Stephen in good time, but now he had a battle to fight. All of these unexpected obstacles that Washington met on the road to Trenton had the same effect on him. They deepened his determination to see the operation through.[29]

THE SURPRISE

∾ The Agony of Colonel Rall

> Here succeeded a scene of war, which I had often
> conceived, but never saw before. The hurry, fright,
> and confusion of the enemy was [not] unlike that
> which will be when the last trump shall sound.
>
> —Colonel Henry Knox, December 28, 1776[1]

THE AMERICAN COLUMNS were now about two miles from Trenton, and the time was about 7:30 in the morning. George Washington urged his men forward, hoping to salvage something from his ruined plan. They had already passed the hour of sunrise, which was 7:20 local time, but no sun was in sight that day. The nor'easter was raging more violently than ever, and the clouds were very thick. One American remembered that the weather was "dark and stormy so that we could not see very far ahead." Sleet and snow were falling heavily again, with intervals of heavy rain. The men struggled to keep their flints and powder dry. Some wrapped their weapons in the blankets that Robert Morris had brought them.[2]

As the Americans moved closer to the town, scouts came up to Washington and reported the location of Hessian outposts. The German commanders had established a ring of forward positions about a mile outside the center of Trenton. One large outpost (in company strength) was on the River Road to the west. Another with twenty-four men was near the intersection of the Scotch Road and the Pennington Road to the northwest. A third guarded the Princeton Road to the northeast, and others protected the bridge over Assunpink Creek south of the town, and the ferry landing. Many "night sentries" were posted in between, five or seven from each outpost. At first light they were replaced by "day pickets."

Colonel Rall had been thorough in his precautions. German outguards covered every major approach by land into Trenton, and other men were in place along the Delaware river. Behind the outposts were duty companies that could offer support. In the center of town, one Hessian regiment was always on alert in "alarm houses," and the others were ready to muster quickly.[3]

George Washington was well informed about the German dispositions in Trenton. His tactical intelligence was excellent this day. After hearing from his scouts, Washington halted the American left wing on the Pennington Road, behind a screen of woods. They were about eight hundred yards from the Hessian guardhouse, a small wood-frame cooper shop that belonged to Richard and Arthur Howell, a mile from the town center. Senior American officers deployed their brigades in three attacking columns: Mercer's New Englanders and Maryland men on the right; Stephen's Virginians with Stirling's Delaware men in the center; and Fermoy's Pennsylvanians on the American left. The vanguard were Virginia infantry, led by Captain William Washington and Lieutenant James Monroe.[4]

On command the three columns started forward in a thick flurry of snow. George Washington himself led the attack in the center. As the men emerged from the woods into open fields on both sides of the road, Washington picked up the pace. One soldier remembered that he led them forward at a "long trot" across the fields.[5] Peering ahead through dense clouds of swirling snow, they saw a door open at the cooper shop, and a Hessian emerged. An American raised his weapon, fired at long range, and missed. Other Hessians ran out of the cooper shop, pulling on their coats and equipment. The Americans managed to get off a ragged volley in the storm, then a second and a third. The Hessians formed and fired back.

The time was a little past eight o'clock. Three minutes later, the heavy boom of American artillery was heard from the lower River Road. In the center of the town, German kettledrums suddenly began to beat the urgent call to arms. George Washington could scarcely believe it. Both American wings attacked at nearly the same moment, through a heavy squall of snow that masked their approach. Against all expectation, they had taken the Hessians by surprise.[6]

The Hessian who appeared in the door of the cooper shop on the upper road was Lieutenant Andreas von Wiederholdt. He had been sent to take command of the outpost after the raid on Christmas night. The strength of the outpost was doubled, and Wiederholdt's orders were very clear. With his twenty-four men he was told to put out night sentries beyond the cooper shop to give warning of a surprise attack, to send out a dawn patrol before first light, and to put day pickets in position from sunrise to sunset.

Wiederholdt had followed his instructions, and even exceeded them. Later he wrote that he "sent out seven posts, as well as I could during the night, and sent out one patrol after another to prevent being surprised." His night sentries made a chain that stretched from Wiederholdt's position in the cooper shop to the outguards from the River Road to his left and to the outpost on the Princeton Road to his right. Other outpost commanders did the same thing on that Christmas night.[7]

Then came the storm. Wiederholdt remembered that "the night passed quietly." At first light he recalled his sentries and sent out a dawn patrol. By now the weather was very bad, and the patrol appears not to have ventured far beyond the cooper shop. Wiederholdt remembered that before eight o'clock "my day patrol was already back for a while, reporting that everything was silent and quiet."[8]

After a week of constant alarms, and the American raid on Christmas evening, Wiederholdt's men were very tired. Many had been on sentry duty or patrol through the night, and again at dawn. In the morning, as the storm grew more violent than ever, they relaxed their vigilance a little. Wiederholdt testified that his seven day pickets were all in place, but he complained that they were not very alert, and they saw nothing in the storm. The lieutenant allowed his seventeen men who were not on picket to get warm and dry in the cooper shop, as any good officer would have done.

Inside the building the air must have grown very stale, with so many men who bathed so seldom in so small a space. At about eight o'clock Wiederholdt decided to step outside. He stood for a moment by the door and looked across the frozen fields toward the woods along the Pennington Road. As he peered through the storm, he dimly saw something moving in the distance. Wiederholdt looked again through a white veil of snow and made out the shapes of men coming toward him. He first thought that they were the patrol of Captain Johann Brubach, the inspector of the guard, who made his rounds every morning, checking each outpost and sentry outside the town. Brubach sometimes approached from that direction.

As Wiederholdt studied the distant figures in the storm, they began to multiply. He counted sixty, too many to be Captain Brubach's small party. Then one of the figures stopped and raised a weapon. Wiederholdt saw the muzzle flash, then another, and a third. He turned to his men and shouted, "*Der Feind!* The Enemy!"[9]

The Hessians came running out of the cooper shop, tugging on their equipment. "We were quickly under arms," Wiederholdt remembered, "and we waited to give the enemy a firm challenge, thinking they were merely a roaming party. They fired three volleys at me and my seventeen men, who held their fire. After the third volley I gave the order to fire." They were at extreme range; nobody on either side appears to have been hit in the first exchange.[10]

Wiederholdt began to see the full size of the American attack. This was no raiding party. Hundreds of men were now visible, advancing through the fields on both sides of the road. He was seeing Mercer's brigade southwest of the Pennington Road, Stephen and Stirling in the middle, and Fermoy to the east. Together they threatened a double envelopment of the small Hessian outpost. Wiederholdt later wrote, "We fought with them until we were almost surrounded by several battalions. I therefore retreated, under constant fire."

The American brigades pressed forward. Washington ordered Fermoy's troops to move east across the country to block the Princeton Road. That task went to Edward Hand's veteran regiment of Pennsylvania Riflemen and Haussegger's battalion of German-speaking infantry from Pennsylvania and western Maryland. They responded quickly and attacked the Hessian outguard on the Princeton Road. Wiederholdt looked to the right, and saw the Hessians fall back. His men were doing the same thing.[11]

The two Hessian detachments withdrew in good order toward the town in a fighting retreat. They converged on the high ground at the north end of Trenton where the main streets came together. There a duty company of Lossberg troops under Captain Ernst von Altenbockum came forward to help them. Wiederholdt remembered, "While we had been engaging the enemy this company formed a line in the street in front of the captain's quarters. I took a position on their right wing and together we fired at the enemy. But soon we were forced to retire in the same manner as before so that we would not be cut off from the garrison."[12]

The American infantry were closer now, and some were able to fire their muskets in the storm. Wiederholdt remembered that Hessians began to fall. Captain Altenbockum's company fought stubbornly against heavy odds, with the outguards at their side. The Hessians fell back slowly toward the village, using houses and outbuildings

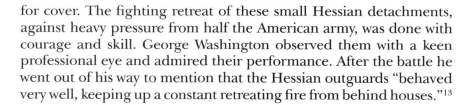

General Nathanael Greene, portrait by
Charles Willson Peale (1793), the
commander of the American left
wing that approached Trenton on
the Pennington Road.
Independence National
Historical Park.

for cover. The fighting retreat of these small Hessian detachments, against heavy pressure from half the American army, was done with courage and skill. George Washington observed them with a keen professional eye and admired their performance. After the battle he went out of his way to mention that the Hessian outguards "behaved very well, keeping up a constant retreating fire from behind houses."[13]

On the River Road, the other wing of the American army advanced toward the lower end of the town at the same time. General Sullivan led from the front, with Captain John Flahaven's New Jersey troops in the van and Colonel John Stark's New Hampshire brigade close behind. Just ahead of the Americans was a small house close to the road where the Hessians had posted a day picket. Beyond it was the Hermitage, General Philemon Dickinson's home. The Hessians made it their main outpost on the River Road and held it with a company of Jägers under Lieutenant Friedrich von Gröthausen.[14]

As the Americans came forward along the River Road, a Hessian picket fired at them. Lieutenant von Gröthausen heard the shot, mustered his Jägers at the Hermitage, and led them forward to support his picket. The Americans moved into the fields on both sides of the road and brought their artillery into action. Major James Wilkinson remembered, "It was now broad day, and the storm beat violently in our faces. The attack had commenced on the left, and

General John Sullivan, a painting by Richard Morrell Staigg, after John Trumbull (1876), the commander of the American right wing, which marched on the River Road. Independence National Historical Park.

was immediately answered by Colonel Stark in our front, who forced the enemy's picket."[15]

John Stark had a reputation as a fighter. He was devoted to the Revolutionary cause and wrote to his wife that he was determined to "live free or die," a phrase that his state later made its motto. Stark had trained his New Hampshiremen to use the bayonet, and he led them forward through the fields along the River Road. The Hessians were astonished to see the despised American rebels running toward them through the storm with "fixed bayonets." Lieutenant von Gröthausen retrieved his pickets and ordered his men to fall back.[16]

As the Hessian Jägers retreated toward Trenton, the Americans launched yet another part of their attack. Massed artillery on the Pennsylvania side of the Delaware began firing into the town. That part of the battle does not appear in most American accounts, but Hessians remembered it well and testified that they came under heavy fire from seven batteries across the river. Solid shot smashed the ice along the waterfront, and shells "from the Howitzers on the other side of the Delaware" exploded around the Hessian positions. German troops near the water's edge were forced to leave their posts "on account of the cannonade." Trenton was now under heavy attack from three sides.[17]

In the center of town, the three Hessian regiments came running out of their quarters at the first sound of firing at the Hessian outposts.[18] They were alert and responded quickly to the attack. Boston fifer John Greenwood was there and wrote later in his memoir, "I

Colonel Rall's Headquarters on King Street, the residence of Stacy Potts, a prosperous manufacturer in Trenton. William S. Stryker (1898), *Battles of Trenton and Princeton*, 92.

am willing to go upon oath, that I did not see even a solitary drunken soldier belonging to the enemy,—and you will find, as I shall show, that I had an opportunity to be as good a judge as any person there."[19]

The German responses to the American attack were not those of intoxicated revelers. When the alarm sounded, the three Hessian regiments in the center of town formed rapidly near their quarters. There was no single alarm post for the entire garrison, but every unit had its own place and went to it, as they had done the day before. The Rall regiment was the "*regiment du jour*" and had been on full alert in their alarm houses all that night, ready to march at a minute's warning. They assembled in a few moments on lower King Street and moved up the street to pick up their colors at Colonel Rall's headquarters. The other two regiments had been sleeping in full uniform, with cartridge boxes strapped on. They also assembled very quickly. The Regiment von Lossberg formed on King Street, and the Regiment von Knyphausen gathered near the lower Queen Street, by the Quaker meetinghouse.[20]

When the first shots rang out, the Hessian brigade adjutant, Lieutenant Jakob Piel, sprinted to Colonel Rall's headquarters on King Street and shouted, "*Der Feind! Der Feind! Heraus! Heraus!* The enemy! Turn out!" Piel ran to alert others, then returned to find Rall standing at a window in his nightshirt.

"*Was ist los?*" Rall shouted. "What's the matter?"

"Do you not hear the firing?" Piel asked.

"I will be there immediately!" Rall answered. He dressed quickly, ran out of his headquarters, and mounted his horse.[21]

As the Hessian regiments began to form, the American infantry converged on Trenton from two directions. On the River Road, John Stark and his New Hampshiremen continued their attack from the west and "pressed it into the town." Wilkinson remembered that "the enemy made a momentary shew of resistance by a wild and undirected fire from the windows of their quarters which they abandoned as we advanced, and made an attempt to form in the main street, which might have succeeded."[22]

Greene's division approached the upper part of the town from the north, with Washington in the lead. The American troops were running forward in open order through the snow. Colonel Clement Biddle wrote, "Indeed I never could conceive that one spirit should so universally animate both officers and men to rush forward into action." They occupied the high ground at the head of King and Queen streets and could see the entire town below.[23]

Lieutenant Wiederholdt's retreating Hessian outguards and Captain Altenbockum's company of Lossbergers resisted bravely, but the larger American force flowed around them on both flanks. To avoid being cut off, the Hessians retreated to another position "in the town at the first houses and fired at the enemy, who were forming for battle on the heights above."[24] The Hessian outpost troops were very tired. They also felt very much alone. Wiederholdt wrote that "no one came to see what was happening, or to reinforce and assist us. But they did their duty."[25]

A few moments later Colonel Rall rode up and asked for a report. It was a fateful conversation. Wiederholdt told him that this not another small raid, that "the enemy was strong, that they were not only above the town but were already around it on both the left and the right." Rall inquired about numbers. Wiederholdt answered that he did not know but had seen four or five battalions "moving out of the woods."[26]

Wiederholdt was accurate in most ways, but he was mistaken in one vital fact. The American troops were not yet around the town "on both the left and the right." They were attacking from the west and north of Trenton. The Hessians still held the stone bridge across Assunpink Creek, which led to good defensive ground southeast of the city. Had Colonel Rall made a fighting retreat across the bridge, he could have put his brigade in a strong position on rising land behind the creek, with his front and flanks protected. In that position his three regiments would not have been easy to defeat. They

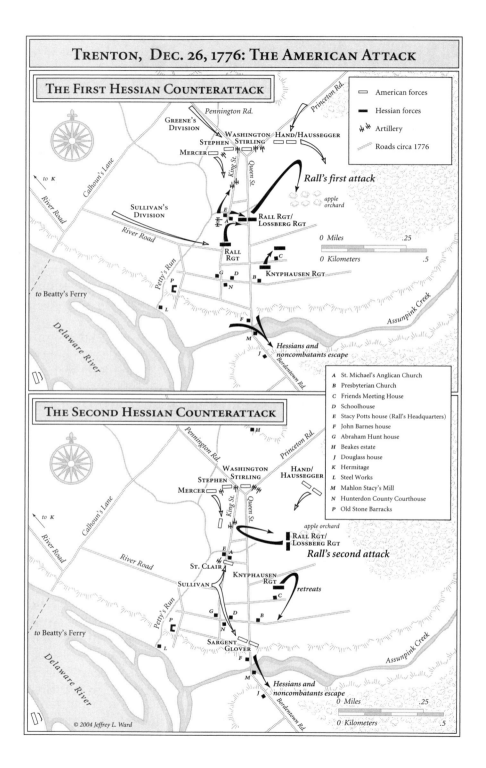

TRENTON, DEC. 26, 1776: THE AMERICAN ATTACK

THE FIRST HESSIAN COUNTERATTACK

Legend:
- American forces
- Hessian forces
- Artillery
- Roads circa 1776

Princeton Rd.

Pennington Rd.

GREENE'S DIVISION

WASHINGTON · HAND/HAUSSEGGER
STEPHEN STIRLING
MERCER

Rall's first attack

apple orchard

SULLIVAN'S DIVISION

River Road

RALL RGT/ LOSSBERG RGT

E
A

RALL RGT

0 Miles .25

0 Kilometers .5

G D
P N
B

KNYPHAUSEN RGT

to Beatty's Ferry

Petty's Run

Delaware River

L

F

M

J

Hessians and noncombatants escape

Assunpink Creek

Bordentown Rd.

- **A** St. Michael's Anglican Church
- **B** Presbyterian Church
- **C** Friends Meeting House
- **D** Schoolhouse
- **E** Stacy Potts house (Rall's Headquarters)
- **F** John Barnes house
- **G** Abraham Hunt house
- **H** Beakes estate
- **J** Douglass house
- **K** Hermitage
- **L** Steel Works
- **M** Mahlon Stacy's Mill
- **N** Hunterdon County Courthouse
- **P** Old Stone Barracks

THE SECOND HESSIAN COUNTERATTACK

H

Pennington Rd.

Princeton Rd.

WASHINGTON
STEPHEN STIRLING
MERCER

HAND/ HAUSSEGGER

to K

River Road

River Road

apple orchard

RALL RGT/ LOSSBERG RGT

E
A

ST. CLAIR

Rall's second attack

SULLIVAN

KNYPHAUSEN RGT

retreats

Calhoun's Lane

Petty's Run

to Beatty's Ferry

G D
P N
B

L

SARGENT GLOVER

F

C

Delaware River

M

J

Hessians and noncombatants escape

0 Miles .25

0 Kilometers .5

© 2004 Jeffrey L. Ward

Bordentown Rd.

Assunpink Creek

would also have had an open line of communication with Donop's Hessians at Mount Holly, Stirling's Highlanders at Blackhorse, and Leslie's troops at Princeton, by way of Crosswicks, which was guarded by a Hessian detachment.

That response might have caused major trouble for George Washington, who knew the desperate risk that he was running. If the initial American assault did not succeed quickly, the small Continental army would be in grave danger. Even a drawn battle at Trenton would put it in a perilous situation, surrounded by four British and Hessian brigades, which greatly outnumbered the Americans. An awakened enemy who moved with energy and decision could trap them against an ice-choked river. The result could be another heavy defeat for Washington's army, even its destruction.

And what if the Continental army were destroyed? After so many defeats around New York, another disaster could end Washington's command. The recruitment of another American army would become difficult, perhaps impossible. Without an army, the American Revolution could become yet another failed rebellion, much like the Scottish rising of 1745, or the Irish insurrection of 1798. American independence could have been lost on the banks of the Delaware.

In that multitude of might-have-beens, several facts are clear enough. Lieutenant Wiederholdt reported erroneously that the Americans had enveloped the town, nearly an hour before they succeeded in doing so. Colonel Rall responded with a decision not to retreat across the creek, but to counterattack the Americans in the town. The Hessian commander seemed not to know that a line of retreat was still open to good ground just beyond the creek. Later in the battle, Colonel Rall discovered what had happened. A Hessian officer remembered that Rall "sent Lieutenant Piel to the Bridge in order to see if they could still get through." By then it was too late.[27]

Colonel Rall was also misled in another way, by his own contempt for the American attackers. His attitude was not unreasonable, given the conduct of American troops in the battles around New York. In Trenton, Rall often remarked that a ragtag force of rebels could never stand against German Regulars. He also had a habit of responding to an attack with a strong counterattack, which was German tactical doctrine in many wars. For all of these reasons, Colonel Rall decided to fight the Americans by attacking directly against their main strength inside the town of Trenton. It was a mistake of historic consequence.

While Wiederholdt and Rall discussed the situation, the American artillery unlimbered on the heights that commanded the town, and the infantry deployed into line. With them on the high ground (very near the present battle monument) was George Washington. He had a clear view of the town below, the river beyond, and Assunpink Creek to his left. To his right he could see Sullivan's division marching toward the town along the River Road. Just below him to the right, Mercer's brigade was moving down the hill along the west side of the town and entering the village through house lots and alleys. Some American troops were getting into the houses and outbuildings and taking positions that commanded the street.[28]

Inside the town, Washington could see the Rall regiment as it formed by the alarm house, marched up King Street to Rall's headquarters, and brought out its regimental colors. He saw the Lossberg Regiment join them and the Knyphausen Regiment form in the lower part of Queen Street below the Friends meetinghouse and move to the right into an open field east of the meetinghouse. Washington remembered, "we presently saw their main body formed, but from their motions they seemed undetermined how to act."[29]

Colonel Rall observed the Americans on the heights and called to his men, "Artillery Forward!" The German artillerymen ran to their guns by the Hessian headquarters on King Street and brought out their heavy horses, which had been kept permanently in harness for such an emergency. Rall ordered his artillery officers to take two guns up King Street and to go into action against the Americans on the heights above. With great speed, Artillery Lieutenants Johann Englehardt and Friedrich Fischer collected eighteen men, hitched eight horses to the two guns, and led them up the hill to "the first houses in the street."[30] In a few minutes they opened fire on the Americans above them and got off twelve quick rounds against the American artillery. One Hessian shot hit the fore-horse on an American three-pounder. Sergeant John Greenwood saw the animal "struck in its belly and knocked over on its back. While it lay there kicking the cannon was stopped."[31]

Under fire, the American artillery came into action on the high ground above the Hessian gunners. General Stirling watched as they "soon got two field pieces at play and several others in a short time." Captain Thomas Forrest's large Pennsylvania battery opened fire with its two big six-pounders and two five-and-a-half-inch howitzers. The New York batteries joined in. Captain Alexander Hamilton brought two guns into action, and Captain Sebastian Baumann's New York battery added three guns more. The gunners bent over their pieces in a heavy fall of wet snow, sheltering their powder and touchholes as best they could. The storm was beating down more

Captain Thomas Forrest, a painting by
Charles Willson Peale (1820).
Forrest's battery of Pennsylvania
artillery went into action on the
high ground above Trenton with the
New York batteries of Sebastian
Baumann and Captain Alexander
Hamilton. Independence National
Historical Park, Philadelphia.

violently than ever. Visibility was poor, and the guns were very wet.
Merely to fire any weapon in that weather was an achievement.

The American artillery overpowered the Hessian guns and laid
down a concentration of fire at the vital center of the battle. Solid
iron shot bounded down King Street, toward the German artillery.
Five horses were hit and fell terribly wounded in the street. Eight
Hessian gunners went down. The rest were driven away from the
guns by grapeshot and by heavy musketry from American infantry,
who were firing from houses on their flank. The German artillerymen
remembered that the American musketry was even more destructive than the batteries on the hill. Finally these brave Hessian gunners could stand no more. German Lieutenants Fischer and
Engelhardt ordered their men to fall back. They abandoned the
guns, retreated to the bottom of the town, and led their men across
the bridge over Assunpink Creek to the hill beyond.[32]

Behind the German guns, the grenadiers of the Rall regiment
in King Street were now exposed to the American artillery. Ensign
Carl Wilhelm Kleinschmidt remembered that "the enemy were firing on them with their cannon, and many men of the regiment had
already been wounded." They recoiled in disorder. Colonel Rall
appeared, always in the thick of the fight. He led them out of the
line of fire, took them east through the house lots and a churchyard,
and rallied the infantry behind the English Church in the center of
the town. The Lossberg regiment gathered there as well.[33]

Rall led both regiments of Hessian infantry east to a large apple orchard just beyond the houses and turned them north. His object was to move against the Americans on the heights above the town and to attack them on their flank. Over the noise of battle, the Hessian troops heard him shout, "Forward! Advance! Advance!" Both the Rall and Lossberg regiments followed him up the hill.[34]

On the high ground above, George Washington saw the Hessian regiments rally in the apple orchard and watched them start up the hill toward his flank. With great speed and presence of mind, he instantly sent an order to Edward Hand's Pennsylvania Rifle Regiment and Haussegger's Pennsylvania and Maryland German regiment. They were told to shift to the east beyond the Hessians, who were advancing up the hill toward the Americans. Hand and Haussegger acted "with Spirit and Rapidity." They moved quickly beyond the Princeton Road and formed a line on the higher ground with a clear field of fire. That counterstroke defeated the Hessian design. If Colonel Rall had led his men forward to strike at what had been Washington's flank, the American regiments beyond the Princeton Road would now be on Rall's flank, and the German troops would be caught between two fires. Washington's quick reaction checked Rall's advance just as it was getting under way.[35]

More bad news was brought to the Hessian commander. Colonel Rall learned that two Hessian guns had been abandoned before the enemy in King Street. Worse, they were the guns of his own regiment. Their loss would be a heavy blow to the honor of his unit. The Hessian colonel turned his men toward the center of the town, and shouted, "*Alle was meine Grenatir seyn, vor werds!* All who are my grenadiers, forward!" The men shared their colonel's concern for the honor of their regiment. Grenadier Reuber wrote proudly that the "grenadiers stormed to recapture the cannons." Many of these men loved and respected their brave colonel. They would have followed him to Hell, and that was where he led them.[36]

With drums beating and colors flying, two regiments of Hessian infantry marched back toward King Street in the center of town, determined to rescue the guns and rout the rebels. They moved straight into a cone of American fire that came at them from three directions. Directly ahead were the infantry of Mercer's brigade, in houses and outbuildings where they were able to dry their muskets and fire from cover. Rall's regiments were in the open. In the rain and snow, many Hessians were unable to return fire with their wet weapons. To the Hessian right, Lord Stirling's American infantry moved down the hill against them, and the American artillery on the heights fired from the flank. On the Hessian left, St. Clair's brigade entered the town by the River Road, moved up King Street, and engaged the German troops from the other side. The American attackers used their artillery brilliantly as shock weapons, just as Henry Knox had intended. At the lower end of town, the New England battery came forward with St. Clair's troops and caught the advancing Hessians in a deadly crossfire.[37]

With great courage, the Hessian infantry drove doggedly forward into King Street and recovered the German guns. "We got them back," Grenadier Reuber wrote triumphantly, but it was another thing to keep them. The Americans were fighting with a determination that the Hessians had not seen before. Sergeant Joseph White's crew worked their gun so hard that they shattered its carriage. White wrote, "The third shot we fired broke the axle tree of the piece,—we stood there some time idle, they firing upon us."[38]

Colonel Henry Knox rode up to Sergeant White's ruined gun, looked toward the Hessian artillery, and said, "My brave lads, go up and take those two held pieces sword in hand. There is a party going and you must join them." The battery commander repeated the order, which was sometimes necessary with these insubordinate Yankees. Captain John Allen said, "You heard what the colonel said, Sergeant White. Now take your men and join the others in the attack."[39]

White's New Englanders joined the party and found that it consisted mainly of Virginians, "commanded by Captain Washington and Lieutenant Monroe." The Virginia infantry and New England gunners charged side by side straight toward the Hessian guns.[40] James Monroe wrote, "Captain Washington rushed forward, attacked and put the troops around the cannon to flight and took possession of them." In the melee, William Washington went down, badly wounded in both hands. James Monroe took over "at the head of the corps" and led it forward. He too was hit by a musket ball, which severed an artery. He was carried from the field, bleeding dangerously. His life was saved by Doctor Riker, who had joined Monroe's company as a volunteer the night before. The New Jersey physician clamped Monroe's artery just in time to keep him from bleeding to death.[41]

At the guns, Sergeant White took command. He remembered, "I hallowed as loud as I could scream to the men to run for their lives right up to the pieces. I was the first that reach them [the Hessian guns]. They had all left it except one man tending the vent." White shouted, "Run, you dog!" He raised his sword above the Hessian's head, who "looked up, and saw it, then run." The American gunners seized the guns and turned one of them toward the

German infantry. White wrote, "We put in a canister of shot (they had put in a cartridge before they left it,) and fired."[42]

On the other side, Hessian grenadier Johann Reuber wrote, "the rebels attacked us ferociously. Near Colonel Rall's quarters there was a barricade of boards and in front of that stood our two company cannon. As the Americans were attempting to reach the cannon we of Rall's Grenadier regiment encountered them, directly in front of Rall's headquarters. The fight was furious. The rebels dismantled the barricade and now we lost the greater part of our artillery and the rebels were about to use them."[43]

The German troops suffered many killed and wounded. The Lossberg regiment lost seventy men in this struggle. The American infantry were aiming at the Hessian officers and brought down four Lossberger captains. Colonel Rall was in the thick of it. As another junior officer went down, Rall turned to console him. Then the colonel himself was hit and "reeled in the saddle," shot twice in the side; both wounds were mortal. The dying German commander was helped off his horse, carried into the church, and laid upon a bench.[44]

In the center of Trenton the battle became a bedlam of sound. The streets echoed with the thunder of artillery, the crash of iron on brick and stone, the noise of splintering wood and shattering glass, the roar of musketry, the clash of steel against steel, the mingled shouts and curses, and the cries of wounded men. On the vast scale of human slaughter this eighteenth-century battle was nothing to compare with other wars, but its very close combat of cold steel, massed musketry, and cannon at point-blank range created a scene of horror beyond imagining.

The Americans were appalled by the carnage that they had caused. Henry Knox wrote, "here succeeded a scene of war of which I had often conceived but never saw before. The hurry, fright, and confusion of the enemy was [not] unlike that which will be when the last trump shall sound."[45] Sergeant Joseph White felt the same way: "My blood chill'd to see such horror and distress, blood mingling together, the dying groans, and 'Garments rolled in blood.' The sight was too much to bear."[46]

The civilian inhabitants of Trenton were caught up in the violence. Among them was little Martha Reed, then a small child, who always remembered the horror of "that awful day," as she called it. "In the grey dawn, came the beating of drums, and the sound of firing," she wrote, "the soldiers quartered in our house, hastily decamped, all was uproar and confusion. My mother and we children hid in the cellar to escape the shots that fell about the house." Her family survived, but others were not so lucky. Martha Reed remembered that "our next door neighbor was killed on his doorstep," and "a bullet struck the blacksmith as he was in the act of closing himself in his cellar, and many other townspeople were injured by chance shots." One young woman was running from one house to another when a musket ball hit the high comb in her hair. She lived to tell the story and said that she was happy not to be half an inch taller.[47] At least one American woman joined the fight. A German recalled that "the inhabitants shot at the Hessians from their houses. In fact even a woman fired out of her window and mortally wounded a captain."[48]

Under heavy fire, the charge of the Hessians failed. They had fought valiantly but were overwhelmed by the weight of American fire. Slowly, grudgingly, the German troops began to give way, and the broken German regiments retreated. Reuber, the Hessian grenadier, believed that the turning point was the loss of Colonel Rall. "If he had not been severely wounded they would not have taken us alive!" he wrote.[49] A Lossberger thought differently. "Our muskets could not fire any more on account of the rain and snow and the rebels fired on us from, within the houses," one of them wrote, "the Regiment von Lossberg lost in this affair 70 men killed and wounded. . . . Our whole disaster was entirely due to Colonel Rall."[50]

Some of the Hessians fled into buildings and basements. Most retreated to the east, away from the town, followed closely by the oncoming Americans, only fifty paces behind. Greenwood remembered that his men ran "after them pell mell. Some of the Hessians took refuge in a church at the door of which we stationed a guard to keep them in, and taking no further care of them for the present, advanced to find more, for many had run down into the cellars of the houses."

Greenwood's regiment advanced through the place where the fighting had been most severe. He wrote, "I passed two of their cannon, brass six-pounders, by the side of which lay seven dead Hessians, and a brass drum. This latter article was, I remember, of great curiosity to me and I stopped to look at it, but it was quickly taken possession of by one of our drummers, who threw away his own instrument." American troops left ranks and scoured the ground for souvenirs. Greenwood wrote that he "obtained a sword from one of the bodies," and "we then ran to join our regiment." He remembered that "General Washington, on horseback and alone, came up to our major and said, 'March on, my brave fellows, after me!' and rode off." Most American soldiers in this battle shared that memory

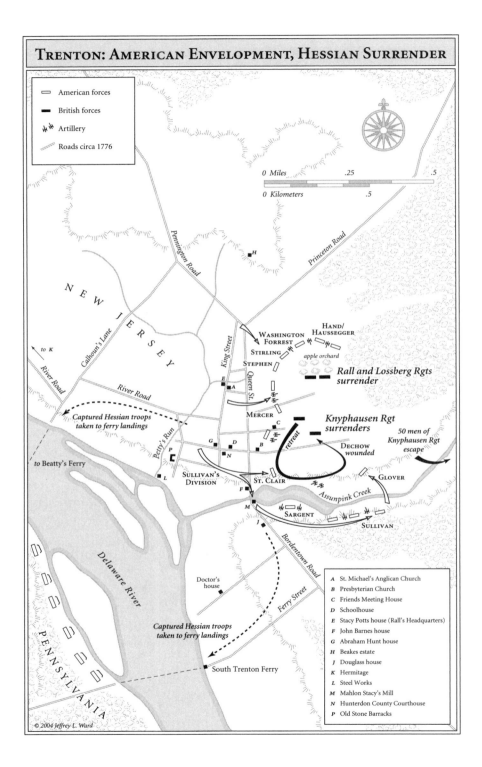

TRENTON: AMERICAN ENVELOPMENT, HESSIAN SURRENDER

American forces
British forces
Artillery
Roads circa 1776

0 Miles .25 .5
0 Kilometers .5

NEW JERSEY

Pennington Road

Princeton Road

H

Calhoun's Lane

to K

River Road

River Road

King Street

Queen St.

H

WASHINGTON
FORREST

HAND/
HAUSSEGGER

STIRLING

STEPHEN

apple orchard

Rall and Lossberg Rgts surrender

E
A

MERCER

Captured Hessian troops taken to ferry landings

Petty's Run

C

Knyphausen Rgt surrenders

50 men of Knyphausen Rgt escape

to Beatty's Ferry

G D

P

B

retreat

DECHOW
wounded

N

L

SULLIVAN'S
DIVISION

F

ST. CLAIR

GLOVER

Assunpink Creek

M

SARGENT

SULLIVAN

J

Delaware River

Bordentown Road

Doctor's
house

Ferry Street

PENNSYLVANIA

Captured Hessian troops taken to ferry landings

South Trenton Ferry

A   St. Michael's Anglican Church
B   Presbyterian Church
C   Friends Meeting House
D   Schoolhouse
E   Stacy Potts house (Rall's Headquarters)
F   John Barnes house
G   Abraham Hunt house
H   Beakes estate
J   Douglass house
K   Hermitage
L   Steel Works
M   Mahlon Stacy's Mill
N   Hunterdon County Courthouse
P   Old Stone Barracks

© 2004 Jeffrey L. Ward

of serving by the side of General Washington. They knew him not only as a leader but a comrade in arms.[51]

The remnants of the Rall and Lossberg regiments retreated to the orchard east of town. They were now without their colonel, and many companies had lost their captains and lieutenants. These highly disciplined men kept some of their cohesion, but they were confused and surrounded. The fight drained out of them, and they did not know what to do.

American infantry and artillery moved forward around them, and the men in Haussegger's Pennsylvania and Maryland German regiment began to call "in German and English to stack their weapons and surrender."[52] An American officer, perhaps Washington's aide George Baylor, rode toward the Hessians and spoke with the senior German officers, Lieutenant Colonel Francis Scheffer of the Lossberg regiment and Major Yost Matthaus of the Rall regiment. He offered them surrender terms and agreed to carry away the brave Captain von Altenbockum, who had been wounded in the head.[53]

The Hessians talked among themselves, then they lowered their proud colors to the snow and grounded weapons. Looking on was George Washington, who was standing with Lord Stirling near Captain Thomas Forrest's battery. Washington had ordered the artillery to shift from round shot to canister. Forrest was about to obey, then turned to the general:

"Sir," he said, "they have struck."

"Struck!" Washington repeated.

"Yes, their colours are down."

"So they are."[54] Washington rode forward toward the Hessians. Forrest's men left their guns and followed him. It was said that the Americans mixed with the Hessians, and "after satisfying their curiosity a little, they began to converse familiarly in broken English and German."[55]

Not part of this surrender was the Knyphausen regiment, the third Hessian unit at Trenton. At the start of the battle the Knyphausen men had marched to join Rall, but perhaps because of a misunderstood order, they countermarched to the southeast of town. They were behind the Quaker meetinghouse when Rall attacked into the center of Trenton. After he fell mortally wounded, and the Rall and Lossberg regiments were repulsed, the Knyphausen regiment tried to escape from the town across Assunpink Creek. Their acting commander, Major Friedrich von Dechow, led them toward the Stone Bridge, with three hundred troops and two guns.[56]

They were too late. The bridge had been held by Hessian troops through the first hour of the battle, and many noncombatants escaped across it. Major von Dechow himself went to the bridge half an hour after the fighting began, found Sergeant Johannes Müller, who commanded the bridge guard, and ordered him to "hold out as long as possible." About half an hour later Müller and his eighteen bridge guards were attacked by "three battalions of the enemy."[57]

These were Sargent's and Glover's brigades, mostly New England Yankees. They came forward quickly, "with their right on the Delaware, and with their left to the town, straight away to the bridge." Sergeant Müller recalled that the Americans carried "two flying colors," probably the Liberty flags that they had used in the New York campaign, or perhaps the Massachusetts and Connecticut flags. They overwhelmed Müller's guard, seized the bridge, and took a blocking position on the far side of Assunpink Creek. Sargent's Continental brigade moved up the Creek on the far bank, and Trenton was completely surrounded.[58]

The Knyphausen regiment turned away from the bridge and marched up the creek in search of a ford. Their two guns sank deep in a patch of soft ground. While they struggled to free their artillery, American troops came up behind them, and others fired from across the creek. The Knyphausen men kept moving up the creek toward another ford, but that crossing was blocked as well. Some of the American infantry were so aggressive that they waded into the freezing creek "about mid-thigh" to attack the Hessians.[59]

More American troops came out of the village and attacked the Knyphausen regiment from the rear and both flanks. The Hessians were trapped. Their acting commander, Major von Dechow, had come on the field still suffering from two wounds received at Fort Washington. Now he was hit again, mortally wounded in the hip. Dechow saw that the situation was hopeless, summoned his officers, and proposed to surrender. One said to him, "Major we cannot give ourselves up like this." Dechow replied, "My dear sirs, do as you like. I am wounded." He was carried off the field, escorted by "a file of sergeants" with "a white handkerchief tied to a musket."[60]

As the Americans gathered around them, the officers and men of the Knyphausen regiment saw that resistance was hopeless. Looking on was Private Jacob Francis, an African American slave who had joined Sargent's brigade. Francis remembered that "the Hessians grounded their arms and left them there and marched down to the old ferry below the Assunpink, between Trenton and Lambertown."[61]

Study for the Capture of the Hessians at Trenton, by John Trumbull. This scene accurately represents the meeting of General Washington with Hessian Major Friedrich von Dechow, acting commander of the Regiment von Knyphausen, who had been mortally wounded in the hip near the end of the battle and was being helped off the field by sergeants in the regiment. Behind him is the high ground south of Assunpink Creek. Trumbull's quick sketch captured the kinetics of the battle. Charles Allen Munn Collection, Fordham University Library.

Washington had heard the firing near the creek and rode to the sound of the guns. One of his officers remembered that "about half-way to the bridge he came upon some German troops who were assisting a badly wounded officer into a church." This was Major von Dechow. Then Sullivan's aide Major Wilkinson came riding up from the bridge with the news that the Knyphausen men had laid down their arms and the last remaining Hessian regiment had surrendered. Washington extended his hand and said, "Major Wilkinson, this is a glorious day for our country."[62]

The victory was not quite complete. After the start of the battle, while the bridge across Assunpink Creek had remained in Hessian hands, some of the Trenton garrison escaped. The first to get away were twenty troopers of the Sixteenth Light Dragoons, the only British unit in Trenton. They mounted their horses, rode rapidly across the bridge, and galloped to Princeton. Close behind were the Hessian

Jägers under Captain von Gröthausen, who had been quartered in the Hermitage west of the town. Another guard of thirteen Jägers at South Ferry also escaped early in the battle.

The surviving Hessian artillerymen under Lieutenants Engelhardt and Fischer retreated through the village and across the bridge after they lost their guns on King Street. Many German noncombatants got away: the Hessian surgeons, musicians and drummers of the Knyphausen regiment, and Hessian women and children. The men at four Hessian outposts south and west of the town escaped, and so did Sergeant Johann Müller's bridge guard, along with a hundred men under Heinrich Boking who were at the Crosswicks Bridge, south of Trenton. Altogether, between four hundred and five hundred men of the Garrison got away.[63]

But of the three Hessian regiments in the town, it was reported that "not a single infantryman came over the bridge." They fought bravely to the end, even knowing that they could not win. Here was a remarkable testament to their creed of obedience and service. Not until the battle was lost did some of these men try to escape. In the final moments, Lieutenant Joachim Baum and fifty Hessian infantry of the Knyphausen regiment fled by swimming across the Assunpink Creek. They nearly drowned in the swift waters of the stream and suffered severely from cold. After a terrible ordeal they reached Princeton ten hours later.[64]

The Americans had won a decisive victory. Altogether, the Hessians lost 918 men. Of that number 22 were killed and 83 were seriously wounded. Many more suffered wounds that were not incapacitating and therefore not recorded, a common pattern in the Revolutionary War on all sides. The Americans captured 896 officers and men, including the wounded, and "as many muskets, bayonets, cartouche boxes and swords." They seized enough material to equip several American brigades. Most prized by the victors were six excellent German cannon, "double fortified Brass three pounders," so strongly made that the Americans rebored them into six-pounders. With the guns came "carriages compleat" and three ammunition wagons. The victors also reported the capture of twenty-five officers' servants, three or four sets of colors (fifteen flags altogether), and a Hessian band, including Colonel Rall's beloved hautboists.[65]

Washington wrote to Congress that American losses were "very trifling indeed, only two officers and one or two privates wounded." In fact the toll was larger than he knew. Many sick and starving men suffered severely, and more than a few died of exhaustion, exposure, and illness. William Dwyer writes that several Continental soldiers sought help in the home of Richard Scudder north of Trenton, and two or three died there on the night after the battle.[66]

We shall never know how many others suffered and died that way. Nobody counted the deaths from all causes during the campaign, but there are many indications that the number was not small. During the winter of 1776–77, the number of "ineffectives" in the entire Continental army rose to 35 percent. Probably it was even higher on December 26–27. Most of these men were ill, and many died of illness, hypothermia, malnutrition, and exhaustion. It is very likely that the number of American deaths from nonbattle causes as a result of the attack on Trenton was larger than the total number of Hessian losses in combat.[67]

After the battle, Washington ordered his men to treat the Hessian prisoners with humanity, and he is said to have met the dying Colonel Rall, perhaps as he was being carried to his quarters. One Hessian remembered that on his deathbed the German commander thought first of his men and asked Washington to allow them to keep their possessions. Rall died of his wounds that night. His adjutant wrote that he was "satisfied that it was not necessary for him to outlive his honor."[68]

Washington called yet another "consultation of officers" in Trenton. Once again he posed a hard question. Should they attack another post, or hold their ground, or retreat across the Delaware? The debate was open and wide-ranging.[69] Some officers wanted to strike again, and quickly. They appealed to historical experience and argued that "Successes & brilliant strokes ought to be pursued— that History shewed how much depended upon improving such Advantages—& that a Pannick being once given no one could ascertain the beneficial Consequences which might be derived from it if it was push'd to all its Consequences."[70]

Others took the part of prudence. They argued that "the enemy was in force both above and below viz. at Princeton & Bordentown," and that "the Stroke being brilliant & successful it was not prudent or politick even to risque the chance of losing the Advantages." Further, some thought that "the weather was so amazingly severe, our arms so wet, and the men so fatigued, it was judged prudent to come off immediately with our prisoners and plunder." In the end, nearly everyone agreed. Even Delaware's bellicose Colonel John Haslet wrote, "We should have gone on, and, panic struck, they would have fled before us, but the inclemency of the weather rendered it impossible."[71]

The Capture of the Hessians at Trenton, painted by John Trumbull (1786–1797). In this imagined scene, Trumbull included careful portraits (many from life), of participants in the battle. The standing figure in white on the far left is Colonel Josiah Parker of Virginia. Behind him are Colonel Edward Wigglesworth and William Shepard. In the center the mortally wounded Hessian commander, Colonel Johann Rall, is supported by Major Stephens Smith, aide to General John Sullivan. The mounted figures behind George Washington are his aides, Robert Hanson Harrison and Tench Tilghman. The severely wounded figure lying behind Rall's extended hand is Lieutenant James Monroe. Holding him is Dr. John Riker, who saved his life on the battlefield. The American officers to the right are John Sullivan, Nathanael Greene (on the white horse), Henry Knox, Philemon Dickinson, John Glover, and George Weedon. Standing in front of them with a bandaged hand is Captain William Washington. Yale University Art Gallery.

While the officers talked, the army found forty hogsheads of rum in Trenton. When Washington found out about it, he ordered the rum destroyed, but the commander-in-chief may have been the last to know. Before his officers could act, more than a few hogsheads had been emptied in another way. The adjutant of the army reported that "the soldiers drank too freely to admit of Discipline or Defence."[72]

In a word, some of the American victors celebrated their own success by getting gloriously drunk and even more disorderly than usual. John Greenwood remembered a wild scene. The men in his regiment "were much pleased with the brass caps which they had taken from the dead hessians." Others began to take them from prisoners. "With brass caps on it was laughable to see how our soldiers would strut,—fellows with their elbows out, and some without a collar to their half-a-shirt, no shoes, etc."[73]

The condition of the army settled the question. Washington's Council of War agreed that they should retreat across the Delaware— if they could get the men into the boats. Washington sent a letter to President John Hancock, laying out some of the reasons for retreat. He explained to Hancock that only half of his army had been able to cross the Delaware. If Putnam, Ewing, and Cadwalader had "passed the river," he wrote, "I should have been able, with their assistance, to have driven the enemy from all their posts below Trenton, but the numbers I had with me, being inferior to those below me, and a strong battalion of Light Infantry being at Princeton above me, I thought most prudent to return the same evening, with the prisoners and artillery."[74] As always, Washington took the opportunity to remind Congress about the perennial problem of supply. He wrote that "the apprehension that we would receive no Succours, and that the difficulty of passing & repassing the river might become greater, led us to conclude our return eligible." Nothing was said to Congress about the rum.[75]

The return across the Delaware proved more difficult for many men than the crossing the day before. The rum did not help. More than a few Americans tumbled into the icy Delaware trying to leap aboard the boats. Others were so cold and exhausted that they could barely move. One of them was William Chamberlin, who left a long account of the march home. "It began to rain," he remembered. "I had got thoroughly wet before we began our retrograde march, and the rain and half-melted snow and water was almost over shoes— our feet was drenched in water every step. I was seized with a kind of ague fit which lasted for half an hour. I went into an house with my teeth chattering in my head, but though my kind host made me a good fire and did everything to favor me, the fire failed to warm me for some time and I expected to have been taken down with a violent fever. After a while, however, I got warm, and made shift to get back to the ferry. Here we had to stand by the river until the prisoners were first got over. The wind by this time had shifted and blew a keen northwestern blast which chilled me to the heart."

The resourceful Chamberlin looked for shelter. He remembered, "I at length went into an house at some distance from the ferry, where was a girl which was called Miss Chamberlin. On the score of namesake I ventured to scrape acquaintance with her, and by her assistance I got a bowl of warm, fresh meat broth, which was of great service to me. I then went down to the river to wait for the boats. The ice was so thick near the shore as to bear for a rod or two. I went on the ice with a view to jump in, but it broke and let me into the river up to my waste, and the boat was filled before I could recover myself. The next boat, however, that struck I waded into the river to meet it, threw my gun into it, made leap with all my strength. I got in and got over to a fire, but almost dead with cold and fatigue."[76]

Some of the artillerymen found the crossing even more difficult. It was specially so for Sergeant Joseph White, who had a gun with a broken axle. Knox ordered him to leave it. White refused. "This piece was called the best in the regiment," he said. "I was determined to get it off. I hired four of our men and one of them had been a mate of a vessel; he contrived it and off we moved."[77]

The men struggled slowly to the river, moving the dead weight of their broken gun. When even the rear guard passed them, Colonel Knox rode back to Sergeant White and told him again, "You had better leave that cannon." White refused again. "I told him I rather ran the risk of being taken, than to leave now we had got so far." As the American army disappeared in front of them, other mounted figures approached from the rear. "Here comes the enemy's light horse," one of the men said. They turned out to be "nothing but a party of old Quakers; they had handkerchiefs tied over their hats, for there had been a snow storm all day."

At last White and his men got their gun across the river. Knox came up to him again with a party of horsemen and said, "Sergeant, what piece is that." White told him that it was "the piece that he ordered to be left," and added, "I wanted victory complete." Knox answered, "You are a good fellow. . . . I will remember you." As the officers put their spurs to their horses, Sergeant White savored a rare moment of "victory complete," not only over the enemy and the broken gun but also his own commanders. "They happened all to be generals, and they rode on," he wrote triumphantly. He was overcome with exhaustion. On the Pennsylvania shore he "lay down upon the snow and took a nap; the heat of my body melted the snow and I sunk down to the ground."[78]

One of the hardest tasks of the American army was to get their Hessian captives across the river to Pennsylvania. The Americans were fascinated by their prisoners. One wrote, "They are of a Moderate Stature rather broad Shoulders their limbs not of equal proportion light complexion with a bluish tinge [probably with cold], hair cued as tight to the head as possible Sticking straight back like the handle of an iron skillet."[79]

The crossing of the Delaware was an ordeal for captors and prisoners alike. John Greenwood was assigned to escort Hessians in a "scow, or flatbottomed boat, which was used in transporting them over the ferry." He remembered that the boat was knee deep in rain and snow, "and some of the poor fellows were so cold that their under-jaws quivered like an aspen leaf."[80]

Elisha Bostwick had another problem in his boat. "The ice continually stuck to the boats driving them down stream[;] the boatmen endeavoring to clear the ice pounded the boat, & stamping with their feet beckoned to the prisoners to do the Same & they all set to jumping at once with their cues flying up & down soon shook off the ice from the boats."[81] For Lieutenant Wiederholdt the worst of it was the landing in Pennsylvania. His boat drifted two miles down the river, and the ice along the bank kept them from coming ashore. He and his men were forced to jump into the river and walk seventy feet through bitter cold water, then break an opening through the ice. They were nearly frozen by the time they got ashore.[82]

While the Hessian prisoners were crossing the Delaware, the news from Trenton began to spread. Its first and greatest impact was in America, where many people received it as a vindication of the Cause. They deeply believed that the battle of Trenton was a Sign of God's Redeeming Providence, and proof that the Continental army was His instrument. This idea of God's all-powerful Providence gave them a sense of agency in the world, as a part of divine purpose. In more secular forms, that attitude was very strong in the army. Captain William Hull of the Seventh Connecticut Regiment wrote, "The Resolution and Bravery of our Men, their Order and Regularity, gave me the highest Sensation of Pleasure. . . . What can't Men do when engaged in so noble a cause?"[83]

Reports of the battle traveled rapidly through the thirteen colonies. In eleven days it reached the frontier settlements of Loudoun County, Virginia, where a British landbuyer named Nicholas Cresswell was being kept under restraint. He wrote on January 6, 1777, "News that Washington had taken 760 Hessian prisoners at Trenton in the Jerseys. Hope it is a lie. This afternoon hear he has likewise taken six pieces of Brass Cannon." The next day he added, "The news is confirmed. The minds of the people are much altered. A few days ago they had given up the cause for lost. Their late successes have turned the scale and now they are all liberty mad again. Their Recruiting parties could not get a man (except he bought him from his master) no longer since than last week, and now the men are coming in by companies."

The more Nicholas Cresswell thought about it, the greater was his anger against both the Americans and the Germans. "Confound the turncoat scoundrels and the cowardly Hessians together," he wrote in his diary. "This has given them new spirits, got them fresh succours and will prolong the War, perhaps for two years. They have recovered [from] their panic, and it will not be an easy matter to throw them into confusion again." Cresswell noticed a sudden surge of military recruiting. "Volunteer Companies are collecting in every County on the Continent and in a few months the rascals will be stronger than ever," he observed. "Even the parsons, some of them, have turned out as Volunteers and Pulpits Drums or Thunder, which you please to call it, summoning all to arms in this cursed babble. Damn them all."[84]

In New York, British leaders were dismayed by the news. Admiral Howe's private secretary Ambrose Serle wrote in his diary on December 27, "Heard the unpleasant news of a whole Brigade of Hessians under Col. Rall being taken Prisoners at Trenton by a large body of Rebels, and at nine o'clock in the morning. I was exceedingly concerned on the public account, as it will tend to revive the drooping spirits of the rebels and increase their force."[85]

As the impact of the defeat came clear, British writers held the Hessian troops responsible. Nicholas Cresswell wrote, "it is the Damd Hessians that has caused this, curse the scoundrel that first thought of sending them here."[86] A British officer added, "They are the worst troops I ever saw. . . . They are voted British pay, [of] which their prince cheats them out of one half. They are extremely dissatisfied at this, so that to make it up they turn their whole thoughts upon Plunder. It was their attention to this plunder, that made them fall a sacrifice to the Rebels at Trenton."[87]

Every British leader denied responsibility and looked for someone else to blame. Whig gazettes in Britain blamed Lord George Germain and other ministers for their conduct of the war. Germain blamed General Howe and declared in Parliament that if only he had attacked Philadelphia, he could have ended the war. Howe and Grant blamed the Hessians, especially the Hessian commander-in-chief in America, General Heister, though he had no role in the critical decisions of the campaign. Hessian officers in the field blamed General Howe for his disposition in New Jersey. In Mount Holly, Colonel Carl von Donop was so shaken by the news that he abandoned his posts and marched with his command to Allentown, twelve miles from Princeton, and then on to Princeton itself. He left behind his own sick and wounded but took with him 150 wagons and carriages filled with plunder, according to the testimony of Hessian Captain Johann Ewald.[88]

In Europe, the news from Trenton stimulated a controversy on the Hessian presence in America, the morality of the *Soldatenhandel*, or soldier trade, and the legitimacy of the government that engaged in it. Before 1776, this commerce had been widely accepted in Europe. After 1777 it came under strong attack. The affair at Trenton was a major factor, for it added the sting of defeat to the stain of moral disgrace.

The leading European critic of the soldier trade was the comte de Mirabeau, then living as an exile in the Netherlands. In 1777, he attacked the soldier trade in the same language that was beginning to be used against the slave trade, as a "*commerce des hommes*" and a trade in human flesh by "sellers of souls." Mirabeau argued that the Hessian soldier trade was all the more odious because it supported English despotism in a failing struggle against American rights. Further, he asked the Hessians to remember the misery it brought to their own sons. In a ringing conclusion he urged that Europeans should be fighting in America, as volunteers on the other side: "Cross the seas," he wrote, "hurry to America, but embrace your brothers there, defend these generous people against the arrogant rapacity of their persecutors. . . . Learn from the Americans the art of living free."[89]

The Hessian Landgraf Friedrich Wilhelm II unwisely responded by attempting to buy up the entire edition of Mirabeau's pamphlet, which gave it wider circulation and encouraged others to join the debate. At Paris in 1777, a writer who was probably Benjamin Franklin concocted a literary hoax, a fictional letter from the Landgraf (with the imaginary name of the count de Schaumbergh) to his commander in America. In this cutting satire, the Landgraf expressed "unspeakable pleasure" on the news of "the courage our troops exhibited at Trenton," and joy on learning that 1,605 men were killed and only 345 escaped. He calculated that Britain would pay 643,500 florins for their deaths. The Hessian count complained that the surgeons had saved a hundred wounded by amputations and urged that "a wiser course" would be "to let every one of them die," which would make them more valuable. He added, "I am about to send you some new recruits. Don't economize them. Remember glory before all things. Glory is true wealth."[90]

The hoax spread swiftly through Europe. It was false in many of its parts, but it was widely believed to be true, especially in its reference to "blood-money clauses," which were not a part of British treaties with Hesse-Cassel but did appear in contracts with other German princes. The Landgraf asked his very able foreign minister Martin von Schlieffen to make a reply, which appeared in French as a pamphlet called *Des Hessois en Amerique*. It celebrated the Landgraf's enlightened rule and defended the soldier trade on the ground that the ancient Greeks had done it and that it increased the wealth and happiness of the Hessian people themselves. Schlieffen pointed out that very few of the Hessians who were captured at Trenton wished to remain in America, which was true before that battle but not afterward. Schlieffen also argued that the American Whigs were more abusive of individual liberty than were the princes of Europe, especially in regard to slaves and Loyalists.[91]

Schlieffen's defense of the soldier trade brought a torrent of criticism. The events on the Delaware did not begin the debate on the soldier trade, but greatly expanded it. They also enlarged the international debate on the American Revolution and raised questions about the legitimacy of Europe's old regime. In all of these ways, the battle of Trenton transformed attitudes toward the War of Independence on both sides of the Atlantic.

HARD CHOICES

~ Associators and Continentals

> This was the time that tried both soul and body. We were standing on frozen ground covered with snow. The hope of the commander-in-chief was sustained by the character of these half frozen, half starved men, that he could persuade them to volunteer for another month. He made the attempt, and it succeeded.
>
> —John Howland, December 31, 1776[1]

ON DECEMBER 27, 1776, the Continental army struggled home to its camps in Pennsylvania. The men were worn out. They had marched and fought for sixty hours through snow, rain, sleet, and hail. Many were ill with fever, catarrh, consumption, and dysentery. Most were suffering from frozen faces, frostbitten hands, and lacerated feet. All were utterly exhausted. Lieutenant James McMichael of the Pennsylvania Line wrote, "after suffering much fatigue we reached our camp, and having obtained comfortable lodgings I found Morpheus had got possession of me."[2]

At the army's headquarters in the Widow Harris's house near Newtown, there was no rest for weary staff officers, who stripped off their swords and sat down at their camp desks, with piles of the army's endless paperwork before them. George Washington toiled at his enormous correspondence, and his letters show that he was wrestling with yet another choice of difficulties. He had won a victory by a bold and lucky stroke, and congratulations were pouring in. But Washington knew that he had awakened a formidable enemy. He could ruin the Cause in a moment if he acted wrongly, or fortune turned against him.

What should he do next? What could he do? Washington believed that at least eight thousand British and German troops were
in New Jersey, and their numbers were likely to grow larger. His own
little army was growing smaller. Many veteran regiments were due
to go home in four days, when their enlistments expired at the end
of the year. The men had done all that he asked of them, and more.
Even before the attack on Trenton, on the morning of December
22, more than 34 percent of them were officially reported as "ineffective." After the battle, the proportion was even higher. How much
more could he ask of these exhausted men?

The weather was another worry. The men had suffered much
on their march to Trenton, and the coldest month lay just ahead. A
weakened American army could be shattered if it tried to fight a
strong enemy on another frozen field. Even without a battle, the
army could be ruined by another winter campaign. The weather
was even more dangerous in another way. If the Delaware River froze
over, as often it did in January, the enemy could march across the
ice to Philadelphia. The Continental army had never been able to
stop them in open combat. After the conquest of New York, New
Jersey, and Rhode Island, the loss of the largest American city would
be a crushing blow to the Cause. Any action was full of danger, but
Washington knew that inaction could be worse. To do anything was
to risk defeat; to do nothing was to court disaster.

Washington reflected on these very hard choices in the quiet of
the Widow Harris's house, with the clocks ticking around him. As he
did so, the American cause had come to yet another crisis, and great
issues were hanging in the balance. But this time the mood was
different in the American headquarters. With all his worries,
Washington's correspondence showed that he was in high spirits.
He had tried his luck by a desperate gamble, and at last fortune had
smiled upon him. Like most Chesapeake gentlemen he was a great
believer in fortune, and success encouraged these men to think that
fate was with them. He was ready to fight the enemy again, and
eager to continue his campaign with another quick stroke, if only he
had the means to do so. To his respected friend John Cadwalader
he wrote, "If we could happily beat up the rest of their quarters
bordering on or near the river, it would be attended with the most
valuable consequences."[3]

As at every difficult moment, Washington decided to convene a council of war. On the afternoon of December 27, he informed his adjutant, "I have called a meeting of the general officers," to discuss

Colonel John Cadwalader, leader of the Philadelphia Associators, from an old print in William S. Stryker, *Battles of Trenton and Princeton* (1898), 81.

"what future operations may be necessary."[4] Just before the council met, a courier arrived with unexpected news. It was a message from John Cadwalader, who reported that he had crossed the Delaware River into New Jersey on the second try, early on the morning of the twenty-seventh with 1,800 troops, mostly Associators. He had done so at the urging of his men, who were always determined to make their own choices. Once on the Jersey shore, they demanded that he remain, even to the point of mutiny. They were in Burlington, south of Trenton, and discovered that the enemy were in a "panic" and had gone off "with great precipitation," some of them all the way to Amboy on the east side of the state. Cadwalader saw an opportunity. "If we can drive them from West Jersey," wrote this merchant-turned-soldier, "the success will raise an army by next Spring, & and establish the Credit of the Continental Money." Here was an unexpected way of turning victory into a larger triumph. Once again the Pennsylvania Associators had acted entirely on their own initiative. With the Jersey militia that Washington complained so often about, they had dropped another opportunity into his lap.[5]

Late on the night of December 27, the council of war held an emergency meeting in the Harris house.[6] Washington reported Cadwalader's surprising news and summarized that officer's suggestion of an opportunity for another campaign in New Jersey. It was typical of Washington's style of leadership to present a promising proposal as someone else's idea, rather than his own. It was his way of encouraging open discussion and constructive debate.

The first response in the council was not enthusiastic, to say the least. The general officers of the army were as weary as the rank and file, and not as resilient as the younger men. Many were appalled by the thought of another desperate cold-weather campaign. According to the one understated account, "Some doubts it is said arose in the general Council on this occasion." We are told that a few spoke out against Cadwalader's suggestion and actively "disapproved the Enterprize." At least one "advised the sending of Orders to the Militia to return" from Jersey to Pennsylvania.[7]

Then the tide of opinion began to turn. Several men declared that "tho' they would not have advised the Movement, yet it being done it ought to be supported." Another officer thought that a bold stroke could liberate a large part of New Jersey, and it would also demonstrate that the success at Trenton was not an accident. After more discussion the council began to agree, and with George Washington's tactful encouragement, it united in consensus. The central question was settled: One victory was not enough. The army should seize the moment and attack again very quickly with all its strength, and "orders were accordingly issued for the troops to prepare to cross the River." The council adjourned in unity and mutual support. It was a remarkable and very instructive success for Washington's maturing style of quiet, consultative leadership. His method was beginning to work in this army of free spirits. It was uniting cantankerous Yankees, stubborn Pennsylvanians, autonomous Jerseymen, honor-bound Virginians, and independent backcountrymen in a common cause.[8]

Having made that decision, Washington resolved to commit all of his resources to the enterprise. Early the next morning, December 28, 1776, gallopers went from his headquarters to generals in the field. To his officers at Morristown, Washington wrote, "I am about to enter the Jersies with a considerable force immediately." They were asked to raise the militia of North Jersey against the enemy and to "harass their flanks and rear." Other letters went to militia generals in West Jersey and Pennsylvania. Another message went to General Heath in Peekskill, on the Hudson River, where his army was guarding the vital lines of communication with New England. Heath was asked to summon the "eastern militia" from Connecticut and Massachusetts and lead them into action as "rapidly as the season will admit." Washington was working more effectively with the militia—listening, responding, encouraging, persuading.[9]

A harder task was to ask his sick and weary Continental troops who had returned from Trenton to march and fight again. They were not fit for it. Even Lord Stirling, one of the bravest hearts in the army, was too ill to march. Even so, the orders went out. The army was told to muster for another campaign. It would cross the Delaware River on December 29. This would be a bigger operation than the last, with eight crossing points for the American army. Sullivan's Continental division and its artillery were to use McConkey's and Johnson's ferry landings, as before. Greene's Continentals were ordered to cross the river downstream at Yardley's Ferry. The militia would go over at Easton, Coryell's, and Trenton ferries, and others downriver.[10]

They worried much about the river. Washington wrote to Cadwalader and other officers along its banks, "Please give me frequent information on the state of the river and whether it is to be passed by boats or whether the ice will admit of a passage."[11] The volatile American weather was another concern, and with good reason. On that day, Saturday, December 28, snow began to fall in the Delaware Valley and rapidly accumulated to a depth of six inches in some places along the river. Then the the air turned clear and dry, and the temperature dropped sharply. The night of December 28 was bitter cold.

At first light on the morning of Sunday, December 29, as the army began to move out, sentries along the Delaware sent an urgent report to headquarters. In the night, the Delaware River had frozen completely over, with a thin covering of ice from bank to bank. Washington wrote to John Hancock, "I am just setting out, to attempt a second crossing over the Delaware. . . . It will be attended with much fatigue and difficulty on account of the ice, which will neither allow us to cross on foot, or give us easy passage with boats."[12]

If the crossing on Christmas night had been a horror, this one was worse. At Yardley's Ferry, Greene's division found that the ice was already two or three inches thick. The infantry stepped gingerly upon it, discovered that it held their weight, and walked across the Delaware. But it was not strong enough to support horses and artillery. Greene's infantry were forced to leave their guns behind, and the heavy wagons that held their tents. In Trenton that night they slept in the open, trying desperately to keep warm by crowding around roaring fires of fence rails, barn boards, and anything else that would burn. The infantry took off their cartridge pouches and huddled so close to the flames that they scorched on one side and froze on the other.

While Greene's troops were struggling at Yardley's Ferry on December 29, Washington was upriver at McConkey's Ferry, trying to cross the Delaware with Sullivan's division. Conditions there were impossible. Washington and Sullivan were not able to get over the river on the ice, or in their boats. The next morning they tried again with more success, and many men crossed that day. Through the next day, both divisions labored at the heavy task of getting some of the guns and wagons over the river. At last they finished as New Year's Eve approached.[13]

Just as the army succeeded in crossing the half-frozen river, another problem threatened to stop it. Commissary officers reported that they were running out of food. The story of supply in the Continental army is a drab subject, much neglected in most histories of these events, but it had a drama of its own. The American Revolution was yet another instance of Rommel's Law that battles are won or lost by the quartermasters before the first shot is fired.

The American army organized its logistics on the British model, with a Commissary Department that looked after food and general supplies. By 1776, it had become the largest economic organization in the colonies. Its head was Commissary General Joseph Trumbull. How he and his staff managed to feed a hungry army in the winter of 1775–76 was a saga in its own right. The army could not forage for itself in Bucks County, Pennsylvania. Commissary officers complained that the farmers would not sell and the millers would not grind for Continental money.[14] Supply was even more difficult in New Jersey. Washington wrote on December 30, "Jersey has been swept so clean that there is no dependence on anything there." The army could not hope to march and fight in the Jersies without carrying its rations.[15]

Joseph Trumbull was able to feed the army only by a continental effort, which operated at the limits of possibility in early America. In the winter of 1776, the staples of army diet were mainly bread or biscuit and salt meat. When supplies were exhausted in the middle states, the commissary general bought his flour from the great Virginia grain plantations along the James, Rappahannock, and Potomac rivers. Salt meat came by wagon from New England, over a long and dangerous route through the New York highlands. To keep that line open, Trumbull moved to New England in the fall of 1776, much to the displeasure of Washington, who wanted him closer at hand. But the "eastern states," as New England was called, remained Trumbull's strongest source of supply for provisions, clothing, and money.[16]

The weakest link in this very long chain was the distribution system in Pennsylvania, which fell into the hands of Carpenter

Wharton, a corrupt and incompetent businessman who volunteered to supply Continental troops in the middle states as deputy commissary general. Wharton ran his office as a private business for the benefit of a small circle of cronies. Complaints were rife that he overcharged Congress, undersupplied the army, and turned a profit in between.[17]

On December 30, 1776, when Washington was moving his regiments across the Delaware, Wharton's commissary office suddenly failed, and food stopped flowing to the army. So severe was the problem that Washington was forced to divide his forces and hold one part of them in Pennsylvania after the rest had moved to New Jersey. He believed that the supply problem was mainly in Philadelphia, and primarily in the office of "Mr. Commissary Wharton."

By hard experience Washington had learned that the best way to deal with a corrupt and incompetent businessman was to ask a bigger businessman to take him in hand. From Trenton, he sent an urgent message to Robert Morris, reporting that "the greatest impediment to our motion is, the want of provisions, some of the troops are yet on the other side of the river [in Pennsylvania], only waiting provisions." Morris summoned the commissary to his office. Within a few hours he replied to Washington, "I gave Mr. Wharton an order for 40 thousand dollars this morning & pressed him to attend most diligently to your supplies. I will Send for him again [to learn] what is done & add Springs to his movements if I can. I wish he was more silent, prudent &c but I fancy he is active."[18]

Morris's intervention worked. Provisions began to flow again that very day, and troops were able to resume crossing the river. Food reached forward units, and the army was united at Trenton, in the nick of time. Its supplies were not abundant, but they were barely enough to feed the troops. Another part of the problem was "Mr. Commissary Wharton." This was postponed until the spring. In the meantime, Robert Morris continued to keep an eye on him.

With another effort, the Continental artillery was brought across the river, more of it than before. Henry Knox and his gunners had repaired broken axles and carriages, added captured Hessian guns, and found others in Philadelphia. Altogether Knox brought "thirty or forty pieces" across the river, twice his strength at Trenton only a few days before. Supplies of powder and shot were ample, and the army brought a large baggage train to New Jersey. It had succeeded in reequipping itself with tents and blankets, and replaced much of the equipment that had been lost at Fort Lee and the retreat from New York.[19]

Still the army suffered from shortages of warm clothing and shoes—especially shoes. A voluntary drive was mounted in the states to collect old clothing for the Continental army as an emergency measure. Families and friends pitched in, and the effort succeeded. A British officer in the First Guards Battalion wrote to Marquis of Rockingham in January 1777, "That the Rebels are in want of every necessary is a language which I have heard, but there is no truth in such an assertion. Some of the prisoners we took at Princeton had exceeding good cloaths, Shoes etc. The Militia which are assembled in considerable numbers . . . are indeed a miserable set of beings almost naked, & as the weather is now setting in severe with a Fall of snow, must soon leave the field."[20]

As the army gathered in New Jersey on December 31, Washington confronted yet another hard question, the most urgent of all. He explained to Robert Morris, "the great and radical Evil which pervades our whole System & like an Ax at the Tree of our safety, Interest and Liberty here again shews its baleful influence—Tomorrow the Continental Troops are all at liberty."[21]

It was not quite all of them, but the enlistments of many experienced troops would expire on December 31. Some of his best regiments seemed the most determined to depart. One of them was Glover's Marblehead mariners, who wanted to go home for a special reason. Many men planned to leave the army so that they could fight at sea. Privateers were "hourly outfitting in the ports of Massachusetts." In 1776, these ships wrought havoc on British shipping. They captured a large part of the Highland regiments at sea and seized ships and cargoes beyond counting. Large sums flowed into Marblehead and Salem and Boston. Fortunes were being made. Here was a way that seagoing men could serve the Cause and enrich themselves at the same time.

Another unit that was ready to go home was Haslet's First Delaware Continental Regiment, one of the best in the army. It had suffered severe losses in six months of service. Of its original 750 men, only 92 were present and fit for duty on December 22. The regiment's term of service was due to expire on New Year's Eve, and nothing could persuade them to stay. On December 30 all but six men left camp. One who remained was Colonel John Haslet, still hobbling on frozen legs after having fallen into the Delaware River on Christmas night. The others were Captain Thomas Holland, Ensign John Wilson, surgeon Reuben Gildre, and two privates. Haslet wrote his friend Caesar Rodney that the departure of his men so infuriated Washington that he "declared his intention of having officers and

Thomas and Sarah Mifflin, a
portrait by John Singleton
Copley (1773). Philadelphia
Museum of Art.

Thomas and Sarah Mifflin, a
portrait by John Singleton
Copley (1773). Philadelphia
Museum of Art.

men bound neck and heel and brought back as an example to the
army." But the departing soldiers were within their rights, and even
dire threats from the commander-in-chief could not deter them.[22]

If Washington hoped to remain in the field, he had to persuade
some of his veterans to stay with him. Finally, a solution was found
by entrepreneurial officers of the Pennsylvania Associators, mostly
Philadelphia merchants. They offered a bounty of ten dollars to
men who agreed to turn out for a few more weeks of winter soldiering. The idea came from Thomas Mifflin, a Pennsylvania merchant
and politician turned militia general. He suggested that Continental troops could be kept by the same means. Mifflin was at Crosswicks
in New Jersey with the Pennsylvania militia and Hitchcock's New
England Continental brigade, mostly veterans from Rhode Island
whose term of service was about to end.

General Mifflin assembled the Rhode Island men. They knew
his history. As early as 1764 this very powerful and wealthy man had
pledged his fortune to the Cause. He had soldiered with them since
the siege of Boston, had shown his courage under fire at Lechmere's
Point in Massachusetts, and had volunteered to serve in the rear
guard at Long Island. Mifflin was a "public man," with much experience of Philadelphia politics. He was so skilled in the arts of political persuasion that he won reelection to the Assembly with 85
percent of the Philadelphia vote.

Now he faced his most difficult test. Thomas Mifflin mustered the New England regiments and rode before them, "mounted on a fine horse, wrapped in a rose colored blanket overcoat and wearing a fur cap." Captain Stephen Olney remembered that "General Mifflin made a harangue." The New Englanders were eager to get home, but they listened to him. He spoke of the Cause, appealed to their conscience, and offered each of them ten dollars hard money if they would stay for six weeks. Mifflin asked them to "poise firelocks" if they were willing to stay. To everyone's amazement the firelocks went up, nearly all of them. John Howland recalled, "The poising commenced by some of each platoon, and was followed by the whole line. . . . We all poised with the rest." Captain Olney recalled that "our regiment, with one accord, agreed to stay to a man; as did also the others, except a few who made their escape by the enemy at Trenton and was not seen in the army afterwards."[23]

The news was carried to George Washington, who was delighted by the result but appalled by the cost. He confided to Congress that a bounty of ten dollars was "a most extravagant Price, when compared to the time of Service, but the example was set by the State of Pennsylvania with respect to their militia, and I thought it no time to stand upon trifles when a body of firm troops, inured to danger, were absolutely necessary to lead on the raw and undisciplined."[24]

Washington agreed to try the same appeal with the Continentals in Greene's and Sullivan's divisions. He mustered the New England regiments and begged them to serve for another six weeks. A sergeant remembered that the general "personally addressed us . . . told us our services were greatly needed, and that we could do more for our country than we ever could at any future date, and in the most affectionate manner entreated us to stay."[25] Then the regimental commanders asked all who would stay to step forward. "The drums beat for volunteers," one remembered, "but not a man turned out." One explained that his comrades were "worn down with fatigue and privations, had their hearts fixed on home and comforts of the domestic circle." The men watched as Washington "wheeled his horse about, rode in front of the regiment," and spoke to them again. Long afterward, a sergeant still remembered his words:

"My brave fellows," Washington began, "you have done all I asked you to do, and more than could be reasonably expected; but your country is at stake, your wives, your houses, and all that you hold dear. You have worn yourselves out with the fatigues and hardships, but we know not how to spare you. If you will consent to stay one month longer, you will render that service to the cause of liberty, and to your country, which you probably can never do under any other circumstances."[26]

The drums rolled again. The sergeant recalled that "the soldiers felt the force of the appeal" and began to talk among themselves. One said, "I will remain if you will." Another said, "We cannot go home under such circumstances." A few men stepped forward, then several others, then many more, and "their example was [followed] by nearly all who were fit for duty in the regiment, amounting to about two hundred volunteers." These were veterans who understood what they were being asked to do. They knew well what the cost might be. One of them remembered later that nearly half of the men who stepped forward would be killed in the fighting or dead of disease "soon after."[27]

An officer asked the general if the men should be enrolled. "No," said Washington, "men who will volunteer in such a case as this, need no enrollment to keep them to their duty."[28] Only a few days before, Washington was infuriated with these men, and ready to clap some of them in irons. Now he was leading them in another way. This gentleman of Virginia was learning to treat a brigade of New England Yankee farmboys and fishermen as men of honor, who were entitled to equality of esteem. That attitude had already begun to spread throughout the army. In 1776, American officers addressed even their lowliest privates as gentlemen. No other army in the world operated on such a principle. Europeans were startled to observe it at work in America; Nicholas Collin observed in 1771, "all are called gentleman and ladies." Here was a new idea of a gentleman, a moral condition rather than a social rank. It was also a new idea of honor, which was not defined by rank or status or gender, but by a principle of human dignity and decency.

Washington invoked this principle when he spoke to his men, and appealed to their conscience and honor. At the same time, he also addressed their material interest. Like General Mifflin he authorized a bounty of ten dollars in hard coin to every Continental soldier who agreed to stay, and he ordered the commanders at Morristown to do the same. It worked. Washington wrote later that day that "the continental regiments from the eastern Governments [New England] have to a Man agreed to stay six weeks beyond their term. . . . I hope this noble example will be followed by the four regiments under your command. . . . Let them know the Militia are pouring in from all quarters and only want Veteran troops to lead them on." The continentals at Morristown also agreed to stay and were promised the same bonus.[29]

Robert Morris, a portrait by Charles Willson Peale (ca. 1782). Independence National Historical Park.

So successful was the solution that it created a problem in its turn. Washington's pay chest was empty. On December 31, 1776, he sent an urgent message to Robert Morris. "Tomorrow the Continental Troops are all at Liberty," he wrote, with some exaggeration. "In order to get their assistance [I] have promised them a bounty of 10 Dollars if they will continue for one Month—But here again a new difficulty presents itself. We have not the money."[30]

Only the day before, Morris had scoured the money chests of Philadelphia for odds and ends of cash to pay Washington's secret agents. Now he had to do it again. According to legend he visited a rich Quaker and persuaded him to unearth a chest of hard money that Morris knew to be buried in his garden. Morris literally dug up the cash and sent Washington "two parcels of hard money," which arrived on New Year's Eve, just in time.[31]

With an idea from Thomas Mifflin and timely help from Robert Morris, George Washington kept many of his veteran regiments for the coming campaign, but their numbers were reduced. Three New England brigades that had counted 2,600 men on December 22 were down to about 1,400 men on the first of January. Mercer's and Stirling's brigades, 1,500 men a week earlier, were now consolidated in one small unit of 325. Stephen's brigade of Virginia Continentals had about 400. Fermoy's Pennsylvanians held their strength at about 610. Altogether, Washington had lost about 2,600 of his Continental veterans to illness and the expiration of enlistments, but he had preserved a veteran force of about 3,300 men.

And as the old Continental regiments were shrinking, the militia entered the field. Mifflin wrote Washington on December 28, "Pennsylvania is at length roused and coming forward to your Excellency's aid." Men were turning out faster than they could be organized into units. They collected their muskets and powderhorns, packed a few provisions into cloth sacks and leather "wallets," bade farewell to their families, and made their way alone and in small parties to the ferry landings on the Delaware River. At the Bristol landing, Mifflin rounded up about 1,500 men from at least twenty-seven Pennsylvania regiments and militia companies, plus a detachment of Continental marines. He led them across the Delaware River to Burlington and formed them into a brigade.[32]

General Cadwalader led another brigade of Philadelphia Associators, mostly shopkeepers, artisans, and dockworkers, perhaps 1,700 or 1,800 men. General Ewing took the field with a third militia brigade, the remains of the old Flying Camp, who were mostly farmers from the counties of York, Cumberland, Lancaster, Chester, and Bucks. The Jersey militia were turning out, all over the state. More men appeared from Cumberland, Gloucester, and Salem counties and joined the South Jersey units that Samuel Griffin had led in early December. Others gathered in the north, at Morristown and Pluckemin. Even centers of Tory strength such as Monmouth County came under Whig control.[33]

In the midst of many troubles, Washington and his officers turned to another question that they judged to be of high importance for their Cause. When they returned to New Jersey, a moral problem came before them. It was about plunder. After the attack on Trenton, Washington had issued a general order that everything taken from the enemy should be divided among the officers and men. On December 27, 1776, he announced that "as a reward to the officers and soldiers for their spirited behavior in such inclement weather, the General will (in behalf of the Continent) have all the Field pieces, the Arms, Accoutrements, Horses and everything else which was taken yesterday, valued and a proportionate distribution of the Amount made among Officers (if they choose to partake) and the Men who crossed the River." The colonels of every regiment were ordered "without delay" to "have the Plunder of every kind (taken by his Reg't) collected and given in to the Quartermaster Gen'l that his men may receive the value of it."[34]

Washington had made a mistake in calling it plunder. He was really thinking about prize money, for items of value captured from an enemy army. He tried to explain to his officers, "the order about Plunder and Stores does not extend to any but that belonging to the Enemy & not to Tory property—had that been allowed, the Effects of many good staunch Worthy persons would have fallen a sacrifice."[35] When the army returned to New Jersey, and patrols began to move widely through a ravaged countryside, plundering of another kind rapidly increased. On January 1 Washington issued new general orders: "His Excellency General Washington strictly forbids all the officers and soldiers in the Continental army, of the militia, and all recruiting parties, plundering any person whatsoever, whether Tories or others." This order was distributed to the troops, and published in the newspapers. It was not always obeyed. Plundering by American troops continued, but on a smaller scale than the organized depredations by German and British Regulars.[36]

The same general orders also established strict standards for treatment of noncombatants, especially women. Washington announced, "It is expected that humanity and tenderness to women and children will distinguish brave Americans, contending for liberty, from infamous mercenary ravagers, whether British or Hessians."[37] Other orders went out for the care of prisoners of war. Washington and his officers set a high standard in their treatment of Hessian captives at Trenton. He issued instructions that "the officers and men should be separated. I wish the former may be well treated, and that the latter may have such principles instilled in them during their Confinement, that when they return, they may open the Eyes of their Countrymen."[38]

Not all Americans wanted to do these things. Always some dark spirits wished to visit the same cruelties on the British and Hessians that had been inflicted on American captives. But Washington's example carried growing weight, more so than his written orders and prohibitions. He often reminded his men that they were an army of liberty and freedom, and that the rights of humanity for which they were fighting should extend even to their enemies. Washington and his officers were keenly aware that the war was a contest for popular opinion, but they did not think in terms of "images" or "messages" in the manner of a modern journalist or politician. Their thinking was more substantive. The esteem of others was important to them mainly because they believed that victory would come only if they deserved to win. Even in the most urgent moments of the war, these men were concerned about ethical questions in the Revolution.

GOOD GROUND

∾ The Midnight Ride of Doctor Rush

> All the Artillery to be Drawn up on the high
> Ground over the Bridge . . . the Troops are to
> form on the Ground in the rear of the Artillery
> to form in three lines . . . Soldiers to hold them-
> selves in compleat readiness to advance at a
> moments warning.
>
> —General Orders for the American army,
> December 30, 1776[1]

AT TRENTON, George Washington made his headquarters in a large two-story house on Queen Street that had belonged to Loyalist John Barnes, the king's high sheriff for Hunterdon County. Here he prepared for the next test. It would be different from the last one. In the Christmas campaign he had mounted a bold offensive, with his slashing attack on the Hessians in Trenton. As New Year's Eve approached he was thinking of a defensive battle against another enemy at the same place. On December 30, he summoned his senior officers to a council of war and reported the latest intelligence. Staff officers believed at least six thousand British and German troops were in New Jersey, and another four thousand or more were marching to their support. The Americans expected an attack in great strength by British and Hessian troops. In council they decided to receive it in Trenton on ground of their own choosing.[2]

After the last battle, these men knew well that Trenton was not easily defensible. Like Colonel Rall, they rejected the idea of fortifying the town itself as an exercise in futility. But the last fight had taught them that a strong defensive position existed on a high open knoll south of Assunpink Creek. It was very good ground: a deep creek in front, the Delaware River on the left flank, and impassable swamps to the right. The twisting bed of Assunpink Creek and its steep banks made a natural moat that could be crossed only at a narrow stone bridge and several fords. Behind the creek a rising slope of open land made a perfect glacis, with broad fields of fire for infantry and artillery. It was a natural fortress against an enemy who approached from the north.[3]

But the position on Assunpink Creek had its weaknesses. In a patch of woods to the right, two fords could be crossed by a determined enemy. The entire position could also be approached from the south by a long and circuitous march. If an opponent could find the fords and cross them, or attack from the rear, the position would become a deadly trap for an unwary defender.

The American commanders decided to accept that risk. Their object was to entice a proud, aggressive, and angry enemy into a costly assault on good ground, much as the French did at Ticonderoga in the last war, and New Englanders at Bunker Hill in 1775. Americans had tried this tactic many times at Dorchester Heights, Guana Heights, Brooklyn Heights, Harlem Heights, White Plains, and Fort Washington. It was a dangerous course for the defenders, as Fort Washington had shown. What if the ground were not so good, or the attackers were better, or something went wrong? In many ways, a defensive battle was a greater risk than the attack on Trenton had been. But if a victory could be won, the reward would be greater too.

After the council agreed, George Washington issued general orders to fortify the position they had selected. All of the artillery was to be "drawn up on the high ground," covering the bridge and the fords. The infantry were ordered to stake out positions in three lines, one behind the other, 250 yards apart. Guards were posted on every road leading toward Trenton, and mounted patrols were sent out in every direction.[4]

The Americans actively collected intelligence on their opponents by every possible means. Deserters and prisoners were questioned separately and at great length. Couriers were intercepted on the road and their letters brought directly to Washington.[5] Much use was made of paid informers. Washington wrote from his Trenton headquarters to Robert Morris on December 30, "We have the greatest occasion at present for hard Money, to pay a certain set of people who are particular use to us. . . . Silver would be most convenient." Morris instantly scraped together a mixed purse of Dutch dollars, English shillings, and French crowns, mainly for espionage.[6]

After the fiasco at New York, Washington had become deeply involved in intelligence-gathering and cultivated many sources. One of the strangest was the *New-York Gazette and Weekly Mercury*. Its printer, Hugh Gaine (1726–1807), was an Irish immigrant from Belfast who strongly supported the American side at the beginning of the Revolution. In the early fall of 1776, Gaine appeared to become a trimmer. He published a Whig edition of his newspaper in Newark, while Ambrose Serle and others issued a Tory edition in New York. In November, Gaine appeared to change sides, returned to occupied New York, and published a gazette so extreme in its Tory rage that it became the favorite target of Whig printers throughout the continent. But probably he was an American secret agent, and he would be protected after the war.[7]

Other intelligence came from mounted officer patrols. Washington now had cavalry with him, the First Troop of Philadelphia Light Horse, twenty-one affluent young gentlemen of "independent means." As a point of honor they insisted on paying their own expenses, and they invested their entire pay in bank shares for a "lying in and foundling hospital" to aid female victims of the war.[8] This silk-stocking outfit must have been jeered by ragged infantrymen when they rode into Trenton on matched chestnut horses. The men wore chocolate brown uniforms with snow-white facings, high-topped riding boots, and small round black hats with silver cords and a jaunty buck's tail. They armed themselves with identical carbines and cavalry swords on blancoed belts and carried horse pistols in saddle holsters marked with the unit's flowery cipher.[9]

Washington had a mission for these elegant gentleman-rebels. He wanted to know what was happening in Princeton, where British forces were gathering only ten miles from his headquarters. On December 30, the general summoned adjutant Joseph Reed, who knew the countryside, having been born and raised in New Jersey and educated in the College at Princeton (class of 1757). Reed was told to lead a mounted patrol of the Philadelphia First Troop, explore the roads, and bring back prisoners. Reed remembered that the Philadelphia cavalrymen were enthusiastic but very green. All but one had "never before seen an enemy."

He led them to Princeton by back lanes from the south, "almost within view of the town." Near an outlying farmhouse they noticed a British soldier, then another and a third. The troopers charged the house, seized a commissary who was foraging in the barn, and surprised twelve hungry British dragoons who were busy "conquering a parcel of mince pyes" inside the house. All of the dragoons were captured except a wily sergeant who slipped away.[10]

The Philadelphia troopers returned in triumph to Trenton with their captives mounted behind, probably to a different reception from the infantry. The prisoners were "separately examined" on the evening of December 30. Reed remembered that "a very perfect account was obtained of British plans and dispositions." Washington learned from these men that British commanders were concentrating eight thousand men at Princeton and were indeed preparing to attack him in Trenton.[11]

More intelligence arrived from Colonel John Cadwalader at Crosswicks. He reported a meeting with a "very intelligent young gentleman" who had been detained overnight in Princeton by the British commander and allowed to leave on the morning of December 30. The "young gentleman" made his way to Colonel Cadwalader's camp and was interviewed by the colonel himself, just as he had been by the British commanders the day before. Both sides were hungry for news of their opponents. The young gentleman had alarmed the British by telling them that the American army was about sixteen thousand strong, nearly three times its actual size. He told Cadwalader that Princeton was rapidly becoming an armed camp, with about five thousand Hessian and British troops. Their commander, Brigadier General Alexander Leslie, made his headquarters in the president's house at the college. The young gentleman described the British defenses in great detail. Eight cannon, all six-pounders, were lined up hub to hub across the west end of Nassau Street. Two other guns faced north, "to sweep the length of the present Witherspoon street," which entered Princeton from that side; four guns more covered the Kingston Road to the east by the Hudibras Tavern. He described breastworks of fascines that were "almost finished" on either side of the Post Road to Trenton. Other fieldworks had been begun on the west and north sides of the town and were nearly finished on the morning of December 31. Outposts and sentries were posted along the Trenton Road from Princeton to Maidenhead.

The young gentleman observed that the town was carefully protected on every side but one. He reported "no Sentries on the east side of town," behind the college, which appeared open and unguarded. The town could be approached by back roads from that direction. Cadwalader drew all this information on a rough map of the town, with a back route from Trenton. He added a note: "This

road leads to the back part of Princeton which may be entered anywhere on this side—the country cleared chiefly for about two miles,"
with "few fences."[12]

One wonders who this "very intelligent young gentleman" might
have been. He knew Princeton intimately. Both the American Colonel and British Brigadier treated him as a noncombatant and a
gentleman "of rank." He appears to have had Whiggish sympathies,
but was not strictly speaking an American spy (as many scholars
have called him). Probably he was an undergraduate at the college,
which had been closed since the British invasion. Whoever he may
have been, this young gentleman from Princeton had a major impact on events.

On the strength of this intelligence, Washington sent a large force
halfway up the Post Road toward Princeton, with orders to delay any
British movement in the direction of Trenton. Major Wilkinson remembered that it included Colonel Charles Scott's brigade of Virginia infantry, Edward Hand's Maryland and Pennsylvania Riflemen,
Colonel Nicholas Haussegger's Pennsylvania German battalion, and
Captain Thomas Forrest's battery of six guns, altogether about a
thousand men.[13]

The Americans advanced under cover of darkness on New Year's
Eve and occupied a formidable position about six miles from Nassau
Hall. They chose a place called Eight Mile Run (today's Shipetaukin
Creek), where the highway crossed a small stream with steep banks,
and hills on both sides of the highway. British and German troops
called it the Pass.[14] The American troops were in position before
sunrise on New Year's Day, and British patrols discovered them very
quickly. At first light on January 1, the First Battalion of British
light infantry and two companies of Hessian Jägers were sent to
clear the road.[15] As the British and Hessians approached, the American troops resisted stubbornly. The fighting continued through the
morning. It took a heavy toll of the attackers, and the Americans
succeeded in defeating the light infantry and Jägers. British commanders sent forward reinforcements of Hessian and British grenadiers and deployed them in great strength, perhaps as many as six
battalions. Captain Johann Ewald of the Hessian Jägers wrote that
the enemy had "defended himself very well, and had not left the
pass until the Grenadiers were brought up against him."[16]

Finally the British and Hessian troops cleared the pass, but at
heavy cost. Ewald, usually very accurate about engagements in which
he was involved, wrote that "140 men [were] lost on both sides." His

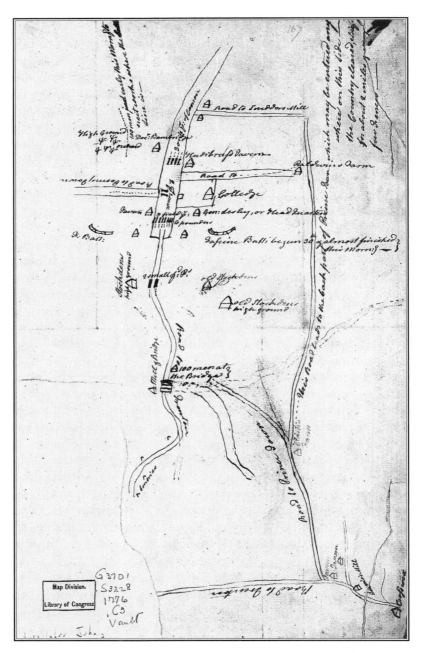

"The Spy Map," a plan of Princeton in the handwriting of John Cadwalader from information supplied by "a very intelligent young gentleman," probably an undergraduate at Princeton, who reported "no sentries on the east side of town, which could be approached by unguarded back roads." Cadwalader sent the map to Washington on December 31, 1776. Library of Congress.

small company of Jägers alone lost seven men, and most of the casualties were British. The Americans were thought to have lost four men killed. Here was a warning for British leaders. The Americans were out in strength, fighting well on good ground, holding their positions, inflicting casualties on picked troops, and taking few losses in return. This was a form of combat that the Regulars could only lose, even when they won the ground.[17]

On the evening of January 1, Washington called another council of war in his headquarters, to talk about the growing information on the enemy's strength and intentions. Joining him were Henry Knox, now promoted to brigadier general of artillery; the two divisional commanders, Nathanael Greene and John Sullivan; brigade commander Arthur St. Clair; adjutant Joseph Reed; and probably others. Washington summarized the disposition of American forces, which were scattered widely in West Jersey. His Continentals were mostly in Trenton or near it. Patrols were out to the northwest, twenty miles up the river; and also to the northeast as far as the outskirts of Princeton. Mifflin's Pennsylvania brigade was in Bordentown seven miles to the south, and some of his militia as far as Burlington, sixteen miles below Trenton. Cadwalader was thought to be at Crosswicks, seven miles southeast of Trenton. Some of his light infantry were reported to be ranging east as far as Cranbury, halfway across the state.[18]

Washington also reported that British reinforcements were marching south along a narrow corridor from New York to Elizabethtown, Amboy, Brunswick and Princeton. Their numbers were uncertain, but larger than the number of American troops, perhaps twice as large. Evidence arrived that the British leaders were preparing to strike at Trenton or Crosswicks. The question was: What should the American army do? Washington posed the problem in an open way, and another "division took place in the council." Joseph Reed remembered that three options were discussed. One proposed that the Continentals should retreat from Trenton and "join Gen. Cadwalader at Crosswick's 7 miles distance." Another idea was to "order [Cadwalader] to join the main body at Trenton." A third was to keep the troops divided and order the division under General Cadwalader to attack Brunswick, capture the British baggage, and release General Lee.[19]

The Council was not able to agree on any of these choices, in part because it did not know enough about Cadwalader's situation. Henry Knox observed that Dr. Benjamin Rush "had just come up from Crosswix" and "was connected with Cadwalader's Corps." Knox

Dr. Benjamin Rush, painting by Charles Willson Peale (1783). A friend to British leaders, a strong supporter of the American cause, a member of the Continental Congress, and an advisor to George Washington in a critical council of war at Trenton on January 1, 1777, Dr. Rush also volunteered his services as a surgeon in the New Jersey campaign. Winterthur Museum.

suggested that Rush be "called into the Council, to give an opinion upon the question." Rush took up the story in his autobiography. He remembered, "I was accordingly sent for, and heard from General Washington a brief state of the controversy. He then asked my advice. I said that I was not a judge of what was proper in the business before the council, but one thing I knew well, that all the Philadelphia militia would be very happy in being under his immediate command, and that I was sure they would instantly obey a summons to join his troops at Trenton. After this information I retired."[20]

Doctor Rush waited outside while the council talked. "A few minutes later," he wrote, "I was called in again and requested by Genl. Washington to be the bearer of a letter to General Cadwalader. I readily consented." The hour was about nine o'clock at night when Washington sat at his desk and drafted orders for Cadwalader. "March your troops immediately to this place," he wrote. "I expect your brigade will be here at five o'clock in the Morning without fail. At any rate do not exceed six." He was asking Cadwalader to muster his militia in the middle of the night, make a forced march of seven miles from Crosswicks to Trenton on muddy roads, and arrive before sunrise.[21]

At about ten o'clock, Rush mounted his horse and set off for Crosswicks with an escort, Sergeant William Hall of the Philadelphia Light Horse. It was a hard ride. "The weather was cold and damp, the roads muddy, and the night extremely dark," Rush remembered. It took them three hours to ride seven miles, with many streams and fences to cross. "When we came within a mile of Crosswicks," Rush wrote, "we met Colonel Delany who had the command of the patroles. He rode up to me and presenting a cocked pistol to my breast, demanded who I was."

"An old friend," Rush answered.

"I don't know you, Sir," said the vigilant officer, Colonel Sharp Delany. "Tell me your name."

"I then told my name and my business," Rush recalled. "He ordered us to be conducted to General Cadwalader's quarters, to whom in his bed I delivered General Washington's letter. It was then about 1 o'clock. He instantly rose and set his brigade in motion."[22]

Cadwalader got his men moving quickly. Sergeant William Young remembered that his Pennsylvania militia mustered at "twelve o'clock or one this morning, joined Battalion and order[ed] to Trentown." The march was difficult and slow. Sergeant Young wrote, "It rained when we set out; on account of the thaw the Road was very muddy and deep. Though we had but eight miles to go it was 9 o'clock before we reached Trentown. I was a good deal fatigued on account of the Deepness of Road, and its being night I could not see my way. The moon gave some light, but it Being on my Back I could not see so as to get the best Road."[23]

The marching brigades came apart on the dark road, and men drifted into Trenton for many hours after daybreak. Captain Charles Willson Peale, of the Philadelphia Associators, wrote in his diary, "The roads are very muddy, almost over our shoe tops. The number of troops, the badness of the roads, so many runs to cross, and fences to remove, make it a tedious march. The sun had risen more than an hour before we reached the town, and afterwards, the difficulty of getting quarters kept us a long time under arms. At last we were provided and had made a fire."[24]

Some had an even harder slog. Cadwalader's light infantry had been scouting as far as Cranbury, ten miles east of Princeton, where they held their own council of war and decided to return. On New Year's Eve, they made a long night march from Cranbury to Allentown on "a very dark night." One remembered the agony of marching on roads halfleg deep which worried the troops exceedingly." When they arrived on January 2, "at daylight we were ordered to march for Trent Town and we came to crosswicks the brigades were gone we got to Trentown about Eleven O'clock."

Lieutenant Rodney remembered that when they reached Trenton, they "found all the troops from our different posts in Jersey

Charles Willson Peale Self-Portrait (1776–77), in the uniform of an Infantry Captain in the Philadelphia Associators. Peale painted this very small image for his wife while he was soldiering in the New Jersey campaigns. He fought in the second battle of Trenton and the battle of Princeton. American Philosophical Society.

collected and collecting there." Washington had succeeded in concentrating his army. Arriving with the militia in Trenton were a veteran brigade of Continentals, Hitchcock's New England men, and several small detachments of about eighty marines. More than two-thirds were from Pennsylvania and New Jersey. They joined Washington's "Continentals," whom militiamen such as Rodney were beginning to call the "Regulars." Altogether their numbers had grown to seven thousand men. It was a different army from the band that had attacked Trenton on the day after Christmas. Morale was rising. "Never were men in higher spirit than our whole Army is," Rodney wrote. "All are determined to extirpate them from the Jerseys; but I believe the enemy's fears will do it before we get up with them."[25]

They were exhausted by their night march. Peale remembered, "I took a short nap on a plank with my feet to the fire; but was suddenly awakened by a call to arms— the enemy approaching, and at a small distance from the town. We soon paraded, and joined the battalion, and appeared on the alarm ground, where I was greatly struck by the appearance of so fine an army." The same thing happened to James Johnston, who marched through the entire night, arrived in Trenton at sunrise, and was sent with his unit to Philemon Dickinson's estate on the river, now vacated by the enemy, and quartered in the general's greenhouse. They were getting breakfast when the drums began to beat.[26]

Many remembered that electric moment. Lieutenant James McMichael in the Pennsylvania Rifle regiment recalled, "At 10 A.M. we received news that the enemy were advancing, when the drums beat to arms, and we were all paraded on the south side of the bridge," behind Assunpink Creek.[27] New England Yankee Stephen

Olney wrote that the Rhode Island regiments "arrived about sunrise, having been all night travelling eleven miles, owing to the badness of the road; we took quarters in the houses and began to prepare for breakfast. But before it was ready, the drums beat to arms." They were surprised, as "the enemy whom we supposed at Princeton, twelve miles off, or at Brunswick, twenty four miles off, were near at hand and double our number." But the commanders of the army had prepared for this moment. Olney's men received clear orders. He wrote, "Our troops paraded on the south side of a small river that passes through the town into the Delaware."[28]

Even as the alarm sounded, many men shared a spirit that was different from the last fight. Among them was Benjamin Rush. After riding all night, he returned to Trenton about seven o'clock in the morning and went to the headquarters of Arthur St. Clair, where he "begged the favor of his bed for a few hours." In this American army, a civilian volunteer did not hesitate to ask a brigadier general if he could borrow the general's bed—and the general agreed. Rush remembered that just as he was falling asleep an alarm gun awoke him. "I started up, and the first creature I saw was a black woman crying and wringing her hands in my room. She was followed by general St. Clair with a composed countenance. I asked him what was the matter. He said the enemy were advancing."[29]

"What do you intend to do?" Rush asked.

"Why, fight them," St. Clair replied, with a smile. Rush remembered that St. Clair than "took down his sword, and girded it on his thigh with a calmness such as I thought seldom took place at the expectation of a battle."[30]

Rush talked with other officers and men, and the word he used repeatedly to describe their mood was "composure." They were veterans of many battles and had defeated some of the most formidable Regulars in the world. The Americans believed that they could do it again, but if not they were determined to fight on. The day before, Rush had talked with General Hugh Mercer and heard him say, again "with great composure," that "he would not be conquered, but that he would cross the mountains and live among the Indians, rather than submit to the power of Great Britain in any of the civilized states."[31] Sergeant William Young found that this spirit was especially strong among the veteran regiments from New England. "The New England Men are a quiet set of men," he wrote on January 1, 1777. There was a growing sense of confidence throughout this American army.[32]

In the British camp, the mood was different. Only a week before, many British leaders had believed that the American rebellion was nearly broken. The disaster at Trenton ended that way of thinking. On December 29, patrols reported that General Washington had crossed the Delaware again, "in two columns not far from Trenton and had encamped behind Trenton Creek." On the same day, a rumor reached the British camp that another American army, "the former Lee corps, now commanded by General Lincoln, was approaching our right flank from the mountains of Morristown." British officers believed that the American armies had grown larger than their own and included sixteen thousand men, the number that the "intelligent young gentleman" had given them.[33]

British commanders in New Jersey had lost the initiative in the span of a single week. They had also lost control of the countryside. Small parties of American militia roamed the roads throughout the state. Even on the highway between the British garrisons at Brunswick and Princeton, an English officer and his servant were shot and killed in an American ambush. That method of attack outraged British officers as an atrocity that was forbidden by the laws of war. It also frightened them. The British army retained control of only a few heavily fortified towns and expected to be attacked at any moment.[34]

Repeated alarms swept through the British and German camps. Ewald remembered that "reports came in almost hourly of the approach of Washington's army." Early on the morning of December 31, the entire garrison was awakened two hours before daylight by another alarm, and the British and Hessian troops stood to arms. "We had information that Washington would attack," Ewald wrote in his diary.[35]

It was only a rumor, but that night another alarm followed in the camp of the Forty-second Highlanders. "In the evening around ten o'clock," one man remembered, an American officer was taken prisoner by a Scottish patrol. This man had sneaked through the outpost and posed as an English adjutant at a Scottish post, from which he demanded the password on the excuse he had forgotten it." The Scots had none of it. They "did not like this story, and held him securely until one of their patrols arrived, to whom they delivered him. When he was brought to Lord Cornwallis, he immediately identified himself and his mission. He was a major of riflemen, who intended to make a surprise attack on the Scottish Regiment as soon as he had succeeded in learning the password."[36]

"Thus had the times changed!" wrote Hessian Captain Ewald. "The Americans had constantly run before us. Four weeks ago we expected to end the war with the capture of Philadelphia, and now we had to render Washington the honor of thinking about our defense. Due to this affair at Trenton, such a fright came over the army that if Washington had used this opportunity we would have flown to our ships and let him have all of America. Since we had thus far underestimated our enemy, from this unhappy day onward we saw everything through the magnifying glass."[37]

THE BRIDGE

❧ Assunpink: The Most Awful Moment

> The bridge looked red as blood, with their killed
> and wounded, and their red coats.
>
> —Sergeant Joseph White, January 2, 1776[1]

LATE ON NEW YEAR'S DAY, General Charles Cornwallis arrived at the British camp in Princeton. He was not in a happy
frame of mind. Five days earlier he had been in New York,
looking forward to a leave in England. He wanted desperately to be
with his wife, Jemima, and was deeply concerned about her health.
General Howe had given him permission to sail home for the winter. On December 27, Cornwallis sent his baggage aboard HMS
Bristol. As the ship was about to sail, a galloper arrived with news of
the disaster at Trenton.[2]

Cornwallis's leave was canceled, and Sir William Howe asked
his most able lieutenant to take the field. The orders were clear and
simple: Find the rebel army, strike quickly, and destroy it. Marching
orders went to British and Hessian forces in New York and New
Jersey, ordering a concentration of ten thousand men at Brunswick
and Princeton. On New Year's Day, Cornwallis made a "forced march"
down the Great Post Road, from New York to Princeton, a distance
of fifty miles. He arrived at Princeton late on that dark and rainy
night, after a long slog on miserable roads knee-deep in mud, with
an escort of three dragoons. For his headquarters, Cornwallis took
over Richard Stockton's Morven at the west end of the village. The
mansion had been occupied by British dragoons, and the estate
had been looted and vandalized. Family paintings had been used

for bayonet practice and sword drill. Books and papers in the library had been burned for warmth. Everything of value had been stolen, and the empty rooms stank of straw and filth.[3]

Even in that dismal setting, Cornwallis introduced an air of complete confidence that instantly animated his command. He "went into council with his generals," not to ask what should be done as Washington did, but to tell his subordinates what he meant to do. Cornwallis "announced his intention to advance toward Trenton in the morning." There was nothing subtle in his plan. He had already decided to commit all of his strength to a single thrust down the main Post Road, directly toward the American army.[4]

At least one of his officers did not agree. Hessian Colonel Carl von Donop spoke against it. Donop knew the countryside well by now, and had learned many painful lessons in the geography of New Jersey. He also knew that the American army was not what it had been only a few weeks ago, and he understood from hard experience how quickly it could move. Donop urged Cornwallis to change his plans and march on Trenton in two columns: one straight down the Post Road as Cornwallis intended, and the other a flanking movement to the British left, south through Cranbury and Allentown to Crosswicks, to turn the American right.

The Hessian officer believed that such an approach would force Washington to abandon Trenton and argued that it would put the American leader in an "unfavorable and precarious situation, since he had no depot for his new army in our vicinity." He asserted that "Lord Cornwallis would have needed only to pursue him steadily, whereby [Washington's] army, lacking everything, would have been destroyed in a few days." Cornwallis rejected that advice. He had made his decision and would stick to it. In the morning he would make a direct march with the concentrated force of his best troops, straight down the Post Road. All of his experience had taught him that a quick, strong stroke was the best course against a weak opponent. Captain Johann Ewald wrote sadly, "The enemy was despised and as usual we had to pay for it."[5]

Cornwallis's army was large, about eight thousand Regulars in the vicinity of Princeton, more than Washington could muster even with all the militia. Another several thousand British, German, and Loyalist troops were in posts throughout North Jersey and could be summoned if necessary. A large train of British artillery had already arrived at Princeton. Supplies were streaming in from Brunswick, Amboy, and New York in wagon convoys. One serial alone included forty-two wagons and arrived in good order. Others were following, and British commissaries ranged through the Jersey countryside with cavalry escorts, "pressing wagons" and taking provisions from farms nearby.

Numbers and resources were not a problem for the British commander. He also had no shortage of quality in his army. Cornwallis had skimmed the cream of the imperial forces. Some of the best regiments in the British army were with him near Princeton that night. The First Battalion of foot guards were there, a second guards battalion was in reserve at Brunswick, and two battalions of Highland infantry. Cornwallis also had six heavy battalions of grenadiers, four Hessian and two British, and two battalions of British light infantry and Hessian Jägers.

With these men was a train of British artillery with "medium" twelve-pounders, the heaviest guns that could be deployed in the field, twice the weight of the largest artillery in Washington's army. Cornwallis also had seven regiments of British infantry in two full brigades, which included some of the best units in the army. In Alexander Leslie's Second Brigade were the Fifth, Twenty-eighth, Thirty-fifth, and Forty-ninth Foot. In reserve was the Fourth Brigade of three infantry regiments, led by Colonel Charles Mawhood and his Seventeenth Foot, one of the best fighting regiments in the British army.

If anything, Cornwallis had an embarrassment of strengths. Command and control of this growing force proved very difficult. Cornwallis had so many troops that they could not all stay at Princeton. They overflowed the town and camped along the roads, as far as five miles away. It would not be easy to march them in a single column on miserable American roads. The main highway from Princeton to Trenton was a narrow muddy track, broken by streams and ravines. Here was another reason for Donop's strategy of several lines of advance on different roads, converging on the enemy. But Cornwallis was adamant. Working in the dark, on the night of January 1–2, he ordered his forces to assemble at Princeton before sunrise on January 2 and to form into a column on the Trenton Road.

The word reached Ewald's company of German Jägers at about eleven o'clock that night, in their camp at Rocky Hill, five miles northeast of Princeton center. They set out for Princeton in the middle of the night. Ewald recalled that "at this time the weather began to break, and since it was raining heavily the march was very unpleasant." Before first light, they were still on the road when the British drums in Princeton began to beat. The Jägers arrived at daybreak, and Captain Johann Ewald found the "entire army under arms."

He was sent to "draw biscuit and brandy from the depot for the men." After a quick meal, they were ordered to continue marching to Maidenhead, five miles down the Trenton Road, where they found the Hessian grenadiers, the rest of the Jägers, and the British Light Infantry, all under the command of Colonel Carl von Donop.[6]

The Hessian officers were angry men, spoiling for revenge against the rebels after the humiliation at Trenton. One of the most violent was their commander. Colonel von Donop ordered his men to take no prisoners, on pain of severe corporal punishment. British Sergeant Thomas Sullivan of the Forty-ninth Foot noted in his diary that the Hessian colonel was "so exasperated against the *Enemy,* especially for the aforesaid Corps being taken Prisoners by them, that he resolved to be revenged; he therefore went thro' the Ranks and declared openly to his men that any of them who would take a *Rebel* prisoner would receive 50 stripes, signifying to them that they were to kill all the *Rebels* they could without mercy."[7]

While the Jägers and the British light infantry waited at Maidenhead, Cornwallis sorted out his main body in Princeton. Ewald recorded the order of march. In the vanguard were a screen of mounted Hessian Jägers, then another company of Jägers on foot with their short German rifles, a hundred Hessian grenadiers, and two troops of light dragoons. Close behind came two battalions of British light infantry and "a number of six pounders." Behind the guns marched the six grenadier battalions, two British and four Hessian. Then came the remnant of Rall's lost Hessian brigade, the British guards, the Highlanders, and the four line regiments of Leslie's Second Brigade, altogether about nine thousand men. In reserve at Princeton was another British brigade of three regiments.[8]

Cornwallis at last mustered most of his men in marching order, but to keep them all together was another problem. Some of the regiments in Leslie's brigade were slow to form. Cornwallis ordered others to start marching before the rest were ready, and large gaps opened between units on the road. Captain-Lieutenant Archibald Robertson wrote, "We lost a great deal of time owing to the whole's not marching in one body from Prince Town, and run a Risque of having been cut up in Detail." It is interesting that Robertson was thinking not of attacking, but being attacked. The confidence that these men shared only a few weeks ago had been severely shaken. They had a new respect for their enemy and were losing faith in their own leaders.[9]

To get the army in motion was one thing; to keep it moving was yet another. The highway was a morass of mud and slush so deep

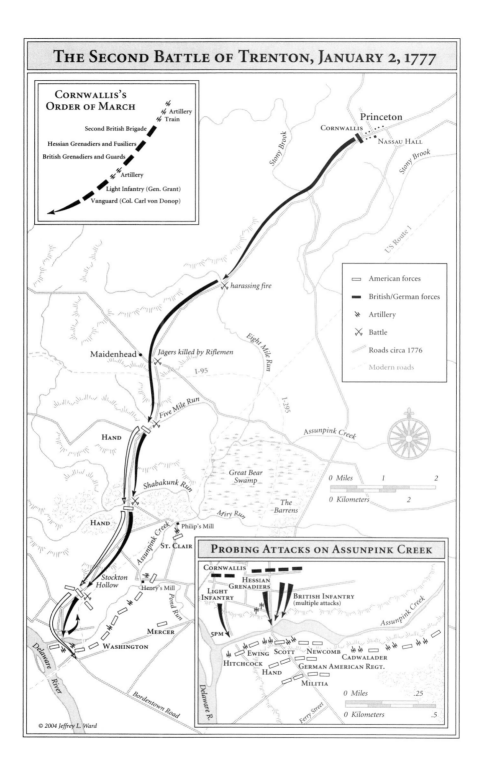

THE SECOND BATTLE OF TRENTON, JANUARY 2, 1777

CORNWALLIS'S ORDER OF MARCH

Artillery Train
Second British Brigade
Hessian Grenadiers and Fusiliers
British Grenadiers and Guards
Artillery
Light Infantry (Gen. Grant)
Vanguard (Col. Carl von Donop)

Princeton
CORNWALLIS
NASSAU HALL

Stony Brook
Stony Brook

US Route 1

harassing fire

Eight Mile Run

Maidenhead · Jägers killed by Riflemen
I-95

I-295

Five Mile Run

HAND

Assunpink Creek

Shabakunk Run

Great Bear Swamp

HAND

Miry Run

The Barrens

Philip's Mill

St. Clair

Stockton Hollow
Henry's Mill

Pond Run

MERCER

WASHINGTON

Delaware River

Bordentown Road

American forces
British/German forces
Artillery
Battle
Roads circa 1776
Modern roads

0 Miles 1 2
0 Kilometers 2

PROBING ATTACKS ON ASSUNPINK CREEK

CORNWALLIS
HESSIAN GRENADIERS
LIGHT INFANTRY
BRITISH INFANTRY (multiple attacks)

Assunpink Creek

5PM

EWING SCOTT NEWCOMB CADWALADER
HITCHCOCK GERMAN AMERICAN REGT.
HAND
MILITIA

Delaware R.

Ferry Street

0 Miles .25
0 Kilometers .5

© 2004 Jeffrey L. Ward

that men sank to their knees and thighs. Every step was a struggle. The men turned out of the highway and marched through fields that became as muddy as the roads. Horses and guns sank deep into a thick sucking ooze. It was heavy labor to advance a few miles, and it was worse for the troops at the end of the column.

Not far from Princeton, the vanguard began to meet armed resistance. Small scattered parties of American pickets took positions in patches of woodland along the road and began a harassing fire. A few Americans had returned to Eight Mile Run (Shipetaukin Creek). As the cavalry screen advanced down the road, the crack of a backcountry rifle was heard, and a British cavalryman fell dead out of his saddle.

It was nearly eleven o'clock in the morning when the British army approached the village of Maidenhead. In the van, the screen of mounted Jägers saw an American on horseback just ahead on the road. He was Elias Hunt, a civilian who lived near the road. When he saw the cavalry, he kicked his horse into a gallop, and the mounted Jägers gave chase. One of them rode a fast horse and rapidly gained ground on Elias Hunt. The Hessian raised his sword to cut down the American. As he was about to strike, the sound of a rifle rang out from a hidden picket near Maidenhead Church. The Jäger was hit but kept galloping after his prey. A bugle was heard from the column, perhaps sounding the recall. Then two more rifle shots were heard. The Jäger and his horse fell dead near the church, both killed by American riflemen.[10]

The American pickets vanished as suddenly as they had appeared, and the British and Hessian vanguard halted at Maidenhead. The main body came up with them. The time was "about noon." At last the British and German forces were united, and they set out together in "a single column." The British officers breathed a sigh of relief. No longer were they concerned about being "cut up in detail." But now they had something else to worry about. Half the day was gone, and Trenton was five miles distant. Less than five hours of daylight remained.[11]

A mile south of Maidenhead, the Trenton Road crossed a stream called Five Mile Run, now Little Shabbakunk Creek. Another mile beyond was a larger crossing of Big Shabbakunk Creek in a patch of woodland. Here the Americans made a stand south of the creek, in a "very close wood a mile in depth," which hid them well. The north side, from which the British and Hessians came, "presented open fields."[12]

American troops were posted in strength. They were the same units who had fought at Eight Mile Creek: Charles Scott's Virginians,

Edward Hand's Maryland and Pennsylvania Riflemen, and Haussegger's Pennsylvania Germans. Supporting them were Captain
Thomas Forrest's Pennsylvania company of six guns. Altogether, they
were about a thousand men.[13]

Their commander was a French officer from Martinique, General Matthias de Roche-Fermoy, who had appeared in America wearing the Croix de St. Louis and claiming the title of chevalier. In
November 1776, he talked his way into a commission as a brigadier
general in the Continental army, and on January 2 he was commanding an American brigade on the Trenton Road. He seemed a
strange fellow, but his American troops had no way of judging him.
As he was of another country, they gave him the benefit of the doubt.
It was a mistake.

As the British and German troops approached from Maidenhead, General Roche-Fermoy mounted his horse and rode off at a
gallop to Trenton. He abandoned his command and did not return
until the battle was over. Major Wilkinson, who knew him a little,
wrote that Roche-Fermoy was a "worthless drunkard." Later in the
war at Ticonderoga he managed to set fire to his quarters and revealed the entire American position just as the British approached,.
He was cashiered from the army.[14]

The sudden flight of General Roche-Fermoy left the American
troops without a leader. Luckily for them, the senior officer present
was Colonel Edward Hand of the Pennsylvania Rifle Regiment, who
stepped into the breach. Hand looked the part of a soldier. He was
tall, lean, and leathery, a natural leader. His tough and undisciplined
backcountry riflemen were devoted to him. With him that day was
Major Henry Miller, a very able officer from Baltimore, "distinguished for his cool bravery wherever he served."[15]

When Roche-Fermoy disappeared down the road, these two leaders assumed command. An eyewitness remembered that Hand "secreted his men some distance within the wood, with Major Miller on
the left and himself on the right." They waited quietly under cover
until the "flank and advanced guards" of the British column came
within close range, then opened "a deadly fire from ambush." So
heavy and accurate was their fire that they broke the British vanguard and "forced them back in great confusion on the main body."
Forrest's artillery joined and stopped the British column.[16]

The Americans along the creek forced Cornwallis to deploy the
main body of his marching column into a line of battle. Wilkinson
wrote that "the boldness of this manoeuvre, menacing a general

Colonel Edward Hand, a nineteenth-century engraving. Elected by backcountry riflemen as their leader, this very able officer served with distinction through the New York and New Jersey campaigns. In the second battle of Trenton he took command on the Maidenhead Road when his superior officer, General Fermoy, a French volunteer, fled as the British approached. Henry P. Johnson, *The Campaign of 1776 around New York and Brooklyn* (1878), facing 114.

attack, induced the enemy to form in order of battle." The British commander also decided "to bring up his artillery and open a battery, with which he scoured the wood for half an hour before he entered it. Altogether, Wilkinson wrote that "this operation consumed two hours, during which time the rifle corps took breath and were ready to renew the skirmish."[17]

Hand's riflemen fell back to another strong position and held their ground with such tenacity that Cornwallis's officers searched for a flanking position to the left. A British officer remembered that "the horse guards and the highlanders were formed and advanced on our left in front," moving closer to the upper fords of Assunpink Creek. As they did so, the New England brigades that were posted there rose up and came forward. British engineer Captain-Lieutenant Robertson wrote, "In order to amuse us they Manoeuver'd 2 or 3,000 men on their right, very well making a Demonstration of Passing the Creek at two Different places in their Possession where it was fordable, so that by that means to turn our left Flank if we advanced towards Trenton." The British flanking movement was stopped, and they turned back to the central axis of their advance.[18]

Hand's men were now under heavy pressure, outnumbered more than six to one. They retreated slowly, filtering back through the woods, and came off in good order with all of their equipment. They had succeeded in stopping the entire British column for two hours. The time was near three o'clock, and the shadows were growing longer. Only two hours of daylight remained before sunset. Trenton was still two miles away.

The Americans fell back another mile and a half to a place where the Trenton Road crossed a ravine called Stockton Hollow.[19] Here they prepared to make a stand in another strong position. Hand's riflemen were on the left. Captain Forrest put his guns behind the ravine overlooking the road.[20] On the American right, Colonel Charles Scott's three small Virginia regiments defended the open ground between the Trenton Road and the upper ford of Assunpink Creek. An observer counted about six hundred Americans.[21]

The defenders were now very close to Trenton, half a mile from the village. George Washington rode out to the position, with Nathanael Greene and Henry Knox. He talked to the men and told them he wanted a little more time to get his army into their defensive position on the south side of Trenton, beyond Assunpink Creek. Washington "thanked the detachment, particularly the artillery, for the services of the day," and "gave orders for as obstinate a stand as could be made on that ground, without hazarding the pieces." He told them "how important it was to retard the enemy's march until nightfall," and then he "retired to marshal his troops for action beyond the Assunpink."[22]

Cornwallis's Regulars marched forward on the Trenton Road. In their accounts, one senses the pressure that they felt, caught between the impatience of their commander and the resolve of their American opponents. When they came within range, Forrest's battery "opened on the column of the enemy." The American roundshot ricocheted down the road, caught the marching troops in enfilade, and stopped them again.

Once more Cornwallis deployed his column into line of battle and brought up his field guns. An artillery duel began, and continued for about "twenty or twenty-five minutes." A long red and blue line of British infantry and Hessian grenadiers came forward, firing volleys of "musketry mingled with the artillery." On the British left, Donop led the Minnegorode battalion and the remnant of the Rall brigade to an elevation overlooking Philip's Ford to prevent a flanking movement by New England brigades guarding the upper fords of the Assunpink.[23]

The American Major Wilkinson watched this engagement from a position with the New England brigade beyond Philip's Ford. "I had a fair flank view of this little combat from the opposite side of the Assunpink," he wrote. It was beginning to get dark. Wilkinson recalled that "the evening was so far advanced that I could distinguish the flame from the muzzles of our muskets." The American troops had held as they were ordered, nearly to nightfall. It was past four o'clock, and sunset was at 4:46 that day, about half an hour away.[24]

Now the full weight of the British army began to make itself felt on the American defenders. Forrest and Hand gave way to avoid being turned and fell back through the village of Trenton. Some of the Virginians retreated to the right toward the upper fords of the Assunpink. The journal of the Hessian Minnegerode battalion noted that the Americans "withdrew in the most perfect order, being attacked by the Linsing and Block battalions."[25]

South of Assunpink Creek, Washington saw Hand's riflemen and Forrest's artillery falling back into the village. He ordered Hitchcock's Rhode Island brigade to advance across Assunpink Creek into Trenton and support them as they retreated. Private John Howland in Lippitt's Rhode Island regiment remembered, "Our brigade was ordered to cross the bridge [over the Assunpink] and march through the main town street, to cover the retreat of the artillery and picket, into and through the north end of the town."[26]

Howland remembered that it was "towards the close of the day. We met them, and opened our ranks to let them pass through. We then closed into a compact and rather solid column, as the street through which we were to retreat to the bridge was narrow, and the British pressed closely on our rear."[27] Hessian Jägers in green coats and British light infantry in their red jackets filtered down the side streets, firing between the houses into the flanks of the New England men. The Americans fell back in growing disorder, and the pace of the British advance increased. Henry Knox, behind his guns, observed that "the enemy, who was Hessians, entered the town pell-mell, pretty much in the same manner we had driven them a few days before." He wrote that they "pushed our small party through the town with vigour, though not with much loss."[28]

There was much confusion in the town. As the Rhode Island men returned to the creek, Howland remembered that "the British made a quick advance in an oblique direction to cut us off from the bridge. In this they did not succeed, as we had a shorter distance." The American troops were now running toward the creek. Most headed for the bridge; some splashed across the stream at the lower fords close to the Delaware. The American artillery began to give them covering fire. Private Howland wrote that the guns "on the south side of the brook" fired on the approaching British and Hessian troops and "played into the front and flank of their column, which induced them to fall back."[29]

A Jersey militiaman remembered that "the enemy were so near that before we crossed the bridge over the Assunpink, some of our troops on the Trenton side of the creek, with a field piece, motioned to us to get out of the street while they fired at the British at the upper end of it."[30]

In the confusion, some Americans were left behind, and a few were caught by the oncoming British and Hessians. One of them was John Rosbrugh, the elderly Scots Presbyterian chaplain from Northampton County, Pennsylvania. As the Americans fell back through the town, Rosbrugh was sitting in Trenton's Blazing Star Tavern. The noise of battle increased, and he ran into the street. He found that somebody had taken his horse, and tried to run down the street toward the creek. He was too late. A "party of Hessians" overtook him and obeyed Colonel von Donop's order: no quarter for rebels. The Hessians made it a game. They took his weapons, stole his money, plundered his watch, stripped off his clothing, and began to torment him with their bayonets. As the chaplain fell on his knees and began to pray, they killed him. Rosbrugh's naked body was found in an open field with thirteen bayonet wounds and many saber cuts to the head. British officers, who hated the "black regiment" of the Presbyterian clergy, celebrated his death.[31]

As the retreating Americans converged on the bridge, their formations came apart. The British light infantry caught the German-American brigade near the lower fords of the Assunpink. Most escaped the across the stream, but some were taken, and they were given quarter. Among the prisoners was their commander, Colonel Nicholas Haussegger.[32]

Nearly all of the Americans got safely across the creek. Howland wrote that "the bridge was narrow and our platoons in passing it were crowded into a dense and solid mass, in the rear of which, the enemy were making their best efforts."[33] George Washington rode up and sat his horse quietly beside the bridge. Every man who crossed the bridge passed close by him. Private Howland wrote, "The noble horse of Gen. Washington stood with his breast pressed close against the end of the west rail of the bridge, and the firm, composed, and majestic countenance of the General inspired confidence and assurance in a moment so important and critical. In this passage across the bridge it was my fortune to be next the west rail, and arriving at the end of the bridge rail, I was pressed against the shoulder of the general's horse and in contact with the general's boot. The horse stood as firm as the rider, and seemed to understand that he was not to quit his post and station."[34]

Again the men spoke of his "composure" in a critical moment, and the infantry rallied to his quiet leadership. Most privates in this little army were very near George Washington in the course of the battle. Many spoke with him. They felt that they were one with him and were inspired by his example. It was a complicated feeling that they had for him: not only trust and loyalty but also confidence and complete approval.

As the men streamed back, Washington directed them to defensive positions. The key to his plan was the terrain and the crossings over Assunpink Creek. After the snow and rain and thaw, the water was high and swift. Henry Knox noted that it was "not fordable" in "most places" and could be crossed only at a few points. A "lower ford" downstream on Washington's left, very near the Delaware River, could be crossed by infantry. In the center of the position was the sturdy stone bridge, strong but very narrow. At a distance to the right were two upper fords. The one at Philip's Mill was easily passable that day. The other, at Henry's Mill, was reported so deep and swift that it was barely usable for horses and nearly impassable for all but strong swimmers.

Washington distributed his strength to cover the crossing places. The vital element in his defense was the American artillery. In the center he put eighteen or nineteen guns, all to cover the bridge, some as close as forty yards. Upstream he put twelve guns "behind the mill" by the upper fords Others were in position to cover the lower fords.[35] He posted his most experienced Continental infantry at the three most critical points. On the American right he placed Arthur St. Clair's New England Continentals, about 1,400 men. Most were at Philip's Mill, where the creek was most easily crossed. On the left he posted Hitchcock's Rhode Island Continentals. Private Howland wrote, "When I was about half way across the bridge, the General addressed himself to Col. Hitchcock, the commander of the brigade, directing him to march his men to *that field* and form them immediately, or instantly, or as quick as possible; which of the terms he used, I am not certain; at the same time extending his arm and pointing to a little meadow at a short distance on the south side of the creek" between the road and the river. "This order was promptly obeyed and then we advanced to the edge of the stream, facing the enemy." They took their positions in "a little meadow . . . between the road and the Delaware," with prepared entrenchments by the lower fords.[36]

Assunpink Bridge, Trenton, wood engraving, published in the *Columbia Magazine* (May 1789). The arch above the bridge was erected to honor George Washington on his inaugural journey as President. He appears as the mounted figure at the right.

In the center Washington sent his Virginia regiments to hold the bridge at the most important point. One man remembered that as they were moving into place, "General Washington came and, in the presence of us all, told Colonel Scott to defend the bridge to the last extremity. Colonel Scott answered with a 'tremendous oath' and repeated, 'to the last man, excellency.'"[37]

Between the Continentals, Washington interspersed militia units. On either side of the bridge he assigned General Ewing's Pennsylvania militia and Colonel Newcomb's New Jersey militia. Cadwalader's Pennsylvania Associators with five guns were "stationed in a field on the right about a mile from town, on the main road to prevent the enemy from flanking." Mercer's brigade was "posted 2 miles up the creek" on high ground south of Pond Run.[38]

The rest of the infantry was drawn up in three lines, one above the other on the rising knoll, with clear fields of fire. A Jersey militia-man wrote that "the troops appeared to cover the whole slope from bottom to top." At the bridge, Scott's infantry was the first line of defense. Hand's Pennsylvania riflemen and what remained of Haussegger's German battalion were behind Scott's infantry. Militia were behind them. Many American muskets were within range of the bridge. The American army was very strong in artillery, much stronger than the British and Hessians. The guns were placed with interlocking fields of fire on the critical crossings of Assunpink Creek.[39]

Altogether, a careful modern count reckons the American strength at nine brigades and about 6,800 men, nearly three times the size of the army that had attacked Trenton in the Christmas campaign.[40] It was holding a position that stretched nearly three miles from the Delaware River to the swamps above Philip's Ford. The New Englander Captain Stephen Olney remembered that "the men were at arms' length apart, so as to make a numerous and formidable appearance." Olney thought that "none but a Yankee would have thought of that."[41] That stratagem did not fool the experienced British officers who were studying the American position through their field telescopes in the deepening twilight. Robertson observed "their main body was drawn up, about 6,000 or 7,000, with the Creek and bridge in front and a number of field pieces."

The American troops also had a clear view of the enemy, and it was a sobering sight. Cornwallis occupied the high ground above the town, which was then fully visible from the other side of Assunpink Creek. He formed his men into long lines in "battalion order" along the crest of the rising ground where they would be most visible. In the town, marching columns of infantry moved forward toward the creek. Americans could see the strength of attacking British and Hessian forces, who outnumbered the defenders.

The American troops long remembered that moment, when the enemy appeared before them in their full strength. Many recorded their feelings in remarkably similar ways. Most shared a deep sense of foreboding, deeper than they recalled at any other battle. One of them was Major James Wilkinson, in St. Clair's brigade on the American right. Writing forty years later, he remembered it as an "awful moment" when "Cornwallis displayed his column, and extended his lines." Wilkinson wrote, "If there ever was a crisis in the affairs of the Revolution, this was the moment; thirty minutes would have sufficed to bring the two armies into contact, and thirty more would have decided the combat; and, covered with woe, Columbia might have wept the loss of her beloved chief and most valorous sons."[42]

A similar thought occurred to Ensign Robert Beale in Scott's Virginia brigade, as he took his post at the center of the line by the stone bridge. "This was the most awful crisis," he wrote, "no possible chance of crossing the River; ice as large as houses floating down, and no retreat to the mountains, the British between us and them."[43]

On the American left, among the Rhode Island Continentals between the bridge and the Delaware River, Private John Howland wrote, "On one hour, yes, on forty minutes, commencing at the moment when the British troops first saw the bridge and creek before them, depended the all-important, the all-absorbing question whether we should be independent States, or conquered rebels!"[44]

This sense of high crisis was tempered by another feeling that emerged in a conversation between two officers in Hitchcock's Rhode Island regiment at the lower fords. One of them was Captain Stephen Olney. He had soldiered through the siege of Boston, the lost battles around New York, and the long retreat across New Jersey, but he always remembered the stand at Assunpink as the critical moment of the war. "It appeared to me then," he wrote, "that our army was in the most desperate situation I had ever known it."

With many others in the army, Olney was keenly aware that "we had no boats to carry us across the Delaware, and if we had, so powerful an enemy would certainly destroy the better half before we could embark." He saw no other line of escape: "To cross the enemy's line of march, between this and Princeton, seemed impracticable," and there was no point in "retreating into the south part of Jersey, where there was no support for an army."[45]

That was "discouraging," he wrote, but "not withstanding all this, the men and officers seemed cheerful, and in great spirits; I asked Lieutenant Bridges what he thought now, of our independence. He answered cheerfully, 'I don't know; the Lord must help us.'" Even in that "awful moment," as they remembered it, another feeling returned, that sense of optimistic fatalism which had appeared before in this American army. These men had a sense of their own strength, a confidence in one another, a feeling that Providence was with them that night.[46]

On the other side, British and Hessian commanders drove their men forward in the gathering darkness, searching for a weakness in the American army, hopeful that one strong blow might send the rebels running as it had done so many times before. In the twilight, they launched probing attacks at the major crossings over Assunpink Creek.

The first attack came at the lower fords. After the Americans retreated across the creek, Cornwallis sent his light infantry and Jägers after them. Captain Ewald, who was in the thick of this fighting, wrote that "the Jägers and Light Infantry immediately attempted to occupy the houses of the town on this side of the bridge. . . . A stubborn outpost fight occurred here whereby many men were killed and wounded on both sides."[47]

At about five o'clock, after sunset but before dark, the British light infantry and Hessian Jägers tried to cross the lower ford on the American left. Washington saw them coming and ordered Hitchcock's Rhode Island Continentals to stop them. The attackers were met by a storm of musketry, and the artillery joined in. Private Howland remembered that "we advanced to the edge of the stream, facing the enemy, who soon found it prudent to fall back under cover of the houses." Stryker added, "the brave New England continentals sent a rain of lead on the attacking party, and they quickly abandoned the project."[48]

A second attack followed at another part of the line. A dense column of Hessian grenadiers came forward to storm the bridge. This was what grenadiers were trained to do, to assault fortified positions with concentrated force. The Hessians brought four guns forward, putting two on Main Street and two more "behind Mr. Waln's house." They posted Jägers with their short rifles in buildings along the creek to pick off the American gunners and more artillery at intervals along the banks of the Assunpink. The Hessian guns began to fire and continued for about twelve minutes, as the American artillery responded.

On the other side, three Virginia regiments were waiting. Their leader (no man commanded them) was Colonel Charles Scott. He turned to his men and lectured them on their musketry. "Well boys," he said, "you know the *old boss* has put us here to defend this bridge; and by God it must be done, let what will come. Now I want to tell you one thing. You're all in the habit of shooting too high. You waste your powder and lead, and I have cursed you about it a hundred times. Now I tell you what it is, nothing must be wasted, every crack must count. For that reason boys, whenever you see them fellows first begin to put their feet upon this bridge do you shin 'em."[49] His men had often heard him explain the reason why. "Take care now and fire low." he said, "Bring down your pieces, fire at their legs, one man Wounded in the leg is better [than] a dead one for it takes two more to carry him off and there is three gone. Leg them dam 'em I say leg them."[50]

The Hessian grenadiers came forward with bravery and determination. Every American in range fired on them, and yet the Hessians kept on, marching into a storm of fire. According to one account they "advanced ab't half way over the bridge when they were repulsed." The Hessians lost thirty-one killed and wounded in that very small space; another twenty-nine came forward to surrender rather than retreat through the heavy fire.[51]

Then came a third set of attacks. A force of British infantry moved forward and tried to seize the bridge. As they approached, Henry Knox's artillery made ready to fire on them, altogether "eighteen or nineteen pieces." Sergeant White remembered, "The enemy came on in solid columns; we let them come on some ways. Then, by a signal given, we all fired together. The enemy retreated off the bridge and formed again, and we were ready for them. Our whole artillery was again discharged at them."[52]

The American infantry joined in, and a torrent of concentrated fire fell on the British troops. The Americans watched in amazement as the British troops kept coming. "They continued to advance," an American militiaman wrote, "though their speed was diminished. And as the column reached the bridge it moved slower and slower until the head of it was gradually pressed nearly over, when our fire became so destructive that they broke their ranks and fled."[53]

Still, it was not over. The broken British columns formed yet again behind the bridge. "Officers reformed the ranks," an American wrote, "and again they rushed the bridge, and again was the shower of bullets pushed upon them with redoubled fury. This time the column broke before it reached the center of the bridge, and their retreat was again followed by a hearty shout from our line." For the Americans it was a moment of triumph and release. One recalled, "It was then that our army raised a shout, and such a shout I never since heard; by what signal or word of command, I know not. The line was more than a mile in length, and from the nature of the ground the extremes were not in sight of each other, yet they shouted as one man."[54]

The British column was broken but still not ready to give up. Reinforcements came up, and they prepared to storm the bridge yet again. Washington responded by committing more of his own troops. He summoned Cadwalader's Associators from the right flank of the army and posted them close to the bridge. Rodney wrote, "In their third and final attempt the British came down in a very heavy column to force the bridge. The fire was very heavy and the light troops were ordered to the support of that important post.... As we drew near, I stepped out of the front to order my men to close up. At this time Martinas Sipple was about ten steps behind the man next in front of him. I at once drew my sword and threatened to cut his head off if he did not keep close. He then sprang froward and I returned to the front."[55]

In the American artillery, Sergeant White wrote, "They came on a third time. We loaded with canister shot and let them come nearer. We fired all together again, and such destruction it made, you cannot conceive. The bridge looked red as blood, with their killed and wounded and red coats."[56]

That was the end of it. The British infantry retreated, and the Americans came forward to the bridge. Among them were two soldiers, Hugh Coppell and William Hutchinson, who remembered that they "passed over the ground which they had occupied during the battle and their attacks on us. Their dead bodies lay thicker and closer together for a space than I ever beheld sheaves of wheat lying in a field which the reapers had just passed."[57]

No definitive report of casualties has survived for this battle. On the Hessian side, Ewald wrote that "many men were killed and wounded on both sides." One Hessian unit alone lost sixty men at the creek. British sources were silent, as often they were after a defeat. Among the Americans, Rodney reckoned that "we lost but a few men, the enemy considerably more." American sources reckoned their own casualties at about fifty. Greene and Washington estimated the enemy's loss at about five hundred killed and captured, in addition to approximately a thousand in the first battle at Trenton. Given the fighting along the Post Road and at Shabbakunk and Stockton Hollow, the street fighting in Trenton, and the probing actions at the bridge, an estimate of 365 British and Hessian killed, wounded, and captured seems not unreasonable.

This was the second battle of Trenton, an event largely missed until the accounts of many individual soldiers and junior officers on both sides emerged to document it in detail. It was not a general engagement, not an all-out assault by the British and Hessian forces, but a series of probing attacks, driven home with high courage by the Regulars. For the American troops it was a great victory. For their general it was a model of a brilliantly managed defensive battle in the same town where Colonel Rall had fought, but with very different results.[58]

TWO COUNCILS

~ A Pride of Lions, a Cunning of Foxes

> Our situation was most critical and our force
> small.... One thing I was sure of, that it would
> avoid the appearance of a retreat, which was
> of consequence.
>
> —George Washington, January 5, 1776[1]

A S NIGHT FELL over Trenton, the infantry fighting sputtered
to an end, but the British artillery continued to fire into the
American formations across the creek. Henry Knox's gunners responded with a barrage of shells, or "bombs," that went shriek-
ing into the town and exploded with great flashes of light in the
gathering darkness. The Americans had no shortage of ammunition. Lieutenant James McMichael of the Pennsylvania Rifle Regiment wrote in his diary, "Our artillery fire was so severe, that the
enemy retreated out of town and encamped on an adjacent hill. We
continued firing bombs up to seven o'clock."[2]

When the guns at last fell silent, men on both sides sank to the
ground in exhaustion, so weary that they could sleep anywhere. Lieutenant McMichael remembered that his Pennsylvania Riflemen were
"ordered to rest, which we very commodiously did upon a number
of rails for a bed. Thus my friend Captain Marshall and I passed the
night until two after twelve o'clock."[3] Other American units were
more hungry than tired. In Hitchcock's New England brigade, Captain Stephen Olney recalled that "after dark, we were dismissed a
little while to get our breakfast, dinner, and supper." It was their
first meal in twenty-four hours.[4]

Behind the lines, the American wounded were carried to homes near the Delaware River "which had been appropriated for a hospital." Doctor Benjamin Rush worked as a volunteer in one of these charnel houses. He remembered that "the first wounded man was a New England soldier. His right hand hung a little above his wrist by nothing but a piece of skin. It had been broken by a cannon ball." Rush toiled into the night with "young surgeons," repairing "about twenty" broken bodies as best they could. When their work was done, Rush recalled that the doctors "all lay down on some straw in the same room with our wounded patients." He wrote, "for the first time war appeared to me in its awful plenitude of horrors. I want words to describe the anguish of my soul, excited by the cries and groans and convulsions of the men who lay by my side. I slept two or three hours."[5]

British and German surgeons were also busy that night. Two battalions of Hessian grenadiers suffered more casualties than the entire American army.[6] The agony of the wounded was beyond description, as they lay alone on filthy straw three thousand miles from home. Most had no anodynes to dull their pain, and no medicines to heal infections in open wounds except vinegar and "tincture of myrrh." Many had little hope of recovery. Mortality from amputations of the upper leg were between 60 and 80 percent in that era. Deaths from hip wounds were above 90 percent. Abdominal wounds were almost always fatal.[7]

The Hessian hospitals at Trenton must have been like the one that Nicholas Collin visited a few months later, after the battle of Red Bank in New Jersey. "The wounded Hessians," he wrote, ". . . were lying on straw in two large rooms, some without arms or legs (outside of the house lay two piles of arms and legs), and others again with their limbs crushed like mush by langrel.[8] Some floated in blood, and told me that some had died for lack of something to bandage their wounds with. While I was there several men died in agony and convulsions. The majority of those who could do so lay and read their little prayer-books."[9]

In the British camp, General Cornwallis made his dispositions for the night. Once again the long-suffering light infantry drew the worst assignment. They were ordered to deploy as "piquets" along Assunpink Creek and to remain in the open without fires all night, as temperatures fell to twenty degrees Fahrenheit. Their assignment was to watch the enemy and to keep American patrols from discovering the positions of British and Hessian units.[10]

The light infantry were a proud elite, but they were also the hard-luck soldiers of the British army. Many of the men who were sent out to stand picket duty along Assunpink Creek on the night of January 2, 1777, had been in America since 1774. Seven of the eighteen light infantry companies at Trenton that evening had led the march to Lexington and Concord in 1775. Eleven had made the assaults at Bunker Hill. Most had fought in the battles around New York.[11] Now they were on the sharp edge at Trenton, after having marched all morning on roads "halfleg deep" in mud and icy water. In the after-noon they were in the thick of nasty street fighting. That evening, some had been wounded in the fighting along the creek. In the Brit-ish army, wounded men were not relieved of duty or counted on casu-alty lists unless their injuries were incapacitating.[12] Through the night, as fresh wounds throbbed and stiffened, these men tugged their short jackets tight against a damp and bitter cold. Infantrymen that they were, they probably generated a little warmth by raging against their commanders, who were snug and safe behind them.[13]

In his headquarters, Lord Cornwallis was preparing a surprise for the morning. He ordered most of his German troops to pull back to the north of town, beyond the range of the American artillery, probably with the intention of bringing them forward the next day in a demonstration against the American front. His British Regulars were sent east of Trenton, into wooded ground along the upper reaches of Assunpink Creek. By ten o'clock that night Cornwallis had as many as two thousand men in the woods close to Philip's Ford. They were in position to cross the creek at "break of day" and attack the right flank of Washington's army. Cornwallis, in his professional way, had been quick to find the fatal weakness in the American position.

The American commanders also had their patrols out and knew exactly what he was doing. Washington ordered field fortifications to be constructed at Philip's Ford. St. Clair's veteran New England brigade were in place there, hard at work with axe and shovel, pre-paring to defend the crossing and the flank of the American army. They were outnumbered five to one by Cornwallis's regiments across the creek.[14]

While those preparations were going forward, both commanders called councils of war on the evening of January 2, 1777. The meet-ings were very different one from another, in ways that revealed what the war was about. Lord Cornwallis had the larger army and the smaller council. His meeting was less a council than a court. It included a tight little group of senior officers, who knew each other very well. They were intelligent and sociable men. Most were of the high aristocracy, with connections to the Crown. All had been bred to the manners of a gentleman, and some had gone to school together at Eton and Westminster. Several sat on the same benches in Parliament. In the army they were officers of long experience, and they had soldiered together on many a foreign field.

Presiding was Earl Cornwallis himself, a figure of greater gravitas than George Washington. Sitting with him was the officer he replaced, Major General James Grant, an irascible Scot who liked to play the Tory to Cornwallis's Whig. Also present was the army's quartermaster general, Sir William Erskine, a British baronet well connected at court, where he had been an aide to the king. A man of ability and intellect, he was thought to have one of the best brains in the army. In America he was dismayed by the management of the British war and increasingly outspoken in his criticism.[15]

The British council of war may have been joined by the commander of the Second Brigade, Alexander Leslie. This officer was of an aristocratic Scottish family, the brother of the earl of Leven. He was a fine officer and a decent man. An English acquaintance described him as "amiable and good . . . of a noble Scotch family, but distinguished more by his humanity and affability."[16] Like Cornwallis and the Howes, the Leslie family were Whiggish in their attitudes and sympathetic to Americans. Before the war they had taken a young American into their home: Benjamin Rush, then a medical student at Edinburgh who became a friend of the earl's son Willie Leslie. When Rush returned to America, the earl of Leven gave him a gift to keep him safe: a golden ring with the Lord's Prayer inscribed in a circle smaller than a dime. On the night of January 2, 1777, Benjamin Rush was a volunteer surgeon with the American army. Willie was Captain William Leslie, company commander in the Seventeenth Foot. The story of their friendship reminds us why so many Britons and Americans thought of the Revolution as a civil war.[17]

In the British council, Lord Cornwallis was not merely a leader but a ruler. The others addressed him as "My Lord," and he called them by their old school nicknames. General Erskine was "Wooly." At one such meeting Cornwallis was overheard saying of Erskine, "Faugh, Faugh! Wooly only wants a junction with Burgoyne that he may crack a bottle with his friend Philips."[18]

These men probably cracked a bottle or two together at Trenton on the night of January 2, and talked of their plans for the morning. They were in high expectation of victory. The Whigs among them sympathized with the American cause, but not to the point of independence, and as professional soldiers they had no respect for their opponents. Grant in his Tory way called them "skulking peasants" who were skilled only in the art of running away. The disaster at Trenton lowered his judgment of the Hessians without raising his opinion of the Americans.

Sir William Erskine's opinions were more temperate than Grant's, but similar in substance. A few months later, Erskine observed that "the rebels were nothing compared with our army in any respect; and that (humanly speaking), we might even now (as we could have done long since) put our foot upon them."[19] And yet behind this display of arrogance, a countercurrent ran through the thinking of many British officers in America. These were men of high physical courage, which they demonstrated on many a bloody field. But they lived in mortal fear of lost honor and reputation, which was everything in their world. After the shock of the Hessian disaster at Trenton, some became more outspoken in their speech and more cautious in their acts. Whatever they said about Colonel Rall in public, they had known him to be a brave soldier and an honorable man. They also knew that what happened to him at Trenton could happen to any of them. In the American war these aristocratic British officers had little reputation to gain by victory, and much to lose if something went wrong. Not much glory could be won by defeating a rabble of "skulking peasants." But all reputation could be lost if the peasants won, and they were dangerously unpredictable.

Cornwallis shared some of these feelings, and they made him cautious on the night of January 2, even as he was confident that he would prevail. He believed that he had Washington in a trap and could defeat him in the morning, but he did not want to take unnecessary risks. One member of the council did not agree. Erskine wanted to dispose of the American army quickly, by a sudden night attack. "My Lord," he said to Cornwallis, "if you trust those people to-night you will see nothing of them in the morning." Erskine did not fear a British defeat, but he was sure that the Americans would run again rather than face the king's troops and would return to fight another day.[20]

Cornwallis rejected this advice. He did not like night attacks, which were unpredictable at best, and the terrain at Trenton was not known to him. The night was "exceeding dark," and the ground had been very soft that day. His troops were exhausted after the mud march from Princeton. Cornwallis told his generals that "the men had been under arms the whole day, they were languid and required rest." Further, the strength of the American artillery had startled him. He wanted to reinforce his strength by bringing more troops and guns from Princeton and had already issued orders to that effect. Cornwallis was sure that "he had the enemy safe enough, and could dispose of them next morning. For all of these reasons he proposed that except for the light infantry, "the troops should make fires, refresh themselves and take repose."[21]

He may also have said of George Washington, "We've got the Old Fox safe now. We'll go over and bag him in the morning." On that note, this chummy British council of fox-hunting men ended exactly as Cornwallis had intended that it should, even before it met. The senior officers of the army deferred to the strong wishes of His Lordship. But Sir William Erskine did so against his better judgment.[22]

On the other side of Assunpink Creek, the Old Fox also summoned his senior officers to an American council of war. It met "immediately after dark" at the quarters of General Arthur St. Clair in the Douglass house on Queen Street (now South Broad Street) in South Trenton. Attending were Washington's two division commanders, Nathanael Greene and James Sullivan, and brigade commanders John Cadwalader, Thomas Mifflin, James Ewing, Arthur St. Clair, Daniel Hitchcock, Hugh Mercer, and Adam Stephen. Also present were his chief of artillery, Henry Knox, adjutant Joseph Reed, and others.[23]

This American gathering was more open and mixed than Cornwallis's small aristocratic circle. Local citizens were invited to attend and speak freely. Nobody doubted that Washington was in charge. His officers deeply respected him, but their conversation was not constrained by deference. The discussion was freewheeling, and its tone suggested that Washington wanted it that way.

Arthur St. Clair remembered how it began. "The General summoned a council of the general officers at my quarters," he wrote, "and after stating the difficulties in his way, the probability of defeat, and the consequences that would necessarily result if it happened, desired advice." Washington did not propose a single course of action as Cornwallis had done. He framed a problem. One officer later remembered what he said. "Encompassed as he was by dangers," Washington spoke quickly and to the point. He "had but a brief statement to submit to his council; the situation of the two armies were known to all; a battle was certain, if he kept his ground until the morning, and in case of an action a defeat was to be apprehended; a retreat by the only route thought of, down the river, would be difficult and precarious." The general concluded by saying that "the loss of the corps he commanded might be fatal to the country: under these circumstances he asked advice."[24]

The American officers were quick to speak. One of them wrote later that "opinions were various—some inclined to retreat, others to hazard all on a general engagement, and it has been suggested to me, that the commander-in-chief, yielding to his natural propensities, favoured the latter proposition."[25] Then Henry Knox spoke in a deep booming voice that brought to mind a battery of his artillery. He believed that a "general engagement" would be "hazardous" in the extreme. If it were to happen, he predicted, the American right wing might well give way, and the "defeat of the left would almost have been an inevitable consequence, and the whole thrown into confusion or push'd into the Delaware as it was impassible by boats." In the homespun language that American officers liked to use, Knox observed that the army was "cooped up" like a flock of chickens.[26]

Several officers pondered these opinions and suggested another course of action: neither a general engagement nor a retreat, but an attack on the enemy's rear. One man who made that suggestion was Arthur St. Clair, their host that night, an officer highly respected by Washington. St. Clair's brigade had been on the extreme right of the American army that day, and his men had patrolled the country lanes beyond their flank. Some of these paths led north by a round-about route to a crossing called Quaker Bridge, near a Friends meeting-house in the woods. St. Clair suggested that "if the army could reach that point unobserved and unopposed, it then could proceed almost due north to Princeton, distant about six miles from the

Arthur St. Clair, portrait by Charles Willson Peale (1782–84). This officer commanded the American right at Assunpink Creek. His men patrolled the back roads toward Princeton. Several officers remembered that at the council of war on the night of January 2, 1777, he suggested the American attack on Princeton. Independence National Historical Park.

bridge." From Princeton the main roads could be used for "turning the left of the enemy, gaining a march upon him, and proceeding with all possible expedition to Brunswick."

Others who knew the country agreed. Adjutant Joseph Reed, who had been raised in Trenton and schooled at Princeton, confirmed the accuracy of St. Clair's suggestion and added his knowledge of the terrain. Reed also reported that when he had led a patrol of Philadelphia Light Horse on a reconnaissance, they had seen no enemy on the back roads as far as Princeton.[27] Once again, as in Washington's other councils of war, the soldiers consulted civilians who lived nearby and listened carefully to their advice. One officer recalled that "two men from the country, near the route proposed, were called to the council for their opinions of its practicability. They offered themselves as guides."[28]

The bold idea of an attack on Princeton and Brunswick began to gather momentum in the council. General Hugh Mercer "immediately fell in with it, and very forcibly pointed out its practicability and the advantages that would necessarily result from it."[29] Washington warmed to the idea. Later he wrote, "One thing I was sure of, that it would avoid the appearance of a retreat, which was of consequence." He was thinking not only of the military problem but also of "popular opinion." One of his many purposes was to "give reputation to our arms." For all of these reasons, the idea of an attack on Princeton won general support from everyone at the meeting. One officer wrote, "General Washington highly approved it, nor was there one dissenting voice in the council." The American meeting ended in complete agreement.[30]

The leadership of Washington and Cornwallis made a striking contrast. The British commanders were highly skilled professionals who affected the amateur style of country gentlemen. They bonded with one another as old boys but were exquisitely sensitive to rank and privilege. Cornwallis arrogated the major decisions entirely to himself and rejected contrary advice from his officers. This system of command was adopted by other senior British commanders in the American War of Independence.

The Americans improvised a different system of command. It was forced upon them by the diversity of cultures in the country, by the pluralism of elites, by a more open polity, by a less stratified society, and especially by expanding ideas of liberty and freedom. The man at the center was George Washington. From much hard-won experience in American politics and war he had learned to work closely with his subordinates. Washington met frequently with them in councils of war and encouraged a free exchange of views. He also listened more than he talked and drew freely from the best ideas that were put before him. In early councils he actually took a vote. Later he worked more skillfully by the construction of consensus. In that way he created a community of open discourse and a spirit of mutual forbearance. He encouraged his lieutenants to join freely in the common effort.

They did so with growing respect for this extraordinary man, despite the errors he had made in the New York campaign. They knew he was fallible, and he felt his limitations more keenly than anyone else. Major decisions were always an agony for him. But Washington knew that nobody else could lead the American army as he was able to do. He had found a way.

While Washington's council of war was meeting on the night of January 2, the weather was changing yet again. The last two days had been unseasonably warm: a classic January thaw with temperatures that rose to forty degrees Fahrenheit. After dark on January 2, a cold front swept across the Delaware Valley, and temperatures fell twenty degrees in a few hours.[31] Shivering soldiers on both sides cursed the weather. John Howland wrote, "The night closed in on us, and the weather, which had been mild and pleasant through the day, became intensely cold."[32]

It was a miserable night for the infantry, but for American commanders it was a stroke of fortune. All that day the roads had been a mass of mud and slush, which marching armies churned into a thick viscous ooze. Cornwallis had been unable to strike quickly at Trenton because his regiments had been mired on the highway from Princeton. In the night, as the American army was preparing to march, the weather changed so suddenly that the ground froze solid within a few hours. Stephen Olney could not believe it. He remembered, "the roads which the day before had been mud, snow and water, were congealed now, and had become as hard as pavement." Rodney added that "the muddy ground was frozen firm by a keen N. West wind."[33]

Even better for the Americans, as they made ready to steal away from their camps, the sky turned very black with little starlight. Wilkinson remembered that "the night, though cloudless, was exceedingly dark."[34] The Americans built up their campfires and kept them burning brightly, hiding their secret intentions behind an open display of effort in the improvement of their positions. Some made noisy use of picks and shovels. Others made a show of guarding the crossings on Assunpink Creek. As many as five hundred men were ordered to continue working at these tasks in the bright circles of firelight. While they did so, others were hard at work in the darkness behind the fires, packing their equipment, wrapping the wheels of their cannon in rags, and preparing to march.[35]

The British light infantry on picket duty across the creek studied this theatrical performance that was elaborately staged for their benefit. Some were not fooled by it. A British officer later wrote, "The sentries who were advanced, heard the rattling of carriages, and patrols, in going their rounds, made their reports of uncommon hurry in the enemy's camp that indicated they were in motion, which was visible also at times thro' the glimmering of their fires."[36]

An observant British engineer, Captain-Lieutenant Archibald Robertson, also saw movement behind the American fires. He believed that the Americans were about to leave their positions and guessed that Washington "meditated a blow on Princeton, which was but weak." Robertson reported the news to General Erskine, who took it directly to Cornwallis. Another British officer remembered, somewhat inaccurately, that "these reports were confirmed and carried to headquarters, where some officers had communicated their suspicions of the enemy's forming some design, yet both the one and the other were disregarded."[37]

What actually happened at the British headquarters was a little different. The warnings were not disregarded but misunderstood. Cornwallis acted energetically upon the information that was brought to him, but in the wrong way. He inferred that the Americans were about to attack him in the night, much as they had attacked Colonel Rall. In his prudent and professional manner he shifted his forces to stop them. Orders went to some of his best troops. The guards, the Second Battalion of British grenadiers, and a battalion of Hessian grenadiers were told to "move into defensive positions at both Henry's Ford and Philip's Ford."[38] In that decision, this highly intelligent commander committed one of the most common fallacies of military reasoning. He prepared to fight the last battle.

Washington had a different battle in mind. He began his preparations by increasing the mobility of his American army, ordering its heavy supply wagons "to be removed silently to Burlington." A soldier with the baggage train remembered, "As soon as night fell our people lined the wood, made large fires. As soon as I could I came to them with the wagon, with the provisions and Blankets, and staid with them till 12 o'clock, then loaded our wagon." Sergeant

William Young jotted a note in his journal: "One o'clock [A.M.] ordered to move out with the Baggage and proceed to Burlington,
such a hurry skurry among all our waggoners. Some of our horses . . .
often got stalled which retarded our march, so much that we didn't
get to Burlington until 12 o'clock [noon]."[39]

While the baggage wagons were moving away, the troops were
instructed to fall in. Sergeant Joseph White wrote, "Orders came by
whispering (not a loud word must be spoke) to form the line and
march." The quiet assembly of so many units in the dark caused
some confusion and much delay. Olney recalled, "The orders for
our march were given in so low a tone that some of the colonels
were at a stand which way to move their regiments." For those in the
ranks, it was the eternal story of hurry up and wait.[40] Rodney remembered that "no one knew what the General meant to do. Some
thought that we were going to attack the enemy in the rear." Pennsylvania militiaman James Johnston wrote that "many of the soldiers, thinking they were about to be led against the enemy, threw
away their knapsacks." Others guessed that "that we were going to
Princeton. The latter proved to be right. We went by a bye-road on
the right hand which made it about 16 miles."[41]

When the army formed in line of march, Johnston recalled,
"General Washington rode back and inquired at the rear of the column, Who commanded here? Major Bell of Colonel Evans's regiment announced himself as in command and received orders to
remain behind for two hours, carefully observing the enemy. Declarant was with Major Bell and was sent forward by him with a party to
reconnoiter the enemy. Moving carefully, they had a full view of the
Hessians sitting round their fires smoking their pipes. A sentinel
challenged. Declarant and the others dropped to the ground and
lay quiet until the sentinel was heard to resume his walk. They then
cautiously retrograded and made report. At the expiration of the
two hours, Major Bell proceeded to join the main army."[42]

Finally the regiments began to move out. Wilkinson remembered
that the troops were ordered "to be silently filed off by detachments."
It was a slow and difficult task to get them moving on a single road in
the dark, and they were several hours getting started. Charles Willson
Peale remembered that his Pennsylvania Associators moved out at
midnight. Others began to march about an hour later, and Rodney's
company did not get under way until two o'clock in the morning.
One part of the army did not know what the others were doing.
Weedon wrote that Washington "filed off in so private a manner that
the rear guard and many of his own centinels never missed him."[43]

The extreme darkness of the night was confusing to some, and frightening to others who were in the field for the first time. Near South Trenton, a regiment of Pennsylvania militia in the rear of the army saw another American unit at a crossroad and mistook it for the enemy. "Panic ensued," one soldier remembered, and it spread to other units.[44] Rodney recalled that "great confusion happened in the rear. There was a cry that they were surrounded by the Hessians and several corps of militia broke and fled towards Bordentown. But the rest of the column remained firm and pursued their march without disorder, but those who were frightened and fled did not recover from their panic until they reached Burlington."[45]

The Quaker diarist Margaret Morris was in Burlington when they arrived. "About noon," she recalled, "a Number of Soldiers, upwards of a thousand, came into town in great confusion, with baggage and some cannon—from these soldiers we learn there was a smart engagement yesterday at Trenton, & that they left them engaged near Trenton Mill, but were not able to say which side was victorious. They were again quartered on the inhabitants."

Good Quaker that she was, Margaret Morris tried to help them. "About bed time," she wrote, "I went in the next house to see if the fires were safe, & my heart was melted with compassion to such a number of my fellow creatures lying like swine on the floor fast asleep, & many of them without even a blanket to cover them. It seems very strange to me that such a number should be allowed to come from the camp at the very time of the engagement, and I shrewdly suspect that they have run away for they give no account why they came, nor where they are to march next." She asked them about it: "Upon my questioning them pritty close, I brought several to confess that they had run away, being scared at the heavy firing on the third. There were several pretty innocent looking lads among them, and I sympathized with their mothers when I saw them preparing to return to the Army."[46]

Washington had lost a large part of the army in that moment of panic, but the rest continued on its march. They began by heading southeast, parallel to the Delaware River, away from the town and the enemy. After about half a mile in that direction, the column turned east on a country road (now Hamilton Avenue in South Trenton) and crossed a little stream called Pond Run that flowed into the Assunpink. Their route took them well clear of British and Hessian positions and led to a new-made path through dense woodland. The trees had been cut away to make a rough passage, but many

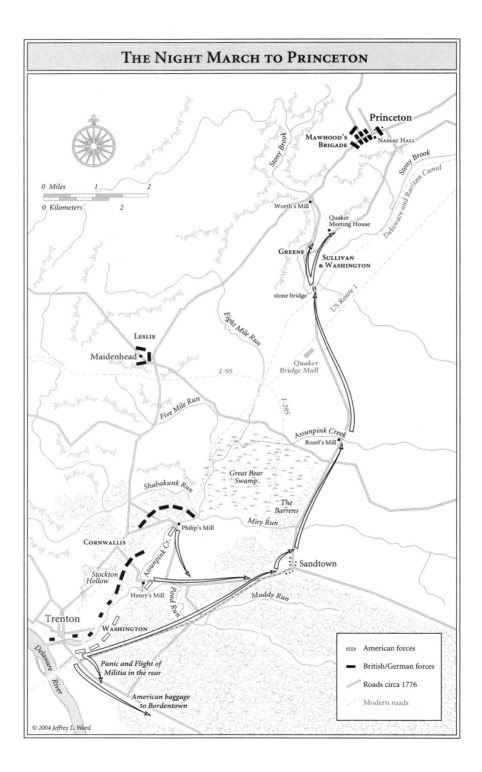

THE NIGHT MARCH TO PRINCETON

Princeton

MAWHOOD'S BRIGADE

NASSAU HALL

Stony Brook

Stony Brook

Delaware and Raritan Canal

Worth's Mill

Quaker Meeting House

GREENE

SULLIVAN & WASHINGTON

stone bridge

US Route 1

0 Miles   1   2

0 Kilometers   2

LESLIE

Maidenhead

Eight Mile Run

I-95

Quaker Bridge Mall

I-295

Five Mile Run

Assunpink Creek

Rozel's Mill

Great Bear Swamp

The Barrens

Miry Run

Shabakunk Run

Philip's Mill

CORNWALLIS

Assunpink Cr.

Sandtown

Stockton Hollow

Henry's Mill

Pond Run

Muddy Run

Trenton

WASHINGTON

Panic and Flight of Militia in the rear

American baggage to Bordentown

Delaware River

	American forces
	British/German forces
	Roads circa 1776
	Modern roads

© 2004 Jeffrey L. Ward

small stubs remained, and men and horses tripped over them in the dark. Some of the stumps in the road were large enough to stop the artillery, and men labored in the darkness to get the guns moving again. John Howland remembered, "we moved slow on account of the artillery, frequently coming to a halt, or stand still, and ordered forward again, one, or two, or three men in each platoon would stand, with their arms supported, fast asleep; a platoon next in rear advancing on them, in walking, or attempting to move, would strike a stub and fall."[47]

Mifflin's and Cadwalader's brigades were making their second night march in two days, with little sleep. Some of the men had made three night marches in a row. In one artillery unit, Sergeant Joseph White and Captain Benjamin Frothingham struggled to stay awake by keeping up a running conversation. "You and I must march together," said Frothingham. Sergeant White remembered that "we marched some ways, I being exceeding sleepy. I pitched forward several times and recovered myself. 'Well,' the captain observed with a laugh, 'that was the first time he'd ever seen anyone sleep while marching.'"[48]

The rough road crossed a stream called Muddy Run, an obstacle for the artillery and ammunition wagons. Then they came to a desolate place called the Barrens, which was a wilderness of small saplings and scrub oak. They continued northeast through the Barrens and around the edge of Great Bear Swamp, a marsh nearly two miles across. The wet ground was frozen solid, and the roads were covered with a glaze of quick-frozen ice and snow. An artillery sergeant remembered that many of his men were "entirely barefooted," and here again "the ground was literally marked with the blood of soldiers feet." The artillery horses also "were without shoes and when passing over the ice would slide in every direction and could advance only by the assistance of the soldiers."

In the artillery, Captain Frothingham turned to Sergeant White and talked of the fight that would probably follow the next day. The captain said, "Did you know that you are to command the left piece tomorrow morning?"

Sergeant White awoke with a start. "That is a job for a commissioned officer," he replied. "Who said so?"

"General Knox," said the captain.

"The responsibility is too great for me," the sergeant answered. "I cannot think why he should pitch upon me."

"Why, he remembers what you did at Trenton."

The sergeant later wrote, "I began to feel my pride rising, and I said no more."[49]

The Old Bridge over Stony Brook on the Quaker Road, a nineteenth-century photograph. This structure still stands today. Historical Society of Princeton.

While they were talking, the column kept moving on in the darkness toward a crossroads hamlet called Sandtown. They skirted the village to avoid detection. Local guides led them through field lanes several hundred yards away from the houses.[50] Beyond Sandtown, they crossed another stream, called Miry Run, and found themselves heading north on a better road, an old route called the Quaker Bridge Road, long used by the Friends to reach Stony Brook Meetinghouse near Princeton.[51]

The marching was easier on the Quaker Bridge Road, and the column began to make better time. Altogether, the army had done remarkably well in the circumstances. They had left their positions on the Assunpink between midnight and two o'clock in the morning. Now they were approaching Quaker Bridge at about first light, which was about 6:50 A.M. that day, half an hour before sunrise. On a roundabout route, they had marched about nine miles in five hours. The average speed of the army was a little less than two miles an hour.[52]

To a modern reader snug in an armchair, the pace may seem painfully slow. But it was no small achievement on a night march in bitter cold and extreme darkness, by an exhausted army with a train of artillery, and on hard-frozen roads full of ruts and stumps. At the time, the march astounded professional soldiers of many nations by its audacity and its celerity. It was a triumph of mind and will over material conditions by George Washington himself, his lieutenants, and most of all the sleep-deprived private soldiers who found the stamina to put one frozen foot in front of another.

As the first streaks of dawn appeared in the eastern sky, the army came to Quaker Bridge. There suddenly it stopped in its tracks. The bridge was strong enough for Quakers on their way to meeting, but it would not bear the army's artillery and ammunition carts. It was necessary to build another, and a party of axemen and carpenters went frantically to work. An eyewitness account tells us that "they were hindered some time in making a bridge over the brook for the Army to pass with the artillery."[53]

While the men toiled at the bridge, Washington reorganized his troops. Rodney's vanguard was ordered "to file off to one side of the road," and the army was led into a large open field. Many units had become separated on the night march, and more than a few stragglers came limping and hobbling up the road to rejoin their regiments. Comrades did what little they could for ruined feet that were swollen, cut, cracked, and bleeding.[54] A soldier remembered that "during this waiting period, one sergeant in Sullivan's division said that his Captain sent round 'a bucket full of [gun]powder and rum, [and said] every man must drink half a jill.'"[55]

Washington split his army into two parts, much as he had done before the first battle of Trenton. The left wing was a small division under Nathanael Greene. The right wing was Sullivan's reinforced division, which became the main body of the army. Both divisions consisted of Continental troops in the lead, followed by militia, and more Continentals in the rear. The officers gave careful thought to the integration of the militia with the veteran Continental regiments.

When the reorganization was complete, and a new bridge was passable for the smaller guns, the army set off again. Rodney remembered that "the sun rose as we passed over Stony Brook," which would have been 7:22 local time. Once again, Washington fretted about the time. He had wanted to strike Princeton just before dawn. Now that plan was gone, and surprise would be more difficult. But still they hurried on, and the spirits of the army rose with the sun. Princeton was only six miles away.[56]

THE BATTLE AT PRINCETON

~ Gallantry against Courage

Washington the dictator has shown himself both a Fabius
and Camillus. His March through our lines is allowed to
have been a prodigy of generalship.
  —Horace Walpole on the American leader at Princeton[1]

This feat [by Colonel Mawhood] was rightly judged to be
one of the most gallant exploits of the war.
  —Sir John Fortescue on the British leader at Princeton[2]

T HE DAY BEGAN with a dawn of spectacular beauty. Major
James Wilkinson remembered that "the morning was bright,
serene, and extremely cold, with an hoar frost that be-
spangled every object." The landscape had a magical appearance,
as the frozen snow reflected the first rays of the sun, and frost crys-
tals on every shrub and tree glittered in the golden light beneath a
pale blue sky.[3]

The American troops crossed over Stony Brook on the old bridge
and the new one they had hastily constructed. On the other side of
the stream, the army divided in two wings and moved in different
directions. Nathanael Greene's small left wing marched to the west.
In the van were Captain John Neil's New Jersey artillery, Hugh Mercer's veteran Virginia Continentals, a small band of Marylanders who
were all that remained of Smallwood's regiment, and a few Delaware
men led by Colonel Haslet. Behind them came the Pennsylvania Rifle
Regiment, perhaps 350 men in all, and Cadwalader's Philadelphia
Associates, about 1,200 men.

They marched west on a sunken road that ran along the bed of Stony Brook, through a deep and narrow ravine about thirty or forty feet wide, to the main highway between Princeton and Trenton. Their orders were to seize control of the highway at a place called Worth's Mill, where the highway crossed a bridge over Stony Brook. Greene's instructions were to "break down the bridge" and put some of his troops in a blocking position, with orders to stop traffic on the highway in both directions. The object was to keep the British garrison at Princeton from fleeing the town, and also to stop reinforcements arriving from Trenton. The rest of Greene's division had a different assignment. They were to follow the Post Road into Princeton. Washington appears to have intended that they should be the first to attack the British garrison on Nassau Street, then as now the main street of the town.[4]

The other wing was Sullivan's division, the main body of the army with about five thousand men. In the vanguard were Lieutenant Colonel Isaac Sherman's infantry and at least two guns, perhaps Alexander Hamilton's New York artillery. Leading from the front was the division commander, General John Sullivan, and Washington's secretary Colonel Richard Harrison. Close behind were St. Clair's New England brigade and Mifflin's Pennsylvania brigade of Continentals and militia, marching "in files without flanking parties."[5]

Beyond the Quaker Bridge, all of these men in Sullivan's long column "wheeled to the right" and headed east on a meandering track called the Saw Mill Road. The route skirted "a small wood south of the Quaker meeting," then turned north toward the rear of the college. There they were to deliver the main attack. The plan was in some ways very similar to the attack on Trenton. In both battles Washington sent his army forward in two columns. One of them drew attention by attacking on the most obvious line, while the other made the main assault from another direction into the back of the town. In both engagements artillery was used as an assault weapon, and green units were placed between veteran Continental troops.[6]

Both divisions of the American army advanced very rapidly. Greene's left wing moved up the sunken road in the Stony Brook ravine. Sullivan's right wing marched toward Princeton on higher ground to the right.

Riding with Sullivan's vanguard was Major James Wilkinson. He remembered admiring the long views across a rolling countryside of open fields and patches of wood, in the early light of a beautiful winter morning. As he looked to his left, he saw a flash of light in the distance, near the highway from Princeton to Trenton. Wilkinson looked again and saw a long red column of British infantry, marching south on the Post Road from Princeton toward Trenton. The flash that had caught his eye was "the reflection of their arms against the rising sun."[7]

The British troops were more than a mile away, near a house called Cochran's, halfway between Princeton and Maidenhead. Wilkinson turned in his saddle to tell Colonel Harrison, Washington's military secretary, but before he could speak, the British column disappeared behind a hill. As the American officers studied the landscape, two red-coated riders appeared on a hill east of Cochran's. They leaped a fence, cantered to the summit of the hill, and observed the American main body for "a minute or two." Then the riders turned away, and the British column came into view again. Wilkinson saw it halt and "come to the right about." It countermarched toward Princeton "in quick time."[8]

The commander of the British column, Lieutenant Colonel Charles Mawhood, discovered the American army at almost the same moment. He was another remarkable character in the British army. Like many of his brother officers, Colonel Mawhood (pronounced Ma-*hoood*) carefully cultivated the manners of an eccentric country gentleman. He delighted in the display of a highly developed air of nonchalance, especially on a field of battle. Americans were amazed to see him riding into combat "mounted on a brown pony," with "a pair of springing spaniels playing before him."[9]

For all of that, Colonel Mawhood was an excellent regimental commander, highly respected by the men who served under him. He was a skilled professional soldier, with twenty-four years of military service, but some described him as "exceeding clever," rarely a compliment in any army. He was a strong Whig. According to a Dutch doctor with whom he boarded during the Jersey campaign, Mawhood "often exprest himself very freely" on politics, "lamenting much the American contest," and he called Lord North "a villain for being the cause" of the war. With others in the British army, Mawhood was beginning to lose confidence in General Howe and other high commanders. The Dutch doctor remembered that "Colonel Mahood on the evening of Christmas day was blaming the English generals for dispersing the army so much in Jersey and said if he was in General Washington's place he would make an attack on several of the principal posts at the same time, that they were all so weak that he might certainly cut them off and be in possession of

Jersey in a few days." Mawhood specifically mentioned Trenton, Burlington, and Mount Holly as ripe targets. The day after that conversation, an officer said to him, "Well Colonel, General Washington has executed your last night's plan already for he has taken Trent Town."[10]

Lord Cornwallis and General Howe both held Colonel Mawhood in high esteem and made him acting commander of the Fourth Brigade at Princeton. When he reached that town on January 2, he was responsible for three infantry regiments: his own Seventeenth, the Fortieth, and the Fifty-fifth Foot. His orders were to hold the town, guard the army's stores, and protect its communications.

That night a courier brought him new orders from Cornwallis to bring two regiments to Trenton early on the morning of January 3, with cavalry, artillery, replacements, and much needed supplies for the army. Mawhood mustered his command two hours before sunrise. Two marching regiments of the line, the Seventeenth and Fifty-fifth Foot, "marked off the parade" at about five o'clock in the morning. The men were cold and hungry. His own regiment had only just arrived in Princeton the evening before after a hard march across the frozen countryside. The regimental ensign, George Inman, wrote that "the season of the year being severe, snow on the ground and for Nights having no other bed than hard frozen earth or Ice and no other covering than a cloak oftentimes induced me to reflect on past times when I used to sleep in soft downy beds and with every comfortable necessary around me."[11]

The British column was slow to form, and it kept growing as other elements were added. At least eight guns were in it, perhaps as many as ten, which Cornwallis wanted in Trenton when he discovered the strength of the American artillery. A convoy of heavy supply wagons assembled, with thirty mounted dragoons as escorts, and another fifty dismounted cavalry.[12] Several detachments of replacements, "convalescents," "draughts," and "details" attached themselves to the column. One large party consisted of Highlanders who were joining the Forty-second Foot. Others were "draughts and recruits" for Cornwallis's battalions of grenadiers and light infantry, which were commonly kept at full strength by transfers from other units. These men were fully armed and organized in provisional companies with their own officers. Grenadier Captain William Hale of the Forty-fifth Foot led one such company of thirty grenadiers and kept a running record of the campaign in a series of letters that have not been used in any published account.[13]

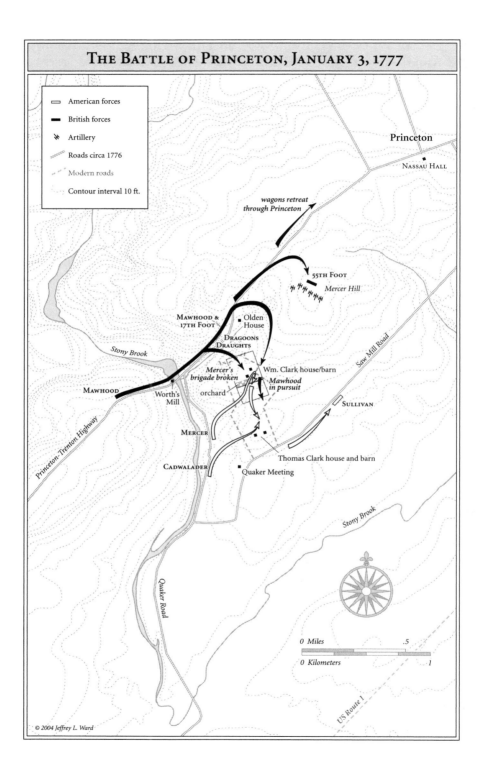

THE BATTLE OF PRINCETON, JANUARY 3, 1777

American forces
British forces
Artillery
Roads circa 1776
Modern roads
Contour interval 10 ft.

Princeton

NASSAU HALL

wagons retreat
through Princeton

55TH FOOT
Mercer Hill

MAWHOOD &
17TH FOOT

Olden
House

DRAGOONS
DRAUGHTS

Stony Brook

Saw Mill Road

Mercer's
brigade broken

Wm. Clark house/barn

Mawhood
in pursuit

MAWHOOD

Worth's
Mill

orchard

SULLIVAN

MERCER

Thomas Clark house and barn

CADWALADER

Quaker Meeting

Princeton-Trenton Highway

Stony Brook

Quaker Road

0 Miles   .5

0 Kilometers   1

US Route 1

© 2004 Jeffrey L. Ward

The British column numbered at least seven hundred men, perhaps more. They made a colorful display: the Royal Artillery in dark blue, light dragoons in short red jackets and brown riding breeches, and red-coated infantry with white facings for the Seventeenth, buff for the Fifty-second, and green for the Fifty-fifth. The Highlanders were prominent in their kilts and feather bonnets. The grenadiers were visible in their high caps, and the light infantry in their short jackets and small helmets. Altogether it was a strong force.

Colonel Mawhood's column began to march a little before sunrise. By about eight o'clock they had crossed the bridge at Stony Brook, and they were near the summit of the hill by Cochran's house when they saw the American troops about a mile away, heading for Princeton. Ensign Inman reported that "a large body of enemy were seen on our left." Some thought that they were Hessians, but Captain William Hale wrote, "We discovered the Rebel Army in two columns, entering a wood on the other side of a Rivulet we had just passed."

Colonel Mawhood considered his options. Clearly the American army was heading toward Princeton and Brunswick. Not so clear was what he should do about it. "We drew up on a woody eminence and looked at them for a considerable time," Hale remembered. "Colonel Mawhood had two choices, either to retire back to Princetown, where . . . we might have defended the works about it, or push on to Maidenhead where the 2d Brigade lay."[14]

In that moment of uncertainty, he decided to do exactly what was expected of a British officer in such a situation. Inman wrote, "Colonel Mawhood immediately determined to attack." He ordered the Fifty-fifth regiment and the artillery to occupy Mercer Hill and sent the wagons back through Princeton to safety. Mawhood led the rest of his column across the countryside, directly toward the American main body.

With him were his own Seventeenth Foot, the dismounted dragoons, and the details from other regiments, including Highlanders, light infantry, grenadiers, and artillery, with two guns in the van. An American eyewitness, Captain Rodney, counted another eight British guns deploying on Mercer Hill, a thousand yards behind the infantry.[15] The speed of the British reaction was remarkable. A medley of many units came instantly together as a strong fighting force, a testament to Mawhood's leadership and the discipline of the British Regulars.

The British force advanced east across the snow-covered fields toward the American main body in the distance. Nathanael Greene's division, still on its sunken road in the deep ravine of Stony Brook, could not see them and continued marching toward the Post Road. Mercer's brigade was leading with Neil's New Jersey artillery, followed by Cadwalader's brigade with two guns. Both Mawhood and Greene were unaware of one another, even as they were very close, and moving on converging lines. In the distance, Washington could see clearly what was happening. He sent a galloper to warn Greene about the British force and ordered him to deal with it while the American main body continued toward Princeton.

Washington's messenger arrived a few minutes later. Greene ordered General Mercer to lead his brigade out of the ravine, directly toward the oncoming British force. Mercer thought that he was facing a small enemy detachment and committed only part of his brigade. About a hundred Pennsylvania Riflemen and twenty Virginians climbed the bank of the ravine. The rest of Mercer's command prepared to follow with artillery. In the rear of Greene's division, Cadwalader saw what was happening, halted his brigade, and waited for orders.[16]

As Mercer's men came out of the ravine, they discovered "a light-horseman looking directly towards us, as we view an object when the sun shines directly in our faces." Mercer ordered his riflemen to "pick him off." Before they could fire, the British trooper wheeled about and was gone. American and British forces were now fully aware of one another. Both advanced toward the high ground on the farm of William Clark. The point of intersection was an orchard surrounded by a fence.

Mawhood sent his fifty dismounted dragoons toward the orchard. About four hundred yards behind them, the Seventeenth Foot were ordered to strip off their packs and form a line of battle with two guns. The regiment had about 224 rank and file that morning, plus the cavalry, artillery, Highlanders, light infantry, and grenadiers, about 450 men in all.[17]

From the other side, Mercer's vanguard of about 120 Americans hurried toward the orchard. Several hundred yards behind them were the rest of Mercer's brigade, another 200 men. To their rear were Cadwalader's brigade of Pennsylvania militia, Rodney's Delaware light infantry, the Philadelphia Redfeather Company of light infantry, and a few marines under Major Samuel Nicholas. Altogether these Americans were about 1,500 strong, roughly three times the size of Mawhood's troops.

The two sides collided in William Clark's orchard, in a classic meeting engagement. The fifty dismounted British dragoons advanced to the edge of the fruit trees and were ordered to lie down behind a fence. As the Americans entered the orchard, the dragoons rose and fired. An American sergeant remembered, "their first shot passed over our heads," clipping limbs and twigs off the apple trees. Mercer's men pushed forward and discharged a volley. The out-numbered dragoons fell back under heavy fire. The Americans drove forward to a low bank of earth that gave them some protection. One remembered that he "fell on one knee and loaded my musket with ball and buckshot. Our fire was most destructive. Their ranks grew thin and victory seemed nearly complete."[18]

More troops were arriving on both sides. Mawhood's British infantry marched forward in line of battle: the Seventeenth Foot with the replacement companies of grenadiers, light infantry, and Highlanders. The rest of Mercer's American infantry were coming up fast. When the two sides were forty yards apart, Captain John Fleming shouted an order in a Virginia accent to his Continentals of his First Virginia Regiment, "Gentlemen, dress before you make ready." An angry British voice replied, "Damn you, we will dress you." The British regiment fired a volley: a great sheet of flame and a ripping sound that sounded like the tearing of a sheet. Again it went high. Mercer's Virginians, Marylanders, and Pennsylvanians fired their own volley into the faces of the Regulars, and their aim was better. An American wrote that "the enemy screamed as if many devils had got hold of them."[19]

The British troops suffered terribly. On the receiving end was Captain Hale, who wrote that the American volley was "a heavy dis-charge, which brought down seven of my platoon at once, the rest being recruits, gave way." He ran to stop them. "I rallied them with much difficulty, and brought them forward with bayonets," he wrote.[20] The Americans fired another volley. "The rebels poured in a second fire," a British soldier wrote. They were aiming at the officers. In the grenadier detachment Captain Williams was killed. Captain Hale had a bullet through his coat, and another caused a "contusion in the leg." In the Seventeenth Foot, many officers fell. One of them was Captain William Leslie, Dr. Benjamin Rush's friend, mortally wounded.[21]

The British infantry returned volley for volley, and now their fire struck home. Half a mile away, an American with the main body watched in horror and fascination as "the smoke from the discharge of the two lines mingled as it rose, and went up in one beautiful cloud," which made a melancholy contrast with the carnage below. An American sergeant looked around in the midst of the fight and saw "my old associates were scattered about groaning, dying and

The Death of General Hugh Mercer, a sketch by John Trumbull (1786). The defiant American leader refused British orders to surrender and was bayoneted on the battlefield. Here again Trumbull's sketches were more dynamic and more true to the event than his finished paintings. Princeton University Library.

dead. One officer who was shot from his horse lay in a hollow place in the ground rolling and writhing in his blood, unconscious of anything around him." Blood was everywhere in the orchard and fields, flowing bright across the icy surface of the snow. Veterans of many battles had never seen it that way. One remembered that "the ground was frozen and all the blood which was shed remained on the surface." It added to the horror of this scene.[22]

Mawhood watched for the right moment, then ordered his regiment to charge bayonets. The British infantry came forward into the orchard, emerging from clouds of white powder-smoke with their blood-red coats and long bayonets, full of rage and fury. Mercer's riflemen had no bayonets. They had stood bravely against musketry and artillery, but in the face of a British bayonet charge they recoiled in confusion. Mercer's gray horse was hit, then Mercer himself. As he went down, he cried, "Retreat!" Many of his men fell back, but Mercer was caught by British troops. One knocked him down with a musket-butt, inflicting a mortal blow. Mercer was handsomely uniformed, even to a cravat, and the British infantry thought they had taken Washington. They gathered round him, and one shouted, "Call for Quarters, you damned rebel." Mercer replied defiantly, "I am no rebel." He refused to surrender and lunged at the British troops with his sword. They bayoneted him many times, and one cried, "Damn him he is dead. Let us leave him."[23]

Delaware's Colonel Haslet stepped forward to replace Mercer and tried to rally the brigade. He was shot dead with a bullet through his brain. Captain Fleming of Virginia was killed, and Captain Neil of the New Jersey artillery died working his gun. The American infantry lost their leaders and were shattered by the bayonet charge. They broke and ran, with the British infantry after them. British Captain William Hale remembered, "at length we drove them through the railings, barns and orchards."[24]

More Americans were now coming on the field. Cadwalader's Pennsylvania Associators hurried forward and began to deploy from a marching column to a fighting line. As they did so, the retreating survivors of Mercer's brigade ran headlong into them, and Cadwalader's line came apart. Some of the Associators began to fall back; others broke and ran. The British Captain Hale saw that Cadwalader's entire command "fell into confusion." He wrote, "I am convinced that had the other [British] brigade been with us we might have defeated the whole American army."[25]

Study for the Battle of Princeton, detail from a pen-and-ink drawing by John Trumbull (ca. 1786). This shows the British attack on the American artillery and the death of Daniel Neil of the Eastern Company, New Jersey State Artillery. Art historians have misidentified this figure as Lieutenant Charles Turnbull. Princeton University Library.

But some of Cadwalader's Philadelphia Associators stood fast and started fighting. Among them was a small battery of Philadelphia artillery. Its commander, Captain Joseph Moulder, brought his guns quickly into action. His two long-barreled four-pounders fired deadly rounds of grape and canister into the British infantry and stopped it. Mawhood quickly brought up two British guns. His men had also captured one of Mercer's guns and used it against the Americans. Hale remembered that "we kept possession of the orchard for twenty minutes, turning one of their own guns upon them."[26]

More American troops streamed into the battle. On the American left, the remnants of Mercer's brigade and a company of Smallwood's Maryland Continentals rallied and returned to the battle. They were supported by Rodney's Delaware light infantry, who took a position among haystacks very near to Moulder's guns and protected them from the British infantry. Other guns arrived on the American left. A New England battery extended the line beyond the small British force. One of the guns was commanded by Sergeant Joseph White, who loaded with canister and fired it into the enemy. White recalled that the canister "made a terrible squeaking noise." In the line of fire were the British grenadiers of Captain Hale. He wrote, "During this time they discovered our weakness, and brought three pieces of cannon in play to our right with grape and case," but the British were so close that the American gunners fired over them. "Our nearness, nearly 100 yards, saved us greatly," Hale wrote.[27]

The Philadelphia Associators, even those who had broken a moment before, formed again into line. It was an extraordinary feat for these untrained soldiers to rally under heavy fire. John Cadwalader gave them strong leadership, but it was the men themselves who decided to stand and fight, Philadelphia artisans, mechanics, merchants, laborers side by side. In that critical moment Washington arrived on the field and took control of the battle. He rode among Cadwalader's Associators and shouted, "Parade with us, my brave fellows! There is but a handful of the enemy, and we will have them directly." Washington led his men straight into the center of the battle, within thirty paces of the British line. He was mounted on a white horse, an easy mark for any British soldier, and yet none shot him.

The American troops were deeply moved by his courage. A young Philadelphia naval officer wrote afterward, "O, my Susan! It was a glorious day, and I would not have been absent from it for all the money I ever expect to be worth." Most of all, he remembered Washington's example. "I shall never forget what I felt at Princeton

Battle of Princeton, oil painting by William Mercer after James Peale (ca. 1786). This very careful reconstruction of the event shows the moment when George Washington came on the field. In the center left are Colonel Cadwalader's Philadelphia Associators. Coming up with Washington are Hitchcock's New Englanders. Behind Washington is a trooper of the Philadelphia Light Horse and Washington's headquarters standard, a blue flag with thirteen white stars. Behind the fence on the right is Colonel Mawhood with the British Seventeenth Foot, the Sixteenth Light Dragoons, and detachments from other regiments. The Historical Society of Pennsylvania Collection, Atwater Kent Museum of Philadelphia.

on his account, when I saw him brave all the dangers of the field and his important life hanging as it were by a single hair with a thousand deaths flying around him. Believe me, I thought not of myself."[28]

Washington led other American units into the fight. Mifflin's brigade came up, and Hand's Pennsylvania Rifles. Hitchcock's "quiet men" from New England advanced with bayonets fixed. Other American units hurried into action, running forward toward the British infantry. Some of them ran past the gun of Sergeant White, who wrote, "I never saw men looked so furious as they did running by us with their bayonets charged." Mawhood's British infantry fired a volley, but again it went high. Washington halted all of his troops and settled them. Then he led them deliberately forward and ordered them to fire "a heavy platoon fire on the march."

Mawhood's British troops were outnumbered and outflanked. Hale wrote, "I expected their flanks would wheel in and attack our rear, which had they done every man must have been cut to pieces." The British infantry continued to fight with a dogged courage that impressed their enemies. Ten British artillerymen died at their guns. Then at last they gave way. Hale wrote that "a resolution was taken to retreat, i.e. run away as fast as we could."[29]

The British line broke, but even then these Regulars kept their discipline. As the Americans moved forward, some groups of British infantry formed yet again and "cut their way through the closing American circle" and escaped toward the Trenton road. Hale was with them as they fled south, then west, and finally north. He remembered that "we went twenty miles round that day to join our troops and marched all the following night to Brunswick, in all upwards of forty miles without halting two hours."[30]

Washington urged his men to go after them. He shouted, "It is a fine fox chase, my boys!"[31] The general himself galloped after the fleeing enemy, until his aides urged him to rein in. Some Americans continued the pursuit. The backcountry riflemen were relentless; they hunted the British Regulars across the countryside and took many prisoners. Other American troops "came into a house on the battlefield, looking for something to eat or drink, and hoping to get warm." A civilian observed that "they were both hungry and thirsty," but in high spirits, "some of them laughing outright, others smiling, and not a man among them but showed Joy in his Countenance."[32]

As the surviving British troops ran to the west, Colonel Mawhood went in a different direction. He ordered the Fifty-fifth Foot and the artillery to retreat from Mercer Hill. Conscious of his responsibility for the defense of Princeton, he turned north with "a few files of infantry" and headed back to the town to take command of what remained of his brigade. To the bemusement of the Americans, he rode defiantly across the front of their army, still with his two playful spaniels gamboling around him. The American riflemen could have shot him, but they let him pass. One would like to believe that it was a tribute to his gallantry.

The Americans were awed by the discipline, skill, and sheer effrontery of their British opponents. Colonel Mawhood's regiment and a pickup force of replacements and convalescents had attacked the entire American army and stopped its advance for a critical moment. After the battle, Washington passed a wounded British soldier and "paused to praise a gallant defence and to assure the man that everything the camp could give the victims of the action

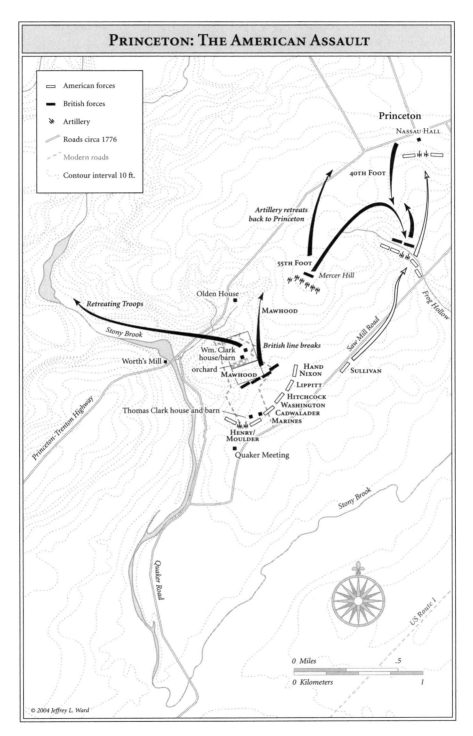

PRINCETON: THE AMERICAN ASSAULT

American forces

British forces

Artillery

Roads circa 1776

Modern roads

Contour interval 10 ft.

Princeton

NASSAU HALL

40TH FOOT

*Artillery retreats
back to Princeton*

Frog Hollow

55TH FOOT

Mercer Hill

Olden House

Saw Mill Road

MAWHOOD

Retreating Troops

Stony Brook

British line breaks

Wm. Clark
house/barn

Worth's Mill

orchard   MAWHOOD

HAND
NIXON   SULLIVAN

Thomas Clark house and barn

LIPPITT

HITCHCOCK

WASHINGTON

CADWALADER
MARINES

Princeton-Trenton Highway

HENRY/
MOULDER

Quaker Meeting

Stony Brook

Quaker Road

US Route 1

0 Miles   .5

0 Kilometers   1

© 2004 Jeffrey L. Ward

would be issued." He posted sentries on the battlefield to keep stragglers from robbing the wounded British soldiers.[33]

While the battle was raging in the orchard, the British troops in
Princeton prepared to defend the town. The Fifty-fifth Foot did not
wait to be attacked. Their commander decided to meet the oncoming
Americans west of the town by advancing toward them. He was outnumbered more than ten to one, but his first thought was to carry the
fight to the enemy. Southwest of the town, there was good defensive
ground behind a deep ravine, very near the old Princeton Inn on
Alexander Street. Here the Fifty-fifth took up a strong position. In
front of them the ground fell away into a ravine still called Frog Hollow, which had been cut into the countryside by a small stream. The
ravine was steep on the British left and gave it some protection.

As the Americans approached, the commander of the Fifty-fifth
Foot showed the same offensive spirit that Cornwallis's army displayed throughout the campaign. He detached a "heavy platoon"
and sent it to attack the flank of the oncoming American column.
As the small British force approached, Sullivan deployed two regiments and broke it by weight of numbers. Part of Sullivan's force
climbed down into the ravine and scrambled up the icy slope on the
other side, beyond the flank of the Fifty-fifth. Other American troops
advanced on the other flank.[34]

When the Americans were within eighty yards, the Fifty-fifth found
its flanks in danger and withdrew on command. The Regulars remained firmly in hand and fell back to another prepared position in
their rear, a formidable breastwork complete with a sally port. Here
they made another stand against heavy odds. Sullivan's men unlimbered their artillery and brought the guns into action on the British
right flank. Two of the American guns fired on a dike or dam upstream of them, at the upper end of Frog Hollow. A few well-placed
rounds smashed the dam, and the rushing water swept it away.[35]

Sullivan had managed a double envelopment, and the British
position was untenable, "owing to the manner of the attack." But
the Fifty-fifth Foot retreated in good order to yet another breastwork near the college. Sullivan's column advanced to within fifty or
sixty feet and made ready to storm the position. A British officer
"came through a sally port, with a white handkerchief on the point
of his sword." Sullivan accepted his surrender.[36]

The Americans advanced to the grounds of the college, where
a small number of British troops knocked the windows out of Nassau
Hall with their muskets and prepared to defend the building. The

Nassau Hall and the Home of John Witherspoon, engraving by Henry Dawkins (1764). On the morning of January 3, 1777, British troops occupied the buildings. General Sullivan's American troops attacked it from the right rear, captured the defenders, and released many American prisoners who were confined in the basement. Princeton University Library.

American artillery deployed and opened fire on Nassau Hall. The battery commander was reported to be Alexander Hamilton. As always he was in the thick of the fighting. It was said that "the ball recoiled" and nearly killed Major Wilkinson. According to a legend long cherished in the college, another American ball was said to have beheaded a portrait of King George II. More likely, the painting was attacked by an American infantryman with bayonet or sword.

The British resistance at the Clark farm, Frog Hollow, the redoubts in Princeton, and Nassau Hall was a series of delaying actions that allowed the larger part of Colonel Mawhood's garrison to escape from Princeton. Most of the supplies and guns were removed from the town, in a big British baggage train that departed for Somerset and Brunswick. Even so, the British defenders suffered heavy losses in the fighting around Princeton. George Inman, the young ensign of the Seventeenth Foot, recorded that his regiment took 224 rank and file into battle and lost 101 dead and severely wounded: a casualty rate of 45 percent. The officers suffered worse. Inman noted he was "the only officer in the right wing of the battalion that was not very much injured, receiving only a buckshot through my crossbelt which just entered the pit of my stomach and made me sick for a moment." Among the detachments of recruits and replacements, casualties were even heavier. Hale's grenadier company suffered seventeen out of thirty-two killed or wounded, a loss rate of 53 percent. The Royal Artillery lost ten men, about half of the crews for the guns that were engaged.[37]

Assuming the same rate of loss in the dismounted cavalry, the Highlanders and light infantry, Mawhood lost 222 men killed and wounded in the battle out of 446 engaged, nearly half of his strength. Many others were captured. General Howe reported 187 rank and file missing, as always an undercount. The Americans reported taking between 200 and 300 prisoners. Part of the difference derived from the failure of British staff officers in New York to include the many draughts and replacements in their estimates. Altogether, the total loss to British forces at Princeton was approximately 450 killed, wounded, captured, and missing.[38]

Mawhood's gallant resistance succeeded in stopping the Americans long enough to disrupt a major part of Washington's operation. The American commander wrote candidly to Congress, "my original plan when I set out from Trenton was to have pushed on to Brunswick." He hoped to seize the biggest British base in New Jersey, "with all their stores and magazines," and a "military chest" of seventy thousand pounds sterling.[39]

But it was not to be. The fight at Princeton drained the energy out of the American army. Washington noted that many of his men "had no rest for two nights and a day," even before the battle began. The American commanders were also thinking about Cornwallis, who could be expected to come after them as rapidly as his men could move. Trenton was only about five hours' march away, and two hours had already been lost. Washington decided to keep his choices open. To gain more time he ordered his men to destroy the bridge at Stony Brook and set up roadblocks with artillery.

The British heard the firing in Trenton, and Cornwallis ordered them to rush toward Princeton. In the lead were Leslie's troops, who were at Maidenhead when Washington attacked Princeton. Sergeant Thomas Sullivan wrote, "Brigadier General Leslie sent an immediate express to lord Cornwallis, who was [in Trenton] with the advance troops; and our brigade and the guards got on the march."[40] Cornwallis drove his men up the Princeton Road in a forced march. Two hours after the British surrender at Nassau Hall, Cornwallis's vanguard were near the bridge at Worth's Mill.

Among them were the Hessian Jägers. Captain Johann Ewald wrote, "at daybreak on the morning of the 3d we suddenly learned that Washington had abandoned his position. At the same time we heard a heavy cannonade in our rear, which surprised everyone. Instantly we marched back at quick step to Princeton, where we found the entire field of action from Maidenhead on to Princeton and vicinity covered with corpses."[41]

As the British army approached Stony Brook, the American drums in Princeton began beating the long roll. The troops formed up at the run, and the army moved out to the east. The American rear guard made a stand at the bridge, and Washington wrote that Cornwallis was "so long retarded" at Stony Brook as "to give us time to move off in good order." From Princeton, the American army marched northeast from Princeton to the hamlet of Kingston. There the road divided. One fork went to Somerset Court House, another to Brunswick. At the intersection, Washington convened a council of war on horseback. The general officers considered several possibilities. One was a quick strike at the big British base in Brunswick. Another possibility was an attack on Somerset Court House, where it was thought that the British baggage train was ripe for capture.[42]

The American army was weary from a night march and battle. The roads were snowy north of Princeton. Wilkinson remembered, "the exclamation was general, 'O that we had 500 fresh men to beat up their quarters at Brunswick.'" Washington himself later wrote, "the harassed state of our own troops (many of them having had no rest for two nights and a day) and the danger of losing the advantage we had gained by aiming at too much, induced me, by the advice of my officers, to relinquish the attempt. . . . Six or eight hundred fresh troops upon a forced march could have . . . put an end to the war."[43]

The army marched instead for Somerset. The van arrived at dusk, and the inhabitants reported that the British baggage trains had left only an hour before, but no unit in the American army had "strength left in it to organize pursuit." The army camped at Somerset the night of January 3–4, and on the morning of January 4 marched to Pluckemin. "We got plenty of beef, pork, etc, which we had been starving for a day or two, not having time to draw or dress victuals." On the fifth and sixth the army was on the road again for Morristown.[44]

When the Americans were well clear of Princeton, the British arrived from Trenton, in what was described as "a most infernal sweat—running, puffing, and blowing, and swearing at being so

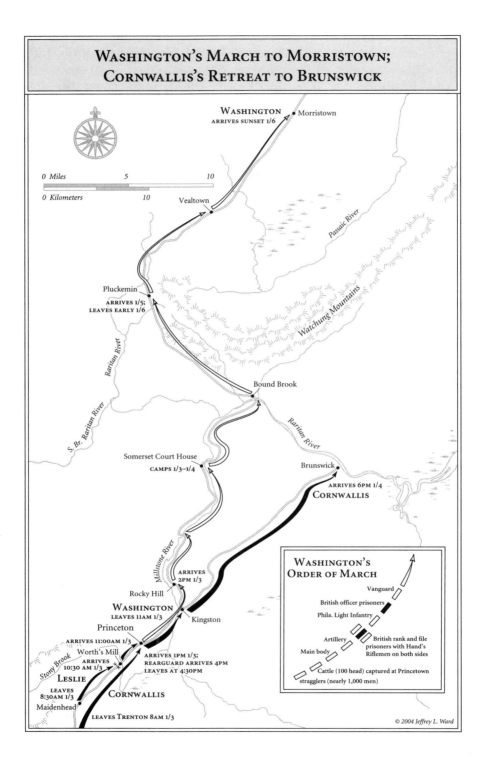

Washington's March to Morristown; Cornwallis's Retreat to Brunswick

WASHINGTON
ARRIVES SUNSET 1/6
Morristown

Passaic River

0 Miles   5   10

0 Kilometers   10

Vealtown

Watchung Mountains

Pluckemin
ARRIVES 1/5;
LEAVES EARLY 1/6

Raritan River

Bound Brook

S. Br. Raritan River

Raritan River

Somerset Court House
CAMPS 1/3–1/4

Brunswick
ARRIVES 6PM 1/4
CORNWALLIS

Millstone River

ARRIVES
2PM 1/3

Rocky Hill

WASHINGTON
LEAVES 11AM 1/3

Kingston

Princeton
ARRIVES 11:00AM 1/3
Worth's Mill
ARRIVES
10:30 AM 1/3

ARRIVES 1PM 1/3;
REARGUARD ARRIVES 4PM
LEAVES AT 4:30PM

Stony Brook

LESLIE
LEAVES
8:30AM 1/3

CORNWALLIS

Maidenhead
LEAVES TRENTON 8AM 1/3

Washington's Order of March

Vanguard
British officer prisoners
Phila. Light Infantry

Artillery
Main body
British rank and file
prisoners with Hand's
Riflemen on both sides

Cattle (100 head) captured at Princetown
stragglers (nearly 1,000 men)

© 2004 Jeffrey L. Ward

outwitted."[45] Ewald was in the van again; he wrote in disgust, "In the afternoon the entire army reached Princetown, marching in and around the town like an army that is thoroughly beaten. Everyone was so frightened that it was completely forgotten even to obtain information about where the Americans had gone. Now the enemy had wings, and it was believed he had flown toward Brunswick to destroy the main depot, which was protected only by one English regiment."[46]

Hurriedly the British army was issued three days' rations of biscuit and brandy. "It left behind its sick and wounded, and moved with such haste toward Brunswick that, although it was only a five-hour march, above one thousand wagoners reached Brunswick toward the evening of the 4th. If the enemy had pursued them with only a hundred horsemen, one after another would have been captured."

On the night of January 3–4, the British army also missed a chance to strike at the Continental army when it was exposed, exhausted, and unable to defend itself. In the Hessian camp, Captain Ewald wrote, "several days later it was learned that after the coup at Princetown, General Washington and his army had camped in the woods at Rocky Hill, two hours from Princetown, until the morning of the 4th—completely exhausted, without ammunition or provisions." Something fundamental had changed. The thoughts of British commanders were no longer about attacking but being attacked. Cornwallis ordered his army to retreat from Princeton to Brunswick, abandoning many posts in New Jersey.[47]

When the news of the battle reached New York City, some American Loyalists refused to believe that it had happened. Others persuaded themselves that the British army had actually won the fight at Princeton. A writer in Hugh Gaine's *New-York Gazette and Weekly Mercury* announced that the battle at Princeton was a British victory, in which Colonel Mawhood's regiment defeated the "entire Rebel army" and inflicted four hundred casualties. It added, "This has been one of the most splendid Actions of the whole campaign, and has given convincing Proof that British Valour has not declined from its antient Glory."[48]

In New York, General Howe's staff distributed casualty lists that grossly undercounted losses. Similar attitudes appeared in Britain when the news arrived. Horace Walpole wrote that the court denied it.[49] In London, Lord North tried to suppress the first reports. But commanders in the field knew what had happened. As the news sank in, the recriminations began. No British or German leader on

any level accepted responsibility. Every senior officer blamed someone else. General Howe found a way to blame the Hessians again
for the battle of Princeton, even though no major unit was engaged.
General Clinton blamed General Cornwallis. "His Lordship, thinking that Washington would wait for him till the next day, deceived
by his fires &c into this belief, neglects to patrole to Allentown—
over which Washington's whole army and the last hope of America
escaped. I am sure no hessian corporal would have been so imposed
upon. 'Tis a wonder Washington did not march to Brunswick."[50]

While the generals were blaming each other, junior officers condemned them all. Lieutenant Colonel Allan Maclean wrote to
Alexander Cummings on February 19, 1777, "Poor devils as the
rebel generals are, they have out generaled us more than once, even
since I have been here, which is only six weeks. . . . Lord Cornwallis
is, I believe, a brave man, but he allowed himself to be fairly outgeneralled by Washington, the 4th of January last at Trenton, and
missed a glorious opportunity when he let Washington slip away in
the night."[51]

Throughout the British and Hessian armies, morale was another casualty of the battle. John Bowater, a British captain of marines, wrote from New York, "The Business was done if it had not
been for this affair, but the rebels exposed their Prisoners and Trophies of War. Many Orations was spoke at Philadelphia and other
places to explain to the people, what a Contemptible Enemy they
had to Cope with. By these and other artfull methods, they prevail'd
on their People to reinlist, and they have now got a very Considerable Army together, and you may depend upon it, they will beat the
Hessians every time they meet (the Grenadiers and Chassures only
excepted)."[52]

The battles at Trenton and Princeton both had a profound effect on the British conduct of the war. Historian Ira Gruber writes
that "in a week's time, Washington had spoiled the work of many
months. Since mid-August the Howes had, it appeared, been following a strategy of careful advances, designed to create the impression of British invincibility, destroy the colonists' faith in the
Continental army, and produce a genuine reconciliation. To ensure
the success of their strategy they had not only declined opportunities to trap the Continental army and to press the war at sea but
also, in spite of the criticism of their subordinates, made repeated
overtures to Congress and the colonists."

Through the fall, the policy of the Howe brothers had been
working. Gruber observes that "by mid-December it seemed that

they had nearly ended the rebellion. The colonists had not been won by the Howes' rhetoric, but they were beginning to respond to the overwhelming display of British power." Then suddenly the momentum was broken. From long study of the Howes' career in America, Gruber concludes that "Trenton and Princeton were supremely important, [in] destroying the illusion of British invincibility, making patriots of potential loyalists, and spoiling the Howes' hopes for an end to the war and a start to a lasting reunion."[53] The Howe brothers were forced to rethink their entire plan. "I do not now see a prospect for terminating the war but by a general action," General Howe wrote, "and I am aware of the difficulties in our way to obtain it."[54]

Americans took heart. New Englanders, responding in their ancestral way, saw the battles as a Sign. General Nathanael Greene wrote to Governor Nicholas Cooke of Rhode Island, "the Lord seems to have smote the enemy with a panic." New Jersey's Governor William Livingston thought about it in another way. He cursed the criminal folly of British leaders and wrote that "their blunders, if possible, are equal to their cruelty." Governor Livingston found a meaning in his classical learning at Princeton. He believed that cause of the British defeat was the hubris of an arrogant "prince and people" whom "God Almighty . . . seems determined to destroy."[55]

A Virginia planter responded in yet another spirit that was more practical and even profane. Thomas Nelson wrote to his friend Thomas Jefferson, "Our affairs have had a black appearance for the two last months, but they say the Devil is not so black as he is painted. We have at last turned the Tables upon these scoundrels by surprise. . . . Could we but get a good Regular army we should soon clear the Continent of these damned invaders."[56]

AFTERMATH

∿ The Forage War

> The season . . . is not yet closed; neither do I intend it
> shall unless the Enemy quit the Jerseys.
>
> —George Washington, January 20, 1777[1]

> Washington this whole winter never had more than
> 7,000 men in the Jersies, where we had 16,000, yet we
> have been tossed and kicked about most amazingly,
> all our forage parties constantly attacked, and tho' we
> generally beat them we lost a great many good men.
>
> —British Colonel Allan Maclean, February 19, 1777[2]

AFTER THE BATTLE at Princeton, the fighting continued in
New Jersey for many weeks. While George Washington led
the Continental army to winter quarters in Morristown, small
parties of Jersey militia took the field. They attacked larger forces
of British and German Regulars with an aggressive spirit that amazed
the enemy and astonished their friends. It started on January 4,
1777. Twenty mounted militia of Captain John Stryker's Somerset
Horse cut off a British supply convoy on the King's Highway near
Ten Mile Run and captured "numerous wagons" full of warm woolen
clothing that American troops urgently needed. Sharp skirmishes
followed near Newark and Rahway on January 5, and at Bound Brook
on January 6. Wherever red coats and brass caps appeared in the
countryside, they were attacked.[3]

The success of these small engagements inspired larger attacks
on British and German posts. A ripe target was Elizabethtown, which

was held in strength by a German regiment of Waldeck Infantry, with several companies of the Seventy-first Highlanders and a troop of British Dragoons. It had been a soft billet until the "bad news from Trenton" arrived and the garrison began to feel very much exposed. Then came reports of a second British failure at Trenton and an American victory at Princeton. "Our pleasure in Elizabeth has passed," German chaplain Philipp Waldeck wrote on January 3. "One can no longer lie down to sleep without thinking this is the last night, the last night of freedom. Instead of undressing in the evening as usual, one becomes accustomed to dress completely, and to go to bed in this manner."[4]

The chaplain's forebodings were well founded. On January 4, Americans ambushed a small patrol of British dragoons outside Elizabethtown and shot two troopers out of the saddle in what Philipp Waldeck called "a dastardly fashion." The next day German Captain Georg von Haacke led a larger force of fifty or sixty Waldeck infantry and an escort of British dragoons, with orders to clear the countryside. Heavy firing was heard in the distance, and a few hours later the dragoons came limping back on bloody horses. They reported that the Jersey militia had attacked them near Springfield, six miles west of Elizabethtown. All of the Waldeck infantry were killed or captured. Only the British cavalry got away.[5]

The response of British commanders was very different from only a week before. After the events at Trenton and Princeton, General Howe was beginning to think defensively. On January 6, he ordered British and German troops at Elizabethtown to abandon the town immediately and pull back to Amboy "as quietly as possible." It was almost too late. As the Regulars retreated in haste, American militia swarmed after them. George Washington reported to Congress that the enemy "evacuated Elizabeth Town with so much precipitation that we made 100 prisoners and took the baggage of two regiments, besides a quantity of provision."[6]

The remnants of the garrison reached Amboy, a fortified seaport only a few miles from New York. Even there they were not safe. The Jersey militia launched bold attacks on the defenses of the town. Sergeant Thomas Sullivan of the Forty-ninth Foot was shocked by the sudden change that had come over the Americans. "Our Army's leaving Trenton and Princetown greatly animated the Enemy," Sergeant Sullivan wrote. "They crowded from all parts of the country to our suburbs, and drove the Waldeckers from Elizabethtown to Amboy, where the 4th brigade British lay. They made an attempt to surprise the town twice but in vain."[7]

This was yet another kind of war, which Regulars called the *petite guerre*. Small parties of militia—sometimes much larger ones—attacked where they saw an opening, killed a few Regulars, and disappeared into the countryside. Each success encouraged more militia to take the field. On January 7, 1777, Colonel Lambert Cadwalader reckoned that "our army in the Jersies must amount altogether to nearly twelve thousand." Most were militia and volunteers. Washington complained endlessly about them. Their indiscipline and stubborn independence infuriated the commander-in-chief. The worst of it, in Washington's words, was that "they come and go when they please."[8]

But in January 1777, it pleased the militia to turn out. Winter was a good campaigning season for an army of citizen-farmers. These men were inspired by the American victories at Trenton and Princeton, and they were angry about the occupation of New Jersey. John Adams had long predicted that General Howe would "repent his mad march through the Jersies." Now Adams observed that the people of New Jersey "begin to raise their Spirits exceedingly, and to be firmer than ever. They are actuated by Resentment now, and Resentment coinciding with Principle is a very powerful motive."[9]

Continental officers did not start this *petite guerre*, but once again George Washington was quick to see an opportunity. His resources for any sort of military operation were severely limited. The Continental army was shrinking yet again. The one-year regiments that had agreed to remain for a few weeks were now departing, and Washington sent some of his best men home to recruit a new three-year army. In their absence, a few small units came forward to keep the army in being. On January 6, 1777, Pennsylvania troops from Bedford and Westmoreland County arrived in the Continental camp after a long and terrible march across the mountains in deep snow and bitter cold. It is a forgotten event in the war, but it was an American anabasis that caused great suffering and took many lives.[10] Six mounted troops of Virginia light horse under Major Theodorick Bland reached Morristown in early January.[11] Maryland infantry came in from Frederick and Hagerstown, and Benjamin Lincoln's New England volunteers marched into camp from Connecticut and Massachusetts. These welcome reinforcements kept the army in being, but barely so. By mid-March only 2,500 Continental troops remained with Washington, fewer than in the dark days of December, but enough for a *petite guerre*. They were sent into the field to work with the militia.[12]

The most active Continental officer in this work was General William Maxwell, an extraordinary character and a combat leader of true genius. His campaigns in the winter war were models of the military art. Maxwell was a Scotch-Irish immigrant, born and raised in County Tyrone, with an Ulster accent so thick that his troops called him "Scotch Willie." He settled in northwestern New Jersey in 1747, became a frontier teacher and trader, took an Indian woman for his common-law wife, and soldiered in the Indian wars with the Jersey Blues and later the Royal Americans. He strongly supported the Revolution, saw much active service on the northern frontier, and joined the Continental army in New Jersey and stayed with it through the winter. In January Washington sent him into the field, with orders to work with the Jersey militia, and to "annoy and harass" the enemy at every opportunity, but to avoid a general engagement. The object was to keep British and Hessian forces on the defensive and to gain control of the New Jersey countryside.[13]

British commanders had no wish for a cold-weather campaign, in which they had little to gain and much to lose. General Howe wanted to gather his resources for a major effort in the spring and summer of 1777. Under growing pressure from the New Jersey militia, he ordered his garrisons in central New Jersey to withdraw to a small enclave along the Raritan River, from Brunswick to Amboy. The same thing happened in north Jersey, where he instructed the Sixth, Seventh, and Twenty-sixth Foot to withdraw from Hackensack and New-Bridge to the coast, where they could be protected by the guns of the Royal Navy.[14] As they retreated, New York's Whig General George Clinton quickly sent American troops to take possession of Hackensack and reported happily that the British regiments had "left the town with the utmost precipitation and fright." Nearly all of northern New Jersey returned to American control.[15]

Clinton also ordered his troops at Hackensack to "bring in the Tories," whom he described as "much dejected and distressed." Throughout New Jersey, retreating British and Hessian troops abandoned the Loyalists to the wrath of their Whig neighbors. In Bergen County, Colonel Abraham Buskirk's Fourth New Jersey Loyalists were handled very roughly. In Monmouth County, Colonel John Morris's Second New Jersey Loyalists were caught near Middletown, and twenty-seven were killed or captured. Many a score was settled with all the rage and cruelty of a civil war. Many frightened Loyalist families packed a few possessions and fled to New York. Others disappeared into the Pine Barrens of South Jersey. The Whigs of New Jersey had no sympathy for the suffering of these unhappy people.[16]

The fate of the Jersey Loyalists dealt another heavy blow to the Howes' policy of amnesty and reconciliation. The British government was unable to protect its American supporters, after asking them to come forward. The Loyalists began to wonder if imperial loyalty flowed only from the bottom up, not from the top down. More than a few men of military age were so angry that they changed uniforms of Loyalist green and red for Continental buff and blue. Others who had taken an oath of loyalty to the Crown in 1776 swore a second oath to Congress in 1777. Some found new uses for their Loyalist certificates. A correspondent reported that "many of the inhabitants of Monmouth County who received written protections, are now determined to return them to his Britannic Majesty's Commissioners in Cartridges."[17]

While the Jersey Loyalists struggled against their fate, British and German Regulars at Brunswick and Amboy had troubles of their own. In early January, Captain Ewald wrote that "the entire army had been stripped bare of shoes and stockings by the constant marching during the bad weather. Uniforms were torn and the officers, especially those of the Jäger companies, had almost nothing on their bodies." After a hard campaign they began to resemble the American tatterdemalions they had been fighting.[18]

More than ten thousand of these ragged Regulars crowded together in a few small towns and surrounding villages. Brunswick was a town of about four hundred houses, "partly deserted and partly destroyed." It overflowed with two battalions of British grenadiers, four battalions of Hessian grenadiers, two full brigades of British infantry, the artillery train, and the Sixteenth Light Dragoons. The Highlanders were packed into the village of Piscataway. Cornwallis's brigade went to Bonhamtown; Leslie's brigade and the guards went to Raritan Landing. The light infantry and Jägers were kept in the field on picket duty and lived in rough huts on the roads to Hillsborough and Bound Brook. There was little left to plunder. Ewald recalled that "this whole region had been completely sacked during the army's march in the past autumn, and had been abandoned by all the inhabitants." The troops subsisted "almost entirely on salt provision," and one officer reported that "everything is very scarce in the country here."[19]

Conditions grew worse when General Howe decided that these troops were not strong enough to keep the Americans at bay and transferred six regiments from Rhode Island to Brunswick and Amboy. Among the reinforcements was Grenadier Captain John Peebles of the Forty-second Foot. He found the towns so congested that his men lived aboard dirty transports in the Raritan River, with nothing to eat but "a little bit of salt pork." Peebles sent his men ashore at every opportunity and "got the ship a little clean'd," but living conditions grew worse through the winter, and "an ugly fever seized a good many both in town and transports."[20]

Peebles visited other units and discovered that the "British regiments here (vizt) the 4th brigade and 71[st Highlanders] are very weak in numbers, having lost a good many by the Enemy in that affair at Princetown." He also found that the entire army was "very sickly." Worse than the toll of battle was illness, which rapidly increased. Soon his own men "turned sick," and Peebles took them to hospitals, which were overflowing with sick and wounded. He was shocked by the misery he saw there. "Several of the wounded very bad. . . . I never saw men more patient and resign'd," he wrote in his diary. "Our company very sickly, two men that were orderly in the hospital on different days were taken suddenly ill, owing they think to the putrid stench in the rooms."[21] Some of the worst suffering was among the women of the British army. A woman with Captain Peebles's company fell ill, and he tried to get help for her. "Sent Ms. Gennes to the Hospital," he wrote, "but they would not admit a sick woman." The women of the army looked after their men, but when they fell ill, nobody looked after them.[22]

The miserable conditions in the garrison towns had an impact on British morale. Spirits had been very high in the summer and autumn. They started to slip in the early winter and fell rapidly after the battles at Trenton and Princeton. Diaries and letters from Brunswick and Amboy overflowed with frustration. The weather was a trial, living conditions were bad, the food was worse, illness was increasing, and the rebels whom these regulars despised had gained the upper hand. The writings of officers and men were full of anger against their remote commanders, who had been outgeneraled three times running by the rebel army.

While the beleaguered garrisons at Brunswick and Amboy overflowed with human misery, General Howe sponsored lavish parties in New York for British staff officers and wealthy Loyalists and kept the small capital in a social whirl. On January 18, 1777, his staff organized a grand festival to celebrate the Queen's Birthday and General Howe's investiture into the Order of the Bath. At a moment when ammunition was short and resupply from England overdue, Captain Montresor of the Royal Engineers was ordered to organize a "very splendid exhibition of fire works" in Manhattan. Rear echelon officers joined in balls and banquets, while the rank and file in New Jersey were reduced to salt rations and hard service.[23]

Lord Cornwallis, now the British commander in Brunswick, did what he could for his men, even supporting them from his own personal fortune. On January 9, he visited the Jägers and told them that "plentiful provisions would arrive any day." He even promised that "each jäger would be clothed at his expense." Two weeks later he was as good as his word. The Jägers received "the promised gift from Lord Cornwallis . . . a complete uniform for each man."[24] He also got the commissary system working. Abundant stocks of food had accumulated in New York, and Cornwallis made sure that some of it got to men in the field. Ewald wrote that his men "lacked for nothing," and "excellent provisions of salted beef and pork, peas, butter, rice and flour for bread, along with the best English beer, were continually supplied." Peebles's men fared not so well, but most had enough to eat.[25]

But the army had one critical shortage. It lacked feed for its animals. Forage and fodder were vital to an eighteenth-century army, as important as oil and gas in the twentieth century. Without forage the army could not move or fight. It could not have artillery in the field, or supply wagons for the infantry, or mounts for cavalry. An army of ten thousand men needed a large and steady flow of forage, especially in winter. General Howe ordered the troops in New Jersey to find their own supplies by foraging on the countryside.

Lord Cornwallis promptly sent out small foraging parties, and they met strong resistance from an armed and hostile population. On January 5, 1777, New Jersey militia attacked at Spanktown (now Rahway) a few miles from Brunswick and killed or wounded four men. British commanders responded with forage parties in regimental strength. One American observed that "they do not pretend to send a foraging party less than 500 or 600 men."[26] Americans attacked these larger forces, too, carefully choosing the time and place. The skirmishes grew into small battles, and British losses began to mount. Near the town of Chatham on January 10, Colonel Charles Scott's Virginia troops captured a foraging party of seventy Highlanders, along with "a large number of baggage wagons," which were in short supply.[27] At Connecticut Farms, a large force of 100 German foragers lost 71 killed and captured to Colonel Oliver Spencer and 300 Jersey militia. On January 16, a column of 350 Americans boldly attacked a forage party at Bonhamtown, very near Brunswick. British troops were reported to have lost 21 killed and 30 or 40 wounded. These three small engagements alone cost the British army the equivalent of one of its shrunken regiments.[28]

George Washington was quick to see that small numbers of his men could do real damage to his opponent. He informed Congress that intelligence reports on the enemy "confirm their want of forage. . . . If their Horses are reduced this Winter it will impossible for them to take the Field in the spring." Washington also recognized that many small engagements could severely reduce the fighting strength of British and German regiments.[29] He ordered most of his Continental troops to reinforce the Jersey militia and placed them in a ring of interlocking positions around Amboy and Brunswick. By the seventeenth of January, his headquarters reported to Congress that American forces were engaged in "daily skirmishes," which took a steady toll of men and morale in Howe's army. They also reduced the flow of food and forage into the British garrisons.

It is interesting to see how Washington worked with his army. He remained at Morristown and did not himself take the field. Through the winter he was busy with the recruitment of the new three-year regiments and the expansion of the army for the spring campaign. Much of his time and energy went into relations with members of Congress and leaders of the states. He was beginning to function not only as a military commander but as a leader of the republic.

Within the army, he was learning to delegate authority. Continental brigadiers and trusted militia generals such as Philemon Dickinson received independent commands and very broad instructions. They were told to be "constantly harassing the enemy" and to "remove out of their reach, all the horses, waggons and fat cattle." Again and again, every officer was instructed to avoid a general engagement but to keep the initiative.

Washington urged his officers always to be the drivers of events and never allow themselves to be "drove." To one of his field commanders he explained the reason why. "Our affairs at present are in a prosperous way," Washington wrote to John Sullivan. "The country seems to entertain an idea of our Superiority—Recruiting goes on well—& a Belief prevails that the enemy are afraid of Us. If then you should be drove, which nothing but the Enemy's want of Spirit can prevent—the Tables will be turned, the country get dispirited, & we shall again relapse into our former discredit." Washington was thinking not only of the war but of the Cause. He was mindful of popular opinion and attentive to its sudden swings of mood.[30]

Washington's lieutenants, like Nelson's captains, knew what was wanted of them. A few asked for more specific directions, but most were comfortable in an independent command and did very well. Adam Stephen wrote that the men of his Continental brigade were in action "eight or ten times a week" and that "fighting is now so familiar that unless it is a very great affair we do not think it worth

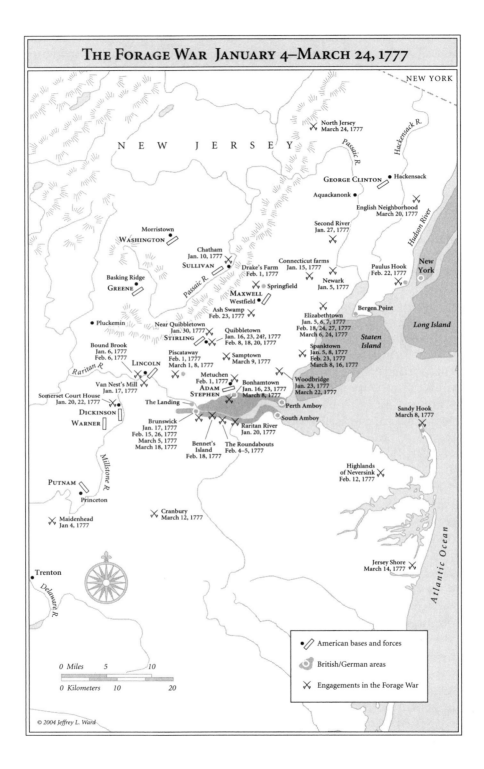

The Forage War January 4–March 24, 1777

NEW YORK

NEW JERSEY

North Jersey
March 24, 1777

Passaic R.

Hackensack R.

GEORGE CLINTON • Hackensack

Aquackanonk •

English Neighborhood
March 20, 1777

Hudson River

Second River
Jan. 27, 1777

Morristown
WASHINGTON

Chatham
Jan. 10, 1777

Connecticut farms
Jan. 15, 1777

SULLIVAN

Drake's Farm
Feb. 1, 1777

Paulus Hook
Feb. 22, 1777

New
York

Basking Ridge
GREENE

Passaic R.

Springfield

Newark
Jan. 5, 1777

MAXWELL

Westfield •

Bergen Point

• Pluckemin

Ash Swamp
Feb. 23, 1777

Elizabethtown
Jan. 5, 6, 7, 1777
Feb. 18, 24, 27, 1777
March 6, 24, 1777

Long Island

Near Quibbletown
Jan. 30, 1777

STIRLING

Quibbletown
Jan. 16, 23, 24?, 1777
Feb. 8, 18, 20, 1777

Staten
Island

Bound Brook
Jan. 6, 1777
Feb. 6, 1777

Piscataway
Feb. 1, 1777
March 1, 8, 1777

Spanktown
Jan. 5, 8, 1777
Feb. 23, 1777
March 8, 16, 1777

LINCOLN

Samptown
March 9, 1777

Raritan R.

Metuchen
Feb. 1, 1777

Woodbridge
Jan. 23, 1777
March 22, 1777

Van Nest's Mill
Jan. 17, 1777

ADAM
STEPHEN

Bonhamtown
Jan. 16, 23, 1777
March 8, 1777

Somerset Court House
Jan. 20, 22, 1777

DICKINSON
WARNER

The Landing

Perth Amboy

Sandy Hook
March 8, 1777

South Amboy

Brunswick
Jan. 17, 1777
Feb. 15, 26, 1777
March 5, 1777
March 18, 1777

Raritan River
Jan. 20, 1777

Bennet's
Island
Feb. 18, 1777

The Roundabouts
Feb. 4–5, 1777

Millstone R.

Highlands
of Neversink
Feb. 12, 1777

PUTNAM

Princeton

Cranbury
March 12, 1777

Maidenhead
Jan. 4, 1777

Jersey Shore
March 14, 1777

Atlantic Ocean

Trenton

Delaware R.

0 Miles   5   10

0 Kilometers   10   20

● / American bases and forces

British/German areas

✕ Engagements in the Forage War

© 2004 Jeffrey L. Ward

mentioning." He observed that the winter war was an "excellent school for a young soldier" and that his regiments were "in such spirits—that they only ask when the enemy come out and where they are—without enquiring their numbers and so fall on."[31]

These operations were well matched to the strengths of the Jersey militia, and they fought in a manner that continued to surprise British and American commanders. A remarkable event occurred on Monday, January 20, 1777, near Abraham Van Nest's mill, two miles from Somerset Court House. General Philemon Dickinson led four hundred Jersey militia and fifty Pennsylvania Riflemen against five hundred or six hundred British troops at a bridge over the Millstone River. An eyewitness reported that "the enemy had placed three field pieces on a hill about 50 yards from the bridge; when our men found it impossible to cross there, they went down the river, broke through the ice, waded across the river up to their middles, flanked the enemy, routed them, and took 43 baggage wagons, 104 horses, 115 head of cattle and about 60 or 70 sheep." The British suffered twenty-four or twenty-five killed and wounded and twelve prisoners. Americans lost four or five men.

The Americans showed such spirit in that fight that British officers were "absolutely certain they were not militia, they were sure that no militia would fight in that way." Washington reported to Congress, "General Dickinson's behaviour reflects the highest honour upon him, for tho' his troops were all raw, he led them thro' the River, middle deep, and gave the enemy so severe a charge, that although supported by three field pieces, they gave way and left their convoy."[32]

The Jersey militia took heart from that success. An American reported, "the militia here are in high spirits, and I hope they will continue so." Other engagements followed, day after day. On January 23, the militia gained another victory when they attacked two British regiments on the road near Brunswick and inflicted "considerable" casualties of thirty to forty killed and "a proportion wounded.[33] Sometimes British and German troops won these skirmishes, but usually they lost more men. On January 24, American Continentals were defeated by six hundred British Regulars near Quibbletown, but the British suffered larger losses.[34] Washington thought that the Americans were learning to use their weapons more skillfully. He wrote to his brother, "our Scouts and the Enemy's Foraging Parties, have frequent Skirmishes, in which they always sustain the greatest loss in killed and wounded, owing to our superior skill in Fire Arms."[35]

British and German officers in the field understood what was happening and tried to recover the initiative that was slipping away from them. They attempted to entice American troops into head-long attacks on small parties that were covered by full regiments, and even brigades. On February 1, 1777, Sir William Erskine baited a cunning trap with a small party of British foragers who were sent to collect hay at Drake's Farm near Metuchen. The Fifth Virginia Continentals were quick to bite and found themselves fighting two crack British brigades, including battalions of the Forty-second High-landers, light infantry, and grenadiers, plus a large Hessian force with eight field pieces. The Virginians were heavily outnumbered, but to the surprise of the enemy they charged the British line and broke a battalion of grenadiers. The British artillery stopped the Americans, but the Continentals rallied under heavy fire and fought stubbornly until the British retreated. Washington described the result as a "sort of drawn battle" in which "the Enemy after suffer-ing considerably went off with so much precipitation that the Hay &c which they had on their waggons was in the greater part strow'd on the Road." Jersey farmers found thirty-six British dead in their fields, and "upwards of 100 wounded." Americans reckoned their losses at between thirty and forty.[36]

On February 8, another British force attempted to draw Ameri-can troops into a general engagement. Cornwallis himself and six British generals led a force of twelve battalions into the field. The American militia and Continentals refused to engage in a pitched battle, but hung stubbornly on the British flanks and rear and in-flicted heavy casualties as Cornwallis's force retreated to Brunswick. The British commanders were outgeneraled in the field.[37]

On Sunday morning, February 23, 1777, the British tried again. Colonel Charles Mawhood, one of the most able British officers, led a large force that included the British Third Brigade, reinforced by a battalion of grenadiers and another of light infantry. Mawhood's primary purpose was to "surprize, surround and extirpate the Rebel army, or at least a large piece of it."[38] Mawhood was a highly aggres-sive officer, as he had demonstrated at Princeton. He ordered his men to "make a sweep into the Country," and they soon found what they were looking for: a group of Jersey militia "driving off some cattle and sheep," and behind them an American force on a hill. Mawhood sent a strong force forward to take the Americans on their flank. Leading the assault was Captain John Peebles's elite grena-dier company of the Forty-second Highlanders. The Scots moved into position and were about to roll up the American line when a hidden American force rose behind a fence on the Highlanders' flank and discharged a devastating volley. The American commander, General William Maxwell, had turned the tables, and outflanked Cornwallis's flankers. Now Peebles's Highlanders were caught by surprise. They fought with dogged courage but were much "gall'd by fire" and began "dropping down fast." As the American musketry increased, Captain Peebles looked around and discovered to his shock that he was the only man left standing. In his own words he "took to his heels" and fell back with his men hobbling and crawling for cover as best they could.[39]

As the Highlanders retreated, more Americans appeared. General Maxwell skillfully led a strong force of the New Jersey brigade, with Colonel Edward Hand's ubiquitous Pennsylvania regiment, Stricker's Maryland regiment, and Brodhead's Eighth Pennsylvania Regiment. The American general had taken full advantage of his British opponent's aggressive leadership to set a trap with great skill. Much of the American force had been kept out of sight. Maxwell brought it forward at the right place and time and broke the Scottish grenadiers in a stand-up fight. Peebles lost twenty-six men in his grenadier company alone.

The entire British force retreated toward Amboy under heavy fire, with its wagons empty of forage and full of wounded men. It was a long road home. Altogether the British infantry marched "at least 28 or 30 miles over fences, woods and ditches, every step up to the ankles in mud or snow, and some of it at the run." The Americans followed closely, with "small parties keeping up a constant fight from all quarters." At last the British reached Amboy at eight o'clock that night, having lost between seventy-five and a hundred men. The Americans lost five men killed and nine wounded in this engagement, which was remembered as the battle of Rahway. They had outmaneuvered one of the most able British brigadiers and outfought one of the best battalions in the British army. After the battle, Captain Peebles visited the wounded, some with mortal injuries. "Poor fellows," he wrote, "what a pity it is to throw away such men as these on such shabby ill-managed occasions."[40]

Two weeks later, on March 8, 1777, Maxwell's men did it again when two thousand British troops appeared in the field at Bonhamtown, incautiously attacked the Americans, and ran into what a British officer called "a nest of American hornets" and were defeated. Maxwell concentrated much of his strength against part of the British force, which "gave way with great confusion." The Americans lost about twenty men; the British, near sixty.[41]

In these engagements, the American army was gaining strength in ways that could not be measured by numbers alone. A British colonel observed that "the rebel soldiers, from being accustomed to peril in their skirmishes, begin to have more confidence. . . . The wounding and killing of many of our rear guards, gives them the notion of victory, and habituates them to the profession."[42] Another British officer agreed. He wrote that "the Rebels have the whole winter gone upon a very prudent plan of constantly harassing our quarters with skirmishes and small parties, and always attacking our foraging parties. By this means they gradually accustom their men to look us in the face, and stand fire which they never dared to attempt in the field."[43]

By the end of the winter, the British commander of the Sixteenth Light Dragoons, Colonel William Harcourt, observed of the American troops that "they are now become a formidable enemy." Harcourt wrote that the Americans "seem to be ignorant of the precision and order, and even of the principles, by which large bodies are moved," but "they possess some of the requisites for making good troops, such as extreme cunning, great industry in moving ground and felling of wood, activity and a spirit of enterprise upon any advantage."[44]

The fighting continued for three months. British Colonel Charles Stuart wrote on March 29, 1777, "the neglect of those high in office, who omitted making magazines of every species of forage when we were in possession of the greater part of the province of New York, has made it absolutely necessary for us to enter into a kind of 'petit guerre' which has kept the army the whole winter in perpetual harassment."[45] The Germans suffered in the same way. Ewald wrote, "not only did the men have to stay dressed day and night, but they had to be kept together, the horses constantly saddled and everything packed." He thought that "the army would have been gradually destroyed through this foraging," a judgment that was shared by his commanders. General Howe arranged that "forage was procured from New York," but never enough of it. The Forage War continued until the greening of the grass in the spring of 1777.[46]

In three months, these many small engagements had a large impact on the material strength of British and German forces. A steady flow of captives streamed into Philadelphia, where, a correspondent wrote, "scarce a day passes without their bringing in some prisoners."[47] As early as January 9, 1777, American General Nathanael Greene reckoned that "within a fortnight past we have taken or killed of Howe's army between two and three thousand men."

Washington agreed. To Rhode island Governor Nicholas Cooke he wrote on January 20, "we have killed wounded and taken prisoners between two, and three thousand; I am very confident the Enemies loss here will oblige them to recall their force from your state." These judgments have not been credited by historians, who continue to underestimate the cost of the Revolutionary War, but Greene and Washington were correct.[48]

In addition to the German and British losses at Trenton and Princeton, more than nine hundred men were killed, wounded, captured, or missing in action during the Forage War, from January 4 to March 21, 1777. This estimate comes from incomplete casualty estimates for some but not all engagements. The true numbers were higher. Altogether, from the Christmas campaign to the beginning of spring, Howe's army suffered at least 2,887 killed, captured, and seriously wounded, after losing 1,510 men in the New York Campaign.[49]

Battle casualties were the smaller part of British and German losses in the winter campaign. On August 27, 1776, General Howe began the campaign in New York with 31,625 rank and file, of whom 24,464 were "effectives fit for duty." On January 8, 1777, the total strength of his forces in Rhode Island, New York, and New Jersey was reckoned at 22,957 rank and file, of whom only 14,000 were "effective men." In five months he had lost about 40 percent of his army, and more losses followed in January, February, and March. By the end of the winter campaign more than half of all British and Hessian troops who had joined Howe's army in 1776 were killed, wounded, captured, missing, dead of disease, or so severely ill as to be officially reported as ineffective.[50] Losses were heaviest in the best and most experienced units: Hessian grenadiers and British light infantry, Highlanders, and veteran line units such as the Seventeenth Foot. As always, the best were the first to go.[51]

The battles at Trenton and Princeton and the Forage War were not small symbolic victories, as many historians have regarded them. The winter campaign inflicted severe damage on British and Hessian forces. Altogether Colonel Charles Stuart estimated that the fighting in the winter of 1776–77 "upon a modest computation has lost us more men than the last campaign."[52] Howe had already sought more troops. In late fall he wrote that another 15,000 Germans or Russians would give him 35,000 effectives. On January 31 he asked for 20,000, and the numbers revealed that his effectives had fallen from 19,000 before Christmas to 14,000. His request caused shock in London. The British government had severely strained its resources to provide 32,000 men for the campaign of 1776. Howe was informed that he could expect only 7,800 men. The result was a chronic shortage of strength in the British army that continued throughout the American war. The campaign that followed in 1777 might have had a different outcome if the British and Hessian regiments had not lost so many of their best troops before it began.[53]

All of these events made a difference in the conduct of the war. General Howe wrote to London, "the unfortunate and untimely defeat at Trenton has thrown us further back than was at first apprehended, from the great encouragement it has given to the rebels. I do not now see a prospect for terminating the war, but by a general action, and I am aware of the difficulties in our way to obtain it, as the enemy moves with so much more celerity than we possibly can."[54] In the late winter of 1776–77, senior British military commanders expressed growing pessimism and even despair. By the spring of 1777, Colonel Charles Stuart wrote home to his father, the earl of Bute, "our leaders wrote more for the eye of the Publick than for the information of the Minister. . . . I am sorry to inform you that as yet we have effected nothing."[55] Much of this feeling centered on the sinking reputation of Sir William Howe. Colonel Allan Maclean wrote, "General Howe is a very honest man, and I believe a very disinterested one. Brave he certainly is, and would make a very good executive officer under another's command, but he is not by any means equal to a C. in C. He has, moreover, got none but very silly fellows about him—a great parcel of old women—most of them improper for American service; I could be very ludicrous on this occasion, but it is truly too serious a matter that brave men's lives should be sacrificed to be commanded by such Generals. For excepting Earl Percy, lord Cornwallis, both Lt. generals, and the Brigadier Generals Leslie and Sir William Erskine, the rest are useless."[56]

Some of the most able British officers looked for a way to get clear of the war. General Percy resigned and returned home after a series of collisions with Howe in the winter of 1776–77, to the consternation of the ministers in London. Other officers shared Percy's feelings. One of them was Colonel William Harcourt, the brilliant commanding officer of the Sixteenth Light Dragoons. In the spring of 1777, Colonel Harcourt wrote privately from New Brunswick to his father, Earl Harcourt, "You may be assured that we are almost without a friend (I mean from principle) on this side of the Atlantic; that the supplies the rebels have received from France and other Powers have been very considerable; and lastly there does not appear the least defection amongst their leaders."[57]

Colonel William Harcourt, later Third Earl Harcourt, an undated miniature by Richard Collins. National Portrait Gallery, London.

Harcourt concluded, "America is never to be regained without making an absolute conquest of her," and given "the nature and constitution of the Country, in which every man is, to a certain degree, a soldier, a victory . . . can seldom prove as decisive as it would be in Europe." He informed his father that he wanted to ask "his Majesty's leave to return to England," if he could do it with honor.[58]

On the other side, Americans were gaining new confidence in their leader. The Jersey campaign transformed the reputation of George Washington. Americans had begun to think highly of him as a man and a soldier during the siege of Boston. Doubts about his leadership grew during the battles around New York, and even Washington shared them. Then came the campaign in New Jersey, and Washington gained the reputation of a leader who won great victories and deserved them. Even his enemies sang his praises. Hessian officers were full of professional admiration for his skill, especially after the second battle of Trenton. Colonel von Donop wrote of Washington that he "retired behind the creek which cuts the town in two, and made such a clever march that he not only turned our left, but defeated the 71st [17th] English regiment on his way, burned our forage depot and made prisoners of our invalids,—one of whom was my aide-de-campe Lt. Donop."[59]

British writers celebrated him as superior to any of their own commanders. In London, the news of Trenton and Princeton spread rapidly, all the more so because of attempts by the government to deny or suppress it. On April 4, 1777, Horace Walpole observed, "It is now the fashion to cry up the manoeuvre of Washington, who has beaten two British regiments, and obliged General Howe to contract his quarters." Even Loyalists praised him in the same way.[60]

One of the most handsome tributes came from the general he defeated. After the British surrender at Yorktown in 1781, Charles Cornwallis and George Washington dined together. A toast was proposed to the victor. Cornwallis rose and said, "When the illustrious part that your Excellency has borne in this long and arduous contest becomes a matter of history, fame will gather your brightest laurels rather from the banks of the Delaware than from those of the Chesapeake."[61]

Americans celebrated George Washington in another spirit. He became the symbol of a new moral order in the world. An acrostic "By a Young Lady" was published widely throughout the continent.

> W itness, ye sons of tyrant's black womb,
> A nd see his Excellence victorious come!
> S erene, majestic, see he gains the field!
> H is heart is tender, while his arms are steel'd.
> I ntent on virtue, and her cause so fair,
> N ow treats his captive with a parent's care!
> G reatness of soul his ev'ry action shows,
> T hus virtue from celestial bounty flows,
> O ur GEORGE, by heaven, destin'd to command,
> N ow strikes the British yoke with prosp'rous hand.[62]

The cost of it to George Washington himself was greater than anyone knew except members of his family. Twenty years after the event, when Washingon had retired to his beloved Mount Vernon, his stepson remembered that in the night, "he would frequently, when sitting with his family, appear absent; his lips would move, his hand be raised, and he would evidently seem under the influence of thoughts which had nothing to do with the quiet scene around him." To the end of his life, George Washington continued to relive the desperate struggle of the dark days in 1776, and the crossing of the Delaware.[63]

CONCLUSION

∾ The War and the American Revolution

> We have a very difficult card to play. We often
> have to act by the moon or twilight and leave
> the World to judge it in the clear sunshine.
>
> —General William Maxwell to
> Adam Stephen, April 10, 1777[1]

O N NEW YEAR'S DAY in 1777, Robert Morris sent George
Washington a letter that rings strangely in a modern ear.
"The year 1776 is over," Morris wrote. "I am heartily glad of
it and hope you nor America will ever be plagued with such another."
Washington shared that feeling, which was very far from our own. We
celebrate 1776 as the most glorious year in American history. They
remembered it as an agony, especially the "dark days" of autumn.[2]

Americans have known many dark days, from the starving times
in early settlements to the attack on the World Trade Center. These
were the testing times and the pivotal moments of our history. It
was that way in 1776, after the decision for independence and the
military disasters in New York. In early December, British commanders believed that they were very close to ending the rebellion, and
American leaders feared that they might be right. Then came a rever-
sal of fortune, and three months later the mood had changed on
both sides. By the spring of 1777, many British officers had concluded that they could never win the war. At the same time, Americans recovered from their despair and were confident that they would
not be defeated. That double transformation was truly a turning
point in the war.[3]

∾ Reprise: A Web of Contingency in History

We have seen how it happened: not in a single event, or even a
chain of events, but in a great web of contingency. This book is mainly
about contingency, in the sense of people making choices, and
choices making a difference in the world. It is not primarily a story
of accidents, though there were many along the way. It is not about
what might have been, though that question is always in the background. This is a story of real choices that living people actually
made. To study an event in these terms is to discover a dense web of
contingency, in which many people made choices within a structure
of relationships. Washington's Crossing is a case in point.

   To summarize in terms of contingency, this story began with
the meeting of three armies in America. Most men who served in
them were volunteers who were there because they chose to be. Many
of them, from generals to privates, made choices that had an impact on events. But what they chose differed very much from one
army to another, and so also did their ways of choosing.

   The American army of 1776 came mostly from middling families who cherished the revolutionary principles of liberty and freedom but understood them in various ways: the collective rights of
old New England, the reciprocal rights of Philadelphia Associators,
the individual rights of backcountry riflemen, and the hegemonic
rights of the Fairfax men. The acts and choices of these men were
an expression of their beliefs. So also were their autonomous ways
of choosing, which made General Washington's job more interesting, to say the least.

   Other patterns of choice appeared among the armies of British
and German Regulars in 1776. These were long-serving volunteers,
trained by modern methods to engage the will actively in the service of others. In ways that varied in detail from English to Scottish
and German regiments, these men shared values of hierarchy, order, discipline, honor, loyalty, duty, and service. Their writings show
that they despised the American rebels and the Revolutionary cause.
The meeting of these armies was more than a clash of weapons and
tactics. It became a conflict of ideas and institutions in which people
made different choices—and chose differently.

   Strategic choices made by leaders on both sides were also very
mixed. In Britain, the drivers of the American war were a small
circle of men in London who meant to break the Revolution by brute
force. Some of their Whiggish commanders in America (the Howe
brothers, Cornwallis, Leslie, Mawhood) were less severe. The Howes

hoped to "conciliate His Majesty's rebellious subjects," by firmness and moderation. But other officers and men were more hostile to the rebels and more predatory toward the inhabitants of what they called "our colonies." These choices did not sit well together—a major weakness in the British cause.

American leaders also made different choices about the conduct of the war. In 1776, George Washington favored a "war of posts." Local leaders demanded a perimeter defense. Charles Lee wanted an active defense by small attacks on British forces. Horatio Gates preferred a Fabian strategy of withdrawal to the Appalachians. Some New Englanders proposed to burn New York and scorch the American earth.

All of these purposes collided in the fighting around New York. The Howe brothers were brilliant in that campaign: firmly in control, clear in their purposes, clever in their military operations, careful not to put things wrong, and highly successful in three months of fighting. The Americans were baffled, indecisive, disorganized, undisciplined, and soundly defeated. In twelve weeks George Washington lost large parts of three states, and 90 percent of the army under his command. In occupied New Jersey the Howes' policy began to work well, as thousands of Americans returned to the Crown, including a signer of the Declaration of Independence. Many supporters of the Revolution gave way to panic and despair.

Other Americans made different choices, and worked to revive a cause that they believed to be near ruin. An inspiration was Thomas Paine's *American Crisis*. In the depth of the December crisis, Congress decided to organize the war effort in a new way, the states redoubled their efforts, and many Americans rallied to a common cause. Washington's army began to grow again. In New Jersey, the brutal acts of occupying troops were at odds with the intentions of their commanders and provoked people to rise against their oppressors. Small groups of Jersey militia decided to launch small attacks by land and water. They exhausted the Hessian garrison at Trenton, gained control of the countryside, and drew British and German troops out of their interlocking positions. This popular rising created an opportunity for George Washington. He made the most of it, in a battle that was itself a war of contingencies.

The American victory at Trenton led to other choices, the most difficult of the campaign. Here again, the process of decision-making differed on the two sides. Some of the critical American decisions were made by privates in the Philadelphia Associators who demanded that their officers cross into New Jersey. Other choices were made by hundreds of sick and weary Continental infantry who decided to stay beyond their enlistments. Indispensable decisions by Robert Morris and his associates in Philadelphia produced the resources that the army urgently needed. Washington and the army had difficult choices about a plan of operations, the design of a defensive battle, and the concentration of the American army at Trenton. Washington was at the center of all these decisions, functioning more as a leader than a commander; always listening, inspiring, guiding; rarely demanding, commanding, coercing.

Generals Howe and Cornwallis also had hard choices to make after the battle of Trenton. They were able and intelligent men of high principle and serious purpose who operated in a more hierarchical world and functioned more as commanders than leaders. They decided to destroy Washington's army by a quick stroke at Trenton and did not listen to the advice of more knowledgeable subordinates. On January 2, 1777, as British and Hessian troops advanced toward Trenton, American troops made a fighting retreat to prepared positions beyond Assunpink Creek and defeated many probing attacks in the second battle of Trenton. That night British and American councils of war made different decisions—and also made them differently. Again Cornwallis imposed his plan from the top down, against the judgment of able inferiors, and prepared to attack in the morning. Washington in his council of war welcomed the judgments of others and presided over an open process of discovery and decision that yielded yet another opportunity. In the night Washington disengaged his forces from an enemy only a few yards away, and an exhausted American army found the will and strength to make another night march toward the British base at Princeton.

As the American army approached Princeton on January 3, 1777, they ran into a British force under Colonel Charles Mawhood. In a classic meeting engagement, Mawhood made the choice to attack with great gallantry, and nearly gained the field. The Americans broke, rallied, and, in a web of tactical decisions by many officers and men, won another victory. Afterward, small parties of Jersey militia chose to attack British and Hessian forces on their own initiative, in small skirmishes that continued for twelve weeks. Washington did not initiate this *petite guerre,* but in another critical act of choice he welcomed it and supported it. The Forage War that followed took a toll of Howe's army, which shrank from 31,600 British and Hessian troops in August to 14,000 effectives by February in 1777. At least 4,300 British and Hessian troops were killed in action, seriously wounded, or captured, of which about 1,500 were lost in New York and more than 2,800 in the New Jersey campaign. Many more men were lost to disease, malnutrition, exposure, and the rigors of the winter campaign.

In the New Jersey campaign, American troops repeatedly defeated larger and better trained regular forces in many different types of warfare: special operations, a night river crossing, a bold assault on an urban garrison, a fighting retreat, a defensive battle in fixed positions, a night march into the enemy's rear, a meeting engagement, and a prolonged *petite guerre*. Professional observers judged that entire performance to be one of the most brilliant in military history.

The winter campaign had a major impact on the war. It wrecked the strategy of the Howe brothers for ending the Revolution by moderation and conciliation. American spirits soared; British and Hessian morale plummeted. The Loyalists of New Jersey suffered severely after the British retreat. Their fate was a disaster for the Howe brothers. The news from New Jersey also had an effect on British opinion, much like the Tet offensive on American opinion in 1968. By the spring of 1777, the war was growing unpopular in the United Kingdom. A Press Act would soon be necessary to maintain the army. The price of British government securities (Consols), which had risen to 89 in 1775 and 1776, began to fall in 1777 and kept on falling through the war: 78 in 1777, 66 in 1778, 61 in 1779, and 55 in 1784.

This war between two opening societies was always a contest for the opinion of free people. The Trenton-Princeton campaign made a difference in the choices of many people in Britain and America. It also had an impact in Europe, where the Hessian disaster at Trenton quickened an angry controversy over the soldier trade in 1777. As we have seen, that dispute in turn raised questions of the competence and legitimacy about the old regime.[4]

    ~ Inventing an American Way of War

In the United States, the winter campaign of 1776–77 also had other consequences. Its many exigencies prompted American leaders to invent a new way of war. The disasters of the New York campaign had been a hard school for them. Through the summer and fall of 1776, they had been unable to find a way to win against a powerful opponent. Part of the problem rose from weaknesses in their cause. They had created a nation without a nation-state, and an army without discipline. Americans had trouble reconciling the ideals of the

Revolution with the realities of government. They were deeply suspicious of power and hated to pay taxes, a major weakness in the War of Independence. Then, as now, sleazy politicians pandered to that prejudice.

But the Americans could draw on other strengths. Their greatest advantage was the moral strength of a just cause. They were fighting on their own ground, in defense of homes and families, for ideas of liberty and freedom. They had a different test of success. Their opponents had to conquer; the Americans needed only to survive. After the occupation of New Jersey, and British maltreatment of prisoners, Americans became highly motivated by the cruel experience of oppression.

Another strength was their religion. The Americans were a deeply spiritual people, with an abiding faith that sustained them in adversity. The free male population was among the most literate in the world. In 1776, the northern states were among the few societies in the world where most people were of middling condition, unlike Europe, where most people were of the "lower orders." In 1775 more than 70 percent of free families in the northern colonies owned their land, and the American economy generated higher incomes per capita than most European nations. In the first year of the Revolution its agriculture was strong, industries were expanding, and privateers were bringing wealth to coastal towns. British and Hessian troops were amazed by the affluence they found in the New World. Americans were also accustomed to govern themselves. In the winter of 1776, the new United States were barely six months old, but Americans had been running their own affairs for six generations.

In the dark days of 1776, Americans reached deep into this reservoir of strength and improvised a new way of managing a war. After many failures, its interlocking parts came together in the winter campaign of 1776–77, with surprising success. Much of this way of war flowed from one fundamental fact. Civil and military leaders were accountable to a free people through their representatives. In 1776, *the people* in a political sense did not mean all the people but included a majority of free adult males. American leaders responded to a new force that their generation was the first to call popular opinion.

To that end, military leaders gave much of their time to working with the members of Congress, consulting leaders in the states, and keeping in touch with the people and their representatives. George Washington set the example. From the start of the war, he worked hard to establish the principle of civil control over military affairs, and always respected it. But there was a problem: Congress intervened actively in military affairs, told the generals how to run the war, and even attempted to make tactical decisions in the defense of New York. John Adams, who had no experience of war, declared that he knew more about military affairs than any American general except Charles Lee. John Hancock believed that he himself should command the Continental army, though his own military experience was limited to drilling a silk-stocking company on Boston Common. He addressed Washington in the imperative, as if the Continental Congress were the House of Hancock and generals were his employees. Washington was remarkably forbearing with these men, but the system was not working well in the dark days of 1776. It was increasingly evident that the Congress could not operate efficiently in an executive role and was ill-qualified to manage the war.

As we have seen, congressmen began to make changes in early December, and on Christmas Eve in 1776 General Nathanael Greene urged them to find a different way of working with the army. After much discussion Congress agreed. On December 26, 1776, the same day as the first battle of Trenton but before the event was known, the Congress granted Washington full authority to direct the war. Critics complained that they betrayed the Revolution and made Washington "dictator" of the American states. But it wasn't so. The general's powers were carefully limited in time and scope, and always subject to congressional oversight. Congress and Army hammered out a typically American compromise, and all the parties understood what it meant. Congress was firmly in charge, but George Washington and his generals were running the war. Always there would be conflicts, mainly over money and appointments. John Adams continued to believe that he knew more about war than George Washington could ever learn, and John Hancock remained as arrogant as ever. But Congress treated Washington with growing respect, and military leaders were very careful to acknowledge the principle of civil supremacy.

This improvised solution to an urgent problem in the dark days of 1776 became a permanent part of the American system. It strongly affirmed the principle of civilian control over the military and also established the practice that military men should direct military affairs, subject to oversight by civil leaders. After the War of Independence, similar ideas spread to many American institutions, including business corporations, colleges, Protestant churches, voluntary associations, and public organizations of many kinds, all with their civil boards and professional managers. It became a model for the separation of powers and the rule of law. This American solution was also a way of dealing with another problem peculiar to a free society and vital to its strength: a growing pluralism of its elites (in this case military and congressional elites), which made American society very different from Britain and Europe.

A critical moment in this American development was the winter crisis of 1776–77. The victories at Princeton and Trenton added stability and legitimacy when most needed, and helped a fragile invention to grow into an American tradition.[5]

ᘓ   An American Way of Fighting: Combat as a Cultural Artifact

At the same time, American military leaders improvised a new way of "war-fighting," which was also a cultural expression of the nation they served. Free Americans in 1776 were a restless, striving, entrepreneurial people, who routinely assumed risk for the sake of profit. They were a practical people who judged actions by results and were highly instrumental in their way of thinking about the world. When they went to war, Americans carried this culture with them. Their attitudes toward fighting were different from those of Europe's feudal and aristocratic elites, who thought of war as a nobleman's vocation and a pursuit of honor. Americans tended to think of war as something that had to be done from time to time, for a particular purpose or goal. They fought not for the sake of fighting but for the sake of winning. From the founding of Jamestown and Sagadahoc in 1607 to our own time, Americans fought at least one major war in every generation—sixteen generations altogether. War was a continuing part of their experience, but they always thought of fighting as an interruption in their lives. They wanted to get it done quickly, so that they could get on with the ordinary business of life.

These attitudes shaped a special way of war-fighting. In general, Americans judged military actions by results, in a highly entrepreneurial spirit. Whether on the offensive or defensive, American generals were expected to be bold, active, quick, and decisive. Public opinion and political leaders were intolerant of generals who failed to get results. This attitude appeared during the War of Independence.

This tendency was amplified by a free press, which demanded quick, clear, and simple results that could be summarized in eighteenth-century broadsides, nineteenth-century telegrams, twentieth-century headlines, and twenty-first-century sound bytes. It was urgently important for military leaders in a free society not merely to act but to give the appearance of action. They were expected to produce results, and to do so in a continuing way. George Washington was keenly aware of this expectation and planned campaigns with public opinion in mind."[6]

This requirement of boldness and activity in war was tempered by another principle, which Washington called prudence. It was always important in an open society and urgently necessary in the winter of 1776. After the disasters around New York, military leaders were acutely conscious that another failure, or even a costly success, could turn the country against them. Washington was mindful of this requirement, and his example helped to establish an American rule. Even when planning bold operations, he reminded his officers about the importance of acting prudently. Benedict Arnold (the least prudent of American generals) received many lectures on that subject. On March 3, 1777, Washington warned, "you must be sensible that the most serious ill consequences may and would, probably result from failure. . . . Unless your strength and circumstances be such as you can reasonably promise yourself a moral certainty of succeeding, I would have you by all means to relinquish the undertaking."[7]

An important measure of prudence for American leaders was the cost of operations in human life. Generals were expected to be very careful with the lives of their men. This was partly a matter of ethics; Americans placed an exceptionally high value on individual life. It was also a matter of politics and public opinion. And it became a military necessity in the fall of 1776, when manpower was short. In consequence, George Washington and his officers designed their operations to minimize losses, with notable success. In the New Jersey campaign, American battle casualties were four killed and eight wounded in the first battle of Trenton, about forty killed and wounded in the second battle of Trenton, and about a hundred killed or seriously wounded at Princeton. The engagements of the Forage War were conducted with much attention to keeping down casualties. In the spring of 1777, for example, General Nathanael Greene worked out an ambitious plan for a "general attack" on the British base at Brunswick. A council of war studied it in detail and returned frequently to the question of numbers and losses. On those grounds, they decided unanimously against it, and even the author of the plan voted no. Throughout the Revolution, American officers gave much attention to minimizing casualties.[8]

The central problem in the American way of war-fighting was to combine boldness with prudence—large gains with small costs. During the winter campaign of 1776–77, Washington and the Continental army found a solution that had many elements. Part of it was flexibility and opportunism in high degree. Throughout the Revolution George Washington's strategic purposes were constant: to win independence by maintaining American resolve to continue the war, by preserving an American army in being, and by raising the cost of the war to the enemy. Washington was always fixed on these strategic ends but flexible in operational means. No single label describes his military operations, though many have been suggested. The diversity of operations in the winter campaign was the first clear example of a style that persisted through the war. He was quick to modify his plans with changing circumstances and adapted more easily than his opponents. Washington was a man of steadfast principle but also a military opportunist. Many American leaders would follow that example: Greene and Morgan, Lee and Jackson, Grant and Sherman, Eisenhower and Bradley, Nimitz and Patton, Schwarzkopf and Franks.

Another element in this American approach to war-fighting was a new way of controlling initiative and tempo in war. After many defeats around New York, American leaders learned the urgent importance of seizing the initiative and holding it. George Washington and his lieutenants did more than merely surprise the Hessian garrison at Trenton on the morning after Christmas. They improvised a series of surprises through a period of twelve weeks. By that method they seized the initiative from their opponents and kept it in their hands for that period. Washington made it a formal principle in the army, when he ordered his generals to drive the campaign and not "be drove."

Initiative was largely about the control of time in campaigning. English historian George Otto Trevelyan wrote that George Washington succeeded at Trenton and Princeton because he "caught the occasion by the forelock."[9] In New Jersey, American leaders learned to make time itself into a weapon. They did it by controlling the tempo and rhythm of the campaign. Day after day through the winter campaign, the Americans called the tune and set the beat. By that method, they retained the initiative for many weeks and kept British commanders off balance. The material and moral impact was very great, especially when a small force was able to control the tempo of war against a stronger enemy. Events happened at a time and place of their choosing. From all this another American tradition developed. It appeared in the Civil War, in both theaters in World War II, and in discussions of tempo by Pentagon planners in the twenty-first century.[10]

To these elements of initiative and tempo, Washington added yet another element, which was speed. On January 20, 1777, William Howe tried to explain to his superiors why he was having so much trouble in New Jersey. He wrote, "the Enemy moves with so much more celerity than we possibly can with our foreign troops who are too much attached to their baggage." Sir William was blaming the Hessians again, which was hardly fair. No man in the army was more attached to his baggage than General Howe, who required an entire "baggage ship" for his needs. But in other ways his observation was correct. In the New Jersey campaign, American troops always moved with "more celerity" than their opponents.[11]

Speed in war is a relative concept. In the world of George Washington and William Howe, celerity meant an army that could keep moving at more than two miles an hour, no small achievement on early American roads with artillery that creaked along on wooden wheels and infantry that hobbled on bloody feet over frozen ground. Small forces could move more quickly, but when it came to the movement of an entire army, George Washington's Continentals were able to outmarch British and German Regulars.

American commanders consciously used "celerity" many times in the New Jersey campaign. Washington did so most dramatically in his first attack on Trenton, and again before the second battle of Trenton, when he concentrated his army overnight with surprising speed on roads "halfleg deep" in mud. Other examples included the fighting withdrawal from Maidenhead to Assunpink Creek on January 2, the night march toward Princeton, and the retreat from Princeton to Pluckemin on January 3. Thereafter, American forces made much use of mobility in the Forage War, when Washington ordered his commanders to be ready to move very quickly, "at an hours warning."[12]

Washington also made a habit of getting the jump on his opponents. British and Hessian commanders were slow getting started in the morning: a problem for Colonel Rall at Trenton, Cornwallis at Princeton, and Mawhood on the road to Maidenhead. Washington made much use of night marches and early morning departures before all his major battles at Trenton and Princeton. At the same time, Americans did all in their power to reduce the mobility of British and Hessian forces. This was their object in the Forage War, when they targeted horses, wagons, and feed. Robert Morris reported to Washington that "the Enemy have since Christmas lost so many Horses, are in such want of forage, and their remaining Cavalry so worn down, that the defects in this department alone would render any movement of their Main body impossible without strong rein-forcements." So successful was this American effort that Morris observed, "General Howe's situation somewhat resembles that of a Strong bull in Trammells, sensible of his own strength he grows mad with rage & resentment when he finds himself deprived of the use of it."[13]

To their use of "celerity," Washington and his lieutenants added another principle, of concentration. Working from weakness, they learned to concentrate a large part of their strength against a small part of the enemy's force. Here again the New York campaign had taught them a lesson, in the fatal consequences of American dispersion and British concentration. Washington changed his ways in the next campaign. Before the first battle of Trenton, Americans encouraged three British and German brigades (five counting the forces in North Jersey) to move away from one another and concentrated their entire force against a single Hessian brigade. At the battle of Princeton, Washington did it again. He concentrated most of his army against a single British brigade and defeated it before superior British forces could arrive. The same thing happened many times in the Forage War, when militia and Continental troops concentrated against exposed outposts, isolated garrisons, and forage parties with much success, slowly wearing down a larger enemy.

A related principle was the use of firepower to magnify the impact of small forces. Contrary to much historical writing, American troops in New Jersey were not short of weapons and ammunition during the winter of 1776–77. Bayonets and weather-tight cartridge boxes were in short supply, but Continentals and even militia were well supplied with infantry weapons.[14] As we have seen, they also had surprising strength in artillery. At the first battle of Trenton, American attackers had twice as many guns in proportion to infantry than did the Hessian garrison. It was the same again at the second battle of Trenton and the fight at Princeton. Heavy use of massed firepower was decisive in the first and second battles of Trenton and the battle of Princeton. American leaders understood that this way of war-fighting meant fewer American casualties. "Force multipliers" of that sort became another enduring element in the American way of war.[15]

The best force multiplier is good intelligence. American leaders learned this lesson in the New York campaign, when British leaders used their control of the waters around the city to mask their intentions and confuse their opponents. American troubles in the New York campaign were largely due to that cause. In New Jersey, American leaders made a major effort to strengthen their intelligence. The central figure was George Washington himself. In the winter campaign of 1776–77, he developed a system of intelligence that became part of his new way of war. Washington personally recruited secret agents, with orders to report to him alone, and employed Nathaniel Sackett, of the New York Committee for Detecting and Defeating Conspiracies, to construct an entire network in New York with agents male and female, of every rank and station. It is impossible to know the full extent of Washington's intelligence operations, for he cloaked them in secrecy, but beyond doubt he was very active in this work.[16]

Washington also asked Continental generals and militia commanders to gather their own intelligence, and even to run their own agents. Many did so, and civilian leaders such as Robert Morris also maintained their own sources. Washington encouraged some degree of separation between these networks for tighter security and broader sources, but he insisted that his officers report promptly what they learned. His attitudes toward intelligence-gathering were different from those of leaders in closed societies, who sought to monopolize intelligence and prohibited efforts they did not control. Washington was comfortable with an open system, in which others were not only permitted but actively encouraged to have a high degree of autonomy. This free and open system of information-gathering engaged the efforts of many people, produced multiple sources, and got better results than closed systems. It was another reason why free societies often have more effective intelligence systems than closed societies.

All of these elements came together in the winter campaign of 1776–77: boldness and prudence, flexibility and opportunism, initiative and tempo, speed and concentration, force multipliers, and intelligence. They defined a new way of war that would continue to appear through the Revolution and in many American wars.

✎ The Policy of Humanity

In 1776, American leaders believed that it was not enough to win the war. They also had to win in a way that was consistent with the values of their society and the principles of their cause. One of their greatest achievements in the winter campaign of 1776–77 was to manage the war in a manner that was true to the expanding humanitarian ideals of the American Revolution. It happened in a way that was different from the ordinary course of wars in general. In

Congress and the army, American leaders resolved that the War of Independence would be conducted with a respect for human rights, even of the enemy. This idea grew stronger during the campaign of 1776–77, not weaker as is commonly the case in war.

In Congress, John Adams took the lead. To his wife he wrote, "I who am always made miserable by the Misery of every sensible being, am obliged to hear continual accounts of the barbarities, the cruel Murders in cold blood, even the most tormenting ways of starving and freezing committed by our Enemies. . . . These accounts harrow me beyond Description."[17] John Adams resolved that the guiding principles of the American Republic would always be what he called the policy of humanity. He wrote, "I know of no policy, God is my witness, but this—Piety, Humanity and Honesty are the best Policy. Blasphemy, Cruelty and Villainy have prevailed and may again. But they won't prevail against America, in this Contest, because I find the more of them are employed, the less they succeed."[18]

Not all American leaders agreed. Others in Adams's generation believed, as do many in our own time, that America should serve its own national self-interest, defined in terms of wealth and power, and seek it by any means. But most men of the American Enlightenment shared John Adams's way of thinking. In the critical period of 1776 and 1777, leaders of both the Continental army and the Congress adopted the policy of humanity. That choice was reinforced when they learned that some British leaders decided to act differently. Every report of wounded soldiers refused quarter, of starving captives mistreated in the prison hulks at New York, and of the plunder and rapine in New Jersey persuaded leaders in Congress and the army to go a different way, as an act of principle and enlightened self-interest. More than any others, John Adams gave words to this policy, and George Washington put it to work.

Attitudes of British leaders and soldiers moved in another direction. Imperial attitudes hardened as the war went on. An example was Marine Captain John Bowater, who wrote, "The Natives are such a Levelling, underbred, Artfull, Race of people that we Cannot Associate with them. . . . Their words come up so slow I frequently long to Shove a Soup ladle down their throat."[19] Captain Bowater added, "I am certain that our troops will act with less humanity this campaign than they did in the last."[20]

Many officers and men in the British army shared Captain Bowater's attitude, and acted upon it. Colonel Charles Stuart wrote candidly to his eminent father, the earl of Bute, in 1778, "Wherever our armies have marched, wherever they have been encamped during the last campaign, every species of barbarity has been executed. We planted an irrecoverable hatred wherever we went, which neither time nor measures will be able to eradicate."[21]

A case in point was the cultural history of quarter. According to the "laws" of European war, quarter was the privilege of being allowed to surrender and to become a prisoner. By custom and tradition, soldiers in Europe believed that they had a right to extend quarter or deny it. If a city resisted a siege, then the attackers had the "right" to kill all its inhabitants. If a fort refused to surrender when closely invested, then the defenders could be put to the sword. In the ethics of European war, quarter was granted to some people and refused to others, according to their conduct and the will of the winner. In these "laws of war," no captive had an inalienable right to be taken prisoner, or even to life itself.

This idea of selective quarter appeared among British troops at the battle of Long Island and the siege of Fort Washington. It was demonstrated again on the battlefield at Princeton, where wounded Americans were denied quarter and murdered by British infantry, with their officers looking on. In the Forage War it happened again. British troops often allowed Americans to surrender and treated them decently, but sometimes they denied quarter and killed captives, and on occasion were ordered to do so. Examples were recorded by Hessian Captain Johann Ewald and British Sergeant Thomas Sullivan.[22]

American attitudes were very different. With some exceptions, American leaders believed that quarter should be extended to all combatants as a matter of right. Sometimes in the heat of battle this was not done, but not in any known action by the American army during the New Jersey campaign. George Washington and high commanders never threatened to deny quarter to an enemy. This difference persisted through the war, with some exceptions in the southern campaign.

Americans were outraged when quarter was denied to their soldiers, as often happened in New York and New Jersey. One of the most notorious incidents occurred during the Forage War at the battle of Drake's Farm. Charles Scott's Virginia infantry was fighting a British force in an open field. At one stage the Americans were driven back and left seven wounded men on the field. The ranking American, Lieutenant William Kelly, was severely wounded in the thigh and attempted to surrender with the other men. British troops refused quarter and murdered them all. They "dashed out their brains with their muskets and ran them through with their bayonets, made them like sieves." As the Americans lay dying, the British troops brutally plundered their bodies with great violence.[23]

The Americans recovered the mutilated corpses and were shocked by what they had found, all the more as it had happened again and again on other fields. After the fight at Drake's Farm, American Brigadier General Adam Stephen engaged in an angry correspondence with Sir William Erskine, the British commander, which received much attention in American newspapers. The British leader denied responsibility, which increased American anger. The words of the British commander, as much as the acts of his men, reinforced the American resolve to run their own war in a different spirit.[24]

Another issue was the treatment of prisoners. After the battles in New York, thousands of American prisoners of war were treated with extreme cruelty by British captors. Some Americans were confined in the churches of New York City, which were desecrated by scenes of cruelty, suffering, and starvation. Other Americans went to prison hulks in New York harbor and died miserably in large numbers. Some escaped, and their reports had the same impact as those of American prisoners of the Japanese in the Second World War.

An American policy on prisoners emerged after the battle of Trenton. Washington ordered that Hessian captives would be treated as human beings with the same rights of humanity for which Americans were striving. The Hessians expected a different fate, with good reason after Long Island and Fort Washington.[25] They were amazed to be treated with decency and even kindness. At first they could not understand it. One of them, Johannes Reuber, thought his good treatment by the rebels must have been the work of Colonel Rall. "With his last breath," Reuber wrote, "he thought about the Grenadiers and asked General Washington to leave his men unharmed."[26]

He learned otherwise when the Hessians were marched to Philadelphia and paraded through the city, where "the old women who were present screamed at us in a terrible manner and wanted to strangle us because we had come to America to steal their freedom."[27] The American army protected the Hessians, and Reuber learned to his surprise that General Washington had issued a broadside declaring that Hessian soldiers "were innocent people in this war, and were not volunteers, but forced into this war." The general asked that the Hessians should be treated not as enemies but friends. Reuber wrote that "conditions improved for us. Old, young, rich and poor, and all treated us in a friendly manner."[28]

Some of the Hessian prisoners from Trenton were sent from Philadelphia to Lancaster, in Pennsylvania, and on to western Virginia in 1777. They were escorted by a company of Pennsylvania militia. When they reached the Pennsylvania state line, all of the militia went home except the captain, who told the Hessians, "whose affections he had won by his humanity," that "they must march on without an escort, as he himself should hurry on to Winchester." When he met them three days later, every Hessian answered the roll call. Afterward, it was said that "the Hessians received many indulgences." Of 13,988 Hessian soldiers who survived the war, 3,194 (23 percent) chose to remain in America. Others later emigrated to the New World with their families.[29]

The same policy was extended to British prisoners after the battle of Princeton. Washington ordered one of his most trusted officers, Lieutenant Colonel Samuel Blachley Webb, to look after them: "You are to take charge of [211] privates of the British Army. . . . Treat them with humanity, and Let them have no reason to Complain of our Copying the brutal example of the British army in their Treatment of our unfortunate brethren. . . . Provide everything necessary for them on the road." There were exceptions on the American side. Loyalists and slaves who joined the British were sometimes treated cruelly by local officials. But Congress and the Continental army generally adopted Adams's "policy of humanity." Their moral choices in the War of Independence enlarged the meaning of the American Revolution.[30]

The most remarkable fact about American soldiers and civilians in the New Jersey campaign is that they did all of these things at the same time. In a desperate struggle they found a way to defeat a formidable enemy, not merely once at Trenton but many times in twelve weeks of continued combat. They reversed the momentum of the war. They improvised a new way of war that grew into an American tradition. And they chose a policy of humanity that aligned the conduct of the war with the values of the Revolution.

They set a high example, and we have much to learn from them. Much recent historical writing has served us ill in that respect. In the late twentieth century, too many scholars tried to make the American past into a record of crime and folly. Too many writers have told us that we are captives of our darker selves and helpless victims of our history. It isn't so, and never was. The story of Washington's Crossing tells us that Americans in an earlier generation were capable of acting in a higher spirit—and so are we.

APPENDICES

APPENDIX A

∼ Strength Estimates of American Forces,
July 27, 1776–March 15, 1777

July 27, 1776: reported totals 21,882; effectives 16,010
   A monthly strength report, including forces under George Washington and the Flying
   Camp in New Jersey under Hugh Mercer but excluding forces in South Carolina and
   other parts of the country. The source is Charles H. Lesser, *The Sinews of Independence*
   (Chicago, 1976), 26–27.

August 27, 1776: estimated totals 28,500 officers and men; effectives 19,000
   This is an historian's careful estimate by Henry P. Johnston, adjusting strength returns
   from August 3 and September 12, 1776. Johnston identifies 71 regiments or parts of
   regiments, of which 25 were Continental. His estimate is very close to Washington's
   report on September 2 that "our number of men at present fit for duty is under 20,000."
   The source is Johnston, *The Campaign of 1776 Around New York and Brooklyn* (Brooklyn,
   1878), 123–25.

September 28, 1776: reported totals 31,748; effectives 20,435
   This report included troops at Fort Lee and Fort Washington. It did not include troops
   on the northern frontier under General Gates. The source is a strength report in the
   National Archives, as tabulated in Lesser, *The Sinews of Independence*, 34–35.

November 28, 1776: estimated totals "less than 3,000 men"
   This was a count of the Continental army at Newark, New Jersey, on November 28,
   1776, made by Lieutenant James Monroe. He wrote in his autobiography, "I happened
   to be on the rear guard at Newark and I counted the force under his [Washington's]
   command by platoons as it passed me, which amounted to less than 3,000 men." The
   source is Monroe, *Autobiography* (Syracuse, 1959), 24.

December 1, 1776: estimated totals "not 3,000 men"
   This is an estimate of the Continental army at New Brunswick, New Jersey, on December 1, 1776. It was made by General Nathanael Greene, who wrote to Governor Nicholas Cooke of Rhode Island, "when we left Brunswick we had not 3,000 men, a very
   pitiful army to trust the liberties of America upon." The source is a letter from Greene
   to Cooke, 4 Dec. 1776, in *Papers of Nathanael Greene*, 1:362.

December 4, 1776: estimated totals "not to exceed 5,000"
   This is an estimate of the Continental army under Washington at Trenton, New Jersey. It
   was made by General Nathanael Greene, who wrote to Governor Nicholas Cooke of Rhode
   Island, "our numbers are still small, not to exceed 5000, but dayly increasing." The source
   is a letter from Greene to Cooke, 4 Dec. 1776, in *Papers of Nathanael Greene*, 1:362.

December 22, 1776: reported totals 11,423; effectives 6,104
   This is a monthly strength report of the Continental army and militia under Washington along the Delaware River. The manuscript is in the National Archives; a facsimile is
   reproduced in Robert K. Wright Jr., *The Continental Army* (Washington, 1989), 96; a
   tabulation is in Lesser, *Sinews of Independence*, 43–45.

December 26, 1776: committed to the Delaware Crossing, 6,500 men
   About 2,400 officers and men crossed the Delaware River at McConkey's Ferry. Three
   other forces were ordered to cross the river: 800 men under General James Ewing at

the South Trenton Ferry, 1,800 men under Colonel John Cadwalader at Bristol Ferry, and 1,000 men under General Israel Putnam at Philadelphia. Putnam's men were to join 500 militia who had been under Colonel Griffin in South Jersey. All three forces were unable to get across to New Jersey on Christmas night, except a few light infantry under Cadwalader and 300 men from Philadelphia who had crossed earlier. The total number of men committed to the operation was 6,500, of which only 2,400 were able to cross the river and engage at Trenton.

   Sources include a report from Washington to John Hancock, December 27, 1776: "I ordered the troops intended for this service which were about 2400 to parade back of McConkey's Ferry." *GW*, 7:454. Henry Knox's estimate was a little higher: "a part of the army consisting of about 2500 or three thousand pass'd the River on Christmas night with almost infinite difficulty, with eighteen field pieces." The source is a letter from Henry Knox to Lucy Knox, 28 Dec. 1776, in William S. Stryker, *The Battles of Trenton and Princeton* (Boston, 1898), 371. Cadwalader wrote to Washington, probably on December 27, "we had about 1800 rank and file including artillery." Cadwalader had first written 1,700, then crossed it out and wrote 1,800. *GW*, 7:445. In another letter dated December 26 at nine o'clock he wrote that "General Putnam was to cross at Philada to day, if the weather permitted. with 1000 men; 300 went over yesterday & 500 Jersey militia are now there as Col. Griffin informs me to day." The source is a letter from Cadwalader to Washington, 2[7?] Dec. 1776. The date of this letter is mutilated in manuscript; editors of the *Washington Papers* believe that it was sent on December 26; I think that it would have been December 27, 1776. *GW*, 7:442.

January 3, 1777: estimated 7,559 effectives
   This is an historian's careful reconstruction of American troops in New Jersey, by Samuel Stelle Smith in *The Battle of Princeton* (Monmouth Beach, N.J., 1967), 36.

January 7, 1777: "nearly 12,000"?
   Colonel Lambert Cadwalader estimated "our Army in the Jersies altogether must amount to near twelve thousand." The source is Cadwalader to Peggy Meredith, 7 Jan. 1777, rpt. in Dennis P. Ryan, ed., *A Salute to Courage* (New York, 1979), 64.

March 15, 1777: 3,870 effectives
   This is from a manuscript titled "Return of the American Forces in New Jersey, Return of Continental troops under the command of his Excellency General Washington at the different posts in the State of New Jersey." The number of "rank and file fit for duty" was 2,543 men in eight posts, of which only 43 were at Morristown. Also listed were 976 militia from Maryland, Virginia, and New Jersey. The total Continentals and militia was 3,519 rank and file; adding 10 percent for officers, 3,870 This strength report is in *GW*, 8:576; it is not included in Lesser, *Sinews of Independence*.

NOTE: These data come from different sources. Some are official monthly strength reports, of which only a few survive for this campaign. They derived from actual enumeration and included officers as well as "rank and file," except for the report of March 15, 1777, to which an adjustment is made, as noted. Other data are estimates by informed contemporary observers, mostly officers in the Continental army, including Washington, Nathanael Greene, and James Monroe. Some are careful reconstructions by historians. Each estimate includes men at arms, but not camp followers, sutlers, women of the army, etc. It counts men serving directly under Washington's command or in detached units such as the Flying Camp which were part of the New Jersey and New York campaigns, but excludes Continental troops in other theaters of the war.

APPENDIX B

❧ Strength Estimates of British and Hessian Forces,
August 27, 1776, and January 8, 1777

I.   Strength Report for British and Hessian troops in New York, August 27, 1776

General Henry Clinton, quoting "Howe's strength reports for this day," estimated "24,464 effectives fit for duty; a total of 26,980, officers not included, who when added amount to 31,625 men." The source is Henry P. Johnston, *Campaign of 1776 Around New York and Brooklyn* (Brooklyn, 1878), 133n.

II.   Distribution of the Army Under the Command of Gen. Sir William Howe, January 8, 1777

		Rank and File	Total
With Commander-in-Chief	British Artillery	380	
	British Cavalry		710
	British Infantry		8,361
	Hessian Infantry	3,300	
	Anspach Infantry	1,043	13,799
New York Island	British Artillery	20	
	British Infantry		1,513
	Hessian Infantry	1,778	3,311
Staten Island	British Artillery	11	
	British Infantry		515
	Waldeck Infantry	330	856
Paulus Hook	British Infantry	360	360
Rhode Island	British Artillery	71	
	British Infantry		1,064
	Hessian Infantry	1,496	2,631
Provincials at King's Bridge			2,000
Total Army			22,957

Wemy's Battn. Rangers not included, 280 rank and file, makes the army full 14,000 effective men.

NOTE: This report does not include officers. Adding 10 percent (the correction used by Henry Clinton, above), yields total strength of 25,253 and 15,400 effectives.

SOURCE: Stephen Kemble, Journal, 8 Jan. 1777, *Kemble Papers*, 1:107.

APPENDIX C

❧ The Women of the Armies

In the spring of 1777, Commissary Daniel Wier of the British army was in trouble with the Treasury Lords in London, who could not square the cost of rations with the number of troops in America. Wier explained that the problem arose from "the Women and Children belonging to each Regiment, which are indeed very numerous beyond any Idea of imagination." Weir reported on May 20, 1777, that General Howe's British units in America included 23,101 men, 2,776 women, and 1,904 children, all "on the ration," a phrase still used in British regiments (half-rations for women, quarter-rations for children). Two excellent books tell their story: Walter Hart Blumenthal's *Women Camp Followers of the American Revolution* (Philadelphia, 1952); and Holly A. Mayer's *Belonging to the Army: Camp Followers and Community During the American Revolution* (Columbia, 1996). The following material draws mainly from their work.

General Howe tried to limit the numbers of women in the New York campaign. At Halifax he allowed no more than six women for each infantry company of about thirty men. The rest were to remain in Halifax, with all the children of the army to remain behind. But a number of children were smuggled aboard the transports, and the number of women increased through the war. Blumenthal reports ration returns for New York City in 1779, where about 4,000 British troops had 1,550 women and 968 children. Others were off rations and were supported by the troops or made their own way (Blumenthal, 39).

German regiments also brought women to America, but in smaller numbers. Wier's ration strength in the spring of 1777 reported only 381 women for 11,192 German troops. Their ratio also increased in America, doubling in proportion to men from 1776 to 1781.

Many American women were attracted to the British armies, and more than a few came down with what was called "scarlet fever." Others were drawn to the Hessians. A German prisoner of war remembered that "at all places through which we passed dozens of girls were met on the road." Some "laughed at us mockingly, or now and then roguishly offered us an apple," in a scene that brought to his mind the eternal Eve (Blumenthal, 31, 37).

Their numbers varied by type of units. In all armies numbers of women were large in the artillery, which also had civilian teamsters. The Royal Artillery in New York reported a ration strength of 515 men, 133 women, and 120 children. In the American army, two of the most prominent women were Margaret Cronin and Molly Pitcher, both in artillery units.

Every army had its own customs. The British and Hessian commanders actively encouraged a carefully limited number of women, who had important and even vital roles. Women "off rations" were also tolerated, as long as they followed the rules. But "irregular women," as General Howe called them, were dealt with differently when they threatened the function of the army. Prostitutes were "turned out of camp," as were women who made a business of selling liquor to soldiers, above the standard rum ration. A woman convicted of a fencing operation was ordered to receive a hundred lashes on her bare back. Other offenders were drummed out of the army, to the sound of the rogue's march.

Practices in the American army were different in the early years of the war. Numbers of women were smaller than in the British and Hessian forces. George Washington did not encourage women camp followers. In August 1777, when he led his army through Philadelphia, women were ordered to move by a different route around the city. New Englanders went further and banned women altogether from camp, though many prostitutes swarmed around it. Lieutenant Jabez Fitch took a friend to a nearby tavern, "to find him some white stockin'd woman." In general, American forces in 1775 and 1776 had few women in their camps and were thought to have suffered for it. Several observers attributed the filthy appearance of the army at Boston and New York and its miserable camp sanitation and very high rates of illness to the absence of women.

By 1777, the number of women with the American army began to increase very rapidly. In 1778, a British intelligent report estimated that "women and waggoners make up near half of their army" (quoted in Mayer, *Belonging to the Army*, 1). Women cooked for the army. They did the washing and cleaned the camps. They were ordered to work as nurses, and after combat they gleaned the battlefield and stripped the dead of clothing and possessions.

They served with the army in the worst campaigns of the war. Several women made the terrible march to Quebec. They were in the worst of the fighting around New York, and some fought at Fort Washington. No women are known to have crossed the Delaware River with Washington, but probably they were there. More than a few dressed as men and bore arms with the infantry. In the battle of Trenton, at least one woman who lived in the town took up arms and brought down a Hessian officer. One wonders if she might have had a personal score to settle with the men who occupied her village.

Women of these armies were a cross-section of their societies. Some were officers' wives, of high social rank in a strongly rank-conscious era. Americans captured several shiploads of "gentle women" and treated them according to their status. American generals brought their wives to camp, especially in the winter. Washington, Greene, and Knox all did so. Many American women were of the yeomanry. They went to war with lovers, husbands, brothers, and friends and demanded to be treated with decency and respect.

Others, increasingly through the war, were very poor and suffered miserably. Hannah Winthrop wrote that "great numbers" of British and German women who were captured at Saratoga "seemed to be the beasts of burthen, having a bushel basket on their back, by which they were bent double, the contents seemed to be pots and kettles, various sorts of furniture, children peeping thro' gridirons and other utensils." Like the men they soldiered with, some women were heroes and some were criminals. Many helped others, with little thought for themselves. Others were famed as the worst of predatory plunderers. There are accounts of women who plundered even the wounded and dying men of their possessions. In these many roles women were an important part of these events, more so than they have been in the historical record.

APPENDIX D

❧ American Order of Battle, New York, ca. August 24, 1776

Commander-in-Chief: George Washington
Secretary: Lt. Col. Robert Hanson Harrison, Virginia
Aides-de-Camp:
    Col. William Grayson, Virginia
    Lt. Tench Tilghman, Maryland
    Lt. Col. Richard Cary Jr., Massachusetts
    Lt. Col. Samuel Blachley Webb, Connecticut
Adjutant General: Col. Joseph Reed, New Jersey and Pennsylvania
Quartermaster General: Col. Stephen Moylan, Pennsylvania
Commissary General: Col. Joseph Trumbull, Connecticut
Paymaster General: Col. William Palfrey, Massachusetts
Muster-Master General: Col. Gunning Bedford, Delaware
Director of the General Hospital: Dr. John Morgan, Pennsylvania
Chief Engineer: Col. Rufus Putnam, Massachusetts

Putnam's Division: Maj. Gen. Israel Putnam
Aide: Maj. Aaron Burr

Read's Brigade: Col. Joseph Read
Brig. Maj. David Henly
13th Mass. Cont., Col. Joseph Read, Massachusetts 505
3rd Mass. Cont., Col. Ebenezer Learned, Massachusetts 521
23rd Mass. Cont., Col. John Bailey, Massachusetts 503
26th Mass. Cont., Col. Loammi Baldwin, Massachusetts 468

Scott's Brigade: Brig. Gen. John Morin Scott
Brig. Maj. Nicholas Fish
N.Y. Militia, Col. John Lasher, New York 510
N.Y. Levies, Col. William Malcolm, New York 297
N.Y. Militia, Col. Samuel Drake, New York 459
N.Y. Militia, Col. Cornelius Humphrey, New York 261

Fellows' Brigade: Brig. Gen. John Fellows
Brig. Maj. Mark Hopkins
Mass. Militia, Col. Jonathan Holman, Massachusetts 606
Mass. Militia, Col. Simeon Cary, Massachusetts 569
Mass. Militia, Col. Jonathan Smith, Massachusetts 551
14th Mass. Cont., Col. John Glover, Massachusetts 365

Heath's Division: Maj. Gen. William Heath
Aides: Maj. Thomas Henly, Maj. Israel Keith

Mifflin's Brigade: Brig. Gen. Thomas Mifflin
Brig. Maj. Jonathan Mifflin
5th Pa. Bn., Col. Robert Magaw, Pennsylvania 480
3rd Pa. Bn., Col. John Shee, 496
27th Mass. Cont., Col. Israel Hutchinson, Massachusetts 513
16th Mass. Cont., Col. Paul Dudley Sargent, Massachusetts 527
Ward's Conn. Rgt., Col. Andrew Ward, Connecticut 437

Clinton's Brigade: Brig. Gen. George Clinton
Brig. Maj. Albert Pawling
N.Y. Militia, Col. Isaac Nichol, New York 289
N.Y. Militia, Col. Thomas Thomas, New York 354
N.Y. Militia, Col. James Swartwout, New York 364
N.Y. Militia, Col. Levi Paulding, New York 368
N.Y. Militia, Col. Morris Graham, New York 437

Spencer's Division: Maj. Gen. Joseph Spencer
Aides: Maj. William Peck, Maj. Charles Whiting

Parsons's Brigade: Brig. Gen. Samuel Holden Parsons
Brig. Maj. Thomas Dyer
17th Conn. Cont., Col. Jedediah Huntington, Connecticut 348
22nd Conn. Cont., Col. Samuel Wyllys, Connecticut 530
20th Conn. Cont., Col. John Durkee, Connecticut 520
10th Conn. Cont., Col. John Tyler, Connecticut 569
21st Mass. Cont., Col. Jonathan Ward, Massachusetts 502

Wadsworth's Brigade: Brig. Gen. James Wadsworth
Brig. Maj. John Palsgrave Wyllys
1st Conn. State Levies, Col. Gold Selleck Silliman, Connecticut 415
2nd Conn. State Levies, Col. Fisher Gay, Connecticut 449
3rd Conn. State Levies, Col. Comfort Sage, Connecticut 482
4th Conn. State Levies, Col. Samuel Selden, Connecticut 464
5th Conn. State Levies, Col. William Douglas, Connecticut 506
6th Conn. State Levies, Col. John Chester, Connecticut 535
7th Conn. State Levies, Col. Phillip Burr Bradley, Connecticut 569

Sullivan's Division: Maj. Gen. John Sullivan
Aides: Maj. Alexander Scammell, Maj. Lewis Morris Jr.

Stirling's Brigade: Brig. Gen. Lord Stirling
Brig. Maj. W. S. Livingston
Smallwood's Md. Cont., Col. William Smallwood, Maryland 600
Haslet's Del. Cont., Col. John Haslet, Delaware 750
Pa. State Rifle Rgt., Col. Samuel Miles, Pennsylvania 650
Pa. State Bn. of Musketry, Col. Samuel John Atlee, Pennsylvania 650
Pa. Militia, Lt. Col. Nicholas Lutz, Pennsylvania 200
Pa. Militia, Lt. Col. Peter Kachlein, Pennsylvania 200
Pa. Militia, Maj. Hay

McDougall's Brigade: Brig. Gen. Alexander McDougall
Brig. Maj. Richard Platt
1st N.Y. Rgt., Late McDougall's New York 428
2nd N.Y. Rgt., Col. Rudolph Ritzeme, New York 434
19th Conn. Cont., Col. Charles Webb, Connecticut 542
Artificers, Col. Jonathan Brewer, 584

Greene's Division: Maj. Gen. Nathanael Greene
Aides: Maj. William Blodgett, Maj. William S. Livingston

Nixon's Brigade: Brig. Gen. John Nixon
Brig. Maj. Daniel Box
1st Pa. Cont. (Riflemen), Col. Edward Hand, Pennsylvania 288
Varnum's R.I. Cont., Col. James Varnum, Rhode Island 391
Hitchcock's R.I. Cont., Col. Daniel Hitchcock, Rhode Island 368
4th Mass. Cont., Col. Nixon, Massachusetts 419
7th Mass. Cont., Col. William Prescott, Massachusetts 399
12th Mass. Cont., Col. Moses Little, Massachusetts 453

Heard's Brigade: Brig. Gen. Nathaniel Heard
Brig. Maj. Peter Gordon
N.J. State Troops, Col. David Forman, New Jersey 372
N.J. Militia, Col. Philip Johnston, New Jersey 235
N.J. Militia, Col. Ephraim Martin, New Jersey 382
N.J. Militia, Col. Silas Newcomb, New Jersey 336
N.J. Militia, Col. Phillip Van Cortlandt, New Jersey 269

Artillery: Col. Henry Knox, Massachusetts 406

Connecticut Militia: Brig. Gen. Oliver Wolcott
Conn. Militia, Col. Thompson, Connecticut 350
Conn. Militia, Col. Hinman, Connecticut 350
Conn. Militia, Col. Pettibone, Connecticut 350
Conn. Militia, Col. Cooke, Connecticut 350
Conn. Militia, Col. Talcott, Connecticut 350
Conn. Militia, Col. Chapman, Connecticut 350
Conn. Militia, Col. Baldwin, Connecticut 350
Conn. Militia, Lt. Col. Mead, Connecticut 350
Conn. Militia, Lt. Col. Lewis, Connecticut 350
Conn. Militia, Lt. Col. Pitkin, Connecticut 350
Conn. Militia, Major Strong, Connecticut 350
Conn. Militia, Major Newberry, Connecticut 350

Long Island Militia: Brig. Gen. Nathaniel Woodhull
Brig. Maj. Jonathan Lawrence
Long Island Militia, Col. Josiah Smith, Long Island 250
Long Island Militia, Col. Jeronimus Remsen, Long Island 200

Flying Camp in New Jersey (Returns of August 20, 1776: effectives/total)
Gen. Hugh Mercer

New Jersey Militia, Maj. Mattias Shipman, 210/214
Delaware Flying Camp, Samuel Patterson 397/486
N.J. Militia, Lt. Col. Jonathan Deare, 180/191
N.J. Militia, Richard Somers, 116/122
N.J. Militia, David Chambers, 248/255
N.J. Militia, Samuel Dick, 133/139
N.J. Militia, Lt. Col. Enos Seeley, 197/211
N.J. Militia, Edward Thomas, 334/334
N.J. Militia, Jacob Ford Jr., 343/343
N.J. Militia, Joseph Beavers, 184/184
Pa. Flying Camp, Lt. Col. Lawrence, 121/121
Pa. Flying Camp, Moore 212/242
Pa. Flying Camp, Jacob Klotz, 376/406
Pa. Flying Camp, Michael Swope, 388/436
Pa. Flying Camp, Lt. Col. Frederick Watts, 443/546
Pa. Flying Camp, William Montgomery, 300/335
Pa. Flying Camp, Richard McAllister, 360/404
Pa. Flying Camp, Lt. Col. William Baxter, 346/390

SOURCES: Henry P. Johnston, *The Campaign of 1776 Around New York and Brooklyn* (Brooklyn, 1878) 126–31; Charles H. Lesser, *The Sinews of Independence: Monthly Strength Reports of the Continental Army* (Chicago, 1976); Robert K. Wright Jr., *The Continental Army* (Army Lineage Series, Washington, 1989).

APPENDIX E

❧ British and Hessian Order of Battle, New York,
   August 22, 1776

Commander-in-Chief: Gen. the Hon. Sir William Howe
Second in Command: Lt. Gen. Henry Clinton
Third in Command: Right Hon. Lt. Gen. Hugh Earl Percy

Brigade of Guards: Maj. Gen. Edward Mathew
1st Battalion Guards
2nd Battalion Guards

1st Brigade: Maj. Gen. Robert Pigot
Brig. Maj. M.B. Smith
4th Foot, Maj. James Ogilvie
15th Foot, Lt. Col. John Bird
27th Foot, Lt. Col. John Maxwell
45th Foot, Maj. Saxton

2nd Brigade: Brig. Gen. James Agnew, killed at Germantown, 1777
Brig. Maj. M. B. Disney
5th Foot, Lt. Col. William Walcott (died of wounds, Germantown)
28th Foot, Lt. Col. Robert Prescott
35th Foot, Lt. Col. Robert Carr (killed at White Plains)
49th Foot, Lt. Col. Sir Henry Calder, Bart.

3rd Brigade: Maj. Gen. Daniel Jones
Brig. Maj. M. B. Baker
10th Foot, Maj. John Vatass
37th Foot, Lt. Col. Robert Abercrimbie
38th Foot, Lt. Col. Wm. Butler
52nd Foot, Lt. Col. Mungo Campbell (killed at Fort Montgomerie, 1777)

4th Brigade: Maj. Gen. James Grant
Brig. Maj. M. B. Brown
17th Foot, Lt. Col. Charles Mawhood
40th Foot, Lt. Col. James Grant (killed at Long Island, 1776)
46th Foot, Lt. Col. Enoch Markham
55th Foot, Capt. Luke

5th Brigade: Brig. Gen. Francis Smith
Brig. Maj. M. B. McKenzie
14th Foot, Lt. Col. Alured Clarke
23rd Foot, Lt. Col. J. Campbell
43rd Foot, Lt. Col. Geo. Clerke
63rd Foot, Maj. Francis Sill

6th Brigade: Brig. Gen. James Robertson
Brig. Maj. M. B. Leslie
23rd Foot, Lt. Col. Benj. Bernard
44th Foot, Maj. Henry Hope
57th Foot, Lt. Col. John Campbell of Starchur
64th Foot, Maj. Hugh McLeroch

7th Brigade: Brig. Gen. Wm. Erskine, Quartermaster General
1st Battalion, 71st Foot, Maj. John Macdonnell of Lochgary
2nd Battalion, 71st Foot, Maj. Norman Lamont of Lamont

16th Light Dragoons, Lt. Col. William Harcourt
17th Light Dragoons, Lt. Col. Samuel Birch

Corps de Reserve: Lt. Gen. Earl Cornwallis
Brig. Gen. the Hon. John Vaughan
1st Battalion Grenadiers, Lt. Col. Hon. Henry Monckton (killed at Monmouth, 1778)
2nd Battalion Grenadiers, Lt. Col. William Medows
3rd Battalion Grenadiers, Maj. Thomas Marsh
4th Battalion Grenadiers, Maj. the Hon. Charles Stuart
33rd Foot, Lt. Col. James Webster (killed at Guilford C.H., 1779)
42nd Royal Highland Regiment, Lt. Col. Thomas Stirling

Light Infantry Brigade: Brig. Gen. the Hon. Alexander Leslie
Brig. Maj. Lewis
1st Battalion Light Infantry, Maj. Thomas Musgrave; Lt. Col. Abernethy
2nd Battalion Light Infantry, Maj. Strawbenzie
3rd Battalion Light Infantry, Maj. the Hon. John Maitland
4th Battalion Light Infantry, Maj. John Johnson

Royal Artillery: Brig. Gen. Samuel Cleaveland
Brig. Maj. Farrington
1st Brigade of Artillery
2nd Brigade of Artillery
3rd Brigade of Artillery

Hessian Division: Lt. Gen. Leopold von Heister

Mirbach's Brigade: Maj. Gen. Werner von Mirbach
Knyphausen Regiment, Col. H. C. von Borck
Rall Regiment, Col. Johann Rall (killed at Trenton, 1776)
Lossberg Regiment, Col. H. A. von Heringen (to Sept. 1776)

Stirn's Brigade: Maj. Gen. J. D. von Stirn
Donop Regiment, Col. D. E. von Gosen
Mirbach Regiment, Col. Johann von Loos
Hereditary Prince Regiment, Col. C. W. von Hachenberg

Donop's Brigade: Col. Carl von Donop
Bloch Grenadier Battalion, Lt. Col. Justus von Bloch
Minnigerode Grenadier Battalion, Lt. Col. Friedrich von Minnegerode
Linsing Grenadier Battalion, Lt. Col. Otto von Linsing

Lossberg's Brigade: Col. A. H. von Lossberg
Ditfurth Regiment, Col. Carl von Bose
Trumbach Regiment, Col. C. E. von Bischausen

Feldjäger Corps, Col. Carl von Donop

SOURCE: David Stewart, *Sketches of the Character, Manners and Present State of the Highlanders. . . ,* 2 vols. (Edinburgh, 1822, rpt. 1977), 2:370; Henry P. Johnston, *Campaign of 1776 Around New York and Brooklyn* (Brooklyn, 1878), 134–36; Rodney Atwood, *The Hessians* (Cambridge, 1980); Orderly Books, 42nd Foot, David Library; "Order Books of Lieut.-Col. Stephen Kemble, Adjutant General and Deputy Adjutant General to the British Forces in America, 1775–1778," *Kemble Papers* 1:249–433.

APPENDIX F

❧ American Order of Battle Before the Attack on Trenton,
December 22, 1776

Commander-in-Chief: Gen. George Washington
    Washington's Life Guard (Capt. Caleb Gibbs) ca. 75 effectives

Secretary: Lt. Col. Robert Hanson Harrison, Virginia
Aides-de-Camp: Col. William Grayson, Virginia
    Lt. Tench Tilghman, Maryland
    Lt. Col. Richard Cary Jr., Massachusetts
    Lt. Col. Samuel Blachley Webb, Connecticut

Adjutant General: Col. Joseph Reed, New Jersey and Pennsylvania
Quartermaster General: Col. Stephen Moylan, Pennsylvania
Commissary General: Col. Joseph Trumbull, Connecticut
Paymaster General: Col. William Palfrey, Massachusetts
Muster Master General: Col. Gunning Bedford, Pennsylvania and Virginia
Director of the General Hospital: Dr. John Morgan, Pennsylvania
Chief Engineer: Col. Rufus Putnam, Massachusetts

Stirling's Brigade, Continental Army, 673 effectives
    1st Regiment, Virginia Continentals (Capt. John Fleming), 185
        Col. James Read was absent; Lt. Col. Francis Eppes (killed at Long Island);
        Maj. John Green (wounded at White Plains), 185
    Haslet's Delaware Continentals (Col John Haslet), 108
    3rd Regiment Virginia Continentals (Col. George Weedon), 181
    1st Pennsylvania Rifle Regiment (Maj. Ennion Williams), 199

Stephen's Brigade, Continental army, 549 effectives
    4th Regiment, Virginia Continentals (Lt. Col. Robert Lawson) 229
    5th Regiment, Virginia Continentals (Col. Charles Scott) 129
    6th Regiment, Virginia Continentals (Col. Mordecai Buckner) 191
        includes an attached remnant of Atlee's regiment

Mercer's Brigade, Continental army, 838 effectives
    20th Regiment, Connecticut Continentals (Col. John Durkee) 313
    1st Regiment, Maryland Continentals, Smallwood's (Lt. Col. Francis Ware) 163
    27th Regiment, Massachusetts Continentals (Col. Israel Hutchinson) 115
    Bradley's Battalion, Connecticut State Troops (Col. Philip Burr Bradley) 142
    Maryland Rifle Battalion Volunteers (Capt. David Harris), 105

Fermoy's Brigade, Continental army, 638 effectives
    1st Regiment, Pennsylvania Continentals (Col. Edward Hand) 254
    German Continentals (Col. Nicholas Haussegger) 374

Glover's Brigade, Continental army (Smith est. 1259 effectives)
    14th (Marblehead) Regiment, Massachusetts Continentals (Col. John Glover)
    3rd Regiment, Massachusetts Continentals (Col. William Shepard)
    19th Regiment Connecticut Continentals (Col. Charles Webb)
    23rd Regiment Massachusetts Continentals (Col. John Bailey)
    26th Regiment Massachusetts Continentals (Col. Loammi Baldwin)

Sargent's Brigade, Continental army (no returns, Smith est. 865 effectives)
    16th Regiment Massachusetts Continentals (Col. Paul Dudley Sargent)
    Ward's Regiment Connecticut Continentals (Col. Andrew Ward)
    6th Battalion, Connecticut State Troops (Col. John Chester)
    13th Regiment Massachusetts Continentals (Col. Joseph Read)
    1st Regiment, MacDougall's New York Continentals (Capt. John Johnson)
    3rd Regiment, Gansevoort's New York Continentals (Lt. Col. Baron Friedrich von Weisenfels)

St. Clair's Brigade (no returns; Stryker est. 500 effectives)
    5th Regiment, formerly 1st New Hampshire Continentals (Col. John Stark)
    8th Regiment, formerly 2nd New Hampshire Continentals (Col. Enoch Poor)
    2d Regiment, formerly 3rd New Hampshire Continentals (Lt. Col. Israel Gilman)
    15th Regiment, Massachusetts Continentals (all field grade officers absent)

Included in the Return for December 22, but not in the attack on Trenton, Dec. 26:

Ewing's Brigade, Pennsylvania Militia of the Flying Camp (Smith est. 826 effectives)
    Cumberland County Regiment (Col. Frederick Watts)
    Lancaster County Regiment (Col. Jacob Klotz)
    Cumberland County Regiment (Col. William Montgomery)
    York County Regiment (Col. Richard McCallister)
    Chester County Regiment (Col. James Moore)

Hitchcock's Brigade (Smith est. 822 effectives)
    Nixon's Regiment, Massachusetts Continentals (Col. John Nixon)
    Varnum's Regiment, Rhode Island Continentals (Col. James Varnum)
    Hitchcock's Regiment, Rhode Island Continentals (Major Israel Angell)
    Little's Regiment, Massachusetts Continentals
    Rhode Island Militia (Col. Christopher Lippitt)

Not included in the Return for December 22, but present with the Continental army:

Knox's Regiment of Continental Artillery (Col. Henry Knox) [ca. 418 effectives?]
    New York Company of Continental Artillery (Capt. Sebastian Baumann)
        3 guns, 80 men [and 5 officers?]
    Massachusetts Company of Continental Artillery (Capt. Lt. Winthrop Sargent)
        2 guns [no return, est. 55 officers and men?]
    New York State Company of Artillery (Capt. Alexander Hamilton)
        2 guns, 4 officers, 32 men
    Eastern Company, New Jersey State Artillery (Capt. Daniel Neil)
        2 guns, 4 officers, 59 men
    Western Company, New Jersey State Artillery (Capt. Samuel Hugg)
        2 guns [no return, est. 55 officers and men?]
    2d Company, Pennsylvania State Artillery (Capt. Thomas Forrest)
        2 brass mounted six-pounders, 2 officers, 50 men
    2d Company of Artillery, Philadelphia Associators (Capt. Joseph Moulder)
        3 guns, 3 officers, 82 men

Other American troops in the campaign but not with the Continental army:

Cadwalader's Brigade, Pennsylvania Associators (Brig. Gen. John Cadwalader)
(Smith est. 1,500)
    Morgan's Regiment, Philadelphia Militia (Col. Jacob Morgan)
    Bayard's Regiment, Philadelphia Militia (Col. John Bayard)
    Cadwalader's Regiment, Philadelphia Militia (Lt. Col. John Nixon)
    Matlack's Rifle Battalion, Philadelphia Militia (Col. Timothy Matlack)
    Kent County Delaware Militia Company (Capt. Thomas Rodney)
    Artillery Company, Philadelphia Militia
    Artillery Company, Philadelphia Militia

Griffin's Brigade, New Jersey Militia (Smith est. 497)
    Cumberland Co. Regiment (Col. Silas Newcomb)
    Cumberland Co. Regiment (Col. David Potter)
    Gloucester Co. Regiment (Col. Enos Seeley
    Gloucester Co. Regiment (Col. Joseph Ellis)
    Gloucester Co. Regiment (Col. Richard Somers)
    Salem Co. Regiment (Col. Samuel Dick)
    Salem Co. Regiment (Col. John Holme)
    Virginia Artillery (2 companies)

Dickinson's Brigade (Brig. Gen. Philemon Dickinson) (Smith est. 500)
    Burlington County Militia Regiment (Col. Joseph Borden)
    Burlington County Militia Regiment (Lt. Col. Thomas Reynolds)
    Hunterdon County Militia Regiment (Col. David Chambers)
    Hunterdon County Militia Regiment (Col. Nathaniel Hunt)
    Hunterdon County Militia Regiment Col. John Mehelm
    Hunterdon County Militia Regiment (Col. Isaac Smith)
    small units of militia from other counties

Marines, recruited at the Tun Tavern, Philadelphia, 1776
    Landlord Robert Mullen was their captain. They served in the Trenton–Princeton campaign. Original uniform facings were white; changed to red in 1779 because of shortage of white cloth.

Cavalry
    Philadelphia Troop of Light Horse (Capt. Samuel Morris) 3/22 (25 effectives)
    Dragoons, Lt. Col. Elisha Sheldon, 1 troop (Smith est. 50 effectives)

NOTE: This list, four days before the first battle at Trenton, derives from an incomplete "Return of the Forces in the Service of the States of America, encamped and in quarters on the banks of the Delaware, in the state of Pennsylvania, under the command of his Excellency George Washington, Esq., Commander-in-Chief of all the Forces of the United States in America, December 22d, 1776," with additions.

DEFINITIONS: "Effectives" in the Continental strength report included officers present, drums and fifes, and rank and file present and fit for duty. They did not include men who were reported as present sick, absent sick, on command, on furlough, deserted, dead, and discharged.

SOURCES: The manuscript strength report is in the National Archives, Washington; reproduced in facsimile in Robert K. Wright Jr., *The Continental Army* (Washington, 1989), 96 and tabulated in Charles H. Lesser, *The Sinews of Independence: Monthly Strength Reports of the Continental Army* (Chicago, 1976), 43–45. Also helpful is Peter Force, *American Archives*, 5th series, 3:1402; William S. Stryker, *The Battles of Trenton and Princeton* (Boston, 1898), 308–9, 344–47, 351–58, 432–33; Samuel Stelle Smith, *The Battle of Trenton* (Monmouth Beach, N.J., 1965), 28–30.

APPENDIX G

∾ British and Hessian Dispositions: New York, New Jersey, and Rhode Island, ca. December 25, 1776

New York (Gen. William Howe, Commander-in-Chief)
    First Brigade (Major Gen. Robertson; Lt. Col. Henry Monckton acting) at New York City
        4th Foot (Maj. James Ogilvie)
        27th Foot (Major Henry Couran)
        45th Foot (Lt. Col. Hon. Henry Monckton)

Hessian Brigades (Gen. Stirn, Gen. Mirbach) at New York City and Fort Washington
    Trumbach's Regiment (Col. Carl Ernest von Bischausen)
    Wissenbach's Regiment (Col. Ludwig von Horn)
    Stein's Regiment (Col. von Seitz)
    Mirbach's Regiment (Col. Johann von Loos)
    Donop's Regiment (Col. David Ephraim von Gosen)
Detached British Regiments
    Two regiments on Long Island
Cavalry
    17th Light Dragoons, two troops

New Jersey (Gen. James Grant)
    Guards Brigade (Brig. Mathew) at Brunswick Landing
        1st Guards Battalion
        2nd Guards Battalion
    Light Infantry (Brig. Alexander Leslie) at Princeton
        1st Light Infantry Battalion (Lt. Col. Thomas Musgrave)
        2nd Light Infantry Battalion (Maj. Strawbenzie)
    Grenadiers, at Brunswick
        1st Battalion Grenadiers
        2nd Battalion Grenadiers (Lt. Col. William Medows)
    Second Brigade (Brig. Alexander Leslie) at Princeton
        5th Foot (Lt. Col. William Walcott)
        28th Foot (Lt. Col. Robert Prescott)
        35th Foot (Lt. Col. James Cockburne)
        49th Foot (Major Thomas Dilkes)
    Fourth Brigade (Lt. Col. Charles Mawhood) at Hillsborough
        17th Foot (Lt. Col. Charles Mawhood)
        40th Foot (Maj. Samuel Bradstreet)
        55th Foot (Maj. Cornelius Cuyler)
    Highland Brigade (Lt. Col. Thomas Stirling)
        42nd Foot, Royal Highland Regiment (Lt. Col. Thomas Stirling) at Black Horse
        71st Foot, The Scotch Regiment (Lt. Col. Archibald Campbell, absent)
            1st Battalion, Aquakenunk
            2nd Battalion, Newark
    Detached British Infantry Regiments
        7th Foot (New-Bridge)
        26th Foot (Hackensack)
        33rd Foot (Lt. Col. Webster) at Amboy
        46th Foot (Lt. Col. Enoch Markham) at Spanktown
        57th Foot at Bergen and Paulus Hook
    Rall's Hessian Brigade (Col. Johann Rall) Trenton
        Rall Regiment (Lt. Col. Balthasar Brethauer)
        Knyphausen Regiment (Maj. Friedrich Ludwig von Dechow)
        Von Lossberg Regiment (Lt. Col. Francis Scheffer)
    Donop's Hessian Brigade (Col. Carl von Donop) Burlington, Bordentown, and vicinity
        Bloch Grenadier Battalion (Lt. Col. Justus von Bloch)
        Minnigerode Grenadier Battalion (Lt. Col. Friedrich von Minnegerode)
        Linsing Grenadier Battalion (Lt. Col. Otto von Linsing)
        Feld Jäger Corps (Col. Carl von Donop)
    Detached German Regiment
        Waldeck Regiment, at Elizabethtown

Cavalry
  16th Light Dragoons (Lt. Col. William Harcourt)
    3 troops at Princeton
    3 troops at Brunswick
    20 dragoons at Trenton
  17th Light Dragoons
    one troop at Elizabethtown
Royal Artillery

Rhode Island Occupation Force (Lt. Gen. Henry Clinton)
  3rd Brigade (Maj. Gen. Daniel Jones)
    Brig. Maj. M. B. Baker
    10th Foot (Maj. Vatass)
    37th Foot (Lt. Col. Robert Abercrimbie)
    38th Foot (Lt. Col. Wm. Butler)
    52nd Foot (Lt. Col. Mungo Campbell)
  5th Brigade (Brig. Gen. B. G. Smith)
    Brig. Maj. Frederick Mackenzie
    14th Foot (Lt. Col. Alured Clarke)
    23rd Foot (Lt. Col. J. Campbell)
    43rd Foot (Lt. Col. Geo. Clerke)
    63rd Foot (Maj. Francis Sill)
  Detached Regiments
    22d Foot
    54th Foot
  Lossberg's and Schmidt's Hessian Brigade (Gen. Friedrich von Lossberg,
      Brig. Gen. Johann von Huyne)
    Wutginau's Regiment (Col. Henrich Julian von Kospoth)
    Bunau's Regiment (Col. Rudolph Bunau)
    Huyn's Regiment (Col. Johann Christophe von Huyn)
    Lieb Regiment (Col. Friedrich Wilhelm von Wumb)
    Ditfurth's Regiment (Col. Carl von Bose)
    Prince Carl's Regiment (Col. Johann Schreiber)
    Regiment du Corps
  Light Infantry
    3rd Battalion Light Infantry (Maj. the Hon. John Maitland)
  Grenadiers
    3rd Battalion Grenadiers (Maj. Thomas Marsh)
  Cavalry
    17th Light Dragoons, 3 troops
  Royal Artillery

NOTE: Smith writes, "Howe had approximately 10,000 men south of the Raritan River: roughly 4,000 at Brunswick, 3,000 at Princeton, then a gap of 12 miles, with 1,500 at Trenton and 1,500 at Bordentown six miles beyond" (Smith, *Trenton*, 27). He missed Stirling.

SOURCES: Montresor, map of British disposition, December 1776, Clinton Papers, Clements Library University of Michigan; Frederick MacKenzie, *The Diary of Frederick Mackenzie*, 2 vols. (Cambridge, 1930) 1:114–15; 123; Friedrich von Münchausen, *At General Howe's Side, 1776–1778: The Diary of General William Howe's Aide-de-Camp, Captain Friedrich von Muenchausen*, trans. Ernest Kipping, ann. Samuel Stelle Smith (Monmouth Beach, N.J., 1974), 8 (report of 26 Dec. 1776); William S. Stryker, *The Battle of Trenton and Princeton* (Boston, 1898), 430–31; Rodney Atwood, *The Hessians: Mercenaries from Hessen-Kassel in the American Revolution* (Cambridge, 1980), 258–65.

APPENDIX H

❧ The Hessian Garrison at Trenton, December 26, 1776

Brigade Rall (Col. Johann Gottlieb Rall)
1,354 effective men "on duty" plus 28 officers; total effectives 1,382

> Grenadier Regiment Rall (Col. Johann Gottlieb Rall)
> Lt. Col. Balthasar Brethauer, acting commander
> Maj. Johann Jost Matthaeus
> Reported strength on December 26: 512 "effective men under arms," 28 wounded and 40 sick in hospitals at New York, 23 sick at Trenton

> Fusilier Regiment von Lossberg (also Alt von Lossberg, after Lt. Gen. Baron Friedrich Wilhelm von Lossberg, commander of a brigade in Rhode Island)
> Lt. Col. Francis Scheffer, acting commander
> Maj. Ludwig August von Hanstein
> "Last Report," 345 effective men "on duty"; no report of ineffectives

> Fusilier Regiment von Knyphausen (after Lt. Gen. Wilhelm von Knyphausen, commander 2d Division, Ländgräflich Hessischen Corps in America)
> Maj. Friedrich Ludwig von Dechow, acting commander
> Strength on December 26, 1776: 429 men effective "on duty," 45 wounded and 17 sick at New York, 8 sick at Trenton

> Artillery (6 guns)
> Lt. Friedrich Fischer
> Lt. Johann Engelhardt
> Strength included with regiments

> Jägers, one company [50 men]
> Lt. Friedrich Wilhelm von Grothausen
> Estimated effectives, 50 men

> Cavalry, British 16th Light Dragoons, [20 men]
> Estimated effectives, 18 men

NOTE: Other estimates vary in detail. Smith estimates the Hessian strength at 1,586, but this is extrapolated from prisoners plus a rough guess of escapees plus killed and captured. Dwyer variously estimated "1,400 hessians in crowded Trenton," and repeated Sullivan's estimate of 1,600 Hessians (*The Day Is Ours!* [New York, 1983], 264, 276).

SOURCES: Rall regiment, testimony in Hessian Court of Inquiry by Maj. Johann Jost Matthaeus, New York, 17 Aug. 1778; Lossberg regiment, Corp. William Hartung, Philadelphia, 22 April 1778; Knyphausen regiment, Lt. Christian Sobbe, regimental adjutant, Philadelphia, 25 April 1778; all LT, ML 591, 200, 377. Secondary accounts include William S. Stryker, *The Battles of Trenton and Princeton* (Boston, 1898), 316, 378, 388–94, 408; bracketed data from Samuel Stelle Smith, *The Battle of Trenton* (Monmouth Beach, N.J.), 30. Regimental reports do not include officers.

APPENDIX I

Delaware River Ferries in 1776

No bridges spanned the middle reaches of the Delaware River in 1776, but many ferries crossed the river, and at least thirteen were used by American troops in the course of the campaign. The ferries were flatboats, in some cases large enough to carry a coach and four, or a heavy Pennsylvania wagon. Most appear to have been rope ferries, which were designed in such a way that the current did much of the work in moving the ferry across the river. On a loose line with a broad catenary, the current pushed the boat halfway across the stream. Then the line could be tightened to pull the ferry to the other bank.

Among the most important in 1776 were the following:

Coryell's Ferry (Lambertville, N.J., New Hope, Pa.), 17 miles above Trenton
The same family operated it on both sides of the river.

McConkey's Ferry (Washington Crossing, Pa.), 9.9 miles above Trenton
Johnson's Ferry (Washington's Crossing, N.J.) Hessians called it John's Ferry.
These two ferries operated side by side.

Beatty's Ferry, 5 miles above Trenton
Dwyer writes: "Some Hessian prisoners made the crossing to Pennsylvania at Beatty's Ferry, about five miles above Trenton. The main body of prisoners was escorted another three miles upstream to the area of Johnson's ferry house, across the river from McConkey's ferry house."

Howell's Ferry, 4.5 miles above Trenton at the Upper Ferry Road near Birmingham (now West Trenton)

Yardley's Ferry, 4 miles above Trenton at the Lower Ferry Road

Upper Trenton Ferry, 0.5 miles above Trenton

Trenton Ferry or Colvin's Ferry, 0.5 miles below Trenton
It ran from Colvin's ferry house in Pennsylvania to the Trenton ferry landing in South Trenton, half a mile downstream from the mouth of Assunpink Creek.

Kirbride's Ferry (Pa.), 7 miles south of Trenton
Bordentown/Burdenton Ferry, N.J.
At the elbow of the river.

Pennsbury Ferry (Pa.), 8 miles below Trenton
A mile below Kirbride's Ferry.

Neshaminy Ferry, 12 miles below Trenton
Bristol, Pa., and Burlington, N.J.

Dunk's Ferry, 13 miles below Trenton
Below Bristol, Pa., and Burlington, N.J.

Cooper's Ferry, 17 miles below Trenton
Philadelphia, Pa., and Camden, N.J.

SOURCES: Christopher Colles, *A Survey of the Roads of the United States of America*, ed. Walter W. Ristow (New York, 1789; rpt. Cambridge, 1961), 58–62; I. J. Hills, *A Complete Plan of Part of the Province of Pennsylvania East and West Jersey with Part of the Adjoining States* (New York, 1778); Samuel Stelle Smith, *The Battle of Trenton* (Monmouth Beach, N.J., 1965), 10, 21; William S. Stryker, *The Battles of Trenton and Princeton* (Boston, 1898), 82, 84; *GW*, 6:440n; Douglas Southall Freeman, *George Washington: A Biography*, 7 vols. (New York, 1948–57), 4:307; John C. Dann, ed., *The Revolution Remembered: Eyewitness Accounts of the War of Independence* (Chicago, 1980), 394–95; William M. Dwyer, *The Day Is Ours!* (New York, 1983), 272.

APPENDIX J

~ Ice Conditions on the Delaware River

A major factor in the winter campaign of 1776 was the formation of ice on the Delaware River. Ice conditions varied by time throughout the Delaware Valley, driven mainly by changes in temperature and precipitation. Conditions also varied by place from one part of the river to another, in a way that made a difference for the military campaign.

During the month of December in 1776, the river was in general free of ice, until the region experienced three days of extremely cold weather, December 20–23. Ice began to form on the river near Trenton on December 23. So rapid was its accumulation on that day that Washington expected the entire river to freeze over, and he feared that British and German troops could cross on the ice to Philadelphia.

On December 24–25, temperatures rose and the ice broke up on the river. On Christmas evening when Washington's army marched to the water's edge, ice conditions varied greatly from one part of the river to another. Above Trenton large quantities of floe ice in flat cakes were drifting down the river. Near McConkey's and Johnson's ferries, the river was passable through the floating ice, and both banks were accessible with difficulty. Washington's two Continental divisions were able to get across the river.

Just south of Trenton, ice conditions were very different. General James Ewing's brigade of Pennsylvania militia also attempted to cross the river at Trenton Ferry, below Trenton Falls. New Jersey state geologist Kemble Widmer writes of that part of the river, "When ice coming down the Delaware meets an incoming tide it piles up at the foot of the rapids called Trenton Falls. It takes only four hours to pile ice five feet deep for nearly a half mile down the river, and across its entire width except for three or four narrow channels of rushing water twenty or thirty feet wide. There is no conceivable way for anyone to cross such an ice jam, much less make a surprise attack." This tidal ice jam below the Trenton Falls was a thick, impenetrable jumbled mass of ice cakes and was impassable.

General John Cadwalader attempted to cross the river at Neshaminy Ferry near Bristol, Pennsylvania, and then at Dunk's Ferry farther south. This force met yet another set of ice conditions. The line of the river and the strong flow of the current tend to drive floe ice against the Jersey shore, where that night it formed a large ice field that extended 150 yards from the bank into the river. Cadwalader's troops were able to get their light infantry across the ice, but they could not move their artillery or horses.

The river was frozen solid in January, to such a depth that General Mercer's body was carried to Philadelphia in a large hearse that crossed the Delaware River on the ice. Had the British and Hessian troops still been close to the river, they could have crossed as well.

The best discussion of ice on the river in relation to the campaign of 1776 is in Kemble Widmer, *The Christmas Campaign: The Ten Days of Trenton and Princeton* (Trenton, 1975), 18–

19. The author was state geologist of New Jersey. For technical questions G. D. Ashton, ed., *River and Lake Ice Engineering* (Littleton, Colo., 1986); an "Ice Jam Primer" is published by the U.S. Army Cold Regions Research and Engineering Laboratory in Durham, N.H., and is available on-line. The U.S. Army Corps of Engineers has compiled an Ice Jam Database, which includes historical materials for the Delaware River through the twentieth century, with scattered data on the nineteenth century.

Much of this material is also available on-line through the USA-CRREL site. The Delaware River Basin Council has an Ice Jam Project for the study of conditions on the river; their work is accessible through their site at www.drbc.net.

APPENDIX K
∾ Weather Records in the Delaware Valley, 1776–77

A major factor in the New Jersey campaign was the weather in the Delaware Valley during the fall and winter of 1776–77. A running record was kept by Phineas Pemberton, a member of the American Philosophical Society, who was very careful and regular in his observations from 1748 to 1778. In 1776, he wrote that he was making his observations at his house "2 mi. westerly of Philadelphia." Every day at eight o'clock in the morning and three o'clock in the afternoon he recorded his observations, sometimes adding a third set of data at nine o'clock at night.

The diary includes a full record of barometric pressure, wind direction, and two temperature readings (outside and inside the house), with comments on sun, clouds, precipitation, storms, and sometimes wind velocity. A note explains that "the thermometer used in the observations is a large one by E. Nairne in Fahrenheit's scale."

Excerpts from the diary were published by the American Philosophical Society in the *American Philosophical Society Transactions*, n.s. 6 (1839), 395. The original is in the collections of the Society and is reproduced from the manuscript with the permission of the Society. Included are the date and time of observation, outside temperature, wind, and comments. The inside temperature and barometric readings are omitted.

Phineas Pemberton Weather Diary, December 1, 1776–January 31, 1777
American Philosophical Society

December, 1776

1	8 am	39	W	Sunsh: & Clouds.
	3 pm	44.5	W	Cloudy & Sunsh: at Int:
2	8 am	36	NW	Fair.
	3 pm	41	NW	Sunsh: & Clouds.
3	8 am	39	NE	Cloudy.
	3 pm	46	S	do. & windy.
4	8 am	52	SW	Rain. Much Rain last Night.
	3 pm	50	NW	Cl. & Sunsh: P.M.
5	8 am	41	NW	Fair.
	3 pm	47	NW	do.

6	8 am	34.5	NE	Sunsh: & Clouds.
	3 pm	44	SW	Fair.
7	8 am	39.5	SW	Cloudy. A Fog early.
	3 pm	47	SW	Fair.
8	8 am	44	SW	Cloudy. A Fog this Morn:
	3 pm	48.5	W	Fair & brisk wind.
9	8 am	41	W	Fair.
	3 pm	47	NW	do.
10	8 am	31	N	Fair.
	3 pm	38.5	NE	Cloudy.
11	8 am	33.5	NE	Cloudy. A little Snow last Ni: & this Morn:
	3 pm	37.5	NE	do.
12	8 am	36	NW	Cloudy. Hail & Rain last Night.
	3 pm	39	NW	Cloudy & Sunsh: p.m.
13	8 am	35	NE	Cloudy Morn:
	3 pm	39	SW	aft. Sunsh: Cloudy.
14	8 am	36	W	Cloudy. A little Snow about 1 p.m.
	3 pm	34	NW	Windy & fair.
15	8 am	23	S	Fair- Hard Frost:
	3 pm	31	SW	do. & a brisk Wind.
16	8 am	31	NW	Cloudy
	3 pm	37	NW	do. Sunsh: at Interv:
17	8 am	25	NW	Fair.
	3 pm	32	NW	do.
18	8 am	29	NW	Cloudy.
	3 pm	36	NW	do. & windy. Sunsh: at Int:
19	8 am	21	N	Cloudy & Sunsh:
	3 pm	29	NE	Fair.
20	8 am	24	NE	Snow the preced: Night & this Morn:
	3 pm	32	NE	Cloudy and Ra: this aftern:
21	8 am	34	NW	Cloudy. Windy with Rain & Snow last Night.
	3 pm	37.5	NW	Flying Clouds Windy & Sunsh:
22	8 am	35	NW	Flying Clouds & Sunsh:
	3 pm	37.5	NW	Sunsh: & Cloudy.
23	8 am	31	N	Fair.
	3 pm	34	NW	do.

24	8 am	23	NW	Fair.
	3 pm	29	NW	do.
25	8 am	19	N	Sunsh: & Clouds.
	3 pm	29	NE	Cloudy.
26	8 am	33	NE	Stormy with much Rain.
	3 pm	35	NW	Hail & Snow at Times. Cleared in the Ev:
27	8 am	32	NW	Cloudy & Sunsh:
	3 pm	35	NW	do.
28	8 am	28	N	Snow
	3 pm	33	NW	Fair.
29	8 am	26	N	Fair.
	3 pm	31.5	N	do.
30	8 am	31	N	Cloudy.
	3 pm	36	N	do.
31	8 am	32	NE	Cloudy.
	3 pm	36	NE	do.

January 1777

1	8 am	41	E	Foggy & Cloudy.
	3 pm	51	S	Cloudy & Rain at Times.
2	8 am	39	NW	Fair & windy. Rain & wind the preced: Night.
	2 pm	39	NW	Clouds, Sunsh: & windy.
3	8 am	21	NW	Fair & frosty.
	3 pm	—	SW	Fair.
4	8 am	25	SW	Fair.
	3 pm	—	W	Sunsh: & flying Clouds.
5	8 am	26	W	Overcast. A little Snow about Noon.
	3 pm	—	W	Fair.
6	8 am	25	W	Fair.
	3 pm	—	W	Sunsh: & flying Clouds.
7	8 am	25	WbS	Sunsh: & Clouds.
	3 pm		WS?	do.
8	8 am	23.5	W	Sunsh: & Clouds.
	2 pm	30	W	Cloudy.
9	8 am	23	W	Sunsh: & Cloudy.
	3 pm	29	W	Flying Clouds & windy with Snow at Times.
10	8 am	18	SW	Overcast. Delaware full of Ice.
	3 pm	27.5	SW	do.

11	8 am	18	NW	Overcast.
	2 pm	25	N	do. Calm all Day.
12	8 am	15	NW	Fair.
	3 pm	27	W	do.
13	8 am	15	NW	Fair.
	3 pm	26	NW	Overcast.
14	8 am	19	NW	Fair.
	2 pm	28	NW	do.
15	8 am	16	SW	Clouds & Sunsh:
	2 pm	—	SW	Fair.
16	8 am	31	SE	Snow.
	2 pm	35	S	Cloudy.
17	8 am	27	NW	Fair.
	2 pm	31	NW	Cloudy.
18	8 am	14	NW	Fair. High Wind last Night.
	3 pm	—	NW	Fair P.M.
19	8 am	19	SW	Fair.
	2 pm	29	SW	Overcast.
20	8 am	35	SW	Clouds & Sunsh: Windy the preced: Night.
	2 pm	42	SW	Fair & Windy.
21	8 am	30	W	Fair.
	2 pm	—	W	do.
22	8 am	31	N	Sunsh: & Clouds.
	2 pm	—	N	do.
23	8 am	29	NE	Cloudy.
	2 pm	33	NE	do. & Hail.
24	8 am	41	Calm	Foggy & Rainy. Rain most of the preced: Night.
	3 pm	53	SE	About half past 9 a.m. the Wind sprung up strong at SE & continued till near 5 P.M. attended with much Rain, when the wind chang'd to SW & soon after cleared.
25	8 am	38	SW	Fair Morn: afterw:
	3 pm	—	NW	Flying Clouds & Sunshine at Intervals.
	9 pm	40		
26	8 am	35	W	Flying Clouds.
	2 pm		WSW	Do. Sunsh: at Interv:
27	8 am	33	NW	Cloudy. Snow last Night.
	2 pm	38.5	NE	Cloudy.

28	8 am	33	NW	Fair.
	2 pm	—	NW	Clouds & Sunsh:
29	8 am	28	E	Overcast.
	2 pm	35	NE	Cloudy. Snow most of the afternoon.
30	8 am	32	NW	Fair Morn:
	2 pm	—	NW	afterw: flying Clouds and Sunsh: at Interv:
31	8 am	33	NW	Clouds & Sunsh:
	2 pm	—	NW	do.

APPENDIX L

❧ The American March on Trenton, December 26, 1776:
Distance and Time

In reckoning distances marched before the first battle of Trenton, most modern histories have followed Stryker, who believed that "an hour later and a march a mile farther would probably have changed the condition of affairs" (*Battles of Trenton and Princeton*, 146). He reckoned that the marching distance from the river to the Bear Tavern was "about a mile," and from Bear Tavern to Birmingham was "somewhat more than three miles" (140). The two American divisions followed different routes from Birmingham (now West Trenton). Stryker believed that "the distance from Birmingham to Trenton by either route was nearly equal, being between four and five miles, with perhaps a little advantage for General Sullivan's division on the River Road" (143).

Stryker was correct in his first statement but mistaken about the distances. The following estimates are derived by walking the roads, driving modern highways with an odometer, and measuring routes on Topographical Survey Maps in the Pennington and Trenton West Quadrangles. The results indicate that Sullivan's division marched 9.86 miles by the River Road, and Greene's Division marched 11.05 miles by the Scotch Road and Pennington Road. These numbers should be taken as lower-bound estimates, for they follow modern roadlines, which tend to be straighter and therefore shorter than eighteenth-century roads over the same route.

Washington also reckoned the distance from McConkey's Ferry to Trenton at "about nine miles" (Washington to Hancock, *Washington Papers*, 7:454). He estimated the march began at "near four," that Greene's division reached the enemy's advanced post "exactly at eight o'clock," and that he heard firing begin on the River Road "three minutes after." Lieutenant Wiederholdt's advanced post was in Howell's cooper shop, one mile north of the present Battle Monument. Lieutenant Wilhelm von Grothausen's outpost on the River Road was at the Hermitage, one mile northwest of Trenton.

The elapsed marching time (including rests) from McConkey's Ferry to the Hessian outposts was approximately four hours. Average speed was 2.21 miles per hour for Sullivan's brigade and 2.5 miles an hour for Greene's brigade. By all accounts, the last half of the march was more rapid than the first, and Greene's column was "running" or "trotting" as it approached Trenton. The march was a remarkable feat, given the weather, darkness, road conditions, terrain, and trouble with the artillery.

The American March from McConkey's Ferry to Trenton (Statute Miles)

Route	Stryker's Estimate	Roadline Distance
Delaware River to Bear Tavern	1 mi.	1.40 mi.
Bear Tavern to Birmingham	3 mi.	3.75 mi.
Birmingham to Broad Street (via River Road)	4–5 mi.	4.71 mi.
Birmingham to Monument (via Scotch Road)	4–5 mi.	5.90 mi.
Total (via River Road)	8–9 mi.	9.86 mi.
Total (via Scotch Road)	8.9 mi.	11.05 mi.

APPENDIX M

✎ Ratios of Artillery and Infantry in the Battles at Trenton and Princeton

Army and Action	Field Guns	Infantry	Ratio
TRENTON I			
Hessians	6	1,500	1:250
Americans	18	2,400	1:133
TRENTON II			
British and Hessians	28	8,000	1:286
Americans	40	6,000	1:150
PRINCETON			
British	6–8?	1,200	1:200–150?
Americans	35	4,500	1:129

NOTE: Primary sources are variant for the second battle of Trenton and on Princeton. At Trenton II, Knox reported "30 or 40" guns in action at Assunpink Creek. It is reasonable to assume that his high estimate was the total number of guns in the army, and the lower number was his guess of the guns in action at the creek. Many historians believe that Mawhood had two guns at Princeton, but Rodney in his memoir reported eight, probably including six guns on Mercer Hill.

SOURCES: Jac Weller, "Guns of Destiny: Field Artillery in the Trenton-Princeton Campaign, 25 December 1776 to 3 January 1777," *Military Affairs* 29 (1956), 1–15; Henry Knox, Papers, at Boston Athenaeum and MHS; Thomas Rodney, *The Diary of Captain Thomas Rodney, 1776–1777*, ed. Caesar A. Rodney, *Papers of the Historical Society of Delaware*, vol. 1, paper 8 (Wilmington, 1888; rpt. New York, 1974); J[oseph] White, *A Narrative of Events, as They Occurred from Time to Time, in the Revolutionary War, with an account of the Battles of Trenton, Trenton-Bridge, and Princeton* (Charlestown, Mass., 1833; rpt. *American Heritage*, June 1956), 74–79.

APPENDIX N

❧ Casualties in the First Battle of Trenton,
December 26, 1776

1. Hessian Losses: American Estimates

Killed in action	22
Severely wounded	84
Captured and returned to Philadelphia	868
Captured and left in Trenton on parole	28
Captured total (including wounded)	896
Total killed, wounded and captured	918

NOTE: The American count of prisoners of war included wounded men. The total list counts each man only once: 22 killed, 84 severely wounded, and 812 captured and not severely wounded. Of the wounded Hessians, 28 were thought to be too ill to move and were left in Trenton on parole; 56 were carried to Philadelphia. Sources include Stryker, 196.

Washington to John Hancock, 27 Dec. 1776, with attached list in the handwriting of Tench Tilghman not published in *GW* 7:454–61.

2. Hessian Losses: Hessian Estimates

	Killed	Wounded	Captured	Total
Officers	5	5	23	28
Noncoms	1	3	84	85
Privates & Music	16	75	784	800
Total	22	83	891	913

NOTE: "Captured" includes wounded; "Killed" includes missing. The source is Smith, *Trenton*, who follows the Hessian estimates; and Stryker, *Battles of Trenton and Princeton*, 195–96, 408–9; a variant Hessian estimate (Atwood, *Hessians*, 95) reports 939 casualties (20 killed and 919 captured).

3. Hessian Losses: British Estimates

Sir George Osburn, muster master general of the British army, reported in official returns that total losses at Trenton were 700, a gross undercount typical of official British casualty reports during the American War of Independence. General Howe in his reports was more honest and adopted the American estimate of 918 casualties as his own. The source is Stryker, *Battles of Trenton and Princeton*, 195–96, 408–9.

4. Hessian Officers Killed and Severely Wounded

Colonel Johann Rall (brigade commander), severely wounded, was carried to the Trenton church, then to his quarters, where Washington visited him; he died on December 27, 1776, and is said to have been buried in Trenton. The site of his grave is lost.

Major Friedrich Ludwig von Dechow (acting commander, von Knyphausen Regiment), mortally wounded in left hip, died on December 27, 1776.

Captain Johann Casper von Riess (Lossberg), killed in action by musket or rifle fire.

Captain Friedrich Wilhelm von Benning (Lossberg), killed in action.

Captain Ernst Eberhard von Altenbockum (Lossberg), severely wounded in the head.

Lieutenant Georg Christoph Kimm (Lossberg), killed in action.

Lieutenant Hermann Zoll (Lossberg), seriously wounded in the spine.

Lieutenant Ernst Schwabe (Lossberg), seriously wounded in the thigh.

Lieutenant Harnickel (Rall), seriously wounded.

Lieutenant Kuehnen (Rall), mortally wounded.

Ensign Ludwig Ferdinand von Geyso (Lossberg), lightly wounded, not counted in casualty lists.

Ensign Christian August von Hobe[n?] (Lossberg), lightly wounded in the leg.

SOURCES: Jakob Piel, Diary, 28 Dec. 1776; Slagle, "Von Lossberg Regiment," 95–96; Richard C. Barth, William E. Dornemann, and Mark Schalm, "The Trenton Prisoner List," *JSHAJ* 3 (1985), 1; Smith, *Trenton*, 27.

5.   American Losses

George Washington wrote to Colonel John Cadwalader on December 27, 1776: "not more than a private or two killed, One or two wounded, & Captn Washington." To John Hancock on the same day, Washington reported, "Our loss is very trifling indeed, only two officers and one or two privates wounded." Tench Tilghman wrote, "Only Capt. Washington and his Lieutenant slightly wounded and two privates killed and two wounded." Leven Powell added, "Ensign [James] Buxton wounded, in the 4th Virginia Regiment." A New Jersey resident, Richard Scudder, reported that "two or three" American soldiers died in his house of illness or exposure. Greenwood reported that two soldiers froze to death on the road to Trenton. Sources include *GW* 7:450, 454; Tilghman, *Memoir*, 460; Powell, *Leven Powell*, 41–43; Dwyer, *The Day Is Ours!*, 271; Smith, *Princeton*, 27. In summary, the evidence indicates that two privates were killed in action, at least four or five died of exposure or illness, and three officers and two privates were wounded. A variant estimate by Peckham estimated American losses at four killed and eight wounded (Howard H. Peckham, *The Toll of Independence* [Chicago, 1974], 27).

APPENDIX O

❧ Hessian Plans for Trenton and the Surrounding Countryside

Valuable sources for the first battle of Trenton, and also for American social history, are "plans" that Hessian troops made of the town and the surrounding countryside. Three officers who fought in the battle submitted sketch-maps to the Hessian court of inquiry in 1778. They were Lieutenant Jakob Piel, Rall's brigade adjutant at Trenton; Lieutenant Andreas Wiederholdt of the Knyphausen regiment, who commanded the outpost on the Pennington Road where the battle began; and Lieutenant Friedrich Fischer of the Hessian artillery. The three officers also testified before the court; Piel and Wiederholdt wrote journals, which are important sources. The originals of these sketch-maps are in the Hessian archives at Marburg; photocopies are in the Library of Congress at Washington. William Stryker thought that Fischer's map was "in some particulars the best in the series." It is reproduced from photoengravings in Stryker's *Battles of Trenton and Princeton*, 123ff. Fischer's plan included a key, retranslated here:

Plan

Of the affair at Trenton, on the 26th of December 1776, between the American Provincial Troops under the command of General Washington, and three Hessian Regiments under the command of the fallen Colonel Rall, which were compelled to surrender as prisoners of war.

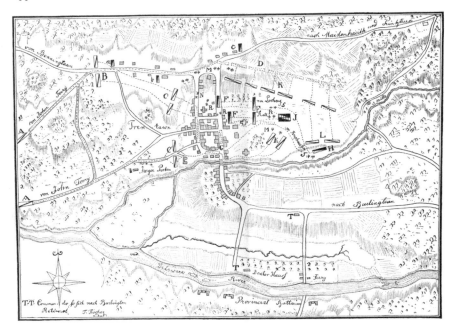

The Fischer Plan of Trenton. Plan of Trenton, December 26, 1776, drawn by
Lieutenant Friedrich Fischer, Hessian Artillery. Photoengraving for William
Stryker, *The Battles of Trenton and Princeton* (1898), 128–29.

Explanation

AA. The march of the Provincial troops in two columns from John's Ferry [the Hessian
name for both McConkey's and Johnson's ferries]

B. Advance on Picket a and Captain v. Altenbockum's company b.

CC. Attack on Trenton after the picket and Captain von Altenbockum's company, and the
captain's picket retreated to Trenton

D. Deployment of the Provincial Troops in line of battle

E. Formation of the Hessian Regiments after leaving Trenton

FF. Attack of the two regiments, von Losberg and Rall, toward Trenton

G. Provincial Troops who seized the bridge

H. Retreat of the von Knyphausen Regiment at the time when the von Losberg and Rall
Regiments attacked [into] the town

J. Retreat of the Regiments von Losberg and Rall

KK. Attack of the Provincial Troops on J.

L. Attack on H after the two Regiments von Losberg and Rall surrendered

M. Provincial Artillery

N. Rall Cannon which were defeated early in the battle

RRR. Von Knyphausen Cannon

SS. Von Losberg Cannon

TT. Forces that retreated to Burlington

The sketch was done with great care, but contains some inaccuracies. Stryker noted as an error that "there was no church near the creek, in the line of march of the von Knyphausen regiment." Fischer was trying to represent the Quaker meetinghouse; his error was not in the location of the church symbol itself, but in the proportions of the town and the lines of the streets. All sketches misrepresented the angle that Queen Street made after it crossed Assunpink Bridge, because the orientation of the town, the river, and the creek are not quite correct. It is interesting that this minor error was common to all three maps: evidence of cooperation (even collusion) before the court of inquiry. In the same spirit, Hessian deponents also agreed that they were attacked by six thousand Americans (a gross error), which suggests that they tried to get their story straight before they testified. The maps reflect this effort. But in general the sketches are accurate and truthful, and give us much information about the battle, the town, and the countryside.

APPENDIX P

❧ American Dispositions in New Jersey, January 1, 1777

Continental Army (General George Washington)

North Trenton Force: Sullivan's Division (Maj. Gen. John Sullivan), 1200–1400 men
    St. Clair's Brigade (Brig. Gen. Arthur St. Clair), remnants of 13 New England regiments under St Clair's command; Washington estimated their strength at less than 100 men per regiment:
        Stark's New Hampshire Continental Regiment (Col. John Stark)
        Reed's New Hampshire Continental Regiment (Col. James Reed, absent)
        Poor's New Hampshire Continental Regiment (Col. Enoch Poor)
        Paterson's 1st Massachusetts Continental Regiment (Col. John Paterson)
    Glover's Brigade remnants combined with St. Clair's Brigade
        Shepard's 4th Massachusetts Continentals, remnant
        Webb's 19th Massachusetts Continentals, remnant
        Glover's 14th Massachusetts Continentals, remnant
        Bailey's Massachusetts Continentals, remnant
    Sargent's Brigade remnants combined with St. Clair's Brigade
        Sargent's 16th Massachusetts Continental Regiment (Col. Paul Dudley Sargent)
        Ward's Connecticut Regiment (Col. Andrew Ward)
        Connecticut State Troops (Col. John Chester)
        Read's 13th Massachusetts Continentals (Col. Joseph Read)

Central Trenton Force: Greene's Division (Maj. Gen. Nathanael Greene), 1,400 men
    Mercer's Brigade (Brig. Gen. Hugh Mercer), 300 men
        Smallwood's Maryland Continental Regiment (Capt. John Stone), 50? men
        Miles's Pennsylvania Rifle Regiment (Maj. Ennion Williams), 200 men
        Rawling's Maryland and Virginia Rifle Regiment (Col. Moses Rawlings), 75 men
        New Jersey State Artillery (Capt. John Niel), 2 guns
    Stirling's Brigade (remnants attached to Mercer's Brigade), 50 men
        Haslet's Delaware Continental Regiment (Col. John Haslet), 5 men
        Read's 1st Virginia Continental Regiment (Capt. John Fleming), 20 men
        Weedon's 3rd Virginia Regiment (Col. George Weedon), departing
        Williams's 6th Maryland Regiment (Col. Otho Holland Williams), departing

Stephen's Brigade (Col. Charles Scott), 400 men
  Scott's 5th Virginia Continental Regiment (Maj. Josiah Parker)
  Elliott's 4th Virginia Continental Regiment (Lt. Col. Robert Lawson)
  Buckner's 6th Virginia Continental Regiment (Maj. Richard Parker)
Fermoy's Brigade (Brig. Gen. Mathias-Alexis Roche-Fermoy), 610
  Pennsylvania and Maryland German Regiment (Col. Nicholas Haussegger), 410
  Hand's 1st Pennsylvania Rifle Regiment (Col. Edward Hand), 200

South Trenton Force (Brig. Gen. James Ewing), 600 men
  Ewing's Brigade, Pennsylvania Militia (Brig. Gen. James Ewing)
    Cumberland County Militia (Col. Frederick Watts)
    Lancaster County Militia (Col. Jacob Klotz)
    Cumberland County Militia (Col. William Montgomery)
    York County Militia (Col. Richard McAllister)
    Bucks County Militia (Col. Joseph Hart)

Crosswicks Force (Brig. Gen. John Cadwalader), 1500 men
  Cadwalader's Brigade, Philadelphia Associators (Brig. John Cadwalader), 1,150 men
    Morgan's Philadelphia Militia Regiment (Col. Jacob Morgan)
    Bayard's Philadelphia Militia Regiment (Col. John Bayard)
    Nixon's Philadelphia Militia Regiment (Col. John Nixon)
    Matlack's Philadelphia Rifle Battalion (Col. Timothy Matlack)
    Henry's Philadelphia Light Infantry (Capt. George Henry)
    Chester County Militia (Commander Unknown)
    Kent County Delaware Militia (Capt. Thomas Rodney)
    Marines (Maj. Samuel Nicholas)
    Pennsylvania Artillery (Capt. Joseph Moulder), 2 six-pounders; 2 three-pounders
  Hitchcock's Brigade (Maj. Israel Angell), 353 men
    Lippitt's Rhode Island Regiment (Col. Christopher Lippitt), 160
    Hitchcock's Rhode Island Continental Regiment (Col. Daniel Hitchcock), 120
    Varnum's Rhode Island Continental Regiment (Col. James Varnum), 7
    Nixon's 4th Massachusetts Continentals (Col. John Nixon), 63
    Little's 12th Massachusetts Continentals (Col. Moses Little), 3

Bordentown Force (Gen. Thomas Mifflin), 1,800 men
  Mifflin's Brigade Pennsylvania Continentals (Brig. Thomas Mifflin), 1,500 men
    De Haas's 2nd Pennsylvania Continental Regiment (Col. Philip De Haas)
    Brodhead's 4th Pennsylvania Continental Regiment (Col. Daniel Brodhead)
    Penrose's 10th Pennsylvania Continental Regiment (Col. Joseph Penrose)
    Humpton's 11th Pennsylvania Continental Regiment (Col. Richard Humpton)
    Cooke's 12th Pennsylvania Continental Rifle Regiment (Col. William Cooke)

South Jersey Force, 500 men
  Griffin's Brigade, New Jersey Militia (Col. Silas Newcombe), 500 men
    Cumberland County Militia (Col. Silas Newcomb)
    Cumberland County Militia (Col. David Potter)
    Ellis's Gloucester County Militia (Col. Joseph Ellis)
    Somers' Gloucester County Militia (Col. Richard Somers)
    Dick's Salem County Militia (Col. Samuel Dick)

New Jersey troops not concentrating at Trenton:
Morristown and Pluckemin Force (Brig. Gen. Alexander McDougall), 750 men
  McDougall's Brigade (Brig. Gen. Alexander McDougall), 750 men
    Greaton's Massachusetts Continentals (Col. John Greaton)

Bond's Massachusetts Continentals (Col. William Bond)
Porter's Massachusetts Militia (Col. Elisha Porter)
New Jersey Militia at Morristown (Col. Jacob Ford)
New Jersey Militia at Pluckemin (Col. William Winds)

Total assembled at Trenton January 1, 1777, 6,900 men
Total at Trenton and Morristown, 7,750 men

NOTE: Washington himself did not know how many men he had under his command on January 1, 1777. He wrote to Hancock that day, "I have not been able to procure returns of our force owing to our situation; I suppose that about two or three and twenty hundred passed with me, which number is now reduced to Fifteen or Sixteen hundred. No estimate of our force can be formed from the number of Regiments; many of 'em by reason of sickness cannot turn out more than a hundred men." His count of 2,200 to 2,300 included some of Greene's and Sullivan's divisions who crossed at McConkey's and Yardley's ferries, but not all of them. See Washington to John Hancock, 1 Jan. 1777, *GW* 7:491–95, 503–5.

SOURCES: These estimates derive from data gathered from muster rolls and ration strengths by Samuel Stelle Smith, *The Battle of Princeton* (Monmouth Beach, N.J., 1967), 34–36; corrected by Lesser, *The Sinews of Independence: Monthly Strength Reports of the Continental Army* (Chicago, 1976), 43–45; Cadwalader to Washington, 31 Dec. 1776, and Washington to John Hancock, 1 Jan. 1777, *GW* 7:491–95, 503–5; and materials from Thomas Rodney, James Wilkinson, Sergeant R——, Howland, Olney, and St. Clair.

APPENDIX Q

~ British and Hessian Order of March, Princeton to Trenton, January 2, 1777

Cornwallis's Division (Lt. Gen. Charles Cornwallis)

Vanguard (Col. Carl von Donop)
    Hessian Jäger Corps, Foot, 1 company (Capt. Johann Ewald)
    Hessian Jäger Corps, Mounted, 1 company (Capt. Friedrich Lorey)
    Hessian Grenadiers (100 picked men)
    16th Light Dragoons, 2 troops
Light Infantry Brigade (General Grant)
    1st Light Infantry Battalion (Maj. Thomas Musgrave)
    2nd Light Infantry Battalion (Maj. John Maitland)
    Grenadier Battalion Köhler (Lt. Col. Johann Köhler)
    42nd Foot (Royal Highland Regiment), Lt. Col. Thomas Stirling
    71st Foot (Scotch Regiment)
Artillery
    "a number of six-pounders"
British Grenadiers and Guards Brigade (Lt. Col. the Hon. Henry Monckton)
    1st British Grenadier Battalion (Lt. Col. William Medows)
    2nd British Grenadier Battalion (Lt. Col. Henry Monckton)
    2nd British Guards Battalion (Lt. Col. James Ogilvie)

Hessian Brigade Grenadiers and Fusiliers
    Grenadier Battalion Linsing (Lt. Col. Otto von Linsing)
    Grenadier Battalion Block (Lt. Col. Henrich von Bloch)
    Grenadier Battalion Minnigerode (Lt. Col. Friedrich von Minnegerode)
    Fusilier Battalion Loos (Col. Johann von Loos)
    (Remnants of the Former Hessian Garrison at Trenton)
Second British Brigade (Brigadier Alexander Leslie)
    5th Foot (Lt. Col. William Walcott)
    28th Foot (Lt. Col. Robert Prescott)
    35th Foot (Lt. Col. James Cockburne)
    49th Foot (Major Thomas Dilkes?)
Artillery Train

Reserve at Princeton:

Fourth British Brigade (Lt. Col. Charles Mawhood)
    17th Foot (Lt. Col. Charles Mawhood)
    40th Foot (Maj. Samuel Bradstreet)
    55th Foot (Maj. Cornelius Cuyler)
    Royal Artillery, 6 guns
Cavalry
    16th Light Dragoons, 1 troop mounted
    16th Light Dragoons, 3? troops, dismounted)
Miscellaneous Regimental Draughts and Details (Captain Philips, Captain Hale)

NOTE: The strength of Cornwallis's force on the march to Trenton was estimated by Münchausen at 7,000 men. A modern estimate by Samuel Stelle Smith makes it approximately 8,000 men in Cornwallis's divisions, plus 1,500 men in Leslie's Fourth Brigade, for a total of 9,500 men. The troops at Princeton were approximately 1,500 men. Washington believed that he was facing an attacking force of 8,000 men, with 4,000 men in reserve—evidence of the growing efficiency of his intelligence.

Other British and German troops in New Jersey included 4,000 men in seven garrisons: the Brunswick and Raritan Landing Garrison of the 46th Foot and the 1st and 2nd Guards Battalions (Brig. Gen. Mathew), some of which marched with the Elizabeth Garrison of the Waldeck Regiment and elements of the 71st Foot (Gen. Vaughan); the Amboy Garrison of the 33rd and 57th Foot; and the Hackensack–New Bridge Garrison of the 7th and 26th Foot. The New York Garrison included the 4th, 27th, and 45th Foot of the First British Brigade, and Hessian troops. The 3rd and 5th Brigades and seven Hessian battalions continued in Rhode Island.

SOURCES: Johann Ewald, *Diary of the American War: A Hessian Journal*, ed. Joseph P. Tustin (New Haven, 1979), 48; *Kemble Papers*, vol. 1; Friedrich von Münchausen, *At General Howe's Side, 1776–1778: The Diary of General William Howe's Aide-de-Camp, Captain Friedrich von Muenchausen*, trans. Ernest Kipping, ann. Samuel Stelle Smith (Monmouth Beach, N.J., 1974), 8–10; Samuel Stelle Smith, *The Battle of Princeton* (Monmouth Beach, N.J., 1967), 37; William S. Stryker, *The Battles of Trenton and Princeton* (Boston, 1898), 430–31.

APPENDIX R

❧ Casualties in the Second Battle of Trenton,
January 1–2, 1777

This engagement was a series of actions along the Princeton-Trenton Road, through the town of Trenton, and at Assunpink Creek, where British and Hessian troops launched a series of probing attacks. No official British casualty reports have been found, but participants on both sides left many records of losses on both sides.

On the Princeton-Trenton Road, Captain Johann Ewald recorded a stubborn engagement on January 1, 1777, at "the pass," with "about 140 men lost on both sides." He recorded that seven Jägers were lost in his corps (Ewald, 48).

On January 2, Ewald wrote that Lieutenant von Grothausen was shot dead on the Trenton highway, "along with several Jägers" (49). At Shabakunk Creek, another action took place, with many troops involved on both sides, but no record of casualties survives. At Stockton Hollow, Howard Peckham counted American losses in that action at 6 killed and 10 wounded; and British and German and British casualties of "at least" 10 killed, 20 wounded, and 25 captured (Peckham, 29).

In the fighting along Assunpink Creek, many participants recorded major casualties on both sides. Ewald observed that "many men were killed and wounded on both sides" (49). A Connecticut officer counted "150 British casualties" (Bill, 87); Captain Thomas Rodney of the Delaware light infantry wrote, "We lost but a few men, the enemy considerably more," and "were repulsed each time with great slaughter" (Rodney, 31). William Hutchinson wrote of the fighting near Assunpink Bridge that "a certain Hugh Coppell and myself passed over the ground which they had occupied during the battle and their attacks upon us. Their dead bodies lay thicker and closer together for a space than I ever beheld sheaves of wheat lying in a field which the reapers had just passed" (in Dann, 146). Dr. Benjamin Rush reported that American houses in South Trenton were made into a hospital, "filling steadily with wounded men" (Rush, Autobiography).

Hessian Grenadier battalions reported losing 61 men in one attack at the Creek (8 killed, 24 wounded, and 29 captured). The Block battalion reported lost 6 dead or dying and 13 wounded; the Minnegerode battalion reported 14 dead and dying with no estimate of wounded (Smith, 17).

Several historians have tried to make a general estimate of casualties for the entire engagement. Alfred Hoyt Bill reported an estimate of "British killed and wounded in this 'second battle of Trenton' at not less than five hundred" (Bill, *The Campaign of Princeton*, 87). Dwyer favored a range and wrote that "overall British losses were heavy, and possibly for that reason never revealed. Estimates would range from 150 to 500" (Dwyer, 326). Ketchum agreed (p. 290).

This historian believes that American losses were heavier than historians have recognized. Adding casualties on the Trenton Road, fighting in the town of Trenton, and prisoners taken there, especially among Maryland and Pennsylvania Germans, the fighting along the creek, and losses to artillery that Dr. Rush reported, American losses in killed, wounded, and prisoners would have been at least 100 killed, wounded, and captured, probably more.

Among Hessian troops, especially Jägers and grenadiers, a minimum of 140 casualties can be identified in the sources listed above, as killed, wounded, and captured along the Princeton Road and Assunpink Creek. British casualties were at least 75 on the Trenton Road and 150 at Assunpink Creek. Overall this would yield total losses of 100 Americans, 140 Hessians, and 225 British troops in the second battle of Trenton.

SOURCES: Johann Ewald, *Diary of the American War: A Hessian Journal*, ed. Joseph P. Tustin (New Haven, 1979); Thomas Rodney, *The Diary of Captain Thomas Rodney, 1776–1777*, ed. Caesar A. Rodney, *Papers of the Historical Society of Delaware*, vol. 1, paper 8 (Wilmington, 1888; rpt. New York, 1974), ms. diary, 1776–77, LC; William Hutchinson, Pension Narrative, in John C. Dann, ed., *The Revolution Remembered: Eyewitness Accounts of the War of Independence* (Chicago, 1980); Benjamin Rush, *Autobiography*, ed. George W. Corner (Princeton, 1948); Howard H. Peckham, *The Toll of Independence: Engagements and Battle Casualties of the American Revolution* (Chicago, 1974); Alfred Hoyt Bill, *The Campaign of Princeton, 1776–1777* (Princeton, 1948); Samuel Stelle Smith, *The Battle of Princeton* (Monmouth Beach, N.J., 1967); William M. Dwyer, *The Day Is Ours!* (New York, 1983).

APPENDIX S

☙ Casualties in the Battle of Princeton, January 3, 1777

1. British Losses, Killed and Wounded:

     For the battle at the Clark farm, we have the following evidence from two British officers, Inman in the 17th Foot and Hale with the drafts of replacements for other units. Together they give a very full and accurate report of British losses, which is consistent with American reports and much higher than the official British casualty figures.

Unit	Strength	Killed and Wounded	Source
17th Foot	224 r&f	101	Inman
	[246 all]	[121]	Smith
Grenadiers	32 all	17	Hale
Light Infantry	50 all	[25?]	Rodney
Dragoons (foot)	50 all	[25?]	White
Highlanders	[50 all?]	[25?]	Fischer
Artillery	[20 all?]	[10]	Smith
Total	[446]	[232]	Fischer

NOTE: "r&f" is rank and file; "all" includes officers; estimated by historians are in brackets.

SOURCES: See below, 414.

2. Official British Casualty Reports
   General Howe's staff reported lower numbers of killed and wounded

Unit	Killed	Wounded	Total
17th Foot all	13	53	66
40th Foot all	0	1	1
55th Foot all	5	4	9
Total	18	58	76

     Howe reported overall 1 captain, 1 sergeant, 16 rank and file killed; 1 captain, 2 lieutenants, 2 ensigns, 5 sergeants, 48 rank and file wounded, 1 captain, 1 lieutenant, 2 ensigns, 5 sergeants, 4 drummers, 187 rank and file missing, total 276.
     He reported losses by regiment for the 17th Foot of 13 killed, 53 wounded, 35 missing; for the 40th Foot, 1 wounded, 93 missing; for the 55th Foot, 5 killed, 4 wounded, 72 missing. Stryker (458) adds 10 killed in the Royal Artillery.

Official British estimates undercounted killed and wounded in the 17th Foot and omitted other units engaged in the battle at Princeton who took nearly half of the British casualties.

SOURCE: *Kemble Papers*, 1:107; and "Returns of Killed, Wounded, and Missing," 3 Jan. 1777, PRO.

3. American Estimates of British Losses
    American leaders reported much greater British losses. Washington wrote to Hancock, "These three Regiments, especially the Two first, made a gallant resistance, and in killed, wounded, and Prisoners must have lost 500 men; upwards of 100 were left dead on the field, and, with what I have with me & what were taken in the pursuit and carried across the Delaware, there are near three hundred prisoners, fourteen of which are Officers, all British" (*GW* 8:521).
    A letter from the American army reported "one hundred of their wounded prisoners in the town, which together with those who surrendered and were taken in small parties endeavoring to make their escape, I think must amount to the number of 400, chiefly British troops."
    Rodney wrote that the enemy left "about 100 men killed" (36).

4. Estimates by Historians
    Peckham estimated that British losses were 28 killed, 58 wounded, and 129 "or more" captured of forces totaling 1,200 (for the entire brigade, not counting other detachments, apparently). Peckham appears to have followed the inaccurate estimates of Howe's staff, with a copying error for the number of killed (Peckham, 29). Smith and Dwyer followed the official estimates and were not aware of Hale's account.

5. Burials at the Princeton Stone Quarry
    The Lawrence narrative (*Ravages at Princeton*, 33) reports that "there was thirty Six dead men the next day buried in a Stone Quarry, among whom was 15 of Genl. Washington's men, the other 21 were Regulars, besides three of them that lay dead in or near the main road." Men from both sides were also "buryed in other places."

6. British Troops Captured
    Howe reported 187 British troops missing. Washington reported capturing between 200 and 300 men, all British. One draft alone included 211 British privates, "lately taken in the Jersies," who were sent as prisoners of war to Connecticut (Washington to Samuel Blachley Webb, 8 Jan. 1777, *GW* 8:16). Robert Beale guarded "about 260" prisoners after the battle (57).

7. Total British Losses: Killed, Wounded, Captured, Missing
    Howe estimated 276 at Princeton (17th, 40th, and 55th Foot only), omitting other detachments who suffered circa 102 casualties; Washington, 500 at Princeton for the entire British force. Our best estimate is approximately 450 casualties.

8. American Losses: Estimates by Participants
    Washington reported, "Our loss in slain is 6 or 7 officers and about 25 or thirty privates; the number of wounded is not ascertained." In another letter he raised the number of officers killed to nine, and in a third he wrote, "Our whole loss cannot be ascertained, as many who were in pursuit of the enemy (who were chased three or four miles) are not yet come in."
    Rodney estimated "we lost about 20 killed."

9. American Losses: Estimates by Historians

Peckham estimated American losses at 23 killed, 20 wounded, 1 captured; Smith and Dwyer reported Washington's estimate of between 31 and 37 killed. Sources include Peckham, 29; Smith, 32; Dwyer, 353.

Our best estimate is 31 to 37 killed, probably about the same number or more wounded, and 1 captured.

10. American Losses: Officers Killed or Mortally Wounded

American officers known to have been killed or mortally wounded include:

General Hugh Mercer; Colonel John Haslet; Captain Daniel Neil, New Jersey Artillery; Captain John Fleming, 1st Virginia Infantry; Captain William Shippin, Marines; Lieutenant Bartholemew Yates, 1st Virginia Infantry; Ensign Anthony Morris Jr., Philadelphia Associators; Lieutenant Morgan, Philadelphia Associators. One American reported killed by Washington, Colonel James Potter, was wounded and captured (Smith, 32).

SOURCES: George Inman, "Ensign George Inman's Narrative of the American Revolution," *PMHB* 7 (1883), 237–48; John William Hale, "Letters Written During the American War of Independence," in H. C. Wylly, ed., *1913 Regimental Annual, The Sherwood Foresters . . .* (London, 1913), 9–59; Thomas Rodney, *The Diary of Captain Thomas Rodney, 1776–1777*, ed. Caesar A. Rodney, *Papers of the Historical Society of Delaware*, vol. 1, paper 8 (Wilmington, 1888; rpt. New York, 1974); ms. diary, 1776–77, LC; John Smith, "Sergeant John Smith's Diary of 1776," ed. Louise Rau, *Mississippi Valley Historical Review* 20 (1933), 247–70; Joseph White, *A Narrative of Events . . .* (Charlestown, Mass., 1833, rpt. *American Heritage*, June 1956), 74–79; Stephen Kemble, *The Kemble Papers*, 2 vols., NYHS *Collections* (New York, 1884–85); *GW*; [Robert Lawrence], *A Brief Narrative of the Ravages of the British and Hessians at Princeton in 1776–77*, ed. Varnum Lansing Collins (Princeton, 1906; rpt. New York, 1968); Howard H. Peckham, *The Toll of Independence: Engagements and Battle Casualties of the American Revolution* (Chicago, 1974); Samuel Stelle Smith, *The Battle of Princeton* (Monmouth Beach, N.J., 1967); William M. Dwyer, *The Day Is Ours!* (New York, 1983).

APPENDIX T

↩ The Forage War: Engagements and Casualties, January 4–March 30, 1777

The King's Highway near Ten Mile Run, Jan. 4: British convoy attacked by Stryker's Somerset Horse; 3 British and "numerous wagons" captured; American losses unknown (Peckham, 29)

Elizabethtown, Jan. 5: British cavalry attacked by militia; 1 trooper killed, 1 wounded; American casualties unknown (Alden et al.)

Spanktown (Rahway, N.J.), Jan. 5: Jersey militia attacked a British forage party; British, 1 killed, 3 wounded; American losses unknown (Peckham, 29)

Newark, Jan. 5 (Alden et al.)

Bound Brook, Jan. 6 (Alden et al.)

Elizabethtown, Jan. 6: Jersey militia attacked a patrol of 50 Waldeck Infantry, who lost 8 or 10 killed and wounded, 40 or 42 captured; American losses unknown (Peckham, 29)

Elizabethtown, Jan. 7: rear guard of retreating garrison attacked; 100 killed or captured

Spanktown (Rahway), Jan. 8 (Alden et al.)

Chatham, Jan. 10: Scott's Virginia Continentals intercepted a British foraging party, captured 70 Highlanders, and took "a large number of baggage wagons" (Ward, 28)

Connecticut Farms, ca. Jan. 15: 300 Jersey militia (Col. Oliver Spencer) attacked 100 Germans, who lost 1 killed, 70 captured; American losses unknown (Peckham, 29)

Bonhamtown, Jan. 16: 350 Americans attacked a larger British force; British losses, 21 killed, 30–40 wounded; American losses unknown (Peckham, 29)

Quibbletown, Jan. 16 (Alden et al.)

New Brunswick, Jan. 17: 200 American troops attacked picket guard and were driven off; American losses, 3 killed, 30 captured; British losses unknown (Peckham, 29)

Van Nest's Mill, Millstone River, Jan. 20: 400 Jersey militia and 50 Pennsylvania Riflemen under Gen. Philemon Dickinson against 500 or 600 British troops, who lost 24 or 25 killed and wounded and 12 prisoners. American casualties were 4 or 5 men (George Washington to John Hancock, 22 Jan. 1777, *GW* 8:125; an accurate British report is Robertson, 20 Jan. 1777; a grossly inaccurate account at Howe's headquarters appears in *Kemble Papers* 1:108; newspaper reports include *Pennsylvania Journal and Weekly Advertiser*, 29 Jan. 1777; *Pennsylvania Packet*, 18 Feb. 1777; Lobdell, "Six Generals," 35)

Somerset Court House, Jan. 20 (Alden et al.)

Raritan River, Jan. 20 (Alden et al.)

Somerset Court House, Jan. 22 (Alden et al.)

Woodbridge, Jan. 23: About 200 of Maxwell's Continental Brigade attacked two British regiments; British losses, 7 killed, 12 wounded; American losses, 2 wounded (Washington to Hancock, 26 Jan. 1777, Washington to William Livingston, 3 Feb. 1777, *GW* 8:161, 234; report of an anonymous American officer in Williamsburg *Virginia Gazette* (Purdie), 28 Feb. 1777; for a British account, *Kemble Papers* 1:108, 22 Jan. 1777; Ward, 55; Peckham, 30)

Bonhamtown, Jan. 23 (Alden et al.)

Morristown, Jan. 23: 200 Virginians led by Col. Charles Scott attacked British and Germans; American losses, 8 killed; British suffered "several casualties" (Peckham 30; Ward)

Quibbletown (Newmarket), Jan. 23/24?: 350 Virginia troops attacked 600 British troops; American losses, 4 wounded; British losses, "heavy" (Peckham, 30)

Second River, Jan. 27 (Alden et al.)

Near Quibbletown, Jan. 30: 300 American troops fought a British foraging party; Americans lost 7 killed; British lost "several casualties" (Peckham, 30)

Drake's Farm, Feb. 1: Sir William Erskine set a trap for 5th Virginia Continentals; in hard fighting, the British forces left 36 killed on the field and "upwards of 100 wounded"; Americans reckoned their losses at between 30 and 40 (Washington to William Livingston, 3 Feb. 1777, Washington to John Hancock, 5 Feb. 1777, *GW* 8:234–35, 250; and *Pennsylvania Evening Post*, 6 Feb. 1777. Many eyewitness accounts appeared in Virginia newspapers, including Purdie's *Virginia Gazette*, 28 Feb., 14 Mar. 1777, and Dixon and Hunter's *Virginia Gazette*, 21 Feb. 1777; for British accounts, see *Kemble Papers* 1:109 (1 Feb. 1777) and *New-York Gazette*, 10 Feb 1777. For a history, Lobdell, "Two Forgotten Battles," 226–30.)

Piscataway, Feb. 1 (Alden et al.)

Metuchen, Feb. 1 (Alden et al.)

The Roundabouts, Raritan River below New Brunswick, Feb. 4–5: A detachment of riflemen from the Bedford (Pa.) Associators, sent from Gen. Israel Putnam's command in Princeton, attacked British boats "waiting for the tide" and killed at least three men (Putnam to Washington, 8 Feb. 1777, *GW* 8:278–80; the report of the Bedford commanders, Capt. William Macalevy, William Parker, and Samuel Davidson, to Putnam, 7 Feb. 1777, is in the Washington Papers, LC)

Bound Brook, Feb. 6 (Alden et al.)

Quibbletown, Feb. 8: A force of 12 British and German battalions fought American militia and Continentals; British losses unknown; Americans lost 12 killed, 6 captured (for British accounts, Robertson, 124 (8 Feb. 1777; *New-York Gazette*, 17 Feb. 1777; for American accounts, Philemon Dickinson to Washington, 9 Feb. 1777, *GW* 8:286; Lobdell,"Six Generals," 35)

Highlands of Neversink, Feb. 12 (Lobdell, "Six Generals," 35)

Brunswick, Feb. 15 (Alden et al.)

Quibbletown, Feb. 18 (Alden et al.)

Elizabethtown, Feb. 18 (Alden et al.)

Bennet's Island, Feb. 18 (Alden et al.)

Quibbletown, Feb. 20: 2 British soldiers killed (Lobdell,"Six Generals," 36; Peckham, 31; Alden et al.)

Paulus Hook, Feb. 22: HMS *Dependence* (Lt. Clark) moored to avoid ice; Americans attempted to cut mooring lines; a fight followed; casualties unknown (Peckham, 31)

Spanktown, Feb. 23: A reinforced British brigade (Col. Charles Mawhood) fought American militia and Continentals (Gen. Wm. Maxwell); British losses, 69 killed and wounded, 6 missing (100 by American count); American losses, 5 killed, 9 wounded. (Peeble, 24 Feb. 1777, 98; Lobdell, "Two Forgotten Battles," 230–34)

Ash Swamp, Feb. 23 (Alden et al.)

Elizabethtown, Feb. 24 (Alden et al.)

Brunswick, Feb. 26 (Alden et al.)

Elizabethtown, Feb. 27 (Alden et al.)

Piscataway, March 1 (Lobdell, "Six Generals," 36)

Brunswick, March 5: German outpost attacked and picket guards "drove in"; losses unknown (Peckham, 31)

Elizabethtown, March 6: Loyalists (Maj. Robert Timpany) attacked American troops; 2 Americans killed, 4 captured; Loyalist losses unknown (Peckham, 31)

Bonhamtown, March 8: Large British force of 2,000 attacked by Gen. William Maxwell; British losses, 20 killed, 40 wounded; 3 Americans wounded (Ward, 57; *Pennsylvania Journal*, 19 March 1777; *Pennsylvania Evening Post*, 15 March 1777; *New-York Gazette*, 24 March 1777; Doremus, 43; Lobdell, "Six Generals," 36; Peckham, 31)

Spanktown (Rahway), March 8 (Alden et al.)

Sandy Hook, March 8: Americans attacked British-occupied lighthouse; losses unknown (Peckham, 31)

Piscataway, March 8 (Alden et al.)

Samptown, March 9: An American force (Maj. Butler) attacked a British outpost; British losses, 4 killed.

Cranbury, March 12: Militia attacked and defeated a British forage party; losses unknown (Peckham, 31)

Jersey Shore, March 14: Loyalists (Maj. Robt. Timpany) fought American troops; losses unknown (Peckham, 31)

Spanktown (Rahway), March 16: A large British force under Gen. John Vaughan attacked American troops; 15 Americans captured.

Brunswick, March 18: Fight between British and Americans; British losses unknown; Americans lost 4 killed, 8 wounded (Peckham, 32)

English Neighborhood, March 20: Loyalists under Col. Joseph Barton attacked a post held by American troops under Col. Levi Pawling; Americans lost 4 captured (Peckham, 32)

Woodbridge, March 22: New Jersey Continentals (Maj. Joseph Bloomfield) fought a big British force; British losses 150; Americans lost 5 killed, 5 wounded (Peckham, 32)

North Jersey, March 24: Maryland troops fought British forces; losses unknown (Peckham, 32)

Strawberry Hill, near Woodbridge, March 28: Skirmish between American and British troops; losses unknown.

Elizabethtown, March 24 (Alden et al.)

Total British and Germans killed, wounded, and captured in New Jersey, 954. This is a lower-bound estimate for 23 engagements; many others left no record of casualties.

SOURCES: Johann Ewald, *Diary of the American War: A Hessian Journal*, ed. Joseph P. Tustin (New Haven, 1979); Stephen Kemble, *The Kemble Papers*, 2 vols., NYHS *Collections* (New York, 1884–85); John Peebles, *John Peeble's American War: The Diary of a Scottish Soldier, 1776–1782*, ed. Ira D. Gruber (London, 1998); Archibald Robertson, *Archibald Robertson, Lieutenant Colonel, Royal Engineers: His Diaries and Sketches in America, 1762–1780*, ed. Harry Miller Lydenberg (New York, 1930); Thomas Rodney, *The Diary of Captain Thomas Rodney, 1776–1777*, ed. Caesar A. Rodney, *Papers of the Historical Society of Delaware*, vol. 1, paper 8 (Wilmington, 1888; rpt. New York, 1974), ms. diary, 1776–77, LC; *GW*; John E. Alden et al., *Battles and Skirmishes of the American Revolution in New Jersey*, map published by New Jersey State Library (Trenton, 1945, 1965, 1973); Jared C. Lobdell, "Two Forgotten Battles of the Revolutionary War," *NJH* 85 (1967), 225–34; idem, "Six Generals Gather Forage: The Engagement at Quibbletown, 1777," *NJH* 102 (1984), 35–49; Harry M. Ward, *General William Maxwell and the New Jersey Continentals* (Westport, Conn., 1997); idem, *Charles Scott and the Spirit of '76* (Charlottesville, 1988); George Doremus, *The American Revolution in Morris County* (Rockaway, N.J., 1967); Howard H. Peckham, *The Toll of Independence: Engagements and Battle Casualties of the American Revolution* (Chicago, 1974); Samuel Stelle Smith, *The Battle of Princeton* (Monmouth Beach, N.J., 1967); William M. Dwyer, *The Day Is Ours!* (New York, 1983); and other sources listed above.

APPENDIX U

∾ Total British and German Casualties, New York and New Jersey Campaigns

Engagements	Killed	Severely Wounded	Killed and Wounded	Captured Unwounded	Missing	Total
I. The New York Campaign						
Battle of Long Island	63	314				377
Harlem Heights	14	154				168
White Plains Campaign			313			313
Fort Washington	78	374			6	452
Small Engagements (est.)						c. 200
New York Campaign Total						1,510
II. The New Jersey Campaign						
First Battle of Trenton	22	84		834		918
Second Battle of Trenton						365
Battle of Princeton						450
Forage War						954
Other Small Actions						200
New Jersey Campaign Total					2,887	
Grand Total						4,397

SOURCES: Appendices N, Q, R, S above; for the New York campaign, Howard H. Peckham, *The Toll of Independence; Engagements and Battle Casualties of the American Revolution* (Chicago, 1974); Mark M. Boatner III, *Encyclopedia of the American Revolution* (Mechanicsburg, Pa., 1994).

APPENDIX V

∾ Deaths from All Causes in American and British Wars, 1776–1976

In the past three centuries, a major change occurred in the pattern of war losses. During the eighteenth and early nineteenth centuries, for every soldier killed in battle, eight soldiers died of other causes. This pattern began to decline very rapidly in the mid-nineteenth century and kept on declining through the twentieth century. At the same time, crude annual mortality rates in Western armies during wartime declined in roughly the same proportion.

This evidence strongly indicates that mortality from all causes in the American War of Independence was much larger than has been reckoned, even as combat deaths were much below those in later wars fought with more lethal weapons.

WAR	DEATH RATIOS Other Deaths/ Battle Deaths		DEATH RATES Annual Deaths per 1,000 Troops
	I	II	All Deaths
Revolutionary War			
Hessian Army, 1776–84		8.3	
Hessian Army, 1777			114.97
Napoleonic Wars			
British Army		8.2	
Mexican War			
U.S. Army		7	100
Crimean War			
British Army		4	
Civil War			
Union Army		1.60	68.7
Spanish War			25.9
World War I	.93	.85	15.4
World War II	.35	.39	3.0
Korea	.62	.61	2.0
Vietnam	n.a.	.22	n.a.

NOTE: For Death Ratios, estimate I is calculated from the ratio of annual death rates. Ratio II is calculated from total deaths through the entire war.

SOURCES: Losses of Hessian troops in the American Revolution, 1776–84, are estimated at 535 deaths in battle and 4,983 deaths from all causes, in a force of 18,970 men. Deaths from all causes for 1777 were reported as 1,477, in a total force of 12,847. Total force estimates for 1777 are computed as total mustered in British service, 12 April–9 Dec. 1777, minus deaths and prisoners of war for 1776. Data are drawn from Rodney Atwood, *The Hessians: Mercenaries from Hessen-Kassel in the American Revolution* (Cambridge, 1980), 254, 255. See also Charles W. Ingrao, *The Hessian Mercenary State: Ideas, Institutions, and Reform Under Frederick II* (Cambridge, 1987), 157. Data for other wars are drawn from Paul E. Steiner, *Disease in the Civil War* (Springfield, Ill., 1968); G. W. Adams, *Doctors in Blue* (New York, 1952; Baton Rouge, 1996), 194–95; *HSUS* (1976), series Y, 856–903; *SAUS* (1984), 579.

APPENDIX W

❦ New Jersey Nomenclature: Place Names in 1776

Alexandria, now Frenchton
Amboy, used interchangeably for South Amboy, Perth Amboy
Acquackanonk Landing, now Passaic
Assunpink Creek, also called Sanpink and Wood Creek (Sgt R, "The Battle of Princeton," 515)
Assunpisk, later Assumption and Clinton
Bergen, now Jersey City
Black Horse, now Columbus, originally called Encroaching Corners after a land dispute; renamed Black Horse after a tavern. When the tavern was renamed Columbus, the name of the town changed with it.

Black River, now Chester
Buskwick or Bushwick, now Middleboro
Brunswick, now New Brunswick
Closter Landing, now Upper Closter and Lower Closter
Cooper's Ferry, now Camden
Coryell's Ferry, now Lambertville, New Jersey, and New Hope, Pennsylvania
Delaware Falls, now Trenton
English Neighborhood, now Leonia
Fairfield, now Fairton
Germantown, now Oldwick
Hillsborough, now Millstone
Hoffs, now Pittstown
King's Highway, English Neighborhood, now Grand Avenue, Leonia
Kirbride's or Kirkbride's Ferry, now Bordentown
The Landing, now West Brunswick
Liberty Pole, now Englewood
Log Gaol, now Johnsonburg
Lower Closter, later Huyler's Landing
Maidenhead, now Lawrenceville
Monmouth Courthouse, now Freehold
New Bridge, now Hackensack
Old Closter Dock landing, now Upper Closter
Petticoat Bridge, near Mount Holly
Paulus Hook or Powles Hook, now Jersey City
Princetown or Prince Town, now Princeton
Quibbletown, now New Market
Raccoon, now Swedesboro
Raritan, now New Brunswick
Recklestown, now Chesterfield
Samptown, now Plainfield
Slabtown, now Jacksonville, renamed in 1863
Spanktown, now Rahway
Upper Closter landing, now Upper Closter
Turkey, now New Providence
Vealtown, now Bernardsville
Walpack, now Newton
White Hill, now Fieldsboro
Yardeley's Ferry, now Yardley

APPENDIX X

❧ Doubtful Documents

Among many primary materials for Trenton and Princeton, several sources of doubtful authenticity have crept into the literature. Some have been repeated from one secondary work to another, and broadcast on the Internet. This is particularly a problem in tertiary writing which does not include documentation, a common practice on the Web.

This inquiry found four major documents that have been used in the histories of the battle to be doubtful at best. All were published by William S. Stryker in *The Battles of Trenton and Princeton* (Boston, 1898). Certainly it was not the case that Stryker himself concocted them. He collected a very large quantity of primary materials, nearly all of high quality. Their origins are not given by Stryker, but nearly all can be identified and confirmed. But a few dubious materials fell into his net.

One of these doubtful sources is a supposed letter from George Washington to General Charles Lee, dated December 1, 1776. It was published by Stryker (326–27), as an "intercepted letter . . . found among the German Records in Marburg, Germany." No such manuscript is known to exist, and no references to it appear in the very full surviving correspondence of George Washington or Charles Lee. One passage about British leaders reads: "The advantages they have gained over us in the past have made them so proud and sure of success that they are determined to go to Philadelphia this winter. . . . Should they now really risk this undertaking then there is a great probability that they will pay dearly for it for I shall continue to retreat before them so as to lull them into security."

In style and substance, this letter is very different from Washington's other writings of the same date. The editors of the *Washington Papers* observe that "the letter differs markedly from other letters that GW wrote during this period in prose style and in opinion." They also report that they have been unable to find the original in the Marburg Archives. No use has been made of it in this work (*GW* 7:249–50).

Another doubtful document is the supposed "Diary of an Officer on Washington's Staff," also published by Stryker (359–64). It is a very colorful and graphic account of the campaign, and of Washington's leadership. No original has been found, no provenance, and no citation. Parts of it closely resemble passages in other printed sources, even word for word. But other parts ring more of the nineteenth century. It refers to the American commander as "Washington" without a title, which rarely happened in eighteenth-century documents. Its very mixed and often anachronistic cadences, vocabulary, and syntax ring wrong in this historian's ear.

Douglas Southall Freeman suspected it on other grounds. He observed that "no officer could have known as much at the time, or could have seen the relative importance of events as clearly as this individual set everything forth." Freeman concluded that this document "has to be rejected as a forgery or later compilation" (Freeman, *Washington* 4:310n). But this judgment was buried in a footnote within a seven-volume work, and many historians have continued to use the "diary" as an authentic source. George F. Scheer and Hugh F. Rankin reproduced it in their documentary history, *Rebels and Redcoats; The American Revolution Through the Eyes of Those Who Fought and Lived It* (1957; New York, 1987), 211–14, as their leading primary source on the battle of Trenton, attributing it to Washington's aide John Fitzgerald. William Dwyer made much use of it in *This Day Is Ours!* (New York, 1983), 228, noting that "the diary is apparently a reconstruction of events." He added that the author is "not definitely identified but believed by many to be Lieutenant Colonel John Fitzgerald."

This document is a source for some of the most scathing and contemptuous comments on German soldiers. It alleges that they were drinking heavily in celebration of Christmas, which other Americans who were present knew to be false. It is also a source of melodramatic quotations attributed to George Washington, which make him appear to be a more Napoleonic commander, both in style and substance.

I believe that parts of this diary are authentic. Some of its passages resemble conversations with Fitzgerald that G. W. Parke Custis reported in his *Recollections and Private Memoirs of Washington* (New York, 1860; rpt. Bridgewater, Va., 1999), 190–92, in particular the passage reporting that when Washington rode between the lines at Princeton, Fitzgerald "drew his hat over his face that he might not see him die" (191). But other passages appear to be later inventions. In short, the "Diary of an Officer on Washington's Staff" is probably a forgery, concocted sometime between the appearance of Custis's *Recollections* in 1860 and Stryker's history in 1898. No use is made of it in this inquiry; events and quotations that appear in it are used only when they can be found in other sources, such as Custis's record of conversations with Fitzgerald.

A third set of source problems centers on the shadowy figure of John Honeyman, a supposed double agent who was said to have visited German commander Johann Rall on the eve of the battle and lulled him into a state of security. This story comes to us from a family legend, and the absence of direct evidence is explained by its adherents as a consequence of the deep secrecy that surrounded Honeyman's work, which they believe was known only to the man himself, his wife, and General Washington. Stryker included this story in his history and published the record of a grand jury which on June 5, 1777, indicted Honeyman for giving "aid and comfort" to the enemy. Stryker thought it significant that no record of punishment could be found, and that its absence proved the authenticity of the legend. But negative evidence is always a weak foundation. Surviving legal records from the Revolution are notoriously incomplete. This document in itself proves nothing about Honeyman's alleged espionage.

The Honeyman legend has found its way into the literature. It appeared in Bill's *Campaign of Princeton*, 26, which reports that Honeyman was "one of the ablest of Washington's spies" and asserts that the absence of evidence is proof of his skill in having "covered his tracks so thoroughly." Honeyman became very prominent in Richard Ketchum's *The Winter Soldiers*, 241–42, 145, 354, and was the subject of Leonard Falkner's "A Spy for Washington," *American Heritage* (August 1957). There is also a John Honeyman Web page on the Internet. Other writers, including Dwyer and Smith, and Freeman, have been doubtful of the legend. It might possibly be true, but in the judgment of this historian, the legend of Honeyman is unsupported by evidence. No use of it is made here.

A fourth document is an undated memorandum in the letterbook of General Robert Anderson, based on memories of conversations with his father, Captain Richard Clough Anderson of the Fifth Virginia Continentals. It has long been used by historians as their primary and even sole source for the American attack on Hessian outposts on Christmas evening, December 25, 1776. The memorandum made Captain Anderson the head of the American party, and his mission a reconnaissance of Hessian positions.

This document has been accepted as accurate by Stryker (373–74), Hall (51–52), Ketcham (253–54), and Dwyer (249–51), but not by Smith (*Trenton*, 20), who omitted the event altogether. Freeman (*Washington* 4:313) began to put things right when he found a letter from Adam Stephen to Jonathan Seaman, dated January 5, 1777, in the Adam Stephen Papers (LC), which confirmed that such an incident actually happened, but not as Anderson remembered. Its leader was not Anderson but Captain Wallis of Stephen's Fourth Virginia Regiment, and its purpose was not a reconnaissance but to take revenge for a man who had been killed. Freeman misread Stephen's handwriting, garbled Wallis's name, and was unable to identify him. Those errors were corrected by Harry M. Ward, *Major General Adam Stephen and the Cause of American Liberty* (Charlottesville, 1989), 278n, who identified Wallis and pieced together the story.

All of these doubtful documents emerged in different ways. The Anderson memorandum was an honest confusion of the sort that often happens in oral traditions within any family. The Honeyman story was a local legend that was hardened into fact, and the absence of documentation was taken as positive proof that the legend was true, and proof that Honeyman was such a brilliant spy that nobody could find evidence of his activities. The officer's diary attributed to Fitzgerald is probably a deliberate concoction, put together between 1860 and 1898, as a nineteenth-century pastiche of eighteenth-century sources. The missing Marburg letter is very much in doubt. Someday it may turn up in the archives, or be found to be a forgery.

Other documents might be added to this list. Some of the Hessian reports before the court-martial in New York and the War Commission in Hesse-Cassel were efforts to escape blame and pin responsibility for the Trenton defeat on Rall, Dechow, and Gröthausen, who were killed in the fighting and could not defend themselves. The Donop diary was concocted after the event by an aide, in an effort to rescue Donop's reputation. Similar distortions appear in British accounts of Princeton and Trenton by Grant, Germain, Howe, and other officers. The Grant Papers were culled to absolve that officer of responsibility for the events at Trenton.

On the American side, more than a few "diaries" are actually memoirs, and "memoirs" were often much "improved." My mother, as she grew deaf, often remarked that what she heard was more interesting than what was actually said. In the same way, what was remembered was sometimes much more interesting than what actually happened. These are routine problems in historical scholarship, and the remedies are well understood: primary evidence, critical analysis of documents, and careful attention to provenance. An historian (especially an early American historian) cannot always use the journalist's two-source rule, but multiple sources are often available for these events, and interlocking sources are always helpful here. Common sense helps too.

There is a strong interpretative bias in most of these dubious sources. They tend to make Washington into a more Napoleonic leader, in speech and acts. They also make the Hessians and British appear more contemptuous, and Americans more noble. They reflected the strong nationalism of the nineteenth century, and they have a good deal of what John Roche called retrospective symmetry.

HISTORIOGRAPHY

～ Images and Interpretations of the Event

Washington's Crossing and the battles at Trenton and Princeton have given rise to a very large literature throughout the Western world. They have also inspired more painting and sculpture by major artists than any other event in American history. To the date of this writing, nine generations have taken up the subject, never twice in the same way.

On first impression, the great whirl of opinion might suggest that historical truth is in the eye of the beholder. But to look more closely is to find another pattern. Even the smallest historical event might be interpreted in many ways, but it happened only in one way, and not in any other. As Wittgenstein put it in his ponderous way, "the world is that which is the case." The operative words are "is," and "is" again.

The flow of historical interpretation might be thought of as a continuing conversation, within generations and also between them. When a new interpreter joins the conversation, many things happen. Old errors are corrected. New errors are introduced, and put right in their turn. Through it all, knowledge increases, and the meaning of an event tends to grow. We can observe this process at work in the changing memory of Washington's Crossing.

～ Participant History: American Ideas of a Providential Event

The first interpreters were the participants. By and large, Americans of the Revolutionary generation did not regard the victories at Trenton and Princeton as their own doing. Most were people of deep religious faith, more so than we remember them. They perceived these events to be God's work and evidence of a divine design for the world. An example was Henry Melchior Muhlenberg, a Protestant minister in Pennsylvania. He wrote in his diary on December 28, 1776, two days after Washington's crossing, "It is a sign that the almighty Lord of hosts has heard the cry of the afflicted and sent an angel to help him."[1]

Henry Muhlenberg believed that the battle of Trenton was an act of divine retribution for the sins of British and Hessian troops in New Jersey. He explained, "when the war lords fail to maintain discipline and rather allow fiends the freedom to commit heaven-defying sins (for example, the raping of ten-year-old girls and married women and committing every imaginable wicked deed against old and feeble persons) then the retributive justice of God soon intervenes. The Lord of Sabbath holds the rod of correction and punishment in His hand and directs the whole and all its parts, large and small, and nothing can happen without his sufferance and decree."[2]

In 1776, many Americans shared Henry Muhlenberg's image of an avenging angel in Continental blue and buff, and they agreed with his interpretation of the battles at Trenton and Princeton as Signs of God's Redeeming Providence. Paradoxically, this way of thinking about history gave its believers a greater sense of agency, as instruments of a higher power. That attitude also appeared in more secular forms, in which the American cause itself became an idea of Providence. An example we have noted was Captain William Hull, who fought in the campaign with the Seventh Connecticut Regiment. He wrote, "What can't Men do when engaged in so noble a cause?"[3]

～ "Rall's Affair": British Ideas of an Accidental Event

British and Loyalist participants understood the same events in other ways. Examples appeared in the journals of Stephen Kemble and Ambrose Serle. Kemble was an American Loyalist who served as General William Howe's adjutant, and Serle was private secretary to Admiral Richard Howe. Both men regarded the American victory at Trenton as a regrettable accident, of small importance in the larger scheme of things. Serle called it an "idle affair."[4] Kemble described it as "Rall's Affair." He attributed the entire event to the misconduct of the Hessians in general and Colonel Johann Rall in particular. To that end, Stephen Kemble propagated the story of the drunken Hessians and wrote of them as if they were entirely separate from the British army. He described Colonel Rall as a "man unacquainted with the Language, and a Drunkard." This idea grew rapidly into the legend that Rall was drunk when the Americans attacked and that the entire Hessian garrison had been celebrating Christmas "in the German way" and drinking heavily.[5]

It wasn't so. To repeat, an American soldier, John Greenwood, whose job was to look after the Hessians immediately after the battle, testified in 1809 that the story of the drunken Hessians was totally false: not one of them was drunk or had been drinking heavily. Of the Americans he wrote, "I am certain not a drop of liquor was drunk during the whole night, nor, as I could see, even a piece of bread eaten." As to the Hessians, he declared, "I am willing to go upon oath that I did not see even a solitary drunken soldier belonging to the enemy,—and you will find, as I shall show, that I had an opportunity to be as good a judge as any person there."[6]

Further, the town had been attacked late on Christmas day, and the entire garrison was under arms. On Christmas evening, Colonel Johann Rall led them into the country in search of the American raiders. After the Hessians returned, the garrison remained on high alert, with outposts reinforced. Later in the night, according to local legend, Colonel Rall was alleged to have played a game of cards with his Trenton landlord, Stacy Potts, and may have visited Abraham Hunt, but no strong evidence exists to show that Colonel Rall or any of his men were drunk on Christmas night or the following morning when the Americans attacked. Their actions on both days are evidence to the contrary. But the myth of the intoxicated Hessians began to fly on wings of scandal, and the corrections never caught up.

A variant on this interpretative theme of blaming the Hessians, without reference to alcohol, became the official British explanation. In reports to London, General William Howe wrote of the event as if he were a distant spectator. He attributed the entire disaster to the incompetence of Hessian leaders, principally General Leopold von Heister, the commanding general of the Hessian forces in America. Heister was nowhere near Trenton and was not in the operational chain of command. But this interpretation of the event had a triple appeal in Howe's headquarters. It absolved British leaders from responsibility, diminished the achievement of the Americans, and was an opportunity to get rid of General von Heister, whom they disliked.[7]

British participants responded to the battle at Princeton in another way. Early dispatches represented it as a British victory that kept the Americans from holding Princeton or attacking New Brunswick and compelled them to retreat into the mountains of New Jersey. As the truth emerged, subsequent accounts from General Howe's headquarters interpreted the battle as a moral victory for British arms, distinguished mainly by the gallantry of Colonel Mawhood and the Seventeenth Foot. Elements of this interpretation persisted for many years in histories of the British army such as John Fortescue's majestic work, which described the battle as "one of the most gallant exploits of the war" for British arms, while noting that it was not a victory.[8]

❧ Howe's Affair: American Loyalists and Transatlantic Debate

Another interpretation of Trenton and Princeton appeared in the writings of American Loyalist Joseph Galloway. He believed that the American Revolution could be defeated by strong measures. The Howe brothers rejected this advice and pursued a policy of moderation and reconciliation. Galloway turned furiously against William Howe in particular and attacked him repeatedly as responsible for the loss of the American colonies.

Galloway regarded the campaigns in New Jersey as the pivotal moment, and the battles of Trenton and Princeton as disasters caused by Howe's errors. The American Loyalist condemned the British commander for missing many opportunities to destroy Washington's army, for not pushing on to Philadelphia in early December when the Delaware River could have been crossed, for coddling New Jersey Whigs, and for scattering troops in small outposts which invited attack. Picking up the story of the drunken Hessians, he described Colonel Rall as a man "obstinate, passionate and incessantly intoxicated with strong liquors" and held Howe personally responsible for putting him in command at Trenton. Altogether, Galloway thought of Trenton and Princeton as Howe's affair and a classic example of the process by which British leaders betrayed the Loyalists and lost the American colonies. It was also an explanation that relieved the Loyalists themselves from any responsibility.[9]

As this criticism increased, Parliament launched an inquiry. Sir William Howe defended himself and began to criticize British ministers. Other British generals and American Loyalists joined in. All of them formed a great circle of denial, each pointing to another and insisting that somebody else was to blame. Not a single British officer accepted responsibility for what had happened. The escalating controversy injured the reputation of all parties. It also demonstrated that the British failure to win a decisive victory in America during the critical winter of 1776–77 was more than a chapter of accidents.[10]

✎ Hessian Interpretations, and a Debate on the Soldier Trade

Hessian officers studied the battle at Trenton in exhaustive detail, mainly because their infuriated Prince Friedrich Wilhelm II demanded to know what had happened to his beloved army. From 1778 to 1782, formal Hessian courts-martial convened at Philadelphia and New York. They interviewed returning prisoners, collected written testimony from officers and men, and gathered original documents from the papers of Colonel von Donop and other sources. This evidence was reviewed by a Hessian court at New York in January 1782, and again by the Hessian War Commission in Cassel.

All of these inquiries centered on the question of who was to blame, and all agreed unanimously on the answer. Hessians concluded that "the disaster at Trenton was due to the neglect of Colonel Rall." He was held responsible for underestimating his enemy, refusing to fortify the town, failing to designate alarm posts, and responding to the attack by counterattacking the Americans in the center of town, rather than retreating to safety.

The Hessian court also found that three other officers were culpable: Major Friedrich von Dechow, Captain Ludwig von Löwenstein, and Lieutenant Friedrich von Gröthausen. All were conveniently in their graves. The Hessian courts specifically discussed every surviving officer and acquitted each of them from any culpability in the affair. The official Hessian inquiry was a whitewash, which successfully protected Hessian officers from the wrath of their prince.

The Hessian inquiry created an invaluable archive of detailed eyewitness accounts and primary documents. These materials showed that Colonel Rall clearly had a share of responsibility for the defeat at Trenton, but not as charged. The three Hessian regiments did have alarm posts and rallied to them when attacked the day before. The fortifications that Rall was urged to build would have had little impact on the events. The evidence also showed that three senior officers were more culpable than Rall himself: General William Howe for putting him there in the first place and scattering his garrisons, General James Grant for refusing to respond to repeated warnings and calls for help; and Colonel von Donop for many derelictions.

Privately, Hessian soldiers were scathing in their criticism of Donop, Grant, and Howe. Some were highly sympathetic to Rall. Jäger Captain Johann Ewald believed that Colonel Rall was a brave and resolute soldier and remarked that the men who condemned him were not fit to carry his sword. Ewald wrote in disgust, "Thus the fate of entire kingdoms often depends upon a few blockheads and irresolute men." He shared the belief that Trenton was an accidental event but had a different idea of the "blockheads" who caused it.[11]

While Hessian soldiers discussed their responsibility for the debacle at Trenton, a larger debate developed in Europe on the morality of their presence in America. We have already noted this international exchange, which drew in the French radical comte de Mirabeau, Benjamin Franklin, and Hessian minister Martin Ernst von Schlieffen. It also enlarged the international discussion of the American Revolution and raised questions about the legitimacy of Europe's old regime.[12]

❧ American Interpretations: George Washington and Republican Virtue

While that debate continued in Europe, another interpretation appeared in the United States. Writers began to represent the victories at Trenton and Princeton as a triumph of republican freedom and virtue over monarchical tyranny and corruption. Their interpretations also centered on one man: George Washington, as the leader and symbol of America's republican cause.

On February 19, 1777, the *Pennsylvania Journal* published a "new catechism" in a series of political questions. One of the first questions asked, "What is the chief end of offensive war?" The correct answer was "To gratify the ambition of a tyrannic prince." The last question was "Who is the Best Man Living?" The answer was George Washington: "He retreats like a general and acts like a hero." The catechism explained, "If there are spots on his character, they are like spots on the sun, only discernible by the magnifying powers of a telescope." It added a history of Trenton and Princeton in which Washington rescued the new republic from British tyrants "by a stroke of policy above their comprehension." Washington was perceived to be the military leader of the republic and the moral exemplar of its cause.[13]

This new interpretation of the event appeared in multivolume histories of the Revolution by American writers David Ramsay and John Marshall, English clergyman William Gordon, and the Italian radical Charles Botta. All strongly supported the American Revolution, perceived the events at Trenton and Princeton as pivotal moments, and centered their histories on the strength of the American cause and the greatness of George Washington.

The best of these works was Charles Botta's *History of the War of Independence of the United States of America.* The author was an Italian physician and scholar who supported the French Revolution and joined Napoleon's Italian campaign as a war of liberation. In 1809, he published a history of the American Revolution to inspire the Old World with the example of the New. It is a highly intelligent work, remarkably detailed, and broadly informed by primary materials that the author obtained through Lafayette and Americans in Paris. Adams, Jefferson, and Madison all praised it as one of the best histories of the American Revolution.

Botta's account of the New Jersey campaign is typical of his work. He regarded British and Hessian leaders as formidable opponents and described Colonel Rall as "a Hessian officer of great merit." Botta believed that the American Revolution was very near defeat in December of 1776. The central figure in his interpretation was Washington, and the critical moment was his decision to attack Trenton—not the attack itself but the "heroic resolution" to make it. Botta wrote, "from this moment the war assumed a new face, and victory began at length to incline in favor of the Americans." Botta regarded the battles as decisive events, mainly because they gave America the leader it needed to prevail. "Achievements so astonishing acquired an immense glory for the captain-general of the United States," he wrote. "All nations shared in the surprise of the Americans; all equally admired the prudence, the constancy, and the noble intrepidity of General Washington. An unanimous voice proclaimed him the savior of his country; all extolled him as equal to the most celebrated commanders of antiquity." Botta gave this idea a special twist. He was much interested in parallels between his two heroes, Washington and Napoleon.[14]

Similar approaches without the Napoleonic interpretation appeared in John Marshall's *Life of George Washington* and William Gordon's *History of the Rise, Progress, and Establishment of the Independence of the United States of America* (1788). Both works drew heavily on the *Annual Register* even to the point of plagiarism, a common practice in their time, and added their own primary materials. Gordon interviewed American leaders and conducted a correspondence with Washington himself. Marshall was allowed by Bushrod Washington to take

Washington manuscripts to Richmond (where they suffered much damage) and used them extensively for his work.

Like Botta, John Marshall regarded the Trenton and Princeton campaign as a pivot point and Washington's leadership as critical, but in a different way. He interpreted the battles mainly as events that changed popular opinion. Marshall gave more attention to the role of the American people and wrote that the support of "the great mass" of the people "can alone furnish the solid force of armies." He believed that "the affairs of Trenton and Princeton were magnified into great victories; and were believed by the people to evidence the superiority of their army and their general. The [earlier] opinion that they were engaged in a hopeless contest yielded to a confidence that proper exertions would ensure ultimate success."[15]

The contrast between Botta and Marshall is interesting. An American conservative gave more weight to public opinion, the central role of the "great mass" of the people, and Washington as leader of a free people. A European radical made Washington into a Napoleonic commander and put the people in a subordinate role.[16]

In the United States, republican interpretations of Trenton and Princeton appeared in painting and sculpture as well as in print. Three American artists served with Washington during the war, and that experience became important to their careers. Painter Charles Willson Peale (1741–1827) was a Chesapeake gentleman, born and raised in Maryland, and a frequent visitor at Mount Vernon. He commanded a company of Philadelphia Associators in Cadwalader's brigade and was in the second battle of Trenton and the battle of Princeton. Later he served as an aide to George Washington. In January 1779, the Pennsylvania Council asked him for a portrait of Washington at Trenton or Princeton. Peale was meticulous in matters of historical detail. He visited the battlefields with his brother James Peale and pupil William Mercer, and the three artists did many sketches. Washington agreed to pose for a full-length portrait, and the sitting continued for two weeks between January 20 and February 2, 1779. At Washington's feet the artist placed the captured German colors, and Congress permitted him to use the actual flags as models. Peale also painted Washington's headquarters standard, with thirteen six-pointed stars on a blue field, probable evidence that it was used at Princeton.[17]

The result was a wonderful portrait, with many layers of interpretative meaning. On the surface, it was a literal likeness of Washington in his prime, at the age of forty-seven. At the same time, it celebrated the easy grace of a Chesapeake gentleman, an ideal to which both the artist and sitter were raised. It was also an image of a strong military leader, secure in his mastery of events. Most of all, it represented a man whose character and integrity gave form to the idea of a republic and meaning to the American cause. Altogether, the painting was an interpretation of the event that centered on the greatness of a single leader.

Peale's heroic portrait was a great success, and he was asked to make many copies. One was commissioned by the trustees of the college at Princeton to replace a portrait of George II that had been damaged in the campaign. Peale's studio produced many other versions on request. The details varied with the commission. Sometimes the background scene was the battle at Princeton, and sometimes Trenton. The comte de Rochambeau ordered a copy with the battle of Yorktown, where he and Washington commanded. Buyers in the 1780s asked for the Stars and Stripes rather than Washington's headquarters flag, and the Peale studio was happy to oblige. But the central figure remained the same.[18]

Another American artist who served in the war painted the same subject in a different republican spirit. Colonel John Trumbull (1756–1843) had deep roots in New England. He was descended from the founders of Plymouth Colony and from the leaders of the Puritan Great Migration. After graduating as the youngest member of Harvard's class of 1773, he joined the army as adjutant in the First Connecticut Regiment, became an aide to Washington, rose to colonel at the age of twenty in 1776, and served in three campaigns.

Later in the war, Trumbull left the army and devoted himself to creating an iconography of the American Revolution. He did meticulous life portraits of many leading figures in the war. One of his most interesting works was a portrait of George Washington, painted in

*George Washington at
Princeton*, painting by
Charles Willson Peale
(1779). Pennsylvania
Academy of the Fine Arts,
Philadelphia. Bequest of
Mrs. Sarah Harrison (The
Joseph Harrison, Jr.
Collection).

1792 on a commission from South Carolina. Trumbull chose to represent Washington in what both men believed to be the critical moment of the Revolution. The artist wrote, "I undertook it *con amore* (as the commission was unlimited), meaning to give his military character, in the most sublime moment of its exertion—the evening previous to the battle of Princeton; when viewing the vast superiority of his approaching enemy, and the impossibility of again crossing the Delaware, or retreating down the river, he conceives the plan of returning by a night march into the country from which he had just been driven, thus cutting off the enemy's communication, and destroying his depot of stores and provisions at Brunswick."[19]

Trumbull explained his purpose to Washington, and the president "entered into it warmly." The artist recalled that "as the work advanced, we talked of the scene, its dangers, its almost desperation. He *looked* the scene again, and I happily transferred to the canvass, the lofty expression of his animated countenance, the high resolve to conquer or to perish."[20] Trumbull's portrait was an image of inner strength and moral purpose, much in the tradition of his New England ancestors. He and Washington were pleased with the result, but the South Carolinians who had commissioned the painting were not happy with it and wanted "a more matter of fact likeness . . . calm, tranquil peaceful." Trumbull painted another portrait "agreeable to their taste" and added images of Charleston and palmetto trees. In New England Trumbull's portrait of Washington's character found a more admiring public, and Trumbull made six copies. The original is owned by Yale University.[21]

Trumbull did many large history paintings as a pictorial record of the Revolution. Among them were careful battle scenes of Trenton and Princeton. They combined large republican themes with meticulous portraits of many individual figures. The paintings were meant to

George Washington at the Battle of Trenton, painting by John Trumbull (1792). Yale University Art Gallery.

be an archive of historical images and a record of the birth of the republic. At the same time, they were a New Englander's idea of a collective effort, with a strong moral meaning. Trumbull represents the new republic as young, healthy, strong, virtuous, and victorious. Its enemies appear aged, weak, wounded, and in defeat. This contrast was meant to be a vision of history and the future.[22]

Another artist who fought in the Revolution was William Rush (1756–1833), a figurehead carver of rare talent who became one of America's first and most gifted sculptors. Rush fought with the Philadelphia Associators at the second battle of Trenton and Princeton. After the war he did many sculptures on republican themes. One showed the Goddess of Liberty carrying a torch, surrounded by symbols of law and justice. Another represented the American eagle "destroying the vitals of tyranny." A third was an image of *Liberty Crowning the Bust of Washington*. One of Rush's most successful works was a full-length portrait-sculpture of Washington. He represented the face and figure of Washington as he appeared in the New Jersey campaign, where the artist had frequent opportunity to observe him. Rush wrote, "I have been in battle immediately under his command—I have viewed him walking, standing, sitting—I have seen him at a game of ball, for several hours; exhibiting the most manly and graceful attitudes I ever saw. I have seen him dismount from his horse, a few hours after the battle of Princeton . . . reviewing with great anxiety his little band, which had just taken the English 17th Regiment. At that moment of crisis . . . his likeness was worth more guineas than the British would have given for his person."[23]

William Rush could have put Washington in uniform, or in Roman dress, and he did include conventional elements of neoclassical sculpture in the work, such as a fluted column

Statue of George Washington
by William Rush (ca. 1814).
Independence National
Historical Park, Philadelphia.

and a Roman toga, but in a fresh and imaginative way. The toga was pulled away to reveal Washington as an ordinary citizen of the American republic, with an unbuttoned coat and a casual air in a relaxed hip-shot pose. The head and features have none of the abstract grandeur of neoclassical sculpture in America and Europe. They are highly individuated and very realistic. Washington is holding the Constitution in his hand. For a sculptor who soldiered with him he was a symbol of the Republic itself.

❧ The Romantic Historians: Irving's Washington; Sully's *Passage of the Delaware*

In the nineteenth century, another school of interpretation appeared among artists and writers who brought a new romantic sensibility to the study of history. One of its masters, William H. Prescott, wrote that "the true way of conceiving the subject is not as a philosophical theme, but as an epic in prose, a romance of chivalry."[24] Here was an idea of history as a drama which engages the emotions of a reader or observer in the experience of the event. The romantic artist sought to awaken large thoughts and strong feelings. He also represented an idea of the grandeur of history.

An early example was the work of Washington Irving (1783–1859), a New York lawyer, diplomat, and literary light of the new republic. Irving was deeply inspired by the example of Sir Walter Scott, visited him at Abbotsford, and tried to emulate him in romantic fiction and biography, mostly on historical subjects. In 1825, Irving conceived the idea of a multivolume biography of George Washington, with whom he felt a special personal bond, from a moment in 1789, when his nurse took him to visit the president and he received the blessing of his namesake. Irving worked at his biography for many years and collected British and Hessian primary materials in Europe. In America he was given special access to the Washington papers, which had been moved to the State Department. He was very careful with his sources and exceptionally accurate in small details. By heroic effort, Irving finished the final volume of the work on his deathbed in 1859.[25]

The New York and New Jersey campaign of 1776–77 was a central event that filled twenty-five chapters. Much of it was a work of description, highly evocative of time and place. It was also a story, with a strong narrative tension and sudden reversals of fortune. A major element was the construction of a character for George Washington as a romantic hero of deep feeling, strong emotion, and powerful internal conflicts. In an account of the disaster at Kip's Bay, Washington Irving described his hero in "a transport of rage" and a "paroxysm of passion and despair" in which "the vehement element of his nature was stirred up from its deep recesses."[26]

By the measure of the high romantic style that followed, Irving's rhetoric was comparatively restrained, but its romanticism was highly developed. The author wrote, "I had a great deal of trouble to keep the different parts together, giving a little touch here and a little touch there. . . . I felt like old Lablache when he was performing in a rehearsal of his orchestra . . . bringing out a violin here, a clarinet there, now suppressing a trombone, now calling upon the flutes, and every now and then bringing out a big bass drum."[27] Irving's *Washington* represented a new historical genre. Most historians who came after the romantic movement, even to our own time, were influenced by its methods of setting a scene, constructing a character, building a narrative, and engaging the emotions of the reader.

American painters in Irving's generation were also part of the romantic movement. Among them was Thomas Sully (1783–1872), an English immigrant who learned to paint in America with the tutelage of Gilbert Stuart and the support of Washington Irving. He became a superb artist, best known for his 2,600 romantic portraits, but his highest ambition was to produce big history paintings. In 1818, the North Carolina legislature asked him to paint two large portraits of George Washington. Sully suggested a historical painting called *The Passage of the Delaware*. It was a huge melodramatic work, seventeen feet wide and twelve feet high. In the background the artist painted an ice-choked river, a stormy sky, and a snowy bank. Men are crossing with artillery and horses, in what appear to be authentic Durham boats (Sully studied his subjects with great care).

At the center of this very dark painting is a bright image of Washington on a white horse. Behind him is his slave companion, William Lee, and symbolic figures of an aide, a Continental officer, and a militiaman. The men around Washington appear highly agitated, and the horses are wild with fear. The dark storm and the anxious men and frightened animals create an image of great emotional violence. By comparison Washington appears almost serene.

Romantic artists spoke of the highest emotional pitch of painting as the art of the art of the sublime, in the sense of inspiring feelings of awe and even terror. That idea became the central theme of Sully's painting. He attempted to draw the observer into the experience of an historical event so great and terrible as to approach the sublime.

Other romantic painters were deeply influenced by Sully's painting. It clearly had an impact on Emanuel Luetze. Edward Hicks painted an image of Washington's Crossing that was a very close copy. But it was not what the North Carolina legislature had in mind, and they rejected it. The artist had trouble finding another buyer and finally sold it to a framemaker for five hundred dollars. It is now in Boston's Museum of Fine Arts.

The Passage of the Delaware, painting by Thomas Sully (1819). Gift of the Owners of the old Boston Museum, Museum of Fine Arts, Boston.

❧ Whig History

In the mid-nineteenth century, the romantic and republican schools came together in a third interpretation, which historians call Whig history. Later its practitioners called themselves Liberals, after the Spaniards who fought to free their country from Napoleon and took the name of *Liberales.*[28]

The Liberal idea combined a strong attachment to ideas of liberty and democracy with a consciousness of history as a story of inevitable progress against heavy resistance. It flourished in the nineteenth century, when Whig-Liberals throughout the world were inspired by the example of the American Revolution. In that spirit, leading scholars in the United States, Britain, and Germany all wrote major multivolume histories of events linked to Washington's Crossing.

In America the central figure was George Bancroft (1800–91), an engaging and complex character. He was a Harvard graduate who earned a Ph.D. at Göttingen, a rock-ribbed New Englander who became a Jacksonian Democrat, a moral reformer who joined the cabinet of James K. Polk, a strong supporter of Abraham Lincoln who wrote speeches for Andrew Johnson, and a dedicated scholar who had a major career in politics and diplomacy.[29]

Through much of the nineteenth century Bancroft labored on a ten-volume *History of the United States,* which centered mainly on the origins, conduct, and consequences of the American Revolution. In Germany Bancroft had been trained to new standards of primary research. He knew the sources well and gathered them assiduously in a great collection at the New York Public Library. They include careful transcripts of many Hessian journals and continue to be very useful to American scholars, including this historian.[30]

George Bancroft believed deeply that history was the story of the growth of liberty and democracy. Though his subject was the making of an American nation, a major theme was what he called the "unity of humanity." He wrote that "the authors of the American Revolution avowed for their object the welfare of mankind," and he dedicated his scholarship to the idea that "the world of mankind does not exist in fragments, nor can a country have an insulated experience. All men are brothers; and all are bondsmen for one another. All nations, too, are brothers." He thought that the American Revolution "was designed to organize social union through the establishment of personal freedom, and thus emancipate the nations from all authority not flowing from themselves."[31]

The ninth volume of Bancroft's history gave much attention to Washington's Crossing and the battles of Trenton and Princeton, as the pivotal events in that titanic struggle. "Until that hour," Bancroft wrote, "the life of the United States flickered like a dying flame. . . . That victory turned the shadow of death into the morning." He had high praise for Washington, but the real protagonist was the Cause itself. Bancroft wrote of the New Jersey campaign as a moral collision between right and wrong. He treated individual British and German figures with sympathy and respect, but their conquest of New Jersey appeared in his work as not merely an error but a transcendent evil. Bancroft wrote with real anger of "the indiscriminate rapacity which spared neither friend nor foe, the terrible excesses of their lust, the unrestrained passion for destruction."[32]

Altogether, the Whig-Liberal history of George Bancroft was a vision of modern history as a moral struggle for freedom, democracy, and the right of people to live under laws of their own making. Washington's Crossing was for him an event of the highest importance in world history.

That judgment was shared by Whigs and Liberals in other nations. It inspired another great historical project by an English Liberal, George Otto Trevelyan (1838–1928). He came from the great Liberal dynasty of Wedgwoods, Trevelyans, Mores, and Macaulays, had a prominent parliamentary career, and held high office in Gladstone's governments, resigning from one because it was not liberal enough. In 1898, Trevelyan began to publish a six-volume work which Edmund Morgan calls "easily the most literate history of the Revolution."[33]

His interpretation rested on values similar to those of George Bancroft, but with a different theme and context. Trevelyan believed that the American Revolution was a struggle for liberty and human rights in Britain as well as the United States. With Chatham and Charles James Fox, he believed that "if America were subjugated, Britain would not long be free." Trevelyan argued that the American Revolution delivered England from the tyranny of personal rule and arbitrary government.[34]

Half of his third volume was devoted to the events at Princeton and Trenton. In his interpretation the campaign of 1776–77 appeared as a pivotal point in English history as well as in the American war itself. Some of the most original parts of the work were devoted to the response of British opinion to American events. Trevelyan wrote that "it must never be forgotten that many Englishmen from the first,—and in the end a decided, and indeed a very large majority among them,—regarded the contest which was being fought out in America not as a foreign war, but as a civil war in which English liberty was at stake."[35]

During the First World War, Trevelyan brought out a new edition of the work, with an added preface that his story was meant to be read with "mutual respect both by Englishmen and Americans," in the hope that all "English-speaking peoples" would be "henceforward fighting shoulder to shoulder" in the common cause of liberty and freedom. Trevelyan's work was highly regarded in both countries and played a central role in the Anglo-American rapprochement that became another pivotal event in the twentieth century.[36]

In the mid-nineteenth century, German historians also wrote about the events at Trenton and Princeton. Two major works show the range of interpretation. One was a work by Max von Eelking, *Die Deutschen Hülfstruppen im nordamerikanischen Befreiungskriege 1776 bis 1876* (1864). The author was a serving officer in the Saxon army and a corresponding member of the New-York Historical Society. He was a man of liberal beliefs and sympathized with the American struggle, which he called a war of liberation (*Befreiungskriege*) rather than a war of independence (*Unabhängigkeitskriege*), as other German scholars called it.[37]

But even as the author sympathized with the American Revolution, he felt that an injustice had been done to German soldiers who fought as British allies (*Hülfstruppen*), rather than mercenaries (*Soldner*). Working mainly from primary sources, he explained that his method was to allow these men to "tell their own story." His purpose was "to restore the good name and credit of German soldiers, ruthlessly attacked on all sides." A large part of the work was devoted to the New Jersey campaign and the battle at Trenton. Captain von Eelking was very critical of command decisions by Colonel Rall but judged him to be an able and courageous soldier, and he concluded that the Hessian garrison fought "as well as possible," with great courage and fidelity, "not to save themselves but as a duty, which they fulfilled to the last minute."[38]

His book was an extended argument that German troops conducted themselves with honor and humanity, and it was a useful corrective to much earlier literature in Britain and America. Von Eelking also argued that the experience of German troops in the New World had important consequences for the growth of liberty and nation-building in Germany, when serving officers such as Dömberg, Langen, York, and Gniesenau applied "lessons learned in America" to the struggle for German independence.[39]

At the same time, a very different interpretation was published by Friedrich Kapp (1824–88), a German liberal politician and lawyer who was active in the Revolution of 1848 and came to America in 1850. He became deeply interested in Germans who fought for the American War of Independence and published biographies of Baron von Steuben and Baron de Kalb, who served with the Continental army and supported the cause of liberty. Kapp's best-known book was *Der Soldatenhandel deutscher Fürsten nach Amerika* (1864), a study of the commerce in soldiers by German princes. It rested on extensive research in primary sources. Kapp used George Bancroft's transcripts of Hessian diaries and journals, explored the Hessian archives in Marburg, and collected much British material on the negotiation of treaties for the employment of German troops in America.[40]

Kapp's book is a scathing indictment of the European old regime in Britain and Germany. He was specially severe on aristocratic leaders of those countries who engaged in a commerce that Kapp regarded as a morally akin to the slave trade. At the same time, he condemned the German princes as relentless enemies of liberal, democratic, and national reform in Germany. The author documented the magnitude and materialism of the trade in great detail. A long appendix reproduced the major documents and contracts in which Britain pledged to pay the rulers of some German states (but not Hesse-Cassel) blood money for every soldier who died or was wounded.[41]

In 1871, Kapp returned to Germany and became a Liberal nationalist leader in the Reichstag. He brought out a new edition of his book, adding an indictment of the German princes of the *Soldatenhandel* as enemies of German national unification, as well as the liberty of their own people.[42]

These liberal ideas inspired artists to paint many images of the American Revolution. The most important was Emanuel Leutze, an American immigrant who returned to his native Germany and joined the German Revolution of 1848. We have already looked at his great painting of Washington crossing the Delaware. It was meant to be an image of a world struggle for liberty, democracy, and national independence, very much in the Whig-Liberal tradition. It is also interesting to note Leutze's strong support for the anti-slavery movement throughout the world, and his inclusion of an African figure in the painting. He strongly supported the Union in the Civil War, and his painting was exhibited in a fund-raising campaign for the Northern war effort. Leutze's painting also celebrated the role of ordinary people in this event. Washington was at the center of the painting, but by comparison with earlier paintings on the same subject, Leutze's work was new in its meticulous attention to private soldiers as well as the commander-in-chief.

A similar approach appeared in another Whig-Liberal painting of Washington's Crossing by a major American artist in the mid-nineteenth century. The artist was George Caleb Bingham, a native Virginian whose family had settled in Saline County, Missouri. He became a painter of the Missouri frontier and settlements along the western rivers. Some of his best-known paintings, among them *Stump Speaking* and *County Election*, celebrated American democracy. Other works centered on Americans who lived and worked on the western rivers, such as *The Jolly Flatboatmen* (1846) and *Raftsmen Playing Cards* (1847). *Lighter Reliev-*

Washington Crossing the Delaware, a painting by George Caleb Bingham (1856–71). Chrysler Museum, Norfolk, Virginia.

ing a Steamboat Aground (1847) is an allegory of boatmen in a small craft coming to the rescue of a proud and elegant steamboat.

The success of Leutze's *Washington Crossing the Delaware* inspired Bingham to create his own image of that event. Bingham began to work on it in 1856 and finished the painting in 1871. In some ways his composition closely resembled Leutze's work, with the ice in the foreground, the landscape behind, and a storm in the sky above. But this American painting differed in other elements. Art historian Nancy Rash observes that Bingham did not copy Leutze's "solution of having the boat move boldly across the picture," but "as in his earlier riverboat pictures he placed the boat in the center facing the viewer with a pyramidal group of figures rising to the head of an equestrian Washington silhouetted against the light sky."[43]

Bingham decided to put the general and his horse on a flatboat very similar to the Mississippi and Missouri craft that appeared in paintings such as *Lighter Relieving a Steamboat*, complete even to the boatmen's straps and other equipment in common use on the western rivers. It is interesting that Bingham painted the background figures and Washington himself in eighteenth-century dress, but the Americans in the foreground mostly in nineteenth-century clothing. On the right is a uniformed figure who looks very much like Andrew Jackson. To the left are men in broad-brimmed hats and trousers who resemble the Whigs and Democrats in Bingham's election paintings.

The painting shows images of American democracy in the nineteenth century emerging from an eighteenth-century Revolutionary scene. An image of George Washington and his army crossing the Delaware is embedded in a prophetic image of the Mississippi as well. All the elements of Whig-Liberal history are present. A celebration of liberty and democracy is combined with a teleological idea of history as a progress toward those ends.

❧ A Tory Interpretation: Lord Mahon's Hypothesis

In the mid-nineteenth century, many British Tories and American conservatives wrote major works of history, but few chose the American Revolution for their subject. An exception was Philip Henry Stanhope (1805–75), later the fifth earl of Stanhope. He is better remembered as Lord Mahon, an earlier courtesy title that he used as a pen name.

Mahon was a strong conservative who began his long service in Parliament as an implacable enemy of the Reform Act. He was also an able and very distinguished British scholar who helped establish the Historical Manuscripts Commission, founded the National Portrait Gallery, and became president of the Society of Antiquaries. All of these labors were an effort to preserve a sense of British continuity and tradition, in which he deeply believed.

As a scholar, Mahon specialized in eighteenth-century English history and published many learned volumes, including a still useful biography of Pitt the Elder and a multivolume history of England from the Peace of Utrecht in 1713 to the Peace of Versailles in 1783. Much of the larger work was about the American Revolution, which he discussed at length.[44]

Lord Mahon offered an original interpretation of the battles at Trenton and Princeton. He suggested that the brain behind the American campaign belonged to Benedict Arnold, and wrote of the critical moment before the attack, "it so chanced, that at this very juncture Washington received a visit in his camp from Benedict Arnold, who it is said, first suggested to him the idea of attempting to recross the Delaware and surprise some part of the King's troops." The source was given as "private information." For a conservative English historian who was not enthusiastic about the American Revolution, that interpretation suggested the role of chance rather than destiny in history.[45]

American historians in the nineteenth century rejected his idea as "certainly incorrect." A transatlantic controversy developed between Lord Mahon and American historians including John Gorham Palfrey and Jared Sparks on this and other issues.[46] It is true that Arnold visited Washington's headquarters on December 22, 1776, having marched south from the northern frontier with badly needed reinforcements for the Continental army. Washington asked him to go quickly to New England and help deal with British and German forces that had occupied Rhode Island. Arnold left immediately on December 22. His able biographer, James Kirby Martin, believes he "offered positive counsel on the commander's proposed counterattack against British outposts in New Jersey."[47] But Washington had been thinking and writing about the operation as early as December 14. Intelligence-gathering was well advanced by the time Arnold arrived. It is highly probable that Benedict Arnold was indeed consulted, with many other officers, but he was not the first to propose the operation, had no part in the final decision, and did not participate in detailed operational planning, which happened after he left for New England.[48]

Washington often consulted widely on major decisions and brought many people into the process of decision-making. Many officers and civilian leaders were more actively involved than Arnold. All believed that the operation was Washington's. One can understand why a conservative English historian might have cherished the thought that George Washington's most brilliant campaign was actually the work of the turncoat Benedict Arnold, who has been called the best general on both sides in the American War of Independence. But it wasn't so.

❧ Nationalists

After the American Civil War another generation took up the subject of the American Revolution. Washington's Crossing was an inspiration to them, and they gave the event a new meaning. Abraham Lincoln set the theme. In 1861 he declared, "Of [Washington's] struggles none fixed itself on my mind so indelibly as the crossing of the Delaware preceding the battle of Trenton. I remember these great struggles were made for some object. I am exceeding anxious that the object they fought for—liberty, and the Union and Constitution they formed—shall be perpetual."[49]

In the free states, which included nearly two-thirds of the national population, a distinctive attitude appeared among historians who had taken an active part in the Civil War. They emerged victorious from that great struggle, with a renewed faith in the great republic and a strong national identity. Throughout the North, the younger generation of the Civil War had a sense of confidence in the nation's future, and they rewrote its history in that spirit.

They also tended to believe that the pivotal moments of American history were its major wars, especially the War of Independence and the Civil War. They did not romanticize war; more than any other American generation they knew its horror. But they believed that the suffering in their war had not been in vain.

This new generation in the North developed a distinctive way of thinking about historical inquiry. In general people who deeply believe that the truth of history is on their side tend to be empiricists; those who feel that history is against them become relativists, as did American conservatives in the 1930s and American radicals in the 1980s and 1990s. After the Civil War, most northern writers were empiricists who thought of history as a science, not a natural science but a serious discipline of thought. When they studied history they worked hard at collecting the evidence and were absolutely confident that it would confirm their beliefs.

All of this led to a new generation of scholarship on the American Revolution in general, and the campaign of Trenton and Princeton in particular. A leading example was William S. Stryker's book *The Battles of Trenton and Princeton* (1898). The author came from an old New Jersey family and grew up on the Delaware River. He knew the town of Trenton intimately and much of the surrounding countryside. In his youth he talked with friends and family who had lived through the battles. During the Civil War, William Stryker served with New Jersey troops, and in 1867 he became adjutant general of the state. One part of his job was to compile historical records of military service, which he did with great industry, publishing rosters of New Jersey troops in both the Civil War and the American Revolution. Then he turned to the writing of history, mainly on Revolutionary battles in New Jersey.[50]

His major work was a history of the campaign of Trenton and Princeton. General Stryker modestly described his book as a "simple compilation of facts." It was more than that, a major effort in a lifetime of labor. He wrote that "in my early manhood, I began to take notes from conversations of my mother and her aged friends." More materials came to him in his office as adjutant general, and he organized a research project as if he were mounting a military campaign. In 1877, General Stryker went to Germany and worked in the Hessian archives at Marburg. Later he employed a team of researchers to copy 1,100 pages of German manuscripts. Nearly half of his book reprinted primary documents that he had gathered from American, British, and Hessian sources. General Stryker was not always attentive to their origin and provenance. Some of his materials do not survive tests of authenticity, but in general Stryker did his "compilation of facts" with great accuracy and attention to detail.[51]

The first half of the book was a narrative of the campaign, written in straightforward soldier's prose, with little of the romantic rhetoric that had flourished before the Civil War. The story was high drama about the building of a nation in time of war, with sweeping reversals of fortune. "Nowhere in the life struggle of any nation," Stryker wrote, "can be shown such a rapid contrast from almost total defeat to brilliant victory." He wrote with great pride of the making of an American nation and celebrated the efforts of ordinary Americans. Stryker concluded that the battles at Trenton and Princeton proved that the best generals and armies in the world "could be outgeneralled by their Washington and could be beaten in detail by the division of the young New Hampshire attorney, the battalion of the Rhode Island blacksmith, or the guns directed by the bookseller of Boston." Stryker's ancestors had served in the campaign, and his great-grandfather led the American army on country roads to Trenton. He wrote of the event with a strong sense of kinship, and of the American nation as if it were an extended family.[52]

The same spirit appeared in Henry Phelps Johnston's histories, *The Campaign of 1776 around New York* (1878) and *The Battle of Harlem Heights* (1897). Johnston was a Civil War veteran who became a professor of history at the College of the City of New York and published three major books on the American Revolution. They were very similar to those of Stryker, who was his friend. In spirit and substance both were nationalists and filiopietists who were absolutely confident that history was on their side. Both men did extensive research in Hessian, British, and American materials. Nearly half of their books consisted of

George Washington, bronze
statuette by Daniel Chester
French (ca. 1897, 1919 cast).
Chesterwood, Stockbridge,
Massachusetts.

full texts of primary documents, which were enduring contributions to scholarship. More than a century later, the published works of Stryker and Johnston are still judged by historians to be the most useful books on the battles of Long Island, Harlem Heights, Trenton, and Princeton.[53]

This militant nationalist school of historical interpretation inspired works by major American artists in the same era. One example was Daniel Chester French's equestrian statue of George Washington (1897) for a public site in Paris. French prepared himself by studying carefully the uniforms and equipment of the American Revolution. Washington appeared as a triumphant warrior, rising straight up in his stirrups, with a sword held aloft.[54]

Another work in the same spirit was the Princeton Battle Monument, commissioned by a local association in the town, with public support from the federal and state governments and many private donors. In 1907, the sponsors commissioned a design by Frederick MacMonnies, one of the most distinguished American sculptors of his generation. MacMonnies was a pupil of Augustus St. Gaudens and a student in Paris at the Ecole des Beaux-Arts. He lived as an expatriate in France, and his work was very much in the Beaux-Arts tradition.

The artist's first design was a small and very elegant Nike on a round pedestal, done with great refinement of proportion and detail. The design did not please the local committee, who thought it was too small and not sufficiently American. MacMonnies gave them a second design, a colossal Roman figure of the republic which towered over the small space that had been acquired at the head of Nassau Street, and was still not American. In 1912, MacMonnies offered a third design, with rectangular proportions said to be inspired by the Arc de Triomphe in Paris. The central figure was a tall figure of Washington on horseback. Below him was a pyramidal mass of American soldiers, some wounded and dying. In their midst the sculptor placed an allegorical figure of Liberty Triumphant, who has seized a broken standard from a dying American and raised it in victory.

The Princeton Battle Monument was dedicated on June 9, 1922, by President Warren Harding, who shared its national spirit and said, "I like this monument. I like every memo-

Princeton Battle Monument, limestone sculpture by Frederick MacMonnies (1922). Historical Society of Princeton.

rial to American patriotism and American sacrifices. No land can do too much to cherish with all its heart and soul these great inheritances." The assembled crowd responded with "long applause" and sang the first verse of "My Country, 'Tis of Thee."[55]

❧ Filiopietists

Nationalist historians such as Stryker and Johnston wrote in a spirit of respect for their forefathers. Others went far beyond them and created another school of interpretation in which respect became a form of reverence. They inspired critics to coin a new word: "filio-pietistic," having an excess of filial piety. The earliest recorded use of it was by Charles Francis Adams in 1893, when he complained of "historians of the Massachusetts filio-pietistic school." His own writings gave it a special meaning: an excess of piety for ancestors who were not Adamses. A British writer in 1897 identified the word as an Americanism. Early examples are all from New England.

Filiopietists had an idea of history that Perry Miller called the declension model. It reversed the hopeful teleology of Whigs and believed that change was for the worst. Brooks Adams expressed its spirit when he started every new day in the bathroom by singing a folk song of his own invention, with three words repeated over and over: "God damn it! God damn it! God damn it!"[56]

In some of its forms, filiopietism was benign and highly constructive. It stimulated interest in early American history and supported serious scholarship on the American Revolution. It gave rise to very active organizations such as the Daughters of the American Revolution, the Sons of the American Revolution, the Society of Colonial Wars, even the Daughters of the Barons of Runnymede. Most of these groups actively promoted research and teaching. Many still do so.

Washington Crossing the Delaware, postcard by Raphael Tuck & Sons (undated, ca. 1900). The African American soldier is banished from the boat.

But in other ways filiopietism could become malignant, when it shifted from celebration of one's own forebears to execration of others. When filiopietism went wrong, it became chauvinism and racism. An example appeared in the imagery of Washington's Crossing. An embossed postcard from the early twentieth century reverently reproduced Leutze's *Washington Crossing the Delaware* with one change. The African American was removed from the boat. In this interpretation, America was for whites only. Other versions of filiopietism restricted it to Christians, or Protestants, or even the descendants of Calvinists. It was an absurd error, but very powerful and dangerous in the world. In the great wars of the twentieth century, millions of human beings died as victims of murderous ideologies which might be thought of as malevolent filiopietism.

❧ Debunkers

A year after President Warren Harding dedicated the Princeton Battle Monument, Americans invented another new word to describe a contrarian school of historical interpretation. They called it "debunking," a term that rose from an interview that Henry Ford gave to reporter Charles N. Wheeler of the *Chicago Tribune* in 1916. That great industrialist declared, "History is more or less bunk. It's tradition. We don't want tradition. We want to live in the present. The only history that is worth a tinker's damn is the history that we make today."

The *Tribune* ran an editorial that called Ford an "ignorant idealist," and was sued for libel. In the courtroom, a lawyer for the newspaper cruelly tested Henry Ford's knowledge of history in general and the American Revolution in particular:

"Have there ever been any revolutions in this country?" the lawyer asked.
"There was, I understand," Ford replied.
"When?"

"In 1812."
"Did you ever hear of Benedict Arnold?"
"I have heard the name."
"Who was he?"
I have forgotten just who he is. He is a writer I think."[57]

The jury awarded Henry Ford damages of six cents. But the idea that history was bunk began to grow. With it came a new school of anti-historians called debunkers. A favorite target was the American Revolution and the spirit of filiopietism that flourished in America. Debunking took many forms. Some of it sought to explode national pieties as erroneous myths and legends. Others argued history had no teleology and insisted that it was a series of accidents without a plan or purpose. They rejected large visions and made a mockery of idealism.

Many debunkers in the early twentieth century were conservatives who were hostile to Whig or Liberal history. More than a few were Americans of old family who were not happy about what had happened to their country and felt that they had been displaced by vulgar upstarts. A leading debunker was a prominent Philadelphian, Sydney George Fisher, who attacked what he called "The Legendary and Mythmaking Process in the History of the American Revolution." The members of the Adams family in Massachusetts debunked the story of Paul Revere's Ride and deeply resented the adulation of George Washington.[58]

The history of the battles at Trenton and Princeton began to be debunked in this spirit. An early example was an essay by Charles Kendall Adams, who argued that it all happened because of a small mistake by a British general. Adams wrote, "Cornwallis was so sure of his game that he made the most stupendous blunder of the war, and decided to refresh his men by a night's sleep. . . . It appears to have been simply this mistake that enabled Washington not only to draw his army out of extreme peril, but also to fall upon the enemy at Princeton." Adams concluded that "if the British commander had attacked vigorously on the afternoon of his arrival, as Washington, Grant, Lee, or any other great general would have done, the chances seem to have been more than ten to one that Washington and his whole army would have been taken prisoners." So much for the generalship of George Washington.[59]

A few brave debunkers went after Washington in a more rounded way. One of them was William E. Woodward, the son of a southern tenant farmer, and a writer of strong radical opinions. He first used the verb "debunk" in a novel called *Bunk* in 1923 and defined it as "taking the bunk out of ideas and opinions." In 1926, he published a debunking biography of George Washington, which argued that Washington was a stupid, ignorant, greedy, selfish man who combined the vices of a modern businessmen, a southern slave driver, and a western Indian fighter. Woodward insisted that he was a poor general and owed his successes merely to luck.[60]

Woodward gained a brief notoriety, but the debunking of George Washington was uphill work. The difficulties appeared in the career of English writer Rupert Hughes, who started a multivolume biography to debunk Washington. By the end of volume III, Hughes was celebrating his subject more enthusiastically than the filiopietists did.[61]

A more successful approach was to debunk the filiopietists themselves by comparing them with the Revolutionary leaders of 1776. The leading example was a painting by Grant Wood, in which Washington's Crossing had a part. Wood was an artist of the American Middle West, who lived all his life in Iowa and painted the world he knew with deep affection that was combined with a sharp critical edge. His favorite subjects were the American myths that he loved and celebrated and criticized in paintings such as *American Gothic*, *Paul Revere's Ride*, and *Parson Weems' Fable*.[62]

One of these paintings was about the battle of Trenton and Princeton. It rose from an event in 1929, when Grant Wood installed a handsome stained glass window in the Veterans Memorial Building in Cedar Rapids, Iowa. It combined an allegorical image of the Republic with stained-glass images of soldiers from six American wars. To the artist's amazement, members of the Daughters of the American Revolution attacked him as un-American, for having the window manufactured in Germany. The controversy grew so bitter that the dedication was postponed for twenty-five years, when tempers had cooled.[63]

Daughters of Revolution, oil on masonite by Grant Wood (1932). Cincinnati Art Museum, the Edwin and Virginia Irwin Memorial.

The artist took his revenge in a painting called *Daughters of Revolution*. It was done for the Washington Bicentennial, a flood of filiopietism. Much of it came from the Daughters of the American Revolution who claimed to be the true keepers of the Revolutionary memory. Grant Wood did not agree. He called them "Tory Gals," and condemned them as "the people who are trying to set up an aristocracy of birth in the Republic."[64]

His painting showed three Daughters of the American Revolution, with smug expressions and unseeing eyes. One holds an imported blue willow teacup in an affected way. Behind them Grant Wood painted a faded image of Leutze's *Washington Crossing the Delaware* as a symbol of the true Revolutionary spirit. The artist was not debunking George Washington. He used Leutze's image to debunk the Daughters of the American Revolution.

The painting was widely exhibited and much discussed in the press. The San Francisco chapter of the Daughters of the American Revolution reviled it as "scandalous" and "destructive of American traditions." Grant Wood claimed that the Baltimore chapter of the Daughters of the American Revolution tried to have him deported as a "Red." But other Daughters loved the satire, and the painting gave many Americans a much needed laugh during the Great Depression.[65]

❧ The Conservative Revival

The First World War and the Great Depression did grave injury to the moral certainties of Whigs and Liberals and undercut their confident faith in history as a story of progress. One result was the multiplication of debunkers and disbelievers. Another was the growth of new forms of belief. Throughout the Western world, thoughtful people responded to the stresses of the new century by moving away from the liberal center, to the left and right.

These trends appeared in the writing of history during the 1930s, especially on highly charged subjects such as the American Revolution. One constructive historical consequence was a new and very serious interest in the people who had opposed the Revolution and had received little sympathy or respect from the Whig-Liberal historians. This trend appeared simultaneously in Germany, Britain, and the United States.

A German example was the work of Philip Losch, a Hessian scholar of high seriousness who was deeply unhappy with the Liberal and nationalist writings of Friedrich Kapp in the nineteenth century. After the horror of the First World War, and the political chaos that included the Kapp Putsch in 1920 (led by Friedrich Kapp's son Wolfgang), Losch was one of many Germans who looked back with nostalgia to what they called the *Zopfzeit*, "the age of the pigtails," in the good old times before the French and American Revolutions. In 1923 Losch published a highly sympathetic biography of Landgraf Wilhelm I, a Hessian prince who had been the archvillain of Liberal historians in the nineteenth century. Losch subtitled his book *Ein Fürstenbild aus der Zopfzeit*, a princely portrait from the good old days. He celebrated the positive achievements of the old regime in Hesse-Cassel, and gave his history the warm texture of a Tischbein portrait.[66]

In 1933, Losch published a more strongly argued book on the *Soldatenhandel* and the subsidy treaties that sent Hessian troops to America. It was a forceful revision of Kapp's liberal critique. Losch demonstrated the breadth of the practice throughout the world, its importance in saving Europe from Turkish conquest, its strong support in many parts of the Hessian population, its record of honorable service, its benefits for Hesse in general and its rewards for Hessians in particular. Losch's scholarship was careful and accurate. He contributed a useful corrective to the Whig history of the nineteenth century and encouraged much serious historical research by other scholars of the old regime.[67]

Similar tendencies appeared in British and American historiography during the 1930s. An important work was Troyer Steele Anderson's *The Command of the Howe Brothers during the American Revolution*, published by the Oxford University Press in 1936. It was a work of excellent scholarship, very sympathetic to William and Richard Howe. These two dark figures were a challenge to historical research. They were very taciturn, and their papers were destroyed by an accidental fire in the nineteenth century. Whig and Liberal historians debated whether the Howes were malevolent or merely incompetent. Tories asserted that the Howes were traitorous Whigs who wanted the Americans to win the war. Anderson carefully reconstructed the purposes of the Howe brothers and found them to be much more interesting, intelligent, principled, purposeful, and sympathetic characters. Other historians in the 1930s wrote of George III with new sympathy and respect. Lewis Namier began his anti-Whig work on the structure of politics in Britain during the eighteenth century. Bernard Pares and others strongly attacked Trevelyan's thesis about the dangers to English liberty in the government of Lord North, George Germain, and George III.

A third example of this international trend was a new sympathy for American Loyalists. Several antiquarian scholars had already written sympathetically of them in the nineteenth century, but something new appeared in the 1930s. The leading expert on the subject, Robert Calhoon, writes that "the modern re-evaluation of the Loyalists" began with two books: a monograph by Julian Boyd on Joseph Galloway, and Leonard Labaree's *Conservatism in American History*. Both works attempted to reconstruct the intellectual underpinnings of Loyalism, its social setting, and its political impact. Much historical scholarship followed on the same lines.[68] All of these works contributed new understanding to figures such as Friedrich Wilhelm II, the Howe brothers, and American Loyalists who had appeared in Whig-Liberal history as caricatures. The result was a serious and important contribution to knowledge.

❧ Karl Marx Crosses the Delaware: The Historical Fictions of Howard Fast

In the 1930s, others turned sharply to the left. Among them was Howard Fast, born in 1914 to Jewish immigrants and raised in the poverty and violence of New York slums. He dropped out of high school, worked as a stack boy at the New York Public Library, became a Marxist, and joined the Communist Party. He remained an active member through the Stalin era, went to jail for refusing to testify about his role, and stayed with the Communist Party until 1957, when he broke with it after Khrushchev's speech.[69] Howard Fast remained faithful to his radical principles much longer than most American Communists and promoted them in popular historical novels and screenplays that had a long reach: *Freedom Road* on Reconstruction (1944), *The American* on the Haymarket affair (1946), *Spartacus* (1951), *Citizen Tom Paine* (1943), *April Morning* on the day of Lexington and Concord, and *The Hessian* (1972), which Fast thought his best.[70]

In 1971, Howard Fast published *The Crossing*, a "fact-based novel" about George Washington and the first battle of Trenton. Fast wrote that his sources were mainly the writings of William Stryker and Washington Irving. "I leaned upon them heavily," the author said. The book was written in a style that was simple, lively, and direct. The strength of the work is the pace of its narrative, but it is full of historical howlers, imagined conversations, and casual inventions, all rationalized by a relativist argument that "history is filled with such alternate versions of the 'truth.'"[71]

The characters talk in twentieth-century New York slang, laced with much mild profanity from another era. Some figures appear as heroes and others as villains or fools, without much relevance to who they actually were or what they did. The author approved of "Johnny Stark" and "Billy Smallwood" and the men of "Smallwood's Rifles." He made Henry Knox into a buffoon, "fat and prissy," apparently on the basis of an unflattering painting late in life. The British and Germans are beneath contempt. General Howe appears as a war criminal, and Hessians as "uniformed robots."[72]

The hero is George Washington, who rises above his class origins to serve the Revolution. The novelist improves his credentials by giving him a fictional "personal bodyguard of black soldiers" and creates an imaginary conflict between Washington and evil American capitalists who own the Durham Iron Works and don't want him to use their boats. Altogether, it is a stridently materialist interpretation of the American Revolution. The film version even makes a historical materialist of Nathanael Greene, who is made to say, "Our own cause is, at its heart, a fight against British taxation. In the end, sir, we all kill for profit. The British, the Hessians . . . and us." It was an idea very far from the thinking of the Yankee idealists it seeks to represent.[73]

❧ Washington Remounted: Douglas Southall Freeman's Study of Leadership

While Howard Fast was working in New York, another American writer was hard at work in Virginia. The two represented American cultures so distant that they might have come from different planets. Douglas Southall Freeman (1886–1953) was the son of a Confederate veteran who had soldiered with Robert E. Lee. He was raised in Virginia to the ways of a southern gentleman and trained at Johns Hopkins as a professional historian. Freeman joined the staff of the *Richmond Times Dispatch*, became its editor from 1915 to 1949, and pursued a career as a serious scholar, publishing meticulous calendars and collections of primary documents on the history of Confederacy.[74]

While a graduate student at Johns Hopkins, Douglas Southall Freeman worked out an idea of history that centered on the vital role of individual leaders. "The influence of personality in History cannot be overestimated," he wrote. "While there are always great events that stir humanity, it will always be found that these events center around some one man, and in him have their life."[75]

Freeman developed that idea at length in multivolume biographies of Robert E. Lee and George Washington. Both projects centered mainly on the study of leadership, which Freeman believed to be not primarily a matter of specific techniques or skills but of moral qualities that he called character. Of Washington he wrote, "the great big thing stamped across that man is character." By character Freeman meant integrity, self-discipline, courage, absolute honesty, resolve, and decision, but also forbearance, decency, and respect for others. He believed that character in this sense was not a fixed set of attributes but something that a leader developed in response to changing conditions.[76]

Freeman's biographies of Lee and Washington were studies of character in action, and leadership in the flow of events. To that purpose, he invented a new historical method, which began with a mastery of sources, and centered his research and writing on discovering what his protagonist knew when he was making his leadership decisions, rather than on what we know after the fact.[77] This unusual way of studying and writing history has been called (very inaccurately) the "fog of war technique." There was nothing foggy about it. The object was to be very clear about what Washington knew, and when he knew it, and how he acted on that knowledge. Freeman's account of the battles at Trenton and Princeton were written in that way. The purpose was to learn about leadership from Washington's acts and choices.

Freeman's books were published over a span of twenty-five years. His *R. E. Lee* appeared in the depth of the Great Depression (1934–35), *Lee's Lieutenants* during the Second World War (1942–44), and *George Washington* during the Cold War (1948–57). American leaders were fascinated by his work. Eisenhower, Nimitz, and Marshall read Freeman's books, corresponded with him, and visited his Richmond home. Eisenhower kept a portrait of Freeman's Lee over his desk. All of these American leaders modeled their actions on what they took to be Freeman's idea of leadership as character. When *Washington* began to appear, Freeman was consulted by Truman and Eisenhower and by high-ranking officers of the Central Intelligence Agency. The books were also widely read by leaders in other sectors of American society. Both the Lee and Washington biographies won Pulitzer Prizes. Historians in the late twentieth century criticized them, but today his methods are being studied with renewed respect. In their own time, they had a large impact on American leaders, and a very long reach in the life of an American generation. The special quality of American leadership in the Second World War and the early years of the Cold War owed much to an idea of leadership as character that was personified by Freeman's Lee and Freeman's Washington.

❧ The Revival of Military History

In the aftermath of the Second World War and during the Cold War, military history flourished in the western world. Many Americans, Britons, and Germans had personal experience of military service. They became deeply interested in the history of war, especially in the history of battle.

The result was much new writing on the American Revolution and the campaign of Trenton and Princeton. In the United States, a contribution to those subjects was made by military historian Samuel Stelle Smith, with *The Battle of Trenton* (1965) and *The Battle of Princeton* (1967). Both were published by the Philip Freneau Press in Monmouth Beach, New Jersey, in a series that included other books by Smith on Monmouth and Brandywine, studies of Saratoga and Bunker Hill by Colonel John Elting, and other works. The books received little attention from academic historians and at the date of this writing are out of print, but serious students of military history hold them in high respect, and they both bring high prices on the antiquarian book market.[78]

Samuel Smith's books on Trenton and Princeton are highly accurate monographs, based on careful research in American primary materials and excellent use of Hessian transcripts in the Lidgerwood collection at Morristown National Historic Park. For readers who want to know how the battles actually happened, the books are valuable for their careful construction of events. The inquiry is tightly centered on questions of descriptive fact. Interpretative statements are carefully balanced, and judgments are mature and restrained.

On a research trip to the New York Public Library, Smith met a German military historian, Ernst Kipping, who did a dissertation at the University of Bonn on Hessian troops in the American Revolution. With Smith's help, part of Kipping's dissertation was published in an English translation as *The Hessian View of America, 1776–1783*. Kipping took an institutional, social, and cultural approach to military history. He studied the social and institutional structure of Hessian forces in America, as well as Hessian accounts of American culture. He also offered a new interpretation of the first battle of Trenton, writing that "the complete victory of Washington here was due mostly to the fact that the Hessian commander in chief at Trenton, Colonel Rall, was unable to reconnoiter the country with any degree of security." This author believes that judgment to be correct, more so than the results of the Hessian courts of inquiry.[79]

Kipping and Smith were deeply interested in making primary sources broadly available and published a translation of the letters of Captain Friedrich von Münchausen, Hessian aide to General William Howe. Another military historian who shared that interest was Joseph P. Tustin. While serving in the U.S. Air Force during the Berlin Airlift in 1948, he bought the manuscript diary of Hessian Jäger Captain Johann Ewald. Other publications by Ewald had been known to scholars, but this was a new source, extraordinary in its detail of the American war. Tustin published an English translation in 1979. It greatly increased knowledge of major events in the war.[80]

In some ways the work of Smith and Kipping and Tustin was similar in substance and tone to a school of military studies called "official history." After the Second World War, every combatant nation sponsored official military histories, which differed very much from one country to another. Some of it was propaganda, as in the old Soviet Union; but in the English-speaking world, official history developed into a distinct subdiscipline of history. Its purpose was to collect primary sources and to conduct accurate, fair, and objective research, centered mainly on command decisions and the administrative history of modern institutions.[81]

In the United States, the armed services established very active centers for military history. After they completed major publications on the Second World War, they turned to other subjects, including the American War of Independence, and some were very helpful for an understanding of the Trenton-Princeton campaign. An example was Erna Risch's *Supplying Washington's Army* (1981), a very able monograph on supply problems, a subject much discussed by academic historians, who offered various explanations for logistical failure. Erna Risch's research yielded evidence that no major American operation in the War of Independence was lost because of logistical failures, even as "military plans were certainly frustrated by supply deficiencies," a more balanced interpretation and a useful corrective to earlier work.

Robert Wright's *The Continental Army* (1983, 1989) was a painstaking reconstruction of the organizational history of every unit in the Continental army. Its thesis was summarized on the frontispiece, which showed Howard Pyle's painting of the American assault on Redoubt 10 at Yorktown. The author added the caption: "Military professionals launched this bayonet attack. . . . Only an army with thorough training, sophisticated organization, esprit de corps, and courage could have attempted this assault. The Continental Army had become such an army." Wright told the story of the creation of the professional Continental army, and its importance to the republic it served.[82]

The Navy Department's major contribution was a vast compendium called *Naval Documents of the American Revolution*, a collection of primary sources so comprehensive that it touched every part of the war and became a major contribution to scholarship. The Office of Air Force History sponsored symposia on command decisions for the bicentennial of the American Revolution.[83]

History-minded military officers also produced their own studies of the Revolution. They tended to be highly professional in their approach and were specially interested in leadership and decision-making. Among the most useful works that dealt with the subject of Washington's Crossing were two books by General Dave R. Palmer, who wrote from long experience of military leadership in two tours of duty in Vietnam and four in Europe. He also commanded the First Armored Division, headed the Army's Command and General Staff College, and became superintendent of West Point. General Palmer published several books and essays about George Washington, notably *The Way of the Fox* and *George Washington, First in War* (2000). He came away from his inquiries with a strongly positive assessment of Washington's generalship. Some academic critics thought he was too positive, but in the judgment of this historian, General Palmer got it right.[84]

ᴈ The Flowering of Academic Historiography

A very strong movement in the twentieth century was the growth of historical scholarship in the universities. History did not emerge as a separate academic discipline in American colleges until the late nineteenth century, at the same time as economics, biochemistry, anthropology, and most major disciplines. Then it grew very rapidly, with the expansion of American higher education.

Academic history in the mid-twentieth century was highly eclectic, more so than most disciplines, but it had a distinct character. Its practitioners were formally trained in graduate programs as specialists in particular subjects. In the 1950s, 1960s, and early 1970s, most academic historians tended to be liberal Democrats or progressive Republicans, centrist in the larger scheme of things, and trained to an idea of balance in interpretation, restraint in judgment, and tolerance of other views. A particular purpose was to respect the historicity of the past. They tended to be very conscious of its distance from the present and were hostile to works that stress elements of continuity in history or similarities between the present and the past. They were mostly interested in problems of change, especially revolutionary change, and the American Revolution became a favorite subject.

Academic scholars were trained to study the history of large structures, long processes, major institutions, material conditions, and systems of value, which they believed to be the determinants of history. But they were organized as a cottage industry and mostly worked alone. Here was a structural problem for their own work. How could a cottage industry deal with large historical problems? One solution was the academic monograph, which attempted to put large problems to small tests. Another was the academic essay, which increasingly became historiographical, a study of writing about history rather than history itself.

Academic historians produced many thousands of publications on the American Revolution in the second half of the twentieth century. The work tended to share important substantive patterns. It was not much interested in the history of events. Battle books passed out of fashion, along with *histoire evenimentielle* in general. No academic historian has ever published a book explicitly on the battles of Trenton and Princeton.[85]

In other ways academic historians made many contributions. Much of their work consisted in case studies of small groups and individuals, not as actors who made a difference but as people who were caught up in large historical processes. Examples included a large biographical literature of high quality: Ira Gruber on the Howe brothers; George Billias on John Glover; Paul David Nelson on many figures both British and American. Other academic historians published excellent one-volume histories of the Revolution, notably Don Higginbotham and Robert Middlekauff. Monographs examined many aspects of the Revolution and the war: the problem of origins, patterns of thought and belief, social change, political structure, religion, cultural history, and much more.

Academic scholars tended to work within a specific period and a national frame, but they shared a common culture throughout the Western world. Many European historians began to write American history, and vice versa. In Britain, Eric Robson and Piers Mackesy contributed important analyses of military strategy, with particular attention to constraints upon it in the American war. Rodney Atwood wrote an excellent Cambridge dissertation, *The Hessians, Mercenaries from Hessen-Kassel in the American Revolution* (1980); part of the book was a helpful and informed study of the battle of Trenton, with a carefully "balanced view," sympathetic to the Hessians.

German historians also made contributions to American history. Among them are Horst Dipple's *Deutschland und die amerikanische Revolution*, a dissertation at the University of Cologne in 1970, translated as *Germany and the American Revolution, 1770–1800: A Sociohistorical Investigation of Late Eighteenth-Century Political Thinking* (1977). It is a major work on the European Press, and German responses to the American Revolution. Americans and Britons have been writing German history: Charles Ingrao's *The Hessian Mercenary State* (1987); Charles Taylor's book on peasant life and the Hessian military state.[86]

Other academic disciplines are increasingly doing historical research. Economist Fritz Redlich published *The German Military Enterpriser and His Work Force: A Study in European Economic and Social History* (1964–65). It analyzes the *Soldatenhandel* as an early capitalist enterprise. The result of all this activity was a huge outpouring of historical knowledge.[87]

❧ Popular History

Another new approach to history emerged in the late twentieth century, partly as a reaction to academic historiography, in which professional scholars wrote increasingly for one another. It called itself popular history, and its primary purpose was to reach a very large public. It attempted to write a history of ordinary people, allowed them to speak in their voices and turned up many sources that had been neglected. And it was popular in its rhetoric.

Much of it was scholarship of very high quality. A distinguished example was Richard Ketchum's *The Winter Soldiers* (1973). The author went to Yale, commanded a subchaser in the Second World War, and played a major role in the development of the American Heritage Publishing Company, which worked to make history more attractive and accessible to a broad public. Ketchum reached a large public with many volumes on the history of the American Revolution. His work centered on individual experiences, and his books showed a flair for vivid images and fluent narrative.[88]

Another first-rate work in this genre was William Dwyer's *This Day Is Ours!* (1983). The author served as a war correspondent in five campaigns during the Second World War, then became a journalist for the *Trentonian* and a resident of Lawrenceville, New Jersey. His book was a popular history of the New Jersey campaign from the fall of Fort Washington on November 16, 1776, to the battle at Princeton on January 3, 1776. Its great strength was its attention to the individual accounts by soldiers in three armies and by citizens in New Jersey. Dwyer turned up sources that had not been used before and made a major contribution that way. For example, his materials brought out the scale of the second battle of Trenton more clearly than ever before. Reviewers celebrated the book for its vignettes of individual experience as "intimate, personalized and vivid." It was a well-balanced work, with genuine sympathy for Hessian, British, and American troops, as well as the people of New Jersey. Not so strong were its larger frame and its narrative line. A real weakness was a lack of rigor and accuracy in its use of sources. But altogether it was an engaging and important work.

American artists in this generation took a similar approach in images of the American Revolution. A lively result is an essay by Bill Mauldin, called *Mud and Guts: A Look at the Common Soldier of the American Revolution*. It was commissioned by the National Park Service for the Bicentennial of the American Revolution and published in 1978. Bill Mauldin's images of the Revolution were in the tradition of his immortal cartoon characters from the Second World War, Willie and Joe. He took a dim view of officers in general, and George Washington in particular as a smug, self-righteous martinet. Mauldin wrote, "As for Washington, I find myself comparing him in many ways to Douglas MacArthur. Both loved their creature comforts . . . both were austere and anti-egalitarian, and both managed to win their wars."[89]

But generals were not the important men in Bill Mauldin's army. Each of his drawings on the Revolution argued a thesis that the spirit of '76 was "best embodied by unlettered, unshaven, sardonic riflemen, whose aim was to get the unpleasantness over and head back to a wilderness full of uncut logs and uncooked game." Bill Mauldin illustrated this idea with cartoons that put Willie and Joe into cocked hats and Revolutionary rags. In one drawing, two ragged soldiers emerge from the paymaster's hut. One studies a Continental dollar he had just received. The other says, "Well, no one can accuse us of being mercenaries." Another drawing shows the weary army slogging through deep mud. One filthy, unshaven soldier attempts to scrape his foot-rags with a bayonet. Another says, "I forget . . . Are we advancing or retreating?"[90]

"*I forget . . . are we advancing or retreating?*" cartoon by Bill Mauldin, *Mud and Guts: A Look at the Common Soldier of the American Revolution*. Washington: National Park Service, 1978, frontispiece, 8. Courtesy of the Mauldin Estate.

"*I forget . . . are we advancing or retreating?*"

These miserable men were Bill Mauldin's anti-heroes of the American Revolution. He concluded, "I had the honor of knowing some of their descendants a couple of centuries later. The offspring weren't much of an improvement, cosmetically speaking, but their attitudes were still healthy—to my way of thinking. I trust they haven't become an endangered species."[91]

❧ History for an Age of Anxiety

Another historical mood appeared after the Second World War. The poet Wystan Hugh Auden called the postwar era an "Age of Anxiety." In a long poem of that name, set in a Manhattan Bar, he explained, "When the historical process breaks down and armies organize with their embossed debates the ensuing void . . . when necessity is associated with horror and freedom with boredom, it looks good for the bar business."[92] The year was 1947. Auden's poem won a Pulitzer Prize in 1948, and found a sympathetic public oppressed by the memory of world wars and great depressions, and troubled by the world to come. A young professor of music at Brandeis, Leonard Bernstein, called his second symphony *The Age of Anxiety*, which in turn inspired a ballet of the same title.

In 1953, the same theme inspired a leading abstract artist to do a painting called *Washington Crossing the Delaware*. He had been born and raised as Larry Grossberg in the Bronx, moved to Manhattan and changed his name to Larry Rivers, studied music at the Juilliard School, and after the war joined a circle of abstract expressionists with Hans Hoffman, Willem de Kooning and Jackson Pollock, who painted their own anxieties.

One day Larry Rivers was reading Tolstoi's *War and Peace* and decided to do a modern painting of a great historical epic on an American theme. He chose the subject of Washington's Crossing. His friend Frank O'Hara thought he was out of his mind. Rivers replied, "What could be dopier than a painting dedicated to a national cliché—Washington Crossing the Delaware," he wrote. "The last painting that dealt with George and the rebels is hanging in the Met and was painted by a coarse German nineteenth-century academician, who really loved Napoleon more than anyone and thought crossing a river on a late December afternoon was just another excuse for a general to assume a heroic, slightly tragic pose."[93]

But Rivers had another image in mind. "What I saw in the crossing was quite different. I saw the moment as nerve wracking and uncomfortable. I couldn't picture anyone getting

Washington Crossing the Delaware, by Larry Rivers (1953). Museum of Modern Art, Estate of Larry Rivers/Licensed by VAGA, New York, New York.

Detail of Study for Washington Crossing the Delaware, by Larry Rivers (n.d.). Museum of Modern Art, Estate of Larry Rivers/Licensed by VAGA, New York, New York.

into a chilly river around Christmas time with anything resembling hand-on-chest heroics." The result was a large painting, seven by nine feet, now in New York's Museum of Modern Art. Its colors are muted shades of brown, orange, and faded red. Washington appears as a small eccentric figure, mounted on a prancing white horse in the upper left corner of the painting. The central character is a forlorn soldier with a bandaged head, standing in a boat. Shadowy figures of individual soldiers and small groups are scattered through the painting and call to mind Auden's Age of Anxiety. "In wartime," the poet wrote, ". . . everybody is reduced to the anxious status of a shady character or a displaced person." In Rivers's painting these men were not working purposefully together but standing apart in what Auden called "their separate sense of themselves." The figures themselves were more clear in quick sketches that Rivers did for the painting. Their mood is dark, withdrawn, brooding, puzzled, bewildered. There are no heroics here and no certainties. Larry Rivers's painting of the Revolution became a mirror for his own troubled time.[94]

The painting got much attention, but not as the artist expected. Frank O'Hara wrote a celebratory poem, "On Seeing Larry Rivers' Washington Crossing the Delaware." Kenneth Koch did a play called *George Washington Crossing the Delaware*. Leading New York painters contributed a pop-art stage set. Patriots and filiopietists scarcely seemed to notice, but the painting caused an uproar among avant-garde artists in New York. Larry Rivers remembered, "In the bar where I can usually be found, a lot of painters laughed." Other abstract expressionists were genuinely outraged that Rivers had actually tried to represent something.[95]

Art critics have perceived the painting as a transitional work between an abstract expressionism that looked within and a pop art that searched for deep meaning in the surfaces of ordinary things. To this historian, the painting has another significance. Larry Rivers's image of *Washington Crossing the Delaware* expressed the stresses that he felt so keenly in his own age, by representing the anxiety of an earlier moment. The artist candidly confessed that he knew very little about the American Revolution and that his "true inspiration derived from patriotic grade school plays he had acted in or watched as a boy." Much of what he believed about Emanuel Leutze and his painting was mistaken, but his artist's intuition was true to an important part of the emotional experience that happened in the "black times" of 1776.

✎ Debunkers Again, and Academic Iconoclasts

In the last half of the twentieth century, the debunkers returned after a long silence during the Second World War. They spoke in different voices, but most shared a common theme. They thought of truth as the underlying fact, and history as the "lowdown," in both senses of that slang word: "inside information" of a nature "low, contemptible and despicable."[96] An early example was Richard Bissell's *New Light on 1776*, which the old respectable firm of Little, Brown and Company thought an appropriate publication for the Bicentennial of the Revolution. One chapter offered the lowdown on the battle of Trenton, in a new version of the old humbug about drunken Hessians. "Across the river in Trenton," Bissell wrote, "the sneering, contemptuous Hessians were essen und fressen und trinken their ponderous way through a heavily Germanic and bibulous Christmas. . . . It was the only American victory in history in which all the prisoners, both officers and men, were found to be suffering from severe heartburn and hangovers." Another chapter offered readers the lowdown on the battle of Princeton: that Washington defeated the "kraut cohorts" there by sending a cannonball through the walls of Nassau Hall. Never mind that the battle was fought mainly in a different place, and against British troops.[97]

A similar mood spread among a troubled generation of academic historians who were born in the baby boom (ca. 1941–57). They came of age in the late sixties and early seventies, when a youth revolution was bright with the promise of a new age. It was a revolution that failed in the era of Vietnam, Watergate, burning cities, and blighted hopes. A conservative revival followed, in which Republicans moved to the right, liberal Democrats shifted

George Washington Crossing the Delaware, acrylic on canvas by Peter Saul (1975).
George Adams Gallery, New York.

toward the center, and many on the left sought sanctuary in American universities as internal exiles from a society that turned away from them.

In the 1980s some of these internal exiles rejected all politics. Others increasingly called
themselves American Marxists and predicted the coming collapse of capitalism. Then came
the unexpected collapse of the Soviet Union instead, and the failure of Marxism throughout the world. It was a double disaster for the American left. The result was an angry generation of academic iconoclasts, disillusioned by the failure of radical movements, alienated
from American institutions, and filled with cultural despair. When the light of their revolution failed, some of them could see nothing but darkness.

More than a few became historians. Some ex-Marxists became historical relativists who
beat their dialectical swords into epistemological ploughshares, and rejected ideals of objective and empirical inquiry. They judged other works mainly by ideological standards of political incorrectness such as racism, sexism, and elitism. Any work with a positive tone about the
United States was condemned as "triumphalism." Their writings expressed intense hostility
to American institutions and alienation from the main lines of American history.[98]

The same iconoclastic mood inspired a new school of academic painting. An example
was *George Washington Crossing the Delaware*, by Peter Saul, an artist on the faculty of the
University of Texas in Austin. In vivid, clashing, Day-Glo acrylic colors, it shows a river
crossing that has been reduced to chaos. Washington, his horse, and his men (all in tie-wigs)
tumble out of the boat into the river while American and British soldiers fire at each other
in a battle on the ice. The values of Emanuel Leutze's painting are inverted as completely as
the capsized boat.[99]

❧ Multiculturalism

While some scholars lost their way in relativism, cynicism, and iconoclastic rage against
their own culture, others found a way forward in the inspirations of the new left and made
more enduring contributions. One was to take seriously an American tradition of radical

thought. Important examples on the subject of the American Revolution included Gary Nash's work on artisans and mechanics in the seaport cities, Eric Foner's biography of Thomas Paine, and many works by Alfred Young.[100]

Another major contribution was to broaden historical inquiry in dimensions of race, ethnicity, class, and gender. Examples that touched the Trenton-Princeton campaign included Steven Russwurm's work on the Philadelphia militia and Charles Patrick Neimeyer's study of the Continental army.[101]

This multicultural work was sometimes marred by strong hostility to one set of cultures in particular: the predominant Anglo-Saxon and north European ways of the great majority of the American population. Another weakness was a tendency to perform rituals of iconoclastic rage as expressions of academic grace. Charles Patrick Neimeyer, for example, began a very useful monograph on the Continental army by attacking "the older, frequently mythic history of 1776." He promised that his "new generation" would "finally set things straight." In his first paragraph he accused John Adams of cowardice and dishonesty, as a man who "talked one way and acted another," a novel way of thinking about John Adams, of all people. After that regrettable beginning, the substance of this work became an important contribution to historical scholarship.[102]

This school of interpretation inspired an American painter to do yet another version of Washington's Crossing. In 1975, Robert Colescott produced a work called *George Washington Carver Crossing the Delaware: Page from an American History Textbook*. It is a new version of Leutze's painting in which George Washington is replaced by George Washington Carver, and every figure in the boat is meant to explode a racist stereotype. The artist explained, "In re-exposing these images I wanted to show the grand-scale stupidity of stereotyping."[103]

George Washington Carver Crossing the Delaware: Page from an American History Textbook, acrylic on canvas by Robert Colescott (1975). Collection of Robert Orchard. Phyllis Kind Gallery, New York, New York.

❧ The Revival of Patriotism and Filiopietism

In the last two decades of the twentieth century, a strong revival of patriotism and filiopietism occurred in many Western cultures and especially the United States. A leader was President Ronald Reagan, and he was riding a powerful wave. One of its many manifestations was a revival of mainstream values among millions of Americans. Another was a resurgence of interest in history. In the United States, that new movement was as broad and diverse as the American population. Some of it was a growth in awareness of ethnic and religious identity. Much of it was an enormous increase in work on family history, often of high sophistication. An example that made a major contribution to knowledge of the Trenton and Princeton campaign was the activity of the Johannes Schalm Historical Association, founded in 1977 by members of the huge Schalm family, many of whom are descended from Hessians who served in America. They are dedicated to "researching, collecting and disseminating data relating to German auxiliaries to the British Crown . . . and their descendants." An important annual journal has published much primary material and many Hessian documents.[104]

Another part of this movement is the rapid growth of reenacting groups. Thousands of these associations exist in America, Britain, and Europe. Many in the United States, and some in Germany, center on the American Revolution. The events of Washington's Crossing are reenacted every year, except in 2002, when it was called off for snow and ice. The events of 2001 included German reenactors from Hesse-Cassel. To meet with groups of reenactors is to form high respect for their interest in history, their concern for historical accuracy, and their large purposes. In Massachusetts, Revolutionary reenactors led by Miles and Rhonda McConnell organized groups called Pickets in 1998. They wore eighteenth-century civilian dress and circulated through the large crowds that turn out for reenactments, functioning as teachers and interpreters. Reenacting groups are increasingly diverse in the United States. They are people of every class, creed, and color, who share a common sense of historical identity and cultural belonging.

❧ Crosscurrents

In the twenty-first century, history is flourishing in the United States, and throughout the Western world. Stories of growing historical illiteracy that appear in the media and in some professional publications are themselves historically inaccurate. In the universities, historical methods are spreading very rapidly to other disciplines. The electronic revolution has made sources more accessible than ever before. An example is Peter Force's old *American Archives* (1837–53), one of the most useful collections of primary documents on the American Revolution. Its nine huge folio volumes are now available on a single compact disc. Nearly all American imprints and newspapers for the Revolutionary era became available in microtext during the late twentieth century. In the early twenty-first century they are in process of electronic publication. Old genres such as letterpress editions of manuscripts have been brought to new levels of refinement. The *Papers of George Washington*, the most important collection of primary materials for the study of the American Revolution, and the campaign of Trenton and Princeton in particular, are being published in an excellent new edition which seeks to include all of Washington's correspondence, including letters to him; more than 140,000 documents, meticulously edited, will soon be available on-line.[105]

History writing and thinking are more eclectic than ever before. Old Marxists are still at work, as if their Revolution is just around the corner. Neoconservatives are publishing with evangelical enthusiasm. Liberals are reviving, and the center is beginning to hold again. The old political and military history is alive and well. Social and cultural and intellectual historians are churning out useful monographs. Popular history is more successful than ever in reaching a broad public by film, cable, magazines, and best-selling books. Debunkers are joyously debunking, and antiquarians delight in escaping to the past. Iconoclasts and filiopietists stimulate one another to new excesses of abuse and adulation. Genealogists, reenactors, collectors,

(North Swell) Washington Crossing the Delaware, painting by Sandow Birk (n.d.).
Oil on canvas, 37-1/2 x 63 inches. Collection of Laguna Art Museum. From the
Stuart and Judy Spence Collection, donated April 1999 by Judy and Stuart
Spence. Courtesy of the artist.

curators, archivists, conservationists, tour guides, filmmakers, park rangers, and public historians have never been so busy, and the best of it is the synergy among these many activities.
    A striking example of expanding interest in history today is the work of Sandow Birk,
one of the most gifted and productive painters in California at the turn of the twenty-first
century. He is known for a large project called *In Smog and Thunder: Historical Works from the
Great War of the Californias*, which links historical images with contemporary realities in a
running commentary on the cultural and ethnic war in Los Angeles and San Francisco
during the late twentieth century. Another group of paintings brings together three of the
artist's passionate interests in surfing, art, and history. One work in that series takes Emanuel
Leutze's painting as its inspiration. It is called *(North Swell) Washington Crossing the Delaware*
and represents surfers in the posture of Washington's soldiers, moving bravely into a great
ocean swell that is driven by a North Pacific storm. The artist explains, "Most Americans will
immediately recognize Leutze's painting and thereby will easily pick up my parody of it,
using California surfers in the same heroic poses." Tyler Stallings observes that the painting
shows surfers "in the throes of both a past and present history." In Sandow Birk's work,
history is a living presence in our own time. He makes that connection in a creative way, and
with deep sympathy.[106]
    Here is one of the great paradoxes of modernity. The more the world changes, the
more important history becomes. A few scholars like to say that the past is a foreign country,
but they could not be more mistaken. The past is our country. Our own kin lived there. The
memory of what they did is becoming ever more important as a part of our lives.

BIBLIOGRAPHY

The best general bibliography of the American Revolution is Ronald Gephart, *Revolutionary America, 1763–1789: A Bibliography*, 2 vols. (Washington, 1984). Dwight L. Smith and Terry A. Simmerman, *Era of the American Revolution: A Bibliography* (Santa Barbara, 1975), is a helpful compilation of 1,400 abstracts from *America, History and Life*. A remarkably comprehensive work is Lawrence H. Gipson, *A Bibliographical Guide to the History of the British Empire, 1748–1776*, published as volume 14 in his *History of the British Empire Before the American Revolution* (New York, 1968). W. J. Koenig and S. L. Mayer, *European Manuscript Sources of the American Revolution* (London and New York, 1974), surveys primary materials in foreign archives.

On the coming of the Revolution, two helpful works by Thomas R. Adams are *American Independence, The Growth of an Idea: A Bibliographical Study of the American Political Pamphlets Printed Between 1764 and 1776 Dealing with the Dispute Between Great Britain and Her Colonies* (Providence, 1965) and *The American Controversy: A Bibliographical Study of the British Pamphlets About the American Disputes, 1764–1783*, 2 vols. (Providence, R.I., 1980).

For the War of Independence, J. Todd White and Charles H. Lesser, eds., *Fighters for Independence: A Guide to Sources of Biographical Information on Soldiers and Sailors of the American Revolution* (Chicago, 1977), lists 538 narratives, diaries, journals, and autobiographies by men and a few women who fought for American independence.

❧ Manuscript Sources

American Philosophical Society, Philadelphia
    Charles Willson Peale Collection
    Thomas Paine Collection
    Phineas Pemberton Weather Diary
British Library, London
    Haldimand Papers Add. Ms. 21665–97
    Graves Papers Add. Ms. 14038–39
    Mackenzie Papers Add. Ms. 39190
Chicago Historical Society, Chicago
    Weedon Papers
Clements Library, University of Michigan
    Clinton Papers
    Gage Papers
David Library, Washington Crossing, Pa.
    Breadalbane Military Manuscripts
    William Legge, Second Earl of Dartmouth, Papers
    Peter Force Papers
    Francis James Jackson Papers
    Robert Clayton Orderly Book
    John Peebles Journal
    American Orderly Books
Harvard University, Houghton Library, Cambridge, Mass.
    Jared Sparks Collection
Library of Congress, Washington, D.C.
    James Grant of Bellindaloch, Papers
    Alexander Hamilton Papers
    Robert Honeyman Diary
    Hugh Percy Papers, film
    Rodney Family Papers, includes Diary of Capt. Thomas Rodney
    Arthur St. Clair Papers

    Jonathan Bayard Smith Family Papers
    Adam Stephen Papers
    John Sullivan Papers
    Consider Tiffany Papers
    Jeremiah Wadsworth Collection
    Washington Papers
    Marburg Hessian Transcripts
    War Office Letters
Morristown National Historic Park, Morristown, N.J.
    William Van Vleeck Lidgerwood Collection (Hessian Transcripts)
    Regimental Orderly Books
National Archives
    Revolutionary Pension Records
New-York Historical Society
    John Lamb Papers
New York Public Library
    Bancroft Transcripts
    Samuel Adams Papers
Princeton University Library
    Ensign Thomas Glyn Journal
    Samuel De Forest Narrative
Public Records Office, London
    Cornwallis Papers PRO 30/11/1-7, 58, 60–110
    Howe-Germain Correspondence CO5/94
    War Office Records
        Letters from Commanders-in-Chief WO 1/2–10
        Regimental Rosters
            16th Light Dragoons WO12/1246
            17th Light Dragoons WO12/1306
            17th Foot WO12/3406
            42nd Foot WO12/5478–79
            55th Foot WO12/6471; 5317–18
Virginia Historical Society
    Richard Clough Anderson Papers
    John Clinton Letters

❧ Published Primary Sources

Collections

    Balderston, Marion, and David Syrett, eds., *The Lost War: Letters from British Officers During the American Revolution* (New York, 1975).
    Crary, Catherine S., ed., *The Price of Loyalty: Tory Writings from the Revolutionary Era* (New York, 1973).
    Dandridge, Danske, ed., *American Prisoners of the Revolution* (Charlottesville, 1911).
    Dann, John C., ed., *The Revolution Remembered: Eyewitness Accounts of the War of Independence* (Chicago, 1980).
    Davies, K. G., ed., *Documents of the American Revolution, 1770–1783, Colonial Office Series*, vol. 12, 14, Transcripts, 1776–77 (Irish University Press, 1976).
    Force, Peter, ed., *American Archives,* 9 vols., 5th ser., vols. 1–3 (Washington, 1837–53).
    Learned, M. D., and C. Grosse, eds., *Americana Germanica* (New York, London, and Berlin, 1902).
    Moore, Frank, ed., *Diary of the American Revolution,* 2 vols. (New York, 1859–60).

Pettengill, Ray W., ed., *Letters from America, 1776–1779: Being Letters of Brunswick, Hessian, and Waldeck Officers with the British Armies During the Revolution* (Boston, 1924).

Ryan, Dennis P., ed., *A Salute to Courage: The American Revolution as Seen Through Wartime Writings of the Continental Army and Navy* (New York, 1979).

Scheer, George F., and Hugh F. Rankin, eds., *Rebels and Redcoats: The American Revolution Through the Eyes of Those Who Fought and Lived It* (1957; New York, 1987).

Smith, Paul H., ed., *Letters of Delegates to Congress* (Washington, 1976–2000).

Stryker, William, ed., *Documents Relating to the Revolutionary History of New Jersey*, in *NJA*, 2d ser., vol. 1 (Trenton, 1901).

Pennsylvania Archives, 1st ser., vol. 5.

Individual American Accounts

Anonymous American reports on the battle of Princeton: Williamsburg *Virginia Gazette* (Purdie), 28 Feb. 1777; and Dixon and Hunter's *Virginia Gazette*, 21 Feb. 1777.

Anonymous Connecticut militiaman, quoted in Dwyer, *The Day Is Ours*, 323; original not seen.

Anonymous, "Diary of an Officer on Washington's Staff," headed "Newtown, Pa., Dec. 22–27, 1776," and published without provenance in Stryker, *Battles of Trenton and Princeton*, 360–64. The original has not been located. Freeman asserts that this document "has to be rejected as a forgery or later compilation. . . . No officer could have known as much at the time, or could have seen the relative importance of events as clearly as this individual set everything forth" (*Washington*, 4:310). Many scholars have reproduced this document and attributed it to Major John Fitzgerald, from whom part of it was cribbed. But Freeman is correct; this source is counterfeit and should not be used. Another source for Fitzgerald (below) can be used with caution. For further discussion, see appendix X, above.

Anonymous, "Editor's Note," *PMHB* (1884), 255–56; accounts of panic in Philadelphia during the "black times."

Anonymous, "Extract from a Letter to a Gentleman in Connecticut," 12 Dec. 1776, in Stryker, *Battles of Trenton and Princeton*, 321.

Anonymous, "Journal of a Pennsylvania Soldier, July–December 1776," *NYPBL* 8 (1904), 547–49.

Anonymous, "Letter from a Gentleman of Great Worth with the American Army. . . ," *Maryland Journal*, 16 Jan. 1777.

Anonymous, "Letter from a Respectable Inhabitant," 22 Aug. 1816, reproduced in Wilkinson, *Memoirs of My Own Times*, 1:136.

Anonymous, "A young naval officer from Pennsylvania who had been granted leave to serve as a volunteer in the Jersey campaign," in Scheer and Rankin, *Rebels and Redcoats*, 219.

Adams, John: *Diary and Autobiography*, ed. Lyman Butterfield, 4 vols. (Boston, 1961, 1964); *Papers of John Adams*, ed. Robert J. Taylor et al., 3 vols. (Cambridge, 1977); *Adams Family Correspondence*, ed. Lyman Butterfield, 2 vols. (Cambridge, 1963).

Adams, Samuel, *Writings*, ed. Harry A. Cushing, 4 vols. (New York, 1904).

Adlum, John, *Memoirs of the Life of John Adlum*, ed. Howard H. Peckham (Chicago, 1968).

Alexander, William (Lord Stirling), "Extract of a Letter from an Officer of Distinction, at Newtown, Bucks County, dated December 27, 1776," *Pennsylvania Evening Post*, 31 Dec. 1776; *NJA*, 2d ser. 1:247–49.

Allen, Daniel. Private, Connecticut state troops. Diary, 1776, in Edward C. Starr, *A History of Cornwall, Connecticut . . .* (Cornwall?, 1926), 252–54.

Anderson, Enoch, *Personal Recollections of Captain Enoch Anderson, an Officer of the Delaware Regiments in the Revolutionary War*, ed. Henry Hobart Bellas (Wilmington: Historical Society of Delaware *Papers* 16 (1896); rpt. New York, 1968).

Anderson, Richard, undated memorandum in the letterbook of General Robert Anderson, based on memories of conversations with his father, Captain Richard Clough Anderson, of the 5th Virginia Continentals. This document was reprinted as authentic by Stryker, *Battles of Trenton and Princeton*, 373–74. It became an important element in many interpretations of the first battle of Trenton, but its account is fundamentally in error. For a discussion see Ward, *Adam Stephen*, below, and text above, 231–33.

　　Avery, David. Chaplain, 15th Massachusetts Regiment. "The Papers of David Avery, 1746–1818," ed. John M. Mulder and Milton J. Coalter, 13 reels of microfilm and transcript in Princeton Theological Seminary; not seen.

　　Baumann, Sebastian. Captain, New York Artillery. *Memoirs of Colonel Sebastian Beauman and His Descendants with Selections from His Correspondence*, ed. Mary C. Doll Fairchild (New York, 1900).

　　Bayard, John, memoir in *PA*, 1st ser., vol. 5.

　　Bedinger, Henry. Sergeant, Virginia Riflemen. In Danske Dandridge, *Historic Shepherdstown* (Charlottesville, 1910), 97–144.

　　Beale, Robert. Ensign, 5th Virginia Regiment. "Revolutionary Experiences of Major Robert Beale," *Northern Neck of Virginia Historical Magazine* 6 (1956), 500–506; partly rpt. in Ryan, *A Salute to Courage*, 55–58.

　　Beatty, William. Captain, Maryland Line. "Correspondence of Captain William Beatty, of the Maryland Line, 1776–1781," *Historical Magazine*, 2d ser. 1 (1867), 147–50. "Journal of Capt. William Beatty, June 1776–January 1781," ibid., 79–85; *MDHM* 3 (1908), 104–19.

　　Bentley, William, *The Diary of William Bentley, D.D., Pastor of the East Church, Salem, Mass.*, 4 vols. (Salem, 1905–14). Bentley is the son of Joshua Bentley. The published edition is incomplete and inaccurate; the original manuscripts should be consulted at the American Antiquarian Society.

　　Biddle, Charles, *Autobiography* (Philadelphia, 1883).

　　Biddle, Clement. Colonel, deputy quartermaster general. Letters in *AA* 5 3:464, 470, 1581, and Stryker, 365, 369.

　　Bloomfield, Joseph, *Citizen Soldier. The Revolutionary War Journal of Joseph Bloomfield*, ed. Mark Lender and James Kirby Martin (Newark, 1982).

　　Bostwick, Elisha, "A Connecticut Soldier Under Washington: Elisha Bostwick's Memoirs of the First Years of the Revolution," ed. William S. Powell, *WMQ* 3 6 (1949), 94–107.

　　Brown, Obediah. Private, Sargent's Regiment. "Military Journal, January 1776–January 1777, Around Boston and New York," *Westchester County Historical Society Bulletin* 4 (1928), 67–72; 5 (1929), 10–20.

　　Burrows, John, *Sketch of the Life of General John Burrows, of Lycoming County* (1837; rpt. Williamsport, Pa., 1917).

　　Boudinot, Elias, *Journal; or, Historical Recollections of American Events During the Revolutionary War* (Philadelphia, 1894; rpt. New York, 1968).

　　[Cadwalader, John]. Colonel commanding Philadelphia Associators. "Extract of a Letter from an Officer of Distinction in General Washington's Army, January 5, 1777," *Pennsylvania Evening Post*, 16 Jan. 1777; rpt. *NJA*, 2d ser. 1:258–62.

　　Cadwalader, Lambert, to Timothy Pickering, May 1822, *PMHB* 25 (1901), 259.

　　Chamberlin, William, "Letter of General William Chamberlin," *MHSP*, 2d ser. 10 (1895–96), 490–504.

　　Clinton, George, *Public Papers*, ed. Hugh Hastings and J. A. Holden (New York, 1899–1914).

　　Collin, Nicholas. Swedish Lutheran pastor. *The Journal and Biography of Nicholas Collin, 1746–1831*, ed. Amandus Johnson (Philadelphia, 1936).

　　Cooley, Eli. Account of the battle of Trenton, manuscript, Princeton University Library; not found.

　　Custis, George Washington Parke, *Recollections and Private Memoirs of Washington, by His Adopted Son . . .* (New York, 1859; rpt. Bridgewater, Va., 1999).

　　Darlington, William. American prisoner of war, escaped from British captivity in New York. Deposition, *AA* 5 3:1234.

　　Dewey, John. Private in St. Clair's Brigade. "Military Journal," April 1776–February 1777, in *Life of George Dewey, Rear Admiral, USN, and Dewey Family History* (Westfield, Mass., 1898), 278–81.

　　Ewing, James. *AA* 5 3:1429, 1444.

Farnsworth, Amos. Enlisted man and officer in Massachusetts Continental regiments. "Diary Kept by Lieut. Amos Farnsworth of Groton, Mass, During Part of the Revolutionary War, April 1775–May 1779," ed. Samuel Greene (Cambridge, 1898); *MHSP,* 2d ser. 12 (1899), 74–107.

Field, Mary Peale, "A Recently Discovered Letter of the American Revolution," ed. Carl Van Doren, *Princeton University Library Chronicle* 4 (June 1943).

Fish, Nicholas, letter to John McKesson, 19 Sept. 1776, *History Magazine,* 2d ser. 3:33; Johnston, *Harlem Heights,* 151–52.

Fisher, Elijah. Private, Massachusetts regiments and Washington's Life Guard. *Elijah Fisher's Journal While in the War of Independence* (Augusta, Me., 1880).

Fitch, Jabez, *The New-York Diary of Lieutenant Jabez Fitch of the 17th (Connecticut) Regiment from August 2, 1776, to December 15, 1777,* ed. W.H.W. Sabine (New York, 1954).

Fithian, Philip Vickers, *Philip Vickers Fithian: Journal, 1775–1776, Written on the Virginia-Pennsylvania Frontier and in the Army Around New York,* ed. Robert Greenhalgh Albion and Leonidas Dodson (Princeton, 1934).

Fitzgerald, Col. John. Recollection of the battle at Princeton, recorded by G.W.P. Custis, *Memoir,* 191–92. Freeman writes, "Custis was prone to be theatrical, and the language he put in Washington's mouth was too formal even for an eighteenth-century leader, in the heat of the action, but there probably was some foundation for the story" (*Washington* 4:354).

Forrest, Captain Thomas, letter to Col. Thomas Proctor, 29 Dec. 1775, in Stryker, *Battles of Trenton and Princeton,* 371–73.

Francis, Jacob. Freed slave and Continental soldier. Pension Narrative in Dann, *Revolution Remembered,* 391–99.

Franklin, Benjamin. "Account of Negotiations" [with Richard Howe], 22 March 1775, in *Writings of Franklin,* ed. A. H. Smyth, 10 vols. (New York, 1905–7), 6:324–59.

Glover, John. Colonel, Marblehead Regiment. "General John Glover's Letterbook," ed. Russell W. Knight, EIHC 112 (1960), 1–55; rpt. as *General John Glover's Letterbook, 1776–1777* (Salem, 1976).

Graham, Michael. Volunteer with the Pennsylvania Flying Camp. Pension narrative in Dann, *Revolution Remembered,* 48–52.

Graydon, Alexander, *Memoirs of His Own Time, with Reminiscences of the Men and Events of the Revolution,* ed. John Stockton Littell (Philadelphia, 1846; rpt. 1969). This work first appeared as *Memoirs of a Life, Chiefly Passed in Pennsylvania, Within the Last Sixty Years, with Occasional Remarks upon the General Occurrences, Character and Spirit of That Eventful Period* (Harrisburg, 1811). It is one of the most perceptive and articulate memoirs of the Revolutionary era but should be used with caution on matters of fact.

Greene, Major General Nathanael. *The Papers of General Nathanael Greene,* ed. Richard K. Showman (Chapel Hill, 1976+).

Greenman, Jeremiah. *Diary of a Common Soldier in the American Revolution, 1775–1783,* ed. Robert C. Bray and Paul E. Bushnell (DeKalb, Ill., 1978).

Greenwood, John. Fifer in Patterson's Massachusetts Regiment. *The Revolutionary Services of John Greenwood of Boston,* ed. Isaac J. Greenwood (New York, 1922), rpt. as *The Wartime Services of John Greenwood: A Young Patriot in the American Revolution* (n.p.: Westvaco Corporation, 1981).

Hale, Nathan. Captain in Knowlton's Connecticut Rangers. *Documentary Life of Nathan Hale,* ed. George D. Seymour (New Haven, 1941).

Hand, Edward, *The Unpublished Revolutionary Papers of Major General Edward Hand of Pennsylvania,* ed. A. J. Bowden (n.p., 1907).

Heath, Major General William, *Memoirs of Major General Heath* (Boston, 1798; rpt. 1904, 1968). Manuscripts in the Massachusetts Historical Society are available on microfilm and are partly published in MHSC, 5th ser. 4 (1878), 1–288; MHSC, 7th ser. 4 (1904), 1–354; 5 (1905) 1–419.

Hamilton, Alexander. Captain, New York Artillery. "Alexander Hamilton Viewed by His Friends: The Narratives of Robert Troup and Hercules Mulligan," ed. Nathan Schachner,

WMQ3 4 (1947), 203–25; also Hamilton to Alexander MacDougall, 17 March 1776, in *Papers of Alexander Hamilton*, ed. H. C. Syrett (New York, 1961), 1:181–82; eyewitness accounts in John C. Hamilton, *Alexander Hamilton*, 2 vols. (New York, 1840), 1:57; *Alexander Hamilton's Pay Book*, ed. E. P. Panagopoulos (Detroit, 1961); and idem, "Hamilton's Notes in His Pay Book of the New York Artillery Company," *AHR* 62 (1957), 310–25. Internal evidence shows that the reading notes were in the same ink and handwriting as the company records and must have been kept during the same period of the war.

Hodgkins, Joseph. Officer in Massachusetts Continental regiments. Letters rpt. in Herbert T. Wade and Robert A. Lively, eds., *This Glorious Cause: The Adventures of Two Company Officers in Washington's Army* (Princeton, 1958), 227–28.

[Houston, William Churchill?]. "Campaign Journal, from November 29, 1776, to May 6, 1777," in Thomas Allen Glenn, *William Churchill Houston (1746–1788)* (Norristown, Pa., 1903).

How, David, *Diary of David How, a Private in Colonel Paul Dudley Sargent's Regiment . . .* , ed. George W. Chase and Henry B. Dawson (Morrisania, N.Y., 1865).

Howland, John, *The Life and Recollections of John Howland*, ed. Edwin H. Stone (Providence, 1857).

Hull, William, account of the first battle of Trenton, in a letter to Andrew Adams, 1 Jan. 1777, in Stryker, *Trenton and Princeton*, 376.

Hunter, Andrew. Presbyterian clergyman, served with Continental army. "Diary, 1776–1779," manuscript, Princeton University Library.

Hutchinson, William. Pennsylvania militiaman. Pension narrative in Dann, *Revolution Remembered*, 145–55.

Jefferson, Thomas, *Papers of Thomas Jefferson*, ed. Julian Boyd (Princeton, 1950), vols. 1–2.

Johnston, James. Pennsylvania militiaman. Pension Narrative in Dann, *Revolution Remembered*, 399–406.

Jones, Judge Thomas, *History of New York During the Revolutionary War* (New York, 1879).

Knox, Henry. Commander of American Artillery. Papers, used at the Boston Athenaeum; also MHS. Not used are Knox Papers at J. P. Morgan Library.

Lacey, John. Captain, 4th Pennsylvania Regiment. "Memoirs," *PMHB* 25 (1901), 1–13, 191–207, 341–54, 498–515; 26 (1902), 101–11, 265–70.

Lardner, John. Private, Philadelphia Light Horse. Account of service with his unit in the Princeton campaign, letter to Capt. John R. C. Smith, 31 July 1824, in Stryker, *Battles of Trenton and Princeton*, 89.

[Lawrence, Robert], *A Brief Narrative of the Ravages of the British and Hessians at Princeton in 1776–77: A Contemporary Account of the Battles of Trenton and Princeton*, ed. Varnum Lansing Collins (Princeton, 1906; rpt. New York, 1968). Misidentified by Stryker as the diary of Thomas Olden.

Lee, Charles, *The Lee Papers*, vols. 4–7 in NYHS *Collections* (New York, 1871–74).

Lee, Henry, *Memoirs of the War in the Southern Department of the United States*, 2 vols. (Philadelphia, 1812).

Livingston, William, *The Papers of William Livingston*, vol. 1, ed. Carl E. Prince (Trenton, 1979).

Lee, Richard Henry, *Memoir of the Life of Richard Henry Lee*, 2 vols. (Philadelphia, 1825); *Letters*, ed. J. C. Ballagh, 2 vols. (New York, 1911–14).

McCarty, Thomas. Sergeant, Virginia Infantry. "The Revolutionary War Journal of Sergeant Thomas McCarty," ed. Jared C. Lobdell, *NJHSP* 82 (1964), 29–46.

McCurtin, Daniel, "Journal," in Thomas Balch, ed., *Papers Relating to the Maryland Line During the Revolution* (Philadelphia, 1857), 11–41.

McDougall, General Alexander, correspondence in *AA* 5 3:1123–1451 passim.

McMichael, James, "Diary of Lieutenant James McMichael of the Pennsylvania Line, 1776–1778," *PMHB* 16 (1892), 129–59; "Diary of Lieutenant James McMichael," *PA*, 2d ser. 15:195–218; the texts vary in small details.

Marrett, John. Minister in Woburn. Interleaved almanac diary entries from 1 Jan. 1775 to 31 Dec. 1776. Published in part in Samuel Dunster, ed., *Henry Dunster and His Descendants* (Central Falls, 1876).

Marshall, Christopher, *Extracts from the Diary of Christopher Marshall, Kept in Philadelphia and Lancaster, During the American Revolution, 1774–178*, ed. William Duane (Albany, 1877).

Martin, Joseph Plumb. Private, Connecticut state troops. *Private Yankee Doodle: Being a Narrative of Some of the Adventures, Dangers, and Sufferings of a Revolutionary Soldier*, ed. George F. Scheer (Boston, 1962).

Maxwell, General William, "General William Maxwell's Correspondence," ed. A. Van Doren Honeyman, *NJHSP*, n.s. 10 (1925), 176–80.

Monroe, James. Lieutenant, Virginia Infantry; future president. *Autobiography*, ed. Stuart Gerry Brown (Syracuse, 1959); James Monroe to George Coleman, 17 Jan. 1809, *Tyler's Quarterly* 9:247–48.

Mott, John, "Recollections," in Amanda Jones, *A Psychic Autobiography*, 11–13 (New York, 1910); "John Mott of New Jersey in the Revolution," www2.crown.net/sspicer/Genealogy/Mott.

Morris, Margaret, *Margaret Morris Her Journal with Biographical Sketch and Notes*, ed. John W. Jackson (Philadelphia: MacManus, 1949); the manuscript journal (not seen) is in the Quaker Collection, Haverford College Library.

Morris, Captain Samuel. Commanding 1st Philadelphia Troop of Light Horse. Letters, *PA*, 5th ser, vol. 1.

Moulder, Joseph. Captain, Philadelphia Artillery. See A. Cuthbert to C. C. Haven, in Haven's *Thirty Days in New Jersey Ninety Years Ago: An Essay Revealing New Facts in Connection with Washington and His Army* (Trenton, 1867), 44–47. Cuthbert's father was an officer in Moulder's battery.

Muhlenberg, Reverend Henry, *The Journals of Henry Melchior Muhlenberg*, 3 vols., ed. Theodore G. Tappert and John W. Doberstein (Philadelphia, 1942).

Nash, Solomon, *Journal of Solomon Nash, a Soldier of the Revolution, 1776–1777*, ed. Charles I. Bushnell (New York, 1861).

Olney, Stephen, "Captain Stephen Olney, Memoir." In *Biography of Revolutionary Heroes: Containing the Life of Brigadier Gen. William Barton, and also Captain Stephen Olney*, ed. Mrs. Williams (Providence, 1839).

Paine, Thomas, *Complete Writings of Thomas Paine*, ed. Philip Foner (New York, 1969). Also "Reply to Cheetham," New York *Public Advertiser*, 22 Aug. 1807, Paine's recollections of the Jersey campaign; copy in Thomas Paine Papers, APS.

Peale, Charles Willson, "Journal by Charles Willson Peale, Dec. 4, 1776–Jan. 20, 1777," *PMHB* 38 (1914), 271–86, 278.

Pennington, William S., "The Diary of William S. Pennington," ed. William A. Ellis, *NJHSP* 63 (1945), 199–218; 64 (1946), 31–42.

Peters, Thomas. Trooper, Philadelphia Light Horse. Account of the Princeton campaign quoted in Dwyer, *This Day Is Ours!*, 304, without citation; not seen.

Polhemus, Captain John. New Jersey officer. "Memoirs," Leach Collection, Genealogical Society of Pennsylvania; partly rpt. in Ryan, *A Salute to Courage*, 58–59; other material is in Clean Hammond's *A Biography of John Hart* (Newfane, Vt., 1977).

Powell, Leven, "Correspondence of Leven Powell," *John P. Branch Historical Papers* 1 (1901),46.

Proctor, General Thomas, "A Sketch of General Thomas Proctor," ed. Benjamin Nead, *PMHB* 4 (1880), 454–70.

R——, Sergeant, "The Battle of Princeton," first published in the Wellsborough, Pa., *Phenix*, 24 March 1832; rpt. as "The Battle of Princeton," *PMHB* 20 (1896), 515–19.

Randolph, Benjamin, diary entries in *Father Abraham's Pocket Almanac* 1775, 1776, 1778, printed by John Dunlap, Philadelphia; at NYPL, not seen.

Reed, Joseph. Colonel and adjutant general, Continental army. "General Reed's Narrative of the Movements of the American Army in the Neighborhood of Trenton in the Winter of 1776–1777," *PMHB* 8 (1884), 301, 391–402; *Life and Correspondence of Joseph Reed*, ed. William B. Reed, 2 vols. (Philadelphia, 1847).

Reed, Martha, "A Grandmother's (Martha Reed, wife of John Shannon) Recollections of the Old Revolutionary Days," 1875, typescript by Susan Pindar Embury, Trenton Public Library, with thanks to Wendy Nardi for helping us find this document.

Rodney, Caesar, *Letters to and from Caesar Rodney, 1756–1784*, ed. George Herbert Ryden (Philadelphia, 1933).

Rodney, Thomas. Captain, Delaware Light Infantry. *The Diary of Captain Thomas Rodney, 1776–1777*, ed. Caesar A. Rodney, *Papers of the Historical Society of Delaware*, vol. 1, paper 8 (Wilmington, 1888; rpt. New York, 1974). The manuscript diary, 1776–77, is in LC; handwriting clearly shows that much of the diary is a memoir.

Rosbrugh, Rev. John. Presbyterian chaplain in the 3rd Northampton Pennsylvania Militia, killed in second battle of Trenton. Letters in John C. Clyde, *Rosbrugh, a Tale of the Revolution; or, Life, Labors, and Death of Rev. John Rosbrugh* (Easton, Pa., 1880).

Rush, Benjamin, *Autobiography*, ed. George W. Corner (Princeton, 1948); *Letters*, ed. Lyman H. Butterfield, 2 vols. (Princeton, 1951).

St. Clair, General Arthur, *The St. Clair Papers . . .* , 2 vols., ed. William Henry Smith (Cincinnati, 1882).

Shaw, Samuel, *The Journal of Major Samuel Shaw* (Boston, 1847).

Slade, William. Private, Connecticut state troops. Diary, in Danske Dandridge, ed., *American Prisoners of the Revolution* (Charlottesville, 1911), 492–502.

Slaughter, Philip. Captain, Virginia Infantry. Memoir and diary., in Rev. Philip Slaughter, *A History of St. Mark's Parish, Culpeper County, Virginia* (Baltimore, 1877; rpt. 1994, 1998), 106–8.

Smith, John. Sergeant, Lippitt's Rhode Island Regiment. "Sergeant John Smith's Diary of 1776," ed. Louise Rau, *MVHR* 20 (1933), 247–70.

Stark, John. General of New Hampshire troops. *Memoir and Official Correspondence of General John Stark*, ed. Caleb Stark (Concord., N.H.?, 1860).

Stephen, Adam. General of Virginia troops. "Letters of Adam Stephen to R. H. Lee," *Historical Magazine*, 1st ser. 9 (1865), 118–22.

Stiles, Ezra. Congregational clergyman; president, Yale College. *Literary Diary of Ezra Stiles*, ed. Franklin P. Dexter (New York, 1901).

Sullivan, General John, *Letters and Papers of Maj. General John Sullivan*, 3 vols., *vol. 1, 1771–1777*, ed. Otis G. Hammond (Concord, N.H., 1930).

Tallmadge, Benjamin, "Major Tallmadge's Account of the Battles of Long Island and White Plains," in Johnston, *Campaign of 1776*, 2:77–81.

Thacher, James, *A Military Journal of the American Revolution* (title varies) (Hartford, 1854, 1862; rpt. New York, 1969).

Tilghman, Tench, *Memoir of Lieut. Col. Tench Tilghman* (Albany, 1876; rpt. N.Y., 1971), includes correspondence.

Trask, Israel. Mansfield's Massachusetts Regiment. Pension narrative in Dann, *Revolution Remembered*, 408–09.

Trumbull, Benjamin. Chaplain, Connecticut troops. "Diary," *CTHSC* 7:195.

Van Cortlandt, Philip, *Philip Van Cortlandt's Revolutionary War Correspondence and Memoirs*, ed. Philip Judd (Tarrytown, 1976).

Washington, George, *The Papers of George Washington, Revolutionary War Series*, ed. W. W. Abbott, Dorothy Twohig, Philander D. Chase, and Beverly H. Runge. Charlottesville, 1988+. Especially useful for this inquiry were vols. 3–8. Still useful for references in earlier works is *The Writings of Washington*, ed. John C. Fitzpatrick (Washington, 1932), vol. 6, Sept. 1776–Jan. 1777.

Webb, Samuel Blachley. Colonel; aide to Washington. *Correspondence and Journals*, 3 vols., ed. Worthington Chauncey Ford (New York, 1893; rpt. New York, 1969).

Weedon, George, Letter to John Page, 29 Dec. 1776, account of Trenton battle, manuscript in CHS; "Calendar of the Correspondence of Brigadier General George Weedon," *APSP* 38 (1899), 81–114.

White, J[oseph], *A Narrative of Events, as They Occurred from Time to Time, in the Revolutionary War, with an Account of the Battles of Trenton, Trenton-Bridge, and Princeton* (Charlestown, Mass., 1833; rpt. *American Heritage*, June 1956, 74–79).

Williams, Ennion. Major in acting command, Pennsylvania Rifle Regiment. Correspondence in *PA*, 1st ser., vol. 5.

Wilkinson, James. Major; aide to Gates and St. Clair. *Memoirs of My Own Times*, 3 vols. including a very rare and valuable atlas (Philadelphia, 1816; rpt. 1973).

Young, William, "The Journal of Sergeant William Young," *PMHB* 8 (1884), 255–78.

British and Loyalist Accounts

Anonymous British soldiers, reports of the engagement at Princeton, *New York Gazette and Weekly Mercury*, 13 Jan. 1777.

Anonymous, "Extract of a Letter received in London," Nov. 30, 1776, *AA* 5 3:928.

Auchmuty, Robert, letter to the Earl of Huntingdon, 8 Jan. 1777. British Historical Manuscripts Commission, *Report on the Manuscripts of the Late Reginald Rawdon Hastings*.

Bamford, William, "Bamford's Diary." *MDHM* 27 (1932), 240–59, 296–314; 28 (1933), 9–26.

Barker, John. Lieutenant, 4th (King's Own) Foot. Diary, published as *The British in Boston*, ed. Harold Murdock and Elizabeth E. Dana (Boston, 1924).

Bowater, John. Captain, British Marines. Correspondence with the Earl of Denbigh, in Marion Balderston and David Syrett, eds., *The Lost War: Letters from British Officers During the American Revolution* (New York, 1975).

Carleton, Gov. Sir Guy. Governor and military commander in Canada. Microfilm in MNHPL.

Carter, William. Lieutenant, 40th Foot. Letters dated 1775–76, published as *Genuine Detail . . .*, (London, 1784), copy in Houghton Library, Harvard University.

Clinton, Major General Sir Henry, *The American Rebellion: Sir Henry Clinton's Narrative of His Campaigns, 1775–1782*, ed. William B. Willcox (New Haven, 1954).

Cornwallis, General Charles, *Correspondence of Charles First Marquis Cornwallis*, 3 vols., ed. Charles Ross (London, 1859). Full and enlightening except on the American Revolution, where it is very thin. A helpful calendar is George H. Reese, comp., *The Cornwallis Papers, Abstracts of Americana* (Charlottesville, 1970), strong on the period from 1779 to 1781.

Cresswell, Nicholas, *The Journal of Nicholas Cresswell*, ed. Samuel Thornely (New York, 1924).

Dowdeswell, Thomas. 1st Battalion, Brigade of Guards. "The Operations in New Jersey: An English Officer Describes the Events of December 1776," ed. J. E. Tyler, *NJHSP* 70 (1952), 133–36.

Evelyn, William Glanville, Captain, 4th Foot. *Memoir and Letters of Captain W. Glanville Evelyn . . .*, ed. G. D. Scull (Oxford, 1879).

Galloway, Joseph, *Historical and Political Reflections on the Rise and Progress of the American Rebellion* (London, 1780); *Letters to a Nobleman, on the Conduct of the War in the Middle Colonies* (London, 1780); *A Letter from Cicero to the Right Hono. Lord Viscount H——e* (London, 1781); *An Extract from a Reply to the Observations of Lieut. Gen. Sir William Howe, on a Pamphlet Entitled Letters to a Nobleman* (London, 1781); "Examination of Joseph Galloway Before the House of Commons, June 18, 1779," *AA* 5 3:1343; *A Reply to the Observations of Lt. Gen. Sir William Howe* (London, 1780).

Germain, (Lord) George, *Historical Manuscripts Commission, Report on the Manuscripts of Mrs. Stopford-Sackville of Drayton House, Northamtonshire*, 2 vols. (London, 1904, 1910).

Glyn, Ensign Thomas. 1st Battalion, Brigade of Guards. "Ensign Glyn's Journal on the American Service with the Detachment of 1,000 Men of the Guards Commanded by Brigadier General Mathew in 1776," manuscript, Princeton University Library.

Grant, Major General James, letters in LT/MNHPL; MHT/LC; partly pub. in Stryker, *Battles of Trenton and Princeton*, 51, 67, 70, 115, 334, 425; James R. Hutson, "Revolutionary America: The Papers of Gen. James Grant," *Library of Congress Information Bulletin* 62 (April 2003), 71–74; Robert D. Clyde, *James Grant of Ballindalloch: A Register of the Microfilm Edition . . .* (Washington, 2003).

Hale, John William. Lieutenant, 45th Foot. "Letters Written During the American War of Independence," in H. C. Wylly, ed., *1913 Regimental Annual, The Sherwood Foresters . . .* (London, 1913), 9–59; also in W. H. Wilkin, *Some British Soldiers in America* (London, 1914).

Hanger, George, Baron Coleraine, *The Life, Adventures, and Opinions of Colonel George Hanger,* 2 vols. (London, 1801).

Harcourt, Sir William. Lieutenant colonel, 16th Light Dragoons. Correspondence with his father in vol. 11 of *The Harcourt Papers,* ed. Edward Harcourt (Oxford, 1880–85).

Harris, George. Captain, 5th Foot. Stephen R. Lushington, *The Life and Services of General Lord Harris, GCB* (London, 1840).

Howe, Admiral Richard (Lord Howe), correspondence in *NDAR* 7 (1776–77), 254–57 passim; "By Richard Viscount Howe . . . and William Howe, Esq., General of His Majesty's Forces in America, the King's Commissioners for Restoring Peace . . . Proclamation," 30 Nov. 1776, *AA* 5 3:928.

Howe, General Sir William. The papers of the Howe brothers were destroyed by fires in the nineteenth century, but much material survives in the British Public Record Office and other collections. Published material includes William Howe, *The Narrative of Lieutenant-General Sir William Howe in a Committee of the House of Commons on the 29th of April 1779 . . .* (London, 1780); Orderly Book, 13 Sept. 1776, in *Kemble Papers*; correspondence with Lord George Germain in Stryker, 327–28; orders in MHT and LT; letters in Grans mss, LC.

Hunter, Martin. Ensign, 52d Foot. *The Journal of General Sir Martin Hunter* (Edinburgh, 1894).

Inman, George. Ensign, 17th Foot. "Ensign George Inman's Narrative of the American Revolution," *PMHB* 7 (1883), 237–48.

Kemble, Stephen. Adjutant to General Howe. *The Kemble Papers,* 2 vols. NYHS *Collections* (New York, 1884–85).

Leslie, Alexander. Letters in MHT and LT; partly published in Stryker, *Battles of Trenton and Princeton,* 424, passim.

Mackenzie, Frederick. Major, 23rd Foot. *The Diary of Frederick Mackenzie,* 2 vols. (Cambridge, 1930); original in Regimental Archives of Royal Welch Fusiliers, Canarvon Castle, Wales.

McPherson, John. Capt., 17th Foot. Good letters in Grant Papers, LC.

Montresor, John. Captain, Corps of Engineers. *The Montresor Journals,* ed. G. D. Scull, NYHS *Collections for the Year 1881* (New York, 1882).

Moody, James, *Lieutenant James Moody's Narrative of his Exertions and Suffering* (London, 1783; rpt. New York, 1968).

Odell, Jonathan. Loyalist physician in Burlington, N.J. Extracts of correspondence in Hill, *History of the Church in Burlington, N.J.*

Peebles, John. Grenadier captain, 42d Foot. *John Peebles' American War: The Diary of a Scottish Soldier, 1776–1782,* ed. Ira D. Gruber (London, 1998).

Percy, Hugh (Lord). Brigadier and colonel, 5th Foot. *Letters,* ed. C. K. Bolton (Boston, 1902).

Rawdon, Francis (Lord), correspondence with Francis, Earl of Huntingdon, Historical Manuscripts Commission, *Hastings Manuscripts, Report on the Manuscripts of the late Reginald Rawdon Hastings,* HMC 78, 4 vols. (London, 1928–47), vol. 3.

Robertson, Archibald. Captain-Lieutenant, British Engineers. *Archibald Robertson, Lieutenant Colonel, Royal Engineers: His Diaries and Sketches in America, 1762–1780,* ed. Harry Miller Lydenberg (New York, 1930).

Sandwich, John, Earl of, *The Private Papers of John, Earl of Sandwich,* 3 vols. (London, 1932), correspodence of the First Lord of the Admiralty.

Serle, Ambrose, *The American Journal of Ambrose Serle, Secretary to Lord Howe, 1776–1778,* ed. Edward H. Tatum Jr. (San Marino, Calif., 1940).

Stedman, Charles, *The History of the Origin, Progress, and Termination of the American War,* 2 vols. (London, 1794). For a critique see R. Kent Newmeyer, "Charles Stedman's History of the American War," *AHR* 63 (1957–58), 924–34.

Stirke, Lieutenant Henry, "A British Officer's Revolutionary Journal, 1776–1778," ed. S. Sidney Bradford, *MDHM* 56 (1961).

Stuart, Colonel Charles, correspondence with the Earl of Bute, in Mrs. E. Stuart Wortley, *A Prime Minister and His Son: From the Correspondence of the 3rd Earl of Bute and of Lt.-General the Hon. Sir Charles Stuart, K.B.* (London, 1925).

Sullivan, Thomas. Sergeant, 49th Foot. *From Redcoat to Rebel: The Thomas Sullivan Journal*, ed. Joseph Lee Boyle (Bowie, Md., 1997); the manuscript diary (not used) is in the Historical Society of Pennsylvania.

Tarleton, Banastre. Cornet, 16th Light Dragoons. Letter to his mother, 18 Dec. 1776, Tarleton Family Papers; copy in Hardwicke Papers, BL; the best account of the capture of Gen. Charles Lee; published in Robert Duncan Bass, *The Green Dragoon* (New York, 1957), 20–22.

Van Cortlandt, Mrs. Philip, "A Loyalist's Wife: Letters of Mrs. Philip Van Cortlandt, December 1776 to February 1777," ed. H.O.H. Vernon-Jackson. *History Today*, August 1964.

Williams, Richard. Lieutenant, Royal Welch Fusiliers. *Discord and Civil Wars: Being a Portion of a Journal Kept by Lieutenant Williams of His Majesty's Twenty-third Regiment While Stationed in British North America During the Time of the Revolution*, ed. Jane van Arsdale (Buffalo, 1954); graphic descriptions, but troubling questions of authenticity.

German Primary Accounts

Many individual German accounts of the New York and New Jersey campaigns have long been available to American scholars, most of them in both English and German texts. The largest collections are the Bancroft German Transcripts in the New York Public Library, the Lidgerwood English transcripts in the Library of the Morristown National Historic Park, and the Marburg Collection of German materials (photostats) in the Library of Congress. Film copies of all three sets are in the author's collection. Many of these materials have been published by Bruce Burgoyne and the Johannes Schalm Historical Association. An anthology of short selections for the entire war is Bruce Burgoyne, ed., *Enemy Views: The American Revolutionary War as Recorded by the Hessian Participants* (Bowie, Md., 1996). Among the most valuable sources for the New Jersey campaign (with a few of exceptional interest for the Hessian army in general) are the following materials.

Individual Records

Anonymous officer of Regiment von Lossberg, "Hessian Journal Found at Trenton, in December Last," Philadelphia *Pennsylvania Evening Post*, 26 July 1777; rpt. *NJA*, 2d ser., vol. 1.

Appell, Martin. Sergeant major in Regiment von Rall, killed Stono Ferry, 20 June 1779. "Brief vom Soldat Martin Appell aus Breuna an seine Eldern," not seen, cited in Atwood, *Hessian*, 41.

Bardeleben, Johann von. Lieutenant in Regiment von Donop. *The Diary of Lieutenant von Bardeleben*, ed. Bruce E. Burgoyne (Bowie, Md., 1998).

Baurmeister, Baron Karl Leopold, *Revolution in America: Confidential Letters and Journals 1776–1784 of Adjutant General Major Baurmeister of the Hessian Forces*, ed. Bernard A. Uhlendorf (New Brunswick, 1957).

Döhla, Johann, *Tagebuch eines bayreuther Soldaten* (Bayreuth, 1913), trans. as *A Hessian Diary of the American Revolution* (Norman, Okla., 1990).

Donop, Carl von. Colonel commanding Jäger Corps. "Letters from a Hessian Mercenary" (correspondence with Friedrich Wilhelm, Prince of Prussia), ed. Hans Huth, *PMHB* 62 (1938), 488–501. Another file of Donop's correspondence with Rall, Grant, Leslie, Howe, and other officers was found among his papers after his death, submitted to the Hessian Court of Inquiry, and placed in the Hessian Archives at Marburg, MHT; idem, "Report on Ft. Lee," MNHPL; see also Wagner; and Generals Leslie, Grant, Colonel Rall, and others. Hessian Manscripts no. 36, Bancroft Collection at NYPL; other material appears in the Marburg Collection, Bancroft Collection at NYPL, and LT. A deathbed interview with Colonel von Donop appears in François–Jean, Marquis de Chastellux, *Travels in North America in the Years 1780, 1781 and 1782*, ed. Howard C. Rice Jr., 2 vols. (Chapel Hill, 1963).

Ewald, Johann. Captain, Jäger Corps. *Diary of the American War: A Hessian Journal*, ed. Joseph P. Tustin (New Haven, 1979). A translation of Ewald's "Tagebuch von dem amerikanischen Kriege," four manuscript volumes with many drawings. At least two manuscript copies are known to exist: one in the Library of His Highness Friedrich Ferdinand, Prince of

Schleswig-Holstein, Germany; the other in private possession in America. It is the most useful Hessian account of the American War of Independence. Ewald also published books and essays in the professional literature very actively after 1783.

Heinrichs, Johannes. Captain, Jäger Corps. "Auszug as dem Hand Journal," trans. as "Extract from the Private Journal of Staff Captain Heinrichs of the Jaeger Corps," in Bernhard A. Uhlendorf, *Siege of Charleston* (Ann Arbor, 1938), 107–363; selections also published as "Extracts from the Letterbook of Captain Johann Heinrichs of the Hessian Jager Corps, 1778–1780," *PMHB* 22 (1898), 137–43.

Heister, Lieutenant General von. Commanding general, Hessian forces in America. "Darstellung der Affaire in Trenton durch den Gen. Lt. v. Heister," Hessian State Archives, Marburg, Germany; LT; correspondence with British officials is in the Public Record Office, CO5 PRO.

Hille, J. F. von, *The American Revolution: Garrison Life in French Canada and New York* (Westport, Conn., 1995).

Krafft, Johann, *Journal of Lieutenant John Charles Philip von Krafft, of the Regiment von Bose, 1776–1784*, ed. Thomas H. Edsall, NYHS *Collections for the Year 1882* (New York, 1883).

Münchausen, Friedrich von. Captain, Leib Regiment; aide to General Howe. *At General Howe's Side, 1776–1778: The Diary of General William Howe's Aide-de-Camp, Captain Friedrich von Muenchausen*, trans. Ernest Kipping, ann. Samuel Stelle Smith (Monmouth Beach, N.J., 1974).

Piel, Jakob. Adjutant, Rall Brigade. "Diary of the Hessian Lieutenant [Jakob] Piel, 1776 to 1783," ed. Bruce E. Burgoyne, *JSHAJ* 4 (1989), 14.

Reuber, Johannes. Grenadier, Rall Regiment. Journal. This is a difficult document, in a rough Kasseler dialect, and the dates are commonly one day off, but it is an invaluable account by a private soldier in the New Jersey campaign. Reuber left two copies for his sons. One remained in Germany; the other is now in the Special Collections of the Rutgers University Library. A German transcript is in the Bancroft Collection at the New York Public Library, and on film in the author's collection. An English translation, "Diary of the Revolutionary War," trans. and ed. Herbert H. Freund, is in *JSHAJ* 1, nos. 2, 3 (1977).

Reuffer, Carl Friedrich. Ensign, Regiment von Mirbach. Diary, in Burgoyne, *Enemy Views*, 38, 46.

Riedesel, Frederike Charlotte Louise, Freifrau von. *Die Berufsreise nach Amerika* (Berlin, 1801), trans. as *Baroness von Riedesel and the American Revolution*, ed. Marvin L. Brown Jr. (Chapel Hill, 1965).

Schubart, Martin Christian Friedrich Daniel, *Deutsche Chronik auf das Jahren 1774–1777*, not seen; Atwood calls it "one of the best," by "an intelligent subaltern in the 1776 campaign."

Specht, J. F. *A Military Journal of the Burgoyne Campaign* (Westport, Conn., 1995).

Seumes, J. G., "Memoirs of a Hessian Conscript: J. G. Seumes' Reluctant Voyage to America," ed. Margarete Woelfel, *WMQ3* 5 (1948), 553–70.

Wagner, Johann Emanuel. Captain and adjutant to Colonel von Donop. A journal commonly called "Donop's Diary" and titled "Journal found in the Despatch box of the late Col. Von Donop, it being written in the hand of Captain Wagner," German transcript in NYPL, English translation in LT.

Waldeck, Philipp. Chaplain, Waldeck Regiment. *A Hessian Report . . . The Diary of Chaplain Philipp Waldeck (1776–1780)*, ed. Bruce Burgoyne (Bowie, Md., 1995).

Wasmus, J. F., *An Eyewitness Account of the American Revolution and New England Life: The Journal of J. F. Wasmus, German Company Surgeon, 1776–1783* (New York, 1990).

Wiederholdt, Andreas. Lieutenant, Regiment von Knyphausen. Wiederholdt compiled a record that he called a *Tagebuch*, or journal, but internal evidence suggests that much of it was a memoir. A German transcript is in the Bancroft Collecticion at NYPL, and a microfilm copy in the author's collection. Excerpts were published as "Tagebuch des Capitains Andreas Wiederholdt von 7 October 1776 bis 7 Dezember 1780," *AG* 4, no. 1 (1902), 25–33; "Colonel Rall at Trenton," *PMHB* 23 (1899) 462–67; "The Capture of Fort Washington, New York, Described by Captain Andreas Wiederhold of the Hessian Regiment Knyphausen," *PMHB* 22 (1898) 95–97; Burgoyne, *Enemy Views*, 91, 117, 346. Illustrations from his diary are in the Rare Book Collections of the Historical Society of Pennsylvania and are published in *JSHAJ* 2 (1982), 1–2.

Individual Testimony at the Hessian Courts of Inquiry

On orders from Landgraf Friedrich Wilhelm II, Hessian commanders in America conducted courts of inquiry on the first battle of Trenton, after the Hessian prisoners were exchanged. The courts convened in 1778 at Philadelphia and in New York from 1779 to 1782 and were reviewed in New York and Germany. The records are in Hessian archives, titled "Affaire von Trenton," and copies are available both in German (MHT) and English (LT).

The inquiry was carefully conducted to protect Hessian officers from the wrath of their prince, but the testimony is very full and was taken from many officers and men. When used in a careful and critical way, it is a very valuable source. Every officer, noncom, and private soldier who appeared before the court was required to identify himself and give a brief record of service, and was asked many questions about conditions in New Jersey, the size and state of his unit, the decisions that were made, and the course of the battle. The answers ran to between five and ten pages or more for each man. Many soldiers who kept their own journals and collections of correspondence also gave testimony separately, which allows comparison of sources. Testimony by the following men was used:

Lieutenant Andreas Wiederholdt, 352–63, 463–67, ML 3
Lieutenant Jacob Bill, ML 87
Lieutenant George Zoll, ML 193
Lieutenant Christian von Hoben, ML 223
Ensign Friedrich Henndorf, ML 256
Captain Ernst Eberhard von Altenbockum, ML 263–76
Corporal Wilhelm Hartung, ML 184–187
Captain Adam Steding, ML 211
Jäger Sergeant George William Hussell, ML 136–52
Jäger Corporal Franz Bauer, ML 152–56
Corporal Nicholas Fenner, ML 168–71
Sergeant Johannes Müller, ML 344–50
von Boeking, ML 484–92
Ensign Heinrich Zimmerman, ML 322–30
Sergeant Christian Diemar, ML 344–50
Lieutenant Jakob Piel, ML 80–98, 124–25
Ensign Carl Wilhelm Kleinschmidt, ML 534–45
Lieutenant Johannes Engelhardt, ML 502–17
Sergeant Jakob Dietzel, ML 518–21
Bombardier Johannes Westerberg, ML 522–26
Bombardier Heinrich von Zelle, ML 528–34
Lieutenant Friedrich Fischer, ML 331–43
Captain August Steding, ML 205–20
Lieutenant August von Hobe, ML 221–31
Lieutenant Gregorius Saltzmann, ML 546–54
Staff Captain Jacob Baum, ML 379–90
Lieutenant Nicholas Vaupell, ML 391–401
Captain Ludwig Wilhelm von Löwenstein, ML 402–12, 483
Lieutenant Ludwig von Geyso, ML 413–20
Ensign Wilhelm Drach von Ellershausen, ML 421–26
Staff Captain Barthold Helfrich von Schimmelpfennig, ML 27–37, 467–73
Lieutenant Werner von Ferry, ML 438–46
Captain Wilhelm von Biesenrodt, ML 447–62
Lieutenant Wilhelm Ludwig von Romrodt, ML 314–21
Sergeant Johannes Müller, 22 April 1778, ML 347–50
Bombardier Volprecht, 13 Aug. 1778, ML 276–79

Major Johann Jost Matthaeus, 17 Aug. 1778, ML 105–110, 578–92
Corporal William Hartung, 22 April 1778, ML 184–87
Lieutenant Christian Sobbe, 25 April 1778, ML 364–78, 474–82

American Public Records

American records include the published *Journals of the Continental Congress, 1774–1789,* ed. Worthington C . Ford, 34 vols. (Washington, 1904–37). This very thin source is supplemented by *Letters of Members of the Continental Congress,* 8 vols. (Washington, 1921–38). A much larger and more complete set, of great value, is Paul H. Smith et al., *Letters of Delegates to Congress, 1774–89* (Washington, 1976+). This immense collection is now available online.

The published records are only a small part of the papers of the Continental Congress in the National Archives (Record Group 360). They include committee reports and investigations such as "Report of the Committee appointed to inquire into the conduct of the enemy," 18 April 1777, published in the *Pennsylvania Evening Post,* 24 April 1777, rpt. *NJA,* 2d ser. 1:347–53; the original manuscripts survive in the papers of the Continental Congress, item 53, pp. 29–39, National Archives.

State records include *Journal of the House of Delegates of Virginia,* October 1776 (Richmond, 1828); *Delaware Archives, Revolutionary War,* 3 vols. (Wilmington, 1911–19); *Pennsylvania Archives,* a vast collection of 138 volumes in nine series (Harrisburg, 1852–1949), of which the first series contains much material on the New Jersey campaign, especially in volume 5. Documents and reports of *Pennsylvania Council of Safety* were published in Pennsylvania newspapers and appear in *NJA,* 2d ser., vol. 1. Among these materials are reports of investigations of British and Hessian atrocities in New Jersey.

British Public Records

For the American Revolution, British public records survive in great profusion at the new Public Record Office, Kew. Materials relevant to this inquiry are mainly to be found in three broad record groups: the Colonial Office, the War Office, and the Admiralty.

Colonial Office records on military affairs in CO5/92–93 include reports from General Howe to his superiors. Also helpful are Colonial Office records on admiralty matters in CO5/120–21.

Military records in the Public Record Office include Secretary at War, In-Letters, Wo1; Out-Letters, Wo4; Commander in Chief, WO3; Marching Orders, Wo5; Headquarters Papers, WO28; and Troop Movements, WO379. The Amherst Papers, WO34, contain much on America. Service records of officers and printed Army Lists are in WO65, and a reference set was used on open shelves in the Public Record Office; the Army Lists include officers of the marines for this period. For individual regiments, the surviving Monthly Returns, WO17, hold much material before 1773 and after 1783, but very little in between. A large collection of regimental rosters, muster books, and paylists is in WO12. These are huge red-bound elephant folios with separate sheets for each company in every regiment. They identify by name, rank, and record of service most men who served in most regiments in the American war.

Parliamentary debates were published in many forms; one of the most important for this period is William Cobbett, *Parliamentary History of England from the Earliest Period to the Year 1803,* 36 vols. (London, 1806–20). A very large set of parliamentary papers has been published in a sumptuous edition by the Irish University Press.

Military Orderly Books

These very useful documents include general orders, regimental orders, morning reports, returns of strength, entries on discipline, clothing, equipment, supplies, promotions, records of engagements, casualties, and whatever else interested the adjutants who kept them.

For American orderly books, a large collection at the New-York Historical Society has been published in a microfilm edition by Research Publications, Inc. (Woodbridge, Conn.,

1977). A set in the author's collection includes orderly books for Lippitt's Rhode Island Regiment, Lamb's Continental Artillery, and Nixon's Sixth Massachusetts Regiment.

Another large collection was published by the Connecticut Historical Society as *Orderly Books and Journals Kept by Connecticut Men . . . , 1775–1778* (Hartford, 1899). Of special interest were the records of Captain William Copit's Company, 1775–76.

Many orderly books are in the Historical Society of Pennsylvania and have been published in the *Pennsylvania Magazine of History and Biography*. Among them is "The Orderly Book of Captain Sharp Delany," for 1776, in the Third Battalion of Philadelphia Associators, *PMHB* 32 (1908), 302–8; and the Orderly Book for the Fourth Battalion, ibid. 29 (1905), 470–78 and 30 (1906) 91–103, 206–19.

The Virginia Historical Society published *The Orderly Book of Captain George Stubblefield*, 5th Virginia Regiment, 1776 (Richmond, 1887).

Another very large collection, in manuscript, bound volumes, and microfilm, is in the library of Morristown National Historic Park Library. Used there were the orderly books of Continental Artillery (Knox's Brigade) 1777–78; Connecticut Light Horse (1776); and Heard's Brigade, New Jersey Militia. A guide is available: Alan Stein, ed., *Orderly Books of the American Revolution in the Morristown National Historical Park Library* (Morristown, 1994).

British orderly books survive in large number. The Morristown library and the David Library at Washington Crossing, Pa., have large collections on film. We used the records of the 17th Foot (manuscripts in the NYHS); 42d Foot (manuscripts in the National Archives of Scotland); 1st Battalion Guards (manuscripts in the Clements Library); 1st Battalion of Marines (from MHS); 4th Battalion of Grenadiers (Public Record Office). Gen. William Howe's Order Books for the period of the Jersey campaign are published in *Kemble Papers*, 1:249–433.

Hessian regimental journals include those for the Regiment von Knyphausen, Regiment von alt-Lossberg, Regiment von Mirbach, Grenadier Battalion Block, Platte Grenadier Battalion Journal, and Hesse-Hanau regiment. These and many others are available in the Lidgerwood Transcripts at Morristown.

Naval Records and Logbooks

William James Morgan, ed., *Naval Documents of the American Revolution* (Washington, 1970), is a vast compilation of great value, thorough in its coverage of its subject, and helpful for many aspects of the American Revolution. It includes logbooks and journals of HMS *Phoenix*, HMS *Rose*, HMS *Greyhound*, HM Sloop *Senegal*, and HMS *Pearl*, in the New York and New Jersey campaign (5:895–97 passim).

British Treatises and Manuals

The Manual Exercise as Ordered by His Majesty (London, 1764).

Rules and Articles for the Better Government of Our Horse and Foot Guards, and All Our Other Forces in Our Kingdoms of Great Britain and Ireland, Dominions Beyond the Seas, and Foreign Parts (London, 1778).

Anonymous, *A New System of Military Discipline, Founded upon Principle by a General Officer*, attributed to Richard Lambert, 6th Earl of Cavan, and reprinted in 1776. An electronic variorum edition of the *New System* has been issued on CD-ROM as part of *The Complete Cuthbertson*, ed. Don Hagist and Mark Tully (n.p., 2000).

Bland, Humphrey, *A Treatise of Military Discipline, 8th edition revised, corrected, and altered to the present practice of the Army* (London, 1762), an earlier work, first published in 1727.

Cuthbertson, Bennet, *A System of Complete Interior Management and Œconomy of a Battalion of Infantry* (Dublin, 1768; rpt. 1776, 1779). A digital variorum edition of the Cuthbertson treatise has been issued on CD-ROM as *The Complete Cuthbertson*, ed. Don Hagist and Mark Tully (n.p., 2000).

Dalrymple, Colonel Campbell, *A Military Essay: Containing Reflections of the Raising, Arming, Cloathing and Discipline of the British Infantry and Cavalry* (London, 1761).

Fage, Edward, *A Regular Form of Discipline for the Militia, as It Is Performed by the West-Kent Regiment* (London, 1759).

Grant, George, *The New Highland Military Discipline* (London, 1757; rpt. 1967).

Howe, William, "Manoeuvres for Light Infantry," in Fuller, *British Light Infantry*, 247–52.

Muller, John, *A Treatise of Artillery*, 3d ed. (London, 1780; rpt. Bloomfield, Ont., 1977).

Simes, Thomas, *The Military Medley* (London, 1768). Reenacting groups have created a website for eighteenth-century drum signals; see www.cvco.org/sigs/reg64/music.html. Idem, *The Military Guide for Young Officers*, 3d ed. (London, 1781).

American Treatises and Manuals

Brattle, William, *Sundry Rules and Directions for Drawing Up a Regiment, Posting the Officers, etc.* (Boston, 1773).

Draper, Richard, *A Plan of Exercise for the Militia of the Province of Massachusetts-Bay, Extracted from the Plan of Discipline for the Norfolk Militia* (Boston, 1772).

Lyman, Phineas, *General Orders of 1757*, ed. William S. Webb (New York, 1899).

Pickering, Timothy Jr., *Easy Plan of Discipline for a Militia* (Salem, 1775).

Newspapers

Maryland Journal, 1776–77
New York Gazette and Weekly Mercury, 1776–77
Philadelphia *Pennsylvania Evening Post*, 1776–77
Philadelphia *Pennsylvania Gazette*, 1775–77
Philadelphia *Pennsylvania Journal*, 1776–77
Philadelphia *Pennsylvania Packet*, 1776–77
Williamsburg *Virginia Gazette* (Purdie), 1777
Williamsburg *Virginia Gazette* (Dixon and Hunter), 1777

Maps

Among modern maps, the most useful for terrain are U.S. Geological Survey maps for the following quadrangles: Bristol, Lambertville, Pennington, Princeton, Trenton East, Trenton West (1995) NIMA 6064 1-SW-ser. V822.

Early American road maps include Christopher Colles, *A Survey of the Roads of the United States of America*, ed. Walter W. Ristow (New York, 1789; rpt. Cambridge, 1961), 58–62; I. J. Hills, *A Complete Plan of Part of the Province of Pennsylvania East and West Jersey with Part of the Adjoining States* (New York, 1778).

For military movements in the Revolution, many contemporary maps were published in London. Among them are "A Plan of New York with Part of Long Island" (London, 1776); Claude Joseph Sautier, "A Topographical Map of the North Part of New York Island, Exhibiting the Plan of Fort Washington, now Fort Knyphausen, with the Rebel Lines to the Southward" (Philadelphia, 1777); and William Faden, "Plan of the Operations of General Washington Against the King's Troops in New Jersey, from the 26th of December to the 3d January 1777" (London, 1777). Most of these maps are reprinted in Kenneth Nebenzahl, ed., *Atlas of the American Revolution* (Washington, 1984), 92–93.

Manuscript maps for the New Jersey campaign by participants in three armies include, for the British, Captain John Montresor, Map of British Garrisons in New Jersey, December 1776, ms. with marginalia in the hand of Gen. Henry Clinton, Clinton Papers, Clements Library, University of Michigan; another copy is in LC.

An American manuscript "Spy Map of Princeton, December 30, 1776," in the hand of Colonel John Cadwalader, accompanies Cadwalader's report to General Washington, LC.

Three German manuscript maps of Trenton were drawn by Hessian officers for the Court of Inquiry. They are Friedrich Fischer's Plan of Trenton, Andreas Wiederholdt's Plan of Trenton, and Jakob Piel's Plan of Trenton, all for December 26, and very detailed. Photocopies are in LC, and the maps are reproduced in Stryker, *Battles of Trenton and Princeton*, facing 128.

❧ Meteorological and Ecological Materials

Weather Diaries

The Phineas Pemberton Weather Diary, Philadelphia, 1776–77. Excerpts from the diary were published by the American Philosophical Society in *APST.* n.s. 6 (1839), 395. Entries for December 1776 and January 1777 are reproduced in the appendix above, with the permission of the American Philosophical Society.

The Delaware River

On the history of ice on the Delaware River, for technical questions there is G. D. Ashton, ed., *River and Lake Ice Engineering* (Littleton, Colo., 1986); an "Ice Jam Primer" is published by the U.S. Army Cold Regions Research and Engineering Laboratory in Durham, N.H., and is available online. The U.S. Army Corps of Engineers has also compiled an Ice Jam Database which includes historical materials for the Delaware River through the twentieth century, with scattered data on the nineteenth century. Much of this material is also available online through the USA-CRREL site. The Delaware River Basin Council also has an Ice Jam Project for the study of conditions on the river. Their work is accessible through their site at www.drbc.net.

Ecological Studies

The Philadelphia Support Office, Northeast Region, National Park Service, commissioned a study titled *Crossroads of the American Revolution in New Jersey: Special Resource Study; National Heritage Feasibility Study, Environmental Assessment*, draft (Philadelphia, Aug. 2002).

A pioneering work by an antiquarian scholar with an interest in geography is Benson J. Lossing, *Pictorial Field-Book of the Revolution*, 2 vols. (New York, 1851, rpt. ed. Terence Barrow, Rutland, 1972).

❧ Secondary Sources

General Works

Surveys of the historical literature include Edmund S. Morgan, ed., *The American Revolution: Two Centuries of Interpretation* (Englewood Cliffs, N.J., 1965), with the author's excellent essay, "The American Revolution: Revisions in Need of Revising," *WMQ3* 14 (1957), 3–15; many essays and edited works by Jack P. Greene, including *The Reinterpretation of the American Revolution, 1763–1789* (New York, 1968); Don Higginbotham, "American Historians and the Military History of the Revolution," *AHR* 80 (1964), 18–34; Wesley Frank Craven, "The Revolutionary Era," in *The Reinterpretation of American History*, ed. John Higham (London, 1962).

Mark M. Boatner III, *Encyclopedia of the American Revolution* (Mechanicsburg, Pa., 1994), is very full and accurate on the military history of the War of Independence. Jack P. Greene and J. R. Pole, eds., *The Blackwell Encyclopedia of the American Revolution* (Cambridge., Mass., and Oxford, 1991), is a helpful survey of the academic literature.

On numbers and losses, Howard H. Peckham, *The Toll of Independence: Engagements and Battle Casualties of the American Revolution* (Chicago, 1974), is a useful corrective to the gross incompetence of the *Historical Statistics of the United States* and estimates by the Department of Defense. But Peckham's estimates, which were deliberately cautious and conservative, are themselves grossly incomplete and largely undocumented.

For general interpretations see "Historiography," above.

Bibliography

George Washington, Biographical Studies

The rate of publication on George Washington is accelerating, with many recent publications, and more promised. A survey of his image and reputation is Marcus Cunliffe, *George Washington: Man and Monument* (Boston, 1958).

Books by men who knew him include G.W.P. Custis, *Recollections and Private Memoirs of Washington, by His Adopted Son . . .* (New York, 1860; rpt. Bridgewater, Va., 1999); also idem, "Washington a Sportsman," *American Turf Register and Sporting Magazine*, Sept. 1829, 7–8.

Major biographies of high quality include John Marshall's excellent *Life of George Washington*, 5 vols. with atlas (Philadelphia, 1804–7); also 2 vols. (Philadelphia, 1833); Washington Irving, *The Life of George Washington* (1854–58; rev. ed, 4 vols. in 2, New York, 1976). A very careful and still useful book is Paul Leicester Ford, *The True George Washington* (Philadelphia, 1899).

A debunker took a turn in William E. Woodward, *Bunk* (New York, 1923); and idem, *George Washington, The Image and the Man* (New York, 1926). Another debunker who became a filiopietist was Rupert Hughes, *George Washington*, 3 vols. (New York, 1926–30).

In the twentieth century, an important work is John C. Fitzpatrick, *George Washington Himself: A Common-Sense Biography Written from His Manuscripts* (Indianapolis, 1933), very informative, by the editor of the bicentennial edition of Washington's writings. A major work of scholarship is Nathaniel Wright Stephenson and Waldo Hilary Dunn, *George Washington*, 2 vols. (New York, 1940).

Douglas Southall Freeman, *George Washington: A Biography*, 7 vols. (New York, 1948–57), is a work of great strengths and weaknesses, discussed on pp. 446 above. James Thomas Flexner, *George Washington, The Forge of Experience* (Boston and Toronto, 1965), is lively and vivid.

More recent biographies of high quality include John E. Ferling, *The First of Men: A Life of George Washington* (Knoxville, 1988); Richard Brookhiser, *Founding Father: Rediscovering George Washington* (New York, 1996); Richard Norton Smith, *Patriarch: George Washington and the New American Nation* (Boston, 1993), centering on Washington's presidency.

On Washington's upbringing, the best study is still Samuel Eliot Morison, "Young Man Washington," in *By Land and By Sea* (New York, 1966), 161–81. On the ideal of honor to which Washington was raised, see Bertram Wyatt-Brown, *Southern Honor* (New York, 1982). On the Northern Neck, see David Hackett Fischer and James Kelly, *Bound Away: Virginia and the Westward Movement* (Charlottesville, 2000). The definitive work on Washington's home is Robert F. Dalzell and Lee Baldwin Dalzell, *George Washington's Mount Vernon* (New York and Oxford, 1998).

On Washington and slavery, see Worthington C. Ford, *Washington as an Employer and Importer of Labor* (Brooklyn, 1889); Walter Z. Mazyck, *George Washington and the Negro* (Washington, 1932).

Important studies of his generalship are Dave R. Palmer, *The Way of the Fox* (Westport, Conn., 1975); idem, *George Washington, First in War* (Mount Vernon, 2000); and John Shy, "George Washington Reconsidered," in *The John Biggs Cincinnati Lectures in Military Leadership and Command*, ed. Henry S. Bausem (Lexington, Va., 1986), 39–52.

Biographies, Alphabetical by Subject

Two general works are very helpful, both edited to a high standard by George A. Billias: *George Washington's Generals* (New York, 1964), is a collection of twelve biographies of American military leaders, by distinguished historians; *George Washington's Opponents* (New York, 1994), does the same for British commanders. Among an outpouring of individual studies, the following works were especially helpful for an understanding of the New York and New Jersey campaigns

Adams, John: David McCullough, *John Adams* (New York, 2001).

Arnold, Benedict: James Kirby Martin, *Benedict Arnold, Revolutionary Hero* (New York, 1997).

Burgoyne, John: Edward B. de Fonblanque, *Political and Military Episodes . . . the Life and Correspondence of the Right Hon. John Burgoyne* (London, 1786); James Lunt, *John Burgoyne of*

Saratoga (London, 1976); Michael Glover, *General Burgoyne in Canada and America: Scapegoat for a System* (London, 1976); Gerald Howson, *Burgoyne of Saratoga: A Biography* (New York, 1979).

Clinton, Henry: William B. Willcox, *Portrait of a General: Sir Henry Clinton in the War of Independence* (New York, 1964).

Corbin, Margaret Cochran: *Margaret Corbin: Heroine of the Battle of Fort Washington, 16 November 1776* (New York, 1932).

Cornwallis, Charles: Franklin and Mary Wickwire, *Cornwallis and the War of Independence* (London, 1970); idem, *Cornwallis, the Imperial Years* (Chapel Hill, 1980).

Galloway, Joseph: John E. Ferling, *The Loyalist Mind: Joseph Galloway and the American Revolution* (University Park, 1977).

Gates, Horatio: Paul David Nelson, *General Horatio Gates: A Biography* (Baton Rouge, 1976); Samuel W. Patterson, *Horatio Gates, Defender of American Liberty* (New York, 1941).

Germain, (Lord) George: Gerald S. Brown, *The American Secretary; The Colonial Policy of Lord George Germain, 1775–1778* (Ann Arbor, 1963).

Glover, John: George A. Billias, *General John Glover and His Marblehead Mariners* (New York, 1960).

Grant, James: Paul David Nelson, *General James Grant: Scottish Soldier and Royal Governor of East Florida* (Gainesville, 1993); Alistair Macpherson Grant, *General James Grant of Ballindalloch, 1720–1806* (privately published, London, 1930).

Greene, Nathanael: Theodore Thayer, *Nathanael Greene: Strategist of the Revolution* (New York, 1960); George W. Greene, *Life of Nathanael Greene*, 3 vols. (New York, 1867–71).

Hamilton, Alexander: Broadus Mitchell, *Alexander Hamilton, Youth to Maturity*, vol. 1 (New York, 1957).

Hand, Edward: Michel [*sic*] Williams Craig, *General Edward Hand: Winter's Doctor* (n.p., 1984?).

Howe, Richard: Among biographies, still informative is George Mason, *The Life of Richard Earl Howe* (London, 1805). Mason was joint-proprietor of Richard Howe's country estate, Porters, in Hertfordshire. Also helpful when used with caution is Sir John Barrow, *The Life of Richard Earl Howe, K.G.* (London, 1838); an excellent short sketch of Richard Howe in the *Dictionary of National Biography* makes corrections of Barrow's work.

Howe, William: Bellamy Partridge, *Sir Billy Howe* (New York, 1932), is a popular biography with much helpful material.

The Howe brothers: Troyer Steele Anderson, *The Command of the Howe Brothers During the American Revolution* (New York, 1936), was a serious, important, and pathbreaking attempt to analyze the leadership of the Howe brothers in a scholarly and sympathetic way, and to correct many inaccurate and hostile judgments. Ira D. Gruber, *The Howe Brothers and the American Revolution* (New York, 1972), is the best modern study, carefully balanced in judgment and informed by extensive primary research. Still useful is Charles Francis Adams, "Contemporary Opinion of the Howes," MHSP 44:118–20.

Knox, Henry: North Callahan, *Henry Knox; General Washington's General* (New York, 1958).

Lee, Charles: John R. Alden, *Charles Lee, Traitor or Patriot?* (Baton Rouge, 1951).

Legge, William, 2d Earl of Dartmouth: B. D. Bargar, *Lord Dartmouth and the American Revolution* (Columbia, 1965).

Leslie, Alexander: William Fraser, *The Melvilles, Earls of Melville, and Leslies, Earls of Leven* (Edinburgh, 1890); as a helpful corrective to pejorative interpretations that are without foundation, see the vignettes in Ann Hulton to Mrs. Adam Lightbody, 25 Nov. 1773, in Harold Murdock, ed., *Letters of a Loyalist Lady* (Cambridge, Mass., 1927), 63.

Leslie, Capt. William: American website at www.silverwhistle.free-online.co.uk/lobsters/will-leslie.html.

Loring, Mrs. Elizabeth: Eva Phillips Boyd, "Jamaica Plain by Way of London," *Old Time New England* 49 (April–June 1959).

McDougall, Alexander: Roger J. Champagne, *Alexander McDougall and the American Revolution in New York* (Schenectady, 1975); Anna Madeline Shannon, "General Alexander McDougall: Citizen Soldier, 1732–1786" (diss., Fordham, 1957).

Maxwell, William: Harry M. Ward, *General William Maxwell and the New Jersey Continentals* (Westport, Conn., 1997), is very helpful on the central figure in the Forage War.

Mercer, Hugh: Frederick English, *General Hugh Mercer: Forgotten Hero of the American Revolution* (New York, 1979); Joseph M. Waterman, *With Sword and Lancet: The Life of General Hugh Mercer* (Richmond, 1941).

Monroe, James: Harry Ammon, *James Monroe: A Biography* (New York, 1971); Richard Hanser, *The Glorious Hour of James Monroe* (New York, 1976).

Morris, Robert: Clarence L. Ver Steeg, *Robert Morris, Revolutionary Financier* (New York, 1976).

Moylan, Stephen: Martin I. J. Griffin, *Stephen Moylan* (Philadelphia, 1909).

Paine, Thomas: David Freeman Hawke, *Paine* (New York, 1974) 182–83. Two other excellent biographies are Eric Foner, *Tom Paine and Revolutionary America* (New York, 1976), and John Keane, *Tom Paine, A Political Life* (London, 1995). James Cheetham, *Life of Thomas Paine* (New York, 1809), is a strange, often informative book, by Paine's enemy after his death.

Peale, Charles Willson: Charles C. Sellers, *Charles Willson Peale* (Philadelphia, 1947; rpt. New York, 1969); idem, *The Artist of the Revolution: The Early Life of Charles Willson Peale* (Hebron, Conn., 1939).

Phillips, William: Robert P. Davis, *Where a Man Can Go: Major General William Phillips, British Royal Artillery, 1731–1781* (Westport, Conn., 1999).

Rall, Johann: Bruce E. Burgoyne, ed., *The Trenton Commanders, Johann Gottlieb Rall and George Washington* (Bowie, Md., 1997), 9–16.

Rosbrugh, John: John C. Clyde, *Rosbrugh, a Tale of the Revolution; or, Life, Labors, and Death of Rev. John Rosbrugh* (Easton, Pa., 1880).

Rush, Benjamin: David Hawke, *Benjamin Rush, Revolutionary Gadfly* (Indianapolis, 1971).

St. Clair, Arthur: *The Life and Public Services of Arthur St. Clair* (1882; rpt. New York, 1971).

Scott, Charles: Harry M. Ward, *Charles Scott and the Spirit of '76* (Charlottesville, 1988), 27, from "Anecdotes of Old General Scott," Draper Coll., Kentucky Manuscripts, 26CC10, State Historical Society of Wisconsin.

Smith, Samuel: Frank Cassell, *A Merchant Congressman in the Young Republic: Samuel Smith of Maryland, 1752–1839* (Madison, 1971).

Stephen, Adam: Harry M. Ward, *Major General Adam Stephen and the Cause of American Liberty* (Charlottesville, 1989).

Lord Stirling: Alan Valentine, *Lord Stirling* (New York, 1969).

Sullivan, John: Charles P. Whittemore, *General of the Revolution: John Sullivan of New Hampshire* (New York, 1961).

Tarleton, Banastre: Robert D. Bass, *The Green Dragoon* (New York, 1957).

Van Hornes, one and all: Francis M. Marvin, *The Van Horn Family History* (East Stroudsberg, Pa., 1929).

Witherspoon, John: Varnum L. Collins, *President Witherspoon*, 2 vols. (Princeton, 1925).

State and Local History

On New York, Thomas Jones, *History of New York During the Revolutionary War*, 2 vols. (New York, 1879) is very informative.

General histories of New Jersey in the Revolution include Leonard Lundin, *Cockpit of the Revolution: The War for Independence in New Jersey* (Princeton, 1940); and Alfred Hoyt Bill, *New Jersey and the Revolutionary War* (Princeton, 1964).

For northern New Jersey, Adrian C. Leiby, *Revolutionary War in the Hackensack Valley: The Jersey Dutch and the Neutral Ground* (New Brunswick, 1962), is excellent. Donald M. Londahl-Smidt, "British and Hessian Accounts of the Invasion of Bergen County," *Bergen County History* (1976), 35–80, is a fine piece of scholarship. T. N. Glover, *The Retreat of '76 Across Bergen County* (Hackensack, 1905), is an older study. Also useful is Ambrose E. Vanderpoel, *History of Chatham, New Jersey* (Chatham, 1959).

For northwestern New Jersey, a leading work is George Doremus, *The American Revolution in Morris County* (Rockaway, N.J., 1976).

For the Raritan Valley and central Jersey: John P. Wall, *Chronicles of New Brunswick* (New Brunswick, 1931); William H. S. Demarest, *A History of Rutgers College, 1776–1924* (New Brunswick, 1924); Andrew Mellick Jr., *The Story of an Old Farm; or, Life in New Jersey in the Eighteenth Century* (Somerville, N.J., 1889); Elizabeth G. C. Menzies, *Millstone Valley* (New Brunswick, 1956); Margaret Cowley, *Exploring the Little Rivers of New Jersey* (New Brunswick, 1971); Hubert G. Schmidt, *Lesser Crossroads* (New Brunswick, 1948); Cornelius C. Vermeule, "Some Revolutionary Incidents in the Raritan Valley," *NJHSP,* n.s. 6 (1921), 74.

Princeton: Thomas Jefferson Wertenbaker, *Princeton, 1746–1896* (Princeton, 1946); Alfred Hoyt Bill et al., *A House Called Morven: Its Role in American History* (Princeton, 1954); Willard Thorp, *The Lives of Eighteen from Princeton* (Princeton, 1946).

Trenton: William S. Stryker, *Trenton One Hundred Years Ago* (Trenton, 1878; rpt. 1893); John Hall, *History of the Presbyterian Church in Trenton, N.J.* (New York, 1859; rpt. 1912).

Burlington: George Morgan, *History of the Church in Burlington, N.J.* (Trenton, 1876).

For Washington's army in Pennsylvania, see W.W.H. Davis, *The History of Bucks County* (Doylestown, Pa., 1876).

Studies of Events, Battles, and Campaigns (in chronological order)

The Siege of Boston: Allen French, *The First Year of the American Revolution* (Boston, 1934); David Hackett Fischer, *Paul Revere's Ride* (New York, 1994).

Long Island: Henry P. Johnston, *The Campaign of 1776 Around New York and Brooklyn* (Brooklyn, 1878); Ira D. Gruber, "America's First Battle: Long Island, 27 August 1776," in *America's First Battles, 1776–1965,* ed. Charles E. Heller and William A. Stofft (Lawrence, Kans., 1986), 1–32.

Manhattan and Harlem Heights: Bruce Bliven, *The Battle for Manhattan* (New York, 1955–56), with wonderful maps; for the battle of Harlem Heights, the first full-scale history is still the best: Henry P. Johnston, *The Battle of Harlem Heights, September 16, 1776: A Review of the Events of the Campaign* (New York, 1897), is a fine work of scholarship, with excellent maps and a long appendix (125–234) that reproduces many primary materials from American, British, and German sources.

The fighting in Westchester, Queen's County, and Dutchess County, New York, is studied in George Athan Billias, "Pelham Bay, a Forgotten Battle," in *General John Glover and His Marblehead Mariners,* 110–23; also William Abbatt, *The Battle of Pell's Point* (New York, 1901); Franklin Delano Roosevelt, ed., "Events on Hudson's River in 1777, as Recorded by British Officers in Contemporary Reports," *Dutchess County Historical Society Yearbook* 20 (1935), an excellent work of history by the president; Joseph S. Tiedeman, "Patriots by Default: Queen's County, New York, and the British Army, 1776–1783," *WMQ3* 43 (1986), 35–63.

The fall of Fort Washington: Secondary works include E. F. Delancey, "Mount Washington and Its Capture on the 16th of November 1776," *MAH* 1 (1877), 63–90; Bolton, *Fort Washington;* Johnston, *The Campaign of 1776;* and Richard K. Showman, in *Papers of General Nathanael Greene,* 1:352–39; for an important British document, see Gen. Samuel Cleaveland, Royal Artillery, "Return of Ordnance and Stores Taken by His Majesty's Troops . . . ," which includes an inventory of artillery taken at Fort Lee, *AA5* 3:1058.

On the British occupation of New Jersey, the best study is Arthur S. Lefkowitz, *The Long Retreat* (Metuchen, N.J., 1998).

For Donop, Stirling, and events in Mount Holly: Joseph P. Tustin, "The Mysterious Widow of the Revolution," *Gloucester County Historical Society Bulletin* 17 (Dec. 1979), 8; William A. Slaughter, "Battle of Iron Works Hill at Mount Holly, New Jersey, December, 1776," *NJHSP* 4 (1909), 19–32.

Military operations on the Delaware are the subject of John W. Jackson, *The Pennsylvania Navy, 1775–1781* (New Brunswick, 1974).

On Washington's crossing, a helpful work is Marion V. Brewington, "Washington's Boats at the Delaware Crossing," *American Neptune* 2 (1942), 167–70.

On the battles of Trenton and Princeton, older works of enduring value include C. C. Haven, *Thirty Days in New Jersey Ninety Years Ago: An Essay Revealing New Facts in Connection with Washington and His Army* (Trenton, 1867). William S. Stryker, *Battles of Trenton and Princeton* (Boston, 1898), is a work of enduring value for its trove of primary documents and its intimate knowledge of places, people, and events. Thomas Jefferson Wertenbaker, "The Battle of Princeton," in *The Princeton Battle Monument* (Princeton, 1922), is an excellent terrain study. Robert G. Albion, *Introduction to Military History* (New York, 1929), includes a stadial analysis of Princeton in five "acts." Alfred Hoyt Bill, *The Campaign of Princeton, 1776–1777* (Princeton, 1948), is a novelist's contribution, strong on drama. Samuel Stelle Smith, *The Battle of Trenton* (Monmouth Beach, N.J., 1965); idem, *The Battle of Princeton* (Monmouth Beach, N.J., 1967), is a meticulous reconstruction of tactical movements and is very attentive to Hessian materials. Richard M. Ketchum, *The Winter Soldiers: The Battles for Trenton and Princeton* (1973; New York, 1991), is a graceful and fluent narrative. William M. Dwyer, *The Day Is Ours!* (New York, 1983), makes a major contribution in its gathering of individual American accounts of the campaign. Kemble Widmer, *The Christmas Campaign: The Ten Days of Trenton and Princeton* (Trenton, 1975), by New Jersey's state geologist, is excellent on the crossing and weather conditions. Jac Weller makes an important contribution to a critical aspect of the battle in "Guns of Destiny: Field Artillery in the Trenton-Princeton Campaign, 25 December 1776 to 3 January 1777," *Military Affairs* 29 (1956), 1–15. Major H. F. Stacke, "Princeton," *Journal of Army Historical Resrach* 13 (1934?), 214–28, rpt. from *The Green Tiger, The Regimental Journal of the Leicestershire Regiment* (May 1932), is an insightful essay on the 17th Foot at Princeton by an experienced officer, in the National Army Museum in London.

The aftermath of the battle at Princeton is the subject of Joshua Doughty, "Washington's March from Princeton to Morristown," *NJHP,* n.s. 5 (1920), 240–46.

On the neglected subject of the Forage War, Jared C. Lobdell has contributed two excellent essays: "Two Forgotten Battles of the Revolutionary War," *NJH* 85 (1967), 225–34; and "Six Generals Gather Forage: The Engagement at Quibbletown, 1777," *NJH* 102 (1984), 35–49. Other works include Mark V. Kwasny, *Washington's Partisan War, 1775–1783* (Kent, Ohio, 1996); and Harry Ward, *Between the Lines: Banditti of the American Revolution* (Westport, Conn., 2002).

Histories of American Military Units

General works on personnel in American armed forces in the War of Independence include Francis B. Heitman, *Historical Register of Officers of the Continental Army* (rev. ed, Washington, 1914; rpt. Baltimore, 1969).

For New Jersey, William S. Stryker, *Official Register of the Officers and Men of New Jersey in the Revolutionary War* (Trenton, 1873; rpt. Baltimore, 1976).

On the militia, an important essay is Don Higginbotham, "The American Militia: A Traditional Institution with Revolutionary Responsibilities," in idem, *Reconsiderations on the Revolutionary War: Selected Essays* (Eastport, Conn., 1978), 83–103. On the New England militia system, see John R. Galvin, *The Minute Men: A Compact History of the Defenders of the American Colonies, 1645–1775* (New York, 1967); David Hackett Fischer, *Paul Revere's Ride* (New York, 1994); idem, ed., *Concord, A Social History* (Waltham, 1983), chaps. 2, 4, 5; and Robert Gross, *The Minutemen and Their World* (New York, 1976; rpt. 2001).

On the Continental army, an excellent work is Robert K. Wright Jr., *The Continental Army* (Washington, 1989). Charles Royster, *A Revolutionary People at War: The Continental Army and American Character, 1775–1783* (Chapel Hill, 1979), is an interpretative social and cultural history of the army. Charles H. Lesser, *The Sinews of Independence: Monthly Strength Reports of the Continental Army* (Chicago, 1976), is a major contribution to the quantitative history of the American army, but missed some strength reports for the New Jersey campaign that are not in the National Archives.

Regarding social origins of American troops in the War of Independence, most research has centered on later years of the war, or on the outbreak of the war in 1775. Patterns of recruitment in 1776–77 were very different from both of those other periods. Cf. Edward C. Papenfuse and Gregory Stiverson, "General Smallwood's Recruits: The Peacetime Career of the Revolutionary Private," *WMQ3* 30 (1973), 117–32; Mark E. Lender, "The Social

Structure of the New Jersey Brigade: The Continental Line as an American Standing Army," in *The Military in America: From the Colonial Era to the Present Time*, ed. Peter Karsten (New York, 1980), 27–44; Charles Patrick Neimeyer, *America Goes to War: A Social History of the Continental Army* (New York, 1996); Joseph A. Goldenberg et al., "Revolutionary Ranks: An Analysis of the Chesterfield Supplements," *VMHB* 87 (1979), 182–89.

Logistics are studied in Erna Risch's *Supplying Washington's Army* (Washington, 1981), by far the best book on the subject. E. Wayne Carp, *To Starve the Army at Pleasure: Continental Army Administration and American Political Culture, 1775–1783* (Chapel Hill, 1984), is an iconoclastic work. Louis Clinton Hatch, *The Administration of the American Revolutionary Army* (New York, 1904), is still useful.

Uniforms are discussed in Charles M. Lefferts, *Uniforms of the American, British, French, and German Armies in the War of the American Revolution* (New York, 1926; rpt. 1971); John Mollo, *Uniforms of the American Revolution* (New York, 1991); Anne S. K. Brown, "Rhode Island Uniforms in the Revolution," *MCH* 10 (1958), 1–10; Harold L. Peterson, *The Book of the Continental Soldier* (Harrisburg, 1968).

For standards and colors, the leading work is Edgar W. Richardson, *Standards and Colors of the American Revolution* (Philadelphia, 1982); see also Frank E. Schermerhorn, *American and French Flags of the Revolution, 1775–1783* (Philadelphia, 1948).

Unit histories of American regiments and battalions in the New Jersey campaign include the following:

New Hampshire: Frederick Kidder, *History of the First New Hampshire Regiment in the War of the Revolution* (Albany, 1868).

Massachusetts: George Athan Billias, *General John Glover and His Marblehead Mariners* (New York, 1960); Samuel Roads, *History and Traditions of Marblehead*, 3d ed. (Marblehead, Mass., 1897).

Rhode Island: Asa B. Gardner, *The Rhode Island Line in the Continental Army* . . . (Providence, 1878); Dan Hitchcock, "So Few the Brave (The Second Rhode Island, 1777–1781)," *MCH* 30 (1978), 18–22.

New York: Asa Bird Gardner, "The New York Continental Line of the Army of the Revolution," *MAH* 7 (1887), 401–19; Worthington C. Ford, "Company of Artillery Commanded by Alexander Hamilton," *NEHGR* 47 (1893), 472–73.

New Jersey: Mark Edward lender, "The Enlisted Line; The Continental Soldiers of New Jersey" (diss., Rutgers, 1975).

Pennsylvania: John B. Trussell Jr., *The Pennsylvania Line: Regimental Organization and Operations, 1775–1783* (Harrisburg, 1977); *History of the First Troop, Philadelphia City Cavalry, 1774–1874* (n.p., n.d.); J. Lapsley, *The Book of the First Troop, Philadelphia City Cavalry, 1774–1915* (Philadelphia, 1915); Steven Rosswurm, *Arms, Country, and Class: The Philadelphia Militia and the 'Lower Sort' During the American Revolution* (New Brunswick, 1987).

Delaware: Christopher Ward, *The Delaware Continentals, 1776–1783* (Wilmington, 1941).

Maryland: "We the Baltimore Independent Cadets," *MDHM* 4 (1909), 372–74; James H. F. Brewer, *History of the 175th Infantry (Fifth Maryland)* (Baltimore, 1955); Rieman Steuart, *A History of the Maryland Line in the Revolutionary War, 1775–1783* (Towson, 1969).

Virginia: John Robert Sellers, "The Virginia Continental Line, 1775–1780" (diss., Tulane, 1968); William E. White, "The Independent Companies of Virginia, 1774–1775," *VMHB* 86 (1978), 149–62.

Backcountry: Captain Philip Slaughter, memoir and diary, rpt. in Rev. Philip Slaughter, *A History of St. Mark's Parish, Culpeper County, Virginia* (Baltimore, 1877; rpt. 1994, 1998), 106–8.

The History of the British Army

General works include Sir John Fortescue, *A History of the British Army*, 13 vols. in 20 (London, 1899–1930); the War of Independence is studied in vol. 3; excellent maps. A lively and intelligent work is Antony Beevor, *Inside the British Army* (London, 1990; rev. ed., 1991). R. M. Barnes, *History of Regiments and Uniforms in the British Army* (London, n.d.), idem, *The British Army of 1914: Its History, Uniforms and Contemporary Continental Armies* (London, 1968), and idem, *The Uniforms and History of the Scottish Regiments* (London, 1956, 1969), are helpful on regimental traditions.

Works in British history on other subjects that contribute to an understanding of the British army include John Cannon, *Aristocratic Century: The Peerage in Eighteenth-Century England* (Cambridge, 1984), 120; E. A. Wrigley and R. S. Schofield, *The Population History of England, 1541–1871* (Cambridge, 1981).

Monographs on various subjects include Anthony A. Bruce, *The Purchase System in the British Army, 1660–1871* (London, 1980); J.F.C. Fuller, *British Light Infantry in the Eighteenth Century* (London, 1925), 124–25; Silvia Frey, *The British Soldier in America: A Social History of Military Life in the Revolutionary Period* (Austin, Tex., 1981), an excellent work; J. A. Houlding, *Fit for Service: The Training of the British Army, 1715–1795* (Oxford, 1981), a very important contribution. On uniforms, Hew Strahan, *British Military Uniforms, 1760–1796* (London, 1975).

On the British army in America, see C. T. Atkinson, "British Forces in North America, 1774–1781: Their Distribution and Strength," *JAHR* 16 (1937), 3–23; and idem, "British Forces in North America, 1774–1781, part II," ibid.,163–66. On logistics in America, Edward E. Curtis, *The Organization of the British Army in the American Revolution* (New Haven, 1926); R. Arthur Bowler, *Logistics and the Failure of the British Army in America, 1775–1783* (Princeton, 1975).

British Unit Histories

Regimental histories of British units that served in the New York and New Jersey campaign include the following works:

16th Light Dragoons: James Lunt, *The Scarlet Lancers: The Story of the 16th/5th The Queen's Royal Lancers, 1689–1992* (London, 1993).

17th Light Dragoons: R.L.V. ffrench Blake, *The 17th/21st Lancers* (London, 1968).

4th Foot (King's Own): L. I. Cowper, *The King's Own: The Story of a Royal Regiment* (Oxford, 1939); one of the best of the British regimental histories.

5th Foot (Northumberland Fusiliers): Lt. Col. R. M. Pratt, *The Royal Northumberland Fusiliers* (Alnick, 1981); H. M. Walker, *A History of the Northumberland Fusiliers, 1674–1919* (London, 1919); Walter Wood, *The Northumberland Fusiliers* (London, Grant Richards, n.d.).

10th Foot: Albert Lee, *History of the Tenth Foot (The Lincolnshire Regiment)* (London, 1911).

17th Foot: Richard Cannon, *Historical Record of the Seventeenth, or the Leicestershire Regiment of Foot* (London, 1848); E.A.H. Webb, *A History of the Services of the 17th (Leicestershire) Regiment* (London, 1911); James Lunt, *The Duke of Wellington's Regiment (West Riding)* (London, 1971).

18th Foot: G. E. Boyle, "The 18th Regiment of Foot in North America," JAHR 2 (1923), 65.

23rd Foot or Royal Welch Fusiliers: A.D.L. Cary and Stouppe McCance, eds., *Regimental Records of the Royal Welch Fusiliers (Late the 23rd Foot)*, vol. 1, *1689–1815* (London, 1921); also *The Regimental Museum of the Royal Welch Fusiliers, 23rd Foot* (n.p., n.d.).

33rd Foot: James Lunt, *The Duke of Wellington's Regiment (West Riding)* (London, 1971).

43rd Foot: Sir Richard G. A. Levinge, *Historical Records of the Forty-third Regiment, Monmouthshire Light Infantry* (London, 1868).

47th Foot: H. G. Purdon, *An Historical Sketch of the 47th (Lancashire) Regiment and the Campaigns Through Which They Passed* (London, 1907); Col. H. C. Wylie, *The Loyal North Lancashire Regiment*, 2 vols. (London, 1933).

52nd Foot: Sir Henry Newbolt, *The Story of the Oxfordshire and Buckinghamshire Light Infantry (The Old 43rd and 52nd Regiments* (London, 1915).

59th Foot: Anonymous, "Notes for a History of the 59th Foot," ca. 1920, Regimental Headquarters, Queen's Lancashire Regiment, Fulwood Barracks, Preston, Lancashire; photocopies in the library of the Minuteman National Historic Park, Concord.

64th Foot: H. G. Purdon, *Memoirs of the Services of the 64th Regiment (Second Staffordshire), 1758 to 1881* (London, n.d.).

Royal Artillery: Francis Duncan, *History of the Royal Regiment of Artillery, 1716–1815,* 2 vols. (London, 1872, 1874; 3d ed., 1879); C.A.L. Graham, *The Story of the Royal Regiment of Artillery* (Woolwich, 1962).

Royal Marines: Col. C. Field, *Britain's Sea Soldiers,* 2 vols. (Liverpool, 1924); Capt. Alexander Gillespie, *Historical Review of the Royal Marine Corps* (Birmingham, 1803); J. L. Moulton, *Royal Marines* (London, 1972); Lt. P. H. Nicolas, *Historical Records of the Royal Marine Forces,* 2 vols. (London, 1845).

Scottish Regiments

The Highland regiments have inspired a large literature of high quality. Philip Howard in *The Black Watch* (London, 1968), 133, estimates that ninety histories have been written on that regiment alone. Among them are David Stewart of Garth, *Sketches of the Character, Manner, and Present State of the Highlanders of Scotland; with Details of the Military Service of the Highlands Regiment,* 2 vols. (Edinburgh, 1822, 1825, 1885); Richard Cannon, *Historical Record of the Forty-second, or, The Royal Highland Regiment of Foot . . .* (London, 1845); Archibald Forbes, *The "Black Watch": The History of the Royal Highland Regiment* (London and New York, 1897); John Stewart, *A Brief History of the Royal Highland Regiment: The Black Watch* (Edinburgh, 1938); Bernard Fergusson, *The Black Watch and the King's Enemies* (London, 1950); Eric and Andro Linklater, *The Black Watch: The History of the Royal Highland Regiment.*

On the regiment in America, John Maclean Patterson, *An Historical Account of the Settlements of Scotch Highlanders in America Prior to the Peace of 1783* (Cleveland, 1900); add Forbes on Ticonderoga; Robert G. Carroon, *Broadsides and Bayonets: The Journals of the Expedition Under the Command of Captain Thomas Stirling of the 42nd Foot, Royal Highland Regiment (the Black Watch) to Occupy Fort Chartres in the Illinois Country, August 1765 to January 1766* (Chicago, 1984).

Other works include Neil McMicking, *The Officers of the Black Watch, 1725–1937* (Perth, 1938); John Stewart, *Royal Highland Regiment, the Black Watch, Formerly 42d and 73rd Foot, Medal Roll* (n.p., n.d.); David Stewart, *Sketches of the Character, Manners and Present State of the Highlanders . . . ,* 2 vols. (Edinburgh, 1822; rpt. 1977).

Histories of Hesse-Cassel and the Hessian Army

On war and society in middle Europe, helpful works include J. Black, *European Warfare, 1660–1815* (London, 1994); J. Childs, *Armies and Warfare in Europe, 1648–1789* (Manchester, 1982); A. Corvisier, *Armies and Societies in Europe, 1494–1789* (Bloomington, 1979).

For the studies of German armed forces in particular states, see C. Duffy, *The Army of Maria Theresa: The Armed Forces of Imperial Austria, 1750–1780* (Doncaster, 1990); idem, *The Army of Frederick the Great,* 2d ed. (Chicago, 1996); P. H. Wilson, *War, State, and Society in Württemberg, 1677–1793* (Cambridge, 1995). An important interpretative work is O. Büsch, *Military System and Social Life: Old Regime Prussia, 1713–1807* (Atlantic Highlands, N.J., 1997).

General works on the history of Hesse-Cassel include Charles W. Ingrao, *The Hessian Mercenary State: Ideas, Institutions, and Reform Under Frederick II* (Cambridge, 1987); Peter K. Taylor, *Indentured to Liberty: Peasant Life and the Hessian Military State* (Ithaca, 1994). An informative traveler's account is John Moore, *A View of Society and Manners in France, Switzerland, and Germany,* 2d ed., 2 vols. (Dublin, 1780).

For the Landgrafs of Hesse-Cassel, see Philipp Losch, *Kurfürst Wilhelm I, Landgraf von Hessen: Ein Fürstenbild aus der Zopfzeit* (Marburg, 1923). For Friedrich Wilhelm II and his values, see Friedrich Wilhelm von Hessen, *Pensées diverses sur les princes,* in *Hessische Blätter* 16, nos. 856–57 (1882).

For Germany and the American Revolution: Horst Dipple, *Deutschland und die amerikanische Revolution* (diss., University of Cologne, 1970), an excellent study of responses in the German press, trans. Bernhard A. Uhlendorf as *Germany and the American Revolution, 1770–1800: A Sociohistorical Investigation of Late Eighteenth-Century Political Thinking* (Chapel Hill, 1977); idem, *Americana Germanica, 1770–1800; Bibliographie deutscher Amerika-literatur*

(Stuttgart, 1976); idem, *Germany and the American Revolution, 1770–1800* (Chapel Hill, 1977); Barbara S. Groseclose, *Emanuel Leutze, 1816–1868: Freedom Is the Only King* (Washington, 1976).

On the Hessian troops in America, an older work, still helpful, is Max von Eelking, *Die Deutschen Hülfstruppen im nordamerikanischen Befreiungskriege 1776 bis 1876*, 2 vols. (Hanover, 1864; rpt. Cassel, 1976); abridged English trans. by J. G. Rosengarten, *The German Allied Troops in the North American War of Independence* (Albany, 1893; rpt. Bowie, Md., 1987). E. J. Lowell, *The Hessians and Other German Auxiliaries of Great Britain in the Revolutionary War* (New York, 1884); Rodney Atwood, *The Hessians: Mercenaries from Hessen-Kassel in the American Revolution* (Cambridge, 1980), an excellent monograph (for the author see *The Independent*, 22 May 1994).

On the culture and values of Hessian troops, see Ernst Kipping, *The Hessian View of America, 1776–1783* (Monmouth Beach, N.J., 1971), 13; Franz Wilhelm Ditfurth, *Historische Volkslieder der Zeit von 1756– 1871* (Berlin, 1872).

A Hessian regimental history is Robert O. Slagle, "The Von Lossberg Regiment: A Chronicle of Hessian Participation in the American Revolution" (diss., American University, 1965).

The German soldier trade is analyzed as an economic system in Fritz Redlich, *The German Military Enterpriser and His Work Force: A Study in European Economic and Social History*, 2 vols. (Vierteljahrschrift für Sozial- und Wirtschaftsgeschichte, 47–48, Wiesbaden, 1964–65). A strong Whig-Liberal indictment of the trade is Friedrich Kapp, *Der Soldatenhandel deutscher Fürsten nach Amerika* (Berlin, 1864, rpt. Munich, n.d.). A revision of Kapp is Philipp Losch, *Soldatenhandel: Mit einem Verzeichnis der Hessen-Kassilischen Subsidienverträge und einer Bibliographie* (1933; rpt. Kassel, 1974).

The growing controversy over the soldier trade after the battle of Trenton appears in Comte de Mirabeau, *Avis aix Hessois et autre peuples de l'Allemagne Vendus par leurs princes à l'Angleterre* (Cleves, 1777); and Martin Ernst von Schlieffen, *Des Hessois en Amerique, de Leur Souverain et des Declamateurs* (n.p., 1782). The original French texts of Mirabeau and Schlieffen with German translations appear in Holger Hamecher, ed., *Mirabeau, Schlieffen und die nach Amerika verkauften Hessen; Zwei zeitgenössische Pamphlete zum 'Soldatenhandel' für den Amerikanischen Unabhängigkeitskrieg* (Kassel, 1991).

On the Hessian hoax, see [Benjamin Franklin?], "From the Count de Schaumbergh to the Baron Hohendorf, commanding the Hessian troops in America," 18 Feb. 1777, commonly called in English and American literature "The Sale of the Hessians." In German literature it is known as the Uriasbrief. The leading study is Philipp Losch, "Der Uriasbrief des Grafen von Schaumberg," *Hessische Chronik. Monatsschrift für Familien- und Ortsgeschichte in Hessen und Hessen-Nassau* 2 (1913), 37–40, 83–88, 99–105.

Weapons and Equipment

In the highly specialized history of firearms, some of the leading works include Anthony D. Darling, *Red Coat and Brown Bess* (Ottawa, 1970); Lindsay Merrill, *The New England Gun* (New Haven, 1975); Howard Blackmore, *British Military Firearms, 1650–1850* (New York, 1968); Warren Moore, *Weapons of the American Revolution . . . and Accoutrements* (New York, 1967); George C. Neumann, *History of the Weapons of the American Revolution* (New York, 1967); George C. Neumann and Frank J. Kravic, *Collectors Illustrated Encyclopaedia of the American Revolution* (Harrisburg, 1975).

For edged weapons, see Charles ffoulkes and E. C. Hopkinson, *Sword, Lance, and Bayonet* (London, 1938); George C. Neumann, *Swords and Blades of the American Revolution* (Harrisburg, 1973); R. J. Wilkinson-Latham, *British Military Bayonets, from 1700 to 1845* (New York, 1969); Graham T. Priest, *The Brown Bess Bayonet, 1720–1860* (Wiltshire, 1968); R.D.C. Evans and F. J. Stephens, *The Bayonet: An Evolution and History* (London, 1985); Robert M. Reilly, *American Socket Bayonets and Scabbards* (Lincoln, R.I., 1990), with a bibliography of the journal literature.

On powder horns, see Madison Grant, *Powder Horns and Their Architecture* (York, Pa., 1987); Nathan L. Swayze, *Engraved Powder Horns of the French and Indian War and Revolution-*

ary War Era (Yazoo City, Miss., 1978); William H. Guthman, *Drums A'beating, Trumpets Sounding: Artistically Carved Powder Horns in the Provincial Manner, 1746–1781* (Hartford, Conn., 1993), with a bibliography of the large journal literature.

Monographs and Specialized Studies

Political aspects of the campaign: Edmund Cody Burnett, *The Continental Congress* (1941; New York, 1964); Jack N. Rakove, *The Beginnings of National Politics* (New York, 1979); H. James Henderson, *Party Politics in the Continental Congress* (New York, 19740); Elisha Douglass, *Rebels and Democrats* (Chapel Hill, 1955). On British politics, outstanding in a large literature is Ira Gruber, "Lord Howe and Lord George Germain: British Politics and the Winning of American Independence," *WMQ3* 22 (1965), 25.

Economic aspects of the campaign: E. James Ferguson, *The Power of the Purse* (Chapel Hill, 1961); Sidney Homer and Richard Sylla, *A History of Interest Rates,* 3d ed. rev. (New Brunswick, 1992); J.E.D. Binney, *British Public Finance and Administration, 1774–1792* (Oxford, 1958).

Maritime and naval history in its relation to the New York and New Jersey campaign is examined in David Syrett, *Shipping and the American War, 1775–83: A Study of British Transport Organization* (London, 1970); and C. Northcote Parkinson, *Britannia Rules* (Gloucester, 1987), 11–12. William Bell Clark, *Naval Documents of the American Revolution* (Washington, 1964), is a major work, a very full collection of documents. For this project, vols. 5–7 (1776–77) were specially useful.

Gender and women in the army are examined in Walter Hart Blumenthal, *Women Camp Followers of the American Revolution* (Philadelphia, 1952); Holly A. Mayer, *Belonging to the Army: Camp Followers and Community During the American Revolution* (Columbia, 1996); and Elizabeth Cometti's article in *NEQ* 20 (1947), 329–46.

Race and African American participation in the New Jersey campaign are discussed in William C. Nell, *The Colored Patriots of the American Revolution* (Boston, 1855), 198–99; Sidney Kaplan and Emma Nogrady Kaplan, *The Black Presence in the Era of the American Revolution* (rev. ed., Amherst, 1989); Graham Hodges, *Root and Branch: African Americans in New York and East Jersey, 1613–1863* (Chapel Hill, 1999). For Captain Tye and other black refugees, see Harry Ward, *Between the Lines: Banditti of the American Revolution* (Westport, Conn., 2002), 61–68; Luther P. Jackson, "Virginia Negro Soldiers and Seamen in the American Revolution," *JNH* 27 (1942), 247–87; Lorenzo Greene, "Some Observations on the Black Regiment of Rhode Island in the American Revolution," *JNH* 37 (1952), 142–72; Sidney S. Rider, *Historical Inquiry Concerning the Attempt to Raise a Regiment of Slaves by Rhode Island During the War of the Revolution* (Providence, 1880); David O. White, *Connecticut's Black Soldiers, 1775–1783* (Chester, 1973).

Medicine in the war is the subject of C. Keith Wilbur, *Revolutionary Medicine, 1700–1800* (Old Saybrook, Conn., 1980). See also Gordon Dammann, *Civil War Medical Instruments and Equipment* (Missoula, 1983).

On military strategy, and elements of continuity in American strategic thinking from the New Jersey campaign to our own time, compare Robert Coram, *Boyd; The Fighter Pilot Who Changed the Art of War* (Boston, 2002), which also republished Boyd's essay "Destruction and Creation," 451–60; also Grant T. Hammond, *The Mind of War: John Boyd and American Security* (Washington, 2001); and General A. M. Gray et al., *Warfighting,* Fleet Marine Force Manual FMF1 (Washington, 1989), an official summary of Marine Corps doctrine, similar in many ways to Boyd's thinking.

Military discipline in its relation to the Enlightenment is explored by Michel Foucault in *Surveiller et punir: Naissance de la prison* (Paris, 1975), trans. as *Discipline and Punish: The Birth of a Prison* (New York, 1978). Conceptual changes occurred in the translation of *surveiller* as *discipline.* A conceptual discussion appears also in Foucault's "Two Lectures," in *Power/Knowledge: Selected Interviews and Other Writings, 1972–1977* (New York, 1980), 78–109; William MacNeill, *Keeping Together in Time* (Cambridge, 1995).

Military science and artillery has spawned a specialized literature that includes William E. Birkhimer, *Historical Sketch of the Organization, Administration, Matériel, and Tactics of the Artillery, United States Army* (Washington, 1884; rpt. 1968); Jac Weller, "Guns of Destiny: Field Artillery in the Trenton-Princeton Campaign, 25 December 1776 to 3 January 1777," *MA* 20 (1956), 1–15; S. James Gooding, *An Introduction to British Artillery in North America* (Bloomfield, Ont., 1965); many works by Adrian B. Caruana, including *Grasshoppers and Butterflies: The Light Three-Pounders of Pattison and Townshend* (Bloomfield, 1979), 8–9; Adrian B. Caruana, *British Artillery Ammunition, 1780* (Bloomfield, Ont., 1979).

Military intelligence in the War of Independence is surveyed in John Bakeless, *Turncoats, Traitors, and Heroes: Espionage in the American Revolution* (1959, New York, 1998); for particular agents and episodes, see Leonard Falkner, "A Spy for Washington," *American Heritage*, August 1957; Catherine Snell Crary, "The Tory and the Spy: The Double Life of James Rivington," *WMQ3* 16 (1959), 61–72; and Morton Pennypacker, *General Washington's Spies on Long Island and in New York* (Brooklyn, 1939); idem, *General Washington's Spies on Long Island and in New York*, vol. 2 (East Hampton, N.Y., 1948).

ABBREVIATIONS

AA4 and AA5	Peter Force, ed., *American Archives*, 4th ser., 6 vols., March 7, 1774, to Aug. 21, 1776, and 5th ser., 3 vols., May 3, 1776, to Dec. 31, 1776 (Washington, 1837–53)
AAS	American Antiquarian Society
AG	*America Germanica*
AH	*American Heritage*
AHR	*American Historical Review*
ADM	Admiralty
AN	*American Neptune*
APS	American Philosophical Society
APST	*American Philosophical Society Transactions*
BCH	*Bergen County History*
BL	British Library
BPL	Boston Public Library
CHS	Chicago Historical Society
CTHSC	*Connecticut Historical Society Collections*
CO	Colonial Office
CRREL	Cold Regions Research and Engineering Laboratory
DCHSY	*Dutchess County Historical Society Yearbook*
DHSP	*Historical Society of Delaware Papers*
DL	David Library, Washington Crossing, Pa.
EIP	*Essex Institute Proceedings*
EIHC	*Essex Institute Historical Collections*
GCHSB	*Gloucester County Historical Society Bulletin*, New Jersey
GW	*The Papers of George Washington, Revolutionary War Series,* ed. W. W. Abbott, Dorothy Twohig, Philander D. Chase, and Beverly H. Runge (Charlottesville, 1988+)
HCMH	*Hessische Chronik. Monatsschrift für Familien- und Ortsgeschichte in Hessen und Hessen-Nassau*
HT	*History Today*
HZ	*Historische Zeitschrift*
JAHR	*Journal of Army Historical Research*
JNH	*Journal of Negro History*
JSHAJ	*Johannes Schalm Historical Association Journal*
LC	Library of Congress
LT	Lidgerwood Transcripts, MNHPL
MA	*Military Affairs*
MAH	*Magazine of American History*
MCH	*Military Collector and Historian*
MDHM	*Maryland Historical Magazine*
MDHS	Maryland Historical Society
MHS	Massachusetts Historical Society
MHT	Marburg Hessian Transcripts, LC
MHSC	*Massachusetts Historical Society Collections*
MHSP	*Massachusetts Historical Society Proceedings*
MNHPL	Morristown National Historical Park Library
MVHR	*Mississippi Valley Historical Review*
NA	National Archives
NAM	National Army Museum, London
NDAR	William Bell Clark, ed., *Naval Documents of the American Revolution* (Washington, 1964+)
NEHGS	New England Historic and Genealogical Society

NEHGR   *New England Historic and Genealogical Register*
NEQ   *New England Quarterly*
NJA   *New Jersey Archives*
NJA2   *New Jersey Archives, Second Series*
NJH   *New Jersey History*
NJHSP   *New Jersey Historical Society Proceedings*
NYHS   New-York Historical Society
NYPL   New York Public Library
NYPLB   *New York Public Library Bulletin*
NYSHAJ   *New York State Historical Association Quarterly Journal*
PA   *Pennsylvania Archives*
PH   *Pennsylvania History*
PMHB   *Pennsylvania Magazine of History and Biography*
PRO   Public Record Office, Kew
PUL   Princeton University Library
VSW   *Viertelsjahrschrift für Sozial- und Wirtschaftsgeschichte*
VHS   Virginia Historical Society
VMHB   *Virginia Magazine of History and Biography*
WCL   William L. Clements Library, Ann Arbor, Michigan
WMQ3   *William and Mary Quarterly,* 3d series
WO   War Office

NOTES

❧ Introduction

1. Mark Twain, *Life on the Mississippi,* ed. Shelley Fisher Fishkin (1883; New York, 1996), 406, 403.

2. Attempts have been made to identify individual figures in the boat, with little success. In 1855, William C. Nell asserted that the African American figure was Prince Whipple of Portsmouth, N.H. But at the time Whipple was probably in Baltimore with his master, a member of Congress. A more likely model for the figure, given his dress and demeanor, would have been one of several seamen in Glover's Fourteenth Massachusetts Regiment. The African American figure in Sully's painting and other early nineteenth-century images was William Lee, Washington's slave companion in the war. Cf. William C. Nell, *The Colored Patriots of the American Revolution* (Boston, 1855), 198–99; Sidney Kaplan and Emma Nogrady Kaplan, *The Black Presence in the Era of the American Revolution* (Amherst, 1989), 49–50.

3. Ferdinand Freiligarth, "Ça Ira" (1846); Barbara S. Groseclose, *Emanuel Leutze, 1816–1868: Freedom Is the Only King* (Washington, 1976), 36.

4. Firsthand accounts by American artists who helped Leutze appear in John I. H. Baur, *Eastman Johnson* (Brooklyn, 1940); and idem, ed., *Worthington Whitridge, Autobiography, 1822–1910* (Brooklyn, 1942), 22–25.

5. In a large literature, leading works include Ann Hawkes Hutton, *Portrait of Patriotism: Washington Crossing the Delaware* (Radnor, Pa., 1959, 1975); Barbara S. Groseclose, *Emanuel Leutze, 1816–1868* (Washington, 1975); Natalie Spassky et al., *American Paintings in the Metropolitan Museum of Art* (Princeton, 1985), 2:13–24; Raymond L. Stehle, "Washington Crossing the Delaware," *PH* 31 (1964), 269–94.

6. Henry James, "A Small Boy and Others" (1913), in F. W. Dupee, ed., *Henry James: An Autobiography* (New York, 1956), 151–52.

7. For some of these images, see the discussion of historiography, 425–57 below.

8. For debunkers see Wesley Frank Craven, *The Legend of the Founding Fathers* (Ithaca, 1956), 187–96, 203–6; for postmodernists, Ron Robin, *Scandals and Scoundrels* (Berkeley, 2004), 222–28, 195–218, 106–7; for iconoclasts, David Hackett Fischer, *Paul Revere's Ride* (Oxford, 1994), 340–42; and see below, 453–54.

9. Thomas L. Livermore, *Numbers and Losses in the Civil War in America: 1861–65* (1900; rpt. Bloomington, 1957); Ezra Carman, "The Maryland Campaign of 1862," unpublished

typescript, Antietam National Battlefield Library, as quoted in James M. McPherson, *Crossroads of Freedom: Antietam* (New York, 2002), 175, 177; personal communication from James M. McPherson, 12 Feb. 2003; Hugh M. Cole, *The Ardennes: Battle of the Bulge* (Washington, 1965, 1994).

10. George Washington to Lord Stirling, 19 Jan. 1777, *GW* 8:110–11; for a discussion of this passage, see John C. Fitzpatrick, *George Washington Himself: A Common-Sense Biography Written from His Manuscripts* (Indianapolis, 1933), 292. This work is rarely read today, but it is one of the best and most useful studies of Washington by the editor of the bicentennial edition of the *Washington Papers*.

❧ The Rebels

1. George Washington to John Hancock, 25? Sep. 1776, *GW* 6:396.

2. For Washington's horsemanship the best sources are the paintings by John Trumbull, who saw him in the field, especially his paintings of the battles at Princeton, Trenton, and Yorktown, in Theodore Sizer, ed., *The Paintings of Colonel John Trumbull*, rev. ed. (New Haven, 1967), figs. 164–96. The experienced riders were Thomas Jefferson to Walter Jones, 2 Jan. 1814, in Adrienne Koch and William Peden, eds., *Life and Selected Writings of Thomas Jefferson* (New York, 1944), 174; and G.W.P. Custis, *Recollections and Private Memoirs of Washington, by His Adopted Son . . .* (New York, 1860; rpt. Bridgewater, Va., 1999), 133; idem, "Washington a Sportsman," *American Turf Register and Sporting Magazine*, Sept. 1829, 7–8. For discussions of Washington and horses see Richard Brookhiser, *Founding Father: Rediscovering George Washington* (New York, 1996), 111; James Thomas Flexner, *George Washington: The Forge of Experience* (Boston and Toronto, 1965), 1:23, 192, 240, 314; Douglas Southall Freeman, *George Washington: A Biography*, 7 vols. (New York, 1948–57), 3:6, 269–70.

3. Mercy Otis Warren, *History of the Rise, Progress, and Termination of the American Revolution*, 3 vols. (Boston, 1805), 1:233; Andreas Wiederholdt, Diary, 28 Dec. 1776 in Bruce Burgoyne, ed., *The Trenton Commanders* (Bowie, Md., 1997), 4. For other descriptions see George Mercer, 1760, in Freeman, *Washington* 3:6; Custis, *Recollections and Private Memoirs*, 527; secondary accounts include Freeman, *Washington* 3:6, 377, 420, 505–6.

4. For Washington's slave William Lee, see below, 18–19.

5. For Washington's movements on March 17, 1776, see *Pennsylvania Evening Post*, 30 March 1776; Frank Moore, ed., *Diary of the American Revolution*, 2 vols. (New York, 1860), 1:222–23; Freeman, *Washington* 4:52–54.

6. George Washington to John Hancock, 19 March 1776, *GW* 3:489; also General Orders, 17 March 1776, ibid., 482.

7. Among several estimates of British strength, a provision return showed 7,579 on the ration list; William Howe reported 8,906 officers and men, and Frederick Mackenzie reported 9,192 men. Allen French favors Howe's numbers. See Allen French, *The First Year of the American Revolution* (Boston, 1934), 672 and appendices.

8. Harvard College, Diploma, 3 April 1776; *GW* 4:23; Salem *Essex Gazette*, 18 Jan. 1776; Moore, *Diary* 1:192.

9. Address from the Massachusetts General Court, 28 March 1776, *GW* 4:555–57.

10. Moore, *Diary* 1:141; Gaine's *New York Mercury*, 2 Oct. 1775; Daniel McCurtin, Journal, 12 Oct. 1775, in *Papers Relating to the Maryland Line During the Revolution*, ed. Thomas Balch (Philadelphia, 1857), 22.

11. Washington to John Augustine Washington, 31 March 1776, *GW* 3:566–71, 569.

12. Washington to John Hancock, 13 March 1776, *GW* 3:461–65.

13. Ibid.

14. George Washington to John Hancock, 25? Sept. 1776, *GW* 6:396.

15. Washington, General Orders, 3 Jan. 1776, and letters to Joseph Reed, 10 Feb. 1776, and Thomas Mumford, 13 Feb. 1776, *GW* 3:14, 286, 305.

16. See David Hackett Fischer and James Kelly, *Bound Away: Virginia and the Westward Movement* (Charlottesville, 2000), 85–87.

17. Washington to Thomas Lord Fairfax, Oct. or Nov. 1749, *The Papers of George Washington*, ed. W. W. Abbot, (Charlottesville, 1983), *Colonial Series* 1:39–40.

18. A letter supposedly written by Lord Fairfax to Washington's mother, complaining, "I wish I could say that he governs his temper," is a literary fiction, concocted by Silas Weir Mitchell. It has found its way into the modern secondary literature. Cf. Nathaniel Wright Stephenson and Waldo Hilary Dunn, *George Washington*, 2 vols. (New York, 1940), 1:33–34; Richard Norton Smith, *Patriarch: George Washington and the New American Nation* (Boston, 1993); Richard Brookhiser, *Founding Father: Rediscovering George Washington* (New York, 1996), 116.

19. For primal honor see Bertram Wyatt-Brown, *Southern Honor* (New York 1982), the best work on the subject.

20. Charles Willson Peale in C. C. Sellers, *Charles Willson Peale*, 108–9; Freeman, *Washington* 4:293.

21. John Armstrong to Congress, 10 Dec. 1776, *AA* 5 3:1151; Freeman, *Washington*, 4:288.

22. Robert F. Dalzell and Lee Baldwin Dalzell, *George Washington's Mount Vernon* (New York and Oxford, 1998), 192.

23. Washington to William Pearce, 18 Dec. 1793, *The Writings of Washington*, ed. John C. Fitzpatrick (Washington 1932) 33:191.

24. Shortly before his death, Washington compiled a list of his major assets, mostly real estate, which he valued at $530,000. This did not include other assets, which have been estimated at about $250,000, nor 331 slaves owned by Washington and his wife whom he intended to emancipate. Together, the total value of the estate in 1799 would come very close to a million dollars. See Dalzell and Dalzell, *George Washington's Mount Vernon*, 221; and Eugene E. Prussing, *The Estate of George Washington, Deceased* (Boston, 1927), a major work of scholarship.

25. George Washington to Lund Washington, 15 Aug. 1778 in Dalzell and Dalzell, *George Washington's Mount Vernon*, 112, 213, 261; also Worthington C. Ford, *Washington as an Employer and Importer of Labor* (Brooklyn, 1889); Walter Z. Mazyck, *George Washington and the Negro* (Washington, 1932); Harvey Wiencek, *An Imperfect God: George Washington, His Slaves, and the Creation of America* (New York, 2003).

26. John C. Fitzpatrick, *George Washington Himself: A Common-Sense Biography Written from His Manuscripts* (Indianapolis, 1933), 53.

27. Ibid., 102.

28. Ibid., 100.

29. Ibid., 92.

30. Washington to George William Fairfax, 31 May 1775, *Papers of George Washington, Colonial Series* 10:367–68.

31. Washington to Joseph Reed, 10 Feb. 1776, *GW* 3:288.

32. John E. Ferling, *The First of Men: A Life of George Washington* (Knoxville, 1988), 103; Freeman, *Washington* 4:436.

33. Emily Stone Whiteley, *Washington and His Aides-de-Camp* (New York, 1936), 9–44, with a roster of all who served, 211–12.

34. Fairfax Independent Company to Washington, 8 July 1775, *GW* 1:77, 24; Freeman, *Washington* 4:549.

35. Freeman, *Washington* 3:183; L. G. Shreve, *Tench Tilghman: The Life and Times of Washington's Aide-de-Camp* (Centreville, Md., 1982), 57–80.

36. For the purchase of William Lee as "'Mulatto Will,'" for £61.15, by promissory note dated 15 Oct. 1767, see Washington's Cash Accounts for May 1768, *Washington Papers, Colonial Series* 8:82–83. Lee was one of the most frequently painted slaves in American history. He appears in John Trumbull's portrait of Washington in 1780, Edward Savage's painting of the Washington family (1796), and Thomas Sully's images of Washington crossing the Delaware. And yet he rarely appears in biographies of Washington. See historiography below, and see also Sidney Kaplan and Emma Nogrady Kaplan, *The Black Presence in the Era of the American Revolution*, rev. ed. (Amherst, 1989), 35–37.

37. George Washington to Lund Washington, 20 Aug. 1775, and Washington to Richard Henry Lee, 29 Aug. 1775, *GW* 1:334–37, 372–75; Ferling, *First of Men*, 127.

38. Elisha Bostwick, "A Connecticut Soldier Under Washington: Elisha Bostwick's Memoirs of the First Year of the Revolution." ed. William S. Powell, *WMQ3* 6 (1949), 94–107; Bostwick's commissions and service record appear in George D. Seymour, ed., *Documentary Life of Nathan Hale* (New Haven, 1941), 320–25.

39. Joseph White, *A Narrative of Events, as They Occurred from Time to Time, in the Revolutionary War, with an Account of the Battles of Trenton, Trenton-Bridge, and Princeton* (Charlestown, Mass., 1833; rpt. *American Heritage*, June 1956, 74–79).

40. Robert Gross, *The Minutemen and Their World* (New York, 1976), 146–47; David Hackett Fischer, *Concord: A Social History* (Waltham, 1983), chaps. 2, 4, 5; idem, *Paul Revere's Ride* (New York, 1994), 149–64.

41. Joseph Plumb Martin, *Private Yankee Doodle: Being a Narrative of Some of the Adventures, Dangers, and Sufferings of a Revolutionary Soldier,* ed. George F. Scheer (Boston, 1962), 17.

42. Ibid., 14.

43. It was authorized as a provincial outfit four days after the fight at Lexington, and reenlisted for one year as a Continental regiment on January 1, 1776. This account follows one of the best regimental histories in the Revolutionary War, George Athan Billias, *General John Glover and His Marblehead Mariners* (New York, 1960), 69–70, passim.

44. Alexander Graydon, *Memoirs of His Own Time, with Reminiscences of the Men and Events of the Revolution* (Philadelphia, 1846), 149; Billias, *Glover and His Marblehead Mariners,* 59–71; John Glover, "General John Glover's Letterbook," ed. Russell W. Knight, *EIHC* 112 (1976), 1–55.

45. Graydon, *Memoirs,* 149.

46. Billias, *Glover and His Marblehead Mariners,* 69; Glover, "Letterbook."

47. Ambrose Serle, *The American Journal of Ambrose Serle, Secretary to Lord Howe, 1776–1778,* ed. Edward H. Tatum Jr. (San Marino, Calif.: Huntington Library, 1940), 56 (7 Aug. 1776).

48. Johann von Bardeleben, *The Diary of Lieutenant von Bardeleben,* ed. Bruce E. Burgoyne (Bowie, Md., 1998), 52 (17 Aug. 1776).

49. Michel [*sic*] Williams Craig, *General Edward Hand: Winter's Doctor* (n.p., 1984?); A. J. Bowden, cat., *The Unpublished Revolutionary Papers of Major General Edward Hand of Pennsylvania* (1907); for black hunting shirts see Christopher Ward, *The Delaware Continentals, 1776–1783* (Wilmington, 1941), 16.

50. Charles K. Bolton, *The Private Soldier Under Washington* (New York, 1902; rpt. 1976, 1997), 91–93.

51. Captain Philip Slaughter, Memoir and Diary, in Rev. Philip Slaughter, *A History of St. Mark's Parish, Culpeper County, Virginia* (Baltimore, 1877; rpt. 1994, 1998), 106–8.

52. The evidence for this flag is doubtful. It first appeared as a drawing in Benson J. Lossing, *Pictorial Field-Book of the Revolution,* 2 vols. (New York, 1851; rpt. ed. Terence Barrow, Rutland, 1972), 2:299. His source is thought to have been a memoir and a diary by Captain Philip Slaughter, which were destroyed in the Civil War. Excerpts from the memoir are published in Slaughter, *A History of St. Mark's Parish,* 106–8. They include a description of the hunting shirts, but the published passages do not describe the colors. The present members of the Culpeper Minute Men accept the authenticity of Lossing's drawing. For the Westmoreland militia and other Pennsylvania units that adopted the rattlesnake flag, and its subsequent use by the Continental navy and marines, and the difference between the rattlesnake with its "Don't Tread on Me" message and the Franklin-Revere serpent of unity (an old European emblem), see Fischer, *Liberty and Freedom,* forthcoming.

53. George Washington to Samuel Washington, 30 Sep. 1775, *GW* 2:72–74.

54. Israel Trask, of Mansfield's Massachusetts Regiment, Pension Application in John C Dann, ed., *The Revolution Remembered: Eyewitness Accounts of the War of Independence* (Chicago, 1980), 408–9.

55. Benjamin Franklin, *Plain Truth* (Philadelphia, 1747); "Form of Association," *Pennsylvania Gazette,* 3 Dec. 1747, in *The Papers of Benjamin Franklin,* ed. Leonard W. Labaree et al. (Philadelphia, 1961), 2:180–212.

56. Graydon, *Memoirs,* 133–37, 146–52, passim.

57. "To the Associators of the City of Philadelphia," broadside, 18 May 1775; Eric Foner, *Tom Paine and Revolutionary America* (New York, 1976), 63–67.

58. Steven Rosswurm, *Arms, Country, and Class: The Philadelphia Militia and the 'Lower Sort' During the American Revolution* (New Brunswick, 1987), 66–72.

59. George Washington to Col. John Cadwalader, 7 Dec. 1776, and to John Hancock, 8 Dec. 1776, *GW* 7:268–69.

60. Mordecai Gist to Matthew Tilghman, 30 Dec. 1775, Gist Papers, MDHS, published in *MDHM* 4 (1909), 372–74.

61. Ibid.

62. "We the Baltimore Independent Cadets," *MDHM* 4 (1909), 372–74; John Hancock to George Washington, 17 July 1776, *GW* 5:358–59.

63. Graydon, *Memoirs*, 179–80.

64. Maj. Adlum to G.W.P. Custis, n.d., in Custis, *Recollections and Private Memoirs*, 264–66; Samuel Smith, Autobiography (1834), Smith Papers, LC; the best history of the regiment is James H. F. Brewer, *History of the 175th Infantry (Fifth Maryland)* (Baltimore, 1955), 1–54.

65. John Hancock to George Washington, 6 July 1776, *GW* 5:219.

66. Washington, General Orders, 9 July 1776, *GW* 5:245–47.

67. Samuel Blachley Webb, Journal, 9 July 1776, in Worthington C. Ford, ed., *Correspondence and Journals of Samuel Blachley Webb*, 3 vols. (New York, 1893), 1:153.

68. Ibid.; Washington, General Orders, 10 July 1776, *GW* 5:256–57; Isaac Bangs, *Journal, NJHSP* 8 (1859), 109 (10 July 1776); *Philip Vickers Fithian, Journal, 1775–1776, Written on the Virginia-Pennsylvania Frontier and in the Army Around New York*, ed. Robert Greenhalgh Albion and Leonidas Dodson (Princeton, 1934), 188 (13 July 1776).

69. Washington, General Orders, 13 July 1776, *GW* 5:290.

70. Graydon, *Memoirs*, 161.

71. George Washington to John Hancock, 25? Sept. 1776, *GW* 6:396.

❧ The Regulars

1. Bennet Cuthbertson, *A System for the Compleat Interior Management and Œconomy of a Battalion of Infantry* (Dublin, 1768), 143.

2. Daniel McCurtin, "Journal of the Times at the Siege of Boston . . . ," in Thomas Balch, ed., *Papers Relating to the Maryland Line During the Revolution* (Philadelphia, 1857), 127.

3. Stephen Kemble, Journal, 1–5 July 1776, *Kemble Papers*, 2 vols., NYHS *Collections* (New York, 1884–85), 1:79.

4. Journal of HMS *Phoenix*, HMS *Rose*, HMS *Greyhound*, HMS *Chatham*, and HM Sloop *Senegal*, July 1776, ADM 51/693, 805, 420, 192, 885, PRO; William James Morgan, ed., *Naval Documents of the American Revolution* (Washington, 1970), 5:895–97; Harry Miller Lydenberg, ed., *Archibald Robertson, Lieutenant General Royal Engineers, His Diaries and Sketches in America, 1762–1780* (New York, 1930), 85–87; Ambrose Serle, *The American Journal of Ambrose Serle, Secretary to Lord Howe, 1776–1778*, ed. Edward H. Tatum Jr. (San Marino, Calif., 1940), 28–64 (12 July–15 Aug. 1776).

5. David Syrett, *Shipping and the American War, 1775–83: A Study of British Transport Organization* (London, 1970); Ira Gruber, "Lord Howe and Lord George Germain: British Politics and the Winning of American Independence," *WMQ3* 22 (1965), 25; citing monthly dispositions of the Royal Navy, 1 July 1776, ADM 8/52, PRO.

6. Qualitative judgments on the army ca. 1776 appear in Piers Mackesy, *The War for America* (Cambridge, 1964), 86; the number of women in the army is computed from an order by General William Howe that every company was allowed six women. Children were forbidden, but multiplied in defiance of the general's orders. Many more women wanted to come, but were compelled to remain in Halifax with the children. The British army on Staten Island grew by August 14 to forty regiments and battalions, which included approximately 350 companies, which would have brought a total of 2,100 women. Probably there were more, as there were many women who wanted to come, and men who wanted to bring them,

and officers who were happy to look the other way. Other women dressed as men and served in the ranks.

Estimates of years of service for general officers are from a quantitative study by Ira D. Gruber, in "America's First Battle: Long Island, 27 August 1776," in Charles E. Heller and William A. Stofft, eds., *America's First Battles, 1776–1965* (Lawrence, Kans., 1986), 2; service of privates is from quantitative research by Sylvia R. Frey, for eight regiments, which ranged from a mean of 8.2 years in the Forty-fourth Foot to 14.7 years in the Eighth Foot. Most averaged about 9 years. The mean age was 28 or 29 years, except in the Eighth Foot, where it was 37 years. See Silvia Frey, *The British Soldier in America: A Social History of Military Life in the Revolutionary Period* (Austin, Tex., 1981), 22, 23–26.

7. J. W. Fortescue, *A History of the British Army,* 13 vols. in 20 (London, 1899–1930), 2:267–603, 3:1–147; R. M. Barnes, *History of Regiments and Uniforms in the British Army* (London, n.d.), 54–60; Alexander Graydon, *Memoirs of His Own Time, with Reminiscences of the Men and Events of the Revolution,* ed. John Stockton Littell (Philadelphia, 1846), 208.

8. A. Bruce, *The Purchase System in the British Army, 1660–1871* (London, 1980); Stephen Brumwell, *Redcoats: The British Soldier and War in the Americas, 1755–1763* (Cambridge, 2002), 83–85; John Cannon, *Aristocratic Century: The Peerage in Eighteenth-Century England* (Cambridge, 1984), 120; E. A. Wrigley and R. S. Schofield, *The Population History of England, 1541–1871* (Cambridge, 1981), 577.

9. Quoted in Antony Beevor, *Inside the British Army* (London, 1990, updated edition, 1991), 308.

10. For British grenadiers in the American Revolution see John Peebles, *John Peebles' American War: The Diary of a Scottish Grenadier, 1776–1782,* ed. Ira D. Gruber (London, 1998). Peebles was captain of a grenadier company in the Forty-second Foot and adjutant of the Fourth Grenadier Battalion in America. His orderly books for the battalion survive at the PRO, with copies at the David Library.

11. The best study is still J.F.C. Fuller, *British Light Infantry in the Eighteenth Century* (London, 1925), 124–25; Howe's "Manoeuvres for Light Infantry" is reprinted on 247–52.

12. The individual training of light infantry was discussed at length in drill manuals; see, for example, Cuthbertson, *System for the Compleat Interior Management,* 178.

13. For light infantry uniforms see Hew Strachan, *British Military Uniforms, 1768–96: The Dress of the British Army from Official Sources* (London, 1975), 13, 20, 25, 193–95, passim; on green feathers see R. Money Barnes, *The Uniforms and History of the Scottish Regiments* (London, 1956; rpt. 1960, 1969), 274.

14. Each battalion of British light infantry normally included nine companies, on detached duty from their parent regiments. Thus, the First Battalion at Staten Island included the light infantry companies of the 4th, 5th, 10th, 17th, 22d, 23rd, 27th, 35th, and 38th Foot. In the Second Battalion were the 40th, 43rd, 44th, 45th, 49th, 52d, 55th, 63rd, and 64th Foot. These battalions were formed in Nova Scotia on June 7, 1776, from regiments that had served in Boston. Most had marched to Lexington and Concord, and nearly all had fought at Bunker Hill. The Third and Fourth battalions were formed from regiments that came to New York from Britain and other parts of the empire. See *Kemble Papers* 1:353; Samuel S. Smith, *Battle of Princeton* (Monmouth Beach, N.J., 1967), 36; and for companies that served in the fighting around Boston see David Hackett Fischer, *Paul Revere's Ride* (New York, 1994), 314.

15. James Lunt, *The Scarlet Lancers: The Story of the 16th/5th The Queen's Royal Lancers, 1689–1992* (London, 1993), 19–20; idem, *John Burgoyne of Saratoga* (London, 1976); Michael Glover, *General Burgoyne in Canada and America: Scapegoat for a System* (London, 1976); Gerald Howson, *Burgoyne of Saratoga: A Biography* (New York, 1979).

16. Ibid., 24–25; Edward B. de Fonbanque, *Political and Military Episodes . . . the Life and Correspondence of the Right Hon. John Burgoyne* (London, 1786).

17. Lunt, *Scarlet Lancers,* 30.

18. William E. Birkhimer, *Historical Sketch of the Organization, Administration, Matériel, and Tactics of the Artillery, United States Army* (Washington, 1884; rpt. 1968), 4–7.

19. S. James Gooding, *An Introduction to British Artillery in North America* (Bloomfield, Ont., 1965), and many works by Adrian B. Caruana, including *Grasshoppers and Butterflies: The Light Three-Pounders of Pattison and Townshend* (Bloomfield, 1979), 8–9.

20. Adrian B. Caruana, *British Artillery Ammunition, 1780* (Bloomfield, Ont., 1979); F. Duncan, *History of the Royal Artillery, 1716–1815*, 2 vols. (London, 1874), 1:297–393, is a survey of British artillery in the American war.

21. Robert P. Davis, *Where a Man Can Go: Major General William Phillips, British Royal Artillery, 1731–1781* (Westport, Conn., 1999); for Phillips and his batteries at Minden see C.A.L. Graham, *The Story of the Royal Regiment of Artillery* (Woolwich, 1962), 10–11.

22. R. Money Barnes, *The British Army of 1914: Its History, Uniforms, and Contemporary Continental Armies* (London, 1968), 174, 182, 210.

23. James Lunt, *The Duke of Wellington's Regiment (West Riding)* (London, 1971), 14. Later they were called the Dukes.

24. Cuthbertson, *System for the Compleat Interior Management*, 7, 54, 64; Frey, *The British Soldier in America*, 94–111.

25. Barnes, *Regiments and Uniforms*, 215; J. A. Houlding, *Fit for Service: The Training of the British Army, 1715–1795* (Oxford, 1981), the leading work.

26. Quoted in Lunt, *Scarlet Lancers*, 23.

27. Cuthbertson, *System of Complete Interior Management;* and *A New System of Military Discipline, founded upon Principle by a General Officer,* attributed to Richard Lambert, the sixth earl of Cavan, and reprinted in 1776. An electronic variorum edition of the Cuthbertson and the text of the *New System* has been issued on CD-ROM as *The Complete Cuthbertson,* ed. Don Hagist and Mark Tully (n.p., 2000).

Other widely read works included Humphrey Bland, *A Treatise of Military Discipline* (1727), 8th ed. revised, corrected, and altered to the present practice of the Army (London, 1762); Lt. Col. Campbell Dalrymple, *A Military Essay: Containing Reflections of the Raising, Arming, Cloathing and Discipline of the British Infantry and Cavalry* (London, 1761); Edward Fage, *A Regular Form of Discipline for the Militia, as It Is Performed by the West-Kent Regiment* (London, 1759). An excellent general study of training manuals with a very full bibliography is J. A. Houlding, *Fit for Service: The Training of the British Army, 1715–1795* (Oxford, 1981).

28. For a discussion of the relation between discipline and the Enlightenment see Michel Foucault, *Discipline and Punish: The Birth of a Prison* (New York, 1978), 135–69, a translation of *Surveiller et punir: Naissance de la prison* (Paris, 1975). Conceptual changes occurred in, for example, the translation of *surveiller* as *discipline,* at the author's own choice. A conceptual discussion appears also in Foucault's "Two Lectures," in *Power/Knowledge: Selected Interviews and Other Writings, 1972–1977* (New York, 1980), 78–109.

Foucault worked backwards, tracing the development of the prison to Jeremy Bentham's Panopticon, and that conceptual model which he called Pantopticism to new forms of discipline in armies, schools, the Catholic church, and other institutions. These systems he attributed to the values of the Enlightenment. The entire work was an attack on liberal democratic cultures in the West as repressive and dehumanizing, and a Panopticon by another name: an attitude widely shared by French Marxist intellectuals after the Second World War. Foucault was right about a connection between the Enlightenment and new ideas of order and discipline in the early modern era, but mistaken in his understanding of how it worked, and still more about its relationship to ideas of liberty and freedom. The principles that he tried to link were historically opposed, and met in conflict during the American War of Independence.

Foucault's work is also a misconception of military discipline, which sought not to create "docile bodies," as he believed, not a "machine," not an "automaton" (135), but a soldier whose mind and will are actively engaged in his duty.

29. [Cavan], *New System,* "Rules, Maxims and Observations," preface, sec. 3.

30. [Cavan], *New System,* preface.

31. Cuthbertson, *System for the Compleat Interior Management,* 156; Houlding, *Fit for Service,* 259.

32. Houlding, *Fit for Service*, 278–99, quoting MacIntire, *Marine Forces*, 172–77.

33. For the 170 drum signals see [Cavan], *New System*, 237–50; also Thomas Simes, *The Military Medley* (London, 1768). Reenacting groups have created a website for eighteenth-century drum signals; see www.cvco.org/sigs/reg64/music.html.

34. *The Manual Exercise as Ordered by His Majesty* (London, 1764).

35. Some scholars think that locking was done as early as 1708; Houlding finds no references before 1727; see Houlding, *Fit for Service*, 281, and Cavan's discussion in *New System*.

36. Fischer, *Paul Revere's Ride*, 66.

37. Cavan, *New System*, preface; Houlding, *Fit for Service*, 160.

38. Cuthbertson, *System for the Compleat Interior Management*, 85, 105, 106, 108.

39. Peebles, *John Peebles' American War*, 15; Frey, *The British Soldier in America*, 22–51.

40. Franklin Wickwire and Mary Wickwire, *Cornwallis and the War of Independence* (London, 1970), 77.

41. Cuthbertson, *System for the Compleat Interior Management*, 124–25, 111.

42. Frey, *The British Soldier in America*, 71–93.

43. *Rules and Articles for the Better Government of Our Horse and Foot Guards, and All Our Other Forces in Our Kingdoms of Great Britain and Ireland, Dominions beyond the Seas, and Foreign Parts*, (London, 1778).

44. Francis Lord Rawdon to Francis, Earl of Huntingdon, 5 Aug. 1776, Historical Manuscripts Commission, *Hastings Manuscripts* 3:179–80.

45. Much of what follows comes from the historiography of the Black Watch. Philip Howard in *The Black Watch* (London, 1968), 133, estimates that ninety histories have been written of that regiment alone. Among them are David Stewart of Garth, *Sketches of the Character, Manner, and Present State of the Highlanders of Scotland; with Details of the Military Service of the Highlands Regiment*, 2 vols. (Edinburgh, 1822, 1825, 1885); Richard Cannon, *Historical Record of the Forty-second, or, The Royal Highland Regiment of Foot . . .* (London, 1845); Archibald Forbes, *The "Black Watch": The History of the Royal Highland Regiment* (London and New York, 1897); John Stewart, *A Brief History of the Royal Highland Regiment: The Black Watch* (Edinburgh, 1938); Bernard Fergusson, *The Black Watch and the King's Enemies* (London, 1950); Eric and Andro Linklater, *The Black Watch: The History of the Royal Highland Regiment*.

On the regiment in America, John Maclean Patterson, *An Historical Account of the Settlements of Scotch Highlanders in America Prior to the Peace of 1783* (Cleveland, 1900); Robert G. Carroon, *Broadsides and Bayonets: The Journals of the Expedition Under the Command of Captain Thomas Stirling of the 42nd Foot, Royal Highland Regiment (the Black Watch) to Occupy Fort Chartres in the Illinois Country, August 1765 to January 1766* (Chicago, 1984).

Other works include Neil McMicking, *The Officers of the Black Watch, 1725–1937* (Perth, 1938); John Stewart, *Royal Highland Regiment, the Black Watch, formerly 42d and 73rd Foot, Medal Roll*, (n.p., n.d.); David Stewart, *Sketches of the Character, Manners and Present State of the Highlanders . . .*, 2 vols. (Edinburgh, 1822; rpt. 1977).

46. Barnes, *Scottish Regiments*, 78; Howard, *Black Watch*, 36.

47. Howard, *Black Watch*, 136; Barnes, *Scottish Regiments*, 78.

48. Cuthbertson, *System for the Compleat Interior Management*, chap. 2, p. 13.

49. Stewart, *Black Watch*, 34.

50. Ibid., 6.

51. For Colonel Thomas Stirling, a short biography appears in the Marchioness of Tullibardine, *A Military History of Perthshire, 1660–1902* (Perth, 1908), 407–9; Howard, *Black Watch*, 135; Stewart, *Black Watch*, 43.

52. Graydon, *Memoirs*, 205.

❧ The Hessians

1. Ernst Kipping, *The Hessian View of America, 1776–1783* (Monmouth Beach, N.J., 1971), 13; Franz Wilhelm Ditfurth, *Historische Volkslieder der Zeit von 1756–1871* (Berlin, 1872) vol. 1, pt. 2.

2. Johann von Bardeleben, *The Diary of Lieutenant von Bardeleben*, ed. Bruce E. Burgoyne (Bowie, Md., 1998), 50–51.

3. A surprising revelation to this historian, even shocking for what it reveals of purposes in London. Most American and British scholars believe that British leaders decided to hire Hessian troops after the news of Lexington and Concord and Bunker Hill. The evidence from European sources tells us that this is not correct. British leaders were planning to apply massive military force against colonial liberty long before Lexington and Concord. The suspicions of American Whigs to that effect have been dismissed as a paranoid delusion that a conspiracy was directed against them. The events at Hofgeismar indicate that some American Whigs in the eighteenth century may have been more accurate than historians in the twentieth century who diagnosed their concerns as symptoms of a personality disorder. The evidence of the Hofgeismar meetings, unreported in American historiography, is in Charles W. Ingrao, *The Hessian Mercenary State: Ideas, Institutions, and Reform Under Frederick II* (Cambridge, 1987), 136.

4. Captain W. G. Evelyn to Mrs. Leveson-Gower, 15 Jan. 1776, in *Memoir and Letters of Captain W. Glanville Evelyn . . .* , ed. G. D. Scull (Oxford, 1879), 77.

5. Peter K. Taylor, *Indentured to Liberty: Peasant Life and the Hessian Military State, 1688–1815* (Ithaca, 1994), 21–48; Ingrao, *Hessian Mercenary State*, 54–55; Fritz Redlich, *The German Military Enterpriser and His Work Force: A Study in European Economic and Social History*, 2 vols. (Vierteljahrschrift für Sozial- und Wirtschaftsgeschichte, 47–48, Wiesbaden, 1964–65). Friedrich Kapp, *Der Soldatenhandel deutscher Fürsten nach Amerika* (Berlin, 1864; rpt. Munich, n.d.), 11–23; Philipp Losch, *Soldatenhandel: Mit einem Verzeichnis der Hessen-Kassilischen Subsidienverträge und einer Bibliographie* (1933; rpt. Kassel, 1974), 7–14.

6. Friedrich Wilhelm von Hessen, *Pensées diverses sur les princes*, published in *Hessische Blätter* 16 (1882), nos. 856–57; quoted in Ingrao, *Hessian Mercenary State*, 21–22, 48, 50, 66, 69, 73–75, 8 6, 130, 139, 165, 171; Friedrich Kapp, "Friedrich II von Hessen und die neuere Geschichtsschreibung," *HZ* 42 (1879), 304–30.

7. Ingrao, *Hessian Mercenary State*, 87.

8. Ibid., 129–30; for an eyewitness account, John Moore, *A View of Society and Manners in France, Switzerland, and Germany*, 2d ed., 2 vols. (Dublin, 1780), 1:30.

9. Robert O. Slagle, "The Von Lossberg Regiment: A Chronicle of Hessian Participation in the American Revolution" (diss., American University, 1965), appendix C; Rodney Atwood, *The Hessians: Mercenaries from Hessen-Kassel in the American Revolution* (Cambridge, 1980), 46, 49.

10. Correspondence of Donop with the Prince of Prussia, later Friedrich Wilhelm II of Prussia, not to be confused with the Landgraf of Hesse-Cassel; published in Hans Huth, ed., "Letters from a Hessian Mercenary," *PMHB* 62 (1938), 488–501.

11. Donop Papers, correspondence between Donop, Leslie, Rall, and others, 13–29 Dec. 1776; Hessian Transcript no. 36, Bancroft Coll., NYPL; microfilm in the author's possession; microfilm of the original manuscripts in LC, microprint in the author's possession; also Donop correspondence in LT.

12. Bruce E. Burgoyne, ed., *The Trenton Commanders: Johann Gottlieb Rall and George Washington* (Bowie, Md., 1997), 9–16; [Andreas Widerholdt], "Colonel Rall at Trenton," *PMHB* 23 (1899), 462–67; Atwood, *Hessians*, 43, 64, 89, 244.

13. Wiederhold, Tagebuch, post 14 Dec. 1776, Bancroft Transcripts, NYPL; Bruce Burgoyne, ed., *Enemy Views: The American Revolutionary War as Recorded by the Hessian Participants* (Bowie, Md., 1996), 117; Jakob Piel, "Diary of the Hessian Lieutenant [Jakob] Pie, 1776 to 1783," ed. Bruce E. Burgoyne, *JSHAJ* 4 (1989), 14 (26 Dec. 1776); Reuber, Journal, 25 [26] Dec. 1776.

14. Piel, Diary, 26 Dec. 1776; Reuber, Journal, 25 [26] Dec. 1776; Rall to Donop, 17, 18, 20, 21 (2 letters) Dec. 1776 and Rall to Leslie, 22 Dec. 1776 (2 letters), Donop Papers, MHT, LC; LT.

15. Col. Sir William Faucitt to the Earl of Suffolk, 12 April 1776, quoted in Atwood, *Hessians*, 43.

16. Wiederholdt, Journal, transcript in Bancroft Collection at NYPL, microfilm copy in the author's collection. Excerpts are translated as "Colonel Rall at Trenton," *PMHB* 23 (1899), 462–67; "The Capture of Fort Washington, New York, Described by Captain Andreas Wiederholdt of the Hessian 'Regiment Knyphausen,' " *PMHB* 22 (1898), 95–97; and also by Bruce Burgoyne in *Enemy Views: The American Revolutionary War as Recorded by the Hessian Participants* (Bowie, Md., 1996), 91, 117, 346; for his service record see Atwood, *Hessians*, 41, 49. Some illustrations from his diary have turned up in the Rare Book Collections of the Historical Society of Pennsylvania and are published in *JSHAJ* 2 (1982), 1–2.

17. Taylor, *Indentured to Liberty*, 98.

18. Margarete Woelfel, trans., "Memoirs of a Hessian Conscript: J. G. Seumes' Reluctant Voyage to America," *WMQ3* 5 (1948), 553–70.

19. Atwood, *Hessians*, 181, 219.

20. John Peebles, *John Peebles' American War: The Diary of a Scottish Soldier, 1776–1782*, ed. Ira D. Gruber (London, 1998), 58–59 (27 Oct. 1776).

21. Kipping, *Hessian View*, 9.

22. Atwood, *Hessians*, 74.

23. Losch, *Soldatenhandel*, 26.

24. Ibid.

25. Johann Ewald, *Diary of the American War: A Hessian Journal*, ed. Joseph P. Tustin (New Haven, 1979), 118.

26. For assessments that mediate between Kapp and Losch, see Ingrao, *Hessian Mercenary State*, 145–48, 209–210; Taylor, *Indentured to Liberty*, 44; for a helpful and balanced discussion of Hessian plundering, see Atwood, *Hessians*, 171–83.

❧ The Plan of the Campaign

1. William Howe, *The Narrative of Lieutenant-General Sir William Howe in a Committee of the House of Commons on the 29th of April 1779 . . .* (London, 1780).

2. The papers of the Howe brothers were destroyed by fire in the nineteenth century, but much material survives in the British Public Record Office and other collections. Among biographies, Sir John Barrow, *The Life of Richard Earl Howe, K.G.* (London, 1838), is still helpful; Bellamy Partridge, *Sir Billy Howe* (New York, 1932), is a popular biography with much useful material; Troyer Steele Anderson, *The Command of the Howe Brothers During the American Revolution* (New York, 1936), was a serious attempt to analyze the leadership of the Howe brothers in a scholarly and sympathetic way and to correct many inaccurate and hostile judgments; Ira D. Gruber, *The Howe Brothers and the American Revolution* (New York, 1972), is the best modern study, carefully balanced in judgment and informed by extensive primary research. Mary Howe mss are in the Grant Papers, LC.

3. Barrow, *The Life of Richard Earl Howe*, 2–5.

4. Richard Howe is thought to have been a year at Westminster and seven years at Eton. William Howe had four years at Eton.

5. J.K.L. [John Knox Laughton], "Richard Howe, Earl Howe," *Dictionary of National Biography* (microprint ed., 2 vols., Oxford, 1975) 1:1019–20, is an excellent short sketch of Richard Howe with corrections of Barrow's work.

6. Ambrose Serle, *The American Journal of Ambrose Serle, Secretary to Lord Howe, 1776–1778*, ed. Edward H. Tatum Jr. (San Marino, Calif., 1940), 71 (21 Aug. 1776).

7. C. Northcote Parkinson, *Britannia Rules* (Gloucester, 1987), 11–12.

8. Barrow, *Richard Howe*, 76–77; George Mason, *The Life of Richard Earl Howe* (London, 1805). Mason was joint-proprietor of Richard Howe's country estate, Porters, in Hertfordshire.

9. Gruber, *Howe Brothers*, 56, 57n; Partridge, *Sir Billy Howe*, 8–11.

10. Partridge, *Sir Billy Howe*, 4–5, Gruber, *Howe Brothers*, 97; Barrow, *Richard Howe*, 56.

11. Anderson, *Command of the Howe Brothers*, 44; Partridge, *Sir Billy Howe*, 5–9.

12. Gruber, *Howe Brothers*, 47.

13. [Joseph Galloway], *A Reply to the Observations of Lt. Gen. Sir William Howe* (London, 1780), 146–50; Anderson, *Command of the Howe Brothers*, 49.

14. Henry Lee, *Memoirs of the War in the Southern Department of the United States*, 2 vols. (Philadelphia, 1812), 1:55. Many contemporaries agreed with Lee. Howe's biographers and historians are not of one mind on this subject. Anderson, *Command of the Howe Brothers*, shares Lee's judgment and observes that "this explanation has the merit of appearing to furnish a natural explanation for much that has often been attributed to scarcely credible causes" (71). But Anderson also concludes that "difficulties over supplies at Boston had a more lasting influence upon Sir William Howe than his experience upon the slopes of Bunker Hill (97). Piers Mackesy has it right when he observes that "whatever the particular experiences which may have influenced him, the core of his thinking concerned the conservation of his force," *The War for America* (Cambridge, 1964), 83.

15. Gruber, *Howe Brothers*, 190; Partridge, *Sir Billy Howe*, 33–34; Thomas Jones, *History of New York During the Revolutionary War*, 2 vols. (New York, 1879) 2:425; Eva Phillips Boyd, "Jamaica Plain by Way of London," *Old Time New England* 49 (April–June 1959); Richard L. Ketchum, *Decisive Day: The Battle for Bunker Hill* (1962; New York, 1974), 35–37, 270; Philip Young, *Revolutionary Ladies* (New York, 1977), 57–86.

16. Charles Lee, in Partridge, *Sir Billy Howe*, 250.

17. Johann Ewald, *Diary of the American War: A Hessian Journal*, ed. Joseph P. Tustin (New Haven, 1979), 10 (23 Oct. 1776); Serle, *Journal*, 71 (21 Aug. 1776).

18. Benjamin Franklin, "Account of Negotiations," 22 March 1775, in *Writings of Franklin*, ed. A. H. Smyth, 10 vols. (New York, 1905–07), 6:324–59; Gruber, *Howe Brothers*, 54; Barrow, *Richard Howe*, 85–89.

19. [Galloway], *Reply*, 146–50.

20. Marc Egnal, *New World Economies: The Growth of the Thirteen Colonies and Early Canada* (New York, 1998), 37–45; James A. Henretta, *The Evolution of American Society, 1700–1815* (Lexington, 1973), 41ff.

21. William Howe to George Germain, 26 April 1776, Historical Manuscripts Commission, *Manuscripts of Mrs. Stopford-Sackville* 2:30, quoted in Anderson, *Command of the Howe Brothers*, 120. Some of Howe's letters to Germain reflected a more aggressive attitude, but Howe's letters tended to reflect in some degree the views of their recipients. His correspondence with the more moderate Dartmouth showed a different posture.

22. Mackesy, *War for America*, 88.

23. [Galloway], *Reply*, 146–50.

24. Howe to Dartmouth, 16 Jan. 1776, and Howe to Germain, 23 April 1776, in Anderson, *Command of the Howe Brothers*, 118–21.

25. John Adams to George Washington, Jan. 1776, *GW* 3:36–37.

❧ The Fall of New York

1. *Philip Vickers Fithian: Journal, 1775–1776, Written on the Virginia-Pennsylvania Frontier and in the Army Around New York*, ed. Robert Greenhalgh Albion and Leonidas Dodson (Princeton, 1934), 218 (27 Aug. 1776); Percy to his father, The Duke of Northumberland, 1 Sep. 1776, *Letters of Hugh Earl Percy . . .* (Boston, 1902), 67–69.

2. Charles Lee to George Washington, 5 Jan. 1776, *GW* 3:30.

3. Charles Lee to Washington, 19 Feb. 1776, *GW* 4:339–41.

4. Charles Lee to George Washington, 5 Feb. 1776, *GW* 3:250–51.

5. Israel Putnam to John Hancock, 7 April 1776, William Heath to Putnam, 8 April 1776, *NDAR* 4:698, 721; Henry P. Johnston, *The Battle of Harlem Heights, September 16, 1776: A Review of the Events of the Campaign* (New York, 1897), 14.

6. Washington to John Hancock, 13 March 1776, and to Charles Lee, 14 March 1776, *GW* 3:461–64, 467–69.

7. Washington to Congress, 8 Sept. 1776, *GW* 6:27–28.

8. Journals of HMS *Phoenix* and HMS *Rose*, 12 July 1776, ADM 51/594, 51/805, PRO; *NDAR*, 5:1037–38, with much primary material.

9. New York *Gazette*, 15 July 1776; Washington to New York Convention, 17 August 1776, *GW* 6:54.

10. Washington to the Commanding Officer of Pennsylvania Troops, 14 July 1776, *GW* 5:315; Robert Morris to William Bingham, 4 Dec. 1776, *NDAR* 7:368; George Clinton to Washington, 23 July 1776, *GW* 5:433; Mercer to Washington, 16 July 1776, *GW* 5: 345.

11. Washington, General Orders, 30 Aug. 1776, *GW* 6:163.

12. Alexander Graydon, *Memoirs of His Own Time, with Reminiscences of the Men and Events of the Revolution*, ed. John Stockton Littell (Philadelphia, 1846; rpt. 1969), 155–56.

13. Wadsworth to Jonathan Trumbull, 9 July 1776; Thomas Seymour to R. Trumbull, 11 July 1776; Wadsworth to Jonathan Trumbull, 18 July 1776; all in *AA5* 1:142, 205, 417.

14. Samuel Blachley Webb to General Ward, 18 July 1776, *AA5* 1:413; Field officers of the Connecticut Light Horse to Washington and Reply, 16 July 1776, and Washington to John Hancock, 17 July 1776, *GW* 5:335–37, 355.

15. Seymour to Trumbull, 11 July 1776, *AA5* 1:205.

16. Charles H. Lesser, *The Sinews of Independence: Monthly Strength Reports of the Continental Army* (Chicago, 1976), xxx, xxxi.

17. Ships of the Royal Navy on North American Station and in the West Indies reported combined annual morbidity rates of 27, 34, and 38 percent for the years 1778, 1779, and 1779. Maurice Bear Gordon, "Naval and Maritime Medicine During the Revolution," *NDAR* 6:1483–1511; for the British army, see Ambrose Serle, *The American Journal of Ambrose Serle, Secretary to Lord Howe, 1776–1778*, ed. Edward H. Tatum Jr. (San Marino, Calif., 1940), 64; and the examination of Thomas Givens, private of the Sixty-fourth Foot, August 13, 1776, who reported that "the soldiers are healthy but have no fresh provision." *GW* 6:23; Johann Bardeleben, *The Diary of Lieutenant von Bardeleben*, ed. Bruce E. Burgoyne (Bowie, Md., 1998), 52 (15 Aug. 1776).

18. Greene, General Orders, 28 July 1776, *Papers of General Nathanael Greene*, ed. Richard K. Showman (Chapel Hill, 1976+), 1:268.

19. Fithian, *Journal*, 190, 193, 197 (19, 22, 26 July 1776).

20. Greene to Washington, 1 Aug. 1776, *Papers of Nathanael Greene* 1:271; William Heath, *Memoirs of Major General Heath* (Boston, 1798; rpt. 1904, 1968), 61.

21. Washington, General Orders, 20 Aug. 1776, *GW* 6:89; Joseph Reed to Livingston, 30 Aug. 1776, *AA5* 2:1231.

22. Gen. Hugh Mercer to George Washington, 14 July 1776, *GW* 5:309.

23. Fithian, *Journal*, 209 (15 Aug. 1776).

24. Livingston to Washington, 21 Aug. 1776, and Washington to Livingston, 22 Aug. 1776, *GW* 6:98–99, 100.

25. George Washington to Lund Washington, 19 Aug. 1776, and Washington to John Hancock, 12 Aug. 1776, *GW* 6:83, 5:677; "Extract of a letter from New York dated August 22, 1776," *AA5* 1:1111–12.

26. Models are in the British National Maritime Museum, Greenwich; prints of ramped landing craft appear in Donald M. Londahl-Smidt, "British and Hessian Accounts of the Invasion of Bergen County," *Bergen County History* (1976), 38.

27. Serle, *Journal*, 72; Johannes Reuber, Journal 20–22 Aug. 1776; Bardeleben, *Diary*, 52–54 (20–23 Aug. 1776); Jakob Piel, "Diary of the Hessian Lieutenant Piel, 1776 to 1783," ed. Bruce E. Burgoyne, *JSHAJ* 4 (1989), 13–14; journals of HMS *Rose, Phoenix, Preston, Asia, Senegal, Thunder, Galatea*, 20–22 Aug. 1776, ADM 51/67, 380, 720, 805, 887, 985, PRO; *NDAR* 6:267–71; the log of the flaghsip HMS *Eagle* is in the National Maritime Museum, Greenwich. For many other accounts see *AA5*.

28. Col. Edward Hand to Col. John Nixon, three notes all dated 21 Aug. 1776, all enclosed in Washington to Hancock, 22 August 1776. The gathering on Howe's flagship was a meeting of commanders to coordinate the attack, described in Serle, *Journal*, 70–71. See

also Washington to Hancock, 23 Aug. 1776, and Washington to Heath, 23 Aug. 1776, all in *GW* 6:102, 111, 113.

29. George Washington to Jonathan Trumbull Sr., 24 Aug. 1776, *GW* 6:123.

30. Smallwood to Maryland Convention, 12 Oct. 1776, *AA*5 2:1011; Washington, General Orders, 25 Oct. 1776, *GW* 6:125; also ibid., 5:647; *AA*5 1:1159–62.

31. Douglas Southall Freeman, *George Washington*, 7 vols. (New York, 1948–57), 1:157n.

32. Washington to Putnam, 25 Aug. 1776, *GW* 6:126–28.

33. Washington to Hancock, 17 July 1776, *GW* 5:355–57.

34. Lt. Karl Frederick Rueffer, Journal, 25–28 Aug. 1776, ed. Bruce Burgoyne, published in *The Hesse-Cassel Mirbach Regiment in the American Revolution*, 33–123, at 52–55.

35. Smallwood to Maryland Convention, 12 Oct. 1776, *AA*5 2:1011–14.

36. "Extract of a Letter from New York," 1 Sept. 1776, and Smallwood to Maryland Convention, 12 Oct. 1776, *AA*5 2:1007–08, 1011–14.

37. Serle, *Journal*, 79 (27 Aug. 1776).

38. Fithian, *Journal*, 219 (27 Aug. 1776).

39. *AA*5 1:1259–60.

40. Col. Heinrich von Heeringen, in E. J. Lowell, *The Hessians and Other German Auxiliaries of Great Britain in the Revolutionary War* (New York, 1884), 65–67.

41. William Howe, Orderly Book, 13 Sept. 1776.

42. Berdeleben, *Diary,* 69.

43. Von Heeringen, in Lowell, *Hessians,* 64–66.

44. Jabez Fitch, Diary, 27–29 Aug. 1776, in *The New-York Diary of Lieutenant Jabez Fitch of the 17th (Connecticut) Regiment from August 2, 1776 to December 15, 1777,* ed. W.H.W.Sabine (New York, 1954), 30–34.

45. Serle, *Journal,* 79 (27 Aug. 1776).

46. Ira D. Gruber, *The Howe Brothers and the American Revolution* (New York, 1972), 112; Howard H. Peckham, *The Toll of Independence: Engagements and Battle Casualties of the American Revolution* (Chicago, 1974), 22; for an excellent essay on the battle see Ira D. Gruber, in "America's First Battle: Long Island, 27 August 1776," in Charles E. Heller and William A. Stofft, eds., *America's First Battles, 1776–1965* (Lawrence, Kans., 1986), 1–32. An important account, not used in any published history of the battle, is Capt. John McPherson to his father, 2 Sep. 1776, Grant Papers, LC.

47. Bardeleben, *Diary, 75.*

48. Washington to Trumbull, 6 Sept. 1776 *GW* 6:239–40; Reed to Livingston, 30 Aug. 1776, *AA*5 1:1231.

49. Freeman, *Washington* 4:173; Minutes of the Council of War, 29 Aug. 1776, *AA*5 1:1246.

50. Benjamin Tallmadge, "Major Tallmadge's Account of the Battles of Long Island and White Plains," published in Henry P. Johnston, *The Campaign of 1776 Around New York and Brooklyn* (Brooklyn, 1878), pt. 2, pp. 77–81.

51. George A. Billias, *General John Glover and His Marblehead Mariners* (New York, 1960), 100.

52. Tallmadge, "Major Tallmadge's Account," 79; for Governor's Island, Bardeleben, *Diary,* 75.

53. Washington to Hancock, 8 Sept. 1776, *GW* 6:248–54.

54. Ibid.

55. Washington to Abraham Yates, 8 Sept. 1776, *GW* 6:262.

56. General Officers to Washington, 11 Sept. 1776, and Council of War, 12 Sept. 1776, *GW* 2:279, 188–89.

57. Serle, *Journal*, 103–5 (15 Sept. 1776).

58. Joseph Plumb Martin, *Private Yankee Doodle: Being a Narrative of Some of the Adventures, Dangers, and Sufferings of a Revolutionary Soldier,* ed. George F. Scheer (Boston, 1962), 33.

59. Ibid., 34.

60. Frederick Mackenzie, *The Diary of Frederick Mackenzie*, 2 vols. (Cambridge, Mass., 1930), 1:48; logbooks and journals of HMS *Rose, Orpheus, Roebuck, Phoenix,* 13–15 Sept. 1776, ADM 51/805, 650, 1965, 694, PRO; *NDAR* 6:838–41; Bartholemew James, *Journal of Rear-*

Admiral Bartholemew James, 1752–1828, ed. John K. Laughton, Navy Records Society Publications 6 (London, 1896), 15 Sept. 1776, *NDAR* 6:841–42.

61. Martin, *Private Yankee Doodle*, 34.

62. Major Nicholas Fish to John McKesson, 19 Sept. 1776, published in Johnston, *Harlem Heights*, 151–52; George Weedon to John Page, 20 Sept. 1776, Weedon Papers, CHS.

63. George Weedon to John Page, 20 Sept. 1776, Weedon Papers, CHS.

64. Mackenzie, *Diary* 1:48.

65. Ibid.; Major Nicholas Fish to John McKesson, 19 Sept. 1776, in Johnston, *Harlem Heights*, 151–52.

66. James Thacher wrote, "it has since become almost a common saying among our officers, that Mrs. Murray saved this part of the American army." James Thacher, *Military Journal of the American Revolution* (Hartford, 1862), 58. This happy tale has been rejected by historians mainly on the basis of Henry Clinton's memoirs, which insist that the advance stopped on Howe's orders to await the second wave (Henry Clinton, *The American Rebellion: Sir Henry Clinton's Narrative of His Campaigns, 1775–1782*, ed. William B. Willcox [New Haven, 1954], 46–47n). Both accounts could well be true.

67. Martin, *Private Yankee Doodle*, 41; Benjamin Trumbull, "Diary," *CTHSC* 6:195; Freeman, *Washington* 4:196.

68. Greene to Washington, 5 Sept. 1776, and Greene to Samuel Ward Sr., 4 Jan. 1775, *Papers of Nathanael Greene* 1:295, 178; George Washington to Lund Washington, 6 Oct. 1776, and to John Hancock, 2 Sept. 1776, and Hancock to Washington, 3 Sept. 1776, *GW* 6:493–96, 199–201, 207.

69. Mackenzie, *Diary* 1:58–60 (20 Sept. 1776).

70. Kemble, *Journal*, 90 (17–20 Sept. 1776); Mackenzie, *Diary* 1:59 (20 Sept. 1776); Hans Huth, "Letters from a Hessian Mercenary," *PMHB* 62 (1938), 494.

71. Henry P. Johnston's *The Battle of Harlem Heights, September 16, 1776: A Review of the Events of the Campaign* (New York, 1897).

72. Joseph Reed to Mrs. Reed, 1 Sept. 1776, *Life and Correspondence of Joseph Reed*, ed. William B. Reed, 2 vols. (Philadelphia, 1847), 1:237–39.

73. Major Nicholas Fish to John McKesson, 19 Sept. 1776, in Johnston, *Harlem Heights*, 151–52, 180; Capt. John McPherson to his father, 25 Dec. 1776, LC, a major account.

74. British accounts by Captain John Montresor, Major Frederick Mackenzie, and Captain William Bamford; American accounts by Stephen Hempstead, Enoch Hale, Samuel Hale, Isaac Hull, Elisha Bostwick, and an anonymous account in Newburyport *Essex Journal*, 13 Feb. 1777; all rpt. in George Dudley Seymour, ed., *Docomentary Life of Nathan Hale* (New Haven, 1941), 290–325. Another account by Connecticut Loyalist Consider Tiffany has come to light. It confirms the role of Rogers, which was recorded in the diary of British Captain William Bamford. See Consider Tiffany, "Manuscript History of the American Revolution," LC. A report by James Hutson appears in the *Information Bulletin* of the Library of Congress (2003). The words of Cato appear in Joseph Addison, *Cato, a Tragedy* (London, 1772), IV, iv, 63–64.

75. Johnston, *Harlem Heights*, 95; George Washington to Lund Washington, 30 Sept. 1776, *GW* 6:441–43.

76. George Washington to John Hancock, 11[–13] Oct. 1776, and Tench Tilghman to William Duer, 12 Oct. 1776, *GW* 6:535–36; Col. Edward Hand to Kitty Hand, 14 Oct. 1776, in Michel [*sic*] Williams Craig, *General Edward Hand: Winter's Doctor* (n.p., 1984?), 36.

77. David Hackett Fischer, *Paul Revere's Ride* (New York, 1994), 224–25.

78. "Extract of a Letter from Colonel Glover," 22 Oct. 1776, and other documents in *AA* 5 2:1188, 1130–31, 3:594; Loammi Baldwin to Mary Baldwin, 20 Oct. and 21 Dec. 1776, Houghton Library, Harvard; Clinton, *American Rebellion*, 49–50; George Athan Billias, "Pelham Bay, a Forgotten Battle," in *General John Glover and His Marblehead Mariners*, 110–23; also William Abbatt, *The Battle of Pell's Point* (New York, 1901); Howe's casualty reports are an undercount, as always.

79. Bardeleben, *Diary*, 90.

80. Primary sources survive in profusion. Freeman reported six major British and German accounts. Now historians can use accounts by Wiederholdt, Ewald, Reuber, Howe, Kemble, Archibald Robertson, Mackenzie, Glyn, George Hart, Serle, Stirke, Percy, Cornwallis, Lt. William Scott, RN, and the logbook of HMS *Pearl*.

American accounts include Washington's official report dated 16 Nov. 1776, Graydon's *Memoirs,* Lambert Cadwalader to Pickering, May 1822 (25 *PMHB* 25 [1901], 259), Nathanael Greene's correspondence, and accounts by Chaplain Benjamin Trumbull, Ichabod Perry, Joseph White, John Adlum, William Heath, and Parson Shewkirk. Secondary works include E. F. Delancey, "Mount Washington and Its Capture on the 16th of November 1776," *MAH* 1 (1877), 63–90; Johnston, *The Campaign of 1776*; Freeman, *Washington* 4:246–53; Richard M. Ketchum, *The Winter Soldiers: The Battles for Trenton and Princeton* (1973; New York, 1991), 103–32 (the best account); and Richard K. Showman, in *Papers of General Nathanael Greene,* 1:352–39.

81. Thomas Glyn, "Journal on the American Service with the Detachment of 1,000 Men of the Guards Commanded by Brigadier General Mathew in 1776," manuscript, Princeton University Library, 122; Freeman, *Washington,* 4:248.

82. Mackenzie, *Diary* 1:96; Demont had been adjutant to Colonel Robert Magaw; see Ketcham, *Winter Soldiers,* 111–12; Thomas Jones, *History of New York During the Revolutionary War,* 2 vols. (New York, 1879), 1:630; *Papers of General Nathanael Greene* 1:351n, 358n; Delancey, "Mount Washington and its Capture."

83. Graydon, *Memoirs,* 205.

84. Nathanael Greene to Henry Knox, 17 Nov. 1776, *Papers of General Nathanael Greene* 1:351–52.

85. Washington Irving was told of this event by men who were with Washington as he watched the fall of the fort from the Jersey Palisades; "it was said so completely to have overcome him, that he wept, with the tenderness of a child." Washington Irving, *The Life of George Washington,* 5 vols. (New York, 1855–59), 2:424; this passage was removed from later editions and is not mentioned by most of Washington's biographers. I think it is another key to the character of this extraordinary man. Joseph Reed, statement ca. 1779, in Reed, *Correspondence* 1:262; Washington to Reed, 22 Aug. 1779, ibid., 263; Washington to Hancock, 16 Nov. 1776, *GW* 7:162–69.

86. Lee to Reed, 24 Nov. 1776, in Reed, *Correspondence* 1:305–6.

✷ The Retreat

1. Johann Ewald, *Diary of the American War: A Hessian Journal,* ed. Joseph P. Tustin (New Haven, 1979), 18 (20 Nov. 1776).

2. Ibid.

3. William B. Willcox, *Portrait of a General: Sir Henry Clinton in the War of Independence* (New York, 1964), 115–17; Henry Clinton, *The American Rebellion: Sir Henry Clinton's Narrative of His Campaigns, 1775–1782,* ed. William B. Willcox (New Haven, 1954), 55.

4. Clinton, *American Rebellion,* 55.

5. Evidence of Howe's intentions appears in his letters to Lord Germain, 20 Dec. 1776; conversations with Clinton; orders to Grant, Donop, and other officers; and Lord Richard Howe's correspondence with George Germain, Peter Parker, and Philip Stephens. See William S. Stryker, *The Battles of Trenton and Princeton* (Boston, 1898), 327–28; Clinton, *American Rebellion,* 54–57; Donop Correspondence, MHT, LC, and LT; Howe Correspondence in *NDAR* 5:634–35, 690–91, 1044, 1075–76, 1144, 1180, 1239, 1261; *NDAR* 6:145–47, 910–11; *NDAR* 7:530, 553–57, 666, 827, 828, 1188. See also Troyer Steele Anderson, *The Command of the Howe Brothers During the American Revolution* (New York, 1936), and Ira D. Gruber, *The Howe Brothers and the American Revolution* (New York, 1972), the best modern study.

6. Washington to William Livingston, 7 Nov. 1776, and to Nathanael Greene, 8 Nov. 1776, *GW* 7:110–12, 115–17.

7. Washington to Nathanael Greene, 9 Nov. 1776, and Washington to John Hancock, 9 Nov. 1776, *GW* 7:119, 121.

8. George Washington, Instructions to Major General William Heath, 12 Nov. 1776; Robert Hanson Harrison to Lt. Col. William Palfrey, 18 Nov. 1776; Washington to John Hancock, 19–21 Nov. 1776, all in *GW* 6:147, 179–82.

9. A helpful biography is Franklin Wickwire and Mary Wickwire, *Cornwallis and the War of Independence* (London, 1970); idem, *Cornwallis: The Imperial Years* (Chapel Hill, 1980); Charles Ross, *Correspondence of Charles First Marquis Cornwallis*, 3 vols. (London, 1859) is full and enlightening except on the American Revolution, where it is very thin. A helpful calendar is George H. Reese, comp., *The Cornwallis Papers, Abstracts of Americana* (Charlottesville, 1970), strong on the period from 1779 to 1781.

10. Her father, Colonel James Jones, died a few years after the outbreak of the Seven Years' War. His worldly goods were auctioned for £2,805.9.6; Wickwire and Wickwire, *Cornwallis and the War of Independence*, 39.

11. Cornwallis's biographers Franklin and Mary Wickwire refuse to credit this story and write that "the action of Lady Cornwallis is totally alien to the conduct of eighteenth-century aristocrat wives, no matter how much they loved their husbands." Maybe so, but not alien to the conduct of Jemima. Cf. Wickwire and Wickwire, *Cornwallis and the War of Independence*, 407.

12. Cornwallis to Sir William Medows, 3 Aug. 1790, quoted in Wickwire and Wickwire, *Cornwallis and the War of Independence*, 74–78.

13. John Peebles, *John Peebles' American War: The Diary of a Scottish Soldier, 1776–1782*, ed. Ira D. Gruber (London, 1998), 202, 187–87, 353 (17 July 1778).

14. Hugh Rankin, "Charles Lord Cornwallis: Study in Frustration," in George A. Billias, *George Washington's Opponents* (New York, 1969), 195.

15. Admiral Richard Lord Howe to Philip Stephens, 23 Nov. 1776, *NDAR* 7:254–57.

16. General Orders, 19 Nov. 1776, "Gen. Sir William Howe's Orders, 1776," in *The Kemble Papers*, 2 vols., NYHS *Collections* (New York, 1884–85), 1:411; Orderly Book, 1st Battalion, Brigade of Guards, New-York Historical Society, in Arthur S. Lefkowitz, *The Long Retreat* (Metuchen, N.J., 1998), 42; for the numbers see Friedrich von Münchausen, *At General Howe's Side, 1776–1778: The Diary of General William Howe's Aide-de-Camp, Captain Friedrich von Muenchausen*, trans. Ernest Kipping, ann. Samuel Stelle Smith (Monmouth Beach, N.J., 1974), 5.

17. Primary accounts by Ewald, Donop, Glyn, Stirke, Kemble, Münchausen, Robertson, and Baurmeister have been brought together in Donald M. Londahl-Smidt, "British and Hessian Accounts of the Invasion of Bergen County," *Bergen County History* (1976), 37–80. Another account is *The Diary of Lieutenant von Bardeleben*, ed. Bruce E. Burgoyne (Bowie, Md., 1998), 78 (20 Nov. 1776).

18. Henry Stirke, "A British Officer's Revolutionary Journal, 1776–1778," ed. S. Sidney Bradford, *MDHM* 56 (1961), 164–65 (20 Nov. 1776); for the identity of the guides see Lefkowitz, *Long Retreat*, 44, and essays by John Spring and Richard P. McCormick in *Bergen County History* for 1970 and 1975.

19. Lefkowitz, *Long Retreat*, 46.

20. For primary sources of the second wave, see Thomas Glyn, "Ensign Glyn's Journal on the American Service with the Detachment of 1,000 Men of the Guards Commanded by Brigadier General Mathew in 1776," manuscript, Princeton University Library; and Carl von Donop, reports to General Leopold von Heister, 19 Nov., 22 Nov., 3 Dec. 1776, LT; "Letters from a Hessian Mercenary" (correspondence with Friedrich Wilhelm, Prince of Prussia), ed. Hans Huth, *PMHB* 62 (1938), 488–501.

21. Lefkowitz, *Long Retreat*, 41, with other legends.

22. Ewald, *Diary*, 18.

23. Ibid.

24. Gen. Samuel Cleaveland, Royal Artillery, "Return of Ordnance and Stores Taken by His Majesty's Troops . . . ," includes an inventory of artillery taken at Fort Lee; *AA* 5, 3:1058.

25. William Dwyer, *The Day Is Ours!* (New York, 1983), 29; Adrian Leiby, *The Revolutionary War in the Hackensack Valley: The Jersey Dutch and the Neutral Ground, 1775–1783* (New Brunswick, 1962), 72; Lefkowitz, *Long Retreat*, 54; the British officer is quoted in T. N. Glover, *The Retreat of '76 Across Bergen County* (Hackensack, 1905), and Lefkowitz, *Long Retreat*, 67.

26. Innkeeper Archibald Campbell observed that Washington was marching with "his suite, life guard, a company of foot, a regiment of cavalry and some soldiers from the rear of the army." Dwyer estimated his strength at 4,500. Another 7,000 were still with Charles Lee at White Plains, and 4,000 were with William Heath at Peekskill, guarding the Hudson crossings. Dwyer, *The Day Is Ours!* 29.

27. Ewald, *Diary*, 18–19.

28. Quoted in Dwyer, *The Day Is Ours!*, 30.

29. "Large numbers deserted his colors daily, was confirmed during the march, especially in the vicinity of Hackensack, where we found many loyalists." Ewald, *Diary*, 25.

30. Willcox, *Clinton*, 115–21; Gruber, *The Howe Brothers*, 135–36; *Archibald Robertson, Lieutenant Colonel, Royal Engineers: His Diaries and Sketches in America, 1762–1780*, ed. Harry Miller Lydenberg (New York, 1930), 114.

31. Ambrose Serle, *The American Journal of Ambrose Serle, Secretary to Lord Howe, 1776–1778*, ed. Edward H. Tatum Jr. (San Marino, Calif., 1940), 146–47; Gruber, *Howe Brothers*, 138.

32. Carl von Donop to Gen. James Grant, 16 Dec. 1776, Donop Correspondence, MHT; Stryker, *Battles of Trenton and Princeton*, 320.

33. "Journal of Capt. William Beatty, June 1776–January 1781," *MDHM* 3 (1908), 105.

34. Ibid., 106; Washington to John Hancock, 1 Dec. 1776, *GW* 7:244.

35. George Washington to John Hancock, 30 Nov. 1776, and Lee to Washington, 30 Nov. 1776, *GW* 7:232–33; *Diary of David How, a Private in Colonel Paul Dudley Sargent's Regiment . . .*, ed. George W. Chase and Henry B. Dawson (Morrisania, N.Y., 1865), 37–38.

36. The primary sources are published and carefully assessed by Nathan Schachner, ed., "Alexander Hamilton Viewed by his Friends: The Narratives of Robert Troup and Hercules Mulligan," *WMQ3* 4 (1947), 203–25; Broadus Mitchell, *Alexander Hamilton, Youth to Maturity* (New York, 1957), 1:79, 514n; also Hamilton to Alexander MacDougall, 17 March 1776, in *Papers of Alexander Hamilton*, ed. H. C. Syrett (New York, 1961), 1:181–82; eyewitness accounts in John C. Hamilton, *Alexander Hamilton*, 2 vols. (New York, 1840), 1:57; E. P. Panagopoulos, ed., *Alexander Hamilton's Pay Book* (Detroit, 1961); idem, "Hamilton's Notes in his Pay Book of the New York Artillery Company," *AHR* 62 (1957), 310–25. The internal evidence shows that the reading notes were in the same ink and handwriting as the company records and must have been kept during the same period.

37. John C. Hamilton, *The Life of Alexander Hamilton*, 2 vols. (New York, 1840), 1:57.

38. Washington to John Hancock, 1 Dec. 1776, *GW* 7:244.

39. Enoch Anderson, *Personal Recollections of Captain Enoch Anderson, an Officer of the Delaware Regiments in the Revolutionary War*, ed. Henry Hobart Bellas (Wilmington: Historical Society of Delaware Papers 16 [1896]; rpt. New York, 1968), 27; Baron Karl Leopold Baurmeister, *Revolution in America: Confidential Letters and Journals 1776–1784 of Adjutant General Major Baurmeister of the Hessian Forces*, ed. Bernard A. Uhlendorf (New Brunswick, 1957), 74; John P. Wall, *Chronicles of New Brunswick* (New Brunswick, 1931), 207.

40. Anderson, *Personal Recollections*, 27.

41. Wickwire and Wickwire, *Cornwallis and the War of Independence*, 92.

42. Ewald, *Diary*, 24.

43. Howe to Germain, 20 Dec. 1776, in *Documents of the American Revolution*, ed. K. G. Davies (Dublin, 1976) 12:266.

44. Anderson, *Personal Recollections*, 26.

45. Douglas Southall Freeman, *George Washington: A Biography*, 7 vols. (New York, 1948–57), 4:273.

46. Anderson, *Personal Recollections*, 28.

47. Münchausen, *Diary,* 6 (7 Dec. 1776); Thomas Sullivan, *From Redcoat to Rebel: The Thomas Sullivan Journal,* ed. Joseph Lee Boyle (Bowie, Md., 1997), 97 (27 Dec. 1776).

48. Charles Willson Peale, manuscript. Autobiography, APS; Horace Wells Sellers, "Journal by Charles Willson Peale," *PMHB* 38 (1914), 271–73 (5–8 Dec. 1776); Lefkowitz, *Long Retreat,* 121; Dwyer, *The Day Is Ours!,* 102; Ketchum, *Winter Soldiers,* 204.

49. Peale, manuscript. Autobiography, APS; Sellers, "Journal by Peale," 272 (8 Dec. 1776), manuscript autobiography, APS.

50. Reed wrote to Washington, "The river is not and I believe cannot be sufficiently guarded. We must depend upon intelligence of their motions." Joseph Reed to George Washington, 12 Dec. 1776, *GW* 7:317–18; Freeman, *Washington* 4:302–4; Stryker, *Battles of Trenton and Princeton,* 323.

51. George Washington to Col. Richard Humpton, 1 Dec. 1776, *GW* 6:248–49.

52. John W. Jackson, *The Pennsylvania Navy, 1775–1781* (New Brunswick, 1974), 75.

53. Stryker, *Battles of Trenton and Princeton,* 130.

54. Joseph Galloway, "Examination of Joseph Galloway before the House of Commons, June 18, 1779, *AA*5 3:1343; Freeman, *Washington* 4: 304.

55. Jackson, *Pennsylvania Navy,* 11–25, 74–83.

56. Münchausen, *Diary,* 6 (Dec. 8, 1776).

57. Ibid.

58. Ewald, *Diary,* 30; Charles Stedman, *The History of the Origin, Progress, and Termination of the American War,* 2 vols. (London, 1794), as quoted in Dwyer, *The Day Is Ours!,* 109.

59. "Extract from a Letter to a Gentleman in Connecticut," 12 Dec. 1776, in Stryker, *Battles of Trenton and Princeton,* 321.

60. John W. Jackson, *Margaret Morris Her Journal with Biographical Sketch and Notes* (Philadelphia, 1949); the manuscript journal is in the Quaker Collection, Haverford College Library.

61. Ibid.

62. "Editor's Note," *PMHB* (1884), 255–56.

63. Freeman, *Washington* 4:300.

64. Nicholas Cresswell, *The Journal of Nicholas Cresswell,* ed. Samuel Thornely (New York, 1924), 179 (5 Jan. 1777).

❧ The Crisis

1. Christopher Marshall, *Diary* (Albany, 1877), 107; the description of the wooden pen and drumhead are from Paine himself in *Pennsylvania Journal,* 6 Nov. 1776; another account by Paine appears in his "Reply to Cheetham," 21 Aug. 1807, in the Thomas Paine Papers, APS. Other material is in David Freeman Hawke, *Paine* (New York, 1974) 14, 113, 182–83. Two other excellent biographies are Eric Foner, *Tom Paine and Revolutionary America* (New York 1976); John Keane, *Tom Paine: A Political Life* (London, 1995).

2. Paine's eyewitness account of the fall of Fort Washington, is reprinted in *AA*5 2:1266-67; on his service as an aide see Richard K. Showman, ed., *The Papers of General Nathanael Greene* (Chapel Hill, 1976+), 1:364.

3. Paine, "Reply to Cheetham," and Alexander Graydon, *Memoirs of His Own Time, with Reminiscences of the Men and Events of the Revolution,* ed. John Stockton Littell (Philadelphia, 1846; rpt. 1969), 188.

4. "Common Sense and Colonel Snarl are perpetually wrangling about mathematical Problems"; Snarl was another aide, Ezekiel Cornell. See Nathanael Greene to Catherine Greene, 2 Nov. 1776, *Papers of General Nathanael Greene* 1:330

5. Frank Moore, *Diary of the American Revolution,* 2 vols. (New York, 1860), 1:350.

6. Graydon, *Memoirs,* 187n.

7. Thomas Paine to Samuel Adams, 1 Jan. 1803, in Philip S. Foner, ed., *Complete Writings of Thomas Paine,* 2 vols.(New York, 1945), 1:1434. The original is in the Adams Papers, NYPL.

8. New York *Public Advertiser*, 22 Aug. 1807; cf. Hawke, who thinks that Paine was writing a journal on the retreat but did the first number of *The Crisis* later in "a single burst of passion." I see no reason to doubt Paine's account. Cf Hawke, *Paine*, 414n.

9. Paine, "Reply to Cheetham."

10. Thomas Paine to Edmund Burke, 7 Aug. 1768, Paine Papers, APS.

11. On the printing history see Paine to Henry Laurens, 14 Jan. 1779, in Foner, *Complete Writings of Thomas Paine* 2:1164.

12. James Cheetham, *Life of Thomas Paine* (New York, 1809), 56; a strange, often informative book, by Paine's enemy after his death. Foner, *Complete Writings of Thomas Paine* 1:49.

13. Paine, "The American Crisis, Number I," in Foner, *Complete Writings of Thomas Paine* 1:52.

14. Benjamin Rush to John Adams, 13 July 1780, *Letters of Benjamin Rush*, ed. Lyman Butterfield, 2 vols. (Princeton, 1951) 1:253.

15. Oliver Wolcott to Laura Wolcott, 1 Jan. 1777, in Paul H. Smith et al., *Letters of Delegates to Congress, 1774-89* (Washington, 1976+), 6:12; Harrison to Robert Morris, 25 Dec. 1776, ibid., 581; Samuel Adams to John Adams, 9 Jan. 1777; in Edmund Cody Burnett, *The Continental Congress* (1941; New York, 1964), 232.

16. *Journals of the Continental Congress, 1774-1789*, ed. Worthington C. Ford, 34 vols. (Washington, 1904-37), 6:207 (12 Dec. 1776).

17. Nathanael Greene to John Hancock, 21 Dec. 1776, *Papers of General Nathanael Greene* 1:370-72.

18. *Journals of the Continental Congress* 6:1043-46, 27 Dec. 1776; Burnett, *Continental Congress*, 233.

19. Oliver Wolcott to Andrew Adams, 1 Jan. 1777, *Letters of Delegates* 6:11.

20. Burnett, *Continental Congress*, 233.

21. Washington to Hancock, 20 Dec. 1776, *GW* 7:381-89.

22. Ibid.

23. Hancock to Morris, 21 Dec. 1776, *Letters of Delegates* 5:642-43.

24. Rush to Adams, 12 Feb. 1812, *Letters of Benjamin Rush* 2:1120.

25. James Wilkinson, *Memoirs of My Own Times*, 3 vols. (Philadelphia, 1816), 1:126. Did this happen? Wilkinson's account is accepted by Douglas Southall Freeman, *George Washington: A Biography*, 7 vols. (New York, 1948-57), 4:309; Richard M. Ketchum, *The Winter Soldiers: The Battles for Trenton and Princeton* (1973; New York, 1991), 249; and William M. Dwyer, *The Day Is Ours!* (New York, 1983), 230-32. It is challenged in Samuel W. Patterson, *Horatio Gates: Defender of American Liberty* (New York, 1941), 109, who argued that the text of Washington's letter of December 23, 1776, contradicted Wilkinson. Freeman could not find that letter. It is in the Gates Papers and published as Washington to Gates, 23 Dec. 1776, *GW* 6:418, and is entirely consistent with Wilkinson's account. See also Paul David Nelson, *General Horatio Gates: A Biography* (Baton Rouge, 1976), 75-78; *Letters of Delegates* 6:700-703.

26. John Shy, "Charles Lee: The Soldier as Radical," in *George Washington's Generals*, ed. George A. Billias (New York, 1964), 26.

27. Charles Lee to Horatio Gates, 12 Dec. 1776, in *The Lee Papers*, 4 vols. (New York, 1871-74), 2:348.

28. Lee to Washington, 11 Dec. 1776, *GW* 7:301.

29. Washington to Lee, 14 Dec. 1776, *GW* 7:335.

30. This follows five primary accounts by men who were there: a letter from Banastre Tarleton to his mother, Jane Parker Tarleton, dated Prince's Town, 18 Dec. 1776, and printed in its entirety by Robert D. Bass, *The Green Dragoon* (New York, 1957), 20-22; accounts by Lt. Col. William Harcourt to his father and brother in *The Harcourt Papers*, ed. Edward Harcourt (Oxford, 1880-85), 11:184-202; G. D. Scull, *The Evelyns in America* (Oxford, 1879), 226-27, 230; an account by Lee's aide-de-camp William Bradford Jr., in Franklin Bowditch Dexter, ed., *The Literary Diary of Ezra Stiles*, 3 vols. (New York, 1901), 2:105-6; and James Wilkinson, *Memoirs* 1:102-7. Wilkinson had just arrived with a letter from Gates and was inside the tavern when the attack came. These sources vary in detail but are fundamentally consistent, and very different from many secondary and tertiary accounts that have worked their way into the literature.

31. Friedrich von Münchausen, *At General Howe's Side 1776-1778: The Diary of General William Howe's Aide-de-Camp, Captain Friedrich von Muenchausen*, trans. Ernest Kipping, ann. Samuel Stelle Smith (Monmouth Beach, N.J., 1974), 7-8 (14 Dec. 1776).

32. Capt. John Bowater to Earl of Denbigh, 5–11 June 1777, in Marion Balderston and David Syrett, eds., *The Lost War: Letters from British Officers During the American Revolution* (New York, 1975), 131.

33. Sullivan to Washington, 13 Dec. 1776; George Washington to Lund Washington, 17 Dec. 1776; George Washington to Samuel Washington, 18 Dec. 1776; all in *GW* 7:328, 369-72; also Robert Morris to George Washington, 21 Dec. 1776, *Letters of Delegates* 5:565.

34. Münchausen, *Diary*, 7-8 (13 Dec. 1776).

35. Freeman, *Washington* 4:292n.

36. Washington to Robert Morris, 22 Dec. 1776, *GW* 7:412; "Sergeant John Smith's Diary of 1776," ed. Louise Rau, *MVHR* 20 (1933), 247-70, 265-66; *This Glorious Cause . . . The Adventures of Two Company Officers in Washington's Army*, ed. Herbert T. Wade and Robert A. Lively (Princeton, 1958) 227-28.

37. John C. Clyde, *Rosbrugh, a Tale of the Revolution; or, Life, Labors, and Death of Rev. John Rosbrugh* (Easton, Pa., 1880).

38. George Washington to John Augustine Washington, 18 Dec. 1776, *GW* 6:398.

39. Burnett, *Continental Congress*, 231; Robert K. Wright Jr., *The Continental Army* (Washington, 1989).

40. James H. F. Brewer, *History of the 175th Infantry (Fifth Maryland)* (Baltimore, 1955); Wright, *Continental Army*, 109.

41. Wright, *Continental Army*, 97.

42. Ibid.

43. Ibid.

44. Ibid., 94.

45. Benjamin Rush to Richard Henry Lee, 21 Dec. 1776, *Letters of Benjamin Rush* 1:120-21.

46. Harry M. Ward, *Charles Scott and the Spirit of '76* (Charlottesville, 1988), 27, 20, 56.

47. Wright, *Continental Army*, 97.

48. Broadus Mitchell, *Alexander Hamilton, Youth to Maturity* (New York, 1957), 1:96; Irving Washington, *The Life of George Washington* (New York, 1854-58), 3:88. There were many others: Sebastian Baumann of New York, Thomas Forrest of Pennsylvania, Daniel Neil of New Jersey, and Samuel Shaw of Massachusetts, all very able young officers of artillery; see *Memoirs of Colonel Sebastian Beauman and His Descendants with Selections from his Correspondence*, ed. Mary C. Doll Fairchild (New York, 1900); Forrest to Col. Thomas Proctor, 29 Dec. 1775, rpt. in William Stryker, *The Battles of Trenton and Princeton* (Boston, 1898), 371-73; *The Journals of Major Samuel Shaw, the First American Consul at Canton, with a Life of the Author by Josiah Quincy* (Boston, 1847; rpt. 1970).

49. Exceptions were Glover's Marblehead men; *Margaret Morris Her Journal with Biographical Sketch and Notes*, ed. John W. Jackson (Philadelphia, 1949), 55; Thomas Anburey, *Travels Through the Interior Parts of America*, 2 vols. (Boston, 1923), 1:102.

50. Charles Bolton, *The Private Soldier Under Washington* (1902; rpt. Gansevoort, N.Y., 1997), 94.

51. Morris to John Hancock, 21 Dec. 1776, *Letters of Delegates* 5:563; Washington to Morris, 25 Dec. 1776, *GW* 7:439-40.

52. Marine Committee to Capt. Isaiah Robinson, 17 Oct. 1776; Committee of Secret Correspondence to Bingham, 21 and 23 Oct. 1776; Robert Morris to Committee of Secret Correspondence, 16 Dec. 1776; Morris to Washington, 21 Dec. 1776; Morris to Hancock, 23 Dec. 1776; all in *Letters of Delegates* 5:348-49, 358-59, 366, 550, 565; also *NDAR* 7:939-40.

53. Elbridge Gerry to Joseph Trumbull, 2 Jan. 1777, and John Hancock to Robert Morris, 2 Jan. 1777, *Letters of Delegates* 6:17, 19; Log of HMS *Pearl*, 20 Dec. 1776, *NDAR* 7:534-35.

54. Resolution on Blankets and Rugs, *Journal of the House of Delegates of Virginia*, Oct. 1776 (Richmond, 1828), 84.

55. Patrick Henry to Thomas Jefferson, 19 Dec. 1776, endorsed by Jefferson "rec'd Jan. 28 1777," *Papers of Thomas Jefferson*, ed. Julian Boyd (Princeton, 1950), 1:658-59; for Jefferson's service as county lieutenant, see his "Commission as Lieutenant of Albemarle," 9 June 1770, renewed 26 Sept. 1775; and his "Militia Return as County Lieutenant," 1776, ibid. 1:42, 246, 664-68.

56. Freeman, *Washington* 4:421.

57. Ibid.

58. Ibid.

59. Samuel Blachley Webb to Joseph Trumbull, Head Quarters Pennsylvania in Bucks County, 16 Dec. 1776, in *Correspondence and Journals*, 3 vols., ed. Worthington Chauncey Ford (New York, 1893; rpt. New York, 1969), 1:174-75.

60. An officer from Connecticut, quoted in Dwyer, *The Day is Ours!*, 249; Philip S. Foner, *Morale Education in the American Army: War of Independence, War of 1812, and Civil War* (New York, 1944).

❧ The Occupation

1. Nathanael Greene to Catherine Greene, 4 Dec. 1776, *The Papers of General Nathanael Greene*, ed. Richard K. Showman (Chapel Hill, 1976+), 1:364-66.

2. Ira D. Gruber, *The Howe Brothers and the American Revolution* (New York, 1972), 354.

3. Troyer Steele Anderson, *The Command of the Howe Brothers During the American Revolution* (New York, 1936), 216; Gruber, *Howe Brothers*, 345.

4. "By Richard Viscount Howe . . . and William Howe, Esq., General of His Majesty's Forces in America, the King's Commissioners for restoring peace . . . Proclamation," 30 Nov. 1776, *AA* 5 3:928.

5. For the response in London see *House of Commons Debates*.

6. The American response to the Howes' proclamation is reproduced in Richard M. Ketchum, *The Winter Soldiers: The Battles for Trenton and Princeton* (1973, New York, 1991), 161.

7. "Captain Stephen Olney, Memoir," in *Biography of Revolutionary Heroes: Containing the Life of Brigadier Gen. William Barton, and also Captain Stephen Olney*, ed. Mrs. Williams (Providence, 1839), 184.

8. Nicholas Collin, *The Journal and Biography of Nicholas Collin, 1746–1831*, ed. Amandus Johnson (Philadelphia, 1936), 34, 254.

9. Benjamin Rush, *Autobiography*, ed. George W. Corner (Princeton, 1948); Benjamin Rush to James Rush, 22 Dec. 1809, *Letters of Benjamin Rush*, ed. Lyman H. Butterfield, 2 vols. (Princeton, 1951), 2:1029.

10. Varnum L. Collins, *President Witherspoon*, 2 vols. (Princeton, 1925); Thomas Jefferson Wertenbaker, *Princeton, 1746–1896* (Princeton, 1946), 58–66.

11. [Robert Lawrence], *A Brief Narrative of the Ravages of the British and Hessians at Princeton, 1776–77* (Princeton, 1906; rpt. 1968), 4, 34.

12. Rush, *Autobiography*, 147.

13. Andreas Wiederholdt, Diary, 7 Oct.–7 Dec. 1776, ed. M. D. Learned and C. Grosse, *Americana Germanica* (New York, London, and Berlin, 1902) 4, no. 1, pp. 25–33; Johann Ewald, *Diary of the American War: A Hessian Journal*, ed. Joseph P. Tustin (New Haven, 1979), 25; S. Sydney Bradford, ed., "A British Officer's Revolutionary War Journal, 1776–1778," *MDHM* 56 (1961), 165 (22 Nov. 1776).

14. Quoted in William M. Dwyer, *The Day Is Ours!* (New York, 1983), 60.

15. *Journal and Biography of Nicholas Collin*, 238–39.

16. Ibid.

17. Francis M. Marvin, *The Van Horn Family History* (East Stroudsberg, Pa., 1929); for Phill's Hill, *Pennsylvania Post*, 7 Oct. 1778.

18. Alexander Graydon, *Memoirs of His Own Time, with Reminiscences of the Men and Events of the Revolution*, ed. John Stockton Littell (Philadelphia, 1846; rpt. 1969), 264, 279; Leonard Lundin, *Cockpit of the Revolution: The War for Independence in New Jersey* (Princeton, 1940), 251.

19. Graydon, *Memoirs*, 264.

20. Ibid., 265–66; Leonard Lundin, *Cockpit of the Revolution: The War for Independence in New Jersey* (Princeton, 1940), 251.

21. The letters are reprinted in Ewald, *Diary*, appendix 2.

22. Robert P. Davis, *Where a Man Can Go: Major General William Phillips, British Royal Artillery, 1731–1781* (Westport, Conn., 1999), 107; Martin I. J. Griffin, *Stephen Moylan* (Philadelphia, 1909), 83.

23. Washington to Joseph Reed, 12 and 19 Jan. 1777, *GW* 7:51, 109.

24. [Lawrence], *Brief Narrative*, 10–11, 13–14, 20.

25. Graham Hodges, *Root and Branch: African Americans in New York and East Jersey, 1613–1863* (Chapel Hill, 1999), 141–42.

26. Graham Hodges, *Slavery and Freedom in the Rural North: African Americans in Monmouth County, New Jersey* (Madison, 1997); an advertisement for Titus as a runaway slave appears in *Pennsylvania Gazette*, 22 Nov. 1775; for Tye and other black refugees see Harry Ward, *Between the Lines: Banditti of the American Revolution* (Westport, Conn., 2002) 61–68.

27. William S. Stryker, *The Battles of Trenton and Princeton* (Boston, 1898), 122n.

28. Ibid.

29. *Ibid.*

30. Dwyer, *The Day Is Ours!*, 166, 221; Stryker, *Battles of Trenton and Princeton*, 92.

31. Thomas Paine, "The American Crisis," in *The Complete Writings of Thomas Paine*, ed. Philip Foner, 2 vols. (New York, 1969), 1:51.

32. Washington to David Forman, 24 Nov. 1776, *GW* 7:203; Stryker, *Battles of Trenton and Princeton*, 8.

33. Davis, *Where a Man Can Go*, 107.

34. Ambrose Serle, *The American Journal of Ambrose Serle, Secretary to Lord Howe, 1776–1778*, ed. Edward H. Tatum Jr. (San Marino, Calif., 1940), 157 (11 Dec. 1776).

35. "Extract of a Letter received in London, dated New York, November 30, 1776," *AA5* 3:928.

36. William Howe to Colonel Carl von Donop, 13 Dec. 1776, Donop Papers, MHT, partly reproduced in Stryker, *Battles of Trenton and Princeton*, 316–17.

37. Thomas Gamble for the General Commanding, Table of Prices, 24 Dec. 1776, Donop Papers, LC.

38. Donop to Grant, 16 Dec. 1776, Donop Papers, LC; Stryker, *Battles of Trenton and Princeton*, 320.

39. Charles Francis Adams, "Contemporary Opinion of the Howes," *MHSP* 44:118–20.

40. Ibid.

41. Rodney Atwood, *The Hessians: Mercenaries from Hessen-Kassel in the American Revolution* (Cambridge, 1980), 181 (20 June 1777); Atwood has other instances of punishment by Knyphausen, who had ten men run the gauntlet in August 1777; on another occasion, mounted Jägers and grenadiers were sent after Hessian plunderers who were burning a house. Atwood reports that nine Hessians were cut down by their own comrades, and ten were arrested (pp. 181–82.)

42. Louise Rau, ed., "Sergeant John Smith's Diary of 1776," *MVHR* 20 (1933), 252, 263.

43. [Lawrence], *Brief Narrative*, 41.

44. Hessian soldiers also had another source of income from "booty." It came to them in several ways. One was prize money, which was officially sanctioned. Every man received his share, from generals to privates. This was also done in other armies, including Washington's army, which promised each man a share of the value of arms and equipment captured at Trenton. But there was a difference in the definition of booty. Hessians included the personal property of people who opposed them as booty. Washington specifically rejected this idea.

45. *Archibald Robertson, Lieutenant Colonel, Royal Engineers: His Diaries and Sketches in America, 1762–1780*, ed. Harry Miller Lydenberg (New York, 1930).

46. It should be noted that this testimony comes from the Hessian officer who was ordered by his commanding officer Colonel von Donop to protect the wagons and coaches

full of plunder. See Ewald, *Diary*, 43; confirmed by Peale, "Journal by Charles Willson Peale, Dec. 4, 1776–Jan. 20, 1777," *PMHB* 38 (1914), 278.

Rodney Atwood (*The Hessians*, 171–83) defends the Hessians against plundering by demonstrating that other armies did it too, which is true enough, and that some Hessian soldiers were punished for plundering, which is also true. But an abundance of testimony from American, British, and Hessian sources indicates a difference of scale and structure in Hessian plundering; e.g., Robertson, Kemble, Serle, Peale, Ewald, etc.

The literature on Hessian plundering has gone through several revisions. A first generation of American and British literature described plundering as unique to Hessians, and the product of a dark depravity in their nature. A revisionist interpretation by some Hessian writers and descendants of Hessians in America argues that they were no different from every other army. A third, adopted here, finds evidence of similarities in the existence of plundering in every army, but differences in magnitude, form, and function.

47. Peale, "Journal," 377.

48. Susan Pindar Embury, "A Grandmother's (Martha Reed, wife of John Shannon) Recollections of the Old Revolutionary Days," 1875, typescript, Trenton Public Library, with thanks to Wendy Nardi for helping us to find this document.

49. Ewald, *Diary*, 22, 31.

50. Martha Reed, "A Grandmother's Recollections."

51. Ewald, *Diary*, 423n, 63.

52. John Mott, "Recollections," in Amanda Jones, *A Psychic Autobiography* (New York, 1910), 11–13; "John Mott of New Jersey," www2.crown.net/sspicer/Genealogy/Mott.

53. Serle, *American Journal*, 87.

54. Thomas H. Edsall, ed., *Journal of Lieutenant John Charles Philip von Krafft, of the Regiment von Bose, 1776–1784*, NYHS *Collections for the Year 1882* (New York, 1883), 90.

55. [Lawrence], *Brief Narrative*, 15.

56. George Washington to Governor William Livingston, 3 March 1777, *GW* 8:500–502.

57. Reports of rapes in New Jersey were collected by the Pennsylvania Council of Safety and ordered to be printed in the *Pennsylvania Packet*, 27 Dec. 1776, and *Pennsylvania Evening Post*, 28 Dec. 1776.

58. Continental Congress, "Report of the Committee appointed to inquire into the conduct of the enemy," 18 April 1777, published in *Pennsylvania Evening Post*, 24 April 1777, rpt. *NJA* 2 1:347–53; the original manuscripts survive in the papers of the Continental Congress, item 53, pp. 29–39, NA.

59. "Extract of a Letter . . . published by order of the Council of Safety," *Pennsylvania Evening Post*, 28 Dec. 1776; *NJA* 2 1:244–46.

60. Howe, *Observations*, 59–60; Douglas Southall Freeman, *George Washington: A Biography*, 7 vols. (New York, 1948–57), 4:236n.

61. John Peebles, *John Peebles' American War: The Diary of a Scottish Soldier, 1776–1782*, ed. Ira D. Gruber (London, 1998), 74.

62. Friedrich von Münchausen, *At General Howe's Side, 1776–1778: The Diary of General William Howe's Aide-de-Camp, Captain Friedrich von Muenchausen*, trans. Ernest Kipping, ann. Samuel Stelle Smith (Monmouth Beach, N.J., 1974), 7 (14 Dec. 1776).

63. Ibid., 8 (26 Dec. 1776).

64. Ibid., 7 (14 Dec. 1776).

65. *Pennsylvania Evening Post*, 28 Dec. 1776, in *NJA* 2 1:244–45.

66. Howe to James Grant, 24 Dec. 1776, Grant Papers, LC.

❧ The Opportunity

1. Sir William Howe to George Germain, 20 Dec. 1776, Co5/94, PRO.

2. These patterns appear in the Donop Correspondence, MHT.

3. Colonel Charles Stuart to Lord Bute, 22 Sept. 1778, in Mrs. E. Stuart Wortley, *A Prime Minister and His Son: From the Correspondence of the 3rd Earl of Bute and of Lt.-General the Hon.*

Sir Charles Stuart, K.B. (London, 1925), 135; James Weymess in Sparks Manuscripts, 22:216, Houghton Library, Harvard; quoted in Paul David Nelson, *General James Grant: Scottish Soldier and Royal Governor of East Florida* (Gainesville, 1993), 3.

4. Nelson, *General James Grant*; also Alistair Macpherson Grant, *General James Grant of Ballindalloch, 1720–1806* (privately published, London, 1930). Nelson's biography is excellent and balanced, and has made extensive use of manuscripts in Ballindalloch Castle, now available at LC. More of Grant's correspondence in this campaign survives in the Donop Papers, and records of Hessian court of inquiry, in the archives at Marburg. I have used photostats of the originals in MHT, and transcripts in LT.

5. For Howe's breakfast in Trenton, Rodney Atwood, *The Hessians: Mercenaries from Hessen-Kassel in the American Revolution* (Cambridge, 1980), 14; Samuel Stelle Smith, *The Battle of Trenton* (Monmouth Beach, N.J., 1965), 8.

6. For the orders written in copperplate hand, in English and French, William Howe, General Orders dated "Headquarters, Trenton, 13th December 1776," Donop Papers, MHT.

7. Grant to Donop, 17 Dec. 1776 Donop papers, photostats, MHT.

8. Ibid.

9. Johann Ewald, *Diary of the American War: A Hessian Journal,* ed. Joseph P. Tustin (New Haven, 1979), 31.

10. Wiederholdt, Diary, "Colonel Rall at Trenton," *PMHB* 23 (1899), 462–67.

11. Johannes Reuber, Journal, 17 [18?] Dec. 1776.

12. "The Affair at Trenton, Finding of Hessian Court Martial, Colonel's Report," LT.

13. Donop to Rall, 14 Dec. 1776, "I have the honor to receive my brother's brigade under my orders," Rall to Donop, 17–22 Dec. 1776, MHT.

14. Jakob Piel, "Diary of the Hessian Lieutenant [Jakob] Piel, 1776 to 1783," ed. Bruce E. Burgoyne, *JSHAJ* 4 (1989), 14 (26 Dec. 1776).

15. Washington to John Hancock, 13 Dec. 1776, *GW* 7:325.

16. Washington to Gates, 14 Dec. 1776, and Washington to William Heath, 14 Dec. 1776, *GW* 7:333–35.

17. *Lee Papers*, vols. 4–7 in NYHS *Collections* (New York, 1871–74), 2:337; Douglas Southall Freeman, *George Washington: A Biography,* 7 vols. (New York, 1948–57), 4:306.

18. Reed to Washington, 12 Dec. 1776, *GW* 7:317–18.

19. Washington to John Hancock, 12 Dec. 1776; to Thomas Cadwalader, Philemon Dickinson, James Ewing, Lord Stirling, Hugh Mercer, Adam Stephen, and Roche Fermoy, all 12 Dec. 1776, *GW* 7:324–25; 304–8.

20. Dickinson to Washington, 21 Dec. 1776, *GW* 7:394.

21. There appear to have been at least two John Motts in service from New Jersey during the Revolution. One of them joined the New Jersey Continental troops who served on the northern frontier. He was at Fort Ticonderoga during the fall of 1776–77 and appears repeatedly as "Lieutenant Mott" in Mark E. Lender and James Kirby Martin, eds., *Citizen Soldier: The Revolutionary War Journal of Joseph Bloomfield* (Newark, 1982), 108, 114. Later he served through much of the Revolution. Another was Captain John Mott in the Hunterdon County militia, who appears in Philemon Dickinson to Washington, 24 Dec. 1776, *GW* 7:427, which also documents his visit with Washington. For the family story, see Amanda Jones, *A Psychic Autobiography* (New York, 1910), 11–13; for an attempt by a member of the family to sort out the confusion of Motts see "John Mott of New Jersey," www2.cron.net/sspicer/Genealogy/Mott; cf. William Stryker, *Official Register of the Officers and Men of New Jersey in the Revolutionary War* (Trenton, 1872; rpt. Baltimore, 1967), 402. Stryker notes in another work that this Captain Mott lived in a house "on ground owned by the New Jersey Hospital for the Insane, on the west bank of the water power," and his home appears in Hessian records as "the rebel captain's house." William S. Stryker, *The Battles of Trenton and Princeton* (Boston, 1898), 146.

22. American records, the Hessian reports, and correspondence of British officers such as General Grant tell the story. See Col. David Chambers to Washington, 16 Dec. 1776, and Philemon Dickinson to Washington, 21 Dec. 1776, *GW* 7:350, 394; correspondence of Rall, Donop, and Grant, 17–23 Dec. 1776, Donop Papers, MHT; Smith, *Trenton,* 13–15.

23. Washington to Ewing, 12 and 14 Dec. 1776, *GW* 7:306–07, 331–33.

24. Smith, *Trenton,* 13.

25. Piel, "Diary," 14 (26 Dec. 1776).

26. Stryker, *Battles of Trenton and Princeton,* 105.

27. Blackened faces inferred from Grenadier Johannes Reuber's journal, 20 [21?] Dec. 1776. The dating of Reuber's diary is often at least one day off and has Washington's main attack on Trenton on the morning of December 25, when it was in fact December 26. Afterward Scheffer thought that the raid at Trenton Ferry was a design by Washington to draw attention from the ferries upstream, and that Rall allowed himself to be distracted. Stryker and others accepted this judgment, but it is mistaken. The raids began before the Trenton attack was planned. At the same time, sometimes at the same moment, the Hunterdon militia were attacking near the upstream ferries as well. And there is no evidence that Washington ordered these raids; like the Hunterdon raids, they appear to have been undertaken by Ewing's men. For different interpretations, cf. Stryker *Battles of Trenton and Princeton,* 105; William M. Dwyer, *The Day Is Ours!* (New York, 1983), 220.

28. Reuber, Journal, 20 [21?] Dec. 1776.

29. Ibid., 7.

30. Ibid.; Rall to Donop, 21 and 22 Dec. 1776; Smith, *Trenton,* 14.

31. Leslie to [Rall and Donop?], 1 o'clock n.d., Donop Papers, MHT.

32. Reuber, Journal, 24 [25?] Dec. 1776. Washington was informed by "an Officer who with a scouting party, was reconnoitering between Princeton and Trenton on Thursday [19 Dec.]" that "three battalions of British troops were marching from the former to the latter." Washington to Israel Putnam, 21 Dec. 1776, *GW* 7:405.

33. Atwood, *Hessians,* 92.

34. Grant to Rall and Donop, 21 Dec. 1776, Donop Papers, MHT.

35. Grant to Donop, 23 Dec. 1776, Donop Papers, MHT.

36. Report of Barzella Haines to Col. von Donop, 21 Dec. 1776, Donop Papers, MHT.

37. Col. Thomas Stirling to Donop, 21 Dec. 1776, Donop Papers, MHT.

38. Stirling to Donop, 21 Dec. 1776, Donop Papers, MHT.

39. Ewald, *Diary,* 35–40; Margaret Morris, *Margaret Morris Her Journal with Biographical Sketch and Notes,* ed. John W. Jackson (Philadelphia, 1949), 56.

40. Ewald, *Diary,* 39.

41. "[A]t Mount Holly—all the Women removed from the Town except one widow of our Acquaintance." Morris, *Journal,* 54 (22 Dec. 1776).

42. Ewald, *Diary,* 42–45. The major source is the journal of Hessian Captain Johann Ewald, which became generally available to American historians only in 1979. It interlocks with other evidence that had long been available—the journal of Margaret Morris, and Donop's correspondence—but only with Ewald did those materials become intelligible in this context. All accounts of this campaign published before 1979 were unaware of these events, and most gave no attention to the importance of Donop's prolonged stay in Mount Holly. Stryker erroneously placed Donop in Bordentown (map bet. 84–85). One of the first general accounts to make use of this new material was Dwyer, *The Day Is Ours!,* 217.

43. Ewald, *Diary,* 45; the American Loyalist Galloway came to the same conclusion. He wrote that at Mount Holly "the rebel corps immediately fled, and dispersed at his approach; and yet, instead of immediately returning to Bordentown to support Colonel Rall, he [Donop] remained loitering . . . without having a single enemy to oppose." Quoted in Dwyer, *The Day Is Ours!,* 217.

44. John Bakeless, *Turncoats, Traitors, and Heroes: Espionage in the American Revolution* (1959; rpt. New York, 1998), 123, 173, 198, 203, 252–65, 361.

45. Joseph Tustin also identified another possibility. Mrs. Elizabeth Vanderhovan lived at Mount Holly in 1777, and she "passed messages to her husband John Vanderhovan, an acknowledged rebel spy." But she matches no part of the description. For this and the Betsy Ross hypothesis, see Joseph P. Tustin, "The Mysterious Widow of the Revolution," *GCSHB* 17 (Dec. 1979), 8. Major Tustin was chief historian at the headquarters of the U.S. Air Force

in Germany during the Cold War. It was he who found the diary of Captain Johann Ewald, translated it, and published it with the Yale University Press.

46. Smith, *Trenton*, 14; Smith did not include Griffin in the south, perhaps because he was writing before the full publication of Ewald's diary and related sources. His statement is equally true of events in that quarter.

47. Joseph Reed to George Washington, 22 Dec. 1776, *GW* 7:416.

48. Harry M. Ward, *Major General Adam Stephen and the Cause of American Liberty* (Charlottesville, 1989), 150; citing David Griffith to Leven Powell, 27 Dec. 1776, "Correspondence of Leven Powell," *John P. Branch Historical Papers* 1 (1901), 46; Richard M. Ketchum, *The Winter Soldiers: The Battles for Trenton and Princeton* (1973; New York, 1991), 292; Stryker, *Battles of Trenton and Princeton*, 84; Richard Hanser, *The Glorious Hour of James Monroe* (New York, 1976), 124; Smith, *Trenton*, 16; Freeman, *Washington*, 4:306.

49. Ewald, *Diary*, 39.

50. Ward, *Adam Stephen*, 150.

51. Grant to Rall, 24 Dec. 1776, Donop Papers, MHT.

52. Testimony of Lt. Jacob Bill, 24 April 1778; Lt. George Zoll, 27 April 1778; Lt. Christian von Hoben, 7 May 1778; Ensign Friedrich Henndorf, 11 May 11, 1778, Hessian Court of Inquiry, LT, ML 87, 193 223, 256.

53. Testimony of Captain Adam Steding, Hessian Court of Inquiry, Philadelphia, 2 May 2, 1778, LT, ML 211.

54. Stryker, *Battles of Trenton and Princeton*, 100; Dwyer, *The Day Is Ours!*, 222.

55. Dechow to Heister, 17 Dec. 1776, in Atwood, *Hessians*, 89, 90.

56. Baron Karl Leopold Baurmeister, *Revolution in America: Confidential Letters and Journals 1776–1784 of Adjutant General Major Baurmeister of the Hessian Forces*, ed. Bernhard A. Uhlendorf (New Brunswick, 1957), 78.

57. Reuber, Journal, 24 [25?] Dec. 1776; Atwood, *Hessians*, 92, Piel, "Diary," 26 Dec. 1776.

58. Wiederholdt, Diary, "Colonel Rall at Trenton," 462–67; Burgoyne, *Enemy Views*, 91, 117, 346.

59. Ewald, *Diary*, 45.

❧ The River

1. James Wilkinson, *Memoirs of My Own Times*, 3 vols. including atlas (Philadelphia, 1816; rpt. 1973), 1:128.

2. Washington to Joseph Reed, 23 Dec. 1776; Mercer to Durkee, 25 Dec. 1776, in William S. Stryker, *The Battles of Trenton and Princeton* (Boston, 1898), 342, 359; Samuel Stelle Smith, *The Battle of Trenton* (Monmouth Beach, N.J., 1965), 18; for the blankets, Washington to Robert Morris, 25 Dec. 1776, *GW* 7:439; for women in the Continental army, Walter Hart Blumenthal, *Women Camp Followers of the American Revolution* (Philadelphia, 1952), 57–90; Holly A. Mayer, *Belonging to the Army: Camp Followers and Community During the American Revolutions* (Columbia, S.C., 1996); Elizabeth Cometti, "Women in the American Revolution," *NEQ* 20 (1947), 329–46; appendix C.

3. On the weather, see Phineas Pemberton Weather Diary, APS, in appendix K.

4. George Washington to Robert Morris, 25 Dec. 1776, *GW* 7:439–41; the letter is in Tench Tilghman's hand, signed by Washington.

5. John Greenwood, *The Revolutionary Services of John Greenwood of Boston*, ed. Isaac J. Greenwood (New York, 1922), rpt. as *The Wartime Services of John Greenwood: A Young Patriot in the American Revolution* (n.p., Westvaco Corporation, n.p., 1981), 80.

6. Ibid., 79.

7. Ibid., 82.

8. Ibid.

9. Washington, General Orders, 25 Dec. 1775, *GW* 7:437; Robert C. Powell, ed., *A Biographical Sketch of Leven Powell* (Alexandria, Va., 1877), 44–46; Mercer to Colonel John Durkee,

25 Dec. 1776, text reproduced in Stryker, *Battles of Trenton and Princeton*, 358–59; and Smith, *Trenton*, 32.

10. Ibid.

11. Washington had also asked Israel Putnam to collect whatever troops he could find and cross the river at Philadelphia. But Putnam's response suggested that not much could be done in that quarter.

12. Washington to Col. John Cadwalader, 25 Dec. 1776, *GW* 7:439.

13. For the hour of sunset, Smith, *Trenton*, 18.

14. Mercer to Durkee, 25 Dec. 1776; Stryker, *Battles of Trenton and Princeton*, 358; Smith interprets this as the time for assembly behind the ferry. The time of sunrise on December 26 was about 7:20 A.M.; Smith, *Trenton*, 18, 20.

15. Wilkinson, *Memoirs*, 1:127; Greenwood, *Services*, 79–81.

16. Greenwood, *Services*, 80; for Avery, see William M. Dwyer, *The Day Is Ours!* (New York, 1983), 229; for delays downstream, Cadwalader to Washington, 26 Dec. 1776, *GW* 7:442; Thomas Rodney, *The Diary of Captain Thomas Rodney, 1776–1777*, ed. Caesar A. Rodney, *DHSP*, vol. 1, paper 8 (Wilmington, 1888; rpt. New York, 1974), manuscript diary, 1776–77, LC; Charles Willson Peale, "Journal by Charles Willson Peale, Dec. 4, 1776–Jan. 20, 1777," *PMHB* 38 (1914), 271–86, manuscript diary, APS.

17. Wilkinson, *Memoirs*, 1:126.

18. Ibid. Did this happen? Wilkinson's account is accepted by Douglas Southall Freeman, *George Washington: A Biography* 7 vols. (New York, 1948–57), 4:309; and Richard M. Ketchum, *The Winter Soldiers: The Battles for Trenton and Princeton* (1973, New York, 1991), 249. It is challenged in Samuel W. Samuel W. Patterson, *Horatio Gates, Defender of American Liberty* (New York, 1941), 109, who argued that the text of Washington's letter of December 23, 1776, contradicted Wilkinson. Freeman could not find that letter, but it is in the Gates Papers, and has been published as Washington to Gates, 23 Dec. 1776, in *GW* 6:418. It supports Wilkinson's account. See also Paul David Nelson, *General Horatio Gates: A Biography* (Baton Rouge, 1976), 75–78; *Letters of Delegates to Congress, 1774–89*, ed. Paul H. Smith et al. (Washington, 1976+), 5:700–3.

19. Greenwood, *Services*, 80.

20. An excellent guide to the role of river ice in this part of the story is a very thoughtful account of the battle, Kemble Widmer, *The Christmas Campaign: The Ten Days of Trenton and Princeton* (Trenton, 1975), 18; see also appendix J.

21. Widmer, *Christmas Campaign*, 18–19. Historians of the battle have condemned Ewing's militia for their failure to cross the river, sometimes with added aspersions on militia in general. To study the conditions on the river is to discover that these judgments are mistaken and unfair. Washington himself was more understanding, and wrote later of Ewing's failed crossing that "the Quantity of Ice was so great, that tho' he did every thing in his power to effect it, he could not get over." Washington to John Hancock, 27 Dec. 1776, *GW* 7:454. For further discussion of ice on the river, see appendix J.

22. Thomas Rodney, *Diary*, Dec. 25, 1776, Rodney Papers, LC; a published version with some vagaries of detail appears in Caesar A. Rodney's published edition, *Diary of Captain Thomas Rodney* (Wilmington, 1888), 22–23.

23. Ibid.; here again, Widmer, *Christmas Campaign*, is very helpful.

24. Peale, "Journal," 278 (26 Dec. 1776).

25. Thomas Rodney, *Diary*, 23.

26. Joseph Reed, "General Reed's Narrative of the Movements of the American Army in the Neighborhood of Trenton in the Winter of 1776–1777," *PMHB* 8 (1884), 394.

27. Wilkinson, *Memoirs* 1:128.

28. Stryker, *Battles of Trenton and Princeton*, 130; George A. Billias, *General John Glover and His Marblehead Mariners* (New York, 1960), 202n; Marion V. Brewington, "Washington's Boats at the Delaware Crossing," *AN* 2 (1942), 167–70.

29. The best account is Billias, *Glover*, 3–14.

30. The fullest account of their service is a letter without date from A. Cuthbert to C. C. Haven, rpt. in Haven's *Thirty Days in New Jersey Ninety Years Ago: An Essay Revealing New Facts in Connection with Washington and His Army* (Trenton, 1867), 44–47. Cuthbert's father was an officer in Moulder's battery.

31. Wilkinson, *Memoirs* 1:128; George Washington to T. Cadwalader, 26 Dec. 1776, *GW* 7:450; Henry Knox to Lucy Flucker Knox, 28 Dec. 1776, rpt. in Stryker, *Battles of Trenton and Princeton*, 371–72.

32. Wilkinson, *Memoirs*, 1:128.

33. Henry Knox to Lucy Flucker Knox, 28 Dec. 1776, rpt. in Stryker, *Battles of Trenton and Princeton*, 371–72.

34. Both Captain Blackler and Private Russell testified to that effect. They were believed in the nineteenth century, but twentieth-century accounts of the battle forgot them. Russell appears in a heroic pose and the wrong uniform on the Trenton Battle Monument. Samuel Roads, *History and Traditions of Marblehead*, 3d ed. (Marblehead, Mass., 1897), 175; *Salem Evening News*, 27 Dec. 1926; Billias, *Glover*, 203.

35. Washington to Hancock, 27 Dec. 1776, *GW* 7:454; on the beehive, Ketchum, *Winter Soldiers*, 252.

36. Greenwood, *Services*, 80.

37. Ibid., 80–81.

38. General Orders, 25 Dec. 1776, *GW* 7:436; also Harry M. Ward, *Major General Adam Stephen and the Cause of American Liberty* (Charlottesville, 1989), 47.

39. Benjamin Rush, *Autobiography*, ed. George W Corner (Princeton, 1948), 124.

ᔰ The March

1. Richard M. Ketchum, *The Winter Soldiers: The Battles for Trenton and Princeton* (1973; New York, 1991), 253.

2. James Monroe, *Autobiography*, ed. Stuart Gerry Brown (Syracuse, 1959), 22–27; Harry Ammon, *James Monroe: The Quest for National Identity* (New York, 1971), 7–28; Richard Hanser, *The Glorious Hour of James Monroe* (New York, 1976), 9–63.

3. William S. Stryker, *The Battles of Trenton and Princeton* (Boston, 1898), 115, 150.

4. Ibid.

5. Ibid.

6. Ibid.

7. Jac Weller, "Guns of Destiny: Field Artillery in the Trenton-Princeton Campaign, 25 December 1776 to 3 January 1777," *Military Affairs* 29 (1956), 1–15.

8. General Orders, 25 Dec. 1776, *GW* 7:434-36.

9. Ibid. Knox counted eighteen guns altogether; another "officer of distinction," possibly Stirling, reported twenty guns.

10. No side boxes or carts or ammunition wagons were mentioned in the sources on Christmas night, but they must have been brought across the river, and they appear in accounts of other operations during this campaign.

11. Washington to John Hancock, 27 Dec. 1776, *GW* 6:454.

12. Other men of New Jersey who reported having served as scouts and volunteers were Edon Burroughs, Stephen Burroughs, William Green, John Guild, Joseph Inslee, John Mott, John Muirhead, Elias Phillips, John Phillips, Joseph Phillips, Philip Phillips, Henry Simmons, Henry Simonds, Uriah Slack, Ephraim Woolsey, and James Slack of Bucks County, Pa. They were kin to one another and members of the Hunterdon County militia. All this is from William M. Dwyer, *The Day Is Ours!* (New York, 1983) 239, 246 (working from accounts collected by a local clergyman, Eli Cooley); and Stryker, *Battles of Trenton and Princeton*, 138–39 ("from tradition.")

13. Elisha Bostwick, "A Connecticut Soldier Under Washington: Elisha Bostwick's Memoirs of the First Years of the Revolution," ed. William S. Powell, *WMQ3* 6 (1949), 94–107.

14. John Greenwood, *The Revolutionary Services of John Greenwood of Boston,* ed. Isaac J. Greenwood (New York, 1922), rpt. as *The Wartime Services of John Greenwood: A Young Patriot in the American Revolution* (n.p., Westvaco Corporation, 1981), 81; elevations are from U.S. Geological Survey maps, Lambertville and Pennington quadrangles, which show a bench-mark elevation of 195 feet near Bear Tavern. Terrain is drawn from contemporary descriptions with the experience of walking the ground with James McPherson from the ferry landings to Trenton in December 2001. Distances were checked by odometer in 2001 and again in 2003, and compared with geological surveys.

15. "Extract of a Letter from an Officer of Distinction, at Newtown, Bucks County, dated December 27, 1776," *Pennsylvania Evening Post,* 31 Dec. 1776; *NJA*2 1:247–49.

16. The line of the road across Jacob's Creek and its tributary stream must be walked to be understood. Even today after many improvements it presents exceptionally steep grades and sloping surfaces. The topography of the march has been missed in every major historical account of this event, but it is painfully familiar to reenactors who march the route. The terrain is also clearly evident on the Pennington Quadrangle of the U.S. Geological Survey.

17. Bostwick, "Memoirs," 102; Bostwick's account of the sloping bank matches this part of the march better than any other. To walk the route is to be persuaded that the episode he described probably happened near Jacob's Creek. On Washington's horsemanship and its role in his career, see the excellent discussion in Richard Brookhiser, *Founding Father: Rediscovering George Washington* (New York, 1996) 47, 111–12, 119, 154.

18. Samuel Stelle Smith, *The Battle of Trenton* (Monmouth Beach, N.J., 1965), citing *PMHB* 8:394.

19. Greenwood, *Services,* 81.

20. Today this stretch of the road, now much improved, crosses Interstate Route 95 and continues past the Mercer County Airport.

21. As to time, Wilkinson noted that the army arrived in Birmingham (the Howell's Ferry Road) at "about twilight." James Wilkinson, *Memoirs of My Own Times,* 3 vols. including atlas (Philadelphia, 1816; rpt. 1973), 1:128. Birmingham is now West Trenton, and the Howell's Ferry Road is the present Upper Ferry Road.

22. Captain William Hull to Andrew Adams, 1 Jan. 1777, Stryker, *Battles of Trenton and Princeton,* 375. In approximate modern equivalents Sullivan's route on the River Road followed the present line of Grand Avenue and Sullivan Way. Greene's approach went along the present West Upper Ferry Road to Parkway Avenue and Pennington Avenue.

23. Washington to Hancock, 27 Dec. 1776, *GW* 8:454.

24. Wilkinson, *Memoirs* 1:129. The doubtful and very grandiloquent account, allegedly from the "Diary of an Officer on Washington's Staff," has Washington at Birmingham receiving a message from Sullivan about the wet weapons, and replying, "Tell General Sullivan to use the bayonet. I am resolved to take Trenton." Many accounts quote this passage and make heavy use of the diary (Stryker, *Trenton and Princeton,* 362; Dwyer, *The Day Is Ours!,* 238, 252, 348 passim; Ketchum, *Winter Soldiers,* 253). But it rings wrong in many ways and is inconsistent with many facts. At Birmingham, Washington and Sullivan were together. And Washington well knew that many of his men had no bayonets that night. Greenwood (*Services,* 83) recalled that "there was not more than one bayonet to five men." The vainglorious words attributed to Washington in this very dubious document have a different tone from other evidence. Here is yet another reason for distrusting this very strange source.

25. Monroe, *Autobiography,* 25; James Monroe to George Coleman, 17 Jan. 1809, *Tyler's Quarterly* 9:247–48. The sources are variant on the location of this roadblock. Their general orders were to remain three miles out of town, but Monroe estimated that the roadblock was a mile and a half from Trenton. The closer position would have been dangerously near to Hessian alarm posts. Perhaps Monroe meant that they were a mile and a half beyond the alarm posts. Cf. General Orders, Dec. 25, 1776, *GW* 7:434–36.

26. David Hackett Fischer, *Paul Revere's Ride* (New York, 1994), 129–46.

27. Monroe, *Autobiography,* 25–27; James Monroe to George Coleman, 17 Jan. 1809, *Tyler's Quarterly* 9:247–48; Harry Ammon, *Monroe,* 12–14.

28. Ketchum, *Winter Soldiers*, 253; Stryker, *Battles of Trenton and Princeton*, 143.

29. This strange and pivotal event is misunderstood in most histories. The error arose from an undated memorandum in the letterbook of General Robert Anderson, based on memories of conversations with his father, Captain Richard Clough Anderson of the Fifth Virginia Continentals. This document was reprinted as authentic in Stryker, *Battles of Trenton and Princeton*, 373–74. It made Captain Anderson the head of the American party, and the mission a reconnaissance of Hessian positions.

Most historians of the battle followed Robert Anderson, Stryker, and Freeman into error (Ketchum, *Winter Soldiers*, 253–54; Dwyer, *The Day Is Ours!*, 249–51). The only exception was Smith, *Trenton*, 20, who made a deeper error in omitting the event altogether.

Freeman (*George Washington: A Biography*, 7 vols. [New York, 1948–57], 4:313) found a letter from Adam Stephen to Jonathan Seaman, 5 Jan. 1777, in the Adam Stephen Papers, LC, which confirmed that such an incident had actually taken place. But Stephen made clear that its purpose was not reconnaissance but to "take revenge" for a man who had been killed. The letter also revealed that its leader was not Captain Anderson but Wallis of Stephen's Fourth Virginia Regiment, in Stirling's brigade. Freeman could not read Stephen's handwriting, garbled Wallis's name, and was unable to identify him.

The error was corrected by Harry M. Ward, *Major General Adam Stephen and the Cause of American Liberty* (Charlottesville, 1989), 278n, who identified Wallis. Stephen's estimate of Hessian casualties in the raid and the Hessian reports are from Ward, p. 151.

❧ The Surprise

1. Henry Knox to Lucy Flucker Knox, 28 Dec. 1776, William S. Stryker, *The Battles of Trenton and Princeton* (Boston, 1898), 371.

2. John Greenwood, *The Revolutionary Services of John Greenwood of Boston*, ed. Isaac J. Greenwood (New York, 1922), rpt. as *The Wartime Services of John Greenwood; A Young Patriot in the American Revolution* (n.p., Westvaco Corporation, 1981). 83.

3. Testimony of Ensign Franz Friedrich Grebe, Hessian Court of Inquiry, "The Affair at Trenton," LT, ML 172–183.

4. Knox made the distance about eight hundred yards; George Johnston about five hundred yards. Cf. Knox to Lucy Knox, 28 Dec. 28, 1776, in Stryker, *Battles of Trenton and Princeton*, 371; George Johnston to Leven Powell, 29 Dec. 1776, "Correspondence of Leven Powell," *John P. Branch Historical Papers* 1 (1901), 46, 41; for the cooper shop and Richard and Arthur Howell, see Stryker, *Battles of Trenton and Princeton*, 146.

5. George Johnston to Leven Powell, 29 Dec. 1776, "Correspondence of Leven Powell," 41.

6. The time of the American attack was estimated differently by observers on both sides. In the Hessian inquiry, some witnesses thought it happened at 7:00 in the morning. Most testified that the first shots were fired between 8:00 and 9:00, and several thought they were about 8:30. Johnston thought the two attacks on the River Road and the Pennington Road were five minutes apart; Washington estimated three minutes.

7. Andreas Wiederholdt, Testimony, Hessian Court of Inquiry on Trenton, 18 April 1778, ML 352–63, LT; another account appears in Wiederholdt's diary for 26 Dec. 1776, transcript in the Bancroft Collection at NYPL, with microfilm copy in the author's collection; of several English translations the best is Burgoyne's in Bruce Burgoyne, ed., *Enemy Views: The American Revolutionary War as Recorded by the Hessian Participants* (Bowie, Md., 1996), 117–24. Wiederholdt's two accounts differ in detail but are fundamentally consistent.

8. Ibid. Wiederholdt's account is confirmed by two other eyewitness accounts: the testimony of Captain Ernst Eberhard von Altenbockum, 12 May 1778, who commanded a company posted at the north end of the village in support of Wiederholdt's outpost; and Corporal Wilhelm Hartung, 22 April 1778, who was also on outpost duty; ML 184–87, LT.

9. Wiederholdt, Testimony.

10. Ibid.

11. For Hand's regiment see the passage struck out of Washington to John Hancock, 27 Dec. 1776, *GW* 7:454–58: "I suspected [the Hessians] were attempting to gain a road leading to Princetown, upon which I ordered Colo. Hands [*sic*] and the German Battalion to throw themselves before them." See also James Wilkinson, *Memoirs of My Own Times*, 3 vols. including atlas (Philadelphia, 1816; rpt. 1973), 1:131. Other secondary accounts are clearly mistaken in putting Hand with Mercer's Brigade (after Samuel Stelle Smith, *The Battle of Trenton* [Monmouth Beach, N.J., 1965], 28).

12. Wiederholdt, Diary.

13. Washington to John Hancock, 27 Dec. 27, 1776, *GW* 7:454. Dwyer reports another eyewitness, John Barnes the Loyalist sheriff of Hunterdon County, who testified, "From the idea I have of military matters I am clearly of the opinion that Captain Bockum [Ernst Altenbockum] behaved well and made a retreat which redounds to his honor." See William M. Dwyer, *The Day Is Ours!* (New York, 1983), 265.

14. Gröthausen was killed on January 2, 1776. The Hessian Inquiry took depositions from two men who were with him at the outposts on the River Road. See Testimony of Jäger Sergeant George William Hussell, and Jäger Corporal Franz Bauer, Hessian Court of Inquiry, 2 April 1778, ML 136–52, 152–56, LT.

15. Wilkinson, *Memoirs* 1:129.

16. Ibid.

17. Testimony of Corporal Nicholas Fenner, 18 April 1778; Sergeant Johannes Müller, 22 April 1778; Ensign Heinrich Zimmerman, 14 April 1776; Sergeant Christian Diemar, 16 April 1778; all Hessian Court of Inquiry, ML 168–71, 322–30, 344–50, LT.

18. Colonel von Donop wrote that "because of the high wind, the rain and the sleet, no one heard the musketry fire at the outposts." But Donop was not there, and many witnesses at the Hessian Court of Inquiry testified that the musketry and cannon fire were heard clearly throughout the town. Cf Donop, 6 Jan. 1777, "Letters from a Hessian Mercenary," ed. Hans Huth, *PMHB* 62 (1938), 495–96.

19. Greenwood, *Services*, 82.

20. Queen Street is today's Broad Street; the Hessians called it Bridge Street. King Street is now Warren Street; the Hessians knew it as High Street.

21. Testimony of Lt. Jakob Piel to the Hessian War Commission and the Prince of Hesse-Cassel, 15 April 1782, based on Hessian Court Martial, New York, 4–5 Jan. 1782, transcript in LC; rpt. in Stryker, *Battles of Trenton and Princeton*. Variant language less favorable to Rall appears in Dwyer, *The Day Is Ours!*, 265–66.

22. Wilkinson, *Memoirs* 1:129.

23. Clement Biddle, 29 Dec. 1776, Stryker, 365–66.

24. Wiederholdt, Diary, Burgoyne ed., 120.

25. Ibid. For the Altenbockum company, see Rodney Atwood, *The Hessians: Mercenaries from Hessen-Kassel in the American Revolution* (Cambridge, 1980), 89, 93, 116. The stand of Captain Altenbockum's company was praised by Hessian General von Heister, by American Tory John Barnes, who witnessed it, and by American commanders.

26. Wiederholdt, Diary.

27. Testimony of Ensign Carl Wilhelm Kleinschmidt, 26 April 26, 1778, Hessian Court of Inquiry, ML 54, LT.

28. Cf. the American perspective in Douglas Southall Freeman, *George Washington: A Biography*, 7 vols. (New York, 1948–57), 4:317–21; and the German perspective in Smith, *Trenton*, 22–23.

29. Washington to Hancock, 27 Dec. 1776, *GW* 7:454. Two sentences in Tilghman's hand were struck out by Washington.

30. For accounts of Rall artillery see Testimony of Lt. Johannes Engelhard, 15 April 1778; Sgt. Jakob Dietzel, 18 April 18, 1778; Bombardier Johannes Westerberg, 28 April 18, 1778; Bombardier Heinrich von Zelle, 18 April 1778; Lt. Friedrich Fischer, 14 April 1778; ML 502–17, 518–21, 522–27, 528–34, 331–343, MHT. For "Cannons forward," Testimony of Capt. August Steding, ibid., ML 215; Lt. August von Hobe, ibid., ML 226; "first houses in

the street," Testimony of Lt. Gregorius Saltzmann, 13 May 1778, ibid., ML 551. Fischer's map for the Hessian Court of Inquiry locates the guns.

31. Greenwood, *Services*, 83.

32. Henry Knox to Lucy Flucker Knox, 28 Dec. 1776, and Thomas Forrest to Col. Thomas Proctor, 29 Dec. 1776, in Stryker, *Battles of Trenton and Princeton*, 371–73; Monroe, *Autobiography*, 25; George Johnston to Leven Powell, 29 D,ec. 29, 1776, "Correspondence of Leven Powell," 41. Wilkinson, *Memoirs* 1:129 thought that Forrest had six guns, but there were only four in his battery. The others were probably the two guns of Hamilton. Baumann's three guns were described as "on the left." Freeman, *Washington* 4:317.

33. Testimony of Ensign Carl Wilhelm Kleinschmidt, 26 April 1778, ML 541, LT.

34. Wiederholdt, Diary, Burgoyne ed., 120. Other historians of the battle have read this evidence in another way. They have followed Wiederholdt's judgments and ignored his descriptive statements. We should do the reverse.

Wiederholdt's testimony was self-serving and very hostile to Rall. It is an alternation of descriptive statements with pejorative judgments that were meant to exculpate himself and to condemn Rall, who was in his grave and unable to speak for himself. Wiederholdt wrote that Rall "did not know which way to turn" and "staggered back and forth without knowing what he was doing . . . what nonsense this was! . . . An only slightly more clever and less talented but knowledgeable person could see the weakness here" (ibid.).

To separate description from judgment is to discover a different pattern in the evidence, one that is more favorable to Rall and also more consistent with that officer's conduct on other fields. Rall made several major errors, but when the fighting began he acted quickly to attack the enemy on the heights above the town. He did so first up King Street. When that failed he advanced to the right, with the object of taking the Americans from the flank. It was also the case that the Americans achieved tactical surprise at Wiederholdt's outpost. His pickets failed to intercept them as they did on the River Road. Wiederholdt blamed the pickets themselves and his commander, and accepted no responsibility for what had happened.

35. Samuel Stelle Smith, *The Battle of Princeton* (Monmouth Beach, N.J., 1967), 23.

36. Johannes Reuber, Journal, 25 [26] Dec. 1776.

37. Testimony of Lt. Ernst Schwabe, ML 242–53; Smith, *Princeton*, 24.

38. Reuber, Journal, 25 [26] Dec. 1776; J[oseph] White, *A Narrative of Events, as They Occurred from Time to Time, in the Revolutionary War, with an Account of the Battles of Trenton, Trenton-Bridge, and Princeton* (Charlestown, Mass., 1833; rpt. *American Heritage*, June 1956, 74–79), 77. Close students of this battle will be aware that this reconstruction differs from other published accounts in its finding that the Hessian guns were lost on King Street, then retaken by the Hessian infantry, and lost again.

A key to the sequence of events is the diary of Reuber, which was not used by Smith or Stryker. Reuber was not an officer, the diary is very rough, and its dates are often a day off. But Reuber's account of events in Trenton is confirmed by other evidence such as the correspondence of Alexander Leslie. The German grenadier tells us that the motive for Rall's return to the center of the town was the recovery of the guns, which other accounts have missed, and also makes clear that the Hessians briefly recovered the guns and lost them again.

Interlocking with this evidence is the account of an American enlisted man, White's "Narrative of Events," 77, which indicates that the Hessian guns were taken by troops from both wings of the American army, working together. Washington and Monroe came into the town from the north and worked their way down King Street to attack the Rall guns. White's New England battery was with Sullivan's right wing, which entered the town by the River Road, from below. White remembered that his men were ordered by Knox to "go *up* and take those two held pieces," and also wrote that his men "*inclined to the right.*"

The two American forces made a combined assault to retake the Hessian guns: Washington and Monroe and their Virginia infantry came down King Street and attacked on the American left; White and his New England artillerymen came up King Street and attacked on the American right.

This reconstruction of events reconciles the disparate accounts of Monroe, Wilkinson, White, Knox, Reuber, Piel, Wiederholdt, and testimony in the Hessian Court of Inquiry. It fits all of that evidence better than the solutions in Stryker, *Battles of Trenton and Princeton*, who may not have had Reuber's account, or Smith, *Trenton*, who does not use Reuber and does not mention Monroe and Washington, perhaps because he could not square their accounts with the Hessian evidence, to which he was very attentive.

39. White, "Narrative of Events," 77.

40. Ibid.

41. James Monroe, *Autobiography*, ed. Stuart Gerry Brown (Syracuse, 1959), 25–26.

42. White, "Narrative of Events."

43. Reuber, Journal.

44. Testimony of Capt. Ernst Altenbockum, ML 263–76, LT.

45. Henry Knox to Lucy Flucker Knox, 28 Dec. 1776, in Stryker, *Battles of Trenton and Princeton*, 371.

46. White, "Narrative of Events," 77.

47. Mary (Reed) Shannon, "A Grandmother's (Martha Reed, wife of John Shannon) Recollections of the Old Revolutionary Days," 1875, typescript by Susan Pindar Embury, Trenton Public Library, with thanks to Wendy Nardi for helping us to find this document.

48. Henry Muhlenberg, *The Journals of Henry Melchior Muhlenberg*, ed. Theodore G. Tappert and John W. Doberstein, 3 vols. (Philadelphia, 1942), 1:771, 31 Dec. 1776, recording a conversation between his son and a captured Hessian officer in Philadelphia.

49. Reuber, Journal, 25 [26] Dec. 1776.

50. Jakob Piel, "Diary of the Hessian Lieutenant [Jakob] Piel, 1776 to 1783," ed. Bruce E. Burgoyne, *JSHAJ* 4 (1989), 14.

51. Greenwood, *Services*, 83.

52. Smith, *Trenton*, 24.

53. Ibid.

54. Wilkinson, *Memoirs*, 1:129–130. This story is rejected by Stryker, *Battles of Trenton and Princeton*, 180, and Freeman, *Washington*, 4:321. The report of an "unidentified officer of distinction," who most historians agree was probably Lord Stirling, wrote of the Hessians that "as I came in full view of them from the back of the wood with his excellency General Washington, an officer informed him that the party had grounded their arms." Freeman writes, "Unfortunately for a good tale, if Forrest previously had come down from the head of Queen Street as Stryker asserted, the Captain could not have been at the place where Washington is said to have received word of the two regiments' surrender. One story or the other has to be discarded. The report that Forrest moved down the street seems the more probable." The wood was described in the letter as extending "up the creek," and the "back of the wood" might have been nearest the east side of town and not far from Forrest, who was also on the east side of the town and probably brought his battery down Queen Street. In short, both accounts are reconcilable and mutually reinforcing. The officer that Stirling spoke of would appear to be the same that Wilkinson identified as Forrest.

55. Dwyer, *The Day Is Ours!*, 259.

56. Major von Dechow died soon after the battle, but the Hessian Court of Inquiry took testimony from many other officers in the Knyphausen Regiment: Christian Sobbe, Jacob Baum, Nicholas Vaupell, Ludwig Wilhelm von Löwenstein, Luwig von Geyso, Wilhelm Drach von Ellershausen, Barthold Helfrich von Schimmelpfennig, Werner von Ferry, Bernhard von Biesenrodt, and Ludwig von Romrodt, in LT, ML 110–20, 364–462, 314–21.

57. Testimony of Sgt. Johannes Müller, 22 April 22, 1778, ML 348, 350, LT.

58. Ibid.; Müller did not describe the flags. Probably they would not have been the Grand Union Flag, which was little used after the Declaration of Independence. The Stars and Stripes had not yet been adopted. The more likely possibilities were Liberty Flags that were flown in the New York campaign; or the official flag of Massachusetts with a green liberty tree and the slogan "An Appeal to Heaven," or Connecticut's official grapevine flags with the motto "Qui Transtulit Sustinet," which were both used in 1776.

59. Dwyer, *The Day Is Ours!*, 260; quoting Private John Dewey (St Clair's Brigade), Military Journal, April 1776–February 1777, rpt. in *Life of George Dewey, Rear Admiral, USN, and Dewey Family History* (Westfield, Mass., 1898), 278–81.

60. Bombardier Volprecht, testimony, 13 Aug. 1778, ML 276, LT; the sergeants are described in Wilkinson, *Memoirs*, 1:130.

61. Jacob Francis, Pension Narrative, in John C. Dann, ed., *The Revolution Remembered: Eyewitness Accounts of the War of Independence* (Chicago, 1980), 395.

62. Freeman is mistaken in thinking that the wounded officer was Rall. It was more likely to have been Dechow. The error came from Wilkinson, *Memoirs* 1:129–31; Freeman, *Washington* 4:321.

63. Contemporary estimates of those who escaped varied from 345 to 600. Donop reported from Allentown, "I organized all the escaped men from the Rall brigade and made up a force of 292 men." Grant and Leslie reported that 53 escaped to Princeton, plus 20 dragoons, which would total 365. Among historians Stryker reckoned that 412 got away; Smith has the highest estimate at 653. It is possible to identify the following numbers of those who escaped by unit:

British 16th Light Dragoons	20
Engelhardt's Artillery	12
Gröthausen's Jägers	50
Musicians and drummers	20
Guard at Assunpink Bridge	18
Troops at Trent House	30
Guard at South Ferry	15
Outpost at Crosswicks	150
Baum's Knyphausen escapees	53

See Smith, *Trenton*, 25–26, 31; appendix N.

64. Smith, *Trenton*, 26.

65. American and Hessian accounts agree on the numbers killed and seriously wounded but differ in detail on the numbers of prisoners. The Hessians estimated 891 prisoners. Americans counted 918 and identified all of them by name, rank, and regiment. The disparity of 27 might have been caused by different ways of reckoning the wounded, or by the exclusion of musicians or servants, or by a Hessian undercount. Washington to John Hancock, 27 Dec. 1776, with attached list in the handwriting of Tench Tilghman not published in *GW* 7:454–61. Cf. Smith, *Trenton*, who follows the Hessian estimates; and Stryker, *Battles of Trenton and Princeton*, 195–96, 408–9. The British return of Muster Master General Sir George Osborn was 700, a gross undercount as always in Howe's army. Later, Howe reported total losses of 918, which was also an undercount. The Hessians also reported losing fifteen colors, which included flags for each company in every regiment.

66. Dwyer, *The Day Is Ours!*, 271.

67. Washington to John Cadwalader, 27 Dec. 1776, and Washington to Hancock, 27 Dec. 1776; *GW* 7:450, 454; for ineffectives, see monthly strength reports of the Continental army, republished in Charles H. Lesser, *The Sinews of Independence: Monthly Strength Reports of the Continental Army* (Chicago, 1976), xxx–xxxi, passim.

68. Piel, "Diary," 14 (26 Dec. 1776).

69. For the fullest account of the meeting, and arguments on all sides, see Joseph Reed, "General Reed's Narrative of the Movements of the American Army in the Neighborhood of Trenton in the Winter of 1776–1777," *PMHB* 8 (1884), 391–92.

70. Ibid.

71. Haslet to Caesar Rodney, n.d. [1 Jan. 1777?], *Letters to and from Caesar Rodney, 1756–1784*, ed. George Herbert Ryden (Philadelphia, 1933), 152–53; Christopher Ward, *The Delaware Continentals, 1776–1783* (Wilmington, 1941), 565n.

72. Reed, "Narrative," 391–92.

73. Ibid.; Greenwood, *Services*, 26–27.

74. Washington to Hancock, 27 Dec. 1776, *GW* 7:456.

75. Washington to Thomas Cadwalader, 27 Dec. 1776, *GW* 7:450.

76. William Chamberlin, "Letter of General William Chamberlin," *MHSP,* 2d ser. 10 (1895–96), 490–504.

77. White, "Narrative of Events," 77.

78. Ibid.

79. Elisha Bostwick, "A Connecticut Soldier Under Washington: Elisha Bostwick's Memoirs of the First Years of the Revolution," ed. William S. Powell, *WMQ3* 6 (1949), 102.

80. Greenwood, *Services,* 26–27.

81. Bostwick, "Memoirs," 102–3.

82. Wiederholdt diary.

83. Muhlenberg, *Journals,* 2:768 (28 Dec. 1776); William Hull to Andrew Adams, 1 Jan. 1777, in Stryker, *Battles of Trenton and Princeton,* 376.

84. Nicholas Cresswell, *The Journal of Nicholas Cresswell,* ed. Samuel Thornely (New York, 1924), 179–80 (6–7 Jan. 1777).

85. Ambrose Serle, *The American Journal of Ambrose Serle, Secretary to Lord Howe, 1776–1778,* ed. Edward H. Tatum Jr. (San Marino, Calif., 1940), 163 (27 Dec. 1776).

86. Cresswell, *Journal,* 181 (17 Jan. 1777).

87. Capt. John Bowater to Earl of Denbigh, 22 May 1777, in Marion Balderston and David Syrett, eds., *The Lost War: Letters from British Officers During the American Revolution* (New York, 1975), 125–26. A highly meretricious account, by an officer who bore a heavy share of the responsibility, is James Grant's letter of 27 Dec. 1776, Grant Papers, LC.

88. Johann Ewald, *Diary of the American War: A Hessian Journal,* ed. Joseph P. Tustin (New Haven, 1979), 44.

89. Honoré-Gabriel Riqueti, Comte de Mirabeau, *Avis aix Hessois et autre peuples de l'Allemagne vendus par leurs princes à l'Angleterre* (Cleves, 1777), 16.

90. [Benjamin Franklin?], "From the Count de Schaumbergh to the Baron Hohendorf, commanding the Hessian troops in America," 18 Feb. 1777, commonly called in English and American literature "The Sale of the Hessians." In German literature it is known as the *Uriasbrief.* The leading study is Philipp Losch, "Der Uriasbrief des Grafen von Schaumberg," *HCMH* 2 (1913), 37–40, 83–88, 99–105.

91. Martin Ernst von Schlieffen, *Des Hessois en Amerique, de leur Souverain et des Declamateurs* (n.p., 1782); the original French texts of Mirabeau and Schlieffen appear in Holger Hamecher, ed., *Mirabeau, Schlieffen und die nach Amerika verkauften Hessen: Zwei zeitgenössische Pamphlete zum "Soldatenhandel" für den Amerikanischen Unabhängigkeitskrieg* (Kassel, 1991).

❧ Hard Choices

1. *The Life and Recollections of John Howland,* ed. Edwin M. Stone (Providence, 1857), 70.

2. James McMichael, "Diary of Lieutenant James McMichael of the Pennsylvania Line, 1776–1778," *PMHB* 16 (1892), 129–59, 140; Washington made his headquarters in the house of the widow Hannah Stewart Harris. The building, long remembered as the "Old Yellow House," stood five miles southwest of McConkey's Ferry, and no longer survives. See W.W.H. Davis, *The History of Bucks County* (Doylestown, Pa., 1876), 234; *GW* 7:449.

3. Washington to Cadwalader, 27 Dec. 1776, *GW* 7:440.

4. Washington to Joseph Reed, 27 Dec. 1776, and Washington to Cadwalader, 27 Dec. 1776, *GW* 7:463, 449–50.

5. John Cadwalader to Washington, 26 Dec. 1776 (2 letters), and 27 Dec. 1776, 10 o'clock [A.M.], *GW* 7:442–45, 451–52. Reed also stated in his narrative that he had sent the same advice to Washington from Trenton, late on December 27. This letter has not been found, and would in any case have reached Newtown after the decision was made in the Council of War; it might have shaped the subsequent planning. "General Reed's Narrative of the Movements of the American Army in the Neighborhood of Trenton in the Winter of 1776–1777," *PMHB* 8 (1884), 393–95.

6. Washington to Joseph Reed, 27 Dec. 1776, and Washington to Cadwalader, 27 Dec. 1776, *GW* 7:463, 449–50. Freeman notes only that "no minutes of this council were written, or, if taken down, preserved." Douglas Southall Freeman, *George Washington: A Biography*, 7 vols. (New York, 1948–57), 4:329.

But the agenda and the course of the discussion appear in Washington's correspondence with Reed, Cadwalader, and other officers. It was in this council that the critical decisions were taken for a return to New Jersey, and for another strike at the enemy. But the event has been lost in the aftermath of the Hessian surrender. Only very brief accounts appear even in works as strong as Ketchum, Smith, Dwyer and Stryker. Cf. Richard M. Ketchum, *The Winter Soldiers: The Battles for Trenton and Princeton* (1973; New York, 1991), 275; Samuel Stelle Smith, *The Battle of Princeton* (Monmouth Beach, N.J., 1967), 5; William M. Dwyer, *The Day Is Ours!* (New York, 1983), 271; and William S. Stryker, *The Battles of Trenton and Princeton* (Boston, 1898).

7. This was what Joseph Reed heard from members of the council. See "Reed's Narrative," 397.

8. Ibid.

9. Washington to Maxwell, McDougall, and Heath, all 28 Dec. 1776, *GW* 7:468–69, 472–73, 471–72.

10. General Orders, 29 Dec. 1776, *GW* 7:476.

11. Washington to Cadwalader, 27 Dec. 1776; Phineas Pemberton Weather Diary, 26–29 Dec. 1776, APS, appendix K below.

12. Washington to Hancock, 29 Dec. 1776, *GW* 7:477.

13. Smith, *Princeton*, 8–9.

14. Azariah Dunham to Joseph Trumbull, 21 Dec. 1776, *GW* 7:395.

15. Washington to Robert Morris, 30 Dec. 1776, *GW* 7:489.

16. Joseph Trumbull to Washington, 13 Dec. 1776, and Washington to Joseph Trumbull, 16 Dec. 1776. *GW* 7:328–29, 360–61.

17. Joseph Trumbull to Washington, 27 June 1776, *GW* 5:125.

18. Washington to Robert Morris, 30 Dec. 1776, and Robert Morris to Washington, 30 Dec. 1776, *GW* 7:489–90.

19. For the artillery see Henry Knox to Mrs. Knox, 2 and 7 Jan. 1777, in Stryker, *Battles of Trenton and Princeton*, 436–37, 449–52.

20. Captain Thomas Dowdeswell to the Earl of Rockingham, Raritan Landing, N.J., 16 Jan. 1777, "The Operations in New Jersey: An English Officer Describes the Events of December 1776," ed. J. E. Tyler, *NJHSP* 70 (1952), 132–36.

21. Washington to Robert Morris, 31 Dec. 1776, *GW* 7:497.

22. Christopher Ward, *The Delaware Continentals* (Wilmington, 1941) 173, 566; John Haslet to Caesar Rodney, *Letters to and from Caesar Rodney, 1756–1784*, ed. George Herbert Ryden (Philadelphia, 1933), 153.

23. Edwin M. Stone, ed., *The Life and Recollections of John Howland* (Providence, 1857), 71; Stephen Olney, "Memoir," in *Biography of Revolutionary Heroes: Containing the Life of Brigadier Gen. William Barton, and also Captain Stephen Olney*, ed. Mrs. Williams (Providence, 1839), 193. Note that these were three Rhode Island regiments: Varnum's from Kent and Kings County, afterward Washington County; Hitchcock's from Providence; and Lippitt's from Bristol; see ibid., 158, 162. Lippitt's men were bound to serve to January 18, but Howland noted that they "poised firelocks" with the rest.

24. Washington to Executive Committee of Congress, 1 Jan. 1777, and Washington to John Hancock, 1 Jan. 1777, *GW* 7:500, 504.

25. Sergeant R——, "The Battle of Princeton," Wellsborough, Pa., *Phenix*, 24 March 1832, rpt. *PMHB* 20 (1896), 515–19.

26. Ibid.

27. Ibid., 516.

28. Ibid.; quotations are inaccurate in Freeman, *Washington* 4:333.

29. Washington to the Commanding Officer in Morristown, 30 Dec. 1776, *GW* 7:490–91.

30. Washington to Robert Morris, 31 Dec. 1776, *GW* 7:497.

31. Washington to Executive Committee of Congress, 1 Jan. 1777; *GW* 7:499. The story of Robert Morris and the buried money is from a lady of old family in Philadelphia. For Morris's shipment of cash to the army, see *GW* 7:490.

32. Mifflin's brigade included recruits for five new regiments then being raised for the Continental army: the Second, Tenth, Eleventh, and Twelfth Pennsylvania regiments and Colonel Timothy Matlack's Philadelphia Rifle Regiment. Also among Mifflin's men were remnants from at least twelve old regiments of Pennsylvania Associators that had been raised in 1775–76: a regiment from Bucks County, three regiments from Northampton County, six from Lancaster County, one from Cumberland County, and one from Bedford County. Also present were men from four independent militia companies from Pennsylvania and one from Delaware. Other units included marine detachments from the Continental navy, the Pennsylvania Navy, and perhaps crews from privateers in Philadelphia. Cf. Stryker, *Battles of Trenton and Princeton*, 433; Jonathan Trumbull to Washington, 28 Dec. 1776, *GW* 7:475–76.

33. McDougall to Washington, 30 Dec. 1776, *GW* 7:485–88; Lord Stirling to William Livingston, 28 Dec. 1776, *AA* 5 3:1463; *PNJHS* 1 (1847), 37–38; Smith, *Princeton*, appendix A.

34. General Orders, 27 Dec. 1776, *GW* 7:448–49.

35. Washington to William Heath, 31 Dec. 1776, *GW* 7:496.

36. Washington, General Orders, 1 Jan. 1777, *GW* 7:499 *Pennsylvania Evening Post*, 14 Jan 1777; *NJA* 2 1:256–57.

37. Ibid.

38. Washington to Pennsylvania Council of Safety, 29 Dec. 1776, *GW* 7:483.

❧ Good Ground

1. "General Orders, Trentown," 30 Dec. 1776, *GW* 7:484. This critical document, which early on December 30, 1776, laid out the American plan for a defensive battle behind Assunpink Creek four days before it happened, did not survive in Washington's papers. Dr. Carlos Godfrey, head of the New Jersey Public Records, discovered it in the Orderly Book of the German Battalion at the Historical Society of Pennsylvania. For discussions see the note by Philander Chase in *GW* 7:484; and *The Writings of Washington*, ed. John C. Fitzpatrick (Washington, 1932) 37:537–38.

2. For Washington's information and assumptions that Howe was going to attack him see Washington to Hancock, 1 Jan. 1777, *GW* 7:504, and General Orders, 30 Dec. 1776, *GW* 7:484.

3. This ground is today a park in downtown Trenton. It preserves much of its terrain, but with changes. The ground has been raised along the edge of Assunpink Creek with massive retaining walls to control flooding. The slope of the rising ground is not as steep as it was in 1776, and the open area is smaller, but still gives a good sense of the American position.

4. General Orders, Trenton, December 30, 1776, *GW* 7:484.

5. Washington to Robert Morris, 30 Dec. 1776, *GW* 7: 489.

6. Washington to Robert Morris, 25 Dec. 1776, *GW* 7: 439–40. Some historians have written that this money was for bounties, but it was clearly for espionage; cf. Samuel Stelle Smith, *The Battle of Princeton* (Monmouth Beach, N.J., 1967), 10.

7. After the Revolution he was allowed to remain in New York City and ran a flourishing print shop and bookstore. See the note by Philander Chase in *GW* 7:89. Many references to Gaine's activities appear in Ambrose Serle, *The American Journal of Ambrose Serle*, ed. Edward H. Tatum Jr. (San Marino, Calif., 1940), 107 (27 Sept. 1776), 114 (26 Sept. 1776), 134–35 (1 Nov. 1776), 176 (17 Jan. 1776; for American accounts see William S. Stryker, ed., *Documents Relating to the Revolutionary History of New Jersey*, in *NJA* 2 1:130, 130n, 251, 310, 317, 383.

8. James Wilkinson, *Memoirs of My Own Times*, 3 vols. (Philadelphia, 1816; rpt. 1973), 1:150–51.

9. *History of the First Troop, Philadelphia City Cavalry, 1774–1874*; J. Lapsley, *The Book of the First Troop, Philadelphia City Cavalry, 1774–1915* (Philadelphia, 1915); Edward W. Richardson, *Standards and Colors of the American Revolution* (Philadelphia, 1982), 72, 113, 214–15.

10. Joseph Reed, "General Joseph Reed's Narrative of the Movements of the American Army in the Neighborhood of Trenton in the Winter of 1776–77," *PMHB* 8 (1884), 399–400; [Lawrence], *Brief Narrative of the Ravages of the British and Hessians at Princeton in 1776*, ed. Varnum Lansing Collins (Princeton, 1906), 30.

11. Ibid. Beside Reed's and Lawrence's narratives, see William Young, "Journal of Sergeant William Young," *PMHB* 8 (1884), 261; and Wilkinson, *Memoirs of My Own Times*, 1:134, which has the best account of the interrogation. Another account by Thomas Peters appears in William M. Dwyer, *The Day Is Ours!* (New York, 1983), 304.

12. John Cadwalader to George Washington, 31 Dec. 1776, *GW* 7:491–95; the manuscript map survives in the Washington Papers, LC. The informant was in Princeton on the morning of December 30 and reached Cadwalader's camp in Crosswicks by "about 12 or 1 o'clock" that day. Cadwalader met with him, presumably in the afternoon, and "made a rough draught of the Road from this place, the Situation of the Cannon & Works begun and those intended this Morning."
To study Cadwalader's letter and his map and the ground is to discover that it was not a sketch of the road from Trenton to Princeton, but from Crosswicks to Princeton. Cadwalader's letter and the map were sent on to Washington by express and were in his hands by December 31, 1776.

13. Wilkinson, *Memoirs* 1:135; on numbers, Smith, *Princeton*, 11; Wilkinson says that these troops were sent out when orders went to Mifflin and Cadwalader, which by Washington's estimation was nine o'clock on the evening of January 1. But as the fight happened at dawn on January 1, they must have been sent out the night before.

14. The line of the road and its elevation have changed, but the terrain of Eight Mile Run still appears clearly on the topographical maps of the U.S. Geological Survey, Princeton Quadrangle (1995) NIMA 6064 1–SW–series V822, and also on eighteenth-century maps such as William Faden, "Plan of the Operations of General Washington Against the King's Troops in New Jersey, from the 26th of December to the 3d January 1777" (London, 1777), in Kenneth Nebenzahl, ed., *Atlas of the American Revolution* (Washington, 1984), 92–93. The topography of Eight Mile Run shows high ground nearly sixty feet above both sides of the creek where the road crosses it. Five Mile Run has a high ground only ten or twenty feet above the crossing. This suggests that the site was Eight Mile Creek, not Five Mile Creek as other historians have believed.

15. Johann Ewald, *Diary of the American War: A Hessian Journal*, ed. Joseph P. Tustin (New Haven, 1979), 48 (2 Jan. 1777); and Archibald Robertson, *Archibald Robertson, Lieutenant Colonel, Royal Engineers: His Diaries and Sketches in America, 1762–1780*, ed. Harry Miller Lydenberg, (New York, 1930), 118–19 (1 Jan. 1777).

16. Ibid.

17. The fight at Eight Mile Run on January 1, 1777, is a missing event in most histories of the campaign. It has eluded some writers altogether; others have confused it with the fighting on the Trenton-Princeton Road that took place on January 2. This is the case with Stryker, *Battles of Trenton and Princeton*, 258–59; Thomas Jefferson Wertenbaker, "The Battle of Princeton," in *The Princeton Battle Monument* (Princeton, 1922), 60–61; Alfred Hoyt Bill, *The Campaign of Princeton, 1776–1777* (Princeton, 1948), 84–85; Douglas Southall Freeman, *George Washington: A Biography*, 7 vols. (New York, 1948–57), 4:342; and Richard M. Ketchum, *The Winter Soldiers: The Battles for Trenton and Princeton* (1973, New York, 1991). Dwyer, *The Day Is Ours!* (New York, 1983), 313, has an incomplete account. Smith, in his careful *Battle of Princeton*, 12–13, identifies the engagement on January 1 but places it at Five Mile Run (Shabbakunk Creek), well beyond Maidenhead. He does not have Ewald's report on the course of the fight, numbers of casualties, and the location on the road *to* Maidenhead.
One reason why so many able historians missed this event was that the account by Ewald was not published until 1979. Another is that the casualties appear to have been mostly on the German and especially the British side, from which fewer materials have survived. A third is that no New England units were involved on the American side, and they produced

more personal narratives than others. Primary accounts include Ewald, *Diary,* 48; Robertson, *Diaries,* 118; and the Journal of the Grenadier Battalion Minnigerode, MNHPL.

18. The following account of events on the evening of January 1–2, 1777, derives from many of the same primary sources used by Dwyer, *The Day Is Ours!,* 308–13, but with small differences of detail, corrections of fact, and a major difference of interpretation. Dwyer titles his chapter "All was now Hurry, Confusion and Noise," a quotation from Benjamin Rush. It described Rush's impression of the American muster, but it was highly organized hurry, in which the American troops moved quickly to prepared positions, with orders that had been issued earlier.

19. Reed, "General Reed's Narrative," 402; Benjamin Rush, *Autobiography,* ed. George W. Corner (Princeton, 1948), 126; both accounts by participants are consistent.

20. Rush, *Autobiography,* 126.

21. Washington to John Cadwalader (or Thomas Mifflin?), 1 Jan. 1777, *GW* 7:510–11.

22. Rush, *Autobiography,* 126–28.

23. William Young, "Journal of Sergeant William Young," *PMHB* 8 (1884), 255–78, 262–63.

24. Charles Willson Peale, Journal, 1 Jan. 1777, in Charles Horace Wells Sellers, ed., "Journal by Charles Willson Peale, Dec. 4, 1776–Jan. 20, 1777," *PMHB* 38 (1914), 271–86, 278.

25. Thomas Rodney to Caesar Rodney, 30 Dec. 1776, in George Herbert Ryden, ed., *Letters to and from Caesar Rodney, 1756–1784* (1933; rpt. New York, 1970), 150–52. Also *The Diary of Captain Thomas Rodney, 1776–1777,* ed. Caesar A. Rodney, *Papers of the Historical Society of Delaware,* vol. 1, paper 8 (Wilmington, 1888; rpt. New York, 1974); the original manuscript in the Library of Congress clearly shows that much of the diary is a memoir; photocopy in author's possession.

26. Dwyer, *The Day Is Ours!,* 310.

27. James McMichael, "Diary of Lieutenant James McMichael of the Pennsylvania Line, 1776–1778," *PMHB* 16 (1892), 129–59, 140; "Diary of Lieutenant James McMichael," *PA,* 2d ser. 15:195–218, 203; the texts vary in small details.

28. Captain Stephen Olney, "Memoir," in *Biography of Revolutionary Heroes: Containing the Life of Brigadier Gen. William Barton, and also Captain Stephen Olney,* ed. Mrs. Williams (Providence, 1839), 193.

29. Rush, *Autobiography,* 127.

30. Ibid.

31. Ibid., 126.

32. William Young, "Journal," 262 (1 Jan. 1777).

33. Ewald, *Diary,* 44 (30 Dec. 1776).

34. Ibid.

35. Ibid., 45 (31 Dec. 1776).

36. Ibid.

37. Ibid., 44 (30 Dec. 1776).

❧ The Bridge

1. J[oseph] White, *A Narrative of Events, as They Occurred from Time to Time, in the Revolutionary War, with an Account of the Battles of Trenton, Trenton-Bridge, and Princeton* (Charlestown, 1833); rpt. in *American Heritage,* June 1956, 74–79.

2. Robertson noted, "In the middle of the night, Lord Cornwallis arrived from York and superseded General Grant in his command." Lt. Thomas Dowdeswell also wrote of "Lord Cornwallis having joined us in the night." Cf. *Archibald Robertson, Lieutenant Colonel, Royal Engineers: His Diaries and Sketches in America, 1762–1780,* ed. Harry Miller Lydenberg (New York, 1930), 118 (1 Jan. 1777); and Dowdeswell to the Marquis of Rockingham, 16 Jan. 1777, in J. E. Tyler, ed., "The Operations in New Jersey: An English Officer Describes the Events of December 1776," *NJHSP* 70 (1952), 133–36. See also Samuel Stelle Smith, *The Battle of Princeton* (Monmouth Beach, N.J., 1967), 13.

Other accounts are variant. Ewald remembered that Cornwallis reached Princeton by the evening of December 31. His memory appears to be mistaken. Cornwallis's biographers Franklin and Mary Wickwire thought that he arrived "toward evening" on January 1, but their sources are secondary accounts. Cf. Franklin Wickwire and Mary Wickwire, *Cornwallis and the War of Independence* (London, 1970), 95.

3. Alfred Hoyt Bill et al., *A House Called Morven: Its Role in American History* (Princeton, 1954), 41–42; Grant to Rigby, 15 Jan. 1777, Grant Papers, LC.

4. Smith, *Princeton*, 13.

5. Johann Ewald, *Diary of the American War: A Hessian Journal,* ed. Joseph P. Tustin (New Haven, 1979), 50 (2 Jan. 1777).

6. Ibid., 48 (1–2 Jan. 1777).

7. Thomas Sullivan, Journal, 1 Jan. 1777, in Joseph Lee Boyle, ed., *From Redcoat to Rebel: The Thomas Sullivan Journal* (Bowie, Md., 1997), 98.

8. Ewald, *Diary,* 48 (2 Jan. 1777); also Smith, *Princeton,* 13.

9. Robertson, *Diaries,* 119 (2 Jan. 1777).

10. "A letter from a respectable inhabitant," 22 Aug. 1816, reproduced in James Wilkinson, *Memoirs of My Own Times,* 3 vols. (Philadelphia, 1816; rpt. 1973) 1:136.

11. Ewald, *Diary,* 48 (2 Jan. 1777).

12. Wilkinson, *Memoirs* 1:137.

13. Ibid., 135; on numbers, Smith, *Princeton,* 11; Wilkinson says that these troops were sent out when orders went to Mifflin and Cadwalader, which by Washington's estimation was nine o'clock on the evening of January 1. But as a skirmish happened at dawn on January 1, some of them must have been sent the night before.

14. Wilkinson, *Memoirs* 1:135–36.

15. Ibid.; Michel Williams Craig, *General Edward Hand: Winter's Doctor* (Lancaster, 1984), 47–49.

16. Wilkinson, *Memoirs* 1:137.

17. Robertson, *Diaries,* 119 (2 Jan. 1777); Wilkinson, *Memoirs* 1:137.

18. Robertson, *Diaries,* 119.

19. We found the exact site of Stockton Hollow difficult to identify on the ground, as much of the land has been leveled and is densely built. Dwyer places it near the Helene Fuld Medical Center; William M. Dwyer, *The Day Is Ours!*(New York, 1983), 317.

20. Smith writes that "Captain Thomas Forrest had placed the battery of 'two field pieces' very strategically overlooking the hollow, at a position about one third of a mile from the present battle monument, now approximately Bond Street"; Smith, *Princeton,* 16.

21. These were the regiments of Maj. Josiah Parker, Lt. Col. Thomas Lawson, and Maj. Richard Parker. Wilkinson, *Memoirs* 1:138.

22. Ibid.

23. Smith, *Princeton,* 15.

24. Wilkinson, *Memoirs* 1:138; for the time of sunset at 4:46 P.M. local solar time, Smith, *Princeton,* 16.

25. Smith, *Princeton,* 15, citing the Journal of the Grenadier Battalion von Minnigerode; "Letter from a Gentleman of great worth with the American army . . . ," *Maryland Journal,* 16 Jan. 1777; Wilkinson, *Memoirs* 1:138–39; Dwyer, *The Day Is Ours!,* 316.

26. Edwin M. Stone, *The Life and Recollections of John Howland* (Providence, 1857), 73.

27. Ibid.

28. Henry Knox to Mrs. Knox, 7 Jan. 1777, in William S. Stryker, *The Battles of Trenton and Princeton* (Boston, 1898), 449–52.

29. Stone, *Howland,* 72.

30. Quoted in Dwyer, *The Day Is Ours!,* 318.

31. John Witherspoon wrote, "Some of the people at Princeton say they thought they were killing me, and boasted that they had done it when they came back. But this is uncertain. . . . [T]he fact of his death and the manner of it is beyond doubt." John C. Clyde, *Rosbrugh, a Tale of the Revolution; or, Life, Labors, and Death of Rev. John Rosbrugh* (Easton, Pa.,

1880); Stryker, *Battles of Trenton and Princeton*, 266–67; Dwyer, *The Day Is Ours!*, 208–10, 322–23, 379–80.

32. Haussegger was regarded with deep suspicion in the American army and was openly critical of its commanders. Even his friends were convinced that he was not captured but "went over to the enemy." See "Memoirs of Brigadier-General John Lacey of Pennsylvania," *PMHB* 25 (1901), 514. For three variant interpretations, all hostile to Haussegger in different degrees, cf. Smith, *Princeton*, 17; Stryker, *Battles of Trenton and Princeton*, 258, 262, 352; Dwyer, *The Day Is Ours!*, 305–8. He was later convicted of treason.

33. Stone, *Howland*, 73; Robert Beale, "Revolutionary Experiences of Major Robert Beale," *Northern Neck of Virginia Historical Magazine* 6 (1956), 500–506.

34. Stone, *Howland*, 73; for another American account see Dwyer, *The Day Is Ours!*, 318.

35. White, *Narrative of Events*; for other accounts see Stryker, *Battles of Trenton and Princeton*, 479; Smith, *Princeton*, 15.

36. Stone, *Howland*, 74.

37. G.W.P. Custis, *Recollections and Private Memoirs of Washington, by His Adopted Son . . .* (New York, 1859; rpt. Bridgewater, Va., 1999), 413; for other accounts, see Harry M. Ward, *Charles Scott and the Spirit of '76* (Charlottesville, 1988), 27.

38. Thomas Rodney, *The Diary of Captain Thomas Rodney, 1776–1777*, ed. Caesar A. Rodney, *Papers of the Historical Society of Delaware*, vol. 1, paper 8 (Wilmington, 1888; rpt. New York, 1974), 31. Smith puts Cadwalader's brigade (in this, their first position) at the intersection of Hudson Street and Hamilton Avenue. He places Mercer's men south of Pond Run, "just east of current Olden Avenue." Smith, *Princeton*, 15.

39. Smith, *Princeton*, 15; for Johnston, the source is Dwyer, *The Day Is Ours!*, 319. Units in the third line are not identified.

40. From a careful count by unit, Smith makes Washington's "total force at Trenton," 6,809; *Princeton*, appendix A, 34–35.

41. Stephen Olney, "Memoir," in *Biography of Revolutionary Heroes: Containing the Life of Brigadier Gen. William Barton, and also Captain Stephen Olney*, ed. Mrs. Williams (Providence, 1839), 193.

42. Wilkinson, *Memoirs* 1:138.

43. Beale, "Revolutionary Experiences," 500–506; the passage on this battle is reprinted in Dennis P. Ryan, *A Salute to Courage: The American Revolution as Seen through Wartime Writings of Officers in the Continental Army and Navy* (New York, 1979), 55–58.

44. Stone, *Howland*,, 74.

45. Olney, "Memoir," 193–94.

46. Ibid.

47. Ewald, *Diary*, 49.

48. Stone, *Howland*, 74; Stryker, *Battles of Trenton and Princeton*, 266; Smith, *Princeton*, 17.

49. Quoted in Harry M. Ward's excellent biography, *Charles Scott and the Spirit of '76* (Charlottesville, 1988), 27, from "Anecdotes of Old General Scott," Draper Collection, Kentucky Manuscripts, 26CC10, State Historical Society of Wisconsin.

50. William S. Powell, ed., "A Connecticut Soldier Under Washington: Elisha Bostwick's Memoirs of the First Years of the Revolution," *WMQ3* 6 (1946), 106.

51. Smith, *Princeton*, 17; *PMHB* 10 (1887), 263.

52. White, *Narrative of Events*, 77.

53. An "American Militiaman," quoted without attribution in Dwyer, *The Day Is Ours!*, 323.

54. Ibid.

55. Rodney, *Diary*, 31 (2 Jan. 1777).

56. White, *Narrative of Events*, 77.

57. William Hutchinson, Pension Application, in John C. Dann, ed. *The Revolution Remembered: Eyewitness Accounts of the War of Independence* (Chicago, 1980), 146.

58. Greene and Washington estimated British and Hessian losses to be between 2,000 and 3,000 for the campaign from December 26, 1776, to January 9, 1777. That number included 1,000 killed and captured at the first battle of Trenton and about 450 killed and

captured at Princeton. This would yield about 500 killed and captured in the second battle of Trenton, including all the fighting along the Post Road, in the town, and at the creek, both British and Hessians together. Perhaps another 100 were killed or captured in small actions. These estimates do not include lightly wounded or sick, a larger number; very little firm evidence survives to settle the question. Stryker and Smith make no estimates; Dwyer and Ketchum reckon between 150 and 500. Bill estimates 500. See Bill, *Campaign of Princeton*, 87; Dwyer, *The Day Is Ours!*, 326. Howard H. Peckham, *The Toll of Independence: Engagements and Battle Casualties of the American Revolution* (Chicago, 1974), reckons 940 Hessian and British killed and captured at Trenton I; 35 killed and captured at Stockton Hollow; and 157 "or more" killed and captured at Princeton, for a total of 1,137 Hessian and British killed and captured. Peckham misses six engagements altogether: at Five Mile Run on January 1, Shabba-kunk Creek, Trenton, and the three British assaults at Assunpink Creek on January 2. His estimates are not documented, but appear to be based on secondary sources, and mainly Stryker. Peckham was making a heroic effort for the entire Revolution; he acknowledged that his estimates were incomplete; Cf. Greene, *Papers*, 2:5 (10 Jan. 1777). Washington, *GW* 8:114 (20 Jan. 1777).

❧ Two Councils

1. George Washington to John Hancock, 5 Jan. 1777, *GW* 7:520–23.

2. William P. McMichael, ed., "Diary of Lieutenant James McMichael, 1776–1778," *PMHB* 16 (1892), 129–59, 140; for the time of sunset, Samuel Stelle Smith, *The Battle of Princeton* (Monmouth Beach, N.J., 1967), 16.

3. McMichael, "Diary," 140.

4. Stephen Olney, "Memoir," in *Biography of Revolutionary Heroes: Containing the Life of Brigadier Gen. William Barton, and also Captain Stephen Olney,* ed. Mrs. Williams (Providence, 1839), 194.

5. Benjamin Rush, *Autobiography,* ed. George W. Corner (Princeton, 1948), 128.

6. William Dwyer, *The Day Is Ours!* (New York, 1983), 326.

7. C. Keith Wilbur, *Revolutionary Medicine, 1700–1800* (Old Saybrook, Conn., 1980), 13, 38, 44. Mortality from amputations in the Civil War was 38 percent for the lower leg, 54 percent for the middle thigh, and 88 percent for the hip joint. Gordon Dammann, *Civil War Medical Instruments and Equipment* (Missoula, Mt., 1983), 1.

8. Langrel was shot with shackles and cables attached. Naval gunners used it to cut rigging, sails, and yards. Collin probably meant langrage, which was case shot filled with irregular dirty pieces of iron. American artillery employed it against infantry at Redbank and also in the Trenton-Princeton campaign. For a British account on January 3, 1777, see below, Hale, p. 329.

9. Nicholas Collin, *The Journal and Biography of Nicholas Collin, 1746–1831,* ed. Amandus Johnson (Philadelphia, 1936), 241.

10. Archibald Robertson, *Archibald Robertson, Lieutenant Colonel, Royal Engineers: His Diaries and Sketches in America, 1762–1780,* ed. Harry Miller Lydenberg (New York, 1930), 119–20 (2 Jan. 1777).

11. The two light infantry battalions in this campaign consisted of eighteen companies from the following regiments. The first battalion: 4th, 5th, 10th, 17th, 22nd, 23rd, 27th, 35th, and 38th Foot. Second battalion: eleven companies from the 40th, 43rd, 44th, 45th, 49th, 52nd, 55th, 63rd, 64th Foot. At Lexington and Concord, Smith's expedition included light infantry companies from the 4th, 5th, 10th, 18th, 23rd, 38th, 43rd, 47th, 52nd, and 59th Foot, and British marines. The 22nd, 44th, and 45th were also present at Bunker Hill and the Siege of Boston. Cf. Smith, *Princeton*, 36, and David Hackett Fischer, *Paul Revere's Ride* (New York, 1994), 314, 309. For a general study, J.F.C. Fuller, *British Light Infantry in the Eighteenth Century* (London, [1925]).

12. This from British regimental rosters, PRO.

13. In Philadelphia, the temperature fell from 39 to 21 degrees by 8 P.M.; Phineas Pemberton Weather Diary, 2–3 Jan. 1777, APS, appendix K.

14. Smith, *Princeton*, 17, 33; Dwyer, *The Day Is Ours!*, 327–29.

15. Frederick Mackenzie, *The Diary of Frederick Mackenzie*, 2 vols. (Cambridge, Mass., 1930), 1:74; Ambrose Serle, *The American Journal of Ambrose Serle, Secretary to Lord Howe, 1776–1778*, ed. Edward H. Tatum Jr., (San Marino, Calif., 1940), 300–302 (1 June 1778).

16. Ann Hulton to Mrs. Adam Lightbody, 25 Nov. 1773, *Letters of a Loyalist Lady*, ed. Harold Murdoch (Cambridge, 1927), 63.

17. Benjamin Rush, *Autobiography* (Princeton, 1948), 51; William Fraser, *The Melvilles, Earls of Melville, and Leslies, Earls of Leven* (Edinburgh, 1890); Rush, *Autobiography*, 129; Captain William Leslie has an American website at www.silverwhistle.free-online.co.uk/lobsters/will-leslie.html.

18. William B. Wilcox, *Portrait of a General: Sir Henry Clinton and the War of Independence* (New York, 1964), 163.

19. Serle, *Journal*, 301 (1 June 1778).

20. James Wilkinson, *Memoirs of My Own Times*, 3 vols. including atlas (Philadelphia, 1816; rpt. 1973), 1:139.

21. Ibid.

22. Did Cornwallis speak these words? They are repeated by his biographers and by most students of the battle. I have found no firm primary evidence, but one might conclude that the phrase is consistent with Cornwallis's thoughts and acts, and also with his style. Cf. Richard M. Ketchum, *The Winter Soldiers: The Battles for Trenton and Princeton* (1973; New York, 1991), 291; Franklin Wickwire and Mary Wickwire, *Cornwallis and the War of Independence* (London, 1970), 96; William S. Stryker, *The Battles of Trenton and Princeton* (Boston, 1898), 268.

23. Wilkinson, *Memoirs* 1:139.

24. Ibid., 140; Wilkinson was not present at the council of war but reported the account as one he "received from general St. Clair, to whose person I was attached," as aide.

25. Ibid.

26. Henry Knox to Mrs. Knox, 7 Jan. 1777, in Stryker, *Battles of Trenton and Princeton*, 449.

27. In fact the roads behind Princeton had been patrolled by British cavalry, but the day before the patrols had been withdrawn to cover the march to Trenton.

28. Alfred Hoyt Bill, *The Campaign of Princeton, 1776–1777* (Princeton, 1948), 93.

29. Douglas Southall Freeman, *George Washington: A Biography*, 7 vols. (New York, 1948–57), 4:345.

30. George Washington to John Hancock, 5 Jan. 1777, *GW* 7:520–23.

31. Phineas Pemberton Weather Diary, 2–3 Jan. 1777, APS; appendix K.

32. Edwin M. Stone, *The Life and Recollections of John Howland* (Providence, 1857), 74.

33. Olney, "Memoir," 196; Thomas Rodney, *The Diary of Captain Thomas Rodney, 1776–1777*, ed. Caesar A. Rodney, *Papers of the Historical Society of Delaware*, vol. 1, paper 8 (Wilmington, 1888; rpt. New York, 1974), 32; Freeman, *Washington* 4:346.

34. Wilkinson, *Memoirs* 1:140.

35. Freeman, *Washington* 4:346–48, notes the contrast with other campaigns, especially Paoli. Olney wrote, "After dark, we were dismissed a little while to get our breakfast, dinner and supper. As the night advanced it became extremely cold, and it seemed to me extravagant that our men should pull down such good cedar fences to augment our fires, and they were replenished by some stragglers, as we afterwards understood, who were ordered for that purpose." Olney, "Memoir," 195.

36. Hall as quoted in Dwyer, *The Day Is Ours!*, 327.

37. Robertson, *Diaries*, 120–21 (2–3 Jan. 1777).

38. Smith, *Princeton*, 18; Robertson, *Diaries*, 120–21 (2–3 Jan. 1777).

39. Washington to Hancock, 5 Jan. 1777, *GW* 7:521; William Young, "The Journal of Sergeant William Young," *PMHB* 8 (1884), 264.

40. J[oseph] White, *A Narrative of Events, As They Occurred from Time to Time, in the Revolutionary War, with an Account of the Battles of Trenton, Trenton-Bridge, and Princeton* (Charlestown, Mass., 1833; rpt. in *American Heritage*, June 1956, 74–79); Olney, "Memoir," 196–97; Smith, *Princeton*, 18.

41. Rodney, *Diary*, 32.

42. James Johnston, Pension Narrative, in John C. Dann, ed., *The Revolution Remembered: Eyewitness Accounts of the War of Independence* (Chicago, 1980), 399–406.

43. Rodney, *Diary*, 32; Charles Willson Peale, "Journal by Charles Willson Peale, Dec. 4, 1776–Jan. 20, 1777," *PMHB* 38 (1914), 271–86, and manuscript autobiography, APS; Wilkinson, *Memoirs*, 1:140; George Weedon to John Page, 6 Jan. 1777, Weedon Papers, CHS.

44. Smith, *Princeton*, 19.

45. Rodney, *Diary*, 32 (3 Jan. 1777).

46. Margaret Morris, *Margaret Morris Her Journal with Biographical Sketch and Notes*, ed. John W. Jackson (Philadelphia, 1949), 62.

47. Stone, *Howland*, 75; also Freeman, *Washington* 4:348.

48. White, *Narrative of Events*.

49. Ibid.

50. Stryker recorded this account from the testimony of "aged people" in Sandtown; *Battles of Trenton and Princeton*, 276.

51. Bill, *Campaign of Princeton*, 93–97.

52. Distances are difficult to estimate, given the meandering roads, and the uncertainty of the exact route in some parts of the march. Certainly the distance marched was greater than the mileage on more direct modern roads. Freeman's map suggests an estimate of eight miles from South Trenton to Quaker Bridge. Smith's map indicates approximately nine miles for the same part of the march. The distance from Quaker Bridge to Nassau Hall by the route that the American main body followed was between five and six miles. Rodney estimated that overall the army marched sixteen miles from the south side of Trenton to the backside of Princeton. Rodney's estimate was probably one or two miles on the high side. Freeman, *Washington*, 4:347; Rodney, *Diary*, 32 (3 Jan. 1777); Smith, *Princeton*, 14.

53. [Lawrence, Robert], *A Brief Narrative of the Ravages of the British and Hessians at Princeton in 1776–77: A Contemporary Account of the Battles of Trenton and Princeton*, ed. Varnum Lansing Collins (Princeton, 1906; rpt. New York, 1968). This account of twenty-four numbered folio pages was written very soon after the battle, passed down to Charles S. Olden, given to Stryker, purchased after his death by the Princeton University Library, and published by the university's reference librarian. The author was thought to be Thomas Olden, which cannot be the case, as he describes himself as eighty-four and Thomas Olden was born in 1735. More recently Samuel Smith has identified the author as Robert Lawrence, a prominent lawyer and colonial leader who was eighty-four years old in 1777. At the time of the battle he was staying with his son-in-law David Olden, in their house on the battlefield. Smith, *Princeton*, appendix D, 38; John E. Stillwell, *Historical and Genealogical Miscellany* (New York, 1940), 3:400.

54. Rodney, *Diary*, 32; Smith, *Princeton*, 19. On a cold day in December 2001, many reenactors of the battle at Princeton came hobbling painfully up the Quaker Bridge Road, as did this historian, who can testify to the effect of cold on feet, even when shod in modern hiking boots of high quality.

55. Smith explains that "this common 18th century practice was believed to make men brave" (*Princeton*, 19).

56. Rodney, *Diary*, 32 (3 Jan. 1777).

❧ The Battle at Princeton

1. Horace Walpole to Sir Horace Mann, in William S. Stryker, *The Battles of Trenton and Princeton* (Boston, 1898), 304.

2. Sir John Fortescue, *A History of the British Army*, 13 vols. in 20 (London, 1899–1930), 3:201.

3. James Wilkinson, *Memoirs of My Own Times*, 3 vols. (Philadelphia, 1816; rpt. 1973), 1:141.

4. On the terrain in the eighteenth century, with a deeper declivity than today, see Samuel Stelle Smith, *The Battle of Princeton* (Monmouth Beach, N.J., 1967), 20.

5. Ibid., 19, the most successful reconstruction.

6. Ibid.

7. Wilkinson, *Memoirs* 1:142.

8. Ibid.

9. Ibid., 144.

10. The Dutch doctor told this to the American officer Thomas Rodney, who entered it in his diary on January 18, 1777. It is in *The Diary of Captain Thomas Rodney, 1776–1777*, ed. Caesar A. Rodney, *Papers of the Historical Society of Delaware*, vol. 1, paper 8 (Wilmington, 1888; rpt. New York, 1974), 46–47 (18 Jan. 1777); manuscript original in Rodney Family Papers, LC.

11. Ensign George Inman, 17th Foot, "George Inman's Narrative of the American Revolution," *PMHB* 7 (1883), 237–48.

12. American eyewitness accounts suggest that Mawhood had more troops than have been identified in most histories of the battle: more infantry from the "details," in the column, and a larger force of artillery. This comes mainly from American descriptions by Thomas Rodney in his *Diary*, 32ff.; and J[oseph] White, *A Narrative of Events, As They Occurred from Time to Time, in the Revolutionary War, with an Account of the Battles of Trenton, Trenton-Bridge, and Princeton* (Charlestown, Mass., 1833; rpt. in *American Heritage*, June 1956, 74–79). Every secondary account has severely underestimated British strength in this engagement. Cf. Smith, *Princeton*, 21, for one example of many.

13. The letters written by Captain William Hale to his father, Admiral Hale of the Royal Navy, are a very valuable primary source, not used in any published account of the battle at Princeton. They are published as "Letters Written During the American War of Independence," in H. C. Wylly ed., *1913 Regimental Annual, The Sherwood Foresters* . . . (London, 1913), 9–59. The author is grateful to Mark Nichipur for calling them to his attention.

14. Hale, "Letters," 18.

15. Rodney observed that "on the hill behind the British line they had eight pieces of artillery, which played incessantly with round and grape shot on our brigade, and the fire was extremely hot" (*Diary*, 34 [3 Jan. 1777]). This would have been Mercer Hill, about eight hundred yards behind the British line. Most secondary accounts report that Mawhood brought two guns into action on the Clark farm, and he also captured two more. Cf. Smith, *Princeton*, 21; William M. Dwyer, *The Day Is Ours!* (New York, 1983), 338. Rodney's account tells us that the British advantage in artillery was very great in the early stages of the battle.

16. Mercer's brigade included remnants of some of Washington's best regiments which had been virtually destroyed in the fighting around New York, about 350 altogether. The largest unit was 200 Pennsylvania Riflemen of Miles's regiment. Read's regiment of Virginia infantry was reduced to twenty men; Smallwood's Maryland regiment was down to a "fragmant" of "perhaps equal size." Haslet's Delaware regiment had four officers and two privates. Rawling's Marylanders were also very few. Daniel Niel's New Jersey State Artillery was attached. Altogether the brigade included troops from five colonies: New Jersey, Pennsylvania, Maryland, Delaware, and Virginia.

17. Inman estimated the strength of the Seventeenth Foot at 224 rank and file; the dragoons were at least 50; Hale's company of grenadier recruits and draughts were more than 32; the light infantry might be assumed about the same; the Highlanders were a force large enough to be noticed by the Americans. After the departure of the Fifty-fifth Foot and artillery for Mercer's Hill, the British troops who followed Mawhood across the fields would have been between 400 and 500 men. Cf. Wm. Hale to Adm. Hale, 15 Jan. 1777, in Hale, "Letters," 18; Inman, "Narrative."

18. Sergeant R——, "The Battle of Princeton," first published in the Wellsborough *Pennsylvania Phenix*, 24 March 1832, rpt. as "The Battle of Princeton," *PMHB* 20 (1896), 517.

19. Williamsburg *Virginia Gazette*, 14 Jan. 1777.

20. Hale, "Letters," 18.

21. Ibid.

22. Wilkinson, *Memoirs* 1:143; Sergeant R——, "Battle of Princeton," 515–19.

23. On the death of Mercer, see Wilkinson, *Memoirs* 1:147; Benson J. Lossing, *Pictorial Field Book of the Revolution*, 2 vols. (New York, 1851; rpt. ed. Terence Barrow, Rutland, 1972), 2:29–30; Benjamin Rush, *Autobiography*, ed. George Corner (Princeton, 1948), 128–29; {Lawrence, Robert], *A Brief Narrative of the Ravages of the British and Hessians at Princeton in 1776–77: A Contemporary Account of the Battles of Trenton and Princeton*, ed. Varnum Lansing Collins (Princeton, 1906; rpt. New York, 1968), 42–43.

24. Hale, "Letters," 18.

25. Ibid.

26. Ibid.

27. White, *Narrative of Events*, 78; Hale, "Letters," 18.

28. "A young naval officer from Pennsylvania who had been granted leave to serve as a volunteer in the Jersey campaign," in George F. Scheer and Hugh F. Rankin, *Rebels and Redcoats* (Cleveland, 1957, rpt. 1987), 219.

29. Hale, "Letters."

30. Ibid., 18.

31. Wilkinson, *Memoirs* 1:145.

32. [Lawrence], *Brief Narrative*, 38.

33. Dwyer, *The Day Is Ours!*, 352; [Lawrence], *Brief Narrative*, 37.

34. Alfred Hoyt Bill, *The Campaign of Princeton, 1776–1777* (Princeton, 1948), 110–11.

35. Smith, *Princeton*, 27.

36. Bill, *Campaign of Princeton*, 112; Smith, *Princeton*, 27.

37. Hale, "Letters," 18; Inman, "Narrative," 240.

38. For details see appendix R above; also Inman, "Narrative," 240; Hale, "Letters," 18; White, *Narrative of Events*, 78; Rodney, *Diary*, 36; Stryker, *Battles of Trenton and Princeton*, 458.

39. George Washington to John Hancock, 5 Jan. 1777, *GW* 7:519–30.

40. Thomas Sullivan, *From Redcoat to Rebel: The Thomas Sullivan Journal*, ed. Joseph Lee Boyle (Bowie, Md., 1997), 100 (3 Jan. 1777).

41. Johann Ewald, *Diary of the American War: A Hessian Journal*, ed. Joseph P. Tustin (New Haven, 1979), 51 (3 Jan. 1777).

42. Douglas Southall Freeman, *George Washington: A Biography*, 7 vols. (New York, 1948–57), 4:357.

43. Ibid., 357–58; Thomas Glyn, "Ensign Glyn's Journal on the American Service with the Detachment of 1,000 Men of the Guards Commanded by Brigadier General Mathew in 1776," manuscript, PUL.

44. Freeman, *Washington* 4:358.

45. Ibid.

46. Ewald, *Diary*, 50.

47. Ibid.

48. *New-York Gazette and Weekly Mercury*, 13 Jan. 1777.

49. Bill, *Campaign of Princeton*, 125, 136.

50. Stryker, *Trenton and Princeton*, 464.

51. Allan Maclean to Alexander Cummings, 19 Feb. 1777, *A Prime Minister and His Son: From the Correspondence of the 3rd Earl of Bute and of Lt.-General the Hon. Sir Charles Stuart, K.B.*, ed. Mrs. E. Stuart Wortley (London, 1925), 105.

52. Capt. John Bowater to Earl of Denbigh, 22 May 1777, in Marion Balderston and David Syrett, eds., *The Lost War: Letters from British Officers During the American Revolution* (New York, 1975), 126.

53. Ira D. Gruber, *The Howe Brothers and the American Revolution* (New York, 1972), 156.

54. Howe to Germain, 20 Jan. 1777, CO5/95, PRO, as quoted in Gruber, *Howe Brothers*, 157; Bill, *Campaign of Princeton*, 127.

55. William Livingston to General Assembly, 24 Jan. 1777, *The Papers of William Livingston*, ed. Carl E. Prince, vol. 2 (Trenton, 1979), 202–3.

56. Thomas Nelson (Balto) to Thomas Jefferson, 2 Jan. 1777, *Papers of Thomas Jefferson*, ed. Julian Boyd (Princeton, 1950+), 2:3.

❧ Aftermath

1. George Washington, 20 Jan. 1777, *GW* 8:113.

2. Allan Maclean to Alexander Cummings, 19 Feb. 1777, in *A Prime Minister and His Son: From the Correspondence of the 3rd Earl of Bute and of Lt.-General the Hon. Sir Charles Stuart, K.B.*, ed. Mrs. E. Stuart Wortley (London, 1925), 103–7.

3. Andrew Mellick, Jr., *The Story of an Old Farm: or, Life in New Jersey in the Eighteenth Century* (Somerville, N.J., 1889), 387; William S. Stryker, *The Battles of Trenton and Princeton* (Boston, 1898), 301–2; Howard H. Peckham, *The Toll of Independence: Engagements and Battle Casualties of the American Revolution* (Chicago, 1974), 29.

4. Philipp Waldeck, *A Hessian Report . . . The Diary of Chaplain Philipp Waldeck (1776–1780)*, ed. Bruce Burgoyne, (Bowie, Md., 1995), 29 (3 Jan. 1777).

5. Ibid., 29 (5 Jan. 1777). Washington wrote of a report from General Maxwell, "advising that a party of militia attacked sixty Waldeckers this morning; killed ten, took the rest prisoners"; see George Washington to New York Committee of Safety, 5 Jan. 1777; Washington to John Hancock, 7 Jan. 1777; Washington to Pennsylvania Council of Safety, 8 Jan. 1777, *GW* 7:532; *Pennsylvania Evening Post* 14 Jan. 1777, *NJA* 2 1:256–57.
Waldeck reported the militia as four times the strength of the German patrol; American accounts reported that the two sides were of about the same strength. Both sides agreed on the number of Waldeck casualties, at eight or ten killed and wounded, and thirty-nine or forty captured with two officers. The militia were reported to have fought "without receiving the least damage." Washington sent the prisoners to Philadelphia: "45 rank and file of the Waldeck and Hessian troops."

6. George Washington to Jonathan Trumbull Sr., 10 Jan. 1777, *GW* 8:37; Washington to John Hancock, 9 Jan. 1777, ibid., 24, which reports that "Gen. Maxwell fell upon the Enemy's Rear and made seventy prisoners and took a parcel of Baggage."

7. Thomas Sullivan, *From Redcoat to Rebel: The Thomas Sullivan Journal*, ed. Joseph Lee Boyle (Bowie, Md., 1997), 102 (4 Jan. 1777).

8. George Washington to Jonathan Trumbull Sr., 6 March 1777, *GW* 8:531–32.

9. John Adams to Abigail Adams, 17 Feb. 1777, in L. H. Butterfield, ed., *The Adams Family Correspondence* (Cambridge, 1963), 2:162–63.

10. Pennsylvania Council of Safety to Washington, 29 Jan. 1777, and Israel Putnam to Washington, 8 Feb. 1777, *GW* 8:183–84, 278–80. The report of the Bedford commanders, Capt. William Macalevy, William Parker, and Samuel Davidson to Putnam, 7 Feb. 1777, is in the Washington Papers, LC, and on film at Brandeis University.

11. George Washington to Maj. Theodorick Bland, 30 Dec. 1776, *GW* 8:485.

12. "Return of American Forces in New Jersey," n.d. [March 15, 1777], *GW* 8:576. This strength return is missing from Charles H. Lesser, *The Sinews of Independence: Monthly Strength Reports of the Continental Army* (Chicago, 1976).

13. Harry M. Ward, *General William Maxwell and the New Jersey Continentals* (Westport, Conn., 1997), ix–x, 1–3, 16–21.

14. Howe's orders are in the *Kemble Papers*, 2 vols., NYHS *Collections* (New York, 1884–85), 1:434 (5 Jan. 1777).

15. American accounts appear in George Clinton, *Public Papers*, ed. Hugh Hastings and J. A. Holden (New York, 1899–1914), 1:534–537; Adrian C. Leiby, *Revolutionary War in the Hackensack Valley: The Jersey Dutch and the Neutral Ground* (New Brunswick, 1962), 102–7.

16. Philadelphia *Pennsylvania Journal and Weekly Advertiser,* 29 Jan. 1777; Leiby, *Revolutionary War in the Hackensack Valley,* 135.

17. *Pennsylvania Evening Post,* 30 Jan. 1777.

18. Johann Ewald, *Diary of the American War: A Hessian Journal,* ed. Joseph P. Tustin (New Haven, 1979), 51 (ca. 5–6 Jan. 1777).

19. Ibid.

20. Ibid.; John Peebles, *John Peebles' American War: The Diary of a Scottish Grenadier, 1776–1782,* ed. Ira Gruber (London, 1998), 93–94, 102, 104 (16–19 Feb., 2, 11, 19 March 1777).

21. Ibid.

22. Ibid.

23. Kemble, *Journal* 1:108 (11–18 Jan. 1777).

24. Ewald, *Diary,* 52 (Jan. 8–23, 1777).

25. Ibid., 55 (12 March 1777); on ration inventories see Edward E. Curtis, *The Organization of the British Army in the American Revolution* (New Haven, 1926), 172; R. Arthur Bowler, *Logistics and the Failure of the British Army in America, 1775–1783* (Princeton, 1975), 62–70; and David Syrett, *Shipping and the American War, 1775–83: A Study of British Transport Organization* (London, 1970), 121–36.

26. Philadelphia *Pennsylvania Journal and Weekly Advertiser,* 29 Jan. 1777.

27. Harry M. Ward, *Charles Scott and the Spirit of '76* (Charlottesville, 1988), 27–28.

28. Peckham, *The Toll of Independence,* 28–30.

29. Washington to Hancock, 14 Jan. 1777, *GW* 8:64.

30. The commanders included Sullivan at Chatham and Scotch Plains, with orders to patrol the "whole country between Quibbletown and the sound," Maxwell at Westfield, Stirling at Quibbletown, Adam Stephen at Metuchen, Greene at Basking Ridge, Lincoln at Bound Brook, Dickinson at Somerset, Warner at Millstone, and Putnam at Princeton. In addition New York General George Clinton was in Hackensack. See Washington to Joseph Reed, 14 Jan. 1777; Washington to Stirling, 4 Feb. 1777, Washington to Sullivan, 28 Jan. and 3 Feb. 1777; all *GW* 8:66–67, 245, 175, 237; Ward, *Maxwell,* 54.

31. Adam Stephen to Maj. Angus McDonald, 15 March 1777, in Ward, *Scott,* 31; Ambrose E. Vanderpoel, *History of Chatham, New Jersey* (Chatham, 1959), 187.

32. American accounts include George Washington to John Hancock, 22 Jan. 1777, *GW* 8:125; a British report is *Archibald Robertson, Lieutenant Colonel, Royal Engineers: His Diaries and Sketches in America, 1762–1780,* ed. Harry Miller Lydenberg (New York, 1930), 122 (20 Jan. 1777), which estimated British strength at five hundred and agreed on losses; a grossly inaccurate account at Howe's headquarters appears in *Kemble Papers* 1:108; newspaper reports include *Pennsylvania Journal and Weekly Advertiser,* 29 Jan. 1777, and *Pennsylvania Packet,* 18 Feb. 1777.

33. Washington to Hancock, 26 Jan. 1777, and Washington to William Livingston, 3 Feb. 1777, *GW* 8:161, 234; report of an anonymous American officer in Williamsburg *Virginia Gazette* (Purdie), 28 Feb. 1777; for a British account, *Kemble Papers,* 1:108 (22 Jan. 1777).

34. Peckham, *The Toll of Independence,* 30.

35. Washington to John Augustine Washington, 24 Feb. 1777, *GW* 8:439.

36. For American accounts, see Washington to William Livingston, 3 Feb. 1777, and Washington to John Hancock, 5 Feb. 1777, *GW* 8:234–35, 250; and *Pennsylvania Evening Post,* 6 Feb. 1777. Many eyewitness accounts appeared in Virginia newspapers including Purdie's *Virginia Gazette,* 28 Feb. and 14 Mar. 1777, and Dixon and Hunter's *Virginia Gazette,* 21 Feb. 1777; for British accounts, see *Kemble Papers* 1:109 (1 Feb. 1777). Kemble reported that "Colonel Harcourt commanded, not Sir William Erskine," and he estimated losses of "40 rebels" and "a few" prisoners against a loss of "20 men and one officer" on the British side." Another very inaccurate British newspaper account in the *New-York Gazette,* 10 Feb. 1777, reckoned American troops engaged at 4,000 under the command of Sullivan, with American losses at 250 men "killed on the spot," and British losses at 18 killed and wounded. For secondary accounts, Ward, *Scott,* 28–30; Jared C. Lobdell, "Two Forgotten Battles of the Revolutionary War," *NJH* 85 (1967), 225–34.

37. For British accounts see Robertson, *Diaries*, 124 (8 Feb. 1777); *New-York Gazette*, 17 Feb. 1777; for American accounts, Philemon Dickinson to Washington, 9 Feb. 1777, *GW* 8:286.

38. Ward, *Maxwell*, 55.

39. Peebles, *Diary*, 98 (24 Feb. 1777).

40. Ibid.

41. Ward, *Maxwell*, 57; *Pennsylvania Journal*, 19 March 1777; *Pennsylvania Evening Post*, 15 March 1777; *New-York Gazette*, 24 March 1777; George Doremus, *The American Revolution in Morris County* (Rockaway, N.J., 1976), 43.

42. Charles Stuart to Lord Bute, 29 March 1777, in *A Prime Minister and His Son: From the Correspondence of the 3rd Earl of Bute and of Lt.-General the Hon. Sir Charles Stuart, K.B.*, ed. Mrs. E. Stuart Wortley (London, 1925), 103.

43. Allan Maclean to Alexander Cummings, 19 Feb. 1777, ibid., 104.

44. Colonel William Harcourt to Earl Harcourt [his father], 17 March 1777, in Edward W. Harcourt, ed., *The Harcourt Papers* (Oxford, n.d.), 11:208.

45. Charles Stuart to Lord Bute, 29 March 29, 1777, Wortley, *A Prime Minister and His Son*, 101.

46. Ewald, *Diary*, 52 (5 Jan. 1777).

47. *Pennsylvania Gazette*, 5 Feb. 1777.

48. Nathanael Greene to Thomas Paine, 9 Jan. 1777, in *Papers of General Nathanael Greene*, ed. Richard K. Showman (Chapel Hill, 1976+), 2:3; George Washington to Nicholas Cooke, 20 Jan. 1777, *GW* 8:113–14.

49. Incomplete casualty reports from New Jersey in the period from January 4 to March 21, 1777, indicate that 954 British and German soldiers were killed, seriously wounded, and captured in 23 engagements during the twelve weeks that followed the battle of Princeton. That number includes only engagements for which losses were reported. Many other engagements also caused casualties but were not recorded.

Adding a lower-bound estimate of 954 battle casualties in the Forage War after January 3 to losses at Trenton and Princeton, Howe's army lost a minimum of 2,887 battle casualties in New Jersey from December 25 to March 21, 1777. For details, data, and sources, see appendices T and U.

50. Official strength reports; for numbers and sources see appendix B.

51. Some historians have doubted the claims of Greene and Washington, but the evidence is strong. On January 8, 1776, Howe's staff reported a total strength of 22,957, of whom 14,000 were "effective men." Ineffectives, mostly wounded and ill, were 8,957 on that date. In addition, Howe lost approximately 2,900 battle casualties in the Trenton and Princeton campaign and the Forage War, from December 25, 1776, to February 28, 1777, and many more to other causes. Altogether General Howe lost between 40 and 50 percent of his effective strength during the fall and winter campaign, mostly to illness and malnutrition. The source is *Kemble Papers* 1:107 (8 Jan. 1777) and appendices N–U.

52. Charles Stuart to Lord Bute, 29 March 1777, in Wortley, *A Prime Minister and His Son*, 101.

53. Howe to Germain, 17 and 20 Jan. 1777, CO 5/94, PRO; Gruber, *Howe Brothers*, 183, 193.

54. Howe to Germain, 20 Nov., 20 Dec. 1776; 31 Jan. 1777, co 5/94, PRO.

55. Stuart to Bute, n.d. [spring 1777], in Wortley, *A Prime Minister and His Son*, 94.

56. Allan Maclean to Alexander Cummings, 19 Feb. 1777, ibid., 105.

57. Col. William Harcourt to Earl Harcourt, 31 May 1777, *Harcourt Papers* 11:214–16.

58. Ibid.

59. Col. Carl von Donop to Friedrich Wilhelm, Prince of Prussia [not the Landgraf of Hesse-Cassel], 6 Jan. 1777, in "Letters from a Hessian Mercenary," ed. Hans Huth, *PMHB* 62 (1938), 488–501.

60. Horace Walpole to Sir Horace Mann, 27 Feb. and 4 April 4, 1777, in Alfred Hoyt Bill, *The Campaign of Princeton, 1776–1777* (Princeton, 1948), 136; for Loyalists on Washington see Consider Tiffany, "His Story," ms, LC.

61. Bill, *Campaign of Princeton*, 121.

62. *Pennsylvania Evening Post*, 7 Jan. 1777; facsimile in *GW* 8:2.

63. G.W.P. Custis, *Recollections and Private Memoirs of Washington, by His Adopted Son . . .* (1859; rpt. Bridgewater, Va., 1999), 170–71.

❧ Conclusion

1. General William Maxwell to General Adam Stephen, 10 April 1777, Stephen Papers, LC, as quoted in Harry M. Ward, *General William Maxwell and the New Jersey Continentals* (Westport, Conn., 1997), 59, 197.

2. Robert Morris to George Washington, 1 Jan. 1777; similar mood appeared in Washington to Morris, 26 Dec. 1776; both *GW* 8:508.

3. Howe's orders are in the *Kemble Papers*, 2 vols., NYHS *Collections* (New York, 1884–85), 1:434 (5 Jan. 1777).

4. Sidney Homer and Richard Sylla, *A History of Interest Rates*, 3d ed. rev. (New Brunswick, 1992), 161.

5. Among many examples see Washington's deference to New York authorities on a problem concerning Loyalists, and to the Marine Committee on naval questions, in Washington to Heath, 12 Jan. 1777, and Washington to John Hancock, 26 Jan. 1777, *GW* 8:48, 160.

6. Washington to John Hancock, 5 Jan. 1777, *GW* 7:521.

7. Washington to Benedict Arnold, 3 March 1777, *GW* 8:493.

8. "Council of War," 2 May 1777, on a plan docketed "April 1777," *GW* 8:324–25.

9. George Otto Trevelyan, *American Revolution*, 4 vols. (New York and London, 1898–1926), 3:124.

10. For tempo in war, see the work of Colonel John Boyd, a leading architect of American military doctrine in the late twentieth and early twenty-first centuries, and the principles that were put to work in the Gulf War and the Iraq War. Robert Coram, *Boyd: The Fighter Pilot Who Changed the Art of War* (Boston, 2002), which reprints Boyd's essay "Destruction and Creation," 451–60; also Grant T. Hammond, *The Mind of War: John Boyd and American Security* (Washington, 2001); and General A. M. Gray et al., *Warfighting*, Fleet Marine Force Manual FMF1 (Washington, 1989), an official summary of Marine Corps doctrine, similar in many ways to Boyd's thinking.

11. Howe to Germain, 20 Jan. 1777, CO5/95, PRO.

12. Washington to Joseph Reed, 14 Jan. 1776, *GW* 8:67.

13. Robert Morris to George Washington, 27 Feb. 1777, *GW* 8:456–57.

14. On February 12, 1777, the ship *Le Mercure* sailed from France with twelve thousand arms and a thousand barrels of powder and reached Portsmouth, New Hampshire, safely six weeks later. Shortly afterward, the brigantine *Sally* arrived at Philadelphia from France with a cargo of eleven thousand stand of arms "fit for immediate use," plus many gunlocks and flints. Hancock to Washington, 26 March 1777, and Ebenezer Hazard to Washington, 26 March 1777, *GW* 8:637–38.

15. Jac Weller, "Guns of Destiny: Field Artillery in the Trenton-Princeton Campaign, 25 December 1776 to 3 January 1777," *Military Affairs* 29 (1956), 1–15; J[oseph] White, *A Narrative of Events, As They Occurred from Time to Time, in the Revolutionary War, with an Account of the Battles of Trenton, Trenton-Bridge, and Princeton* (Charlestown, Mass., 1833; rpt. in *American Heritage*, June 1956, 74–79); for a quantitative review of this evidence see appendix M.

16. Heath to Washington, 24 Jan. 1777; William Duer to Washington, 28 Jan. 1777; Washington, Instructions to Nathaniel Sackett "for secret service," 4 Feb. 1777; Nathaniel Sackett to Washington, 7 Apr. 1777; all *GW* 8:145–47, 170–72, 242–43, 9:79–82. The legend of Robert Honeyman has inspired a large literature. Honeyman was said to be a man of Scotch-Irish ancestry who was an open Tory and a secret agent for George Washington. Some writers claim that Honeyman moved back and forth between the armies as a double

agent. Others think that he visited Trenton and kept Washington informed about the garrison. Some claim that he was arrested by Washington, then allowed to make his escape to Trenton, where he went to Colonel Rall and reported that the American army was starving, mutinous, and incapable of attacking, which led Rall to relax his guard and have a drunken celebration on Christmas night. Another legend is that Honeyman was protected from persecution as a Tory by the secret intervention of Washington, which is claimed as confirmation.

Some parts of these stories are clearly mistaken, and interlock with myths such as the drunken Hessians. No major element is confirmed by evidence contemporary with the event. It is possible that evidence may turn up to prove that Honeyman may indeed have been one of many people employed by Washington as a spy or agent, but in its absence the story is very doubtful, and no use is made of it here.

Many essays represent the story as fact; none support it with evidence. Compare Thomas Fleming, "George Washington, Spymaster Extraordinary," www.thomasfleming.writer.com/ gwashspy.ht; Leonard Falkner, "A Spy for Washington," *American Heritage*, August 1957; A.V.D. Honeyman, "An Unwritten Account of a Spy of Washington," *Our Home* 1 (1873), rpt. in *NJH* 85 (1967), 219–24; Garrett Husveth, "John Honeyman: Colonial Spy," *AGS Quarterly* (May 2002); C. G. Wolfe, "The Spy Who Came from Lamington," *Black River Journal* 2 (2001), 7–9, 20–23.

17. John Adams to Abigail Adams, 17 Feb. 1777, *Adams Family Correspondence*, ed. Lyman Butterfield, 2 vols. (Cambridge, 1963), 2:163.

18. Ibid.

19. Capt. John Bowater to Earl of Denbigh, 4 April 1777, in Marion Balderston and David Syrett, eds., *The Lost War: Letters from British Officers During the American Revolution* (New York, 1975), 122.

20. Ibid.

21. Charles Stuart to Earl of Bute, 16 Sept. 1778, in *A Prime Minister and His Son: From the Correspondence of the 3rd Earl of Bute and of Lt.-General the Hon. Sir Charles Stuart, K.B.*, ed. Mrs. E. Stuart Wortley (London, 1925), 132.

22. François-Jean, Marquis de Chastellux, *Travels in North America in the Years 1780, 1781, and 1782*, ed. Howard C. Rice Jr., 2 vols. (Chapel Hill, 1963), 1:158.

23. Jared C. Lobdell, "Two Forgotten Battles of the Revolutionary War," *NJH* 85 (1967), 227; Harry M. Ward, *Charles Scott and the Spirit of '76* (Charlottesville, 1988), 29–30.

24. Stephen to Erskine, 4 Feb 1777, and Erskine to Stephen, n.d, in *Pennsylvania Evening Post*, 10 May 1777; *NJA* 2, 1:364–67; affidavits by American surgeons who documented the facts in detail are in the Papers of the Continental Congress.

25. *The Revolutionary Services of John Greenwood of Boston*, ed. Isaac J. Greenwood (New York, 1922), rpt. as *The Wartime Services of John Greenwood: A Young Patriot in the American Revolution* (n.p., Westvaco Corporation, 1981), 91n.

26. Journal, 25 [26] Dec. 1776.

27. Bruce Burgoyne, ed., *Enemy Views: The American Revolutionary War as Recorded by the Hessian Participants* (Bowie, Md., 1996), 131.

28. Ibid.

29. E. J. Lowell, *The Hessians and Other German Auxiliaries of Great Britain in the Revolutionary War* (1884), 107.

30. Washington to Samuel Blachley Webb, 8 Jan. 1777, *GW* 8:16.

❧ Historiography

1. Henry M. Muhlenberg, *The Journals of Henry Melchior Muhlenberg*, trans. Theodore G. Tappert and John W. Doberstein, 3 vols. (Philadelphia, 1942), 2:768 (28 Dec. 1776).

2. Ibid.

3. William Hull to Andrew Adams, 1 Jan. 1777, in William Stryker, *The Battles of Trenton and Princeton* (Boston, 1898), 376; Page Smith, "David Ramsay and the Causes of the American Revolution," *WMQ3* 18 (1960), 51–77.

4. Ambrose Serle, *The American Journal of Ambrose Serle, Secretary to Lord Howe, 1776–1778*, ed. Edward H. Tatum Jr. (San Marino, Calif., 1940), 163, 165–71, 173.

5. Stephen Kemble, *The Kemble Papers*, 2 vols., NYHS *Collections* (New York, 1884–85), *Journal* 1:105 (30–31 Dec. 1776).

6. John Greenwood, *The Revolutionary Services of John Greenwood of Boston*, ed. Isaac J. Greenwood (New York, 1922), rpt. as *The Wartime Services of John Greenwood: A Young Patriot in the American Revolution* (n.p., Westvaco Corporation, 1981), 82.

7. Howe wrote, "This misfortune seems to have proceeded from Colonel Rall's quitting his post and advancing to the attack, instead of defending the village," a miscomprehension of the event. Howe to Germain, 29 Dec. 1776; in later dispatches Howe blamed Donop for marching to Mount Holly, and Hessian generals in America, who had no part of the event, and the Hessian army as a whole. Stryker, *Trenton and Princeton*, 219–20; Nicholas Cresswell, *Journal of Nicholas Cresswell*, ed. Samuel Thornely (New York, 1924), 91; Rodney Atwood, *The Hessians: Mercenaries from Hessen-Kassel in the American Revolution* (Cambridge, 1980), 100, 106.

8. E.A.H. Webb, *A History of the Services of the 17th (the Leicestershire) Regiment* (London, 1911), 70–73; J. W. Fortescue, *A History of the British Army*, 13 vols. in 20 (London, 1899–1930), 3:201.

9. Joseph Galloway, *Letters to a Nobleman on the Conduct of the War in the Middle Colonies* (London, 1780), 51–52; Atwood, *Hessians*, 89, 95.

10. For discussions of this controversy, see Troyer Steele Anderson, *The Command of the Howe Brothers During the American Revolution* (Oxford, 1936), which is strongly supportive of the Howes; and Ira D. Gruber, *The Howe Brothers and the American Revolution* (New York, 1972), the best and most balanced account. Israel Mauduit's set of the pamphlets in this controversy are in the Massachusetts Historical Society.

11. Johann Ewald, *Diary of the American War: A Hessian Journal*, ed. Joseph P. Tustin (New Haven, 1979), 45.

12. Mirabeau, *Avis aix Hessois et autre peuples de l'Allemagne Vendus par leurs princes à l'Angleterre* (Cleves, 1777), 16; [Benjamin Franklin], "From the Count de Schaumbergh to the Baron Hohendorf, commanding the Hessian troops in America," 18 Feb. 1777, commonly called in English and American literature "The Sale of the Hessians." In German literature it is known as the *Uriasbrief.* The leading study is Philipp Losch, "Der Uriasbrief des Grafen von Schaumberg," *Hessische Chronik. Monatsschrift für Familien- und Ortsgeschichte in Hessen und Hessen-Nassau* 2 (1913), 37–40, 83–88, 99–105; Martin Ernst von Schlieffen, *Des Hessois en Amerique, de Leur Souverain et des Declamateurs* (n.p., 1782). The original French texts of Mirabeau and Schlieffen with German translations appear in Holger Hamecher, ed., *Mirabeau, Schlieffen und die nach Amerika verkauften Hessen; Zwei zeitgenössische Pamphlete zum "Soldatenhandel" für den Amerikanischen Unabhängigkeitskrieg* (Kassel, 1991).

13. *Pennsylvania Journal*, 19 Feb. 1777.

14. Charles Botta, *Storia della Guerra dell' Independenza degli Stati Uniti d'America*, 4 vols. (Milan, 1809), trans. George A. Otis as *History of the War of Independence of the United states of America*, 2 vols. (Philadelphia, 1821, 1826, 1837, 1845), 1:422. An electronic edition of the 1826 in CD-ROM and download versions is available from the Brave Electronic Publisher.

15. John Marshall, *Life of George Washington*, 5 vols. (Philadelphia and London, 1804–7); 2 vols. (Philadelphia, 1833), 1:134.

16. William Gordon, *History of the Rise, Progress, and Establishment of the Independence of the United States of America*, 4 vols. (London, 1788); 3 vols. (New York, 1789, 1794). For extensive borrowing from the *Annual Register* see O. G. Libby in *Annual Report of the American Historical Association for the Year 1899* 1:367–88; and Lynn Turner in *American Historical Review*.

17. Peale's son Titian wrote of this flag in the Washington portrait, "I don't know that I ever heard my father speak of that flag, but the trophies at Washington's feet I know he painted from the flags then captured, and which were left with him for the purpose. He was always very particular in matters of historic record in his pictures." David Hackett Fischer, *Liberty and Freedom*, forthcoming.

18. The original painting is in the Pennsylvania Academy of Fine Arts. Copies are at Colonial Williamsburg, Yale, Mount Vernon, Princeton, and New York's Metropolitan Museum of Art (2). Others change the background to Yorktown and are at the Maryland State House in Annapolis and the Château Rochambeau at Vendôme. Another copy by Samuel Smith is in Independence Hall. See Edward W. Richardson, *Standards and Colors of the American Revolution* (Philadelphia, 1982); Samuel Stelle Smith, *The Battle of Trenton* (Monmouth Beach, N.J., 1965); Charles Coleman Sellers, *Portraits and Miniatures by Charles Willson Peale* (Philadelphia, 1952), and *Supplement* (1969); idem, *Charles Willson Peale: A Biography* (New York, 1969).

Richardson believes that Washington's headquarters flag was created "sometime after the flag resolution of June 14, 1777" (*Standards and Colors of the American Revolution*, 19). Whitney Smith thinks that Washington's "personal command flag" might have come first, and describes the hypothesis of its "possible influence" on the flag resolution as one of several "plausible theories." Whitney Smith, *Flags Through the Ages and Around the World* (New York, 1975), 193.

19. Theodore Sizer, ed., *The Autobiography of John Trumbull* (New Haven, 1953), 170–71.

20. Ibid., 171.

21. Theodore Sizer, ed., *The Works of Colonel John Trumbull*, rev. ed. (New Haven, 1967), frontispiece, fig. 95; also engraved by Asher Durant (1834).

22. Garry Wills, *Cincinnatus: George Washington and the Enlightenment: Images of Power in Early America* (Garden City, 1984), 61, on the moral meaning of left and right, which doesn't work for most of Trumbull's paintings, but a moral contrast is always very clear.

23. Ibid., 105–6; Linda Bantel et al., *William Rush: American Sculptor* (Philadelphia, 1982), 26.

24. Quoted in David Levin, *History as Romantic Art* (Stanford, 1959), 3.

25. Citations here are to Washington Irving, *The Life of George Washington* (1854–58; rev. ed., 4 vols. in 2, New York, Crowell, n.d.), 2:235–38.

26. Ibid., vol. 2, chaps 9–35; for Washington's conflicted character, 2:151, 195.

27. Wills, *Cincinnatus*, 246.

28. Herbert Butterfield, *The Whig Interpretation of History* (London, 1959).

29. Russel B. Nye, *George Bancroft: Brahmin Rebel* (New York, 1944).

30. George Bancroft, *The History of the United States from the Discovery of the Continent*, 10 vols. (Boston, 1834–1875); idem, *History of the Formation of the Constitution of the United States of America*, 2 vols. (New York, 1882).

31. Bancroft, *History of the United States*, 4:5–11.

32. Ibid., 9:235, 254.

33. George Otto Trevelyan, *The American Revolution*, 4 vols. (London and New York, 1898–1907); Edmund Morgan, *The American Revolution: Two Centuries of Interpretation* (Englewood Cliffs, N.J., 1965), 180.

34. This theme was specially strong in Trevelyan's *George the Third and Charles Fox: The Concluding Part of the American Revolution*, 2 vols. (London and New York, 1912–14), 1:8–12, 213–28.

35. Trevelyan, *American Revolution*, 3:152–53.

36. Trevelyan, *American Revolution*, new ed. (1917), 3:x.

37. Max von Eelking, *Die Deutschen Hülfstruppen im nordamerikanischen Befreiungskriege 1776 bis 1876*, 2 vols. (Hanover, 1864; rpt. Cassel 1976); abridged English trans. by J. G. Rosengarten, *The German Allied Troops in the North American War of Independence* (Albany, 1893: rpt. Bowie, Md., 1987).

38. Ibid., 74.

39. Ibid., 8–9, 74, 256.

40. Friedrich Kapp, *Der Soldatenhandel deutscher Fürsten nach Amerika* (Berlin, 1864, rpt. Munich, n.d.).

41. Ibid., 231–99.

42. Ibid., 65, 92, 233ff.

43. Nancy Rash, *The Painting and Politics of George Caleb Bingham* (New Haven, 1991), 221.

44. Lord Mahon, *The Life of the Right Honorable William Pitt . . .* , 4 vols. (London, 1861–62), still a valuable life-and-letters biography, and the *History of the War of Succession in Spain, 1702–1714* (London, 1832), drawn from the papers of his ancestor the first Earl of Stanhope, and *The History of England from the Peace of Utrecht to the Peace of Versailles, 1713–1783*, 7 vols. (London, 1836–53), also an abridged American edition. Citations below are to the author's set, of the fifth edition revised (London, 1858).

45. Lord Mahon, *History of England* 6:129 and note.

46. E.g., Stryker, *Battles of Trenton and Princeton*, 90n; John G. Palfrey, "Lord Mahon's History of England," *North American Review* 75 (1852), 185–208; George H. Calcott, "The Sacred Quotation Mark," *The Historian* 21 (1959), 409–20; Frank O. Gatell, *John Gorham Palfrey and the New England Conscience* (Cambridge, 1963), 222–23.

47. James Kirby Martin, *Benedict Arnold: Revolutionary Hero* (New York, 1997), 292.

48. Washington to Arnold, 14 Dec. 1776, and Gates to Washington, 17 Dec. 1776, *GW* 7:331, 361; for references to the decision to attack Trenton, see Robert Morris to Washington, 21 Dec. 21, 1776, and Israel Putnam, 21 Dec. 1776, *GW* 7:403, 405.

49. Quoted in Ann Hawkes Hutton, *Portrait of Patriotism* (Radnor, Pa., 1959), 128–29.

50. Stryker, *Battles of Trenton and Princeton*.

51. Ibid., iii–vi; see appendix X for a discussion of particular source problems.

52. Ibid., 306–7.

53. Henry Phelps Johnston, *The Campaign of 1776 Around New York* (New York, 1878), and *The Battle of Harlem Heights* (New York, 1897). Brief biographies of Johnston appear in the *Fifty Years Meeting of the Yale Class of 1862* (New Haven, 1862); *New York Times*, 3 March 1923; and *Dictionary of American Biography*.

54. Barbara J. Mitnick, *George Washington: American Symbol* (New York, 1999), 47.

55. Allan Marquand et al., *The Princeton Battle Monument* (Princeton, 1922), 7–21, 40–41.

56. David Hackett Fischer, *Historians' Fallacies* (New York, 1970), 139.

57. *Chicago Tribune*, 15 May and 23 June 1916; Carol Gelderman, *Henry Ford: The Wayward Capitalist* (New York, 1981), 177–80.

58. Sydney George Fisher, "The Legendary and Mythmaking Process in the History of the American Revolution," *APSP* 51 (1912), 53–75.

59. Charles Kendall Adams, "Some Neglected Aspects of the Revolutionary War," *Atlantic Monthly* 82 (1898), 174–75, 177–89.

60. William E. Woodward, *Bunk* (New York, 1923); idem, *George Washington, The Image and the Man* (New York, 1926).

61. Rupert Hughes, *George Washington*, 3 vols. (New York, 1926–30), 3:689–990.

62. Wanda M. Corn, *Grant Wood: The Regionalist Vision* (New Haven, 1983), an excellent work from which much of what follows is drawn; also helpful is Darrell Garwood, *Artist in Iowa: A Life of Grant Wood* (New York, 1944), 137.

63. Corn, *Grant Wood*, 98; Thomas Craven, "Grant Wood," *Scribners* 101 (1937), 18.

64. Quoted in Corn, *Grant Wood*, 100.

65. Quoted ibid., 101.

66. Philipp Losch, *Kurfürst Wilhelm I, Landgraf von Hessen: Ein Fürstenbild aus der Zopfzeit* (Marburg, 1923).

67. Philipp Losch, *Soldatenhandel: Mit einem Verzeichnis der Hessen-Kasselischen Subsidienverträge und einer Bibliographie* (Kassel, 1933; rpt. 1974).

68. Julian Boyd, *Anglo-American Union: Joseph Galloway's Plans to Preserve the British Empire* (Philadelphia, 1941); Leonard W. Labaree, "The Nature of American Loyalism," *AAS Proceedings* 54 (1944), 15–58; idem, *Conservatism in American History* (New York, 1948).

69. Howard Fast, *Being Red* (Boston, 1990); idem, *The Naked God* (1957); Adam Wald, "Howard Fast (b. 1914)," in *Encyclopedia of the American Left* (Urbana, 1992).

70. Frank Campenni, "Citizen Howard Fast: A Critical Biography," www.trussel.com/hf/campenni.htm.

71. Howard Fast, *The Crossing*, 201–2.

72. Ibid., 25, 42, 53, 54, 90, 105, 127.

73. Douglas A. Jeffrey, "Fiction Parades as Fact in A&E's 'The Crossing,'" Claremont Institute, 1999, www.claremont.org.

74. I am much in debt to David E. Johnson and his excellent biography, *Douglas Southall Freeman* (Gretna, 2002); also helpful is Dumas Malone, "The Pen of Douglas Southall Freeman," in *George Washington*, vol. 6, *Patriot and President* (New York, 1954), xi–xxxi.

75. As quoted in Johnson, *Freeman*, 103.

76. Ibid., 304.

77. Ibid., 119–20.

78. Samuel Stelle Smith, *The Battle of Monmouth* (Monmouth Beach, N.J., 1964), *The Battle of Trenton* (1965), *The Battle of Princeton* (1967), *The Fight for the Delaware* (1970), *The Battle of Brandywine* (1976); John F. Reed, *Valley Forge, Crucible of Victory* (1970); John Elting, *The Battle of Bunker's Hill* (1975), *The Battles of Saratoga* (1977); Peter J. Guthorn, *American Maps and Mapmakers of the Revolution* (1966), *British Maps of the American Revolution* (1972); and other titles.

79. Ernst Kipping, *Die Truppen von Hessen-Kassel im Amerikanischen Unabhängigkeitskrieg 1777–1783* (Darmstadt, 1965); idem, *The Hessian View of American 1776–1783* (Monmouth Beach, N.J., 1971), 22; Ernst Kipping and Samuel Stelle Smith, eds., *At General Howe's Side, 1776–1778: The Diary of General William Howe's Aide-de-Camp, Captain Friedrich von Muenchausen* (Monmouth Beach, N.J., 1974).

80. Johann Ewald, *Diary of the American War: A Hessian Journal*, ed. Joseph P. Tustin (New Haven, 1979).

81. Robin Higham, ed., *Official Histories: Essays and Bibliographies from Around the World* (Manhattan, Kans., 1970); idem, ed., *Official Military Historical Offices and Sources*, 2 vols. (Westport, Conn., 2000).

82. Robert Wright, *The Continental Army* (Washington, 1983, 1989), ii.

83. William James Morgan, ed., *Naval Documents of the American Revolution*, vol. 5 (American theater: May 9, 1776–July 31, 1776), vol. 6 (American theater: August. 1, 1776–Oct. 31, 1776; European theater: May 26 1776–Oct. 5, 1776), vol. 7 (American theater: Nov. 1, 1776–Feb. 28, 1777; European theater: Oct. 6, 1776–Dec. 31, 1776) (Washington, 1970, 1972, 1976). Stanley J. Underdal, ed., *Military History of the American Revolution* (Washington, 1976).

84. Dave R. Palmer, *The Way of the Fox: American Strategy in the War for America, 1775–1783* (Westport, Conn., 1975); idem, *George Washington, First in War* (Mount Vernon, 2000).

85. Thomas Jefferson Wertenbaker, "The Battle of Princeton," in Allen Marquand et al., *The Princeton Battle Monument* (Princeton, 1922), 51–123, an excellent essay. Fifty years later John Shy delivered a lecture on the same subject for the bicentennial celebration.

86. Horst Dipple, *Deutschland und die amerikanische Revolution* (diss., University of Cologne, 1970), trans. by Bernhard A. Uhlendorf as *Germany and the American Revolution, 1770–1800: A Sociohistorical Investigation of Late Eighteenth-Century Political Thinking* (Chapel Hill, 1977); idem, *Americana Germanica, 1770–1800: Bibliographie deutscher Amerika-literatur* (Stuttgart, 1976); idem, *Germany and the American Revolution, 1770–1800* (Chapel Hill, 1977); Charles W. Ingrao, *The Hessian Military State: Ideas, Institutions, and Refom Under Frederick II, 1760–1785* (Cambridge, 1987); Peter K. Taylor, *Indentured to Liberty: Peasant Life and the Hessian Military State, 1688–1815* (Ithaca, 1994).

87. Fritz Redlich, *The German Military Enterpriser and His Work Force: A Study in European Economic and Social History* 2 vols., *VSW* vols. 47–48 (Wiesbaden, 1964–65).

88. Richard M. Ketchum, *The Decisive Day: The Battle of Bunker Hill* (New York, 1962, 1974); *The Winter Soldiers: The Battles for Trenton and Princeton* (New York, 1973); *Saratoga: Turning Point of America's Revolutionary War* (New York, 1997); *Divided Loyalties: How the American Revolution Came to New York* (New York, 2002).

89. Bill Mauldin, *Mud and Guts: A Look at the Common Soldier of the American Revolution* (Washington, 1978), 33.

90. Ibid., frontispiece, 8.

91. Ibid., 58.

92. W. H. Auden, *The Age of Anxiety* (New York, 1947); also in *Collected Longer Poems* (New York, 1969), 253–353.

93. Brad Gooch, *City Poet: The Life and Times of Frank O'Hara* (1993); Larry Rivers, interview with Frank O'Hara quoted in Marjorie Perloff, *Frank O'Hara: Poet Among Painters* (1977); www.english.uiuc.edui/maps/poets/m_r/ohara/rivers/htm.

94. Perloff, *Frank O'Hara*.

95. Ibid.

96. *Webster's New World Dictionary* (2d college ed., 1970) defined "low-down" as "[slang] the true, pertinent facts; esp., secret or inside information (with *the*); *adj.* [Colloq.] mean; contemptible; despicable."

97. Richard Bissell, *New Light on 1776* (Boston, 1775), 102.

98. E. Wayne Carp, *To Starve the Army at Pleasure: Continental Army Administration and American Political Culture, 1775–1783* (Chapel Hill, 1984), 14.

99. Peter Saul, "George Washington Crossing the Delaware" (Franklin Galleries, 1975).

100. Gary Nash, *The Urban Crucible: Social Change, Political Consciousness, and the Origins of the American Revolution* (Cambridge, 1979); Eric Foner, *Tom Paine and Revolutionary America* (New York, 1976); Alfred F. Young, ed., *The American Revolution* (De Kalb, 1976); idem, *The Shoemaker and the Tea Party* (Boston, 1999).

101. Steven Rosswurm, *Arms, Country, and Class: The Philadelphia Militia and the "Lower Sort" During the American Revolution, 1775–1783* (New Brunswick, 1987); Charles Patrick Neimeyer, *America Goes to War: A Social History of the Continental Army* (New York, 1996); Sylvia Frey, *Water from the Rock: Black Resistance in a Revolutionary Age* (Princeton, 1991); Holly A. Mayer, *Belonging to the Army: Camp Followers and Community During the American Revolution* (Columbia, S.C., 1996).

102. Neimeyer, *America Goes to War*, xiii.

103. Mitnick, *George Washington*, 174, quoting Jim Waltzer, "In Profile: Robert Colescott," *Art and Antiques* 20 (1997), 104; also Sharon Fitzgerald, "Robert Colescott Rocks the Boat," *American Visions* 12 (1997). 14–16.

104. *Journal of the Johannes Schalm Historical Association* 1 (1977)–present.

105. Jared Sparks, ed., *The Writings of George Washington*, 12 vols. (Boston, 1834–37); Worthington C. Ford, ed., *The Washington Papers*, 14 vols. (New York, 1892); John C. Fitzpatrick, ed. *The Writings of George washington*, 39 vols. (Washington, 1931–44); W. W. Abbot, Dorothy Twohig, Philander C. Chase, and Beverly H. Runge, eds., *The Papers of George Washington*, ca. 85 volumes when complete (Charlottesville, 1983+).

106. Sandow Birk, letter to the author, August 22, 2003; Tyler Stallings, ed., *Sandow Birk's "In Smog and Thunder: Historical Works from the Great War of the Californias,"* with commentary on CD-ROM written by Sandow Birk and Paul Zaloom (San Francisco, 2000, 2002), 68; with thanks to the artist.

SOURCES FOR MAPS

Map 1: Friedrich Kapp, *Der Soldatenhandel deutscher Fürsten nach Amerika* (Berlin, 1864; rpt. Munich, n.d.), 266–68; Philipp Losch, *Soldatenhandel: Mit einem Verzeichnis der Hessen-Kassilischen Subsidienverträge und einer Bibliographie* (1933; rpt. Kassel, 1974), 7–16; Charles W. Ingrao, *The Hessian Mercenary State: Ideas, Institutions, and Reform Under Frederick II* (Cambridge, 1987), 27; Peter K. Taylor, *Indentured to Liberty: Peasant Life and the Hessian Military State* (Ithaca, 1994), ii; Rodney Atwood, *The Hessians: Mercenaries from Hessen-Kassel in the American Revolution* (Cambridge, 1980), 256; Ernst Kipping, *The Hessian View of America, 1776–1783* (Monmouth Beach, N.J., 1971), 4.

Map 2: Henry P. Johnston, *The Campaign of 1776 around New York and Brooklyn* (Brooklyn, 1878), map facing 300, documents, 2:5–194; John Ewing, "Draught of the Engagement at Long Island," ibid. 2:50; Ira D. Gruber, "America's First Battle: Long Island, 27 August 1776," in Charles E. Heller and William A. Stofft, eds., *America's First Battles, 1776–1965* (Lawrence, Kan., 1986), 1–32; "A Plan of New York with Part of Long Island" (London, 1776); Douglas Southall Freeman, *George Washington: A Biography*, 7 vols. (New York, 1948–57), 4:160–61, 172, 185, 199, 213, 220, 228; situation maps in Mark Boatner, ed., *Encyclopedia of the American Revolution* (Mechanicsburg, Pa., 1994), 648–53; map by Jeffrey Ward in Barnet Schecter, *The Battle for New York* (New York, 2002), 133.

Map 3: Maps by Rafael Palacios in Bruce Bliven, *Battle for Manhattan* (New York, 1955–56), endpapers; Bernard Ratzer, *Plan of the City of New York, in North America: Surveyed in the Years 1766 & 1767* (London, 1776), NYPL; Henry P. Johnston, *The Campaign of 1776 Around New York and Brooklyn*, 212f.; idem, *The Battle of Harlem Heights, September 16, 1776: A Review of the Events of the Campaign* (New York, 1897), maps opp. 46, 50, 60, 70, 78, 116; documents, 125–234; map by Jeffrey Ward in Schecter, *The Battle for New York*, 192.

Map 4: Claude Joseph Sauthier, "A Topographical Map of the Northn. Part of New York Island, Exhibiting the Plan of Fort Washington, now Fort Knyphausen, with the Rebels Lines to the Southward . . . ," (Philadelphia, 1777); Freeman, *Washington* 4:245; map by Rafael Palacios in Richard M. Ketchum, *The Winter Soldiers: The Battles for Trenton and Princeton* (1973; New York, 1991), 114; map by Jeffrey Ward in Schecter, *The Battle for New York*, 248.

Map 5: Woodbridge, "Seat of War in New Jersey," in Arthur S. Lefkowitz, *Long Retreat* (Metuchen, 1998), plate 8–9; Alfred Hoyt Bill, *New Jersey and the Revolutionary War* (Princeton, 1964); Freeman, *Washington* 4:259; Adrian C. Leiby, *The Revolutionary War in the Hackensack Valley* (New Brunswick, 1962), 67; materials cited on 115–37.

Maps 6–7: Capt. John Montresor, manuscript map of British garrisons in New Jersey, Dec. 1776, Henry Clinton Papers, Clements Library, University of Michigan; sketch maps by Jäger Captain Johann Ewald in *Diary of the American War: A Hessian Journal*, ed. Joseph P. Tustin (New Haven, 1979), 29, 33, 37, 41, 47; modern maps in Ketchum, *Winter Soldiers*, 257; Samuel Stelle Smith, *The Battle of Trenton* (Monmouth Beach, N.J., 1965), 10; *New Jersey Atlas and Gazetteer*, 2d ed. (Yarmouth, Me., 2001); materials cited on 182–205.

Map 8: U.S. Geological Survey maps: Bristol, Lambertville, Pennington, Princeton, Trenton East, Trenton West Quadrangles (1995) NIMA 6064 1-SW-series V822; Smith, *Trenton*, 21; Freeman, *Washington* 4:347; Christopher Colles, *A Survey of the Roads of the United States of America*, ed. Walter W. Ristow (New York, 1789; rpt. Cambridge, 1961), 58–62; I. J. Hills, *A Complete Plan of Part of the Province of Pennsylvania East and West Jersey with Part of the Adjoining States* (New York, 1778); *New Jersey Atlas and Gazetteer*, 2d ed. (Yarmouth, Me., 2001); materials cited on 206–20.

Map 9: U.S. Geological Survey Quadrangles for Pennington, Princeton, Trenton East, Trenton West; Smith, *Trenton*, 18; Rafael Palacios in William Faden, "Plan of the Operations of General Washington Against the King's Troops in New Jersey, from the 26th of December to the 3d January 1777" (London, 1777); Kenneth Nebenzahl, ed., *Atlas of the American Revolution* (Washington, 1984), 92–93; *New Jersey Atlas and Gazetteer*, 2d ed. (Yarmouth, Me., 2001); materials cited on 221–33.

Maps 10, 19: Hessian manuscript maps of Trenton, 26 Dec. 1776, by Friedrich Fischer, Andreas Wiederholdt, and Jakob Piel; photocopies in the MHT; rpt. in William Stryker, *The Battles of Trenton and Princeton* (Boston, 1898), 128ff.; Plan of Trenton in 1776, ibid., 92; Smith, *Trenton*, 23–25; Ketchum, *Winter Soldiers*, 257.

Map 11: U.S. Geological Survey Quadrangles for Trenton East, Trenton West, Princeton; James Wilkinson, *Memoirs of My Own Times*, 3 vols. (Philadelphia, 1816; rpt. 1973), atlas; Samuel Stelle Smith, *The Battle of Princeton* (Monmouth Beach, N.J., 1967), 16; Ketchum, *Winter Soldiers*, 287; Cornwallis's Order of March in appendix Q; *New Jersey Atlas and Gazetteer*, 2d ed. (Yarmouth, Me., 2001).

Map 12: "Spy Map of Princeton, Dec. 30, 1776," ms. in the hand of Col. John Cadwalader, accompanying Cadwalader's report to Gen. Washington, LC.

Maps 13–14: Map from interviews in Stryker, *Battles of Trenton and Princeton*, 278; modern maps in Smith, *Princeton*, 14; Ketchum, *Winter Soldiers*, 287; Freeman, *Washington* 4:347; *New Jersey Atlas and Gazetteer*, 2d ed. (Yarmouth, Me., 2001); accounts by Rodney, White, Morris, Washington, Wilkinson, St. Clair, Olney, Howland, and others cited on 290–307.

Maps 15–16: Primary accounts by Cadwalader, Dewey, Glyn, Greenwood, Hale, Inman, McMichael, Olney, Sergeant R——, Rodney, Rush, St. Clair, Washington, White, Wilkinson, Young; Geological Survey Quadrangle for Princeton; five situation maps in Thomas Jefferson Wertenbaker, "The Battle of Princeton," *The Princeton Battle Monument* (Princeton, 1922), 75, 85, 92, 98, 104; four situation maps in Smith, *Princeton*, 20–25; Rafael Palacios map in Ketchum, *Winter Soldiers*, 302; Stryker, *Trenton and Princeton*, 288; Freeman, *Washington* 4:351; Boatner, *Encyclopedia of the American Revolution*, 892.

Map 17: Accounts by Washington, Rodney, Smith, *Princeton*, 31ff.; Bill, *Campaign at Princeton*, facing 103; Joshua Doughty, "Washington's March from Princeton to Morristown," *NJHSP*, n.s. 5 (1920), 240–46; *New Jersey Atlas and Gazetteer*, 2d ed. (Yarmouth, Me., 2001).

Map 18: Primary accounts of individual engagements listed in appendix T; John D. Alden et al., *Battles and Skirmishes of the American Revolution in New Jersey* (Trenton: N.J. Dept. of Environmental Protection, Bureau of Geology and Topography, 1945, 1965, 1973); Jared C. Lobdell, "Two Forgotten Battles of the Revolutionary War," *NJH* 85 (1967), 225–34; idem, "Six Generals Gather Forage: The Engagement at Quibbletown, 1777," *NJH* 102 (1984), 35–49.

ACKNOWLEDGMENTS

This book has grown from the same seed that produced *Paul Revere's Ride* and the Oxford series *Pivotal Moments in American History*. It centers on an idea of historical contingency as a web of choices, and historical writing as a braided narrative.

Appropriately, the acts and choices of many people shaped the book itself. First on a long list is James M. McPherson, my co-editor and friend of forty years. He and I have been talking about contingency for as long as I can remember, and Jim helped with this project in many ways. We walked the ground together in the Delaware Valley, explored the battlefields, and followed the routes of marching armies in cold December weather. The "Ordeal at Jacob's Creek" emerged directly from that experience, and much else besides. Jim also read the manuscript twice, and was very generous with his time and advice amid many contingencies in his own career.

At the Oxford University Press, our series owes its origin to Keith Thomas. When he was Secretary of the Press and I was an American Delegate, Keith asked for a paper on American history at the Press, and encouraged a proposal that led to the series called *Pivotal Moments in American History*.

In its development, Jim and I have been privileged to work with two of the best editors in America today. Sheldon Meyer long urged me to do a book on Washington's Crossing, and the book grew from his suggestions. He read the manuscript in several drafts, improved the text in many ways, and kept me centered on the work at hand. I am very grateful for his thoughtful criticism, wise advice, and friendship of many years.

Peter Ginna has been a wonderful editor in every way. He brings to his work a unique combination of sympathy and rigor, warm support and tough criticism, high seriousness and a happy sense of humor. Peter gave the book a very intelligent reading, and in the midst of many responsibilities at the Press he found the time to do line editing of a sort that is said (mistakenly) to be extinct in publishing houses today. I have come to value his judgment, and to cherish his friendship.

At Oxford, Joellyn Ausanka and Ruth Mannes shepherded the book through the press with skill and patience. India Cooper copy-edited the manuscript in a very skillful way, and greatly improved it.

Jeffrey Ward did the maps to a very high standard of excellence. His work combines accuracy, clarity, and grace with imagination and creativity—a unique combination of strengths that makes him one of the best cartographers in the world. It was a pleasure to work with him.

Many people on both sides of the Atlantic helped to find materials and offered advice and support and suggestions. In New England, Peter Harrington helped us at the Anne S. K. Brown Military Collection in the John Hay Library, Brown University. Marc Nichipur at the Minuteman National Historic Park at Concord shared some British materials on the battle of Princeton that had not been used in any published account. The reference staff at Brandeis University never failed to find helpful answers to hard questions. Others who helped were Sinclair Hitchings at the Boston Public Library, Suzanne Warner at Yale, Linda Jackson at Chesterwood, Peter Drummey and Nicholas Graham at the Massachusetts Historical Society, and Danielle Catera at the Museum of Fine Arts in Boston. George Billias and I have been talking about the Revolution for many years, and I've learned much from him.

In New York, Thomas Fleming and the Revolutionary Roundtable at Fraunces Tavern offered helpful criticism early in the project. Andrea Mihalovic at VAGA solved a sticky problem in a graceful way. Others who helped were Liz Larson at the New-York Historical Society, Kathleen Stocking at the New York State Historical Association, Patrice Kane in

Special Collections at the Fordham University Library, and the staff of the Phyllis Kind Gallery in New York City.

In New Jersey, David J. Veechioli and his staff made us welcome in his extraordinary Library at Morristown National Historic Park and helped with the Lidgerwood transcripts and their manuscripts and rare books. Marisa Moriga at the Historical Society of Princeton was very generous with her time. Anna Lee Pauls and the staff of the Princeton University Library turned up some uncatalogued materials; Wendi Nardi at the Trenton Public Library found the memoir of Martha Reed. Karen Richter helped us at the Princeton Art Museum when her own office was in process of creative destruction. Clay Craighead at the Washington's Crossing State Park answered many questions on the river and ice conditions. Also helpful were Celia Yao at the Monmouth County Library, Peggy Carlsen at Historic Rockingham State Park, John Mills at the Princeton Battlefield State Park, and the staff of the Gloucester County Historical Society.

In Pennsylvania, Valerie Lutz at the American Philosophical Society went far out of her way to help us find manuscripts and weather diaries. Richard Ryerson and his staff could not have been more helpful and hospitable in opening the amazing resources of the David Library, one of our leading institutions for the study of the American Revolution. Andrea Ashby Leraris was a model of efficiency at Independence Hall National Historic Park; every demagogue who runs for office by reviling the federal bureaucracy should spend some time with Andrea. Hilary Krueger, curator at Washington Crossing State Park in Pennsylvania, went far beyond the call of duty to help us with Durham boats. I am also grateful to Kerry McLaughlin at the Historical Society of Pennsylvania, Diana Peterson at the Haverford College Library, Sally Bacon at the Johannes Schalm Historical Association, and Kristen Froelich at the Atwater Kent Museum.

Susan Newton helped us at the Winterthur Museum, Delaware; and Nadine Shapiro at the Maryland State Archives in Annapolis.

In Washington, Jennifer Jones gave us the benefit of her knowledge of the armed forces collection at the Smithsonian. On questions of weather in 1776, we were helped by the staff of the National Climatic Data Center, National Oceanic and Atmospheric Administration.

In the Library of Congress, the expert staff of the manuscript division was very helpful, especially Jeffrey Flannery and Fred Bauman. Division chief James Hutson allowed us to see Consider Tiffany's manuscript history of the American Revolution and gave us a draft of his forthcoming essay on the capture and execution of Nathan Hale.

David McCullough called my attention to new manuscript materials that have recently become available, and shared his thoughts on Washington and the Revolution with extraordinary generosity.

In Virginia, Harry Ward and his colleagues and students at the Center for Leadership studies at the University of Richmond offered very helpful criticism, as did Roger Ekirch and his students at Virginia Tech. We also had expert assistance from Dawn Bonner at Mount Vernon; David Voelkel at the James Monroe Museum and Memorial Library; Claudia Jew at the Mariner's Museum in Newport News; Sarah Beth Walsh at the Chrysler Museum of Art, Norfolk; Mark Underwood at the Alexandria Memorial; and James Kelly at the Virginia Historical Society.

In the West, thanks go to John Dann, Clayton Louis, and John Shy at the William L. Clements Library in the University of Michigan; Cathy Grosfils at the Cincinnati Art Museum; Leo Kelly at the Terra Museum in Chicago; Bolton Colburn and Janet Blake at the Laguna Art Museum in Laguna Beach, California; and Sandow Birk in Long Beach, California.

In England, we were helped by the staff of the British Library and the Public Record Office at Kew; Emma Butterfield at the National Portrait Gallery; Mathew Buck at the Royal Artillery Museum, Woolwich; Fleur Mainwaring at the National Army Museum in Chelsea; and Lucy Waitt at the National Maritime Museum in Greenwich. In Scotland, we are grateful to Lt. Col. S. J. Lindsay of the Black Watch in Perth; Allan Carswell at the National War Museum of Scotland; and Helen Nicoll at the National Museums of Scotland. In Germany,

Marianne Heinz helped us with materials at the Staatliche Museum in Kassel, as did Anke Killing at the Westfalisches Landesmuseum in Munster.

In Baltimore long ago, Fraulein Rosalie Lephardt was my high school German teacher at City College (1949–51) and generously loaned me her own books and papers. Despite her best efforts my German is a poor and miserable thing, but I hope she might find pleasure in knowing that her teaching was put to work fifty years later, even if the translations are what she would call *ungeschicht*, or was it *ungeschlacht?*

Marianne Litty at Pure Imaging in Watertown, Mass., created digital images of eighteenth-century materials with skill and grace. Joshua Itzkowitz-Shifrinson helped with New Jersey place names.

At Brandeis University, my greatest debt is to my students, who continue to teach their teacher. Many thanks go to Dona Delorenzo and Judy Brown for running the office with high efficiency. I am very grateful to our excellent President, Jehuda Reinharz, for his friendship and continuing support.

My family helped with this project in many ways. My father, John Fischer, at the age of ninety-three is my most valued critic and trusted advisor; he read two drafts of the manuscript and gave very wise and constructive suggestions. My greatest debt as always is to my wife, Judith. The Internal Revenue Service thinks that she and I are a small business. If so, she is the Chief Executive Officer and keeps the entire enterprise afloat. She also found time to help with the illustrations and index, and supported the project in many ways. My brother, Miles Fischer, offered helpful advice. Susanna Fischer gave generously of her time and helped solve a difficult problem in Washington. Fred Turner led me into the work of Foucault, and Erik Mueller took us to Mount Vernon on a happy spring day. Our granddaughter, Thea, didn't work on this project, but she brightened the days of those who did. Anne Fischer turned up some wonderful art on Washington's Crossing. This book is dedicated to Anne, with a father's love.

Wayland, Massachusetts, and Bar Harbor, Maine   D. H. F.
14 September 2003

Additional thanks go to Sam Abrams, Peter Albertsen, Ed Belding, James F. Davis, Michael A. Davis, Richard Gamble, Read Scott Martin, James McPherson, Bill Poole, Joseph Rubenfine, and David Witham for corrections that are added to the fifth hardcover printing and the paperback edition of the book. Thanks go to the staff at National Public Radio, who called to my attention an error in the Introduction of *Washington's Crossing*, which inaccurately described a report on the Emanuel Leutze painting by NPR correspondent Ina Jaffe. I apologize for the error.

7 September 2004   D. H. F.

INDEX